Florence & Tuscany

THIS EDITION WRITTEN AND RESEARCHED BY

Virginia Maxwell, Nicola Williams

PLAN YOUR TRIP

ON THE ROAD

MEDIOIMAGES / GETTY IMAGES ©

FLORENCE P56

DARRELL GULIN /GETTY IMAGES ©

TUSCANY P120

Contents

UNDERSTAND

SURVIVAL GUIDE

SPECIAL FEATURES

Welcome to Florence & Tuscany

Travel writers tend to deploy the word 'idyllic' far too often, devaluing it in the process. But here in Tuscany, it really does apply.

Living History

Tuscany has been enticing visitors ever since the Etruscans arrived here to party and decided to stay. The Romans came to stock their grain silos, Christians came to walk the stages of a medieval pilgrimage route, Napolean came to plunder art and British aristocrats came to complete their Grand Tour. Once here, these and many other visitors swiftly fell into the local swing of things, partaking of the food and wine with gusto, admiring the diverse landscapes and soaking up the region's incredibly rich historical and cultural heritage. You're sure to enjoy following in their footsteps.

An Artistic Powerhouse

Then there's the art. And oh, what art! The Etruscans indulged their fondness for a classy send-off with exquisite funerary objects that are still being excavated to this day, and the Romans, always partial to puffing up their own importance, left their usual legacy of monumental sculptures. But it was during the medieval and Renaissance periods that Tuscany really hit its artistic stride, with painters, sculptors and architects creating the masterpieces that now entice visitors into churches, museums and galleries across the region.

Sensational Slow Food

The local obsession with food and wine trumps every other regional characteristic, and then some. Three of Italy's greatest wines – Brunello di Montalcino, Vino Nobile di Montepulciano and Vernaccia di San Gimignano – are produced here, and gastronomic gems such as *bistecca alla fiorentina* (chargrilled T-bone steak), *cacciucco* (Livornese fish stew) and *pici con ragù di cinghiale* (hand-rolled pasta with wild-boar sauce) are just some of the region's signature dishes. Tour here and you'll develop a true understanding of what Slow Food is, and how truly delectable locally sourced and simply prepared Tuscan cuisine can be.

Postcard-Perfect Landscapes

Yes, the scenery really *is* that gorgeous. Central Tuscany is dotted with medieval hilltop fortresses, vine-planted hillsides and sculptural stands of cypress trees; the northwest and east harbour boast dramatic mountain ranges and fecund forests; and the central and southern coasts feature a garland of islands floating tantalisingly close to a shoreline teeming with wildlife. The range of outdoor activities on offer is equally diverse, contributing to the region's reputation as a repository of grand-slam sights and experiences unmatched anywhere in the world.

Why I Love Florence & Tuscany

By Virginia Maxwell, Author

Why do I love Tuscany? Let me count the ways. I love the bejewelled artistic treasure chest that is Florence, the Gothic gem of Siena and the multiplicity of miraculously preserved medieval hill towns. I love the food, which is made with love and local produce, and I adore the Sangiovese-slanted local wines. I love the locals, who protect their traditions with an almost fanatical zeal and are careful custodians of their rich cultural heritage. But most of all, I love the fact that in this refined pocket of Italy, an extraordinary experience awaits around every corner.

For more about our authors, see page 352

Above: Landscape near Monticchiello (p227), Val d'Orcia

Florence & Tuscany

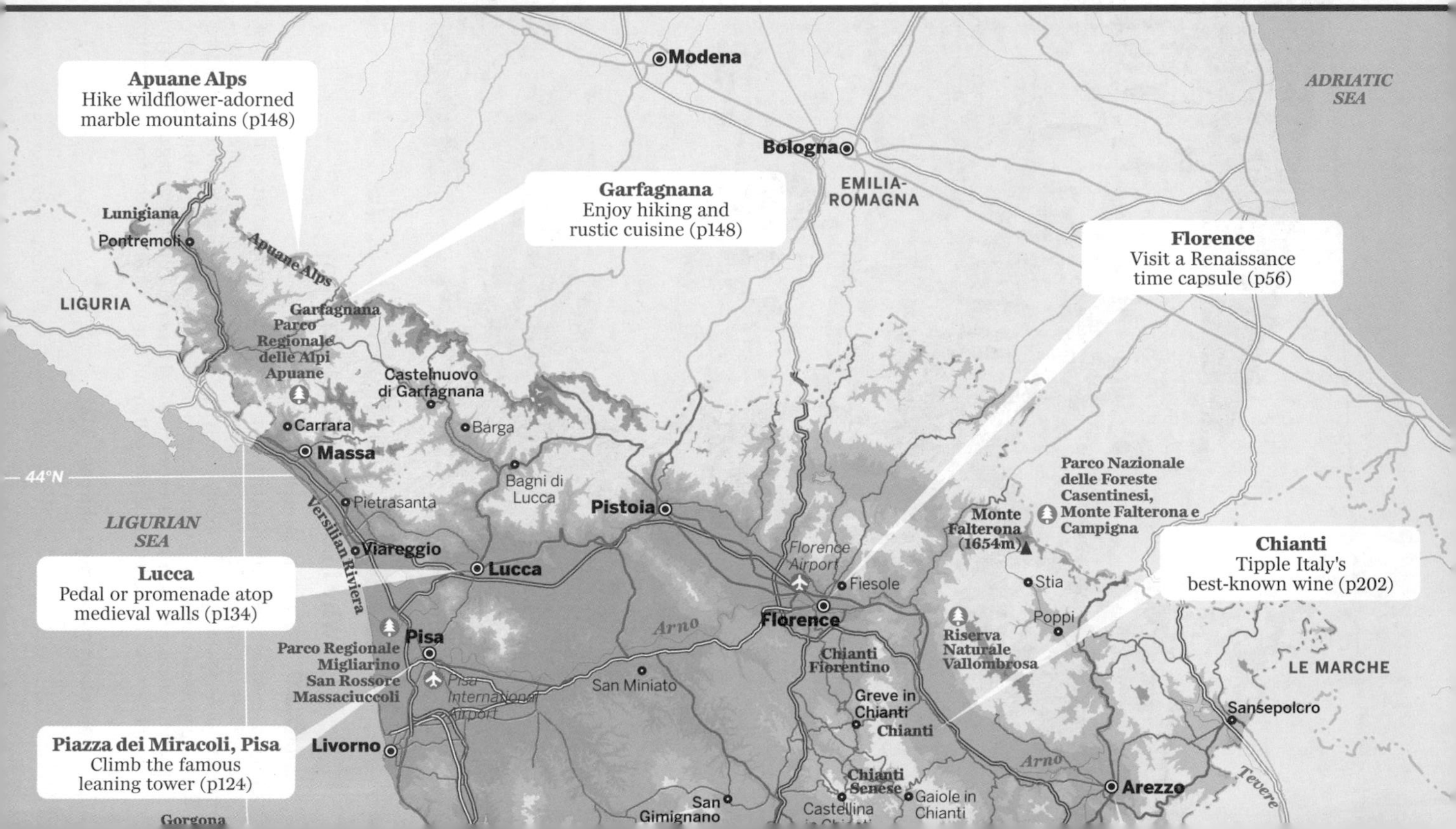

Apuane Alps
Hike wildflower-adorned marble mountains (p148)

Garfagnana
Enjoy hiking and rustic cuisine (p148)

Florence
Visit a Renaissance time capsule (p56)

Chianti
Tipple Italy's best-known wine (p202)

Lucca
Pedal or promenade atop medieval walls (p134)

Piazza dei Miracoli, Pisa
Climb the famous leaning tower (p124)

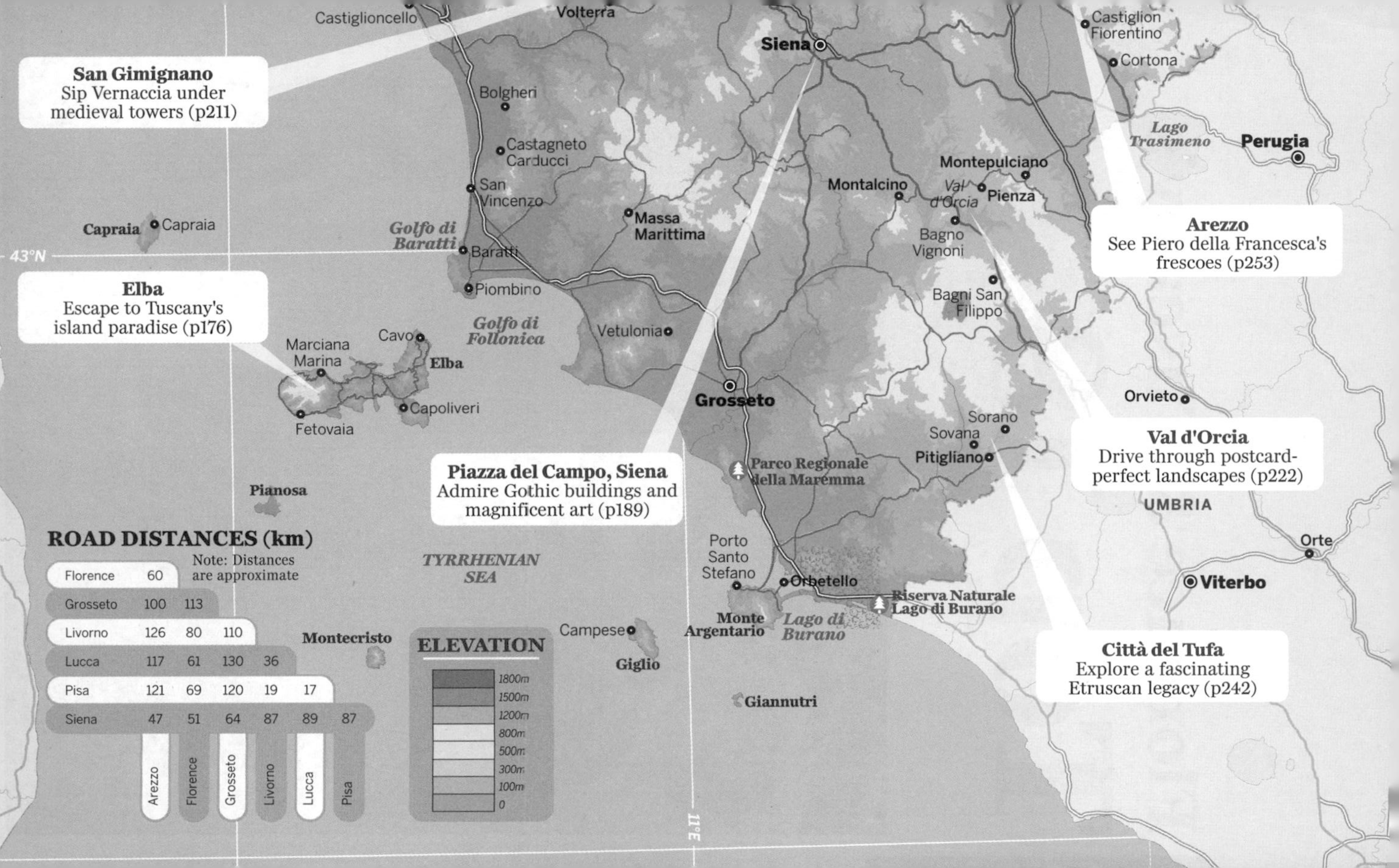

ROAD DISTANCES (km)

Note: Distances are approximate

	Arezzo	Florence	Grosseto	Livorno	Lucca	Pisa
Florence	60					
Grosseto	100	113				
Livorno	126	80	110			
Lucca	117	61	130	36		
Pisa	121	69	120	19	17	
Siena	47	51	64	87	89	87

Florence & Tuscany's Top 18

Uffizi Gallery, Florence

1 Visiting this magnificent art gallery (p64) twice or even three times during your stay in Florence is highly recommended. In fact, we'll go on record to say that limiting yourself to a mere morning – as many visitors do – could almost be described as criminally negligent. Chock-full of Renaissance masterpieces, this Medici-built palace is home to major works by Giotto, Botticelli, Michelangelo, da Vinci, Raphael, Titian and Caravaggio, and is one of only a few cultural institutions in the world that deserves a life-long program of revisits. Below: Botticelli's *Birth of Venus*

Piazza del Campo, Siena

2 Horses race around it twice a year, local teenagers treat it as an impromptu picnic spot and tourists inevitably gasp on seeing it for the first time – Siena's strangely sloping and perfectly paved central piazza (p189) is where the city's geographical and historical heart lies. Presided over by the graceful Palazzo Comunale and fringed with bustling cafe terraces, it's where you should come to promenade, take photographs and experience this magically intact Gothic city in all its glory.

DEA / G. NIMATALLAH / GETTY IMAGES ©

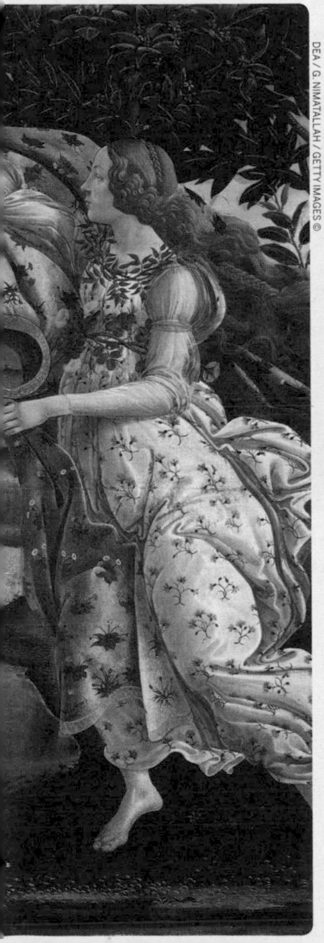

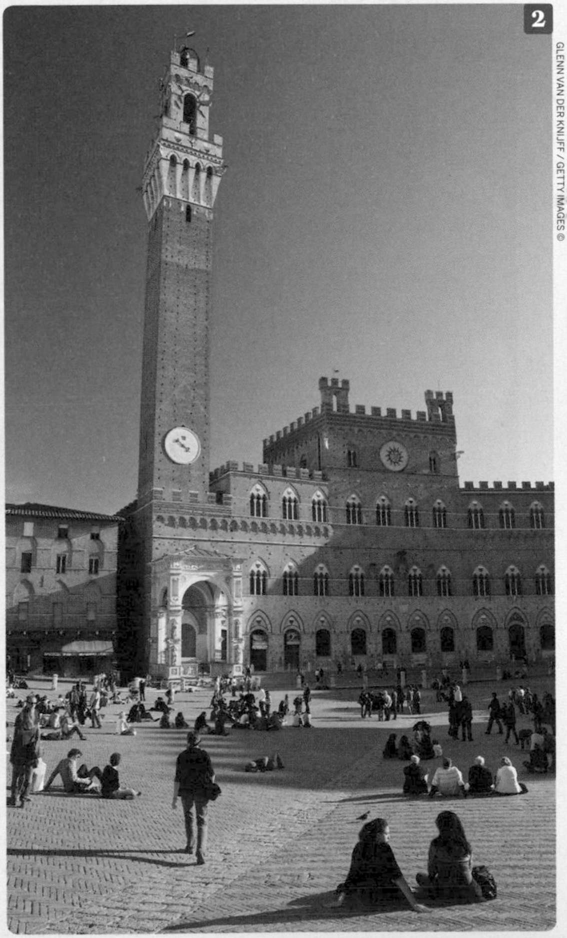

2

GLENN VAN DER KNIJFF / GETTY IMAGES ©

Chianti

3 'A jug of wine, a loaf of bread and thou': the Persian poet Omar Khayyam could well have been extolling the joys of Chianti (p202) when he wrote the *Rubáiyát*'s oft-quoted stanza. Come to Tuscany's most romantic destination and you'll end up waxing lyrical, too – luxurious accommodation, stunning scenery and the very best of modern Tuscan cuisine provide the ingredients for an idyllic short escape, particularly when accompanied by generous pourings of Italy's best-known wine, the ruby-red, violet-scented Chianti Classico.

Flavours of Tuscany

4 'To cook like your mother is good, but to cook like your grandmother is better', says the Tuscan proverb. Here, age-old recipes passed between generations form the backbone of the cuisine and make any visit a gastronomic delight. Forget foams, foraging and other culinary claptrap beloved of celebrity chefs from Copenhagen, London and New York – in Tuscany (p290), cooking is dictated by the season, is packed full of flavour and is locovore to the letter. *Buon appetito*!

5

6

Relaxing in an Agriturismo

5 Do something for both the local economy and your soul – stay in an *agriturismo* (accommodation on a working farm or wine estate; p34). These provide an insight into traditional Tuscan country life and the chance to relax in idyllic rural surrounds. Popular with families, *agriturismi* offer opportunities to do everything from helping to bring in the grape or olive harvest to feeding the farm animals. Usually with amenities such as swimming pools and home-cooked dinners, they're havens of Tuscan tranquillity. Top: Countryside near Pienza (p224)

Hunting for Truffles

6 The most precious product in the Italian pantry is sourced east of Pisa, in the woods surrounding the hilltop town of San Miniato (p146). Here, the loamy soil yields precious white truffles – lots and lots of them. Come here between mid-October and mid-December to join the excitement of a truffle hunt, or follow your nose to San Miniato on the last three weekends of November, when the Mostra Mercato Nazionale del Tartufo Bianco (National White Truffle Market; p147) takes over the town.

PETER ZELEI / GETTY IMAGES ©

Medieval Festivals

7 Tuscans have more than a few peculiarities. They won't eat foreign food (and that includes dishes from the neighbouring regions of Lazio and Emilia-Romagna), they never eat pizza at lunch, and they adore dressing up in medieval costumes and playing with giant crossbows or lances. Almost every town hosts an annual festival (p26) in which locals don fancy dress and join neighbourhood teams battling for trophies such as golden arrows and silk banners. Between May and September you'll be able to join in the fun. Top left: Florence's Scoppio del Carro parade (p93)

Val d'Orcia

8 Home to the medieval abbeys of Sant'Antimo (p225) and San Galgano (p222), the Renaissance splendour of Pienza (p224) and the relatively modern and oh-so-drinkable wonder that is Brunello di Montalcino (p294), the Val d'Orcia (p222) is so extraordinary that it is one of the Italian inclusions on Unesco's World Heritage List. Visit one of the abbeys in the morning, drive some of the valley's scenic secondary roads and then linger over a Brunello-fuelled lunch for the rest of the day – life doesn't get much better. Top right: Farm and vineyard, Val d'Orcia

The Duomo, Florence

9 A building that graces a million postcards (and then some), the *duomo* (p69) isn't just the most spectacular structure in Florence – it's also one of Italy's most recognisable icons. The polychrome marble facade is wonderful, but what makes the building so extraordinary is Filippo Brunelleschi's massive red-brick dome, one of the greatest architectural achievements of all time.

9

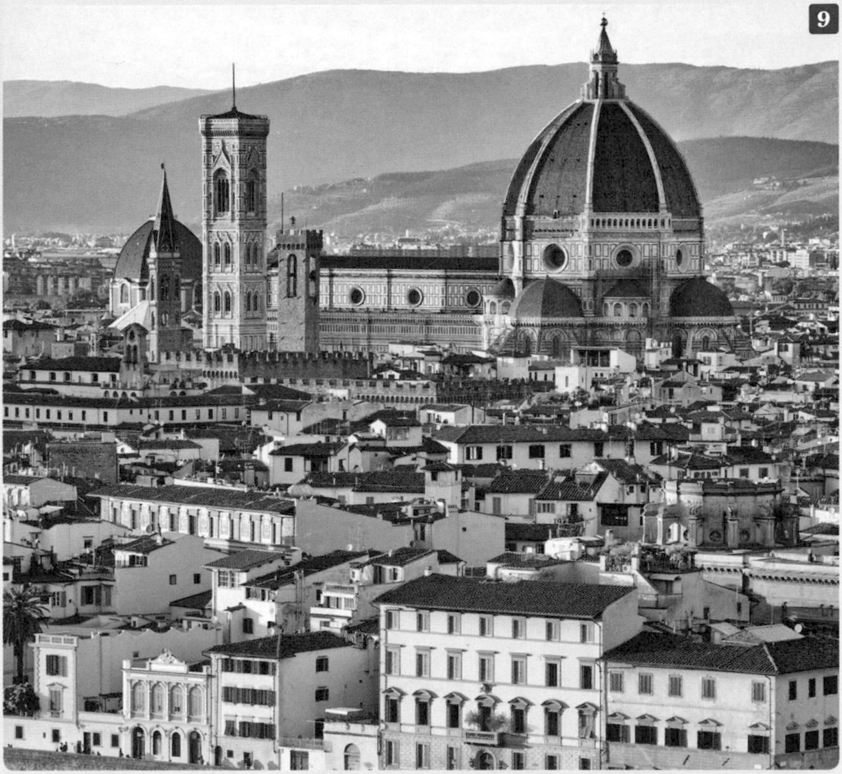

Garfagnana

10 Head to the hills (p148) north of Lucca to feast on fruits of the forest (chestnuts, honey and mushrooms), hike through wildflower-festooned fields and make a leisurely progress from one laid-back medieval mountain village to another. Base yourself in an *agriturismo* and spend your days hiking, mountain biking and eating wonderfully well. From here, the beaches and artistic enclaves of the Versilian coast aren't too far away, but most visitors find that once they've discovered this off-the-beaten-track corner of Tuscany, they never want to leave.

Right: Serchio river, Garfagnana

UNIVERSAL IMAGES GROUP / DEAGOSTINI / ALAMY ©

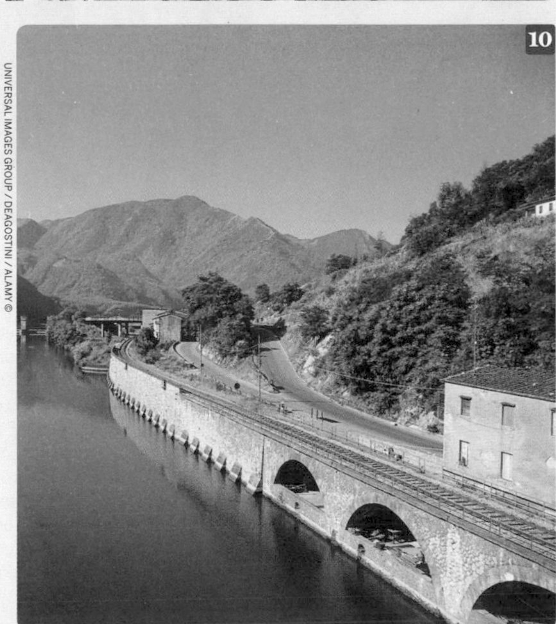

10

Piazza dei Miracoli, Pisa

11 History will come alive when you stand in the middle of this piazza (p124). Showcasing structures built to glorify God and flaunt civic riches (not necessarily in that order), this cluster of Romanesque church buildings possesses an architectural harmony that is remarkably refined and very rare. Hear the acoustics in the baptistry, marvel at Giovanni Pisano's marble pulpit in the *duomo* and confirm that, yes, the famous tower (p125) really does lean. It truly is a field full of miracles.

Art in Arezzo

12 Though way off the well-trod tourist trail, eastern Tuscany's major city (p253) has loads to offer the visitor. Chief among its attractions is Piero della Francesca's fresco cycle of the *Legend of the True Cross* in the Basilica di San Francesco, but there are also three other churches and four museums housing significant works of art. Come here on the first weekend of the month and you may even be able to purchase a masterpiece of your own – the city's antiques fair is one of the most famous in Italy.

Above: Piero's *Legend of the True Cross*

Touring by Vespa

13 What could be more Italian than hopping on a Vespa (p133) and cruising the countryside, stopping to visit wine estates, medieval *pieve* (rural churches) and hilltop towns along the way? The famous scooter – nicknamed a *vespa* (wasp) by its original manufacturer Enrico Piaggio – is ubiquitous throughout the region and ideally suited to slow travel. If you hire one, the only accessories you'll need for a perfect day or two of touring are a road map and gourmet picnic provisions.

Pedalling through Lucca

14 The Lucchesi version of the Giro d'Italia is shorter and considerably less strenuous. Hire a bike, provision yourself with picnic supplies and freewheel along the city's cobbled streets (p134), zooming through a progression of piazzas and stopping to pay your respects at the city's clutch of architecturally important churches. Next, hit the popular bicycle path atop the city walls (p135; such fun!) or head into the surrounding countryside to visit opulent villas surrounded by formal gardens and scenic parkland. Above: Piazza Anfiteatro, Lucca

15

16

Exploring the Apuane Alps

15 This rugged mountain range within the Parco Regionale delle Alpi Apuane (p148), beckons hikers, bikers and drivers with a trail of isolated farmhouses, medieval hermitages and hilltop villages. Its most spectacular sights are the slopes providing a backdrop to the town of Carrara (p153), which are scarred with marble quarries that have been worked since Roman times. Come here to sample *lardo di colonnata* (thinner-than-wafer-thin slices of local pig fat), one of Tuscany's greatest gastronomic treats, in the tiny village of Colonnata (p154).

Aperitivo

16 Tuscans love a tipple or two, and who's to blame them? While you're here, be sure to join them in the age-old ritual of *aperitivo* (pre-dinner drinks accompanied by cocktail snacks; p40) or in the more recent phenomenon of *apericena* (drinks with a snack buffet so generous that it can double as dinner). Best enjoyed after a leisurely *passeggiata* (early evening stroll), *aperitivo* is most seductive in the larger cities and towns, when people-watching is an important component. *Salute!* Top right: Bruschetta

The Franciscan Pilgrim Trail

17 Offering a heady mix of scenery, art, history and religion, the Santuario della Verna (p266) in eastern Tuscany and the hilltop town of Assisi (p267) in neighbouring Umbria are two of the most important Christian pilgrimage sites in the world. Visit the windswept monastery in the Casentino where St Francis is said to have received the stigmata, and then move on to his birthplace, where Giotto's famous fresco series in the upper church stuns every beholder with its beauty and narrative power. Opposite top: Basilica di San Francesco (p267), Assisi

BUENA VISTA IMAGES / GETTY IMAGES ©

Medieval Towers, San Gimignano

18 They form one of the most enchanting skylines in the world, house everything from local families to contemporary art, and bring history alive for every visitor – San Gimignano's medieval towers (p211) are one of Tuscany's signature sights. You can't climb many these days (the exception is the Torre Grossa in the Palazzo Comunale), but you can explore in their shadow and reflect on the civic pride and neighbourhood rivalry that prompted their construction and have given this diminutive hilltop town its unique appearance.

Need to Know

For more information, see Survival Guide (p320)

Currency
Euro (€)

Language
Italian

Visas
Not needed for residents of Schengen countries or for many visitors staying for less than 90 days.

Money
ATMs widely available. Credit cards accepted in most hotels and many restaurants; exceptions are noted in reviews.

Mobile (Cell) Phones
Local SIM cards can be used in European and Australian phones. Other phones must be set to roaming.

Time
One hour ahead of GMT/UTC; clocks are put forward one hour during daylight saving time (late-March–late October).

When to Go

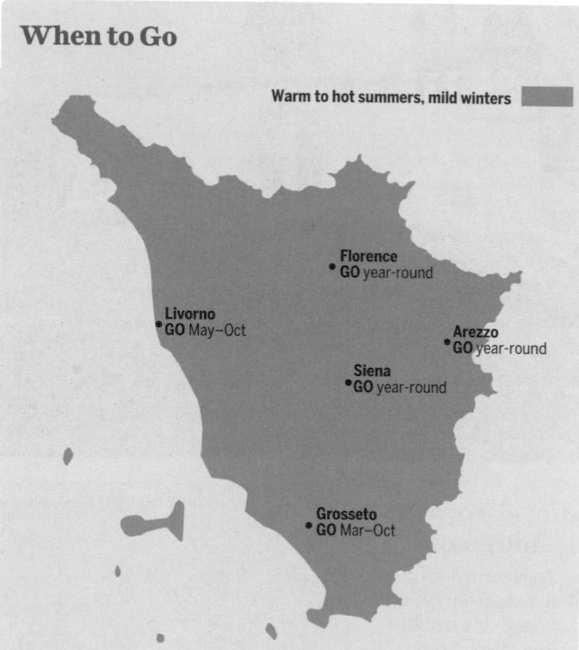

High Season
(May, Jun, Sep, Oct)

➡ Accommodation prices rise by up to 50%.

➡ Perfect weather for travelling, but it can be crowded.

➡ Major festivals are held from June to September.

Shoulder
(Apr, Jul & Aug)

➡ In April the weather is pleasant and prices are reasonable.

➡ High summer can be hot away from the coast and crowded on the coast.

➡ Most attractions stay open to sundown during summer.

Low Season
(Nov–Mar)

➡ Accommodation bargains abound, but many hotels close for the season.

➡ Some tourist information offices close.

➡ Many restaurants close for annual holidays.

Websites

Turismo in Toscana (www.turismo.intoscana.it) Official Tuscan tourism authority site.

Toscana & Chianti News (www.toscanaechiantinews.com) News and listings.

Firenze Made in Tuscany (www.firenzemadeintuscany.it, in Italian) Design-driven guide.

Informacittà Toscana 24hr (www.informacitta.net, in Italian) Events listings.

Artrav (www.arttrav.com) Florence-based blog.

Lonely Planet (www.lonelyplanet.com/italy/tuscany) Loads of practical information.

Important Numbers

Italy country code	☎39
International access code	☎00
Ambulance (free from landline)	☎118
Local police (free from landline)	☎113
Pan-European emergency & emergency from mobile phone	☎112

Exchange Rates

Australia	A$1	€0.70
Canada	C$1	€0.73
Japan	¥100	€0.76
New Zealand	NZ$1	€0.61
UK	UK£1	€1.19
USA	US$1	€0.75

For current exchange rates see www.xe.com.

Daily Costs

Budget: Less than €70

- Dorm bed: €20–40
- Sandwich: €4
- Many sights have free entry
- Trattoria dinner: €20
- Coffee drunk at the bar: €1

Midrange: €70–200

- Midrange-hotel double room: €100–200
- Restaurant meal: €35
- *Aperitivo*: €8
- Average museum entry: €5
- Walking tours: €10–50

Top End: Over €200

- Top-end-hotel double room: €200 and over
- Dinner of Modern Tuscan cuisine: €50
- Coffee sitting on a cafe terrace: €4
- Tour guide for three hours: €150

Opening Hours

As a general rule:

Banks 8.30am to 1.30pm and 3.30pm to 4.30pm Monday to Friday

Restaurants 12.30pm to 2.30pm and 7.30pm to 10pm

Cafes 7.30am to 8pm

Bars & pubs 10am to 1am

Shops 9am to 1pm and 3.30pm to 7.30pm (or 4pm to 8pm) Monday to Saturday

Arriving in Tuscany

Pisa International Airport Buses cost €1.10 to central Pisa, and €5 to central Florence. Trains are €2.50 to Pisa's Stazione Pisa Centrale, and €7.80 to Florence's Stazione di Santa Maria Novella (often with change of train at Pisa Centrale). A taxi to central Pisa will cost €10.

Florence airport Buses cost €6 to central Florence. Taxis to central Florence have a €20 flat rate, plus €1 per bag; there are surcharges at night and on Sunday and holidays.

Getting Around

Car Undoubtedly the best option, allowing you to explore scenic countryside and small hill towns. Drive on the right, overtake on the left, give way to the right at roundabouts. Many towns and cities have a *Zona a Traffico Limitato* (ZTL; Limited Traffic Zone) in their historic centre; keep your car outside the ZTL or be hit with a hefty fine.

Bus There's a reasonably extensive regional bus network. *Corse rapide* (express) services link Florence and Siena; other routes can involve long trips.

Train High-speed trains link Florence, Arezzo and Cortona, as well as Grosseto, Livorno and Pisa. *Regionale* (regional) trains link Florence, Lucca and Pisa.

For much more on **getting around**, see p327

First Time Florence & Tuscany

For more information, see Survival Guide (p320)

Checklist

- Check the validity of your passport
- Check if you need a visa
- Organise a youth, student or teacher card if applicable
- Book ahead for accommodation and major sights
- Book ahead to attend music and cultural events
- Organise international roaming on your phone if needed
- Organise travel insurance

What to Pack

- Driving map and GPS for the car (the latter can be rented with car hire)
- Travel plug (adaptor)
- Sunscreen, sunhat and sunglasses – it can get hot under the Tuscan sun!
- Umbrella and/or raincoat – except in high summer
- Corkscrew – Italian winemakers don't approve of screw-tops
- Sturdy walking shoes – cobbled streets and uneven country paths abound

Top Tips for Your Trip

- Always carry some cash. Unattended gas stations don't always accept foreign credit cards, and some restaurants and hotels operate on a cash-only basis.
- Don't rely solely on a GPS – it's always safest to cross-check your route on a printed road map.
- You will often find that there is free wi-fi access in or around *palazzi comunale* (town halls) and tourist offices.
- Foodies should consider purchasing a copy of the *Osterie d'Italia* Slow Food guide or the Gambero Rosso *Ristoranti d'Italia* or *Bar d'Italia* guides; available in bookshops throughout the region (Italian only).

What to Wear

A sense of style is vital to Tuscans, who take great pride in their dress and appearance. Here, maintaining *la bella figura* (ie making a good impression) is extremely important. Steer clear of shorts and flip-flops unless you're at the beach and always dress up, not down, at restaurants, clubs and bars. Smart-casual outfits will cover you in most situations; trainers and jeans are frowned upon for evening wear.

Cover yourself when entering a church (no shorts, short skirts or sleeveless or off-the-shoulder tops) and note that topless and nude bathing are unacceptable at most beaches.

Sleeping

Always try to book your accommodation in advance. This is especially important in spring, summer and autumn (fall), when good hotel and *agriturismi* (farm stay accommodation) rooms can be hard to find. See p33 for more accommodation information.

- **Agriturismi** Accommodation on working farm or wine estates; a fantastic option if you have a car and especially if you are travelling with children.
- **Boutique Hotels** Trending in Tuscany as we write, and the option of chóice for cashed-up travellers visiting Tuscan towns and cities.
- **B&Bs** Often old-fashioned, inevitably comfortable and well priced.

Money

Credit and debit cards are widely accepted. Visa and MasterCard are the most popular options; American Express is only accepted by international chain hotels, luxury boutiques and major department stores, and few places take Diners Club and JCB. Always check if restaurants take cards before you order; most bars and cafes do not. Chip-and-pin is the norm for card transactions.

Bancomats (ATMs) are everywhere; most offer withdrawal from overseas savings accounts and cash advances on credit cards. Both transactions will incur international transaction fees. If you don't want to rely on plastic, you can usually change cash and travellers cheques at a bank, post office or *cambio* (exchange office).

For more information, see p323.

Bargaining

Tuscans don't bargain, so neither should you.

Tipping

➡ **Taxis** Round the fare up to the nearest euro.

➡ **Restaurants** Many locals don't tip waiters, but most visitors leave 10% to 15% if there's no service charge.

➡ **Cafes** Leave a coin (as little as €0.10 is acceptable) if you drank your coffee at the counter or 10% if you sat at a table.

➡ **Hotels** Bellhops usually expect €1 to €2 per bag; it's not necessary to tip the concierge, cleaners or front-desk staff.

Language

Tourism is an extremely important part of the Tuscan economy, so most locals speak at least one language other than Italian. English is the most common, but many locals also speak French. That said, your travels will be easier if you master a few basic phrases in Italian.

See p332 for more information.

What's the local speciality?
Qual'è la specialità di questa regione?
kwa·*le* la spe·cha·lee·*ta* dee *kwes*·ta re·*jo*·ne

A bit like the rivalry between medieval Italian city-states, these days the country's regions compete in speciality foods and wines.

Which combined tickets do you have?
Quali biglietti cumulativi avete?
kwa·lee bee·*lye*·tee koo·moo·la·*tee*·vee a·*ve*·te

Make the most of your euro by getting combined tickets to various sights; they are available in all major Italian cities.

Where can I buy discount designer items?
C'è un outlet in zona? che oon *owt*·let in *zo*·na

Discount fashion outlets are big business in major cities – get bargain-priced seconds, samples and cast-offs for *la bella figura*.

I'm here with my husband/boyfriend.
Sono qui con il mio marito/ragazzo.
so·no kwee kon eel *mee*·o ma·*ree*·to/ra·*ga*·tso

Solo women travellers may receive unwanted attention in some parts of Italy; if ignoring fails have a polite rejection ready.

Etiquette

➡ **Greetings** Shake hands, make eye contact and say *buongiorno* (good morning/afternoon), *buonasera* (good evening) or *piacere* (pleased to meet you). If you know someone well, air-kissing on both cheeks (starting on their left cheek) is standard.

➡ **Polite Language** Say *mi scusi* to attract attention or say 'I'm sorry', *grazie (mille)* to say 'thank you (very much)', *per favore* to say 'please', *prego* to say 'you're welcome' or 'please, after you' and *permesso* if you need to push past someone in a crowd.

➡ **Cafes** Don't hang around at an espresso bar; drink your coffee and go. It's called espresso for a reason.

➡ **Body Language** Be wary of making a circle with two hands ('I'll kick your ass'), an A-OK signal ('You might be gay'), or the devil horns with your hand ('Your wife is cheating on you').

➡ **In churches** Never intrude on a mass or service.

What's New

Antinori nel Chianti Classico, Bargino, Chianti

Designed by Florentine architect Marco Casamonti and opened to great acclaim in 2013, this stunning wine estate features an all-glass tasting room suspended above barrels in the ageing cellar. (p208)

La Bandita Townhouse, Pienza

The owners of the acclaimed La Bandita rural retreat in the Val d'Orcia have remodelled a Renaissance-era convent in Pienza's Unesco-listed historic centre to create an alluring boutique hotel and cafe. (p226)

Grande Museo del Duomo, Florence

After taking almost three decades to restore, Lorenzo Ghiberti's gilded brass doors from the Battistero di San Giovanni are now on show in the *duomo*'s revamped museum. (p71)

Gucci Museo & Caffè, Florence

Fashionistas are flocking to the fashion label's super-chic museum and caffè, which were recently unveiled in the 14th-century Palazzo della Mercanzia on Piazza Signoria. (p74)

Museo di San Mamiliano, Sovana

In 2004 archaeologists unearthed the exciting cache of 498 gold Roman coins that are on show in this new museum on Sovana's Roman-era main street. (p244)

Giardino Torrigiani, Florence

Take a guided tour with a marquis and his wife in Europe's largest private walled garden. (p89)

Slow Food Office, San Miniato

Cementing the town's foodie credentials is this newly opened office, which can help with tastings, tours, cellar visits, wine itineraries and other tastebud-tempting activities. (p147)

Surfer Joe's Diner, Livorno

This 1950s-style diner has added dynamism and a dose of Californian surf culture to Livorno's seafront. (p168)

LAB Pasticceria, Arezzo

Sweet confections are served in the ultra-stylish surrounds of this courtyard cafe just off Arezzo's sophisticated shopping strip, Corso Italia. (p258)

Relais Baia Bianca, Elba

These dazzling white, designer-chic apartments fringe the golden sandy beach of La Biodola. (p183)

Hotel Alma Domus, Siena

Still home to six Domenican nuns, this convent hotel has been refurbished and now offers stylish and comfortable budget rooms with wonderful views. (p197)

For more recommendations and reviews, see lonelyplanet.com/italy/tuscany

If You Like...

Food

Bistecca alla fiorentina Chargrilled T-bone steak comes rare, unadorned and packed full of flavour. Sample it in the Val di Chiana, where it's a local art form.

Chianti The home of Italy's signature wine and the incubator of modern Tuscan cuisine should top every foodie's must-do list.

Antipasto Toscano Follow the local lead and start your meal with a plate of cured meats, *pecorino* (sheep's-milk cheese) and toasts topped with chicken liver pâté.

Fruits of the forest Foraging here really pays off, particularly in autumn when truffles, porcini mushrooms and chestnuts are harvested. Join the fun of a truffle hunt.

Wine

Aperitivo Florentines love indulging in *aperitivi* (pre-dinner drinks with snacks) and *apericena* (drinks with snacks so generous that they can double as dinner). See what the fuss is about in the city's fabulous wine bars.

Strade del Vino For a road trip with a difference, follow a regional wine itinerary, visiting vineyards, *cantine* (cellars) and local artisan food producers.

IGTs To taste what the international wine press has dubbed 'Super Tuscans', head to Bolgheri on the Etruscan Coast, home of the groundbreaking Sassicaia.

Montalcino Be there for the release of the new vintage of Brunello in February. Bliss.

Architecture

Siena The city's historical centre is a showcase of the Gothic style, with the *duomo* (cathedral) being the jewel in its crown. (p194)

Florence Climb to the top of Brunelleschi's dome to survey the city's skyline in all its Renaissance splendour. (p69)

Insider Florence Everyone sees the *duomo*, but true architecture buffs head to Brunelleschi's more modest commissions: the Ospedale degli Innocenti (p81) and Cappella de' Pazzi (p82).

Pisa The Piazza dei Miracoli lives up to its name, delivering a monumental arrangement of Romanesque buildings that have battled the threat of subsidence and stood the test of time. (p124)

Renaissance Art

Uffizi Gallery It doesn't get any better than this. The repository of the Medici art collection is so wonderful that even superlatives seem inadequate when trying to describe it. (p64)

Museo Civico Secular art takes centre stage in Siena's town hall, courtesy of Ambrogio Lorenzetti's *Allegories of Good and Bad Government* fresco cycle. (p192)

Piero della Francesca Follow a trail of the great painter's works in eastern Tuscany, marvelling at the tenderness of the *Madonna del Parto* and the masterful storytelling of the *Legend of the True Cross*. (p263)

Collegiata Decipher a medieval cartoon strip and be enchanted by Domenico Ghirlandaio's tribute to Santa Fina at San Gimignano's *duomo*. (p211)

IF YOU LIKE... OPERA

Visit Lajatico for the once-a-year performance staged by locally born operatic superstar Andrea Bocelli. It's held in the purpose-built, evocatively named Teatro del Silenzio in July. (p149)

Contemporary Art

Castello di Ama Works by some of the art world's biggest names are showcased in the formal gardens of this wine estate in Chianti. (p211)

Fattoria di Celle Industrialist Giuliano Gori has commissioned an extraordinary collection of site-specific artworks at his vast family estate outside Pistoia. (p146)

Galleria Continua One of Europe's most impressive contemporary art galleries is located in the medieval time capsule of San Gimignano. Go figure. (p212)

Giardino dei Tarocchi A whimsical labour of love by Franco-American artist Niki de Saint Phalle, this sculpture garden south of Grosseto brings the tarot card pack to life. (p250)

Natural Landscapes

Parco Nazionale dell'Arcipelago Toscano Europe's largest marine protected area covers the whole of the Tuscan archipelago and has at its centre the magical island of Elba. (p176)

Parco Regionale Migliarino, San Rossore, Massaciuccoli Climb Pisa's Leaning Tower and you'll be able to see this haven of bird life west of the city. Explore it on foot, by bicycle, on horseback or in a horse-drawn carriage. (p46)

Apuane Alps The snowy-white mountain peaks forming the backdrop to the town of Carrara aren't capped with snow – they're topped with vast quarries where marble has been gouged out of the landscape since Roman times. (p148)

The Casentino Dense forests, crystal-clear river streams and

(Top) Cappella de' Pazzi (p82), Florence
(Bottom) Autumn hues in Chianti (p202)

hidden medieval monasteries await in the northeastern corner of the region. (p263)

Scenic Drives

Hit the road to see the real Tuscany – the provincial variety rather than the autostradas. Most of these can be explored by 2WD and offer opportunities galore for cultural stops, nature walks and great meals.

The Passo del Vestito Ascend this spectacular mountain pass from Castelnuovo di Garfagnana to Massa on the Versilian coast. (p152)

Elba off season Wait until the crowds have gone home, then wind your way along the stunning road on the island's southwest coast, stopping for a seafood lunch at the enchanting hilltop town of Capoliveri. (p185)

The Val d'Orcia Explore the gently rolling, cypress-topped hills of this postcard-perfect pocket of Tuscany. (p222)

Chianti Every road seems to lead to vineyards and olive groves, honey-coloured stone farmhouses, graceful Romanesque *pieve* (rural churches) and imposing castles. (p202)

IF YOU LIKE... LIBRARIES

Prepare to be mighty impressed by two magnificent Renaissance examples: Florence's Biblioteca Medicea Laurenziana (p77) and Siena's Museo delle Tavolete di Biccherna (p196).

Gardens

Giardino Torrigiani In a secret location in the centre of Florence, this 19th-century garden includes rare tree species, wide English-style lawns, herb and vegetables gardens, sculpted lions, a beautifully restored greenhouse, and remains of the city walls built under Cosimo I in 1544. (p89)

Villa Grabau The sweeping English- and Italian-styled gardens of this neoclassical villa near Lucca feature splashing fountains, more than 100 terracotta pots planted with lemon trees and a postcard-pretty lemon house. (p135)

Orto de' Pecci This Sienese oasis is home to a cooperative organic farm, medieval garden and experimental vineyard planted with clones of medieval vines. (p197)

Giardino di Boboli This prime example of a formal Florentine garden dates back to the 16th century. (p88)

Pilgrimage Sights

Via Francigena Walk parts of this medieval pilgrimage route, stopping at evocative destinations including the Abbazia di Sant'Antimo along the way. (p216)

Santuario della Verna Visit the windswept monastery in the Casentino where St Francis of Assisi is said to have received the stigmata. (p266)

Cattedrale di San Martino Pay your respects to the *Volto Santo*, a simply fashioned image of a dark-skinned, life-sized Christ that is Lucca's most revered religious icon. (p135)

Assisi The Birthplace of St Francis and St Clare is Italy's second most important pilgrimage destination (after Rome). (p267)

Month by Month

TOP EVENTS

The Palio, July and August

Carnevale, February to March

Puccini Festival, July to August

Maggio Musicale Fiorentino, April to June

Giostra del Saracino, June and September

February

It's only towards the end of this month that locals are coaxed out of their winter hibernation. Weather conditions can be bone-chillingly cold in mountainous areas and windswept hill towns can appear all but deserted.

Carnevale di Viareggio

Kicking off 40 days before Ash Wednesday and the restrictions of Lent, Viareggio's month-long street party involves fireworks, floats, parades and revelry galore. (p158)

March

Locals start to get into the springtime swing of things in the weeks leading up to Easter. Many regular visitors time their trips for this period to take advantage of low-season prices and uncrowded conditions.

Settimana Santa

Easter Week is celebrated in neighbouring Umbria with processions and performances in Assisi. Other Easter celebrations in the region include Florence's Scoppio del Carro (Explosion of the Cart) on Easter Sunday.

April

Wildflowers carpet the countryside, market stalls burst with new-season produce and classical music is staged in wonderfully atmospheric surrounds. Easter sees the tourist season kicking off in earnest.

Maggio Musicale Fiorentino

This arts festival – Italy's oldest – is held in Florence's Teatro del Maggio Musicale Fiorentino and stages world-class performances of theatre, classical music, jazz and dance from April to June (www.maggiofiorentino.com). (p93)

May

Medieval pageants take over the streets of towns and cities across the region from late spring to early autumn, highlighting ancient neighbourhood rivalries and the modern-day love of street parties.

Balestro del Girifalco

In Massa Marittima, crossbow teams from the town's three *terzieri* (districts) dress in medieval costumes and compete for trophies, including a painted banner. Held on the first Sunday after 20 May and again in July or August. (p236)

Giostra dell'Archidado

More crossbows, this time in Cortona, when a full week of medieval merriment in late May or June culminates in an exciting competition between representatives from the town's five residential quarters. (p269)

June

It's summertime and, yes, the living is easy. The start of the month is the perfect time to tour the

(Top) The Palio parade (p199), Siena
(Bottom) Parade float at Carnevale di Viareggio (p158)

paradisaical isle of Elba, and any time is right to gorge on seafood and strawberries.

Luminaria

On the night of 16 June, Pisans honour their city's patron saint with thousands of candles and blazing torches along the banks of the Arno, as well as a spectacular fireworks display.

Giostra del Saracino

A grand, noisy affair involving extravagant fancy dress and neighbourhood rivalry, this medieval jousting tournament is held in Arezzo on the third Saturday in June and first Sunday in September. (p257)

San Gimignano Estate

The town's streets, piazzas and historic buildings host a popular summer program of opera, films, concerts, theatre and dance. Held between June and September (www.sangimignano.com).

July

Cyclists and walkers take to the mountains but everyone else heads to the beach, meaning that accommodation prices in inland cities and towns drop as a result. Summer music festivals abound.

Festivals in Cortona

The hill town of Cortona is alive with the sound of music at its annual Festival of Sacred Music, held early in the month, and Cortona Mix

Festival, held late July to early August. (p269, p269)

Music in Montalcino

Sip a glass or two of Brunello while mingling with Montalcino's winemakers at the town's refined International Chamber Music Festival. (p223)

Puccini Festival

Opera buffs from around the world make a pilgrimage to the small town of Torre del Lago for this annual event in July and August (www.puccinifestival.it). Performances are staged in an open-air lakeside theatre next to the great man's house. (p138)

The Palio

The most spectacular event on the Tuscan calendar is held on 2 July and 16 August in Siena. Featuring colourful street pageants, a wild horse race and generous doses of civic pride, it exemplifies the living history that makes this region so compelling. (p199)

Lucca Summer Festival

This month-long music festival (www.summer-festival.com) lures big-name international pop, rock and blues acts to lovely Lucca, where they serenade crowds under the stars in some of the city's most atmospheric piazzas.

August

Locals take their annual holidays and the daily tempo of life in the cities slows to a snail's pace. Be warned: the weather can be oppressively hot and beaches are inevitably crowded.

Volterra AD 1398

On the third and fourth Sundays of August, the citizens of Volterra roll back the calendar some 600 years, take to the streets in period costume and participate in this medieval festival. (p218)

Bravio delle Botti

Members of Montepulciano's eight *contrade* (districts) race to push 80kg wine barrels uphill in this race held on the last Sunday in August (www.braviodellebotti.com).

September

Autumn/fall is when La Vendemmia (the grape harvest) is celebrated and when the forests proffer their highly anticipated harvests of intensely scented porcini mushrooms and creamy chestnuts.

Grapes in Greve

The major town in the Chianti wine district holds its annual wine fair in the first or second week of September.

Palio della Ballestra

Sansepolcro's party-loving locals don medieval costumes and peacock around town on the second Sunday of September while hosting a crossbow tournament between local archers and rivals from the nearby Umbrian town of Gubbio.

November

This is when restaurateurs and truffle tragics come from every corner of the globe to sample and purchase Tuscany's bounty of strong-smelling and utterly delicious white truffles.

Mostra Mercato Nazionale del Tartufo Bianco

The streets of San Miniato are filled with one of the world's most distinctive aromas at the National White Truffle Market, held on the last three weekends in November. (p147)

Itineraries

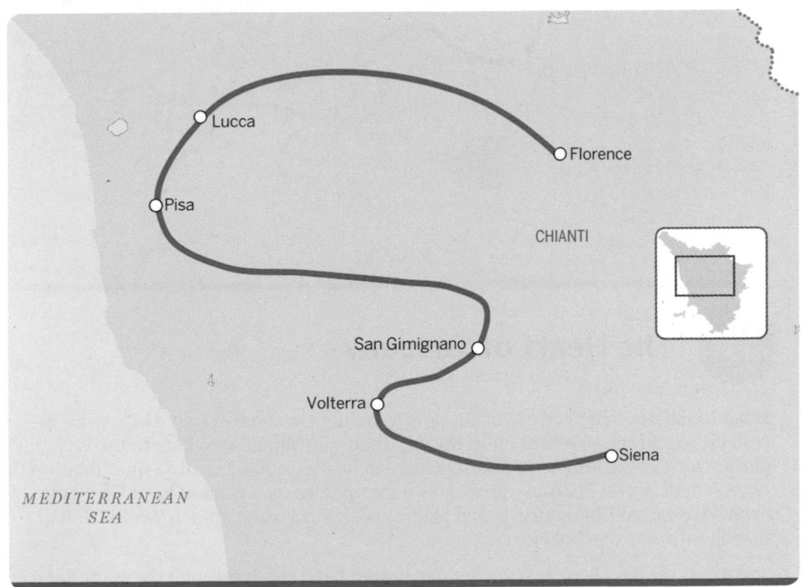

Only the Best

Florence anchors any 'best of' tour. You'll need at least three days to do this magnificent city justice – any less and you'll be selling both it and yourself short. Spend one day visiting the Uffizi Gallery, another wandering through the San Marco and San Lorenzo neighbourhoods, and the third crossing the Arno to explore the artisan's neighbourhood of Oltrarno. After having eaten, drunk, shopped and seen more Renaissance masterpieces than you would previously have thought possible, it's time to slow down the pace and move on to the enchanting walled city of **Lucca** for two days. Hire a bike and use pedal power for a leisurely exploration of its cobbled city streets and villa-studded surrounding countryside. On day six, pop into **Pisa** to scale its Leaning Tower, leaving after lunch to arrive at a Tuscan farmhouse in **Chianti** before dusk. Check-in for three nights, visiting wineries, taking a day trip to **San Gimignano** or **Volterra**, exploring sculpture gardens and feasting on modern Tuscan food during your stay. On day nine, head to gloriously Gothic **Siena**, home to museums, restaurants and churches that will supply a truly fabulous two-day finale to your trip.

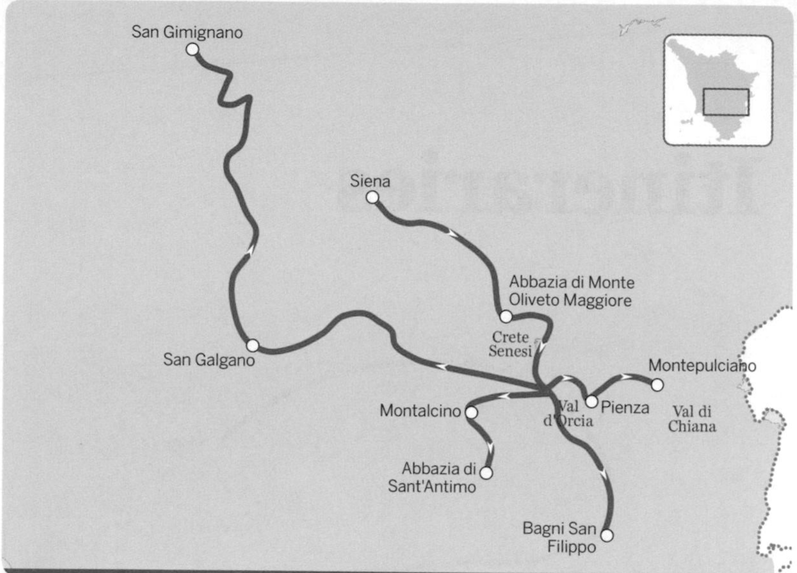

The Heart of Tuscany

Head to the sun-kissed centre of Tuscany to indulge in some of Italy's best wine, architecture and scenery. Kick off in **Siena**, where you should gravitate towards Gothic glories such as the Museo Civico and Opera della Metropolitana di Siena. Nibble on the city's famous sweet biscuits – preferably accompanied by a glass of local Vin Santo – and explore the atmospheric streets and piazzas of the incredibly intact, World Heritage-listed *centro storico* (historic centre).

After three days here, tear yourself away and head south through the stunning scenery of the Crete Senesi, visiting the **Abbazia di Monte Oliveto Maggiore**, and then continuing southeast to base yourself in or around the towns of **Pienza** or **Montepulciano** for three nights – there are plenty of impressive accommodation options to choose from, including chic boutique hotels, atmospheric *agriturismi* (farm or wine estates offering accommodation) and idyllic villa retreats. From your base, you'll be able to explore the Val d'Orcia and Val di Chiana, visiting the wine country around **Montalcino**, listening to Gregorian chants at the **Abbazia di Sant'Antimo,** wandering through the ruined Cistercian abbey of **San Galgano**, soaking in hot cascades at **Bagni San Filippo** and sampling the gastronomic products that this part of Tuscany is known for – Chianina beef, *cinta senese* (indigenous Tuscan pig), fresh *pecorino* (sheep's milk cheese), fragrant olive oil and two of Italy's greatest wines: Brunello di Montalcino and Vino Nobile di Montepulciano. If you are travelling during summer, you may be lucky enough to witness a medieval-themed neighbourhood festival or attend a musical performance in an abbey, *palazzo* (mansion) or piazza.

End your sojourn in this idyllic area by looping back along scenic secondary roads to romantic **San Gimignano**, home to medieval tower houses, a lavishly frescoed *duomo* (cathedral) and a small but charming municipal museum and art gallery. Dine on delicate pasta dishes scented with locally grown saffron, and celebrate Tuscany's manifold charms with a glass or two of the town's golden-hued Vernaccia wine – life doesn't get much better than this!

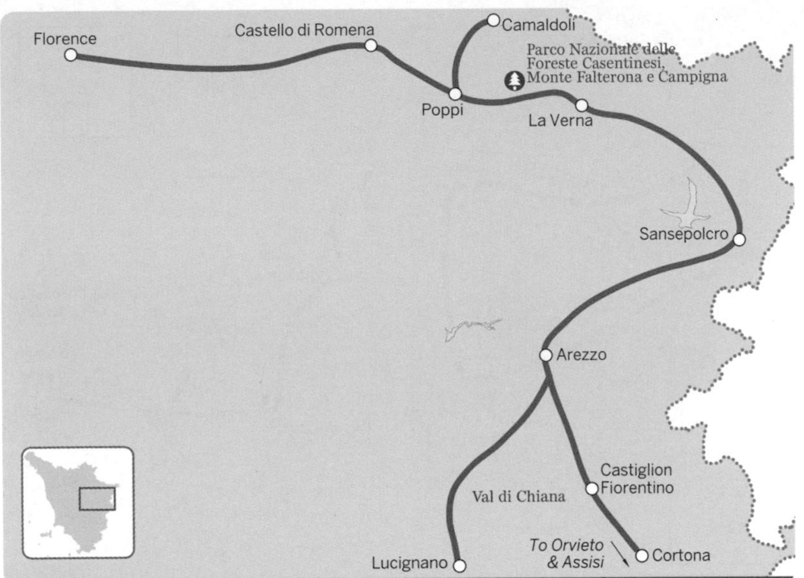

12 DAYS Into the East

Mix it up a bit by balancing well-known destinations with some intriguing off-the-beaten-track alternatives. Spend three days admiring the Renaissance splendour of **Florence** before branching out east into the little-visited Casentino region, home to the idyllically isolated **Parco Nazionale delle Foreste Casentinesi, Monte Falterona e Campigna**. Base yourself around the fortified hill town of **Poppi** for three days, sampling the area's rustic and delicious cuisine, visiting the isolated medieval monasteries of **Camaldoli** and **La Verna**, wandering around the evocative ruins of the **Castello di Romena** and walking a few trails in the national park. Next, meander southeast to **Sansepolcro**, proud possessor of charming medieval churches, great restaurants and a museum showcasing works by the great Renaissance painter, Piero della Francesca.

Tear yourself away after two nights and continue to your final destination, the Val di Chiana, where you can spend a few days eating, drinking and sightseeing your way around the valley. While here, pop into the provincial capital, **Arezzo**, where locals outnumber tourists by a healthy margin and where churches are the highlight – don't miss the Cappella Bacci, Pieve di Santa Maria and *duomo*, and be sure to follow your church visits with a *passeggiata* (evening stroll) along glamorous Corso Italia.

A number of nearby medieval hilltop towns are also well worth visiting – **Castiglion Fiorentino** and **Lucignano** are extremely pretty, but both pale in comparison with **Cortona**, which deserves a half-day visit at the very least. Be sure to walk up the steep cobbled streets to its Fortezza Medicea, and also check out the collections at the Museo dell'Accademia Etrusca and the Museo Diocesano.

When your time runs out, consider heading south towards Rome on the A1 autostrada, stopping to visit the stunning cathedral at **Orvieto** en route to admire Luca Signorelli's famous fresco cycle of *The Last Judgment*. Alternatively, head into the neighbouring region of Umbria to visit one of Italy's most famous pilgrimage centres, **Assisi**, home to the Basilica di San Francesco, where Giotto's extraordinary frescoes portraying the life of St Francis stun all beholders.

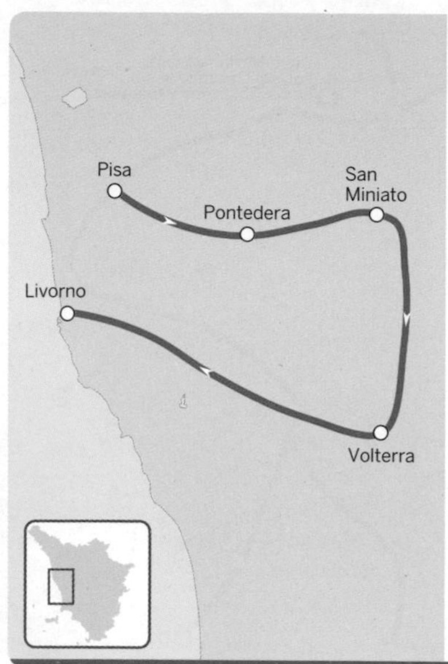

Pisa & its Provinces

Start your peregrination in **Pisa**, spending two days admiring the marble pulpits in the Baptistry and *duomo*, the paintings and sculpture in the Museo Nazionale di San Matteo and the exquisite exterior decoration of the Chiesa di Santa Maria della Spina. Conclude your visit at the Piazza dei Miracoli, home to that famous engineering project gone horribly wrong, the Leaning Tower. On day three, spend the morning paying homage to Italy's famous Vespa scooter at the Museo Piaggio in **Pontedera** before driving (or maybe scootering!) through gently rolling hills covered in olive groves and vineyards to hunt truffles and sleep in style at the gourmet destination of **San Miniato**. From here, head to spectacularly sited **Volterra** in the Val di Cecina, where visits to alabaster ateliers and an extraordinary museum of Etruscan art await. Spend two nights here and then finish your tour in the neighbouring province and city of **Livorno**, home to an atmospheric central market, the delectable seafood stew known as *cacciucco* and the world-famous Sassicaia wine.

The Maremma

To make the most of the great outdoors, head to the region's south. Start in the little-visited but utterly delightful medieval town of **Massa Marittima** and spend a couple of days visiting its museums and sampling Maremmese food and wine in its rustic eateries. On day three, check out an archaeological dig, Etruscan tombs and an impressive museum at the ancient hilltop settlement of **Vetulonia** and stay in a local *agriturismo* for the night. From here, head down the coast to the wild and wonderful **Parco Regionale della Maremma** to walk, canoe, cycle or horse ride alongside the famous cowboys known as the *butteri*. End your journey inland amid the stunning surrounds of the Città del Tufa (City of the Tufa), where you should visit the towns of **Pitigliano**, **Sovana** and **Sorano**. Here you can sample the local Morellino di Scansano wine at Società Agricola Terenzi; explore the amazing Etruscan necropolises at the Parco Archeologico 'Città del Tufa'; and spend a day taking an 8km walk along the enigmatic sunken roads known as *vie cave*.

Plan Your Trip

Staying in Tuscany

Tuscany is blessed with accommodation styles and options to suit every taste and budget. Most cities and large towns offer family-run pensioni (guest houses), B&Bs and boutique hotels; in rural areas, agriturismi (accommodation on working farms or vineyards) reign supreme. Luxury options are also common.

Choosing Your Accommodation

Visitors to Tuscany are spoiled for choice when it comes to finding places to stay, so it pays to research thoroughly. Always check hotel websites for special deals. We use the following pricing system in this book. Unless otherwise stated, prices quoted are for a double room with private bathroom and breakfast:

€ up to €110

€€ €110 to €200

€€€ €200-plus

Accommodation Types

- **Affittacamere** A budget room in a private house. Tourist offices can often provide lists.
- **Agriturismo** A working farm or vineyard offering rooms; many have restaurants.
- **Albergo** A hotel; these include business hotels, luxury hotels and characterful midrange choices.
- **B&B** A small guesthouse offering bed and breakfast at a reasonable price. Most offer double rooms with a private bathroom.
- **Boutique hotel** A growing trend in Tuscan cities, where they often occupy magnificent *palazzi* (palaces). The Ferragamo fashion empire is a major player in this sector, operating seven

Accommodation Highlights

Best Agriturismi

La Cerreta (p172)
Fattoria San Martino (p230)
Podere San Lorenzo (p218)
Agriturismo Due Palme (p181)
Montebelli Agriturismo & Country Hotel (p241)
Podere dell'Orso (p171)

Best Boutique Hotels

Antica Torre di Via de' Tornabuoni 1 (p97)
La Bandita (p223)
Villa Sassolini (p203)
Campo Regio Relais (p199)
Albergo Pietrasanta (p156)
Hotel al Teatro (p168)
Villa Fontelunga (p258)
Il Salviatino (p99)

Best on a Budget

Academy Hostel (p98)
Hotel Scoti (p96)
La Casa di Adelina (p227)
Hotel Alma Domus (p197)
Pensione Bartoli (p170)
Al Pozzo dei Desideri (p214)
La Primavera (p218)

properties in Tuscany under its Lungarno Collection brand (www.lungarnocollection.com), as is the Florence-based Whythebest group (www.whythebesthotels.com).

- **Country hotel** Tuscan rural retreats come in many varieties. As well as *agriturismi* and villas, you'll find self-catering apartments in a *borgo* (farm hamlet), spa hotels and resort-style hotels.
- **Foresteria** These offer rooms and dorm beds in religious communities such as monasteries and convents. Though catering predominantly for pilgrims or people on religious retreats, they are also popular with families and budget travellers.
- **Locanda** A country inn offering B&B in rustic surrounds; most will provide dinner if you request this in advance.
- **Ostello** A hostel offering dorm beds and rooms to budget travellers.
- **Pensione** A small, family-run guesthouse offering B&B. The owners usually live on site.
- **Rifugio** A mountain hut kitted out with bunk rooms sleeping anything from two to a dozen or more people. Many offer half-board and are open from mid-June to mid-September.
- **Villa** The stuff of which dreams are made. Historic villas and *fattorie* (farmhouses) can be rented in their entirety or sometimes by the room. Most have swimming pools and are set in idyllic landscapes.

Booking Your Accommodation

It is wise to book well ahead for all accommodation, particularly in Florence and Siena and along the coast in summer. Note that in busy periods, some hotels may impose a multinight stay (this usually applies at beach hotels over July and August, and always applies in Siena during the Palio). Country hotels, *locande* (inns), villas and *agriturismi* often close in winter.

Most hotels will give you the choice of a *camera doppia* (room with twin beds) or a *camera matrimoniale* (room with double bed). Many hotels do not have *camera singola* (single rooms); instead, lone travellers will pay a slightly reduced price for a double room.

Credit cards are accepted at many – but not all – places to stay. MasterCard and Visa are more widely accepted than American Express or Diners Club International. When booking directly with the hotel, a deposit of up to 30% may be requested.

Useful Resources

Associazione Italiana Alberghi per la Gioventù (Association of Italian Youth Hostels | AIG; www.aighostels.com) Affiliated with Hostelling International (HI).

Campeggi e Villaggi Turistici (Camping & Holiday Villages in Italy | TCI) An annually published list (in Italian) of all Italian camping grounds published by Touring Club Italiano (TCI). Available from bookshops throughout the region.

Camping.it (www.camping.it) Useful website listing camp sites across the region.

Club Alpino Italiano (CAI; www.cai.it) Has a database of CAI-operated *rifugi* (mountain huts).

Locande d'Italia (Slow Food Editore) Compendium of Slow Food–recommended accommodation. Published in Italian only; available from bookshops throughout the region.

MonasteryStays.com (www.monasterystays.com) A well-organised online booking centre for monastery and convent stays.

AGRITURISMI

Agriturismi (farm stay accommodations) have long been popular in Tuscany. By definition, an *agriturismo* is required to grow at least one commercial crop, but beyond this common thread they can run the gamut from a rustic country house with a handful of olive trees to a luxurious country estate with an attached vineyard to a fully functioning farm where guests can help with the harvest. They are vital to small communities, as they inject money into local economies, provide employment and often cross-subsidise the production of artisanal farm produce. In many ways, they embody the concept of Slow Travel – we love them to bits, and have recommended many of them in this book.

What to Expect

You can expect a warm welcome, particularly when staying in rural areas. Whether they be cosy *pensioni,* grand villas or sleek boutique hotels, Tuscan sleeping choices inevitably have personable and professional staff and offer clean and comfortable rooms.

Hotels are non-smoking by national law and many offer accommodation for mobility-impaired guests. Most offer free wi-fi and/or an internet kiosk (indicated by wi-fi and internet symbols in reviews).

Leisure Facilities

Country hotels will usually offer one or two leisure activities. Swimming pools are commonplace (usually open May to September), and many hotels have mountain bikes for guest use. Tennis courts, horse stables and wellness centres are less common, but can be found reasonably regularly. Of these, horse-riding usually incurs an extra charge, as do certain treatments in wellness centres (massage etc).

Dining

The vast majority of hotels include breakfast in their room rate; this can take the form of anything from a simple coffee and *cornetto* (croissant) to a full Western-style buffet. Many *agriturismi,* country hotels and boutique hotels also offer in-house dining, usually in the form of a set dinner menu that changes daily. Options with the best in-house dining:

- Podere San Lorenzo (p218), Volterra
- La Bandita (p223), Pienza
- La Cerreta (p172), Castagneto Carducci
- Locanda Vigna Ilaria (p139), Lucca
- Villa Sassolini (p203), Moncioni
- Locanda Gavarini (p160), Pontremoli
- Grand Hotel Palazzo (p168), Livorno

Handy Hints

- Print out location information from your hotel's website; many places in cities are secreted in hard-to-find laneways, and country retreats are often in obscure locations that don't appear on standard road maps. Don't rely on GPS, either.
- If driving, check with the hotel as to the most convenient and cost-effective place to park. And beware the infamous *Zona a Traffico Limitato* (ZTL; Limited Traffic Zones).
- Ask hotel staff for restaurant recommendations – they often know about great local eateries and will usually be happy to make reservations for you.
- If you're allergic to animals, mention this when booking. Many country hotels have cats and dogs.
- It's often possible to negotiate a discount if you stay five nights or more.

ON-THE-GROUND ASSISTANCE

Tourist offices throughout the region can help you to source accommodation. Check their websites, email them or visit offices on the ground for advice and recommendations.

Hotel Tax

In recent years a number of Italian cities, including Florence, Siena, San Gimignano, Montepulciano and Cortona, have introduced a hotel occupancy tax (*tassa di soggiorno*). This is charged on top of your regular hotel bill and must generally be paid in cash. The exact amount, which varies from city to city, depends on the type of place you stay in and the time of year, but as a rough guide expect to pay €1 per person per night in a one-star hotel or hostel, €2 in a B&B, €2 to €3 in a three-star hotel and €4 to €5 in a four- or five-star hotel. Children under 10 or 12 are generally not taxed; those aged 11-16 are usually charged 50% of the adult tax. Prices quoted in this book do not include the tax.

Florentine delicatesse

Plan Your Trip

Eat & Drink Like a Local

For Tuscans, eating and drinking is as much a fine art as their masterpiece surrounds. And exceedingly well around a shared table is how they eat, thanks to an ancient cuisine sourced in the family farmstead from seasonal fruits of the land and sea. Titillate tastebuds with these food-trip essentials.

The Year in Food

Feasting is year-round, with foodie festivals galore. For details on specific food events see p36.

Spring (Mar-May)

Markets burst with baby violet artichokes, asparagus, fresh garlic and – towards the season's end – cherries, figs and courgette flowers begging to be stuffed.

Summer (Jun-Aug)

Strawberries, peppers and the start of San Gimignano's saffron harvest (July to November). Beat the heat by the sea with seafood, elsewhere with a gelato – chestnut, fig and honey, or saffron and pine-nut flavour.

Autumn (Sep-Nov)

Olives and grapes are harvested, forest fruits such as chestnuts and *porcini* mushrooms (August to October) gathered, and game hunted for. Oenophiles head to Greve in Chianti in September for Chianti's biggest wine fair. Mid-October opens the white truffle season near Pisa.

Winter (Dec-Feb)

The truffle season, which continues until mid-December, peaks with San Miniato's truffle market. Montalcino wine producers crack open the new vintage at February's Benvenuto Brunello.

Food Experiences

Meals of a Lifetime

Enoteca Pinchiorri, Florence (p104) Tuscany's only Michelin three-star address, stratospheric and smug in a 16th-century Florentine *palazzo* (palace).

Peperino, San Miniato (p148) Dinner for two at the world's smallest, and possibly most romantic, restaurant.

Barbialla Nuova, Montaione (p147) Hunt white truffles in musky woods, then head to a village trattoria to eat it shaved over steak.

Il Pellicano, Monte Argentario (p250) Sensational seafood dishes and glorious sea views.

Il Leccio, Sant'Angelo in Colle (p224) Simple but spectacular cuisine sourced from the garden, washed down with extraordinary Brunellos.

Cheap Treats

Pecorino Ewe's-milk cheese perfect in fresh, crunchy *pane* (bread).

Porchetta rolls Warm sliced pork (roasted whole with fennel, garlic and pepper) in a crispy roll.

Torta di ceci Savoury chickpea pancake.

Castagnaccio Hybrid cake-crêpe, sweet and made from chestnut flour.

Gelato The best Tuscan ice cream uses seasonal, natural ingredients: figs, chestnuts, pine nuts, honey, saffron, wild strawberries...

Dare to Try

Bistecca alla fiorentina Blue and bloody is the only way to eat Florence's iconic T-bone steak; Trattoria Mario (p102) is the address.

Lampredotto Cow's fourth stomach, chopped, simmered and cooked up at every Florentine *trippaio* (cart or mobile stand; p100).

Trippa alla fiorentina Tripe in tomato sauce, once eaten, never forgotten at Da Nerbone (p102) in Florence's Mercato Centrale.

Lardo di colonnata Carrara's luscious pig lard, aged in marble vats, keeps cardiologists in the black (p154).

Biroldo Local version of haggis, included in tastings at Osteria Vecchia Mulino (p149) in Castelnuovo di Garfagnana.

Mallegato San Miniato's Slow Food–accredited blood sausage, always on the menu at Podere del Grillo (p147).

Local Specialities

Spicy green olives, extra-virgin olive oils, full-bodied red wines, smoky *porcini* mushrooms and bags of beans are culinary trademarks across the Tuscan board, but delve deeper to discover geographic differences every gourmet will revel in.

Florence

Tuscany's leading lady is a born-and-bred gourmet. Be it slow food or fine dining, *panino* (sandwich) in a piazza or tripe at a street cart, Florence meets every gastronomic taste with style and panache.

The day's end ushers in **aperitivi** (pre-dinner drinks), a sacrosanct ritual big and buzzing in Tuscany's largest city: so copious are the complimentary buffets of snacks and nibbles laid out to accompany drinks that savvy young Florentines increasingly forgo dinner for **apericena** (aperitivi and dinner rolled into one).

The icon of Tuscan cuisine is **bistecca alla fiorentina,** a chargilled T-bone steak legendary for its gluttonous size and rebel reputation as former outlaw.

Black truffles

Northwestern Tuscany

Wedged between wind-whipped sea and mountain, this unexpected culinary nest-egg is known for its fresh *pecorino* (sheep's milk cheese), *zuppe di cavolo* (cabbage soup) and other humble farm fare. Slow Food town San Miniato, near Pisa, is the source of Tuscany's exceptional white truffles.

In **Castelnuovo di Garfagnana**, fresh porcini, chestnuts and sacks of farm-grown *farro* (spelt) fill autumnal markets. Sweet *castagnaccio* (chestnut cake) is to locals in Garfagnana what *buccellato* (a sugared bread loaf studded with sultanas and aniseed) is to those in Lucca.

TRUFFLES

They're not a plant, they don't spawn like mushrooms and cultivating them is impossible. Pig-ugly yet precious, these wild knobs of fungus excite and titillate. Said to have aphrodisiacal qualities, one whiff of their pungent aroma is enough to convince: the smell of truffles, especially the more pungent white truffle, is seductive. Or rather, the smell is the taste (think fresh mint without its smell).

Truffles grow in symbiosis with oak trees and are *bianco* (white – actually a mouldy old yellowish colour) or *nero* (black – a gorgeous velvety tone). They are sniffed out by dogs from mid-October to late December, in San Giovanni d'Asso near Siena, and San Miniato, between Florence and Pisa. Truffles are typically served raw and thinly shaved over simple, mild-tasting dishes to give the palate full opportunity to revel in the subtle flavour. Our favourite truffle tastings:

➡ **Barbialla Nuova, Montaione** (p147) Tuscany's golden ticket for hunting white truffles.

➡ **Pepenero, San Miniato** (p148) Celebrity chef Gilberto Rossi gives truffles a creative spin.

➡ **Ristorante Da Ventura, Sansepolcro** (p262) Nothing beats a simple omelette sprinkled with fresh truffle shavings.

➡ **I Sette Consoli, Orvieto** (p230) Special dishes of the day celebrate the truffle season.

Olio & Convivium (p105), Florence

Not far from the coast, pig fat is aged in Carrara-marble vats and eaten 12 or 24 months later as wafer-thin, aromatic slices of *lardo di Colonnata*.

Central Coast & Elba

Two words: sensational seafood. The grimy port of **Livorno** is the place to feast on superb affordable dining and **cacciucco,** a zesty fish stew swimming with octopus, rock fish and a shoal of other species.

Inland, vineyards around the village of **Bolgheri** produce Super Tuscan Sassicaia and other full-bodied reds – a perfect match for *cinghiale* (wild boar). On **Elba**, sweet red Aleatico Passito DOCG is the nectar amid the raft of sun-drenched wines grown on the island; spunky olive oils, too.

Siena & Central Tuscany

Siena is the GPS coordinate where Tuscan cuisine originates, say locals, for whom *caffè* (coffee) and a slice of *panforte* (a rich cake of almonds, honey and candied fruit) is a mandatory part of their weekend diet.

Chianti is for serious foodies: cheery, dry, full red wines; butcher legend Dario Cecchini; tip-top Chianti Classico DOP olive oils; *finocchiona briciolona* (pork salami made with fennel seeds and Chianti) from Antica Macellerìa Falorni (p205); and some of Tuscany's most exciting, modern Tuscan cuisine.

Montalcino is famed for red Brunello wine, the consistently good Rosso di Montalcino and prized extra-virgin olive oils. **Montepulciano**, home of Vino Nobile red and its equally quaffable second-string Rosso di Montepulciano, also produces fine beef and Terre di Siena DOP (protected origin) extra-virgin olive oil.

Cheese aficionados make a beeline for **Pienza**, where some of Italy's finest *pecorino* is crafted; and the **Val di Chiana** where sheep cheese is wrapped in fern fronds to become *ravaggiolo*. The same gorgeous rolling green valley is also where the world-famous Chianina beef comes from, making it the perfect place to sample *bistecca alla fiorentina*, perhaps after a tasty *primo* (first course) of *pici* (a type of local hand-rolled pasta).

Something of a culinary curiosity, fiery red **San Gimignano** saffron was the first in Europe to get its own DOP stamp of quality.

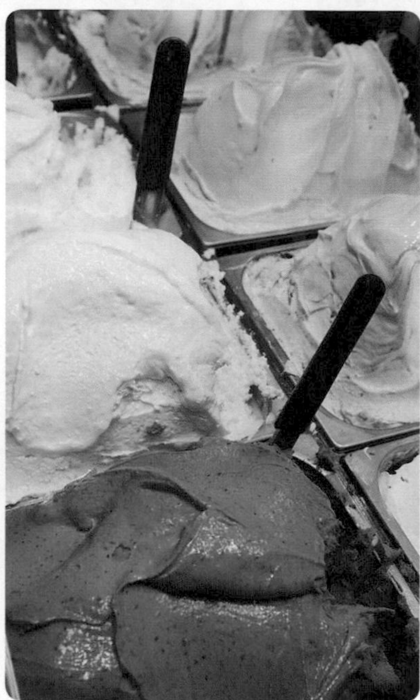

LONELY PLANET / GETTY IMAGES ©

Different flavours of gelato

Southern Tuscany

When it comes to quality-guaranteed beef, chicken and game, Maremma is the byword. **Grosseto** is the mecca for the sweet-toothed thanks to handmade biscuits (including traditional Jewish honey-and-walnut pastry, *lo sfratto*) from Dolci Tradizioni dalla Maremma Toscana (p247).

How to Eat & Drink

It pays to know what and how much to eat, and when – adopting the local pace is key to savouring every last exquisite gastronomic moment of the Tuscan day.

BEST COOKING CLASSES

- Pepenero (p148)
- Scuola di Arte Culnaria Cordon Bleu (p92)
- In Tavola (p92)

When to Eat

- **Colazione** (breakfast) is a quick dash into a bar or cafe for a short sharp espresso and *cornetto* (croissant) or *brioche* (pastry) standing at the bar.
- **Pranzo** (lunch) is traditionally the main meal of the day, though Tuscans now tend to share the main family meal in the evening. Standard restaurant times are noon or 12.30pm to 2.30pm; locals don't lunch before 1pm.
- **Aperitivo** (aperitif) is the all-essential post-work, early-evening drink that takes place any time between 5pm and 10pm when the price of your cocktail (€8 to €10 in Florence) includes a copious buffet of nibbles, finger foods, or even salads, pasta and so on.
- **Cena** (dinner) has traditionally been lighter than lunch. The traditional Tuscan belt-busting, five-course whammy only happens on Sunday and feast days. Standard restaurant times are 7.30pm to around 10pm (often later in Florence and across the board in summer).

Where to Eat

In a **ristorante** (restaurant) expect to find crisp linen, classic furnishings, formal service and refined dishes. A **trattoria** is a restaurant, often family-owned with cheaper prices, more relaxed service and classic regional specialities. Intimate and relaxed, the **osteria** has its origins in a traditional inn serving wine with a little food on the side; these days it's hard to differentiate between an *osteria* and trattoria. For a cheap feed, cold beer and a buzzing, convivial vibe, head for a **pizzeria**.

Enoteca (wine bars) are increasingly casual, atmospheric places to dine and taste Tuscan wines by the glass.

Dining on a farm at an **agriturismo** (farm stay) is the best of Tuscany – a copious, never-ending feast of homemade cooking with local produce against a quintessential Tuscan backdrop of old stone farmhouse, cypress alley and pea-green rolling hills.

At the **gelateria** (ice-cream shop), rain, hail or shine, a queue outside the door marks the best of ice-cream shops. The astonishing choice of flavours will have you longing for an Italian ice cream long after you've left Tuscany.

Above: Ingredients for *ribollita*, a thick vegetable, bread and bean soup

Right: A selection of cheeses for sale

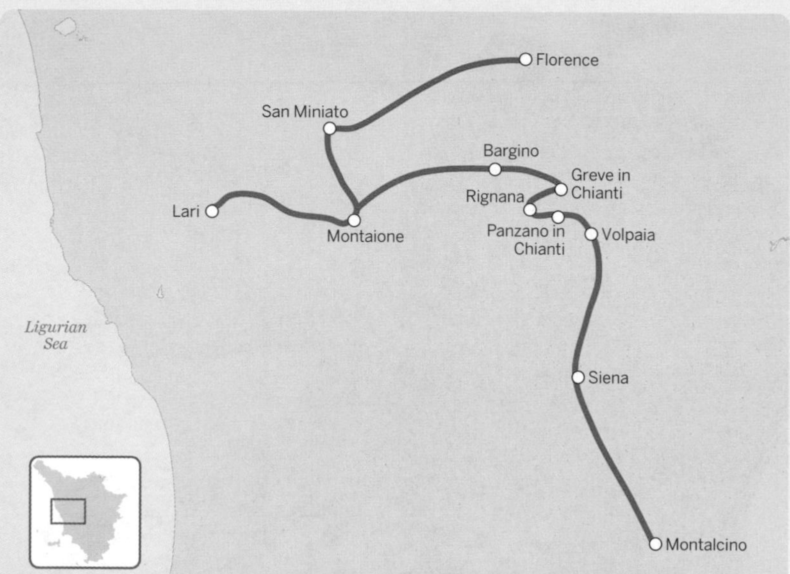

Foodie Itinerary: Florence to Siena

No city plays the gourmet better than **Florence**: shop for olive oils at **Mercato Centrale** (p79), lunch at **Trattoria Mario** (p102), and indulge in chocolate *degustazione* (tasting) with local foodie Alessandro Frassica at **Ino** (p101). At dusk join Florentine gastronomes for *aperitivo* (pre-dinner drinks) at **Il Santino** (p106), followed by a light mozzarella and violet artichoke supper at **Obikà** (p101); or super modern Tuscan dinner at **iO Osteria Personale** (p105).

Day two, motor 30km into rolling hills around **San Miniato**, a Slow Food town with superb lunch options. Afterwards, pick up an afternoon tasting itinerary from **Slow Food** (p147). Dine at **Podere del Grillo** (p147) and overnight on white-truffle estate, **Barbialla Nuova** (p147) in **Montaione**.

Next morning, drive one hour west to **Lari** to watch artisan pasta makers at work; or dive into Chianti for a cellar visit and lunch at the flagship **Antinori nel Chianti Classico** (p208) in **Bargino**. Eat and overnight at **Rignana** (p203).

It's a short drive next day to **Greve in Chianti**'s **Museo del Vino** (p205). Buy *finocchiona briciolona* (fennel seed-studded pork salami) for a picnic lunch at **Antica Macelleria Falorni** (p205) and end the day at **Badia a Passignano** (p208).

Day five, drive south to **Panzano in Chianti**. Lunch with Tuscany's celebrity butcher Dario, and take a cooking class at wine and olive oil estate **Castello di Volpaia** (p210). Overnight in **Siena** where **Enoteca I Terzi** (p200) beckons for dinner. Next day, shop for *panforte* (a rich cake of almonds, honey and candied fruit) to take home at **Panificio Il Magnifico** (p201), then drive to **Montalcino** for a cellar tour and lunch with award-winning Brunellos at **Ristorante di Poggio Antico** (p224). End on a culinary high at **La Bandita** (p223).

Menu Decoder

➡ **Menù di degustazione** Tasting menu.

➡ **Coperto** Cover charge, €1 to €3 per person, for complimentary bread.

➡ **Piatto del giorno** Dish of the day.

➡ **Antipasto** A hot or cold appetiser; for a mix of appetisers go for *antipasto misto* (mixed antipasto).

➡ **Primo** First course, usually pasta, rice or *zuppa* (soup).

➡ **Secondo** Second course, *carne* (meat) or *pesce* (fish).

➡ **Contorno** Vegetable side dish.

➡ **Dolce** Dessert, often *torta* (cake) or *cantucci* (dry almond-studded biscuits) dunked into a glass of sweet Vin Santo wine.

BEST WINES

➡ Brunello di Montalcino

➡ Vino Nobile di Montepulciano

➡ Chianti

➡ Vernaccia di San Gimignano

➡ Super Tuscan Sassicaia

➡ **Acqua minerale** (mineral water) Jugs of tap water aren't in, but a bottle of *frizzante* (sparkling) or *naturale* (still) with a meal is a Tuscan standard.

➡ **Vino della casa** (house wine) Wine in restaurants is reasonably priced and good; the cheapest is house wine, ordered in carafes of 25cl, 50cl, 75cl or a litre.

Plan Your Trip

Outdoor Experiences

When Renaissance man's brilliance gets too much, flee into the open arms of Mother Nature. This green region has mountains of natural beauty to savour, the only prerequisite being go slow: to skip the myriad of outdoor activities underscoring Tuscany's natural splendour is to zap the essence of Tuscany.

Top Outdoor Experiences

Best Short Walks

Vie Cave, along Etruscan sunken roads below **Pitigliano** (p242)

Guided nature walks in hills around **San Gimignano** (p214)

Montalcino to Abbazia di Sant'Antimo, **Val d'Orcia** (p225)

Best Easy Bike Rides

With elegance atop the city walls of **Lucca** (p134)

Around **Chianti** (p202) vineyards and olive groves

Elba (p176) island touring

Best at Sea

Sea kayaking and diving offshore from **Elba** (p176)

Slicing silent waterways with a canoe, **Parco Regionale della Maremma** (p248)

Best Spa Towns

Old English literati fave **Bagni di Lucca** (p152)

Ancient Roman soak **Terme di Saturnia** (p246)

Montecatini Terme (www.termemontecatini.it) of Puccini fame

On Your Marks

Efficient pre-trip planning of your outdoor adventures ensures you can revel in the Tuscan thrills without any unexpected spills once in situ.

When to Go?

Lapping up all that fresh mountain and sea air, heady with the scent of wild sage and maritime pine, is an integral part of the Tuscan outdoor experience. Spring and autumn with their abundance of warm dry days, wild flowers and forest fruits, are the prettiest times to be outdoors. July (not as hot or crowded as August) is the best month for water-sports on the Med and hiking in the Apuane Alps. Autumn, when the harvests start in the vineyards and olive groves, has a particularly mellow appeal and, with summer's warmth lingering well into October, there is plenty of daylight for mellow hikes through dewy mornings, crunchy leaves and mushroom-rich forests.

Avoid

Easter The first key holiday period of the year for Italians, this two-week slot in late March or April sees too many people jostle for too little picnic-table and trail space.

August Italians take their summer holidays, crowding trails, cycling routes and roads. On lower terrain, the intense heat of August can be oppressive.

Autumn Often means slippery wet roads and poor visibility for cyclists.

Where to Go

Whatever outdoor activity rocks your boat, there is a part of Tuscany with your name on it. For token outdoor activists, essentially urban at heart, plump for Florence as a base – the city has bags of bike-tour operators running two-wheel day trips to Chianti.

Chianti Tuscany's key wine-growing area means easy walking and cycling between achingly pretty vine and olive groves.

Apuane Alps & Garfagnana Ruggedly scenic and off the mainstream tourist radar, with the region's most dramatic mountains, marble quarries and forested valleys: hiking, caving, mountain biking and horse-riding.

Etruscan Coast Hit the beach, July and August, for sand, sea, sailing and water-sport action. Inland, cycling is dirt track to silky smooth.

Elba A summer island idyll with stunning sea kayaking, sailing, diving and snorkelling; beautiful family walks from cove to cove, through scented *macchia* (herbal scrub) and parasol pines.

Val d'Orcia Family walking and cycling near Siena.

Maremma Hiking, biking, horse riding and backwater canoeing on Tuscany's southern coast.

Get Set

Before diving into Tuscany's ethereal landscape, get set with the necessary nuts-and-bolts info and gear to ensure a silky-smooth ride.

Information

The **Region of Tuscany** (www.turismo.intoscana.it) is a one-stop resource for background information, interactive maps and inspiring routes on foot, by bike or horseback. Caving, spas and water sports are other activities it covers.

Throughout Tuscany, tourist offices and national-park offices have mountains of information on outdoor activities, including lists of guides and accommodation options en route. Printed brochures detailing trails are increasingly scarce – buy maps and guides online before leaving home.

Various actiivity operators and specialists are listed throughout this guide; **Toscana Adventure Team** (☎0571 99 32 52, 3487 91 12 15; www.tateam.it; Casa Carbonaia, Via di Santa Lucia 11, Vinci) is a great all-rounder, organising everything from mountain-biking and horse-riding to coasteering, canyoning, helibiking, abseiling, trekking and caving. Also try **Hedonistic Hiking** (☎Australia 61 3 5755 2307, UK 44 1858 565148; www.hedonistichiking.com.au), which offers treks around Volterra, Pisa, Elba, Lucca, Chianti and Siena with luxurious villa accommodation and gourmet meals.

Maps

Florentine cartographer **Edizioni Multigraphic** publishes maps for walkers and mountain-bike riders with *sentieri* (walking trails), *mulattiere* (mule tracks, especially good for mountain bikes), mountains huts and so on superimposed on the map. Its *Carte dei Sentieri* (1:25,000) and *Carte Turistica e dei Sentieri* (1:25,000 or

BEST WALKS IF YOU LIKE ...

- **Etruscan ruins** Golfo di Baratti (p173), Pitigliano (p242)
- **Birdwatching** Riserva Naturale Provinciale Diaccia Botrona (p248); Laguna di Orbetello (p249); Parco Regionale Migliarino, San Rossore, Massaciuccoli (p46)
- **Cowboys** Parco Regionale della Maremma (p248)
- **Geology** Monterotondo Marittimo (p240)
- **Wine** Chianti (p202), Montalcino (p222), Montepulciano (p227)
- **Pilgrim paths** Marciana (p183), Abbazia di Sant'Antimo (p225)
- **Coastal panoramas** Monte Capanne (p184), Marciana (p184)
- **Art & Sculpture** Parco Sculture del Chianti (p211) and Fattoria di Celle (p146)

1:50,000) map series are both available online at **Omnimap** (www.omnimap.com).

What to Take

Generally you'll only need the minimum of items – for easy walks or bike rides, a pair of trainers and small daypack containing an extra layer of clothing and wet-weather gear. Sunblock, sunglasses and a hat (helmet for cyclists) are essential. Budget at least one bottle of water, calculating for at least 1.5L per walker or cyclist for a summertime day. A fistful of high-nutrition, easily assimilated food, such as cereal bars, dried fruit or nuts, can impart a quick energy kick.

Map and compass are obviously essential off the beaten track. Wild camping is not permitted in the high mountains; plan overnight stops around the availability of beds in *rifugi* (mountain huts); bring a sleeping bag.

Go

Pretrip planning done: go, do Tuscany. But don't expect machine-gun adrenalin rushes and life-changing palpitations of the heart. In typical Tuscan style, outdoor action is beaded with serenity – a lazed, go-slow experience designed wholly with appreciation of masterpiece landscape and cuisine in mind.

Caving

Typically it's a sport completely inaccessible without the gear and expertise. But deep in the Apuane Alps, seasonal three-hour tours of the Grotta del Vento (p152) – 1200 steps past subterranean rivers and crystal-brimmed lakes – are an extraordinary experience.

Walking

People have been criss-crossing Tuscany for millennia, creating paths and trails as they went. One of the most important pilgrim routes in Europe during the Dark Ages was the **Via Francigena**, in its time a veritable highway across Tuscany. Starting in the Magra river valley and winding through the wild Lunigiana territory of the northwest, the trail hugged the coast for a while before cutting inland to Siena via San Gimignano and then turning south to Rome. Parts of the route can be walked today. *Via Francigena in Toscana* (1:50,000) is an excellent hiking map.

The other extreme is the 24-stage **Grande Escursione Appenninica** that goes from the Due Santi pass above La Spezia southeast to Sansepolcro in eastern Tuscany.

Chianti is the big walking favourite and is the essence of what Tuscan walking

NATIONAL & REGIONAL PARKS

Created to protect a diverse booty of land, river, lake and marine ecosystems, Tuscany's national parks and nature parks are naturally rich in outdoor experiences.

PARK	FEATURES
Parco Nazionale dell'Arcipelago Toscano	Europe's largest marine park, covering 18,000 hectares of land and 60,000 sq metres of sea; typical Mediterranean island flora and fauna
Parco Nazionale delle Foreste Casentinesi, Monte Falterona e Campigna	source of the river Arno and Italy's most extensive, best-preserved forest: ancient pines, beech, five maple types and the rare yew; deer, wild boar, mouflon, wolves and 97 nesting bird species
Parco Alpi Apuane	mountainous regional park cascading to the sea from the Garfagnana; golden eagles, peregrine falcons, buzzards and the rare chough (the park's symbol)
Parco Regionale Migliarino, San Rossore, Massaciuccoli	coastal reserve stretching from Viareggio to Livorno; extraordinary birdlife (over 200 species) in its marshes, dunes and wetland
Parco Regionale della Maremma	regional park comprising the Uccelllina mountains, pine forest, agricultural farmland, marshland and 20km of unspoiled coastline; oak and cork oak, herbal maquis (scrubland); Maremma cows, horses and chickens

is about – rambling from vineyard to wine cellar to century-old farm where the day ends with a feast of homemade pasta, salami, meat and other tasty farm products enjoyed with gusto. Several atmospheric overnights in farmstay accommodation punctuate the classic walk from Florence to Siena. **Il Mugello**, northeast of Florence, is another area within easy reach of Florence for half- and full-day walks.

On Elba – a prime hiking spot, more for its dramatic scenery than challenging peaks – the only real stiff hike is up **Monte Capanne**.

Alpine Practicalities

More serious hikers head to the **Apuane Alps** and the **Garfagnana** on the spine of the Apennines in northwest Tuscany. Main town Castelnuovo di Garfagnana is the choice base camp and the place to pick up information on *rifugi* found at higher altitudes on hiking trails in the Apuane Alps. Most can only be reached on foot from June to September, and have basic kitchen facilities and/or serve meals. Some are privately run; many are part of Italy's national alpine association **Club Alpino Italiano** (CAI; www.cai.it).

Cycling

Whether you're out for a day's gentle pedal around Florence, a sybaritic weekend winery tour in Chianti with friends, or a serious workout with a week or more of pedal power, Tuscany cooks up bags of cycling scope.

The most versatile bicycle for Tuscan roads is a comfortable all-terrain bike capable of travelling over paved and country roads and, more importantly, able to climb hills without forcing you to over-exert yourself.

The picturesque **Strada Chiantigiana** (SS222) waltzes through Chianti wine country on its way from Florence to Siena, while **Le Crete** and **Val d'Orcia** in central Tuscany wheels out a fanfare of golden wheat fields and cypress alleys for passing cyclists.

Back roads and trails are an interesting option for the fairly fit with a multigear mountain bike – rural Tuscany is mainly hilly. **Monte Amiata** is the perfect goal for aspiring hill climbers, while **Chianti** and **Le Crete** sport ample hilly itineraries with short but challenging climbs.

For those seeking a gentler ride, the **Etruscan Coast** and **south of Livorno** along the scenic wine and oil road are favourites; ask at Livorno tourist office for the *Costa degli Etruschi: Cycling Itineraries* booklet detailing 20 cycling routes.

WEBSITE	ACTIVITIES	BEST TIME TO VISIT
www.islepark.it	sea kayaking, sailing, diving, snorkelling, water sports, walking, cycling, wine tasting	spring and summer
www.parcoforestecasentinesi.it	walking, hiking, birdwatching	spring and autumn
www.parcapuane.toscana.it	hiking, mountain biking, caving	summer and autumn
www.parcosanrossore.org	easy walking, cycling, horse-riding, birdwatching, canoeing	spring, summer and autumn
www.parco-maremma.it	walking, hiking, cycling, horse-riding, canoeing	spring and autumn (mid-Jun–mid-Sep visits by guided tour only)

BEST ONE-DAY BIKE TOURS

Florence and Siena are hubs for hooking up with a cycling guide. One-day tours (23km) only need to be booked a day or two in advance. Everything is supplied, including bike, helmet, route map, water bottle and quite often lunch and/or wine tasting.

In Florence try Florence by Bike (p118) if you're wanting the bike and itinerary but no guide; and FiesoleBike (p96) to pedal from Fiesole to Florence at sunset.

If bringing your own bike from home, check with your airline whether there's a fee and how much, if any, disassembling and packing it requires. Bikes can be transported by train in Italy, either with you or to arrive within a couple of days.

Practicalities

For those not willing or able to haul their bikes from home, there are plenty of places in Tuscany to rent a pair of wheels and buy the colour-coordinated lycra. Book through **EcoRent** (www.ecorent.net), or upon arrival at bike-rental outlets in Florence, Pisa, Lucca, Siena and other towns. Many hotels and *agriturismi* (farm stay accommodation) also organise bike rental.

While most historic town and city centres are closed to cars, cyclists are free to enter at will. But the real joy is once you head out into Tuscany's green belt of wildflower meadows, sage-scented hedgerows and kilometre after kilometre of traffic-free road.

Horse-Riding

The rhythmic crunch of hooves as you saunter serenely on horseback through chestnut and cork oak wood, past fields of bright yellow sunflowers and wild red poppies, and between vines, is hypnotically calming, aromatic – and oh-so-Tuscan.

Riding is big region-wide, with plenty of *agriturismi* having horses for guests to ride. Several farms, especially in southern Tuscany's **Parco Regionale della Maremma**, specialise in equestrian holidays and offer treks of one or several days. Combining the intimacy of *agriturismi* and meals around a shared table with the formality of a riding school, these equestrian farms are the most atmospheric way of experiencing Tuscany on horseback; Circolo Ippico Uccellina (p249) and Il Gelsomino (p249) are recommended horse-riding centres. Then there's the Maremma cowboy experience.

On the **Etruscan Coast**, a horseback itinerary takes riders from Livorno 170km southeast to Sassetta along a melody of sun-scorched coastal paths (best in spring and autumn), agricultural cart tracks, and summer-cool shady tracks through the forested hinterland (best in summer). It recommends accommodation en route for both horses and riders, and several half- and one-day loops feed off the main trail creating ample choice for riders of all abilities.

Across the water, on the island of Elba in the **Parco Nazionale dell'Arcipelago Toscano**, old military or forest tracks between trees double as equestrian pathways; Portoferraio tourist office has maps, brochures and complete trail details.

Ballooning

Drifting noiselessly over pea-green vineyards and silvery olive groves is the essence of Tuscan travel – slow, serene and cinematic.

The ballooning season is late spring to early autumn. Take-off is around 6am, flights last 1¼ hours, and cost around €240 per person, often including a champagne breakfast.

Jump in a basket and take to the skies with:

Tuscany Ballooning (☎055 824 91 20; www.tuscanyballooning.com; Via del Masso 14 , San Casciano in Val di Pesa) Near Florence.

Ballooning in Tuscany (☎338 146 29 94; www.balloonintuscany.com) South of Siena.

Chianti Ballooning (☎055 807 79 40; www.chiantiballooning.com) Chianti-based.

Water Sports

Most can easily imagine Tuscany's signature cypress trees and medieval hilltop villages, but few imagine the shimmering blue wedge of water on the horizon speckled with islands. Add a sea kayak or surfboard, and a secret sandy cove perhaps – reached only from the sea – and you

BEST EQUESTRIAN FARMSTAYS

- La Cerreta (p172), Sassetta
- Montebelli Agriturismo & Country Hotel (p241), near Vetulonia
- Il Gelsomino (p249), Alberes

have the real picture: the Tuscan coast and its offshore islands are the source of great outdoor action.

Diving & Snorkelling

The island of **Elba** is among Italy's top year-round diving spots (although you'll shiver without a semidry wetsuit between November and May): if you're into wrecks, you can plunge into blue waters at Pomonte, where the *Elvisco* cargo boat sits on the seabed 12m deep, or gawp through a mask at the German WWII plane *Junker 52,* wrecked at a more challenging depth of 38m near Portoferraio.

Otherwise, aquatic flora and fauna is protected and dramatic. Diving facilities are generally of a high standard and several diving schools on the island rent all the gear and organise guides, courses and so on. Less intrepid water lovers can snorkel.

Back on the mainland, you can also dive along the **Etruscan Coast** and further south in Porto Ercole on **Monte Argentario**.

Kayaking & Canoeing

Hot sultry summer afternoons are best spent lapping up the slow, natural rhythm of Tuscan travel in a sea kayak or canoe – from beach to beach along **Elba's** magnificent cove-clad coast (bring provisions along given it will just be you, kayak, sand, sea and one or two monumental wind-sculpted rocks) or past sand dunes in the **Parco Regionale della Maremma** (where there's a fabulous guided canoe trail).

Sailing & Surfing

The coves of the Tuscan archipelagos and around **Monte Argentario** are superb for sailing, as well as windsurfing, kite surfing and sea kayaking. Rent equipment and receive instruction at all the major resorts. **Viareggio** holds several annual sailing regattas.

White-Water Rafting

A handful of outfits in the spa town of **Bagni di Lucca** in northwestern Tuscany organise white-water rafting expeditions on the Lima River.

Plan Your Trip

Travel with Children

If you're looking for a family-friendly destination, Tuscany fits the bill. Your children might whinge about the number of churches and museums on the daily itinerary, but they'll be quickly appeased by gelato (yay!), pizza and pasta (yay again!) and the huge number of kid-friendly activities waiting to be discovered.

Best Regions for Kids

Florence

Interactive museums, fantastic *gelaterie* (ice-cream shops) and public gardens make Tuscany's major city a top choice for families.

Northwestern Tuscany

Head to the hills (in this case the Apuane Alps and Garfagnana) for the opportunity to see marble miners at work in a mountain quarry, and run up and down wildflower-carpeted hillsides. Down on the plain, the city of Lucca has lots to offer the little ones.

Central Coast & Elba

Beaches and boats. Enough said.

Southern Tuscany

This pocket of the region is full of nature reserves, national parks and archaeological sites where kids can play hide and seek in the ruins. It's the perfect place for them to run off their frightening reserves of excess energy.

Tuscany for Kids

Are We There Yet?

Most visitors tend to drive around Tuscany. Fortunately, distances between destinations aren't particularly long and there are inevitably plenty of 'spot the sheep' and 'count the churches' opportunities.

When in cars, remember that children under 12 are not allowed to sit in the front passenger seat, and that child restraints and seatbelts are mandatory.

If you're travelling on public transport, note that a seat on a bus costs the same whether you're an adult or child (you don't need to pay for toddlers and babies who sit on your lap, though). On trains, children under 12 receive a 50% discount.

Teenagers

The only family members who might not be thrilled about your choice of holiday destination are teenagers – there are no malls or theme parks here and PlayStations and Xboxes aren't among the usual amenities in hotel rooms. This means that they'll have to join the rest of the family in enjoying the huge number of outdoor and cultural activities on offer. But guess what? In the process, they might even enjoy themselves.

Discounts

If they are EU citizens, your kids will almost always be eligible for discounted or free entry to museums and other attractions. These discounts don't always apply to non-EU citizens, though. There are usually three tiers of discount: free entry for all kids under six years of age and a 50% discount for EU students aged 25 and under. A few museums and attractions offer discounted family passes; we have included details in the relevant reviews.

Beaches

Families from North America and Australasia may find Tuscan beaches disappointing, with little surf, not much sand and hardly any room in summer. Many tracts of beach have been privatised – you may have to pay for a chair and beach umbrella.

While sunblock is used by some locals, protective beachwear with an Ultraviolet Protection Factor (UPF) – recommended by skin cancer organisations in Australia and North America – are not readily available here. Bring your own and expect your kids to attract a few strange looks when they enter the water wearing them.

For the best beach experiences in the region, head to Elba.

Museums & Churches

Hmm. What's the solution when the adults can't wait to visit churches and museums, but the kids can't imagine anything worse (and are quick to say so)? Bribery inevitably works, but there's also the possibility of visiting museums with interactive displays or child-oriented tours. When all else fails in an art gallery or church, we've been known to play 'Spot a realistic-looking Baby Jesus painting'. It's never going to happen (one of the great mysteries of Renaissance art), but there's nothing like a challenge to keep kids engaged!

Children's Highlights

For experiences that keep your kids active and engaged and that you might enjoy too, consider the suggestions below.

Towers to Climb

➡ **Torre del Mangia, Siena** Steep steps (lots of them) and awesome views at the top. (p189)

➡ **Duomo and Campanile, Florence** Climb up Giotto's *campanile* (bell tower) or into Brunelleschi's dome. (p69)

➡ **Leaning Tower, Pisa** Yes, it really does lean. And yes, it's loads of fun to take photographs simulating your kids holding it up. (p125)

➡ **Torre d'Arnolfo, Florence** Clamour up 418 steps to reach the Palazzo Vecchio's battlements. (p72)

➡ **Torre Civica delle Ore, Lucca** See if you meet the resident ghost in this 13th-century clock tower. (p134)

BRIBERY: A PARENT'S BEST FRIEND

Maybe you're trying to coax the junior members of the family to accompany you to a museum or church. Or perhaps you're keen to ensure a low whine factor on car trips. Whatever the situation, there's nothing wrong with a spot of parental bribery. Consider the following:

Agriturismi Book into a farm stay and you'll usually be able to ensure a full morning's sightseeing by promising that the afternoon will be spent by the pool or patting the resident dogs, cats and farm animals.

Gelato Anywhere, any time. It almost always works.

Pizza Usually pizzerias only open in the evening. This means that the prospect of a pizza dinner can sometimes ensure a full day's good behaviour.

Hot Chocolate A deliciously smooth and sweet version awaits at Caffè Rivoire, conveniently close to the Uffizi Gallery.

Pinocchio Tuscany is the birthplace of the cute wooden boy with the long nose, and souvenir stalls everywhere sell Pinocchio marionettes, wooden figures and other toys that little kids love.

PLANNING

Travelling with children involves little extra predeparture planning. Your most important decisions will be about accommodation. We highly recommend that you consider staying in *agriturismi* (farm stay accommodation) and country villas, as these often offer kid-friendly activities such as swimming, tennis, horse-riding and mountain biking. Many also have restaurants, which can be a godsend after a big day out and about.

Gardens to Explore

➡ **Parco Sculture del Chianti, Central Tuscany** A 1km walking trail and lots of peculiar artworks to gawk at. (p211)

➡ **Giardino dei Tarocchi, Southern Tuscany** If you thought the Parco Sculture del Chianti's artworks were strange, wait until you see the giant sculptures at this place! (p250)

➡ **Giardino di Boboli, Florence** Statues, hidden paths and a really weird 'face' sculpture. (p88)

Cool Stuff

➡ **Cava di Fantiscritti, Carrara** Take a Bond-style 4WD tour of the open-cast quarry or follow miners into the core of a marble mountain. (p154)

➡ **Museo Piaggio, Northwestern Tuscany** Scooters. Way cool. (p133)

➡ **City walls, Lucca** Hire a bike and ride along the top of the walls, stopping for a picnic along the way. (p135)

➡ **Grotta del Vento, Northwestern Tuscany** Explore a world of underground abysses, lakes and caverns. (p152)

➡ **Museo Galileo, Florence** Astronomical and mathematical treasures collected by the Medicis, with plenty of hands-on opportunities to explore how they work. (p74)

➡ **Cabinovia Monte Capanne, Elba** Take a cable car up Elba's highest peak. (p184)

➡ **Pistoia Sotteranea, Pistoia** Discover subterranean rivers underneath a 13th-century hospital. (p144)

➡ **Martelli, Lari** They love to eat it, so it's not surprising that kids enjoy watching spaghetti being made, too. (p170)

Wildlife Encounters

➡ **Museo di Storia Naturale del Mediterraneo, Livorno** Check out the skeleton of Annie the whale. (p167)

➡ **Parco Regionale Migliarino, San Rossore, Massaciuccoli, Northwestern Tuscany** Take a horse-drawn carriage ride around this natural reserve just outside Pisa.

➡ **Riserva Naturale Provinciale Diaccia Botrona, Southern Tuscany** Spot flamingos and herons on a boat tour through the marshes. (p248)

➡ **Parco Regionale della Maremma, Southern Tuscany** Hike, cycle or canoe through this huge coastal park. (p248)

➡ **Acquario di Livorno, Livorno** Meet Cuba, the huge green resident turtle. (p166)

Knights & Castles

➡ **Fortezza Medicea, Cortona** Your kids won't have any trouble walking uphill to the town's highest point. The same, alas, cannot be said for all parents; it's really steep, so consider yourself warned. (p269)

➡ **Museo Stibbert, Florence** Lifesized figures of horses and their riders in all manner of suits of armour from Europe and the Middle East. (p77)

➡ **Castello dei Conti Guidi, Eastern Tuscany** A real castle, complete with dungeons and a suit of armour. (p263)

➡ **Palazzo Vecchio, Florence** Not really a castle (it's a palace), but there are secret staircases, hidden rooms and you can meet the original residents. Well, sort of... (p72)

Kid-Friendly Walks

➡ **'Le Biancane' Monterotondo Marittimo, Southern Tuscany** A two-hour walk through a strange geothermal landscape full of belching steam and sulpher crystals. (p240)

➡ **Vie Cave, Pitigliano to Sorano** Excite young historians with a trail along sunken Etruscan roads. (p242)

➡ **Parco Archeologico di Baratti e Populonia, Golfi di Baratti** Incredible trails around quarries and ruined tombs. (p173)

➡ **Elba** The largest island in the Tuscan archipelago is especially well geared for short walks, with lots of capes and beaches. (p178)

Regions at a Glance

Florence

Food
Art
Shopping

Gourmet Paradise

The city's exceptional dining scene encompasses everything from fast food (eg tripe *panini* from old-fashioned street carts) to no-nonsense trattorias, bustling food markets and the only restaurant in Tuscany to possess three Michelin stars.

Renaissance Beauty

The Uffizi is one of the world's most famous art galleries, but it's not the only repository of artistic masterpieces in the city. Churches, chapels and a bevy of lesser-known museums showcase masterpieces galore.

Fashion & Artisan Crafts

From the designer boutiques on the chic shopping strip of Via de' Tornabuoni to tiny artisan workshops hidden down laneways in the traditional craft district of Oltrarno: the city where Gucci was born really is the last word in quality shopping.

p56

North-western Tuscany

Food
Mountains
The Outdoors

White Truffles

No single food is lusted over as much as the perfectly perfumed fresh white truffle – here, they're hunted in dew-kissed forests around San Miniato and eaten with gusto during autumn truffle season.

Majestic Marble

Take a drive from the Garfagnana through rugged peaks and richly forested valleys laced with walking trails to witness the majestic marble mountains of the Apuane Alps in their full glory.

On Your Bike!

The trio of valleys that form the Garfagnana region perfectly suits holiday-makers keen on hiking, biking and eating. Trails criss-cross chestnut woods and forests rich in berries and porcini mushrooms.

p120

Central Coast & Elba

Food
Beaches
History

Seafood in Livorno

The feisty locals in this gritty waterside city are staunchly proud of *cacciucco,* a remarkable seafood stew swimming with at least five types of fish. It's best enjoyed with a glass of local Sassicaia wine.

Coastal Capers

Visit Elba, the palm tree–clad paradise where Napoleon was banished. This bijou island offers a sensational mix of sunbathing, seakayaking, snorkelling and swimming.

Etruscan Heritage

Exploring the remains of ancient Etruscan tombs and temples hidden beneath sky-high parasol pines on the Golfo di Baratti's sandy shoreline is an extraordinary experience. Pair it with gentle walking and a picnic lunch.

p162

Siena & Central Tuscany

Food
Wine
Hill Towns

Sweet Temptations

Sample the biscuits and cakes that Siena is famous for, accompanied by a coffee or dunked in a glass of sweet Vin Santo wine at the end of a meal.

In Vino Veritas

When it comes to wine, it doesn't get any better than this. Brunello, Vino Nobile, Chianti Classico and Vernaccia all hail from here, and estates throughout the region produce the stuff that makes international wine buffs happy.

Take to the Hills

Explore scenic hilltowns such as Montalcino, Montepulciano, Volterra and San Gimignano where the intact medieval architecture is as impressive as the views – and that's really saying something.

p187

Southern Tuscany

Food
Archaeology
Nature

Slow Food

This is a no-fuss zone when it comes to cuisine. Local chefs buy local, stick to the season and subscribe to the concept of Slow Food. And you've gotta love that.

Waves of Civilisation

The Etruscans certainly left their mark here, and the countryside of the extraordinary Città del Tufa (City of the Tufa) is littered with their tombs. The Romans didn't shirk in this respect either, as a visit to the archaeological sites of Roselle or Vetulonia will attest.

Land of the Big Sky

Europe's bird species stop here on their migration to North Africa for good reason – huge tracts of pristine landscape boast an impressive range of flora and fauna.

p232

Eastern Tuscany

Food
Holy Sites
Art

The Real McCoy

Come to the Val di Chiana to eat Italy's best *bistecca alla fiorentina,* the succulent, lightly seared piece of locally raised Chianina beef that is Tuscany's signature dish.

Holy Places

St Francis is closely associated with this part of Tuscany. Born in nearby Assisi, he is said to have received the stigmata at the Santuario della Verna in the wonderfully wild Casentino forest.

Arty Itineraries

The old adage 'quality before quantity' applies here. Follow a trail highlighting the works of Piero della Francesca, but also look out for works by Cimabue, Fra' Angelico, Signorelli, Rosso Fiorentino, the Lorenzettis and the della Robbias.

p251

On the Road

Elba

Florence

POP 357,300

Includes ➡

Best Places to Eat

- Il Santo Bevitore (p105)
- Trattoria Mario (p102)
- Obikà (p101)
- Antica Trattoria da Tito (p103)
- iO Osteria Personale (p105)

Best Places to Stay

- Hotel Scoti (p96)
- Antica Torre dei Via de' Tornabuoni 1 (p97)
- Palazzo Guadagni Hotel (p100)
- Villa Landucci (p99)
- Academy Hostel (p98)

Why Go?

Return time and again and you still won't see it all. Stand on a bridge over the Arno river several times in a day and the light, mood and view changes every time. Surprisingly small as it is, this riverside city is like no other. Cradle of the Renaissance and of tourist masses that flock here to feast on world-class art, Florence (Firenze) is magnetic, romantic and busy. Its urban fabric has hardly changed since the Renaissance, its narrow streets evoke a thousand tales, and its food and wine are so wonderful the tag 'Fiorentina' has become an international label of quality assurance.

Fashion designers parade on Via de' Tornabuoni. Gucci was born here, as was Roberto Cavalli who, like many a smart Florentine these days, hangs out in wine-rich hills around Florence. After a while in this absorbing city, you might want to do the same.

Road Distances

	Florence	Pisa	Lucca	San Miniato
Pisa	69			
Lucca	61	23		
San Miniato	37	47	70	
Siena	51	87	30	77

Getting Around

Regular buses link Florence and Pisa airports with Florence's central train station, Stazione di Santa Maria Novella, from where the city centre is a 10-minute walk. Florence itself is small and best navigated on foot, with most major sights within easy walking distance. There are bicycles for rent and an efficient network of buses and trams. Unless you're mad, forget a car.

THREE PERFECT DAYS

Day 1: David Tour

Follow the world's most famous naked man: start with Michelangelo's original in the Galleria dell'Accademia, saunter past Piazza della Signoria's famous copy, then hit Museo del Bargello to see versions by Donatello and Andrea Verrocchio. Enjoy other Michelangelo creations in the Biblioteca Medicea Laurenzia and Basilica di Santo Spirito; watch the sun set from Piazzale Michelangelo.

Day 2: Both Sides of the Arno

Spend the morning at the Uffizi, followed by a gourmet sandwich at 'Ino, or a wine-bar lunch at Cantinetta dei Verrazzano or La Canova di Gustavino. Should you have organised it in advance, take a guided tour of the Vasarian Corridor, or take our Walking Tour (p90) with a detour along Via de' Tornabuoni for window-shopping and a truffle *panino* at Procacci. Come evening, cross the Arno for an *aperitivo* at Le Volpe e L'uva or Il Santino, and dinner at Il Santo Bevitore or Il Guscio.

Day 3: No Art Please!

Begin on Piazza della Signoria with breakfast at Caffè Rivoire, then visit the Gucci Museo and have a coffee in its cafe. Walk to the river, where Museo Galileo enthrals. Cross Ponte Vecchio for lunch at Il Ristoro or Olio & Convivium, then walk to Palazzo Pitti, behind which the city's loveliest green space, Giardino di Boboli, unfolds. Indulge in afternoon tea with a view in Giardino Bardini, then head east to San Niccolò. Savour the sunset from Piazzale Michelangelo and dinner at a Piazza Santo Spirito eatery.

Where to Stay

- Florence is unexpectedly small, rendering almost anywhere in the centre convenient.
- Budget hotels are clustered around the Santa Maria Novella train station and Mercato Centrale in neighbouring San Lorenzo.
- Hip Santa Croce and the Oltrarno are packed with great dining addresses.

DON'T MISS

No frescoes better portray the humanist spirit of the Renaissance than those by Fra' Angelico in Florence's Museo di San Marco (p80). The climax is his superb *Annunciation* (c 1440).

Best Frescoes

- Chiesa di Santa Trinita (p75)
- Basilica di Santa Maria Novella (p76)
- Palazzo Medici-Riccardi (p78)
- Museo di San Marco (p80)
- Cappella Brancacci (p85)

Best City Panoramas

- Dome & Campanile, Duomo (p69)
- Torre d'Arnolfo, Palazzo Vecchio (p72)
- Piazzale Michelangelo (p92)
- La Terrazza, Continentale Hotel (p107)

Resources

- **Florentine** (www.theflorentine.net) English-language newspaper
- **Florence Museums** (www.firenzemusei.it)
- **Florence Tourism** (www.firenzeturismo.it)
- **Art Trav** (www.arttrav.com) Penned by a Florence-based art historian
- **Firenze Spettacolo** (www.firenzespettacolo.it) City entertainment guide

Florence Highlights

❶ Visit the world's most extraordinary collection of Renaissance paintings at the **Uffizi Gallery** (p64).

❷ Admire sculptural tombs of Florentine luminaries and a Brunelleschi chapel at the **Basilica di Santa Croce** (p81).

❸ Scale new heights inside the **duomo** (p69): climb its dome and bell tower.

❹ Contemplate the artistic genius of Fra' Angelico at **Museo di San Marco** (p80).

❺ Explore artisan workshops, where real Florentines live, work and meet for *aperitivi* (pre-dinner drink), in **Oltrarno** (p84).

❻ Hike uphill to meet a copy of *David* and the most magnificent city panorama at the **Piazzale Michelangelo** (p92).

❼ Escape the city heat for a day between olive groves and Roman ruins in hilltop **Fiesole**; lunch at **La Reggia degli Etruschi** (p96) and cycle back to Florence with the setting sun and local guide Giovanni.

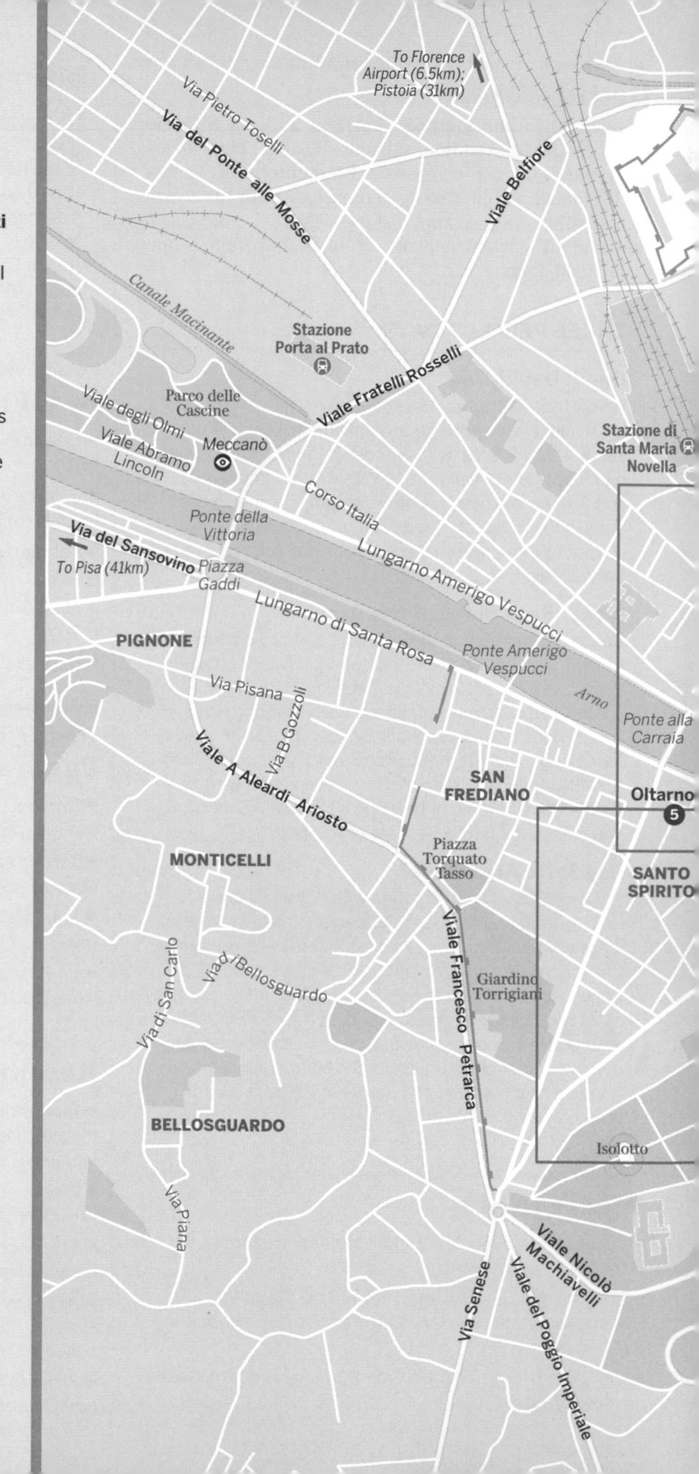

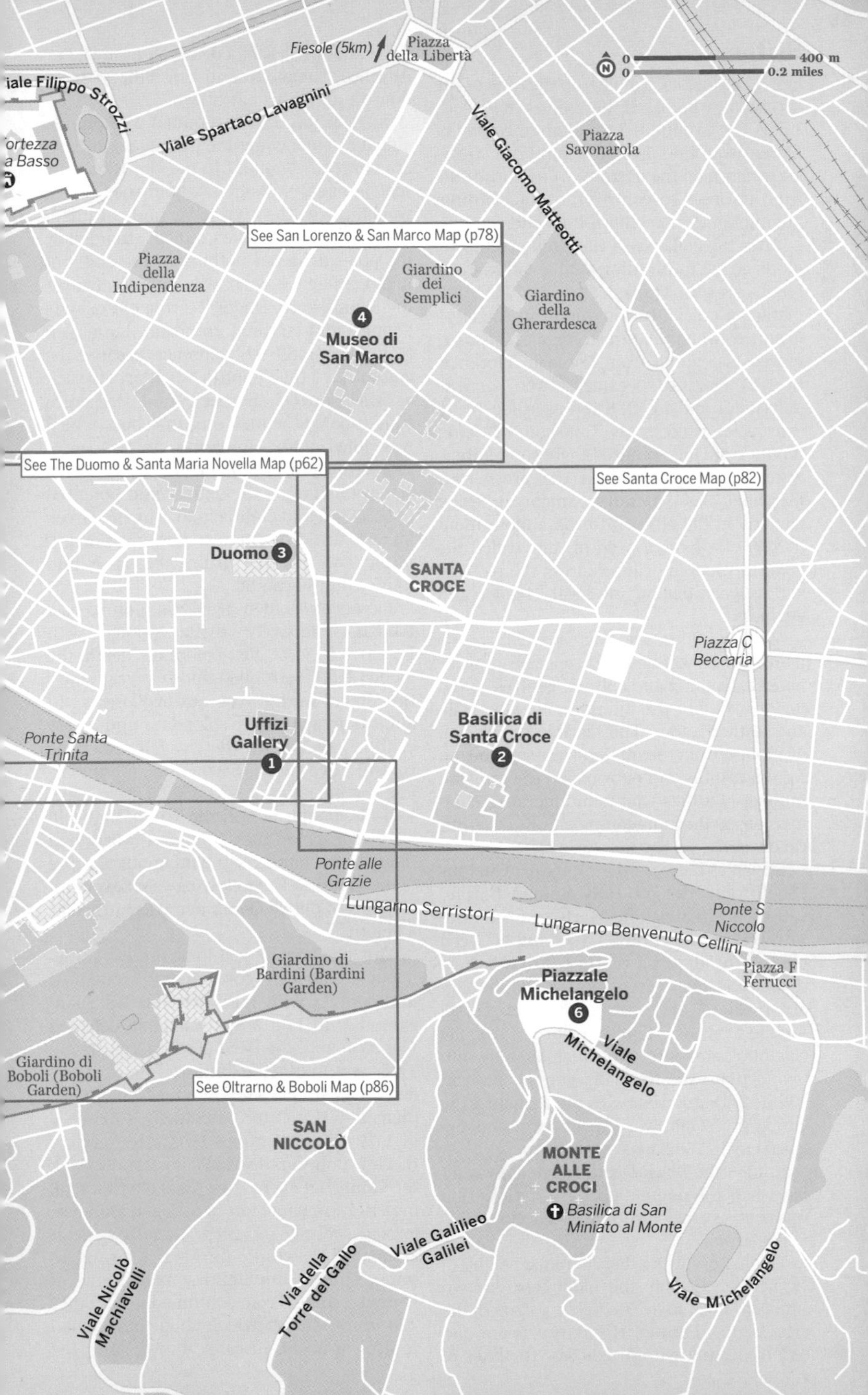

Fiesole (5km)
Piazza della Libertà
0 400 m
0 0.2 miles
Viale Filippo Strozzi
Viale Spartaco Lavagnini
Fortezza da Basso
Viale Giacomo Matteotti
Piazza Savonarola
See San Lorenzo & San Marco Map (p78)
Piazza della Indipendenza
Giardino dei Semplici
Giardino della Gherardesca
4
Museo di San Marco
See The Duomo & Santa Maria Novella Map (p62)
See Santa Croce Map (p82)
Duomo 3
SANTA CROCE
Piazza C Beccaria
Basilica di Santa Croce
2
Uffizi Gallery
1
Ponte Santa Trìnita
Ponte alle Grazie
Lungarno Serristori
Lungarno Benvenuto Cellini
Ponte S Niccolo
Piazza F Ferrucci
Giardino di Bardini (Bardini Garden)
Piazzale Michelangelo
6
Viale Michelangelo
Giardino di Boboli (Boboli Garden)
See Oltrarno & Boboli Map (p86)
SAN NICCOLÒ
MONTE ALLE CROCI
Basilica di San Miniato al Monte
Viale Galilieo Galilei
Via della Torre del Gallo
Viale Nicolò Machiavelli
Viale Michelangelo

History

Florence's history stretches to the time of the Etruscans, who based themselves in Fiesole. Julius Caesar founded the Roman colony of Florentia around 59 BC, making it a strategic garrison on the narrowest crossing of the Arno in order to control the Via Flaminia linking Rome to northern Italy and Gaul.

After the collapse of the Roman Empire, Florence fell to invading Goths, followed by Lombards and Franks. The year AD 1000 marked a crucial turning point in the city's fortunes, when Margrave Ugo of Tuscany moved his capital from Lucca to Florence. In 1110 Florence became a free *comune* (city-state) and by 1138 it was ruled by 12 consuls, assisted by the Consiglio di Cento (Council of One Hundred), whose members were drawn mainly from the prosperous merchant class. Agitation among differing factions in the city led to the appointment in 1207 of a foreign head of state called the *podestà,* aloof in principle from the plotting and wheeler-dealing of local cliques and alliances.

Medieval Florence was a wealthy, dynamic *comune,* one of Europe's leading financial, banking and cultural centres, and a major player in the international wool, silk and leather trades. The sizeable population of moneyed merchants and artisans began forming guilds and patronising the growing number of artists who found lucrative commissions in this burgeoning city. But a political crisis was on the horizon.

Struggles between the pro-papal Guelphs (Guelfi) and the pro-Holy Roman Empire Ghibellines (Ghibellini) started in the mid-13th century, with power yo-yoing between the two for almost a century. Into this fractious atmosphere were born revolutionary artist Giotto and outspoken poet Dante Alighieri, whose family belonged to the Guelph camp. After the Guelphs split into two factions, the Neri (Blacks) and Bianchi (Whites), Dante went with the Bianchi – the wrong side – and was expelled from his beloved city in 1302, never to return.

In 1348 the Black Death spirited away almost half the population. This dark period was used as a backdrop by Boccaccio for his *Decameron.*

The history of Medici Florence begins in 1434, when Cosimo the Elder (also known simply as Cosimo de' Medici), a patron of the arts, assumed power. His eye for talent and tact in dealing with artists saw the likes of Alberti, Brunelleschi, Luca della Robbia, Fra' Angelico, Donatello and Fra' Filippo Lippi flourish under his patronage.

In 1439 the Church Council of Florence, aimed at reconciling the Catholic and Eastern churches, brought to the city Byzantine scholars and craftsmen, whom they hoped would impart the knowledge and culture of classical antiquity. The Council, attended by the pope, achieved nothing in the end, but it did influence what was later known as the Renaissance. Under the rule of Cosimo's popular and cultured grandson, Lorenzo il Magnifico (1469–92), Florence became the epicentre of this 'Rebirth', with artists such as Michelangelo, Botticelli and Domenico Ghirlandaio at work. Lorenzo's court, which was filled with Humanists (a school of thought begun in Florence in the late 14th century affirming the dignity and potential of mankind and embracing Latin and Greek literary texts), fostered a flowering of art, music and poetry, turning Florence into Italy's cultural capital.

Florence's golden age was not to last though, effectively dying (along with Lorenzo) in 1492. Just before his death, the Medici bank had failed and two years later the Medici were driven out of Florence. In a reaction against the splendour and excess of the Medici court, the city fell under the control of Girolamo Savonarola, a humourless Dominican monk who led a stern, puritanical republic. In 1497 the likes of Botticelli gladly consigned their 'immoral' works and finery to the flames of the infamous 'Bonfire of the Vanities'. The following year Savonarola fell from public favour and was burned as a heretic.

The pro-French leanings of the subsequent republican government brought it into conflict with the pope and his Spanish allies. In 1512 a Spanish force defeated Florence and the Medici were reinstated. Their tyrannical rule endeared them to few and when Rome, ruled by the Medici Pope Clement VII, fell to the emperor Charles V in 1527, the Florentines took advantage of this low point in the Medici fortunes to kick the family out again. Two years later though, imperial and papal forces besieged Florence, forcing the city to accept Lorenzo's great-grandson, Alessandro de' Medici, a ruthless transvestite whom Charles made Duke of Florence. Medici rule continued for another 200 years, during which time they gained control of all of Tuscany, though after the reign of Cosimo I (1537–74), Florence drifted into steep decline.

The last male Medici, Gian Gastone, died in 1737, after which his sister, Anna Maria, signed the grand duchy of Tuscany over to the House of Habsburg-Lorraine (at the time effectively under Austrian control). This situation remained unchanged, apart from a brief interruption under Napoleon from 1799 to 1814, until the duchy was incorporated into the Kingdom of Italy in 1860. Florence briefly became the national capital a year later, but Rome assumed the mantle permanently in 1871.

Florence was badly damaged during WWII by the retreating Germans, who blew up all of its bridges except the Ponte Vecchio. Devastating floods ravaged the city in 1966, causing inestimable damage to its buildings and artworks. However, the salvage operation led to the widespread use of modern restoration techniques that have saved artworks throughout the country. In 1993 the Mafia exploded a massive car bomb, killing five, injuring 37 and destroying a part of the Uffizi. Just over two decades later and amid a fair amount of controversy, this world-class gallery is in the midst of its biggest-ever expansion, end date yet to be confirmed.

Sights & Activities

Florence seriously overwhelms. Its wealth of museums and galleries house many of the world's most important and exquisite examples of Renaissance art, and its architecture is unrivalled. Yet the secret is not to feel pressured to see and do everything on offer here: combine your personal pick of the major sights with ample meandering through the city's warren of narrow streets.

Most churches enforce a strict dress code for visitors: no shorts, sleeveless shirts or plunging necklines.

Duomo to Piazza della Signoria

Florence's big-hit sights lie in the geographic, historic and cultural heart of the city – the tight grid of streets between Piazza del Duomo and cafe-strung Piazza della Signoria. Along **Via de' Tornabuoni** you hit Florence's main concentration of luxury designer boutiques, strung along both sides of the street like jewels on a particularly precious necklace. Prada, Gucci, Ferragamo, Gianfranco Ferre, Armani, Pucci and McQueen are all here. Two streets radiating west off

MUSEUM TICKETS

In July, August and other busy periods such as Easter, unbelievably long queues are a fact of life at Florence's key museums – if you haven't prebooked your ticket, you could well end up standing in line queuing for four hours or so.

For a fee of €3 per ticket (€4 for the Uffizi and Galleria dell'Accademia), tickets to nine *musei statali* (state museums) can be reserved, including the Uffizi, Galleria dell'Accademia (where *David* lives), Palazzo Pitti, Museo del Bargello and the Medicean chapels (Cappelle Medicee). In reality, the only museums where prebooking is vital are the Uffizi and Accademia – to organise your ticket, go online or call **Firenze Musei** (Florence Museums; 055 29 48 83; www.firenzemusei.it; telephone booking line 8.30am-6.30pm Mon-Fri, to 12.30pm Sat), with ticketing desks (open 8.30am to 7pm Tuesday to Sunday) at the Uffizi, Palazzo Pitti and outside Chiesa di Orsanmichele (open 9am to 4.30pm Monday to Friday).

At the Uffizi, signs point prebooked ticket holders to the building opposite the gallery where tickets can be collected; once you've got the ticket you go to Door 1 of the museum (for prebooked tickets only) and queue again to enter the gallery. It's annoying, but you'll still save hours of queuing time overall. Many hotels in Florence also prebook museum tickets for guests.

For one week of the year (usually sometime in spring), admission to state museums is free of charge; dates change, making it impossible to plan a trip around this, so keep your eyes open. One date that doesn't shift is 18 February, the day Anna Maria Louisa de' Medici (1667–1743) died. In honour of the last of the Medici family, who bequeathed the city its vast cultural heritage, admission to all state museums is free on this day.

EU passport holders aged under 18 and over 65 get into Florence's state museums for free, and EU citizens aged 18 to 25 pay half-price. Have your ID with you at all times. Note that museum ticket offices usually shut 30 minutes before closing time.

The Duomo & Santa Maria Novella

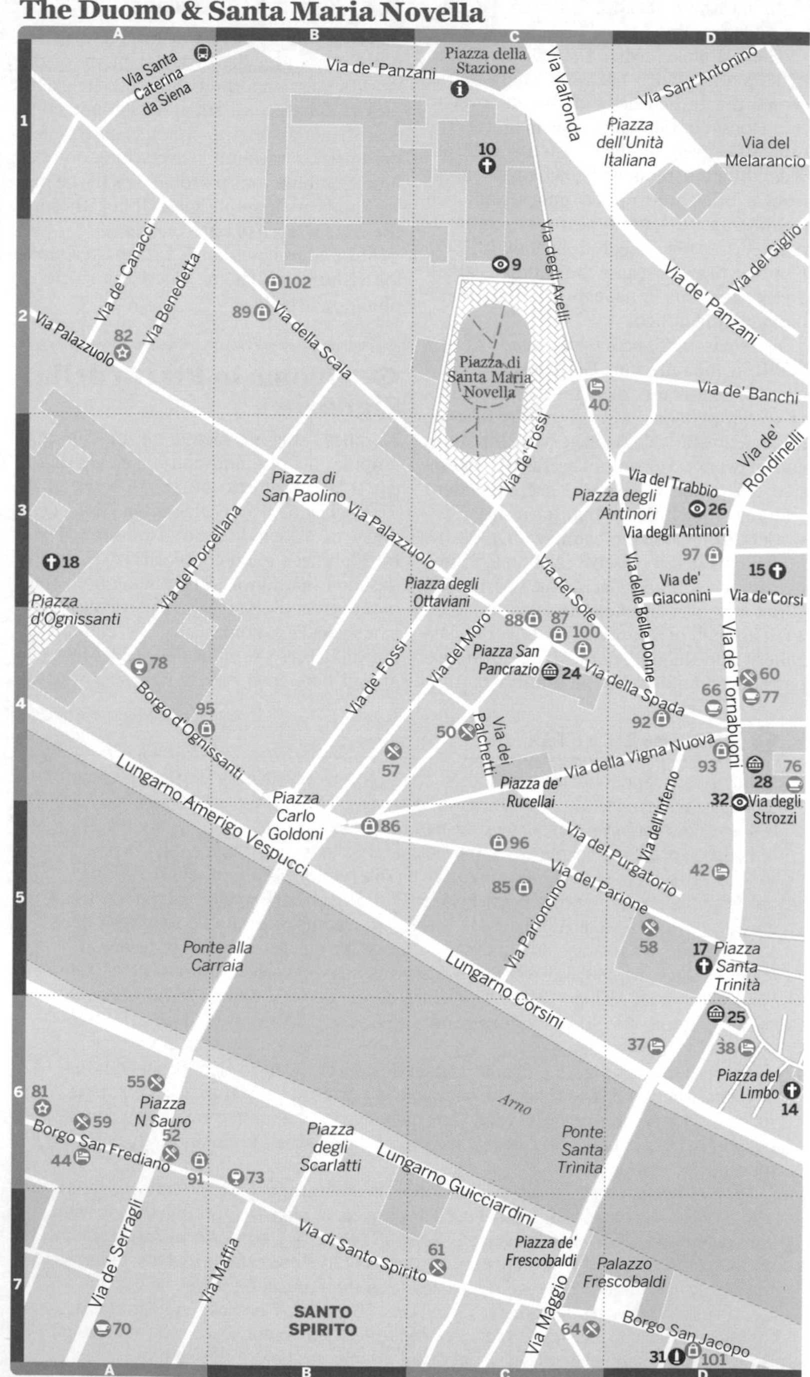

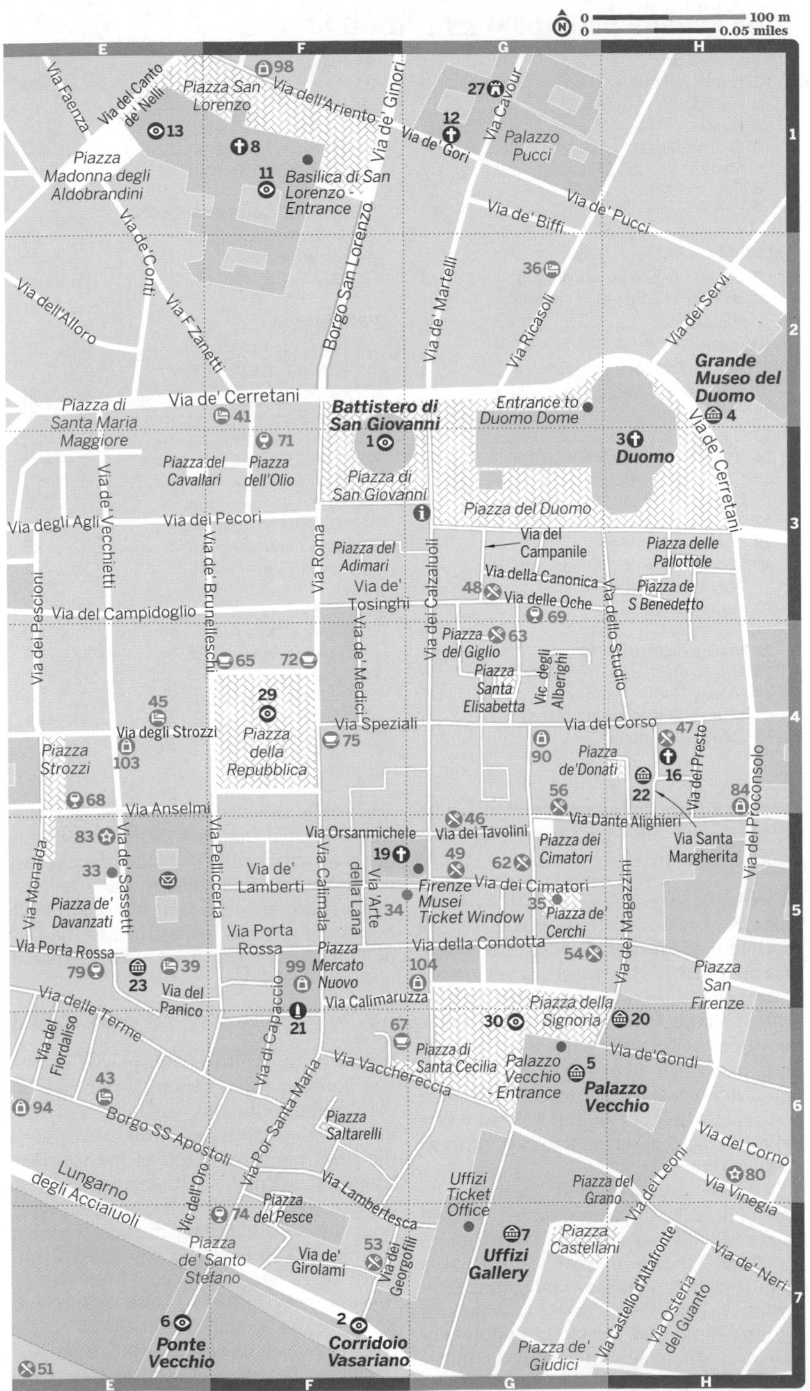

0 100 m
0 0.05 miles
Piazza San Lorenzo
Via dell'Ariento
Via de' Ginori
Via Cavour
Palazzo Pucci
Via de' Gori
Via Faenza
Via del Canto de' Nelli
Piazza Madonna degli Aldobrandini
Basilica di San Lorenzo - Entrance
Via de' Pucci
Via de' Biffi
Via de' Conti
Via dell'Alloro
Via F Zanetti
Borgo San Lorenzo
Via de' Martelli
Via Ricasoli
Via dei Servi
Grande Museo del Duomo
Piazza di Santa Maria Maggiore
Via de' Cerretani
Battistero di San Giovanni
Entrance to Duomo Dome
Duomo
Piazza del Cavallari
Piazza dell'Olio
Piazza di San Giovanni
Piazza del Duomo
Via degli Agli
Via dei Pecori
Via de' Vecchietti
Via de' Brunelleschi
Via Roma
Piazza del Adimari
Via del Campanile
Piazza delle Pallottole
Via della Canonica
Via de' Tosinghi
Via dei Calzaiuoli
Via delle Oche
Piazza de S Benedetto
Via dei Pescioni
Via del Campidoglio
Via dello Studio
Piazza del Giglio
Via de' Medici
Piazza Santa Elisabetta
Vic degli Alberighi
Via degli Strozzi
Piazza della Repubblica
Via Speziali
Via del Corso
Piazza de'Donati
Piazza Strozzi
Via del Presto
Via del Proconsolo
Via Anselmi
Via Dante Alighieri
Via Santa Margherita
Via Orsanmichele
Via dei Tavolini
Piazza dei Cimatori
Via Pellicceria
Via Calimala
Via de' Sassetti
Via Monalda
Via de' Lamberti
Via dell'Arte della Lana
Firenze Musei Ticket Window
Via dei Cimatori
Piazza de' Cerchi
Piazza de' Davanzati
Via Porta Rossa
Via dei Magazzini
Via della Condotta
Piazza Mercato Nuovo
Via del Panico
Via Calimaruzza
Piazza San Firenze
Via delle Terme
Via di Capaccio
Piazza della Signoria
Via del Fiordaliso
Piazza di Santa Cecilia
Via Vaccherecia
Palazzo Vecchio - Entrance
Via de'Gondi
Palazzo Vecchio
Borgo SS Apostoli
Via Por Santa Maria
Piazza Saltarelli
Via del Corno
Lungarno degli Acciaiuoli
Vic dell'Oro
Via Lambertesca
Uffizi Ticket Office
Piazza del Grano
Via dei Leoni
Via Vinegia
Piazza del Pesce
Uffizi Gallery
Piazza Castellani
Via de' Neri
Piazza de' Santo Stefano
Via de' Girolami
Via dei Georgofili
Via Castello d'Altafronte
Via Osteria del Guanto
Ponte Vecchio
Corridoio Vasariano
Piazza de' Giudici

The Duomo & Santa Maria Novella

Top Sights
1 Battistero di San Giovanni F3
2 Corridoio Vasariano F7
3 Duomo H3
4 Grande Museo del Duomo H2
5 Palazzo Vecchio G6
6 Ponte Vecchio E7
7 Uffizi Gallery G7

Sights
8 Basilica di San Lorenzo F1
9 Basilica di Santa Maria Novella - Entrance C2
10 Basilica e Chiostri Monumentale di Santa Maria Novella C1
11 Biblioteca Medicea Laurenziana F1
12 Cappella dei Magi G1
13 Cappelle Medicee E1
14 Chiesa dei Santissimi Apostoli D6
15 Chiesa di San Gaetano D3
16 Chiesa di Santa Margherita H4
17 Chiesa di Santa Trìnita D5
18 Chiesa d'Ognissanti A3
19 Chiesa e Museo di Orsanmichele F5
Fontana di Nettuno ..... (see 30)
20 Gucci Museo H6
21 Il Porcellino F6
22 Museo Casa di Dante H4
23 Museo di Palazzo Davanzati E5
24 Museo Marino Marini C4
25 Museo Salvatore Ferragamo D6
26 Palazzo Antinori D3
27 Palazzo Medici-Riccardi G1
28 Palazzo Strozzi D4
29 Piazza della Repubblica F4
30 Piazza della Signoria G6
31 Torre dei Marsili D7
32 Via de' Tornabuoni D4

Activities, Courses & Tours
33 ArtViva E5
34 Florence Town G5
35 Italy by Segway G5

Sleeping
36 Academy Hostel G2
37 Antica Torre di Via de' Tornabuoni 1 ..... D6
38 Hotel Cestelli D6
39 Hotel Davanzati E5
40 Hotel L'O C2
41 Hotel Perseo F2
42 Hotel Scoti D5
43 Hotel Torre Guelfa E6
44 Palazzo Magnani Feroni A6
45 Palazzo Vecchietti E4

Eating
46 Cantinetta dei Verrazzano G5
47 Da Vinattieri H4
48 Grom G3
49 I Due Fratellini G5
50 Il Latini C4
51 Il Ristoro E7

Tornabuoni, **Via della Spada** and **Via Della Vigna Nuova**, are where more edgy boutiques are found.

★Uffizi Gallery ART MUSEUM

(Map p62; www.polomuseale.firenze.it; Piazzale degli Uffizi 6; adult/reduced €6.50/3.25; ⏲8.15am-6.50pm Tue-Sun) The jewel in Florence's crown, the Uffizi fills the vast U-shaped **Palazzo degli Uffizi**. Its collection spans the gamut of art history, but its core is the masterpiece-rich Renaissance collection – Botticelli works fill an entire room. Visits are best kept to three or four hours. When it gets too much, head to the rooftop cafe for fresh air and fabulous views.

Cosimo I commissioned Vasari to design and build the gargantuan U-shaped palace in 1560 – a government office building (*uffizi* means offices) for the city's administrators, judiciary and guilds. Following Vasari's death in 1564, architects Alfonso Parigi and Bernando Buontalenti took over. Buontalenti modified the upper floor of the palace to house the works of art keenly collected by Francesco I, a passion inherited from his father. In 1580 the building was complete. By the time the last of the Medici family died in 1743, the family's private art collection was enormous. Fortunately, it was bequeathed to the City of Florence on the strict proviso that it never leave the city.

➡ Tuscan Masters: 13th Century to 14th Century

Works in the Uffizi are displayed on the 2nd floor in a series of numbered rooms off two dramatically long corridors. Arriving in the **Primo Corridoio** (First Corridor), the first room to the left of the staircase (Room 2) highlights 13th-century Sienese art and is designed like a medieval chapel (look up to admire those great wooden ceiling trusses) to reflect its fabulous contents: three large altarpieces from Florentine churches by Tuscan masters Duccio di Buoninsegna, Cimabue and Giotto. These clearly reflect the transition from the Gothic to the nascent Renaissance style.

52 Il Santo Bevitore.......... A6
53 'Ino.......... F7
54 La Canova di Gustavino.......... G5
55 La Carraia.......... A6
56 L'Antico Trippaio.......... G4
57 L'Osteria di Giovanni.......... B4
58 Mariano.......... D5
59 Momoyama.......... A6
60 Obikà.......... D4
61 Olio & Convivium.......... C7
62 Osteria Il Buongustai.......... G5
63 Tic Toc.......... G4
64 Trattoria Camillo.......... C7

Drinking & Nightlife
65 Caffè Concerto Paszkowski.......... F4
66 Caffè Giacosa.......... D4
67 Caffè Rivoire.......... F6
68 Colle Bereto.......... E4
69 Coquinarius.......... G3
70 Cuculia.......... A7
71 Fiaschetteria Nuvoli.......... F3
72 Gilli.......... F4
Gucci Museo Caffè.......... (see 20)
73 Il Santino.......... B6
74 La Terrazza.......... F7
75 La Terrazza.......... F4
76 Le Renaissance Café.......... D4
77 Procacci.......... D4
78 Sei Divino.......... A4
79 Slowly.......... E5

Entertainment
80 Blop Club.......... H6
81 La Cité.......... A6
82 Space Club.......... A2
83 YAB.......... E5

Shopping
84 A Piedi Nudi nel Parco.......... H4
85 Alberto Cozzi.......... C5
86 Alessandro Gherardeschi.......... B5
Angela Caputi.......... (see 43)
87 Aprosio & Co.......... C4
88 Desii Lab.......... C4
89 Dolce Forte.......... B2
90 Fabriano Boutique.......... G4
91 Francesco da Firenze.......... A6
92 Grevi.......... D4
93 Gucci.......... D4
94 La Bottega dell'Olio.......... E6
95 Le Gare 24.......... A4
96 Letizia Fiorini.......... C5
97 Loretta Caponi.......... D3
98 Mercato de San Lorenzo.......... F1
99 Mercato Nuovo.......... F5
100 Mio Concept.......... C4
101 Obsequium.......... D7
102 Officina Profumo-Farmaceutica di Santa Maria Novella.......... B2
103 Patrizia Pepe.......... E4
104 Pineider.......... G5

Note the overtly naturalistic realism overtones in Giotto's portrayal of the *Madonna and Child* among angels and saints, painted some 25 years after that of Duccio and Cimabue (c 1306–10).

The next room stays in Siena but moves into the 14th century. The highlight is Simone Martini's shimmering *Annunciation* (1333), painted with Lippo Memmi and setting the Madonna in a sea of gold. Also of note is *Madonna with Child and Saints* (1340) by Pietro Lorenzetti, which demonstrates a realism similar to Giotto's; unfortunately both Pietro and his artistic brother Ambrogio died from the plague in Siena in 1348.

Masters in 14th-century Florence paid as much attention to detail as their Sienese counterparts, as works in the next room demonstrate: savour the depth of realism and extraordinary gold-leaf work of *San Remigio Pietà* (1360–65) by gifted Giotto pupil, Giottino (otherwise known as Giotto di Stefano).

➡ International Gothic

Rooms 5 and 6 (actually one large room) are dedicated to works of the International Gothic style, with the knockout piece being Gentile da Fabriano's *Adoration of the Magi* (1423), originally commissioned by Palla Strozzi for Santa Trìnita.

➡ Renaissance Pioneers

A concern for perspective was a hallmark of the early-15th-century Florentine school (Room 7) that pioneered the Renaissance. One panel (the other two are in the Louvre and London's National Gallery) from Paolo Uccello's striking *Battle of San Romano* (1436–40), which celebrates Florence's victory over Siena, shows the artist's efforts to create perspective with amusing effect as he directs the lances, horses and soldiers to a central disappearing point.

In Room 8, Piero della Francesca's famous profile portraits (1465) of the crooked-nosed, red-robed Duke and Duchess of Urbino are wholly humanist in spirit: the former painted from the left side as he'd

The Uffizi

JOURNEY INTO THE RENAISSANCE

Navigating the Uffizi's main art collection, chronologically arranged in 45 rooms on one floor, is straightforward; knowing which of the 1500-odd masterpieces to view before gallery fatigue strikes is not. Swap coat and bag (travel light) for floor plan and audioguide on the ground floor, then meet 16th-century Tuscany head-on with a walk up the *palazzo's* magnificent bust-lined staircase (skip the lift – the Uffizi is as much about masterly architecture as art).

Allow four hours for this journey into the High Renaissance. At the top of the staircase, 2nd floor, show your ticket, turn left and pause to admire the full length of the first corridor sweeping south towards the Arno river. Then duck left into room 2 to witness first steps in Tuscan art – shimmering altarpieces by **Giotto** 1 et al. Journey through medieval art to room 8 and **Piero della Francesca's** 2 impossibly famous portrait, then break in the corridor with playful **ceiling art** 3 . After Renaissance heavyweights **Botticelli** 4 and **da Vinci** 5 , meander past the Tribuna (potential detour) and enjoy the daylight streaming in through the vast windows and panorama of the **riverside second corridor** 6 . Lap up soul-stirring views of the Arno, crossed by Ponte Vecchio and its echo of four bridges drifting towards the Apuane Alps on the horizon. Then saunter into the third corridor, pausing between rooms 25 and 34 to ponder the entrance to the enigmatic Vasari Corridor. End on a high with High Renaissance maestros **Michelangelo** 7 and **Raphael** 8 .

The Ognissanti Madonna
Room 2
Draw breath at the shy blush and curvaceous breast of Giotto's humanised Virgin (*Maestà;* 1310) – so feminine compared with those of Duccio and Cimabue painted just 25 years before.

Portraits of the Duke & Duchess of Urbino
Room 8
Revel in realism's voyage with these uncompromising, warts-and-all portraits (1472–75) by Piero della Francesca. No larger than A3 size, they originally slotted into a portable, hinged frame that folded like a book.

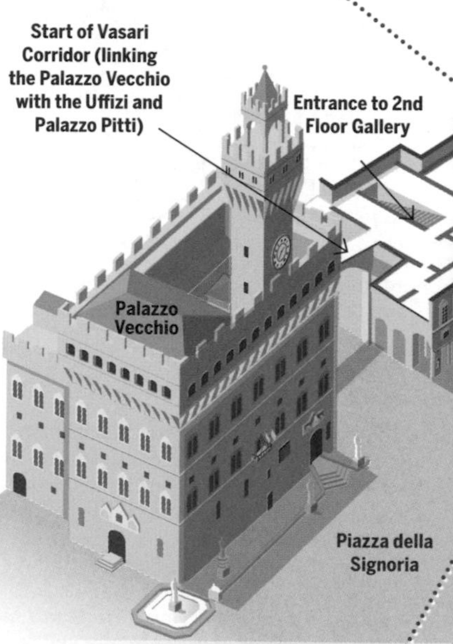

Grotesque Ceiling Frescoes
First Corridor
Take time to study the make-believe monsters and most unexpected of burlesques (spot the arrow-shooting satyr outside room 15) waltzing across this eastern corridor's fabulous frescoed ceiling (1581).

The Genius of Botticelli Room 10–14

The miniature form of *The Discovery of the Body of Holofernes* (c 1470) makes Botticelli's early Renaissance masterpiece all the more impressive. Don't miss the artist watching you in *Adoration of the Magi* (1475), left of the exit.

View of the Arno

Indulge in intoxicating city views from this short glassed-in corridor – an architectural masterpiece. Near the top of the hill, spot one of 73 outer towers built to defend Florence and its 15 city gates below.

First Corridor

Tribuna

No room in the Uffizi is so tiny or so exquisite. It was created in 1851 as a 'treasure chest' for Grand Duke Francesco and in the days of the Grand Tour, the Medici Venus here was a tour highlight.

Entrance to Vasari Corridor

Third Corridor

> **Matter of Fact**
>
> The Uffizi collection spans the 13th to 18th centuries, but its 15th- and 16th-century Renaissance works are second to none.

Doni Tondo Room 35

The creator of *David*, Michelangelo, was essentially a sculptor and no painting expresses this better than *Doni Tondo* (1506–08). Mary's muscular arms against a backdrop of curvaceous nudes are practically 3D in their shapeliness.

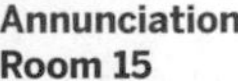

Annunciation Room 15

Admire the exquisite portrayal of the Tuscan landscape in this painting (c 1472), one of few by Leonardo da Vinci to remain in Florence.

> **Value Lunchbox**
>
> Try the Uffizi rooftop cafe or – better value – gourmet *panini* at 'Ino (www.ino-firenze.com; Via dei Georgofili 3-7r).

lost his right eye in a jousting accident, and the latter painted a deathly stone-white, reflecting the fact the portrait was painted posthumously.

Carmelite monk Fra' Filippo Lippi had an unfortunate soft spot for earthly pleasures, eloping with a nun from Prato and causing a huge scandal. Search out the artist's self-portrait as a podgy friar in *Coronation of the Virgin* (1439–47).

Another related pair, brothers Antonio and Piero del Pollaiolo, fill Room 9, where their seven cardinal and theological values of 15th-century Florence – commissioned for the merchant's tribunal in Piazza della Signoria – burst forth with fantastic energy. More restrained are Piero's *Portrait of Galeazzo Maria Sforza* (1471).

The only canvas in the theological and cardinal virtues series not to be painted by the Pollaiolos was *Fortitude* (1470), the first documented work by Botticelli.

➡ Botticelli Room

The spectacular Sala del Botticelli, numbered 10 to 14 but in fact one large hall, is one of the Uffizi's most popular rooms and is always packed. Of the 15 works by the Renaissance master known for his ethereal figures, *Birth of Venus* (c 1484), *Primavera* (Spring; c 1478), the deeply spiritual *Cestello Annunciation* (1489–90), the *Adoration of the Magi* (1475; featuring the artist's self-portrait on the extreme right) and *The Madonna of the Magnificat* (1483) are the best known. True aficionados rate his twin set of miniatures depicting a sword-bearing Judith returning from the camp of Holofernes and the discovery of the decapitated Holofernes in his tent (1495–1500) as being among his finest works.

➡ Leonardo Room

Room 15 displays two early Florentine works by Leonardo da Vinci: the incomplete *Adoration of the Magi* (1481–82), drawn in red-earth pigment (removed for restoration wotrks at the time of writing), and his *Annunciation* (c 1472).

➡ La Tribuna

The Medici clan stashed away their most precious masterpieces in this exquisite octagonal-shaped treasure trove (Room 18), created by Francesco I between 1581 and 1586. Designed to amaze and perfectly restored to its original exquisite state, a small collection of classical statues and paintings adorn its walls, upholstered in crimson silk, and 6000 mother-of-pearl shells painted with crimson varnish encrust the domed ceiling.

➡ Flemish & German Masters

Rooms 20 to 23 house works by Northern Renaissance painters including Abrecht Dürer *(Adoration of the Magi;* 1504), and Lukas Cranach the Elder *(Adam and Eve;* 1528).

➡ High Renaissance to Mannerism

Passing through the loggia or **Secondo Corridoio** (Second Corridor) visitors enjoy wonderful views of Florence before entering the **Terzo Corridoio** (Third Corridor), rooms 25 to 34 were closed at the time of writing as part of the massive ongoing expansion and reorganisation of the Uffizi.

Michelangelo's dazzling *Tondo Doni,* a depiction of the Holy Family, hangs in room 35. The composition is unusual and the colours as vibrant as when they were first applied in 1504–06. It was painted for wealthy Florentine merchant Agnolo Doni (who hung it above his bed) and bought by the Medici for Palazzo Pitti in 1594.

Beautifully renovated Room 42, the **Niobe Room,** was built to house a group of statues representing Niobe and her children. Discovered in a Roman vineyard in 1583 and brought to Florence in 1775, the works are 4th century BC Roman copies of Greek originals.

The work of Venetian masters graces Room 43, where eight Titians are displayed. Masterpieces include the sensual nude *Venus of Urbino* (1538), and the striking portrait of Eleonora Gonzaga, Duchess of Urbino (1536–37). The next room, No 44, features works by Paolo Veronese and Tintoretto, the latter's famously ink-black *Portrait of a Man* (c 1555–60) being a dark highlight. Tintoretto's *Leda and the Swan* (c 1550) also hangs here.

ℹ LESSER-KNOWN GEMS

When the Uffizi, *David* and Ponte Vecchio crowd gets too much, flee to one of Florence's faintly lesser-known gems: Palazzo Strozzi (blockbuster art exhibitions), Museo del Bargello (early Michelangelos), Chiesa di Orsanmichele (medieval statuary), Biblioteca Medicea Laurenziana (Michelangelo staircase) and Museo Marino Marini (Rucellai Chapel).

➡ 'New Uffizi' 1st Floor Galleries

As part of the ongoing 'New Uffizi' expansion project, the Uffizi added an astonishing 1800 sq m of gallery space to its already vast repertoire in 2012, and expansion continues well into 2014. Head downstairs to the 1st floor where the **Sala Blu** (Blue Room), aka rooms 46 to 55, display the Uffizi's collection of 16th and 17th century works by foreign artists, including Rembrandt (room 49); Rubens and Van Dyck share room 55.

The next nine rooms, walls painted a deep crimson red to reflect their 16th-century focus, include two key players in ushering Florence from the High Renaissance to Mannerism: Andrea del Sarto (rooms 56 to 59) and Räphael (room 66). The latter's charming *Madonna of the Goldfinch* (1505–06), which he painted during his four-year sojourn in Florence, is the star piece of the red Räphael room (No 66).

To check the latest new rooms to have opened as part of the €65 million 'New Uffizi' expansion project, in the making since 1997, check the 'News' section of www.uffizi.org. When complete (end date unknown) the Uffizi will count over 100 rooms and a lovely new exit on Piazza Castellani designed by Japanese architect Arato Isozaki. In the meantime, expect to find rooms temporarily closed and the contents of others dramatically changed.

SAVVY ADVANCE PLANNING

- ➡ Cut out the queue by booking tickets in advance for the Uffizi and Galleria dell'Accademia.
- ➡ Work out which museum pass suits and buy online.
- ➡ Reserve a tour of the Vasarian Corridor and Palazzo Vecchio; also reserve for Cappella Brancacci and Cappella dei Magi.
- ➡ Buy tickets for springtime's Maggio Musicale Fiorentino.
- ➡ The Uffizi, Galleria dell'Accademia and most other state museums are shut on Monday. But it's the perfect day for visiting hidden-gem museum Museo di Orsanmichele, above the church of the same name.
- ➡ Thursday is the day to catch an evening of contemporary art (for free) at Palazzo Strozzi.

★Duomo — CATHEDRAL

(Cattedrale di Santa Maria del Fiore or St Mary of the Flower; Map p62; www.operaduomo.firenze.it & http://museumflorence.com; Piazza del Duomo; free admission Duomo, combined ticket to dome, baptistry, campanile, crypt and museum adult/child under 14 €10/free; ⏲10am-5pm Mon-Wed & Fri, to 4pm Thu, to 4.45pm Sat, 1.30-4.45pm Sun; dome 8.30am-6.20pm Mon-Fri, to 5pm Sat; crypt 10am-5pm Mon-Fri, to 4pm Thu, to 4.45pm Sat; campanile 8.30am-6.50pm) Florence's *duomo*, the city's most iconic landmark, is among Italy's 'Big Three' (with Pisa's Leaning Tower and Rome's Colosseum). Its red-tiled dome, graceful *campanile* (bell tower) and breathtaking pink, white and green marble facade have the wow factor in spades. Begun in 1296 by Sienese architect Arnolfo di Cambio, the cathedral took almost 150 years to complete.

Its neo-Gothic facade was designed in the 19th century by architect Emilio de Fabris to replace the uncompleted original, torn down in the 16th century. The oldest and most clearly Gothic part of the cathedral is its south flank, pierced by Porta dei Canonici (Canons' Door), a mid-14th-century High Gothic creation (you enter here to climb up inside the dome).

When Michelangelo went to work on St Peter's in Rome, he reportedly said: 'I go to build a greater dome, but not a fairer one.' One of the finest masterpieces of the Renaissance, Florence's famous cathedral dome is indeed a feat of engineering and one that cannot be fully appreciated without climbing its 463 interior stone steps.

The **dome** (combined ticket to dome, baptistry, campanile, crypt and museum adult/child under 14 €10/free) was built between 1420 and 1436 to a design by Filippo Brunelleschi. Taking his inspiration from Rome's Pantheon, Brunelleschi arrived at an innovative engineering solution of a distinctive octagonal shape of inner and outer concentric domes resting on the drum of the cathedral rather than the roof itself, allowing artisans to build from the ground up without needing a wooden support frame. Over four million bricks were used in the construction, all of them laid in consecutive rings in horizontal courses using a vertical herringbone pattern. The final product is 91m high and 45.5m wide.

The climb up the spiral staircase is relatively steep, and should not be attempted if you are claustrophobic. Make sure to pause when you reach the balustrade at the base of the dome, which gives an aerial view of the octagonal *coro* (choir) of the cathedral below and the seven round stained-glass windows (by Donatello, Andrea del Castagno, Paolo Uccello and Lorenzo Ghiberti) that pierce the octagonal drum.

Look up and you'll see flamboyant late-16th-century frescoes by Giorgio Vasari and Federico Zuccari, depicting the *Giudizio Universale* (Last Judgement).

As you climb, snapshots of Florence can be spied through small windows. The final leg – a straight, somewhat hazardous flight up the curve of the inner dome – rewards with an unforgettable 360-degree panorama of one of Europe's most beautiful cities.

After the visual wham-bam of the facade and dome, the sparse decoration of the cathedral's vast interior, 155m long and 90m wide, comes as a surprise – most of its artistic treasures have been removed over centuries according to the vagaries of ecclesiastical fashion, and many are now on show in the Grande Museo del Duomo. The interior is also unexpectedly secular in places (a reflection of the sizeable chunk of the cathedral not paid for by the church): down the left aisle two immense frescoes of equestrian statues portray two *condottieri* (mercenaries) – on the left Niccolò da Tolentino by Andrea del Castagno (1456) and on the right Sir John Hawkwood by Uccello (1436) – who fought in the service of Florence in the 14th century.

Between the left (north) arm of the transept and the apse is the Sagrestia delle

THE EXTRAORDINARY VASARIAN CORRIDOR

Bathed in mystery, this must be the world's most infamous and enigmatic corridor. Look above the jewellery shops on the eastern side of Ponte Vecchio to see – most dramatically at sunset – Florence's **Corridoio Vasariano** (Map p62; ☎055 29 48 83; ⏲by guided tour; 🚌B), an extraordinary elevated covered passageway joining the Palazzo Vecchio on Piazza della Signoria with the Uffizi and Palazzo Pitti on the other side of the river. Around 1km long, it was designed by Vasari for Cosimo I in 1565 to allow the Medicis and court's high dignitaries to wander between the two palaces in privacy and comfort. From the 17th century, the Medicis strung it with self-portraits – a collection of 700-odd art works today that includes self-portraits of Andrea del Sarto (the oldest), Rubens, Rembrandt, Canova and others.

The original promenade incorporated tiny windows (facing the river) and circular apertures with iron gratings (facing the street) to protect those who used the corridor from outside attacks. But when Hitler visited Florence in 1941, his chum and fellow dictator Benito Mussolini had big new windows punched into the corridor walls on Ponte Vecchio so that his guest could enjoy an expansive view down the Arno from the famous Florentine bridge.

On the Oltrarno, the corridor passes by **Chiesa di Santa Felicità** (Map p86; www.santafelicita.it; Piazza di Santa Felicità; ⏲9.30am-noon & 3.30-5.30pm Mon-Sat) FREE – atmospheric host to some wonderful music concerts – thereby providing the Medici with a private balcony in the church where they could likewise attend Mass without mingling with the minions. Stand in front of the small Romanesque church on Piazza di Santa Felicitià and admire the trio of arches of the Vasarian Corridor that runs right above the portico outside the otherwise unnotable church facade. Inside, walk towards the altar and look backwards to see the Medici balcony up high (and imagine the corridor snaking behind it). Oh, and before leaving the church, don't miss Ghirlandaio's *Meeting of St Anne and St Joachim* hung at the end of its right transept.

The Vasarian Corridor is open to just a privileged few – look for spots in the Uffizi and elsewhere where you can get sneak peeks of the corridor. To actually visit it – a memorable experience – either join a guided tour of just five people (in Italian only) organised very occasionally by **Firenze Musei** (€15 including Uffizi admission and booking fee) – tours are advertised in advance on the Uffizi website (www.uffizi.firenze.it). Or, the easier option, hook up with a private English-speaking tour guide; **Florence Town** (Map p62; ☎055 012 39 94; www.florencetown.com; Via de' Lamberti 1; adult/child €125/70 incl Uffizi admission & breakfast; ⏲2 to 3 times weekly) organises morning tours that include two hours in the Uffizi, breakfast in its rooftop cafe and the corridor. Whatever tour you plump for, reserve well in advance.

Messe (Mass Sacristy), its panelling a marvel of inlaid wood carved by Benedetto and Giuliano da Maiano. The fine bronze doors were executed by Luca della Robbia – his only known work in the material. Above the doorway is his glazed terracotta *Resurrezione* (Resurrection).

A stairway near the main entrance of the cathedral leads down to the **crypt** (combined ticket to dome, baptistry, campanile, crypt and museum adult/child under 14 €10/free), where excavations between 1965 and 1974 unearthed parts of the 5th-century Chiesa di Santa Reparata that originally stood on the site.

The steep 414-step climb up the 85m-high **campanile** (combined ticket to dome, baptistry, campanile, crypt and museum adult/child under 14 €10/free), designed by Giotto, offers the reward of a view nearly as impressive as that from the dome. The first tier of bas-reliefs around the base of the campanile are copies of those carved by Pisano, but possibly designed by Giotto, depicting the Creation of Man and the *attività umane* (arts and industries). Those on the second tier depict the planets, the cardinal virtues, the arts and the seven sacraments. The sculptures of the Prophets and Sibyls in the niches of the upper storeys are copies of works by Donatello and others; see the originals in the Grande Museo del Duomo.

★Grande Museo del Duomo MUSEUM

(Cathedral Museum; Map p62; www.operaduomo.firenze.it; Piazza del Duomo 9; combined ticket to dome, baptistry, campanile, crypt and museum adult/child under 14 €10/free; ⏲9am-6.50pm Mon-Sat, 9am-1.05pm Sun) Surprisingly overlooked by the crowds yet one of the city's most impressive, this museum – currently being massively reorganised and enlarged to embrace another 2000 sq m in a former theatre-turned-garage next door – safeguards sacred and liturgical treasures that once adorned the *duomo*, baptistry and *campanile*. Make a beeline for the glass-topped courtyard with its awe-inspiring showpiece encased in glass – Ghiberti's original 15th-century masterpiece, the *Porta del Paradiso* (Gate of Paradise), designed for the eastern entrance to the Baptistry.

After 27 years secreted away in restoration workshops, the gloriously golden, 16m-tall gilded brass doors that took almost three decades to restore were unveiled with much pomp and ceremony in 2012.

In a small room just off the stair landing is the museum's best-known piece, Michelangelo's *La Pietà*, a work he sculpted when he was almost 80 and intended for his own tomb. Vasari recorded in his *Lives of the Artists* that, dissatisfied with both the quality of the marble and of his own work, Michelangelo broke up the unfinished sculpture, destroying the arm and left leg of the figure of Christ. A student of Michelangelo's later restored the arm and completed the figure.

Continue upstairs, where a pair of exquisitely carved *cantorie* (singing galleries) or organ lofts – one by Donatello, the other by Luca della Robbia – face each other. Originally in the cathedral's sacristy, their scenes of musicians and children at play add a refreshingly frivolous touch amid so much sombre piety. Don't miss the same sculptor's wooden representation of a gaunt, desperately desolate Mary Magdalene in the same room, a work completed late in his career.

End on a giddy high with a masterpiece of medieval and Renaissance metalwork: the Altar of St John, crafted by three generations of Florentine silversmiths between 1367 and 1480, was created for the Baptistry. More than 250kg of silver was used to make the altar panels, sculpted to illustrate the life of John the Baptist in the most extraordinary detail. The accompanying cross, also hung originally in the Baptistry, is the work of Antonio del Pollaiolo.

Expansion and restoration work at the musem will continue until the end of 2015; once complete, the museum will double in space and stash away hundreds more treasures (including, for example, Ghiberti's northern Baptistry doors, removed from the Baptistry in 2013 to be restored like their eastern counterparts).

★Battistero di San Giovanni BAPTISTRY

(Map p62; Piazza di San Giovanni; combined ticket to dome, baptistry, campanile, crypt and museum adult/child under 14 €10/free; ⏲11.15am-6.30pm Mon-Sat, 8.30am-1.30pm Sun & 1st Sat of month) Across from the cathedral is Florence's 11th-century Romanesque baptistry, an octagonal striped structure of white-and-green marble with three sets of doors conceived as a series of panels in which the story of humanity and the Redemption would be told. Buy tickets from the ticket office opposite the northern doors at Via de' Cerretani 7.

Andrea Pisano executed the southern doors (1330), illustrating the life of St John the Baptist, and Lorenzo Ghiberti won a public competition in 1401 to design the northern doors, today replaced by copies (the originals were removed in 2013 and are currently being restored for eventual display in the Grande Museo del Duomo). But it is Ghiberti's gilded bronze doors at the eastern entrance, known as the Gate of Paradise (Porta del Paradiso), that are the most celebrated. What you see today is are likewise copies of the panels – the gleaming, polished originals take pride of place in the Grande Museo del Duomo.

Dante counts among the famous dunked in the Baptistry's baptismal font.

Piazza della Signoria PIAZZA

(Map p62; Piazza della Signoria) Edged by historic cafes, crammed with Renaissance sculptures and presided over by magnificent Palazzo Vecchio, this photogenic piazza has been the hub of local life for centuries. Early evening and all day at weekends, Florentines indulge in the sacrosanct *passeggiata* (evening stroll), breaking for a coffee, hot chocolate or *aperitivo*, perhaps at the city's most famous cafe, Caffè Rivoire (p110).

Whenever the city entered one of its innumerable political crises, the people would be called here as a *parlamento* (people's plebiscite) to rubber-stamp decisions that frequently meant ruin for some ruling families and victory for others. Scenes of great pomp and circumstance alternated with those of terrible suffering: it was here that vehemently pious preacher-leader Savonarola set fire to the city's art – books, paintings, musical instruments, mirrors, fine clothes and so on – during his famous 'Bonfire of the Vanities' in 1497, and where he was hung in chains and burnt as a heretic, along with two other supporters a year later.

The same spot where both fires burned is marked by a bronze plaque embedded in the ground in front of Ammannati's **Fontana di Nettuno** (Neptune Fountain; Map p62). With its pin-headed bronze satyrs and divinities frolicking at its edges, this huge fountain is hardly pretty and is much mocked as *il biancone* (the big white thing), not to mention a waste of good marble, by many a Florentine. Far more impressive are the equestrian statue of Cosimo I by Giambologna in the centre of the piazza, the much-photographed copy of Michelangelo's *David* that has guarded the western entrance to the Palazzo Vecchio since 1910 (the original stood here until 1873 but is now in the Galleria dell'Accademia) and two copies of important Donatello works – *Marzocco*, the heraldic Florentine lion (for the original visit the Museo del Bargello) and *Giuditta e Oloferne* (Judith and Holofernes, c 1455; original inside Palazzo Vecchio).

Facing this line-up is the 14th-century **Loggia dei Lanzi**, an open-air museum where works such as Giambologna's *Rape of the Sabine Women* (c 1583), Benvenuto Cellini's bronze *Perseus* (1554) and Agnolo Gaddi's *Seven Virtues* (1384–89) are displayed. The loggia owes its name to the Lanzichenecchi (Swiss bodyguards) of Cosimo I, who were stationed here, and the present day guards live up to this heritage, sternly monitoring crowd behaviour and promptly banishing anyone carrying food or drink.

★ Palazzo Vecchio MUSEUM

(Map p62; ☎055 276 82 24; www.musefirenze.it; Piazza della Signoria; museum adult/reduced/child €10/8/free, tower €6.50, guided tours €2; ⏰museum 9am-midnight Fri-Wed, to 2pm Thu summer, to 7pm Fri-Wed, to 2pm Thu winter; tower 9am-8.30pm Fri-Wed, to 1.30pm Thu summer, 10am-4.30pm Fri-Wed, to 1.30pm Thu winter) Florence's fortress palace, with its striking crenellations and 94m-high tower, was designed by Arnolfo di Cambio between 1298 and 1314 for the *signoria* (city government). Highlights include scaling the tower and admiring the **Salone dei Cinquecento**, created for the Consiglio dei Cinquecento (Council of 500) that ruled Florence at the end of the 15th century. Don't miss Michelangelo's sculpture *Genio della Vittoria* (Genius of Victory).

During their short time in office the nine *priori* (consuls) – guild members picked at random – of the *signoria* lived in the palace. Every two months nine new names were pulled out of the hat, ensuring ample comings and goings.

In 1540 Cosimo I made the palace his ducal residence and centre of government, commissioning Vasari to renovate and decorate the interior. Not too long after the renovation, he and his wife Eleonora di Toledo (famously immortalised in Bronzino's portrait in the Uffizi collection) decided that the newly renovated apartments were too uncomfortable for their large family to live in year-round and he purchased Palazzo Pitti as a summer residence. After the death of Eleonora and their sons Giovanni and Garzia from malaria in 1562, Cosimo moved the rest of his family to Palazzo Pitti permanently. At this time, the building became known as Palazzo Vecchio (it was orignally called Palazzo della Signoria). It remains the seat of the city's power, home to the mayor's office and the municipal council. The best way to discover this den of political drama and intrigue is by thematic guided tour or audioguide (p73).

Sheer size aside, what impresses most about the 53m-long, 22m-wide **Salone dei Cinquecento** are the swirling battle scenes, painted floor to ceiling by Vasari and his apprentices. These glorify Florentine victories by Cosimo I over arch-rivals Pisa and Siena: unlike the Sienese, the Pisans are depicted bare of armour (play 'Spot the Leaning Tower'). To top off this unabashed celebration of his own power, Cosimo had himself portrayed as a god in the centre of the exquisite panelled ceiling – but not before commissioning Vasari to raise the original ceiling 7m in height. It took Vasari and his school, in consultation with Michelangelo, just two years (1563–65) to construct the ceiling and paint the 34 gold-leafed panels, which rest simply on a wooden frame. The effect is mesmerising.

Off this huge space is the **Chapel of SS Cosmas and Damian**, home to Vasari's 1557–58 triptych panels of the two saints depicting Cosimo the Elder as Cosmas (on the right) and Cosimo I as Damian (on the left). Next to the chapel is the **Sala di Leo X**, the private suite of apartments of Cardinal Giovanni de' Medici, the son of Lorenzo Il Magnifico, who became pope in 1513.

Up the stairs and across the balcony (from where you can enjoy wonderful views of the Salone dei Cinquecento), are the private apartments for both Eleonora and her ladies-in-waiting. These bear the same heavy-handed decor blaring the glory of the Medici as the rest of the palace. Of note is the ceiling in the **Camera Verde** (Green Room) by Ridolfo del Ghirlandaio, inspired by designs from Nero's Domus Aurea in Rome, and the vibrant frescoes by Bronzino in the chapel.

Also on the 2nd floor, the **Sala dei Gigli**, named after its frieze of fleur-de-lis, representing the Florentine Republic, is home to Donatello's original *Judith and Holofernes*. Domenico Ghirlandaio's fresco on the far wall in this room, depicting figures from Roman history, was meant to be one of a series by other artists, including Botticelli.

A small study off the hall is the chancery, once Niccolò Machiavelli's office. Another

PALAZZO VECCHIO TOURS

The only way to get the most out of Florence's most dynamic, well-thought-out museum is to join one of its excellent **guided tours** (☎055 276 85 58; info.museoragazzi@comune.fi.it; ⏰reservations 9.30am-5pm).

The best of the adult bunch is probably the 'Secret Passages' tour, in which groups of 12 are led along the secret staircase built between the palace's super-thick walls in 1342 as an escape route for French Duke of Athens Walter de Brienne, who seized the palace and nominated himself Lord of Florence, only to be sent packing back to France by the Florentines a year later. It follows this staircase to the **Tesoretto** (Treasury) of Cosimo I – a tiny room no larger than a cupboard for his private collection – and the equally intimate, sumptuous **Studiolo** (Study) of his introverted, alchemy-mad son Francesco I. Cosimo commissioned Vasari and a team of Florentine Mannerist artists to decorate the study, Francesco appearing in one of the 34 emblematic paintings covering the walls not as a prince, but as a scientist experimenting with gunpowder. The lower paintings concealed 20 cabinets in which the young prince hid his shells, crystals and other treasures. The tour ends in the palace **roof** above the Salone dei Cinquecento, where you can see the huge wooden trusses supporting Vasari's ornate ceiling.

The 'Experiencing the palace first-hand' tours are specifically designed with children and are open to visitors aged 8 (or 10 depending on the tour) to 88 years. Actors dressed in Renaissance costume rope young participants into the performance. A sumptuously attired Eleonora of Toledo, clearly shocked by the casual attire of today's children, has been known to give advice about proper grooming for young ladies, and Cosimo I is happy to lay down the law about the proper age for a Medici to take on duties as a cardinal (the answer is 14, the age of his son Ferdinando when he became a cardinal).

Tours last 1¼ hours and take you into parts of the building otherwise inaccessible; many are in English. Reserve in advance by telephone or email.

room, the **Sala delle Carte Geografiche** (Map Room), houses Cosimo I's fascinating collection of 16th-century maps charting everywhere in the known world at the time, from the polar regions to the Caribbean.

On dry days (closed when raining), end your visit with a breathtaking (literally), 418-step hike up the palace's striking **Torre d'Arnolfo** (tower) and battlements. No more than 25 people are alllowed on the terrace at any one time – in high season expect to wait in line on the 3rd floor – and the panorama of Piazza della Signoria and the city beyond is fabulous. Once up, you have just 30 minutes to lap it up. No children under 6 years; last tickets sold one hour before closing.

Gucci Museo FASHION MUSEUM

(Map p62; www.gucci.com; Piazza della Signoria 10; adult/child €6/free; ⌚10am-8pm) Strut through the chic cafe, bookshop and icon store to reach this surprisingly interesting museum. It tells the tale of the Gucci fashion house, from the first luggage pieces in Gucci's signature beige fabric emblazoned with the interlocking 'GG' logo to the 1950s red-and-green stripe and beyond. Don't miss the gleaming white, 1979 Cadillac Seville with gold Gs on the hubcaps and Gucci fabric upholstery.

Displays continue to present day. In the final room, exhibiting men's loafers, be sure to look in the mirrors (to admire your own feet and inferior footwear).

Piazza della Repubblica PIAZZA

(Map p62) The site of a Roman forum and heart of medieval Florence, this busy civic space was created in the 1880s as part of a controversial plan of 'civic improvements' involving the demolition of the old market, Jewish ghetto and slums, and the relocation of nearly 6000 residents. Vasari's lovely *Loggia del Pesce* (Fish Market) was saved and re-erected on Via Pietrapiana. Today the piazza is known for its concentration of historic cafes.

Museo Galileo SCIENCE MUSEUM

(Map p86; ☎055 26 53 11; www.museogalileo.it; Piazza dei Giudici 1; adult/reduced/family €9/5.50/22; ⌚9.30am-5.30pm Wed-Mon, to 12.30pm Tue) On the river next to the Uffizi in 12th-century Palazzo Castellani – look for the sundial telling the time on the pavement outside – is this state-of-the-art science museum, named after the great Pisa-born scientist who was invited by the Medici court to Florence in 1610 (don't miss two of his fingers and a tooth displayed here).

A visit of the museum unravels a mesmerising curiosity box of astronomical and mathematical treasures (think telescopes, beautiful painted globes, barometers, watches, clocks and so on) collected by Cosimo I and other Medicis from 1562 and, later, the Lorraine dynasty. Allow plenty of time for the interactive area where various hands-on exhibits allow visitors to discover first-hand how and why some of the historic instruments actually work. Temporary exhibitions are equally compelling.

Chiesa e Museo di Orsanmichele CHURCH, MUSEUM

(Map p62; Via dell'Arte della Lana; ⌚church 10am-5pm, museum 10am-5pm Mon) **FREE** This thoroughly unusual and inspirational church, with a splendid Gothic tabernacle by Andrea Orcagna, was created when the arcades of an old grain market (1290) were walled in and two storeys added during the 14th century. A real must-see, its exterior is exquisitely decorated with niches and tabernacles bearing statues.

Representing the patron saints of Florence's many guilds, they were commissioned in the 15th and 16th centuries after the *signoria* ordered the city's guilds to finance the church's decoration.

These statues represent the work of some of the greatest Renaissance artists. Only copies adorn the building's exterior today but all the originals except one are beautifully displayed in the church's little-known, light and airy museum, open only on Monday in two floors above the church.

Via de' Tornabuoni STREET

(Map p62) Renaissance palaces and the flagship stores of Italian fashion houses border Via de' Tornabuoni, the city's most expensive shopping strip. Named after a wealthy Florentine noble family (which died out in the 17th century), it is sometimes referred to as the 'Salotto di Firenze' (Florence's Drawing Room).

From the *duomo,* walk west along Via de' Pecori and its extension, Via degli Agli, crossing three streets before coming to Via de' Tornabuoni. Straight ahead, at the T-intersection, is **Palazzo Antinori** (Map p62; Piazza Antinori 3), built between 1461 and 1469, owned by the Antinori family since 1506. One of Florence's most aristocratic families, the Antinori are known for the wines they produce on their Tuscan estates in Chianti.

Opposite, huge stone steps lead up to 17th-century **Chiesa di San Gaetano** (Map p62).

Palazzo Strozzi ART GALLERY
(Map p62; www.palazzostrozzi.org; Via de' Tornabuoni; variable admission prices; ⏲10am-8pm Tue-Sun, to 11pm Thu) This 15th-century *palazzo* is one of Florence's most impressive Renaissance mansions. It was built for wealthy merchant Filippo Strozzi, one of the Medicis' major political and commercial rivals, and is host today to some of the city's most exciting blockbuster art exhibitions. Contemporary art in its basement Strozzini gallery (free admission after 6pm Thursday) and an imposing internal courtyard are equally alluring.

Art workshops, Family Sundays and other activities aimed squarely at families make Palazzo Strozzi a firm favourite with pretty much everyone. There's always a buzz about the place, with young Florentines congregating in the courtyard Renaissance Café (p109) (run by Florentine designer Roberto Cavalli no less); it's one of the best spots in the city to pick up free wi-fi.

Chiesa di Santa Trìnita CHURCH
(Map p62; Piazza Santa Trìnita; ⏲8am-noon & 4-5.45pm Mon-Sat, 8-10.45am & 4-5.45pm Sun-7pm Sun) FREE Built in Gothic style and later given a Mannerist facade, this 14th-century church shelters some of the city's finest frescoes, including Lorenzo Monaco's *Annunciation* (1422) in the **Cappella Salimbenes/Bartholini** and eye-catching frescoes by Ghirlandaio depicting the life of St Francis of Assisi in the **Cappella Sassetti**, to the right of the altar. They were painted between 1483 and 1485 and feature portraits of illustrious Florentines of the time.

Look out for the crest of the Salimbenes/Bartholini family on the floor of the chapel – it features poppies and the motto 'Per Non Dormire' (For Those Who Don't Sleep), a reference to the fact that the family fortune resulted from the acquisition of an important cargo of wool from Northern Europe, a deal sealed unbeknown to their business rivals, who had been doped with opium-laced wine at a lavish party the night before the cargo was due to arrive in Florence.

Museo Salvatore Ferragamo MUSEUM
(Map p62; www.museoferragamo.it; Via de' Tornabuoni 2; adult/reduced €6/free; ⏲10am-7pm daily) The splendid 13th-century **Palazzo Spini-Feroni** has been the home of the Ferragamo fashion empire since 1938. Anyone with even the faintest tendency towards shoe addiction or with an interest in the socio-historical context of fashion should not miss the esoteric but oddly compelling shoe museum.

Museo di Palazzo Davanzati MUSEUM
(Map p62; Via Porta Rossa 13; adult/reduced €2/1; ⏲8.15am-1.30pm, closed 1st, 3rd & 5th Mon, 2nd & 4th Sun of month) Tucked inside a 14th-century warehouse and residence aka Palazzo Davanzati, home to the wealthy Davanzati merchant family from 1578, this palazzo museum with wonderful central loggia, is a gem. Peep at the carved faces of the original owners on the pillars in the inner courtyard and don't miss the 1st-floor **Sala Madornale** (reception room) with its painted wooden ceiling or the exquisitely decorated **Sala dei Pappagalli** (Parrot Room) and **Camera dei Pavoni** (Peacock Bedroom).

Museo Marino Marini ART GALLERY
(Map p62; Piazza San Pancrazio 1; adult/reduced €4/2; ⏲10am-5pm Wed-Sat & Mon) Deconsecrated in the 19th century, the Chiesa di San Pancrazio is home to this small art museum displaying sculptures, portraits and drawings by the Pistoia-born sculptor Marino Marini (1901–80). But what really stuns is the superbly restored **Cappella Rucellai** and the tiny scale copy of Christ's Holy Sepulchre in Jerusalem – a Renaissance gem by Leon Battista Alberti.

The chapel was built between 1458 and 1467 for the tomb of wealthy Florentine banker and wool merchant, Giovanni Rucellai. Alberti chose white marble from Carrara and green marble from Prato to craft the sepulchre, an exquisite work of art with its classical mouldings, decorative geometric motifs and lantern crown. Abandoned for decades, it was restored and unveiled with much pomp and ceremony in 2013.

⊙ Santa Maria Novella

Radiating west and south from the venerable basilica, the neighbourhood of Santa Maria Novella is blessed with chic boutiques, impressive palaces and art-adorned churches.

Basilica e Chiostri Monumentali di Santa Maria Novella CHURCH, CLOISTERS
(Map p62; www.chiesasantamarianovella.it; Piazza di Santa Maria Novella 18; adult/reduced €5/3; ⏲9am-5.30pm Mon-Thu, 11am-5.30pm Fri, 9am-5pm Sat, 1-5pm Sun) This monumental

complex, fronted by the green-and-white marble facade of the 13th- to 15th-century **Basilica di Santa Maria Novella** (Map p62), secrets romantic church cloisters and a stunning frescoed chapel. The basilica itself is a treasure chest of artistic masterpieces, climaxing with a series of frescoes by Domenico Ghirlandaio. Allow at least a couple of hours to take it all in.

The lower section of the basilica's striped marbled facade is transitional from Romanesque to Gothic; the upper section and the main doorway (1456–70) were designed by Leon Battista Alberti. As you enter, look straight ahead to see Masaccio's superb fresco *Trinity* (1424–25), one of the first artworks to use the then newly discovered techniques of perspective and proportion. Close by, hanging in the central nave, is a luminous painted *Crucifix* by Giotto (c 1290).

The first chapel to the right of the altar, **Cappella di Filippo Strozzi,** features spirited late 15th-century frescoes by Filippino Lippi (son of Fra' Filippo Lippi) depicting the lives of St John the Evangelist and St Philip the Apostle.

Behind the main altar itself are the highlights of the interior – Domenico Ghirlandaio's series of frescoes in the **Cappella Maggiore.** Relating the lives of the Virgin Mary, these vibrant frescoes were painted between 1485 and 1490, and are notable for their depiction of Florentine life during the Renaissance. They feature portraits of Ghirlandaio's contemporaries and members of the Tornabuoni family, who commissioned them.

To the far left of the altar, up a short flight of stairs, is the **Cappella Strozzi di Mantova,** covered in wonderful 14th-century frescoes by Niccolò di Tommaso and Nardo di Cione. The fine altarpiece (1354–57) here was painted by the latter's brother Andrea, better known as Andrea Orcagna.

From the church, walk through a side door into the serenly beautiful **Chiostro Verde** (Green Cloister; 1332–62), part of the vast monastical complex occupied by Dominican friars who arrived in Florence in 1219 and settled in Santa Maria Novella two years later. The tranquil cloister takes its name from the green earth base used for the frescoes on three of the cloister's four walls. On its north side is the spectacular **Cappellone degli Spagnoli** (Spanish Chapel), originally the friars' chapter house and named such in 1566 when it was given to the Spanish colony in Florence. The tiny chapel is covered in extraordinary frescoes (c 1365–67) by Andrea di Bonaiuto. The vault features depictions of the Resurrection, Ascension and Pentecost, and on the altar wall are scenes of the *Via Dolorosa, Crucifixion* and *Descent into Limbo.* On the right wall is a huge fresco of *The Militant and Triumphant Church* – look in the foreground for a portrait of Cimabue, Giotto, Boccaccio, Petrarch and Dante. Other frescoes in the chapels depict the *Triumph of Christian Doctrine,* 14 figures symbolising the Arts and Sciences, and the Life of St Peter.

By the side of the chapel, a passage leads into the **Chiostro dei Morti** (Cloister of the Dead), a cemetery existent well before the arrival of the Dominicans to Santa Maria Novella. The tombstones embedded in the walls and floor date to the 13th and 14th centuries.

On the west side of the Chiostro Verde, another passage leads to the 14th-century **Cappella degli Ubriachi** and a large **refectory** featuring ecclesiastical relics and a 1583 *Last Supper* by Alessandro Allori. Both are currently closed for renovation.

There are two entrances to the Santa Maria Novella complex: the main entrance to the basilica or through the tourist office opposite the train station on Via de' Partzani; Firenze Card holders are obliged to use the latter.

Chiesa d'Ognissanti CHURCH

(Map p62; Borgo d'Ognissanti 42; ⌚7am-12.30pm & 4-8pm Mon-Sat, 4-8pm Sun) Stroll along Borgo d'Ognissanti, from Piazza Carlo Goldoni towards ancient city gate Porta al Prato, past antiques shops and designer boutiques to reach this 13th-century church, built as part of a Benedictine monastery. Its highlight is Domenico Ghirlandaio's fresco of the *Madonna della Misericordia* protecting members of the Vespucci family, the church's main patrons.

Amerigo Vespucci, the Florentine navigator who gave his name to the American continent, is supposed to be the young boy whose head peeks between the Madonna and the old man.

Also here are a *Crucifixion* by Taddeo Gaddi, Ghirlandaio's *St Jerome* (1480) and Botticelli's pensive *St Augustine* (also 1480). Botticelli, who grew up in a house on Borgo d'Ognissanti, is buried here (look for the simple round tombstone marked 'Sandro Filipepe' in the south transept).

DON'T MISS

BACKSTREET FLORENCE: DANTE

Italy's most divine poet was born in 1265 in a wee house down a narrow lane in the backstreets of Florence. Tragic romance was what made him tick and there's no better place to unravel the medieval life and times of Dante than the **Museo Casa di Dante** (Map p62; ☎055 21 94 16; Via Santa Margherita 1; adult/reduced €4/2; ⏱10am-5pm Tue-Sun).

When Dante was just 12 he was promised in marriage to Gemma Donati. But it was another Florentine gal, Beatrice Portinari (1266–90), that was his muse, his inspiration, the love of his life (despite only ever meeting her twice in his life): in *Divina Commedia* (Divine Comedy) Dante broke with tradition by using the familiar Italian, not the formal Latin, to describe travelling through the circles of hell in search of his beloved Beatrice.

Beatrice, who wed a banker and died a couple of years later aged just 24, is buried in 11th-century **Chiesa di Santa Margherita** (Map p62; Via Santa Margherita 4), tucked down an alley near Dante's house; note the wicker basket in front of her grave filled with scraps of paper on which prayers and dedications evoking unrequited love have been penned. The tiny chapel was also where the poet married Gemma in 1295. Dimly lit and atmospherically filled with soft classical background music, it remains much as it was in medieval Florence. No wonder novelist Dan Brown chose it to set a scene in his most recent Dante-themed thriller, *Inferno* (2013), that takes place in Florence.

Top off the old-world experience at neighbouring hole-in-the-wall Da Vinattieri (p100) with a tripe *panino* (sandwich) eaten squatting on a simple wooden stool on this old-fashioned alley in backstreet Florence.

Museo Stibbert MUSEUM
(www.museostibbert.it; Via Federigo Stibbert 26; adult/reduced €8/6; ⏱10am-2pm Mon-Wed, to 6pm Fri-Sun) Anglo-Italian, Florence-born Frederick Stibbert (1838–1906) was one of the grand 19th-century wheeler-dealers on the European antiquities market and amassed an intriguing personal collection, showcased in Villa di Montughi, aka the Stibbert Museum. Take bus 4 from Stazione di Santa Maria Novella to the 'Gioia' stop on Via Fabroni, from where it is a short walk.

Particularly great for kids is the **Sala della Cavalcata** (Parade Room) where life-sized figures of horses and their riders in all manner of suits of armour from Europe and the Middle East rub shoulders. Other varied exhibits include clothes, furnishings, tapestries and 16th- to 19th-century paintings.

San Lorenzo

This is Medici territory – come here to see their palace, church, library and mausoleum, all decorated with extraordinary works of art.

Basilica di San Lorenzo CHURCH
(Map p62; insignebasilicasanlorenzo.wordpress.com; Piazza San Lorenzo; admission €4.50, with Biblioteca Medicea Laurenziana €7; ⏱10am-5.30pm Mon-Sat, 1.30-5pm Sun Mar-Oct) In 1425 Cosimo the Elder, who lived nearby, commissioned Brunelleschi to rebuild the basilica on this site, which dated to the 4th century. The new building would become the Medici parish church and mausoleum – many members of the family are buried here.

Considered one of the most harmonious examples of Renaissance architecture, the basilica has never been finished – Michelangelo was commissioned to design the facade in 1518 but his design in white Carrara marble was never executed, hence the building's rough unfinished appearance.

In the austere interior, columns of *pietra serena* (soft grey stone) crowned with Corinthian capitals separate the nave from the two aisles. Donatello, who was still sculpting the two bronze pulpits (1460–67) adorned with panels of the Crucifixion when he died, is buried in the chapel featuring Fra' Filippo Lippi's *Annunciation* (c 1450). Left of the altar is the **Sagrestia Vecchia** (Old Sacristy), designed by Brunelleschi and decorated in the main by Donatello.

Biblioteca Medicea Laurenziana LIBRARY
(Medici Library; Map p62; www.bml.firenze.sbn.it; Piazza San Lorenzo 9; admission €3, incl basilica €7; ⏱9.30am-1.30pm Mon-Fri) Beyond the basilica ticket office lie peaceful cloisters framing a pretty garden with buxom orange trees. Stairs lead up to the loggia and the Biblioteca Medicea Laurenziana, commissioned by Giulio de' Medici (Pope Clement VII) in 1524

San Lorenzo & San Marco

San Lorenzo & San Marco

Top Sights

1 Galleria dell'Accademia C2
2 Mercato Centrale B2
3 Museo di San Marco C1

Sights

4 Chiesa della Santissima Annunziata D2
5 Museo Archeologico D2
6 Ospedale degli Innocenti D2
7 Piazza della Santissima Annunziata D2

Activities, Courses & Tours

8 City Sightseeing Firenze A2

Sleeping

9 Antica Dimora Johlea C1
10 Hotel Azzi A1
11 Hotel Morandi alla Crocetta D2
12 Ostello Archi Rossi A1

Eating

13 Carabé C2
14 Clubhouse B2
15 Da Nerbone B2
16 La Cucina del Garga B1
17 Trattoria Mario B2

Entertainment

18 Be Bop Music Club C2

to house the extensive Medici library (started by Cosimo the Elder and greatly added to by Lorenzo il Magnifico).

The extraordinary staircase in the vestibule, intended as a 'dark prelude' to the magnificent **Sala di Lettura** (Reading Room), was designed by Michelangelo.

Cappelle Medicee MAUSOLEUM
(Map p62; ☎055 29 48 83; www.polomuseale.firenze.it; Piazza Madonna degli Aldobrandini; adult/reduced €6/3; ⏰8.15am-1.20pm, closed 2nd & 4th Sun & 1st, 3rd & 5th Mon of month) Nowhere is Medici conceit expressed so explicitly as in their mausoleum, the Medician Chapels. Sumptuously adorned with granite, the most precious marble, semiprecious stones and some of Michelangelo's most beautiful sculptures, it is the burial place of 49 members of the dynasty.

Francesco I lies in the grandiose **Cappella dei Principi** (Princes' Chapel) alongside Ferdinando I and II and Cosimo I, II and III. Lorenzo il Magnifico is buried in the stark but graceful **Sagrestia Nuova** (New Sacristy), Michelangelo's first architectural work and showcase for three of his most haunting sculptures: *Dawn and Dusk* on the sarcophagus of Lorenzo, Duke of Urbino; *Night and Day* on the sarcophagus of Lorenzo's son Giuliano; and *Madonna and Child,* which adorns Lorenzo's tomb.

Palazzo Medici-Riccardi PALACE
(Map p62; ☎055 276 03 40; www.palazzo-medici.it; Via Cavour 3; adult/reduced €7/4; ⏰9am-6.30pm Thu-Tue summer, to 5.30pm winter) Cosimo the Elder entrusted Michelozzo with the design of the family's townhouse in 1444. The result was this palace, a blueprint that influenced the construction of Florentine family residences such as Palazzo Pitti and Palazzo Strozzi for years to come. The upstairs chapel, **Cappella dei Magi** (Map p62; ☎055 276 03

40; www.palazzo-medici.it; Palazzo Medici-Riccardi, Via Cavour 3; adult/reduced €7/4; ⌚9am-7pm Thu-Tue summer, to 6pm winter), houses one of the supreme achievements of Renaissance painting and is an absolute must-see for art lovers.

The tiny chapel is covered in a series of wonderfully detailed and recently restored frescoes (c 1459–63) by Benozzo Gozzoli, a pupil of Fra' Angelico. His ostensible theme of *Procession of the Magi to Bethlehem* is but a slender pretext for portraying members of the Medici clan in their best light; try to spy Lorenzo il Magnifico and Cosimo the Elder in the crowd. The chapel was reconfigured to accommodate a baroque staircase, hence the oddly split fresco. The mid-15th-century altarpiece of the *Adoration of the Child* is a copy of the original (originally here) by Fra' Filippo Lippi. Only 10 visitors are allowed in at a time; in high season reserve in advance at the palace ticket desk.

The Medici lived at Palazzo Medici until 1540, making way for the Riccardi family a century later. They gave the palace a comprehensive remodelling and built the sumptuously decorated **Sala Luca Giordano**, a masterpiece of baroque art, on the 1st floor. Giordano adorned the ceiling with his complex *Allegory of Divine Wisdom* (1685), a rather overblown example of late baroque dripping with gold leaf and bursting with colour. The palazzo now houses the offices of the Florence Provincial Authority and hosts various temporary exhibitions in its public rooms.

★Mercato Centrale MARKET
(Central Market; Map p78; Piazza del Mercato Centrale; ⌚7am-2pm Mon-Fri, to 5pm Sat) Housed in a 19th-century iron-and-glass structure,

WHO'S THAT BLOKE?

Name *David*

Occupation World's most famous sculpture.

Vital statistics Height: 516cm tall, weight: 19 tonnes of mediocre-quality pearly white marble from the Fantiscritti quarries in Carrara.

Spirit Young biblical hero in meditative pose who, with the help of God, defeats an enemy more powerful than himself. Scarcely visible sling emphasises victory of innocence and intellect over brute force.

Commissioned In 1501 by the Opera del Duomo for the cathedral, but subsequently placed in front of the Palazzo Vecchio on Piazza della Signoria where it stayed until 1873.

Famous journeys It took 40 men four days to transport the statue on rails from Michelangelo's workshop behind the cathedral to Piazza della Signoria in 1504. Its journey from here, through the streets of Florence, to its current purpose-built tribune in the Galleria dell'Accademia in 1873 took seven long days.

Outstanding features (a) His expression which, from the left profile, appears serene, Zen and boy-like, from the right, concentrated, manly and highly charged in anticipation of the gargantuan Goliath he is about to slay; (b) the sense of counterbalanced weight rippling through his body, from the tension in his right hip on which he leans to his taut left arm.

Why the small penis? In classical art a large or even normal-sized packet was not deemed elegant, hence the daintier size.

And the big head and hands? *David* was designed to stand up high on a cathedral buttress in the apse, from where his head and hand would have appeared in perfect proportion.

Beauty treatments Body scrub with hydrochloric acid (1843); clay and cellulose pulp 'mud pack', bath in distilled water (2004).

Occupational hazards Over the centuries he's been struck by lightning, attacked by rioters and had his toes bashed with a hammer. The two pale white lines visible on his lower left arm is where his arm got broken during the 1527 revolt when the Medici were kicked out of Florence. Giorgio Vasari, then a child, picked up the pieces and 16 years later had them sent to Cosimo I who restored the statue, so the story goes.

Florence's oldest and largest food market is noisy, smelly and full of wonderful fresh produce to cook and eat. For a snack while you're here, follow the stream of stallholders making their way to Da Nerbone (p102).

San Marco

This part of the city boasts far more than the city's most famous resident, one Signore *David*. The frescoes in the Museo di San Marco are nothing short of superb.

★Galleria dell'Accademia ART GALLERY
(Map p78; www.polomuseale.firenze.it; Via Ricasoli 60; adult/reduced €6.50/3.25; 8.15am-6.50pm Tue-Sun) A lengthy queue marks the door to this gallery, built to house one of the Renaissance's greatest masterpieces, Michelangelo's original *David*. Fortunately, the world's most famous statue is worth the wait. The subtle detail of the real thing – the veins in his sinewy arms, the leg muscles, the change in expression as you move around the statue – *is* impressive.

Carved from a single block of marble already worked on by two sculptors before him (both of whom gave up), Michelangelo's most famous work was also his most challenging – he didn't choose the marble himself, it was veined and its larger-than-life dimensions were already decided.

And when the statue of the nude boy-warrior, depicted for the first time as a man in the prime of life rather than a young boy, assumed its pedestal in front of Palazzo Vecchio on Piazza della Signoria in 1504, Florentines immediately adopted it as a powerful emblem of Florentine power, liberty and civic pride.

Michelangelo was also the master behind the unfinished *San Matteo* (St Matthew; 1504–08) and four *Prigioni (*'Prisoners' or 'Slaves'; 1521–30), also displayed in the gallery. The Prisoners seem to be writhing and struggling to free themselves from the marble; they were meant for the tomb of Pope Julius II, itself never completed. Adjacent rooms contain paintings by Andrea Orcagna, Taddeo Gaddi, Domenico Ghirlandaio, Filippino Lippi and Sandro Botticelli.

★Museo di San Marco MUSEUM
(Map p78; www.polomuseale.firenze.it; Piazza San Marco 1; adult/reduced €4/2; 8.15am-1.20pm Mon-Fri, to 4.20pm Sat & Sun, closed 1st, 3rd & 5th Sun & 2nd & 4th Mon of month) At the heart of Florence's university area sits the **Chiesa di San Marco** and adjoining 15th-century Dominican monastery where both gifted painter Fra' Angelico (c 1395–1455) and the sharp-tongued Savonarola piously served God. Today the monastery showcases the work of Fra' Angelico. It is one of Florence's most spiritually uplifting museums.

Enter via Michelozzo's **Cloister of Saint Antoninus** (1440). Turn immediately right to enter the **Sala dell'Ospizio** (Pilgrims' Hospital) where Fra' Angelico's attention to perspective and the realistic portrayal of nature comes to life in a number of major paintings, including the *Deposition of Christ* (1432), originally commissioned for the church of Santa Trìnita.

Giovanni Antonio Sogliani's fresco *The Miraculous Supper of St Domenic* (1536) dominates the former monks' **refectory** in the cloister; and Fra' Angelico's huge *Crucifixion and Saints* fresco (1441–42) decorates the former chapterhouse. But it is the 44 monastic **cells** on the 1st floor that are the most haunting: at the top of the stairs, Fra' Angelico's most famous work, *Annunciation* (c 1440), commands all eyes.

A stroll around each of the cells reveals snippets of many more fine religious reliefs by the Tuscan-born friar, who decorated the cells between 1440 and 1441 with deeply devotional frescoes to guide the meditation of his fellow friars. Most were executed by Fra' Angelico himself; others are by aides under his supervision, including Benozzo Gozzoli. Among several masterpieces is the magnificent *Adoration of the Magi* in the cell used by Cosimo the Elder as a meditation retreat (Nos 38 to 39). Quite a few of the frescoes are extremely gruesome – check out the cell of San Antonino Arcivescovo, which features a depiction of Jesus pushing open the door of his sepulchre, squashing a nasty-looking devil in the process. After centuries of being known as 'Il Beato Angelico' (literally 'The Blessed Angelic One') or simply 'Il Beato' (The Blessed), the Renaissance's most blessed religious painter was made a saint by Pope John Paul II in 1984.

Contrasting with the pure beauty of these frescoes are the plain rooms that Savonarola called home from 1489. Rising to the position of prior at the Dominican convent, it was from here that the fanatical monk railed against luxury, greed and corruption of the clergy. Kept as a kind of shrine to the turbulent priest, they house a portrait, a few personal items, the linen banner Savonarola carried in processions and a grand marble monument erected by admirers in 1873.

Piazza della Santissima Annunziata PIAZZA

(Map p78) Giambologna's equestrian statue of Grand Duke Ferdinando I de' Medici commands the scene from the centre of this majestic square, dominated by the facades of **Chiesa della Santissima Annunziata** (Map p78), c 1250, rebuilt by Michelozzo et al in the mid-15th century, and the **Ospedale degli Innocenti** (Hospital of the Innocents; Map p78; Piazza della SS Annunziata 12), Europe's first orphanage founded in 1421.

Look up to admire the classically influenced portico, designed by Brunelleschi and famously decorated by Andrea della Robbia (1435–1525) with terracotta medallions of babies in swaddling clothes. At the north end of the portico, the false door surrounded by railings was once a revolving door where unwanted children were left. You can pay €1 to visit its lovely courtyard (open from 10am–3.30pm Monday to Saturday, and to 1.30pm Sunday), but the interior is currently closed for major restoration works; it will reopen in April 2015 as a spanking new **Museum of Childhood**.

Just off the northeast corner of the piazza is the **Museo Archeologico** (Map p78; Piazza Santissima Annunziata 9b; adult/reduced €4/2; 8.30am-7pm Tue-Fri, 8.30am-2pm Sat & Sun) whose rich collection of finds, including most of the Medici hoard of antiquities, plunges you deep into the past and offers an alternative to Renaissance splendour. On the 1st floor you can either head left into the ancient Egyptian collection or right for the smaller section of Etruscan and Graeco-Roman art.

Santa Croce

Presided over by the massive Franciscan basilica of the same name on the neighbourhood's main square, this area has a slightly rough veneer to it.

Piazza di Santa Croce PIAZZA

(Map p82) This square was initially cleared in the Middle Ages, primarily to allow hordes of the faithful to gather when the church itself was full. In Savonarola's day, heretics were executed here.

Such an open space inevitably found other uses, and from the 14th century it was often the colourful scene of jousts, festivals and *calcio storico* matches. Still played in this square in the third week of June each year, *calcio storico* (www.calciostorico.it) is like a combination of football and rugby with few rules (headbutting, punching, elbowing and choking are allowed, but sucker-punching and kicks to the head are forbidden). Look for the marble stone embedded in the wall below the gaily frescoed facade of **Palazzo dell'Antella** (Map p82), on the south side of the piazza; it marks the halfway line on this, one of the oldest football pitches in the world.

Curiously enough, the Romans used to have fun in much the same area centuries before. The city's 2nd-century amphitheatre took up the area facing the western end of Piazza di Santa Croce. To this day, Piazza dei Peruzzi, Via de' Bentaccordi and Via Torta mark the oval outline of the north, west and south sides of its course.

★ **Basilica di Santa Croce** CHURCH

(Map p82; Piazza di Santa Croce; adult/reduced €6/4, family ticket €12; 9.30am-5pm Mon-Sat, 2-5pm Sun) The austere interior of this massive Franciscan basilica is a shock after the magnificent neo-Gothic facade enlivened by varying shades of coloured marble. Though most visitors come to see the tombs of Michelangelo, Galileo and Ghiberti buried inside this church, it's the frescoes by Giotto and his school in the chapels to the right of the altar that are the real highlights.

The basilica itself was designed by Arnolfo di Cambio between 1294 and 1385 and owes its name to a splinter of the Holy Cross donated by King Louis of France in 1258. Some of its frescoed chapels are much better preserved than others – Giotto's murals in the **Cappella Peruzzi** are in particularly poor condition. Fortunately, those in the **Cappella Bardi** (1315–20) depicting scenes from the life of St Francis have fared better. Giotto's assistant and most loyal pupil,

LOCAL KNOWLEDGE

HIDDEN BEHIND DOORS

Just what is behind the average Florentine's front door? Take a peek with Andrew Losowsky's *The Doorbells of Florence* (http://losowsky.com/doorbells), a collection of photographs of doorbells in Florence accompanied by a fictional story about the fun and antics that goes on behind them.

Santa Croce

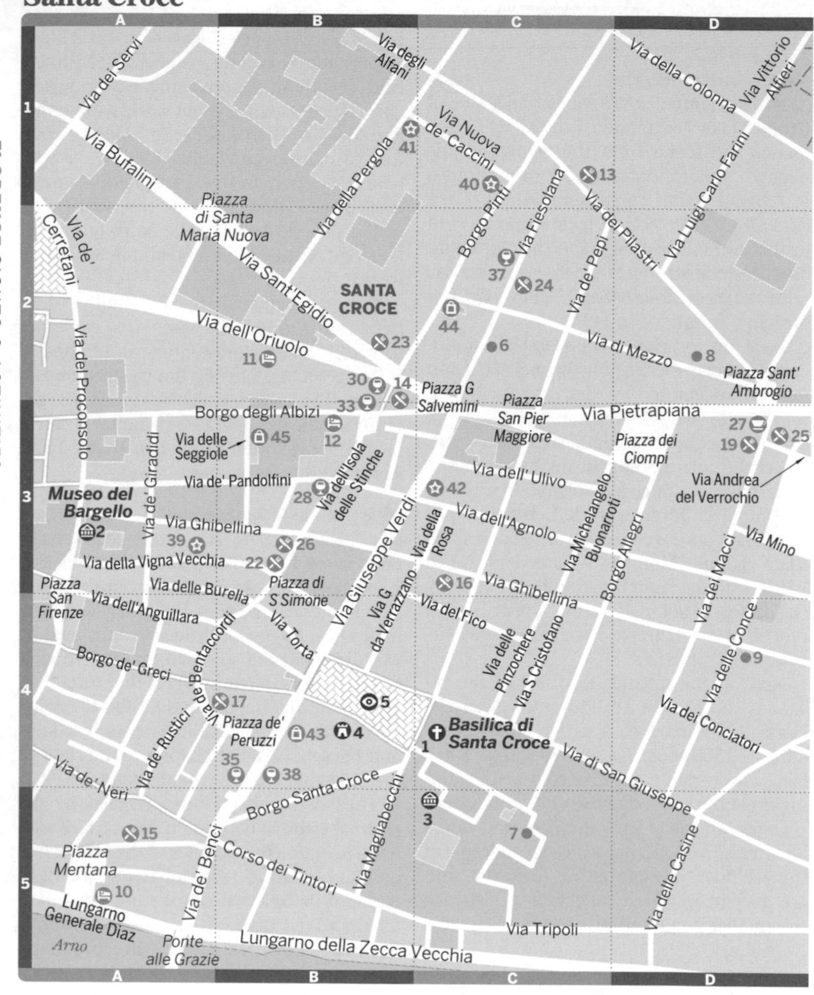

Taddeo Gaddi, frescoed the neighbouring **Cappella Majeure** and nearby **Cappella Baroncelli** (1332–38); the latter takes as its subject the life of the Virgin.

Taddeo's son Agnolo painted the **Cappella Castellani** (1385) with delightful frescoes depicting the life of St Nicholas (later transformed into 'Santa Claus') and was also responsible for the frescoes above the altar.

From the transept chapels a doorway designed by Michelozzo leads into a corridor, off which is the **Sagrestia**, an enchanting 14th-century room dominated on the left by Taddeo Gaddi's fresco of the Crucifixion. There are also a few relics of St Francis on show, including his cowl and belt. Through the next room, the church bookshop, you can access the Scuola del Cuoio (p92), a leather school where you can see bags being fashioned and buy the finished products.

At the end of the corridor is a Medici chapel with a fine two-tone altarpiece in glazed terracotta by Andrea della Robbia.

Brunelleschi designed the second of Santa Croce's two serene cloisters just before his death in 1446. His unfinished **Cappella de' Pazzi** at the end of the first cloister is notable for its harmonious lines and restrained

terracotta medallions of the Apostles by Luca della Robbia, and is a masterpiece of Renaissance architecture. It was built for, but never used by, the wealthy banking family destroyed in the 1478 Pazzi Conspiracy – when papal sympathisers sought to overthrow Lorenzo il Magnifico and the Medici dynasty.

Located off the first cloister, the **Museo dell'Opera di Santa Croce** (Map p82; admission incl basilica adult/concession €5/3) features *Crucifix* by Cimabue, restored to the best degree possible after flood damage in 1966, when more than 4m of water inundated the Santa Croce area.

Other highlights include Donatello's gilded bronze statue St Louis of Toulouse (1424), originally placed in a tabernacle on the Orsanmichele facade; a wonderful terracotta bust of St Francis receiving the stigmata by the della Robbia workshop; and frescoes by Taddeo Gaddi, including *The Last Supper* (1333).

★Museo del Bargello ART MUSEUM

(Map p82; www.polomuseale.firenze.it; Via del Proconsolo 4; adult/reduced €4/2, temporary exhibitions €6/3; ⌚8.15am-4.20pm Tue-Sun & 1st & 3rd Mon of month, to 2pm winter) It was behind the stark exterior of Palazzo del Bargello, Florence's earliest public building, that the *podestà* meted out justice from the late 13th century until 1502. Today the building safeguards Italy's most comprehensive collection of Tuscan Renaissance pieces and some of Michelangelo's best early works.

Michelangelo was just 21 when a cardinal commissioned him to create the drunken grape-adorned *Bacchus* (1496-97), displayed in Bargello's downstairs **Sala di Michelangelo**. Unfortunately the cardinal didn't like the result and sold it to a banker. Other Michelangelo works to look out for here include the marble bust of *Brutus* (c 1539–40), the *David/Apollo* from 1530–32 and the large, uncompleted roundel of the *Madonna and Child with the Infant St John* (1503–05, aka the Tondo Pitti).

After Michelangelo left Florence for the final time in 1534, sculpture was dominated by Baccio Bandinelli (his 1551 *Adam and Eve*, created for the *duomo*, is displayed in the Sala di Michelangelo) and Benvenuto Cellini (look for his playful 1548–50 marble *Ganimede* in the same room).

On the 1st floor, to the right of the staircase, is the **Sala di Donatello**. Here, in the majestic Salone del Consiglio Generale where the city's general council met, works by Donatello and other early-15th-century sculptors can be admired. Originally on the facade of Chiesa di Orsanmichele and now within a tabernacle at the hall's far end, Donatello's wonderful *St George* (1416–17) brought a new sense of perspective and movement to Italian sculpture. Also look for the bronze bas-reliefs created for the Baptistry doors competition by Brunelleschi and Ghiberti.

Yet it is Donatello's two versions of *David*, a favourite subject for sculptors, which really fascinate: Donatello fashioned his slender, youthful dressed image in marble in 1408

Santa Croce

Top Sights
1 Basilica di Santa Croce C4
2 Museo del Bargello A3

Sights
3 Museo dell'Opera di Santa Croce C5
4 Palazzo dell'Antella B4
5 Piazza di Santa Croce B4

Activities, Courses & Tours
6 Florence by Bike C2
7 Scuola del Cuoio C5
8 Scuola di Arte Culinaria Cordon Bleu D2
9 Tuscany Bike Tours D4

Sleeping
10 Hotel Balestri A5
11 Hotel Dalí B2
12 Hotel Orchidea B3

Eating
13 Acquacotta C1
14 Antico Noè B2
15 Brac A5
16 Enoteca Pinchiorri C3
17 Francesco Vini B4
18 Il Giova E3
Il Pizzaiuolo .... (see 19)
19 Il Teatro del Sale D3
20 Le Carceri E4
21 Mercato di Sant'Ambrogio E3
22 Osteria del Caffè Italiano B3
Pizzeria del' Osteria del Caffè Italiano .... (see 22)
Pollini .... (see 25)
Ristorante Cibrèo .... (see 25)
23 The Oil Shoppe B2
24 Touch C2
25 Trattoria Cibrèo D3
26 Vivoli B3

Drinking & Nightlife
27 Caffè Sant'Ambrogio D3
28 Danny Rock B3
29 Drogheria E3
30 Eby's Bar B2
31 Kitsch F3
32 Le Murate Caffè Letterario E4
33 Lion's Fountain B3
34 Monkey Bar E3
35 Moyo B4
36 Nano Caffè E3
37 Rex Caffé C2
38 Soul Kitchen B4

Entertainment
39 Full Up A3
40 Jazz Club C1
41 Teatro della Pergola B1
42 Twice Club C3

Shopping
43 Boutique Nadine B4
44 Mrs Macis C2
45 Vintage di Antonini Alessandra B3

and his fabled bronze between 1440 and 1450. The latter is extraordinary – the more so when you consider it was the first free-standing naked statue to be sculpted since classical times.

Criminals received their last rites before execution in the palace's 1st-floor **Cappella del Podestà**, also known as the Mary Magdalene Chapel, where Hell and Paradise are frescoed on the walls, as are stories from the lives of Mary of Egypt, Mary Magdalene and John the Baptist. These remnants of frescoes by Giotto were not discovered until 1840, when the chapel was turned into a storeroom and prison.

The **2nd floor** moves into the 16th century with a superb collection of terracotta pieces by the prolific della Robbia family, including some of their best-known works, such as Andrea's *Ritratto idealizia di fanciullo* (Bust of a Boy; c 1475) and Giovanni's *Pietà* (1514). Instantly recognisable, Giovanni's works are more elaborate and flamboyant than either father Luca's or cousin Andrea's, using a larger palette of colours.

Oltrarno

Literally 'other side of the Arno', atmospheric Oltrarno is the traditional home of the city's artisanal workshops. It embraces the area south of the river and west of Ponte Vecchio and its backbone is busy Borgo San Jacopo, clad with restaurants, shops and a twinset of 12th-century towers, **Torre dei Marsili** (Map p62) and **Torre de' Belfredelli** (Map p86).

When you reach the stage of museum overload and need to stretch your legs and see some sky, the tiers of parks and gardens behind Palazzo Pitti – not to be missed at sunset when its entire vast facade is coloured a vibrant pink – are just the ticket.

Should you notice something gone awry with street signs in Oltrarno – on a No Entry sign, a tiny black figure stealthily sneaking away with the white bar for example – you can be sure it is the work of **CLET** (Via dell'Olmo 8r; ⏲variable), Florence's most talked-about and admired street artist who quietly beavers away in his Oltrarno studio on Via dell'Olmo creating stickers that end up on street signs all over the city. In 2011 the French-born artist created quite a stir in his adopted city by installing, in the black of night, a life-sized figurine entitled *Uomo Comune* (Common Man) on Ponte alle Grazie (to which the city authorities turned a blind eye for a week before removing it).

★Ponte Vecchio BRIDGE

(Map p62) The first documentation of a stone bridge here, at the narrowest crossing point along the entire length of the Arno, dates from 972. The Arno looks placid enough, but when it gets mean, it gets very mean. Floods in 1177 and 1333 destroyed the bridge, and in 1966 it came close to being destroyed again. Many of the jewellers with shops on the bridge were convinced the floodwaters would sweep away their livelihoods; fortunately the bridge held.

They're still here. Indeed, the bridge has twinkled with the glittering wares of jewellers, their trade often passed down from generation to generation, ever since the 16th century, when Ferdinando I de' Medici ordered them here to replace the often malodorous presence of the town butchers, who used to toss unwanted leftovers into the river.

The bridge as it stands was built in 1345 and was the only one saved from destruction at the hands of the retreating Germans in 1944. What you see above the shops on the eastern side is the infamous **Corridoio Vasariano**, built rather oddly around (rather than straight through) the medieval **Torre dei Mannelli** at the bridge's southern end.

★Basilica di Santo Spirito CHURCH

(Map p86; Piazza Santo Spirito; ⏲8.30am-12.30pm & 4-5.30pm Thu-Tue) FREE The facade of this Brunelleschi church, smart on Florence's most shabby-chic piazza, is most striking in summer when it forms an atmospheric backdrop to open-air concerts and a buzzing social scene. Inside, the basilica's length is lined with 38 semicircular chapels (covered with a plain wall in the 1960s), and a colonnade of grey *pietra forte* Corinthian columns injects monumental grandeur.

Artworks to look for include Domenico di Zanobi's *Madonna of the Relief* (1485) in the **Cappella Velutti**, in which the Madonna wards off a little red devil with a club, and Filippino Lippi's poorly lit *Madonna with Child and Saints* (1493–94) in the **Cappella Nerli** in the right transept.

The main altar, beneath the central dome, is a voluptuous baroque flourish, rather out of place in Brunelleschi's characteristically spare interior.

Don't miss the door next to **Capella Segni** in the left aisle leading to the **sacristy**, where you'll find a poignant wooden crucifix attributed by some experts to Michelangelo. Michelangelo used to visit the hospital inside the neighbouring monastery at night to study the anatomy of corpses yet to be buried, hence his donation of the exquisitely sculptured Christ, or so the story goes.

Cenacolo di Santo Spirito MUSEUM

(Map p86; Piazza Santo Spirito 29; admission €2.50; ⏲10am-4pm Sat-Mon) For a change of pace from the Renaissance, head to this former refectory decorated with a grand fresco by Andrea Orcagna depicting the *Last Supper and the Crucifixion* (c 1370). Inside, a collection of rare 11th-century Romanesque sculpture woos.

★Cappella Brancacci CHAPEL

(Map p86; ☎055 276 82 24; www.musefirenze.it; Piazza del Carmine 14; adult/reduced €6/4.50; ⏲10am-4.30pm Wed-Sat & Mon, 1-4.30pm Sun) Fire in the 18th century all but destroyed 13th-century **Basilica di Santa Maria del Carmine** (Map p86), but fortunately it spared the magnificent frescoes in its Cappella Brancacci, to the right of the church entrance. Visits are by guided tour (20 minutes, every 20 minutes) and advance reservations are recommended in season given only 30 people at a time are allowed in.

This chapel is a treasure of paintings by Masolino da Panicale, Masaccio and Filippino Lippi. Masaccio's fresco cycle illustrating the life of St Peter is considered among his greatest works, representing a definitive break with Gothic art and a plunge into new worlds of expression in the early stages of the Renaissance. *The Expulsion of Adam and Eve from Paradise* and *The Tribute Money*, both on the left side of the chapel, are his best-known works. Masaccio painted these frescoes in his early twenties, taking over from Masolino, and interrupted the task to go to Rome, where he died, aged only 27. The cycle was completed some 60 years later by Filippino Lippi. Masaccio himself

Oltrarno & Boboli

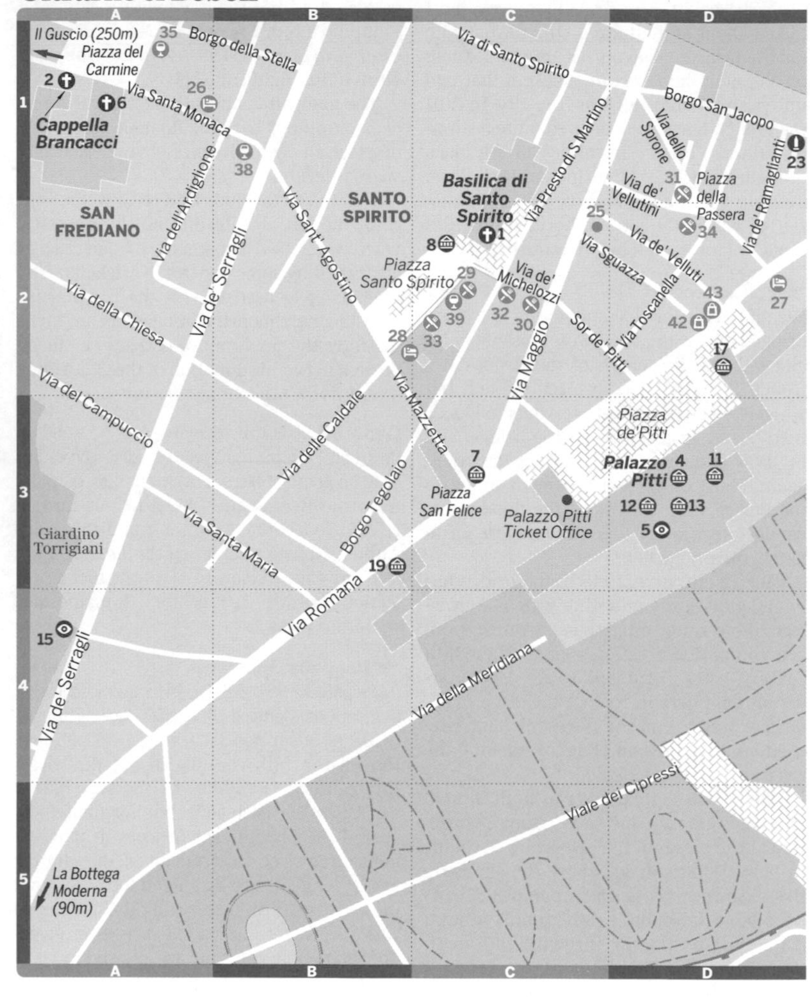

features in his *St Peter Enthroned*; he's the one standing beside the Apostle, staring out at the viewer. The figures around him have been identified as Brunelleschi, Masolino and Alberti. Filippino Lippi also painted himself into the scene of *St Peter's Crucifixion*, along with his teacher, Botticelli.

★Palazzo Pitti MUSEUM

(Map p86; www.polomuseale.firenze.it; Piazza Pitti; adult/reduced Galleria Palentina & Galleria d'Arte Moderna €8.50/4.25, Museo degli Argenti & Galleria del Costume €7/3.50; ⏲8.15am-6.50pm Tue-Sun summer, shorter hr winter) Banker Luca Pitti commissioned Brunelleschi to design this palace in 1457, but by the time it was completed waning family fortunes forced them to sell it to the Medici. It later became the residence of the city's rulers and, from 1865 until 1919, the residence of the Savoy royal family. Several art museums can be found inside.

Exquisite amber carvings, ivory miniatures, glittering tiaras and headpieces, silver pill boxes and various other gems 'n jewels are displayed in the ground-floor **Museo degli Argenti** (Silver Museum; Map p86; ⏲8.15am-6.50pm summer, shorter hr rest of yr,

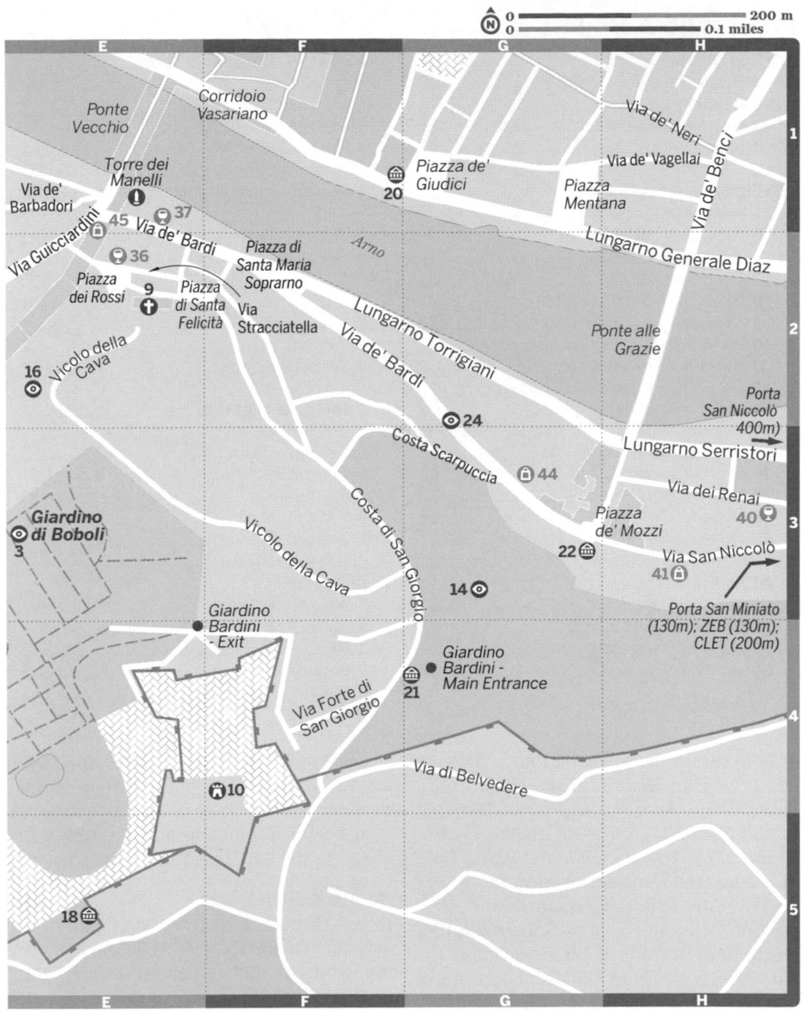

closed 1st & last Mon of month), a series of elaborately frescoed audience chambers, some of which host temporary exhibitions. Notable (but not always open) is the **Sala di Giovanni da San Giovanni**, which sports lavish head-to-toe frescoes (1635–42) celebrating the life of Lorenzo Il Magnifico – spot Michelangelo giving Lorenzo a statue. 'Talk little, be brief and witty' is the curt motto above the painted staircase in the next room, the public audience chamber, where the grand duke received visitors in the presence of his court.

Raphaels and Rubens vie for centre stage in the enviable collection of 16th- to 18th-century art amassed by the Medici and Lorraine dukes in the 1st-floor **Galleria Palatina** (Map p86; ⌚8.15am-6.50pm Tue-Sun summer, shorter hr winter), reached by several flights of stairs from the palace's central courtyard. This gallery has retained the original display arrangement of paintings (squeezed in, often on top of each other) so can be visually overwhelming – go slow and focus on the works one by one.

Highlights include Fra' Filippo Lippi's *Madonna and Child with Stories from the Life*

Oltrarno & Boboli

Top Sights

1 Basilica di Santo Spirito C2
2 Cappella Brancacci A1
3 Giardino di Boboli E3
4 Palazzo Pitti D3

Sights

5 Appartamenti Reali D3
6 Basilica di Santa Maria del Carmine A1
7 Casa Guidi C3
8 Cenacolo di Santo Spirito C2
9 Chiesa di Santa Felicità E2
10 Forte di Belvedere F4
11 Galleria d'Arte Moderna D3
12 Galleria del Costume D3
13 Galleria Palatina D3
14 Giardino Bardini G3
15 Giardino Torrigiani A4
16 Grotta del Buontalenti E2
17 Museo degli Argenti D2
18 Museo delle Porcellane E5
19 Museo di Storia Naturale - Zoologia La Specola B3
20 Museo Galileo F1
21 Museo Roberto Capucci G4
22 Palazzo de' Mozzi G3
23 Torre de' Belfredelli D1
24 Via de' Bardi G2

Activities, Courses & Tours

25 In Tavola C2

Sleeping

26 Hostel Santa Monaca A1
27 Hotel La Scaletta D2
28 Palazzo Guadagni Hotel B2

Eating

29 Gustapanino C2
30 Gustapizza C2
31 Il Magazzino D1
32 La Casalinga C2
33 Tamerò C2
34 Trattoria 4 Leoni D2

Drinking & Nightlife

35 Dolce Vita A1
36 Le Volpi e l'Uva E2
37 Open Bar E1
38 Vivanda B1
39 Volume C2
40 Zoé H3

Shopping

41 Alessandro Dari H3
42 Casini Firenze D2
43 Giulio Giannini e Figlio D2
44 Lorenzo Villoresi G3
45 Madova E1

of St Anne (aka the Tondo Bartolini; 1452–53) and Botticelli's *Madonna with Child and a Young Saint John the Baptist* (c 1490–95) in the **Sala di Prometeo**; Raphael's *Madonna of the Window* (1513–14) in the **Sala di Ulisse**; and Caravaggio's *Sleeping Cupid* (1608) in the **Sala dell'Educazione di Giove**. Don't miss the **Sala di Saturno**, full of magnificent works by Raphael, including the *Madonna of the Chair* (1511) and portraits of Anolo Doni and Maddalena Strozzi (c 1506). Nearby, in the **Sala di Giove**, the same artist's *Lady with a Veil* (aka La Velata; c 1516) holds court alongside Giorgione's *Three Ages of Man* (c 1500).

Past the **Sala di Venere** are the **Appartamenti Reali** (Royal Apartments; Map p86; ⌚8.15am-6.50pm Tue-Sun Feb-Dec) is a series of rooms presented as they were circa 1880–91 during House of Savoy times.

Palazzo Pitti's 2nd-floor **Galleria d'Arte Moderna** (Map p86; ⌚8.15am-6.50pm Tue-Sun summer, shorter hr winter) curates 18th- and 19th-century works. The work of the Florentine Macchiaioli school (the local equivalent of Impressionism) dominates the collection.

Few visitors get as far as the **Galleria del Costume** (Map p86; ⌚8.15am-6.50pm summer, shorter hr rest of yr, closed 1st & last Mon of month), a parade of fashions from the times of Cosimo I to the haute-couture 1990s.

★ Giardino di Boboli — GARDEN

(Boboli Gardens; Map p86; Piazza Pitti; adult/reduced/child €7/3.50/free; ⌚8.15am-7pm summer, shorter hr winter) Behind Palazzo Pitti, the Boboli Gardens laid out in the mid-16th century to a design by architect Niccolò Pericoli are a prime example of a formal Tuscan garden and they are lovely to wander. At the upper, southern limit, beyond the box-hedged rose garden and **Museo delle Porcellane** (Porcelain Museum; Map p86; Giardino di Boboli; adult/reduced €7/3.50 incl Giardino di Boboli, Museo delgi Argenti & Museo del Costume; ⌚Mar 8.15am-5.30pm, Apr-May & Sep-Oct 8.15am-6.30pm, Jun-Aug 8.15am-7.30pm, Nov-Feb 8.15am-4.30pm), fantastic views over the Florentine countryside fan out.

Highlights of this wonderful airy garden, blessed with plenty of statues and hidden paths between trees, include a rather neglected **Cypress Alley**, the walled **Giardino**

del Cavaliere (Knights' Garden), and **Isoletto**, a gorgeous ornamental pool. Typical Renaissance, the 18th-century **orangery** (closed to visitors) is where 500-odd citrus trees keep snug in winter. The 17th-century maze, a Tuscan horticultural standard, was razed in the 1830s to make way for a driveway for carriages. The monumental 'face' sculpture (1998) is by Polish sculptor Igor Mitoraj (b 1944), who lives in Pietrasanta near Carrara today.

By the garden exit, hundreds of seashells decorate the facade of **Grotta del Buontalenti** (Map p86; 11am, 1pm, 3pm, 4pm & 5pm), a fanciful grotto by Giambologna. Peer inside to see Venere (Venus) rising from the waves. The wall, smothered with the foliage of orange trees to the left of the grotto is the outer facade of the final leg of the legendary **Vasarian Corridor** (p70), linking the Uffizi with Plazzo Pitti.

Giardino Bardini GARDEN

(Map p86; www.bardinipeyron.it; entrances at Via de' Bardi 1r & Costa di San Giorgio 2; adult/reduced/child €7/3.50/free; 8.15am-7pm summer, shorter hr winter) This garden was named after art collector Stefano Bardini (1836–1922), who bought the villa in 1913 and restored its medieval garden. Smaller and more manicured than the Boboli, it has all the features of a quintessential Tuscan garden, but not the crowds. Inside the villa, the **Museo Roberto Capucci** (Map p86; www.bardinipeyron.it; Giardini Bardini; adult/reduced €8/6; 10am-9pm Wed-Sun Apr-Oct) hosts a collection of Capucci-designed haute couture and temporary exhibitions.

A springtime stroll past artificial grottos, an orangery, marble statues and fountains is idyllic. Beds of azaleas, peonies and wisteria bloom in April and May, irises in June. The romantic **summer cafe** (open from 10am to 6pm April to September), set in a stone loggia overlooking the Florentine skyline, is a wonderful spot for a *panino* lunch, ice cream or afternoon tea.

Giardino Torrigiani GARDEN

(Map p86; 055 22 45 27; www.giardinotorrigiani.it; Via de' Serragli 144; 1½-hour guided tours by donation; by advance reservation via email) Astonishing. Behind the unassuming facades of Via de' Serragli lies a vast, secret garden – Europe's largest privately owned green space within an historic centre, owned by the Torrigiani Malaspina and Torrigiani di Santa Cristina families. Well-kept and loved, it's possible to visit this leafy retreat in the engaging company of the charismatic Marquis Vanni Torrigiani Malaspina and his wife Susanna.

GARDEN STROLL

An easy footpath leads from Giardino di Boboli to Giardino Bardini; the gate between the two – a mere five-minute walk – shuts at 5pm.

Tours (in English or Italian) are intimate and proffer a rare glimpse into a very different and privileged Florentine world.

Designed at the height of the Romantic movement in the early 19th century, the idyllic oasis of green wrapped around the original 16th-century villa and subsequent early 19th-century house includes rare tree species, wide English-style lawns, herb and vegetables gardens, sculpted lions, a beautifully restored greenhouse, and remains of city walls built under Cosimo I in 1544 (one of six sets of walls to be built around Florence at different times – spot the segment of older, 14th century walls outside the garden).

The garden design is laden with complex Masonic symbology, climaxing with an elegant neo-Gothic tower spiralling to the heavens; the three levels allude to the three stages of the initiation process from the profane world to the initiation of Freemasonry.

In the recently restored greenhouse and Italian garden known collectively as La Serra Torrigiani Vanni, the marquis Vanni and Susanna run horticultural, gardening and painting courses and workshops. In the future they hope to build a trio of treehouses for guests to sleep B&B style.

Casa Guidi MUSEUM

(Map p86; www.browningsociety.org; Piazza San Felice 8; 3-6pm Mon, Wed & Fri Apr-Nov) FREE It was on the ground floor of 15th-century Palazzo Guidi, across from Palazzo Pitti, that Robert and Elizabeth Browning rented an apartment in 1847, a year after their marriage. Robert wrote *Men and Women* in the apartment they called home for 14 years and poetess Elizabeth both gave birth to their only child here and died here.

Museo di Storia Naturale – Zoologia La Specola HISTORY MUSEUM

(Map p86; www.msn.unifi.it; Via Romana 17; adult/child/family €6/3/13; 9.30am-4.30pm Tue-Sun

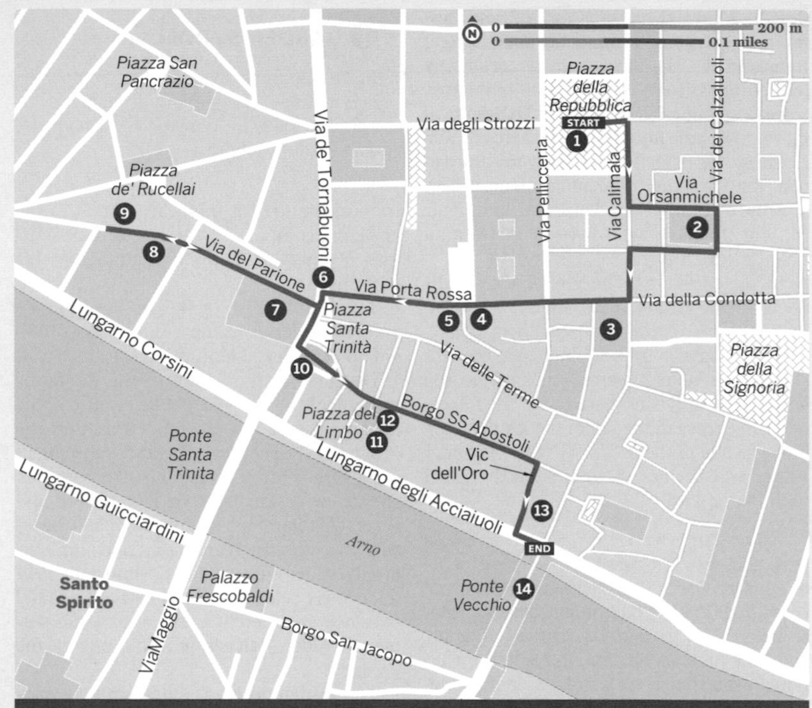

City Walk
Quintessential Florence

START PIAZZA DELLA REPUBBLICA
FINISH PONTE VECCHIO
LENGTH 2KM, TWO HOURS

Start with coffee on ❶ **Piazza della Repubblica** (p74) then walk one block south along Via Calimala and turn left onto Via Orsanmichele to ❷ **Chiesa e Museo di Orsanmichele** (p74), a unique church with ornate statuary adorning its facade and a fascinating museum inside. Backtrack to Via Calimala and continue walking south until you see the loggia of ❸ **Mercato Nuovo** (p112), the 16th-century 'New Market'. Florentines know it as 'Il Porcellino' (The Piglet) after the bronze statue of a wild boar on its southern side. Rub its snout to ensure your return to Florence.

Walk past the market and along Via Porta Rossa to ❹ **Palazzo Davanzati** (p75) with its magnificent studded doors and fascinating museum. A few doors down, next to the ❺ **Slowly** (p108) bar, peep through the sturdy iron gate and look up to admire the ancient brick vaults of this dark alley – this is hidden Florence of 1001 fabulous doors and lost alleys at its best!

Continue to ❻ **Via de' Tornabuoni** with its luxury designer boutiques. Swoon over frescoed chapels in ❼ **Chiesa di Santa Trinita** (p75), then wander down Via del Parione to visit paper marbler ❽ **Alberto Cozzi** (p117) and puppet maker ❾ **Letizia Fiorini** (p113).

Backtrack to Via de' Tornabuoni and turn right, past 13th-century ❿ **Palazzo Spini-Feroni,** home of Salvatore Ferragamo's flagship store, to Borgo Santissimi Apostoli. A short way ahead on Piazza del Limbo is the Romanesque ⓫ **Chiesa dei Santissimi Apostoli** (Map p62), in a sunken square once used as a cemetery for unbaptised babies.

After browsing for Tuscan olive oil in ⓬ **La Bottega dell'Olio** (p116), continue east and turn right into Vicolo dell' Oro, home to the ⓭ **Hotel Continental,** whose sleek rooftop terrace is the perfect spot for a sundowner with a ⓮ **Ponte Vecchio** (p85) view.

Oct-May, to 5.30pm Jun-Sep) One of several sections of Florence's natural history museum dating to 1775, La Specola showcases 5000-odd animals (out of a depository of 3.5 million). The big highlight, not recommended for the squeamish or young children, is the collection of wax models of bits of human anatomy in varying states of bad health.

Via de' Bardi STREET

(Map p86) Walking east from Ponte Vecchio, the first stretch of Via de' Bardi shows clear signs of its recent history. This entire area was flattened by German mines in 1944, and hastily rebuilt in questionable taste after the war. The street spills into Piazza di Santa Maria Soprarno. Follow narrow Via de' Bardi away from the square and you enter a quiet corner of Florence once practically owned by the powerful Bardi family.

By the time Cosimo the Elder wed Contessina de' Bardi in 1415, the latter's family was on the decline. Via de' Bardi ends on Piazza de' Mozzi, surrounded by the sturdy facades of grand residences. Pope Gregory X stayed at **Palazzo de' Mozzi** (Map p86; Piazza de' Mozzi 2) when brokering peace between the Guelphs and Ghibellines.

Forte di Belvedere FORTRESS, GALLERY

(Map p86; ☎055 29 08 32; Via di San Leonardo 1; admission €5; ⏰10am-8pm Fri-Wed summer) Forte di Belvedere is a rambling fort designed by Bernardo Buontalenti for Grand Duke Ferdinando I at the end of the 16th century. From the massive bulwark soldiers kept watch on four fronts – as much for internal security to protect the Palazzo Pitti as against foreign attack. After five lengthy years of renovation works, the imposing fortress is once again open to visitors: it hosts fabulous contemporary art exhibitions and the sweeping panorama from its walls is among the city's most breathtaking.

FLORENCE FOR CHILDREN

Children are welcomed anywhere, anytime, in Florence. Families frequently go out with young children in the evenings, strolling riverside with a *gelato* or dining al fresco on summertime terraces. That said, Florence is not the easiest city to visit with very young children; green spaces and playgrounds are scarce and, while some of the pricier hotels can provide babysitters, there's no organised service for tourists.

For parents with a baby in tow, there is no easier, more central (or more pleasant) spot to stop for a break than the Gucci Museo Caffè (p109). The clean toilets are equipped with changing mats, mums can happily breastfeed without anyone batting an eyelid, and there are plenty of art books and free iPäds in the cafe to amuse tots.

Teems of locally published books help children discover Florence – museum bookshops in Palazzo Vecchio and the Uffizi have tip-top selections.

Tours & Workshops

Florence proffers plenty of guided activities designed with kids in mind, including the engaging themed tours and workshops for children from aged 4 years (some from 8 or 10 years) at Palazzo Vecchio and the monthly two-hour 'Art Weekend' workshops at Palazzo Strozzi (p75). Or consider a pizza-, gelato- or pasta-cooking course for your child.

Museums & Monuments

Hopeless for pushchairs, yes, but older kids love scaling new Florentine heights with an energy-burning hike up Palazzo Vecchio's Torre d'Arnolfo (p72), the Duomo belltower or around the inside of its astonishing dome. Recommended museums for the over six year olds include the Museo di Storia Naturale – Zoologia La Specola (p89), Museo Stibbert (p77) and Florence's state-of-the-art science museum, Museo Galileo (p74).

Parks & Playgrounds

The best playgrounds for under six year olds are near the *duomo* (cathedral) on Piazza Massimo d'Azeglio and across the river on Lungarno Santa Rosa and Piazza Torquato Tasso. The vintage **carousel** on Piazza della Repubblica never stops enchanting.

Children over six never tire of playing hide-and-seek between statues in Giardino di Boboli (p88) or tearing round 118-hectare **Parco delle Cascine** (Viale degli Olmi; 🚌1, 9, 12, 13, 16, 26, 27, 80 & B), which in summer has an open-air **swimming pool** to splash around in.

To get here from Piazza de' Mozzi, turn east down Via dei Renai, past leafy Piazza Nicola Demidoff, dedicated to the 19th-century Russian philanthropist who lived nearby in Via San Niccolò. At the end of Via dei Renai, 16th-century **Palazzo Serristori** was home to Joseph Bonaparte in the last years of his life until his death in 1844; a humble end to the man who, at the height of his career, had been appointed king of Spain by his brother Napoleon. Turn right and you end up on Via San Niccolò; walk east along this street to emerge at the tower marking **Porta San Niccolò**, all that is left of the city walls. To get an idea of what the walls were once like, walk south from Chiesa di San Niccolò Oltrarno through **Porta San Miniato**. The wall extends a short way to the east and for a stretch further west, up a steep hill that leads you to the fortress.

Piazzale Michelangelo VIEWPOINT

Turn your back on the bevy of ticky-tacky souvenir stalls flogging *David* statues and boxer shorts and take in the spectacular city panorama from this vast square, pierced by one of Florence's two *David* copies. Sunset here is particularly dramatic. It's a 10-minute uphill walk along the serpentine road, paths and steps that scale the hillside from the Arno and Piazza Giuseppe Poggi; from Piazza San Niccolò walk uphill and bear left up the long flight of steps signposted Viale Michelangelo. Or take bus 13 from Stazione di Santa Maria Novella.

Basilica di San Miniato al Monte CHURCH

(Via Monte alle Croce; ⌚8am-7pm May-Oct, 8am-noon & 3-6pm Nov-Apr) Five minutes uphill from Piazzale Michelangelo is this wonderful Romanesque church, dedicated to St Minius, an early-Christian martyr in Florence who is said to have flown to this spot after his death down in the town (or, if you want to believe an alternative version, walked up the hill with head tucked underneath his arm).

The church dates to the early 11th century, although its typical Tuscan multicoloured marble facade was tacked on a couple of centuries later. Inside, 13th- to 15th-century frescoes adorn the south wall and intricate inlaid marble designs line the nave, leading to a fine Romanesque crypt. The sacristy in the southeast corner features frescoes by Spinello Arentino depicting the life of St Benedict. Slap-bang in the middle of the nave is the bijou **Capella del Crocefisso**, to which Michelozzo, Agnolo Gaddi and Luca della Robbia all contributed.

OFF THE BEATEN TRACK

TOP 5: LOSE THE CROWD

- Florence can be overwhelming: flee to **Fiesole** (p96) in the Florentine hills for peace, quiet and lunch with a spectacular view.
- Take tea with a panoramic city view in the manicured gardens of **Giardino Bardini** (p89).
- Join the privileged few in an exclusive, cross-river stroll along the enigmatic **Vasarian Corridor** (p70).
- Motor out of the city through vineyards and olive groves in a vintage Fiat 500 with the **500 Touring Club** (p93).
- Lose yourself among rare trees and sculpted lions in Florence's secret garden, aka **Giardino Torrigiani** (p89), Europe's largest private walled garden right in the heart of Florence.

 Courses

Florence has zillions of schools running courses in Italian language, culture and cuisine.

Scuola di Arte Culinaria Cordon Bleu COOKING

(Map p82; ☎055 234 54 68; www.cordonbleu-it.com; Via di Mezzo 55r) Serious cooking school for amateurs and professionals with heaps of short-term, long-term and one-off courses.

Scuola del Cuoio LEATHER WORKING

(Map p82; ☎055 24 45 34; www.scuoladelcuoio.com; Via San Giuseppe 5r) Leather-working courses in a leather school created by Franciscan friars after WWII.

In Tavola COOKING

(Map p86; ☎055 21 76 72; www.intavola.org; Via dei Velluti 18r) Take your pick from dozens of carefully crafted courses for beginners and professionals: pizza and gelato, pasta making, easy Tuscan dinners etc.

 Tours

City Sightseeing Firenze BUS

(Map p78; ☎055 29 04 51; www.firenze.city-sightseeing.it; Piazza della Stazione 1; adult 1/2/3 days

€20/25/30) Explore Florence by red open-top bus, hopping on and off at 15 bus stops around the city. Tickets, sold by the driver, are valid for 24 hours.

Tuscany Bike Tours BIKE TOUR
(Map p82; ☎055 386 04 95; www.tuscany-biketours.com; Via Ghibellina 34r) One-day, 23km-long bike tours in Chianti with lunch, castle tour, wine and oil tasting (€80); transfer to Chianti by minibus.

Italy by Segway SEGWAY TOUR
(Map p62; www.italysegwaytours.com; Via dei Cimatori 9r) Guided Segway tours (€75, three hours) as well as more mainstream bike tours (€35, three hours) in the morning or at sunset. Reserve in advance online.

ArtViva WALKING TOUR
(Map p62; ☎055 264 50 33; www.italy.artviva.com; Via de' Sassetti 1; per person from €25) Marketed as the 'Original & Best', these excellent one-to three-hour city walks are led by historians or art history graduates; tours include the Uffizi, the Original David tour and an Evening Walk/Murder Mystery Tour. ArtViva also runs trips further afield to Chianti (wine tasting) and a Renaissance villa outside Florence (villa lunch and swim).

Freya's Florence Tours WALKING TOUR
(☎349 0748907; www.freyasflorence.com; per hr €70) Australian-born, Florence-based private tour guide; admission fees not included in guiding fee.

Faith Willinger – Lessons & Tours CULINARY
(www.faithwillinger.com) Food lovers' walking tour, a market stroll, gelato crawl and much more by American-born, Florence-based food writer Faith Willinger, who runs cooking courses, hands-on 'market to table' sessions, tastings, demonstrations and culinary visits, including meaty field trips to Panzano in Chianti.

Accidental Tourist WINE, CULINARY
(☎055 69 93 76; www.accidentaltourist.com) Become an Accidental Tourist (membership €10), then sign up for a wine tour (€60), cooking class (€70), gourmet picnic (€35) and so on; tours happen in and around Florence.

Festivals & Events

Festa di Anna Maria Medici HISTORICAL
Florence's Feast of Anna Maria Medici marks the death in 1743 of the last Medici, Anna Maria, with a costumed parade from Palazzo Vecchio to her tomb in the Cappelle Medicee; 18 February.

Scoppio del Carro LIGHT SHOW
A cart of fireworks is exploded in front of the cathedral at 11am on Easter Sunday – get there at least two hours early to grab a good position.

Maggio Musicale Fiorentino ARTS
(www.maggiofiorentino.com) Italy's oldest arts festival, held in Florence's Teatro del Maggio Musicale Fiorentino, stages world-class performances of theatre, classical music, jazz and dance; April to June.

Festa di San Giovanni MIDSUMMER
Florence celebrates its patron saint, John, with a *calcio storico* match on Piazza di Santa Croce and fireworks over Piazzale Michelangelo; 24 June.

Festival Firenze Classica MUSIC
(www.orcafi.it) July sees Florence's highly regarded Orchestra da Camera Toscana performing classical music in the atmospheric settings of the Oratorio di San Michele a Castello and Palazzo Strozzi.

Festa delle Rificolone RELIGIOUS
During the Festival of the Paper Lanterns children carrying lanterns, accompanied by drummers, *sbandieratori* (flag throwers), musicians and others in medieval dress, process through the streets from Piazza di Santa Croce to Piazza della Santissima Annunziata to celebrate the Virgin Mary's birthday; 7 September.

OFF THE BEATEN TRACK

VINTAGE MOTORING

Hook up with Florence's **500 Touring Club** (☎346 8262324; www.500touringclub.com; Via Gherardo Silvani 149a) for a guided tour in a vintage motor – with you behind the wheel! Every car has a name in this outfit's fleet of gorgeous vintage Fiat 500s from the 1960s (Giacomo is the playboy, Anna the feminist girl and so on). Motoring tours are guided – hop in your car and follow the leader – and themed; families love the picnic trip, couples wine tasting. March to November tours need to be booked well in advance.

1

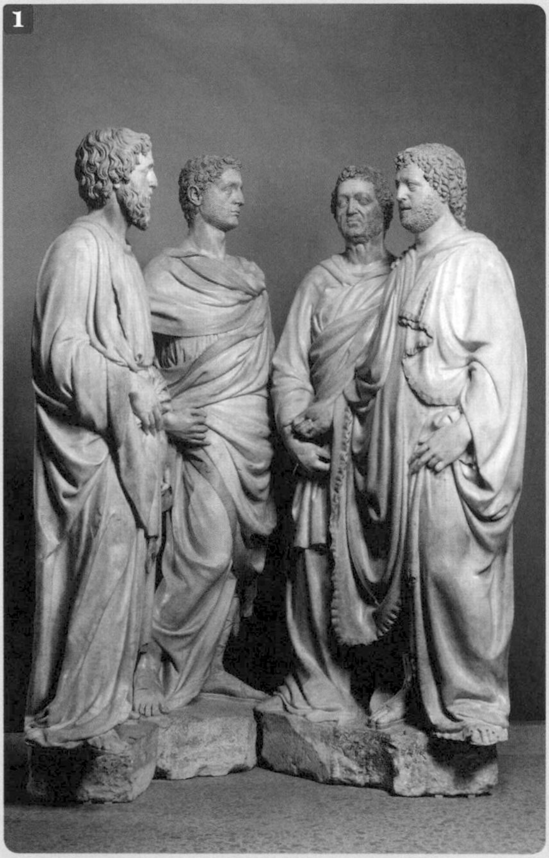

PHOTO SCALA, FLORENCE - COURTESY OF THE MINISTERO BENI E ATT. CULTURALI ©

2

4

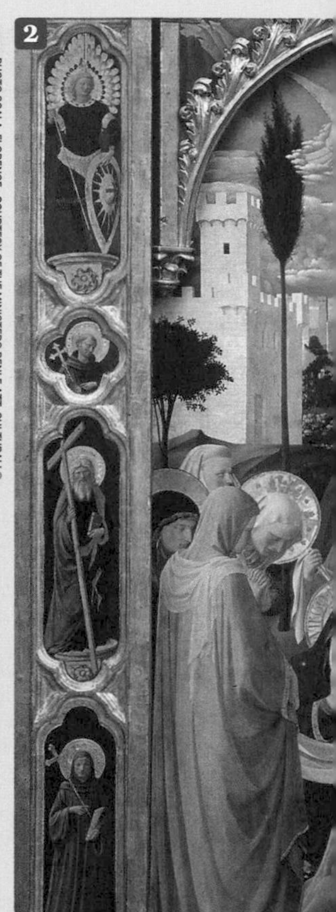

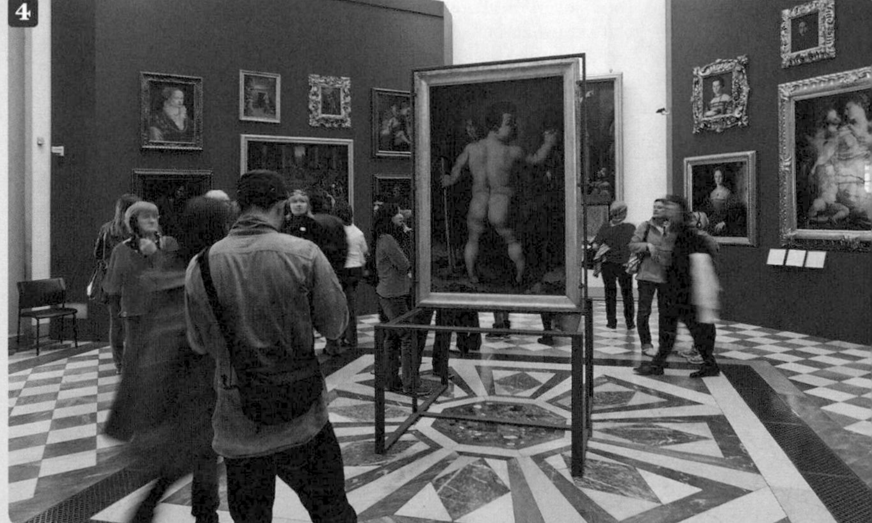

1. Di Banco's *Four Crowned Martyrs*, Chiesa e Museo di Orsanmichele (p74)
This unusual church is decorated with sculptures by some of the greatest Renaissance artists.

2. Fra' Angelico's *Deposition of Christ*, Museo di San Marco (p80)
Previously a monastery where Fra' Angelico served God, the Museo di San Marco is one of Florence's most spiritually uplifting museums.

3. Michelangelo's *David*, Galleria dell'Accademia (p80)
A lengthy queue marks the door to this gallery, but the world's most famous statue is worth the wait.

4. Uffizi Gallery (p64)
The Galleria degli Uffizi is the jewel in Florence's crown. Its collection spans the gamut of art history, but its core is the masterpiece-rich Renaissance collection.

3

FIESOLE DAY TRIPPER

One of the joys of Florence is leaving it behind and Fiesole provides the perfect excuse. Perched in the hills 9km northeast of the city, this bijou hilltop village has seduced for centuries with its cooler air, olive groves, scattering of Renaissance-styled villas and spectacular views of the plain. Boccaccio, Marcel Proust, Gertrude Stein and Frank Lloyd Wright, among others, raved about it.

10am

Founded in the 7th century BC by the Etruscans, Fiesole was the most important city in northern Etruria and its **Area Archeologica** (www.museidifiesole.it; Via Portigiani 1; adult/reduced Fri-Sun €10/6, Mon-Thu €8/4, family €20; ⏲10am-7pm summer, shorter hr rest of yr), off central square **Piazza Mino di Fiesole**, provides the perfect flashback. Buy a ticket from the tourist office a couple of doors away then meander around the ruins of an Etruscan temple, Roman baths and archaeological museum. Later, pause for thought on the stone steps of the 1st-century-BC Roman amphitheatre, summer stage to Italy's oldest open-air festival, **Estate Fiesolana**.

Afterwards pop into neighbouring **Museo Bandini** (www.museidifiesole.it; Via Dupré; adult/reduced €5/3 or free with Area Archeologica ticket; ⏲10am-7pm summer, shorter hr rest of yr) to view early Tuscan Renaissance art, including fine medallions (c 1505–20) by Giovanni della Robbia and Taddeo Gaddi's luminous *Annunciation* (1340–45).

Noon

From the museum, a 300m walk along Via Giovanni Dupré brings you to the **Fondazione Primo Conti** (☎055 59 70 95; www.fondazioneprimoconti.org; Via Giovanni Dupré 18; admission €3, with archives €5; ⏲9am-2pm Mon-Fri) where the eponymous avant-garde 20th-century artist lived and worked. Inside hang more than 60 of his paintings and the views from the garden are inspiring. Ring to enter.

1pm

Meander back to **Piazza Mino di Fiesole,** host to an antiques market on the first Sunday of each month, where cafe and restaurant terraces tempt. The pagoda-covered terrace of **Villa Aurora** (☎055 5 93 63; www.villaurora.net; Piazza Mino da Fiesole 39; meals €30), around

Sleeping

Duomo to Piazza della Signoria

Incredibly, for such a dead-central part of Florence, this area has some excellent budget addresses.

★Hotel Scoti HISTORIC HOTEL €
(Map p62; ☎055 29 21 28; www.hotelscoti.com; Via de' Tornabuoni 7; s/d/tr/q €80/125/150/175; 📶) Wedged between Prada and McQueen, this is a splendid mix of old-fashioned charm and value for money. Run with smiling aplomb by Australian Doreen and Italian Carmello, the hotel is enthroned in a 16th-century *palazzo* on Florence's smartest shopping strip. The 16 rooms are clean and comfortable, but the star is the frescoed lounge from 1780. Breakfast €5.

Hotel Cestelli BOUTIQUE HOTEL €
(Map p62; ☎055 21 42 13; www.hotelcestelli.com; Borgo SS Apostoli 25; d €100-115, s/d with shared bathroom €60/80, extra bed €25; ⏲closed 4 wks Jan-Feb, 3 wks Aug) A stiletto hop and skip from the Arno and fashionable Via de' Tornabuoni, this eight-room hotel in a 12th-century *palazzo* is a gem. Its large, quiet rooms ooze understated style – think washbasin with silk screen and vintage art. Before stepping out, quiz Italian photographer Alessio and gracious Japanese wife, Asumi, on new eating, drinking and shopping openings.

Hotel Torre Guelfa HISTORIC HOTEL €€
(Map p62; ☎055 239 63 38; www.hoteltorreguelfa.com; Borgo SS Apostoli 8; d/tr/q €200/250/300; ❄@📶) If you wanna kip in a Real McCoy Florentine *palazzo* without breaking the bank, this 31-room hotel with fortress-style facade is the address. Scale its 13th-century, 50m-tall tower – Florence's tallest privately owned *torre* (tower) – for a sundowner over-

since 1860, is the classic choice for its view. For rustic Tuscan partaken at a shared table, **Vinandro** (☎055 5 91 21; www.vinandrofiesole.com; Piazza Mino da Fiesole 33; meals €20; ⏰lunch & dinner summer) is popular, but not a patch on **La Reggia degli Etruschi** (☎055 5 93 85; www.lareggiadeglietruschi.com; Via San Francesco; meals €30; ⏰lunch & dinner daily), an outstanding dine with swoonworthy views where knowing Florentines lunch on Sunday.

3pm

Stagger around **Cattedrale di San Romolo** (Piazza Mino di Fiesole; ⏰7.30am-noon & 3-5pm) FREE, begun in the 11th century. A glazed terracotta statue of San Romolo by Giovanni della Robbia guards the entrance inside. Afterwards, make your way up steep walled **Via San Francesco** and be blown away by the staggeringly beautiful panorama of Florence that unfolds from the terrace adjoining 15th-century **Basilica di Sant'Alessandro**. Grassy-green afternoon-nap spots abound and the tourist office has brochures outlining walking trails (1km to 3.5km) from here.

5pm

Enjoy an *aperitivo* (pre-dinner drinks) with Florentines at local hangout **JJ Hill** (☎055 5 93 24; Piazza Mino da Fiesole 40; ⏰6pm-midnight Mon-Wed, 5pm-1am Thu-Sat, to 11pm Sun), an atmospheric Irish pub with a tip-top beer list, excellent burgers and other quality pub grub. Or fire up the romantic in you with in a 2½-hour guided bike ride (€25 to €30 including bike hire) by sunset back to Florence with **FiesoleBike** (☎345 3350926; www.fiesolebike.it; Piazza Mino da Fiesole), a creative bike rental/guiding outfit run with passion by local Fiesole lad Giovanni Crescioli (a qualified biking and hiking guide to boot). His 'sunset' tour departs daily from Piazza Mino di Fiesole at 5pm in season; book in advance online.

Practicalities

The **tourist office** (☎055 596 13 23, 055 596 13 11; www.fiesoleforyou.it; Via Portigiani 3, Fiesole; ⏰10am-6.30pm summer, shorter hr rest of yr) has local information.

ATAF bus 7 (€1.20, 20 minutes, every 15 minutes) runs from Florence's Piazza San Marco uphill to Fiesole's central square, Piazza Mino di Fiesole.

looking Florence and you'll be blown away. Rates are practically halved in low season.

To lose yourself in a mind-blowing Florence panorama from your bed, check into the deluxe suite.

Hotel Davanzati HOTEL €€
(Map p62; ☎055 28 66 66; www.hoteldavanzati.it; Via Porta Rossa 5; s/d/q €132/199/342; ❄@📶) Twenty-odd steps lead up to this swish hotel snug against Palazzo Davanzati. A beguiling labyrinth of enchanting rooms, unexpected frescoes and modern comforts, it has bags of charisma – and that includes Florentine debonair Tommaso and father Fabrizio, who run the show (Grandpa Marcello surveys proceedings). There's a laptop in every room and iPads in reception.

Hotel Perseo HOTEL €€
(Map p62; ☎055 21 25 04; www.hotelperseo.it; Via de' Cerretani 1; s €125, d €147-165, tr €166-195, q €205-230; ❄@📶) Perseo is a perfect family choice with its 20 large rooms, down-to-earth decor and friendly hosts, New Zealander Louise and Italian husband Giacinto. Top-floor rooms smooch with the rooftops and gorgeous views of the *duomo*. Should you have trouble tracking down (black) No 1 on the street, look for red No 23. Low-season rates are more than 50% cheaper.

★ **Antica Torre di Via de' Tornabuoni 1** BOUTIQUE HOTEL €€€
(Map p62; ☎055 21 92 48; www.tornabuoni1.com; Via de' Tournabuoni 1; d from €325; ⏰reception 7am-10pm; 📶) Footsteps from the Arno, inside the beautiful 14th-century Palazzo Gianfigliazzi, is this raved-about hotel. Its 20 rooms are stylish, spacious and contemporary. But what completely steals the show is the stunning rooftop breakfast terrace – easily the best in the city. Sip cappucino and swoon over Florence graciously laid out at your feet.

Palazzo Vecchietti LUXURY HOTEL €€€

(Map p62; ☎055 230 28 02; www.palazzovecchietti.com; Via degli Strozzi 4; d from €285; ❄@📶) This *residenza d'epoca* with 14 hopelessly romantic rooms and loggia in a 15th-century *palazzo* is a buzzword for hotel chic. Tapestries, bookshelves and artworks adorn stone walls and colour schemes mix traditional hues with bolder blues, reds and violets. Three rooms have a terrace to breakfast between rooftops. No surprise: this is the handiwork of Florentine designer Michele Bönan.

Santa Maria Novella

Ostello Archi Rossi HOSTEL €

(Map p78; ☎055 29 08 04; www.hostelarchirossi.com; Via Faenza 94r; dm €28-32, s/d €62/90; ⊙closed 2 wks Dec; @📶) Guests' paintings and artwork brighten up the walls at this private hostel near Santa Maria Novella train station. Bright white dorms have up to 12 beds (those across the garden are quieter); there are washing machines, frozen meal dispensers and microwaves for guests. No curfew (knock to enter after 2am). Free two-hour walking tours for guests, daily at 10am.

Hotel Azzi HOTEL €€

(Locanda degli Artisti; Map p78; ☎055 21 38 06; www.hotelazzi.com; Via Faenza 56/88r; d €105-115, tr/q €130/150; ❄📶) The five-minute walk from the central market and train station only adds to the convenience of this well-kempt hotel. Its old-world style coupled with a lounge, library full of books, terrace and Jacuzzi makes it particularly popular among older travellers (lots of retired couples). The hotel also has cheaper rooms and self-catering apartments in nearby annexes.

Hotel L'O LUXURY HOTEL €€€

(Map p62; ☎055 27 73 80; www.hotelorologioflorence.com; Piazza di Santa Maria Novella 24; d from €315; P❄@📶) The type of seductive address James Bond would feel right at home in, this super-stylish hotel oozes panache. Designed as a showcase for the (very wealthy) owner's (exceedingly expensive) luxury wristwatch collection, L'O (the hip take on its full name, Hotel L'Orologio) has four stars, rooms named after watches and clocks pretty much everywhere. Don't be late…

San Lorenzo & San Marco

★**Academy Hostel** HOSTEL €

(Map p62; ☎055 239 86 65; www.academyhostel.eu; Via Ricasoli 9; dm €32-34, s/d €42/86, d with shared bathroom €76; ❄@📶) Cheap accommodation shouldn't compromise on comfort is the much-appreciated philosophy of this modern 10-room hostel, snug on the 1st floor of Baron Ricasoli's 17th-century *palazzo* with dreamy interior courtyard and terrace. The reception area was once a theatre and 'dorms' sport maximum four or six beds, high moulded ceilings, brightly coloured lockers and chic flower-adorned screens. No credit cards for payments under €150. Rates, unusually for a hostel, include breakfast.

Antica Dimora Johlea B&B €€

(Map p78; ☎055 463 32 92; www.johanna.it; Via San Gallo 80; s €50-160, d €70-220; ❄@📶) This well-established and highly regarded B&B is just one of five historic B&B residences run by Johlea & Johanna in Florence, all scattered on or around Via San Gallo.

Hotel Morandi alla Crocetta BOUTIQUE HOTEL €€

(Map p78; ☎055 234 47 47; www.hotelmorandi.it; Via Laura 50; s €70-120, d €100-170, tr €130-210, q €150-250; P❄📶) This medieval convent-turned-hotel away from the madding crowd in San Marco is a stunner. Rooms are refined, tasteful and full of authentic period furnishings and paintings. A couple of rooms have handkerchief-sized gardens to laze in, but the *pièce de résistance* is frescoed room No 29, the former chapel.

Santa Croce

★**Hotel Dalí** HOTEL €

(Map p82; ☎055 234 07 06; www.hoteldali.com; Via dell'Oriuolo 17; d/tr €85/110, apt from €95, s/d with shared bathroom €40/70; P@📶) This overwhelmingly friendly hotel with 10 spacious homelike rooms is the passion and unrelenting love of world travellers-turned-parents Marco and Samanta ('running the hotel is like travelling without moving'). Rooms are equipped with a kettle, coffee and tea; there is a shared microwave guests can use; and bathrooms are modern.

The icing on the cake is a trio of gorgeous self-catering apartments – one with *duomo* view – sleeping two, four or six. No

OFF THE BEATEN TRACK

FLEE THE CROWD

Should you want to get away from it all and stay out of town, two remarkable 'prince and pauper' addresses leap out.

In a 17th-century villa framed by extensive grounds, HI-affiliated **Villa Camerata** (055 60 14 51; www.ostellofirenze.it; Viale Augusto Righi 2-4; dm €19-21; P @) is among Italy's most beautiful hostels (and oh so typically Tuscan!). Bus 17 from Stazione di Santa Maria Novella stops 400m from the hostel; count on 30 minutes travel time.

Then there's **Il Salviatino** (055 904 11 11; www.salviatino.com; Via del Salviatino 21; d from €475; P @), named after the Salviati family who transformed the 14th-century villa into the ravishing, swoon-worthy 17th-century ode to luxury it is today. Hidden among cypress trees in the hills 3.5km east of Florence, the villa really is the stuff of Tuscan dreams. Italian literati gathered here in the 17th and 18th centuries, and today it is Europe's moneyed hipsters who check in to spoil themselves rotten in the spa, lounge in the cascading infinity pool or perfectly manicured Italian gardens, and ogle smugly at the dome of Florence's cathedral from the terrace bar.

breakfast, but free parking in the leafy inner courtyard. Low season rates are around 30% less.

Hotel Orchidea HOTEL €

(Map p82; 055 248 03 46; www.hotelorchideaflorence.it; Borgo degli Albizi 11; s/d/tr/q with shared bathroom €60/75/100/120) This old-fashioned *pensione* in the mansion where the Donati family roosted in the 13th century (Dante's wife, Gemma, was allegedly born in the tower) is charm personified. Its seven rooms with sink and shared bathroom are simple, but their outlook is five-star. Many guests return each May/June simply to enjoy the 100-year-old wisteria in bloom. No breakfast, but free tea- and coffee-making facilities.

Rooms 5, 6 and 7 have huge windows overlooking a gorgeous garden and No 4 spills out onto an old stone terrace.

Hotel Balestri HISTORIC HOTEL €€

(Map p82; 055 21 47 43; www.hotel-balestri.it; Piazza Mentana 7; d €100-160, tr €140-165; @) Bold on the banks of the Arno, this historic hotel dating to 1888 remains the only riverside place to stay in downtown Florence. As part of the chic, quality-guaranteed Whythebest Florence hotel group (they're the guys behind L'Orologio, Villa Cora and other chic pads), Balestri is comfortably contemporary while retaining a distinct old-world charm.

Villa Landucci B&B €€

(055 66 05 95; www.villalanducci.it; Via Luca Landucci 7; d €100-120; P) Five elegant and refreshingly spacious rooms are named after Tuscan wines at this gourmet-themed B&B, a short walk away from Santa Croce. The best in the house, 'Bolgheri' and 'Chianti', open onto the wonderful back garden – pretty as a picture with its perfect flowerbeds, well-tended veggie patch, magnificent magnolia tree and age-old palm. Kids will love the play area.

Debora, a sommelier, and partner Matteo, who created the place are fonts of knowledge when it comes to dining well, and they can organise wine-tasting and food tours for guests. Breakfast is predominantly organic and the free parking is a rarity in the city. Borrow a bicycle (reserve in advance) to pedal the 500m to Piazza del Duomo.

Oltrarno

Hostel Santa Monaca HOSTEL €

(Map p86; 055 26 83 38; www.ostellosantamonaca.com; Via Santa Monaca 6; dm €18-22, d/q per person €25.50/22; reception 6am-2am; @) A convent until the 1860s, this 112-bed hostel, open since 1966 when it first gave shelter to flood victims, comes warmly recommended. It has a great little terrace the size of a pocket handkerchief from which to contemplate the stars on long summer nights, and guests can rent bicycles to pedal around town (€2/10 per hour/day).

The well-equipped kitchen is bright and jolly with washing machine (€6.50 per wash), free safe deposits, free wi-fi and two computers to surf. Girls-only or mixed dorms sleep four to 22 and are closed for cleaning between 10am and 2pm. Curfew 2am. Low season rates are a couple of euros less.

★**Palazzo Guadagni Hotel** HOTEL €€
(Map p86; ☎055 265 83 76; www.palazzoguadagni.com; Piazza Santo Spirito 9; s €100-140, d €140-180, extra bed €35; ❄📶) Plump above Florence's liveliest summertime square, this hotel, with impossibly romantic loggia, is legendary – Zefferelli shot scenes from *Tea with Mussolini* here. Florentines Laura and Ferdinando are the creative duo behind the transformation of Renaissance palace into brilliant-value hotel. Its 15 spacious rooms tastefully mix old and new, and the loggia terrace with wicker furniture is dreamy.

Hotel La Scaletta HOTEL €€
(Map p86; ☎055 28 30 28; www.hotellascaletta.it; Via Guicciardini 13; s €94-119, d €110-154) An austere air wafts through this maze of a hotel, hidden in a 15th-century *palazzo* near Palazzo Pitti. But rooms – the priciest ones peeping down on Boboli Gardens – are spacious, and the view from the dreamy roof terrace is nothing short of fabulous. Savour a summertime breakfast or early evening drink here and congratulate yourself on finding one of the best deals in town.

Palazzo Magnani Feroni LUXURY HOTEL €€€
(Map p62; ☎055 239 95 44; www.florencepalace.com; Borgo San Frediano 5; d from €379; P❄@📶) This extraordinary old *palazzo* is the stuff of dreams. The 12 suites, which occupy four floors with the family's private residence wedged in between, are vast and ooze elegance, featuring authentic period furnishings, rich fabrics and Bulgari toiletries. The 360-degree city view from the rooftop is magnificent and unforgettable.

Eating

Quality ingredients and simple execution are the hallmarks of Florentine cuisine, climaxing with the *bistecca alla fiorentina*, a huge slab of prime T-bone steak rubbed with olive oil, seared on the char grill, garnished with salt and pepper and served beautifully *al sangue* (bloody).

Other typical dishes include *crostini* (toasts typically topped with chicken-liver pâté), *ribollita* (thick vegetable, bread and bean soup), *pappa al pomodoro* (bread and tomato soup) and *trippa alla fiorentina* (tripe cooked in a rich tomato sauce).

As equally an attractive option as the city's many restaurants is its wealth of *enoteca* – wine bars serving tasting platters of cheese, salami and cold meats as well as, quite often, full meals.

In between meal times, if you're absolutely desperate to dine, the historic cafe-restaurants on Piazza della Repubblica serve food all day (at a price).

Duomo to Piazza della Signoria

★**Osteria Il Buongustai** OSTERIA €
(Map p62; Via dei Cerchi 15r; meals €15; ⏲11.30am-3.30pm Mon-Sat) Run with breathtaking speed and grace by Laura and Lucia, this place is unmissable. Lunchtimes heave with locals who work nearby and savvy students who flock here to fill up on tasty Tuscan homecooking at a snip of other restaurant prices. The place is brilliantly no frills – expect to share a table and pay in cash; no credit cards.

Cantinetta dei Verrazzano BAKERY €
(Map p62; Via dei Tavolini 18-20; focaccia €2.50-3; ⏲noon-9pm Mon-Sat, 10am-4.30pm Sun) A *forno* (baker's oven) and *cantinetta* (small cellar) make a heavenly match. Sit down at a

TRIPE: FAST-FOOD FAVOURITE

When Florentines fancy a fast munch-on-the-move, they flit by a *trippaio* – a cart on wheels or mobile stand – for a tripe *panini* (sandwich). Think cow's stomach chopped up, boiled, sliced, seasoned and bunged between bread.

Those great bastions of good old-fashioned Florentine tradition, *trippai* still going strong include the cart on the southwest corner of Mercato Nuovo; **L'Antico Trippaio** (Map p62; Piazza dei Cimatori), **Pollini** (Map p82; Piazza Sant' Ambrogio) in Santa Croce; and hole-in-the-wall **Da Vinattieri** (Map p62; Via Santa Margherita 4; ⏲10am-7.30pm Mon-Fri, to 8pm Sat & Sun) tucked down an alley next to Dante's Chiesa di Santa Margherita. Pay up to €4.50 for a *panini* with tripe doused in *salsa verde* (pea-green sauce of smashed parsley, garlic, capers and anchovies) or garnished with salt, pepper and ground chilli. Alternatively, opt for a meaty-sized bowl (€5.50 to €7) of *lampredotto* (cow's fourth stomach that is chopped and simmered for hours).

TOP SANDWICH SHOPS

Count on paying between €5 and €8 for a lavishly filled *panino* (sandwich).

★ **Mariano** (Map p62; Via del Parione 19r; ⏲8am-3pm & 5-7.30pm Mon-Fri, to 3pm Sat) Our favourite for its simplicity, around since 1973. Sunrise to sunset this brick-vaulted, 13th-century cellar gently buzzes with Florentines propped at the counter sipping coffee or wine or eating salads and *panini*. Come here for a coffee-and-pastry breakfast, light lunch, *aperitivo* or a *panino* to eat on the move. Look for the green neon 'pizzicheria' up high on the outside facade and the discrete 'alimentari' sign above the entrance.

★ **Gustapanino** (Map p86; Piazza Santa Spirito; focacce €3-3.50; ⏲11am-8pm Mon-Sat, noon-5pm Sun) It's dead simple to spot what many Florentines rate as the city's best *enopaninoteca* (wine and sandwich stop) with no seating but bags of square space and church steps outside – look for the queue out the door.

'Ino (Map p62; Via dei Georgofili 3r-7r; panini €8, tasting platter €12; ⏲11am-8pm Mon-Sat, noon-5pm Sun) Artisan ingredients sourced locally and mixed creatively by passionate gourmet Alessandro Frassica is the secret behind this gourmet sandwich bar near the Uffizi. Create your own combo or pick from dozens of house specials. End with chocolate *degustazione* (tasting) – the chocolate peppered with olive oil and lemon zest is sensational.

I Due Fratellini (Map p62; www.iduefratellini.com; Via dei Cimatori 38r; panini €3; ⏲9am-8pm Mon-Sat, closed Fri & Sat 2nd half of Jun & all Aug) This hole-in-the-wall has been in business since 1875. Wash *panini* down with a beaker of wine and leave the empty on the wooden shelf outside.

Oil Shoppe (Map p82; Via Sant'Egidio 22r; panini €3-4.50; ⏲11am-5pm Mon-Fri) Queue at the back of the shop for hot subs, at the front for cold, at this busy student favourite. Choose your own or let chef Alberto Scorzon take the lead with his 10-filling wonder.

marble-topped table, admire prized vintages displayed behind glass wall cabinets and sip a glass of wine (€4 to €10) produced on the Verrazzano estate in Chianti. The focaccia topped with caramelised *radicchio* is a must – as is a mixed cold-meat platter (ignore the bristly boar legs strung in the open kitchen).

Tic Toc BURGERS €

(Map p62; Via dell' Oche 15r; burgers €10, club sandwiches €7; ⏲11am-11pm Mon-Sat) This new kid on the block, created by the gregarious and charismatic Igor from neighbouring Coquinarius, is worth a pit stop. US diner (albeit it a highly stylish one as only a Florentine could do) is its vibe and burgers made from the finest handcut beef, chicken or vegetables is its culinary lure.

Homemade salsa, bacon and fries are a given, and there's plenty more extra toppings (€0.50) to pick from. Handily, food is served all day and the bar is a hot spot come *aperitivo* hour. Jack Daniels anyone?

★ **Obikà** CHEESE €€

(Map p62; ☎055 277 35 26; www.obika.it; Via de' Tornabuoni 16; 2/3/5 mozzarella €13/20/30, pizza €10-13.50; ⏲noon-4pm & 6.30-11.30pm Mon-Fri, noon-11pm Sat & Sun) Given its exclusive location in Palazzo Tornabuoni, this designer address is naturally ubertrendy. Taste different mozzarella cheeses with basil, organic veg or sundried tomatoes in the cathedral-like interior or snuggle beneath heaters on sofa seating in the elegant, star-topped courtyard. The €9 *aperitivi* comprising a drink and twinset of tasting platters (mozzarella and proscuitto) is copious, as is Sunday brunch.

La Canova di Gustavino WINE BAR €€

(Map p62; ☎055 239 98 06; Via della Condotta 29r; meals €40; ⏲noon-midnight) The rear dining room of this atmospheric *enoteca* is lined with shelves of Tuscan wine – the perfect accompaniment to homemade black tagliolini in a seafood and pesto sauce or grilled quail with polenta and red *radicchio* crème brulée. Yes, cuisine is creative Tuscan and yes, one eats as well as drinks exceedingly well here.

Santa Maria Novella

L'Osteria di Giovanni TUSCAN €€

(Map p62; ☎055 28 48 97; www.osteriadigiovanni.it; Via del Moro 22; meals €35; ⏲dinner Mon-Fri, lunch & dinner Sat & Sun) It's not the decor that stands out at this friendly neighbourhood eatery, it's the cuisine: Tuscan and creative. Think chickpea soup with octopus or pear- and ricotta-stuffed *tortelli* (a type of ravioli) bathed in a leek and almond cream. Throw in the complimentary glass of prosecco and plate of *coccoli* (traditional Florentine salted fritters) as *aperitivo* and you'll return time and again.

Oh, and did we mention the subsequent glass of Vin Santo with home-made *cantucci* (hard, sweet biscuits – to dunk into the wine) at the end of the meal?

Il Latini TRATTORIA €€
(Map p62; ☎055 21 09 16; www.illatini.com; Via dei Palchetti 6r; meals €35; ⏲lunch & dinner Tue-Sun) A veteran guidebook favourite built around melt-in-your-mouth *crostini* (toast), Tuscan meats, fine pasta and roasted meats served at shared tables. There are two dinner seatings (7.30pm and 9pm), with service ranging from charming to not so charming. Bookings mandatory.

San Lorenzo & San Marco

★Trattoria Mario TUSCAN €
(Map p78; www.trattoriamario.com; Via Rosina 2; meals €20; ⏲noon-3.30pm Mon-Sat, closed 3 wks Aug; ❄) Arrive by noon to ensure a stool around a shared table at this noisy, busy, brilliant trattoria – a legend that retains its soul (and allure with locals) despite being in every guidebook. Charming Fabio, whose grandfather opened the place in 1953, is front of house while big brother Romeo and nephew Francesco cook with speed in the kitchen.

Monday and Thursday are tripe days, Friday is fish and Saturday sees local Florentines flock here for a brilliantly blue *bistecca alla fiorentina* (€35 per kilo). No advance reservations, no credit cards.

Da Nerbone MARKET STALL €
(Map p78; Mercato Centrale, Piazza del Mercato Centrale; ⏲7am-2pm Mon-Sat) Forge your way past cheese, meat and sausage stalls in Florence's Mercato Centrale to join the lunchtime queue at Nerbone, in the biz since 1872. Go local and order *trippa alla fiorentina* (tripe and tomato stew) or follow the crowd with a feisty *panini con bollito* (a hefty boiled-beef bun, dunked in the meat's juices before serving). Eat standing up or fight for a table.

La Forchetta Rotta TUSCAN €
(☎055 384 19 98; Via San Zanobi 126r; lunch/dinner €7.50/25; ⏲lunch & dinner Mon-Sat) The restaurant arm of the dynamic duo behind Santa Croce's Monkey Bar, this place is staggeringly good value – and tasty to boot. Its kitchen caters predominantly to workers from surrounding offices and the result is superb: the pick of three or four homespun *primi, secondi* and *contorni* (side dishes) for €7.50. The nibble banquet, laid out from 7pm onwards, for *aperitivo* is equally generous.

TOP GELATERIE

Florentines take gelato seriously and there's healthy rivalry among local *gelaterie artigianale* (makers of handmade gelato) who strive to create the city's creamiest, most flavourful and freshest ice cream. Flavours are seasonal and a cone or tub costs around €2/3/4/5 per small/medium/large/maxi.

Vivoli (Map p82; Via dell'Isola delle Stinche 7; tub €2-10; ⏲7.30am-midnight Tue-Sat, 9am-midnight Sun summer, to 9pm winter) Inside seating makes this ice-cream and cake shop stand out. Pistachio, pear and caramel, and chocolate with orange are crowd favourites. Pay at the cash desk then trade your receipt for ice. No cones, only tubs.

Grom (Map p62; www.grom.it; cnr Via del Campanile & Via delle Oche; ⏲10.30am-midnight Apr-Sep, to 11pm Oct-Mar) Rain, hail or shine, queues run halfway down the street at this sweet address; many ingredients organic. Tasty hot chocolate and milkshakes too.

La Carraia (Map p62; Piazza Nazario Sauro 25r; ⏲9am-11pm summer, to 10pm winter) One glance at the constant line out the door of this bright green-and-citrus shop with exciting flavours (ricotta and pear, English soup, the best mint in town), and know you're at a Florentine favourite.

Carabé (Map p78; www.gelatocarabe.com; Via Ricasoli 60r; ⏲10am-midnight, closed mid-Dec–mid-Jan) Traditional Sicilian gelato, granita (sorbet) and brioche (Sicilian ice-cream sandwich); handy address if you're waiting in line to see *David*.

Clubhouse AMERICAN, PIZZERIA €
(Map p78; ☎055 21 14 27; www.theclubhouse.it; Via de' Ginori 6r; pizza €6-12, meals €20; ⏲noon-midnight) This cavernous American bar, pizzeria and restaurant is handily close to *David* and makes for the perfect dining-drinking hybrid any time of day (including Sunday brunch). Design buffs will appreciate its faintly industrial vibe. Foodies will love its pizza-making courses. Gluten-free menu and €7 cocktail *aperitivi* from 6pm.

Antica Trattoria da Tito TRATTORIA €€
(☎055 47 24 75; www.trattoriadatito.it; Via San Gallo 112r; meals €30; ⏲lunch & dinner Mon-Sat) The 'No well done meat here' sign, strung in the window, says it all: the best of Tuscan culinary tradition is the only thing this iconic trattoria serves. In business since 1913, Da Tito does everything right – tasty Tuscan dishes like onion soup and wild boar pasta, served with friendly gusto and hearty goodwill to a local crowd. Don't be shy to enter.

La Cucina del Garga TUSCAN €€
(Map p78; ☎055 47 52 86; www.garga.it; Via San Zanobi 33r; meals €30) Garga is one of Florence's great culinary legends. La Cucina, a contemporary reincarnation of the original Garga, is the newbie kitchen of Alessandro Gargani, New York chef and son of Giuliano 'Garga' Gargani, whose San Frediano trattoria wooed Florentine tastebuds for more than three decades. Boldly painted walls crammed with modern art is the other Garga trademark.

Alesssandro's kitchen cooks up some of the same great Garga classics – including his father's signature *tagliatelle de magnifico* (pasta ribbons with mint and citrus zest in a creamy brandy sauce) – as well as new creations. Reservations essential at weekends.

✕ Santa Croce

Mercato di Sant'Ambrogio MARKET €
(Map p82; Piazza Ghiberti; ⏲7am-2pm Mon-Sat) Outdoor food market with an intimate, local flavour.

Il Giova TRATTORIA €
(Map p82; ☎055 248 06 39; www.ilgiova.com; Borgo La Croce 73r; meals €25; ⏲lunch & dinner Mon-Sat) Pocket-sized and packed, this cheery trattoria is everything a traditional Florentine eating place should be. Dig into century-old dishes like *zuppa della nonna* (grandma's soup), *risotto del giorno* (risotto of the day) or *mafalde al ragù* (long-ribboned pasta with meat sauce) and pride yourself on finding a place to dine with locals.

Brac VEGETARIAN €
(Map p82; ☎055 094 48 77; www.libreriabrac.net; Via dei Vagellai 18r; meals €20; ⏲noon-midnight, closed 2 wks mid-Aug; ✎) This hipster cafe-bookshop – a hybrid dining-stroke-*aperitivi* address – cooks up inventive, home-style and strictly vegetarian and/or vegan cuisine. Its decor is recycled vintage with the odd kid's drawing thrown in for that intimate homey touch; and the vibe is artsy.

Dine at the front-room bar, in the interior courtyard strung with recycled art, or around a candlelit table between bookshelves in the back dining room. Reserve in advance at weekends. Brac can be tricky to find – there is no sign outside, just an inconspicuous doorway a block back from the river with a jumble of books in the window – but persevere.

Antico Noè OSTERIA €
(Map p82; Volta di San Piero 6r; meals €20; ⏲noon-midnight Mon-Sat) Don't be put off by the dank alley in which this old butcher's shop with white marble-clad walls and wrought-iron meat hooks is found. The drunks loitering outside are generally harmless and the down-to-earth Tuscan fodder served is a real joy. For a quick bite, go for a *panini* from the adjoining *fiaschetteria* (small tavern). No credit cards.

Acquacotta TRATTORIA €
(Map p82; ☎055 24 29 07; Via dei Pilastri 51r; meals €25; ⏲lunch & dinner Tue-Sun) With its red-and-white checked tablecloths, terracota tile floor and lace curtains, Acquacotta is everything a traditional Florentine eatery should be. Cuisine is as traditional as decor and the €12.50 lunch deal – two courses plus water and wine – is a steal. Advance reservations essential for dinner.

★**Il Teatro del Sale** TUSCAN €€
(Map p82; ☎055 200 14 92; www.teatrodelsale.com; Via dei Macci 111r; breakfast/lunch/dinner €7/20/30; ⏲9-11am, 12.30-2.15pm & 7-11pm Tue-Sat, closed Aug) Florentine chef, Fabio Picchi, is one of Florence's living treasures who steals the Sant' Ambrogio show with this eccentric, good-value members-only club (everyone welcome, annual membership €7) inside an old theatre. He cooks up breakfast,

lunch and dinner, culminating at 9.30pm in a live performance of drama, music or comedy arranged by his wife, artistic director and comic actress Maria Cassi.

Dinners are hectic: grab a chair, serve yourself water, wine and antipasti and wait for the chef to yell out what's about to be served before queuing at the glass hatch for your *primo* (first course) and *secondo* (second course). Dessert and coffee are laid out buffet-style just prior to the performance.

Trattoria Cibrèo TRATTORIA €€
(Map p82; www.edizioniteatrodelsalecibreofirenze.it; Via dei Macci 122r; meals €30; ⏲lunch & dinner Tue-Sat, closed Aug) Dine here and you'll instantly understand why a queue gathers outside before it opens. Once in, revel in top-notch Tuscan cuisine: perhaps ricotta and potato flan with a rich meat sauce, puddle of olive oil and grated parmesan (divine!) or a simple plate of polenta, followed by homemade sausages, beans in a spicy tomato sauce and braised celery. No advance reservations, no credit cards, no coffee and arrive early to snag a table.

Francesco Vini TUSCAN €€
(Map p82; ☎055 21 87 37; www.francescovini.com; Piazza de' Peruzzi 8r, Borgo de' Greci 7r; meals €40; ⏲9am-midnight Mon-Sat) Built on top of Roman ruins, this wine specialist has two entrances – one with pavement terrace on people-busy Borgo de' Greci and a second, lovelier one on a hidden, quintessentially Florentine square. Winter dining is between bottle-lined wall and red brick and in summer everything spills outside. But it's the wine list, packed with Tuscan greats, that steals the show.

LOCAL KNOWLEDGE

PIAZZA DEL PASSERA

This bijou square with no passing traffic is a gourmet gem. Pick from cheap wholesome tripe in various guises at **Il Magazzino** (Map p86; ☎055 21 59 69; www.tripperiailmagazzino.com; Piazza della Passera 2/3; meals €30; ⏲lunch & dinner), or pricier Tuscan classics at **Trattoria 4 Leoni** (Map p86; ☎055 21 85 62; www.4leoni.com; Piazza della Passera 2/3; meals €40; ⏲lunch & dinner) known for its *bistecca alla fiorentina* (chargrilled T-bone steak) that it has cooked up since 1550; reservations essential.

Touch MODERN TUSCAN €€
(Map p82; ☎055 246 61 50; www.touchflorence.com; Via Fiesolana 18r; meals €40) Hidden behind an elegant facade with frosted glass and oyster-grey paintwork is this intimate dining space. Chefs use traditional Tuscan ingredients to create thoroughly contemporary dishes, but what really turns heads is the iPad on each table. Flip through the menu, look at images of each dish and enjoy short videos showing how each is prepared before ordering – on the iPad.

Ristorante Cibrèo MODERN TUSCAN €€€
(Map p82; ☎055 234 11 00; www.edizioniteatrodelsalecibreofirenze.it; Via Andrea del Verrocchio 8r; meals €75; ⏲lunch & dinner Tue-Sat, closed Aug) The flagship of the Fabio Picchi empire, this elegant restaurant is an essential stop for anyone interested in modern Tuscan cuisine. Knock-out choices on our most recent visit were a *primo* of spicy fish soup and a *secondo* of roast pigeon with mustard fruits. The wine list is equally impressive.

Osteria del Caffè Italiano TUSCAN €€€
(Map p82; ☎055 28 93 68; www.osteriacaffeitaliano.com; Via dell'Isola delle Stinche 11-13r; meals €45; ⏲lunch & dinner Tue-Sun) The menu at this Florence dining veteran is packed with classics like *mozzarella di bufala* with Parma ham, ravioli stuffed with ricotta and *cavolo nero* (black cabbage), and the city's famous *bistecca alla fiorentina* (per kilo €60). End with the devilish profiteroles, hot chocolate sauce ladled at the table from an old-fashioned copper pot.

Find it on the ground floor of 14th-century Palazzo Salviati.

Enoteca Pinchiorri GASTRONOMIC €€€
(Map p82; ☎055 24 27 77; www.enotecapinchiorri.com; Via Ghibellina 87r; 4-/8-course tasting menu €200/250; ⏲lunch & dinner Tue-Sat, closed Aug) Chef Annie Féolde applies French techniques to her versions of refined Tuscan cuisine and does it so well that this is the only restaurant in Tuscany to brandish three shiny Michelin stars. The setting is a 16th-century palace hotel and the wine list is mind-boggling in its extent and excellence. A once-in-a-lifetime experience.

Oltrarno

★Tamerò PASTA BAR €
(Map p86; ☎055 28 25 96; www.tamero.it; Piazza Santa Spirito 11r; meals €20; ⏲lunch & dinner

Tue-Sun) A happening address on Florence's hippest square: admire pasta cooks at work in the open kitchen while you wait for a table – the chances are you'll have to. A buoyant, party-loving crowd flocks here to fill up on imaginative, fresh pasta dishes (€7.50 to €10), giant salads (€7.50) and copious cheese/salami platters (€9). Decor is trendy industrial and weekend DJs spin sets from 10pm.

La Casalinga TRATTORIA €
(Map p86; ☎055 21 86 24; Via de' Michelozzi 9r; meals €25; ⊙lunch & dinner Mon-Sat) Family run and locally loved, this busy unpretentious place is one of Florence's cheapest trattorias. Don't be surprised if Paolo, the patriarch figure who conducts the mad-busy show from behind the bar, relegates you behind locals in the queue: it's a fact of life, eventually you'll be rewarded with hearty Tuscan dishes, cooked to exacting perfection.

Think *bollito misto con salsa verde* (mixed boiled meats with green sauce), spaghetti *al pomodoro* and *ribollita* just like *nonna* (grandma) and her *nonna* and her *nonna* made.

Il Ristoro TUSCAN €
(Map p62; ☎055 264 55 69; Borgo San Jacopo 48r; meals €20; ⊙noon-4pm Mon, to 10pm Tue-Sun) A disarmingly simple address not to be missed, this two-room restaurant with deli counter is a great budget choice – its two-course €15 lunch deal is a steal. Pick from classics like *pappa al pomodoro* or a plate of cold cuts and swoon at views of the Arno swirling beneath your feet.

★Il Santo Bevitore MODERN TUSCAN €€
(Map p62; ☎055 21 12 64; www.ilsantobevitore.com; Via di Santo Spirito 64-66r; meals €35; ⊙lunch & dinner Sep-Jul) Reserve or arrive dot-on 7.30pm to snag the last table at this raved-about address, an ode to stylish dining where gastronomes dine by candlelight in a vaulted, whitewashed, bottle-lined interior. The menu is a creative reinvention of seasonal classics, different for lunch and dinner: purple cabbage soup with mozzarella cream and anchovy syrup, acacia honey bavarese (firm, creamy mousse) with Vin Santo–marinated dried fruits.

Olio & Convivium TUSCAN €€
(Map p62; ☎055 265 81 98; Via di Santo Spirito 4; meals €35; ⊙lunch & dinner Tue-Sat, lunch Mon) A key address on any gastronomy agenda: your tastebuds will tingle at the sight of the legs of ham, conserved truffles, wheels of cheese, artisan-made bread and other delectable delicatessen products sold in its shop. Dine out the back.

Da Ruggero TUSCAN €€
(☎055 22 05 42; Via Senese 89r; meals €25; ⊙lunch & dinner Thu-Mon, closed mid-Jul–mid-Aug) A 10-minute stroll through Boboli Gardens (or along the street from Porta Romana) uncovers this trattoria, run by the gracious Corsi family since 1981 and much-loved for its pure, unadulterated Florentine tradition. Cuisine is Tuscan simple and hearty – *zuppa di ortiche* (nettle soup), *spaghetti alla carrettiera* (spaghetti in a chilli-fired tomato sauce) and of course the iconic *bistecca*. Delicious.

Trattoria Camillo TRATTORIA €€€
(Map p62; ☎055 21 24 27; Borgo San Jacopo 57r; meals €50; ⊙lunch & dinner Thu-Mon) *Crostini* topped with aphrodisiacal white-truffle shavings, deep-fried battered green tomatoes or zucchini (courgette) flowers and homemade walnut liqueur are a few of the seasonal highlights served beneath a centuries-old red-brick vaulted ceiling at this much-loved trattoria. The quality of products used is exceptional and service is endearingly old-fashioned.

★iO Osteria Personale MODERN TUSCAN €€€
(☎055 933 13 41; www.io-osteriapersonale.it; Borgo San Frediano 167r; meals €45; ⊙dinner Mon-Sat) Persuade everyone at your table to order the tasting menu to avoid the torture of picking just one dish – everything on the menu at this fabulously contemporary and creative 'osteria' is to die for. Pontedera-born chef Nicolò Baretti uses only seasonal products, natural ingredients and traditional flavours – to sensational effect.

Imagine sea bass tartare with ricotta cheese, pine kernels and spinach salad; or sweetbreads with marjoram-scented artichokes. The grand finale is dessert, climaxing with warm white chocolate and olive oil cream served with lavender slush and passion fruit aspic. Culinary heaven on earth. Dinner from 8pm.

Il Guscio TUSCAN €€€
(☎055 22 44 21; www.il-guscio.it; Via dell'Orto 49; meals €40; ⊙lunch & dinner Mon-Sat) Exceptional dishes come out of the kitchen of this family-run gem in San Frediano. Meat and fish are given joint billing, with triumphs such as white bean soup with prawns and fish joining superbly executed mains on the

TIP-TOP PIZZERIE

Expect to pay between €4.50 and €10 for a pizza at this trio of Florentine-recommended addresses:

Gustapizza (Map p86; Via Maggio 46r; pizza €4.50-8; ⌚11.30am-3pm & 7-11pm Tue-Sun) This unpretentious pizzeria near Piazza Santa Spirito gives a new meaning to the word 'packed'. Arrive early to grab a bar stool at a wooden-barrel table and pick from eight pizza types.

Pizzeria del' Osteria del Caffè Italiano (Map p82; www.osteriacaffeitaliano.com; Via dell'Isola delle Stinche 11-13r; pizza €8; ⌚7.30-11pm) Simplicity is the buzz word at this pocket-sized pizzeria that makes just three pizza types – *margherita, napoli* and *marinara*. No credit cards.

Il Pizzaiuolo (Map p82; ☎055 24 11 71; Via dei Macci 113r; pizzas €5-10, pastas €6.50-12; ⌚lunch & dinner Mon-Sat, closed Aug) Young Florentines flock to The Pizza Maker to nosh Neapolitan thick-crust pizzas hot from the wood-fired oven. Bookings essential for dinner.

sophisticated menu, including guinea fowl breast in balsamic vinegar.

Momoyama JAPANESE €€€
(Map p62; ☎055 29 18 40; www.ristorantemomoyama.it; Borgo San Frediano 10r; meals €40; ⌚12.30-2.30pm & 7.30pm-2am; 🚌6 & D) When the urge for a pasta-free evening in a striking minimalist interior kicks in, head here. This thoroughly contemporary, designer noodle bar cooks up beautifully sculpted platters of sushi, sashami, carpaccio, rolls and a creative selection of noodle bowls. Late opening hours cater to the chic party set.

Out of Town

When the summer city heat stifles, do what Florentines – get out of town for an al fresco lunch between flowers or riverside at these recommended addresses.

Targa MODERN TUSCAN €€
(☎055 67 73 77; www.targabistrot.net; Lungarno Colombo 7; meals €30; ⌚lunch & dinner Mon-Sat) 'Friendly food' is the strapline of this sleek address, a modern *bistrot Fiorentino* (Florentine bistro) bursting with green foliage on the banks of the Arno just over 1km east of Ponte San Niccolò. Dining is around Parisian-style wooden bistro tables – in or out on wooden decked verandah – and the wine list is superb. Advance reservations essential.

Trattoria le Cave di Maiano TRATTORIA €€
(☎055 5 91 33; www.trattoriacavedimaiano.it; Via Cave di Maiano 16, Maiano; meals €35; ⌚lunch & dinner, closed Mon winter) Florentines flock to this restaurant in Maiano, a village 8km north of Florence near Fiesole, at weekends to indulge in long leisurely lunches on its outdoor terrace. Huge servings are the rule of thumb, everything is homemade, and the rustic inclination of the chef is reflected in the abundance of rabbit, boar and suckling pig dishes – all of which go wonderfully well with the quaffable house wine.

Trattoria Bibe TRATTORIA €€
(☎055 204 00 85; www.trattoriabibe.com; Via della Bagnese 11r, Galuzzo; meals €35; ⌚lunch & dinner Sat & Sun, dinner Mon, Tue, Thu & Fri Dec-Jan & Mar-Oct) Pigeon, frogs legs, hare and guineafowl are among the roasts (count at least 40 minutes) at this old-fashioned inn – so legendary that Italian poet Eugenio Montale wrote a poem about Grandfather 'Bibe' in 1927. Dine elegantly inside or amid flowers out. Find it 3km south of Florence; bus 46.

Drinking & Nightlife

Florence's drinking scene is split between *enoteche* (increasingly hip wine bars that invariably make great eating addresses too), trendy bars with lavish *aperitivo* buffets and straightforward cafes that quite often double as lovely lunch venues.

Wine Bars

Nothing whets one's appetite for the Florentine way of living better than hanging out in an *enoteca*, glass of Chianti in hand. Eating is a given at most of these addresses – real drinking-dining hybrids.

★ **Il Santino** WINE BAR
(Map p62; Via Santo Spirito 34; glass of wine & crostini €6.50-8; ⌚10am-10pm) Just a few doors down from one of Florence's best gourmet addresses, Il Santo Bevitore, is this pocket-

sized wine bar, run by the same gastronomic folk and packed out every evening. Inside, squat modern stools contrast with old brick walls but the real action is outside, from around 9pm, when the buoyant wine-loving crowd spills onto the street.

Le Volpi e l'Uva WINE BAR
(Map p86; www.levolpieluva.com; Piazza dei Rossi 1; crostini €6.50, cheese/meat platters €8-10; ⌚ 11am-9pm Mon-Sat) The city's best *enoteca con degustazione* bar none: this intimate address with marble-topped bar crowning two oak ageing wine barrels chalks up an impressive list of wines by the glass. To attain true bliss, indulge in *crostini* (€6.50) topped with honeyed speck or *lardo,* or platter of boutique Tuscan cheeses (try the Rocco made by Fattoria Corzano e Paterno).

Coquinarius WINE BAR
(Map p62; www.coquinarius.com; Via delle Oche 11r; crostini & carpacci €4; ⌚ noon-10.30pm) With its old stone vaults, scrubbed wooden tables and refreshingly modern air, this *enoteca* run by the dynamic and charismatic Igor is spacious and stylish. The wine list features bags of Tuscan greats and unknowns, and a substantial *crostini* (toasts with various toppings) and *carpacci* (cold sliced meats) menu ensures you don't leave hungry. Or stay for dinner– it's worth it.

Vivanda WINE BAR
(Map p86; www.vivandafirenze.it; Via Santa Monaca 7r; meals €25; ⌚ lunch & dinner) A first for gourmet Florence, the focus of this bright modern *enoteca* – its small interior packed jaw to jowl with tables – is organic wine. Locally sourced products ensure a delightful lunch, or reserve in advance for an early-evening tasting (€25) – four different organic wines perfectly paired with ash-aged pecorino, bufala ricota cheese and Cienta Senese salami.

Sei Divino WINE BAR
(Map p62; Borgo Ognissanti 42r; ⌚ 10am-2am) This stylish wine bar tucked beneath a red-brick vaulted ceiling is privy to one of Florence's most happening *aperitivo* scenes. From the pale aqua-coloured Vespa parked up inside, to the music, occasional exhibition and summertime pavement action, Sei Divino is a vintage that is eternally good. *Aperitivi* 'hour' kicks in from 5pm to 10pm.

Fiaschetteria Nuvoli WINE BAR
(Map p62; Piazza dell'Olio 15r; ⌚ 7am-9pm Mon-Sat) Pull up a stool on the street and chat with a regular over a glass of *vino della casa* (house wine) at this old-fashioned *fiaschetteria,* a street away from the *duomo.*

ZEB WINE BAR
(www.zebgastronomia.com; Via San Miniato 2r; ⌚ noon-3pm Thu & Sun-Tue, noon-3pm & 7.30-10.30pm Fri & Sat) This modern, minimalist *enoteca* with a lovely choice of cold cuts at the deli-style counter sits at the foot of the hill leading up to Piazzale Michelangelo, in village-like San Niccolò – enter the perfect pit stop post-panorama.

Lounge Bars

These are the addresses for that all-essential *aperitivo* (pre-dinner drinks from around 7pm to 10pm) and/or late-night cocktails (around midnight before clubbing), two trends embraced with gusto by Florentines. Live music is the common denominator.

★ Volume BAR
(Map p86; www.volumefirenze.com; Piazza Santo Spirito 3r; ⌚ 9am-1.30am) Fabulous armchairs, lots of recycled and upcycled vintage furniture, books to read, juke box, crêpes and a tasty little choice of nibbles with coffee or a light lunch give this hybrid cafe-bar-gallery real appeal – all in an old hat-making workshop complete with the tools and wooden moulds casually strewn around. Vintage is the vibe, artisanal creativity the underlying beat.

Watch for various music, art and DJ events and happenings.

La Terrazza BAR
(Map p62; www.continentale.it; Vicolo dell Oro 6r; ⌚ 2.30-11.30pm Apr-Sep) This rooftop bar with wooden-decking terrace accessible from the 5th floor of the Ferragamo-owned Hotel Continentale is as chic as one would expect of a fashion-house hotel. Its *aperitivo* buffet is a modest affair, but who cares with that fabulous, drop-dead-gorgeous panorama of

APERICENA

Apericena, a brilliant cent-saving trick and trend among students and 20-somethings in Florence, translates as an *aperitivo* buffet so copious it doubles as *cena* (dinner). Firm Florentine favourites known for their exceptionally generous buffets include Kitsch (p109), Slowly (p108) and Obikà (p101).

BEST FOR APERITIVI WITH...

Soul-Soaring View Flò (p108), La Terrazza at the Hotel Continentale (p107), La Terrazza (p110)

The Jet Set Flò (p108), Colle Bereto (p108), Open Bar (p108), Slowly (p108), Gucci Museo Caffè (p109)

Stuff-Yourself-Silly Buffet La Forchetta Rotta (p102), Kitsch (p109)

Great Wine by the Glass Le Volpi e l'Uva (p107), Sei Divino (p107), Coquinarius (p107)

Organic Wine Vivanda (p107)

Courtyard Seating Obikà (p101)

one of Europe's most beautiful cities. Dress the part or feel out of place.

Flò LOUNGE BAR

(www.flofirenze.com; Piazzale Michelangelo 84; ⌚7.30pm-late summer) Without a doubt the hottest and hippest place to be seen in the city on hot sultry summer nights is Flò, a truly ab fab seasonal lounge bar that pops up each May or June on Piazzale Michelangelo. Different themed lounge areas include a dance floor, and VIP area (where you have no chance of reserving a table unless you're in the Florentine in-crowd).

Open Bar LOUNGE BAR

(Map p86; www.goldenviewopenbar.com; Via de' Bardi 58; ⌚7.30am-1.30am) Of course it is touristy given its prime location near Ponte Vecchio, but it is worth a pit stop nonetheless – preferably at *aperitivo* hour when chic Florentines sip cocktails, slurp oysters and enjoy the 'golden view' of the Arno swirling below their feet.

Zoé BAR

(Map p86; Via de' Renai 13r; ⌚8am-3am) Bright white and shiny, this savvy Oltrarno bar knows exactly what its hip punters want – a relaxed, faintly industrial space to hang out in all hours (well, almost). Be it breakfast, lunch, cocktails or after-dinner party, Zoé is your woman. Come springtime's warmth, the scene spills out onto a wooden decking street terrace in front. Watch for DJs spinning tunes and parties.

Drogheria LOUNGE BAR

(Map p82; www.drogheriafirenze.it; Largo Annigoni 22; ⌚10am-3am) Be it rain, hail or shine, this is a lovely contemporary address in Santa Croce. Inside, it is a large vintage-chic space with dark wood furnishings and soft leaf-green chairs, perfect for lounging for hours on end. Come spring, the action moves outside onto the terrace, which is on the huge piazza behind Sant' Abrogio market.

The kitchen cooks up various bar-style dishes including burgers – beef, veggie, tofu or falafel.

Nano Caffè CAFE, BAR

(Map p82; www.nanocaffe.info; Largo Annigoni, Piazza Ghiberti; ⌚9am-3am) This L-shape bar behind Sant'Ambrogio market is best-loved by Florentines perhaps for its al fresco terrace, a fantastic twinset of large cream parasols shading an eclectic collection of colourfully painted chairs, stools and benches covered in sackcloth. All ages and types hang out in warm weather. Its interior design seems to be reserved for more of a hip set.

Slowly LOUNGE BAR

(Map p62; www.slowlycafe.com; Via Porta Rossa 63r; ⌚9pm-3am Mon-Sat, closed Aug) Sleek and sometimes snooty, this lounge bar with a candle flickering on every table is known for its glam interior, Florentine Lotharios and lavish fruit-garnished cocktails – €10 including buffet during the bewitching *aperitivo* 'hour' (6.30pm to 10pm). Ibiza-style lounge tracks dominate the turntable.

Caffè Sant'Ambrogio CAFE

(Map p82; www.caffesantambrogio.it; Piazza Sant'Ambrogio 7/r; ⌚10.30-3am Mon-Sat; 📶) One of Santa Croce's original (iconic) hangouts, this cafe-bar has lost none of its street cred over the years. Trendy 30-something Florentines continue to flock here for everything from a morning espresso to snacky lunch, after-work cocktails and late-night drinks.

Moyo BAR

(Map p82; www.moyo.it; Via de' Benci 23r; ⌚8am-2am Mon-Thu & Sun, 9am-3am Fri & Sat; 📶) This trendy all-rounder pulls in a moneyed younger set with its endless stream of DJ sets, themed *aperitivi* and late-night drinks, different types of breakfast and quick-fix lunches. Cocktails are particularly big – cranberry martini with lemon juice and triple sec is the house speciality.

Colle Bereto LOUNGE BAR

(Map p62; Piazza Strozzi 5; ⌚8am-2am Tue-Sun; 📶) The local fashion scene's bar of choice, uberstylish Colle Bereto is where the bold and the beautiful come to see or be seen for breakfast, lunch or at *aperitivo* hour.

Soul Kitchen BAR

(Map p82; www.soulkitchenfirenze.it; Via de' Benci 34r; ⏲11am-3am) Look out for flyers for DJs, live music and various hip happenings at this trendy design bar, footsteps from Piazza Santa Croce.

Kitsch BAR

(Map p82; www.kitschfirenze.com; Viale A Gramsci 5; ⏲6.30pm-2.30am; 📶) This hipster American-styled bar in Santa Croce is known among cent-conscious Florentines for its lavish spread at *aperitivi* time – €8.50 for drink and sufficient nibbles to not need dinner. It sports a dark-red theatrical interior and a bright 20s- to early 30s- crowd out for a good time. DJ sets set the place rocking after dark.

Danny Rock BAR

(Map p82; www.dannyrock.it; Via de' Pandolfini 13r; ⏲10-2am; 🚌A) Around since 1980, Danny Rock was given a new lease of life in late 2012 when new management waltzed in and revamped the place. Artisanal beer from around the globe is its main draw these days, alongside a bright and breezy interior, food all day, and charismatic owner Cosimo Lavacchi behind the bar.

Rex Caffé BAR

(Map p82; Via Fiesolana 25r; ⏲6pm-3am Sep-May) A firm long-term favourite, down-to-earth Rex sports great drinks and an artsy Gaudi-inspired interior.

Dolce Vita BAR

(Map p86; www.dolcevitaflorence.com; Piazza del Carmine 6r; ⏲5pm-2am Tue-Sun, closed 2 weeks Aug) This '80s favourite on the other side of the river hosts live bands and small photography/art exhibitions in its small, design-driven interior. The action spills onto a decking terrace outside in summer.

Pubs

Monkey Bar PUB

(Map p82; Via della Mattonaia 20r; ⏲6pm-2am) Duck behind Sant' Abrogio market to find this busy pub, packed most nights with a mix of Florentine and foreign students downing shots and sipping cocktails. Italian double act Lorenzo and Freddy are the duo behind the place.

Lion's Fountain IRISH PUB

(Map p82; www.thelionsfountain.com; Borgo degli Albizi 34r; ⏲10am-2am) If you have the urge to hear more English than Italian – or local bands play for that matter – this is the place. Plump on a pretty pedestrian square, Florence's busiest Irish pub buzzes in summer when the beer-loving crowd spills across most of the square. Live music.

James Joyce PUB

(☎055 658 08 56; Lungarno Benvenuto Cellini 1r; ⏲6pm-2am Sun-Thu, 6pm-3am Fri & Sat) Neither as Irish nor as literary as the name suggests, this veteran pub with beer garden attracts a gregarious student and post-grad crowd thanks to its fabulous and large riverside terrace, Guinness on tap, table football and requisite U2 soundtrack.

Eby's Bar LATIN BAR

(Map p82; Via dell'Oriulolo 5r; ⏲10am-3am Mon-Sat) A lively student crowd packs out this young, fun, colourful address with wooden benches tucked outside in a covered alleyway. The kitchen is Mexican.

Cafes

Cafes are a dime a dozen in Florence. Prime squares to sit and people-watch from a pavement terrace are Piazza della Repubblica, Piazza Santo Spirito and Piazza della Signoria. A coffee taken sitting down at a table is up to four times pricier than one drunk standing up at a bar: a cappuccino costs around €1.40/5.50 standing up/sitting down and a hot chocolate €2.50/6.

Le Renaissance Café CAFE

(Map p62; Piazza Strozzi; ⏲9am-8pm Fri-Wed, to 11pm Thu) Soul-soaringly high-vaulted ceiling, sleek black Panton chairs and exquisitely low drink prices seduce a mixed crowd at this artsy hangout in Palazzo Strozzi on Florence's most designer-chic street. It's run by the same team as Caffè Giacosa of Roberto Cavelli fame across the road, and the chocolate-swirled cappuccino (€1.40 sitting down) is among the best in town.

Gucci Museo Caffè CAFE

(Map p62; Piazza della Signoria 10; meals €25; ⏲10am-11pm; 📶) Everything from the crockery to G-shaped sugar 'cubes' might be emblazoned with the Gucci monogram. But over-zealous branding aside, this smart, laid-back cafe is one of the city's hippest places to hang over coffee, lunch, *aperitivo*, newspapers, design books or inhouse iPads. A huge table hooked up with plugs makes it a laptop-user favourite.

DON'T MISS

BEST HISTORIC CAFES

Few cafes have seen or heard as much as these fabulous old Florentine beauties.

Caffè Giacosa (Map p62; www.caffegiacosa.it; Via della Spada 10r; ⌚7.45am-8.30pm Mon-Fri, 8.30am-8.30pm Sat, 12.30-8pm Sun) This small cafe is famous for what it was – an 1815 child, inventor of the Negroni cocktail and hub of Anglo-Florentine sophistication during the interwar years – and what it is (hip cafe of local hotshot designer Roberto Cavalli, whose flagship boutique is next door). Giacosa is known for its refreshingly unelevated prices and its hip cafe across the street in the courtyard of Palazzo Strozzi.

Caffè Rivoire (Map p62; Piazza della Signoria 4; ⌚Tue-Sun) The golden oldie to refuel inside or out after an Uffizi or Palazzo Vecchio visit, this pricey little number with unbeatable people-watching terrace has produced some of the city's most exquisite chocolate since 1872. Black-jacketed barmen with ties set the formal tone.

Caffè Gilli (Map p62; www.gilli.it; Piazza della Repubblica 39r; ⌚Wed-Mon) The most famous of historic cafes on the city's old Roman forum, Gilli has been serving utterly delectable cakes, chocolates, fruit tartlets and *millefoglie* (sheets of puff pastry filled with rich vanilla or chocolate Chantilly cream) to die for since 1733 (it moved to this square in 1910 and sports a beautifully preserved art nouveau interior).

Caffè Concerto Paszkowski (Map p62; www.paszkowski.com; Piazza della Repubblica 31-35r; ⌚Tue-Sun) Born as a brewery overlooking the city's fish market in 1846, this Florentine institution with heated terrace and elegant, piano-clad interior lured a literary set a century on. Today it pulls the whole gambit of punters, mobile-touting Florentine youths, suit-clad businessmen and well-dressed old ladies sipping tea.

Procacci CAFE

(Map p62; www.procacci1885.it; Via de' Tornabuoni 64r; ⌚10am-8pm Mon-Sat) The last remaining bastion of genteel old Florence on Via de' Tornabuoni, this tiny cafe was born in 1885 opposite an English pharmacy as a delicatessen serving truffles in its repertoire of tasty morsels. Bite-sized *panini tartufati* (truffle pâté rolls) remain the thing to order, best accompanied by a glass of *prosecco*.

Cuculia CAFE

(Map p62; www.cuculia.it; Via dei Serragli 11; ⌚10am-midnight Tue-Fri, to 1am Sat) This hybrid bookshop-cafe is a wonderfully serene spot to while away a few hours in the company of classical music and shelves loaded with books. The vibe is very much old-world refinement and the tiny candlelit nook out back is perfect for a romantic moment over a *cocktailaperitivo*. Food too.

La Terrazza CAFE

(Map p62; La Rinascente, Piazza della Repubblica 1; ⌚9am-9pm Mon-Sat, 10.30am-8pm Sun) Three canvas parasols and a dozen tables make this hidden terrace on the roof of Florence's central department store a privileged spot. Gloat with the birds over coffee or cocktail at achingly lovely views of the *duomo*, Piazza della Repubblica and Florentine hills beyond.

Nightclubs

To savour the best of Florentine clubs, don't arrive before midnight – dance floors generally fill by 2am. June to September everything grinds to a halt when most clubs – bar Central Park and Meccanò, which have outdoor dance floors – shut. Admission, variable depending on the night, is usually more expensive for males than females and is sometimes free if you arrive early (between 9.30pm and 11pm).

Blop Club NIGHTCLUB

(Map p62; www.blopclub.com; Via Vinegia 21r; ⌚11pm-3am Mon-Wed, to 5am Thu-Sat) No surprise that Florence's trendiest club of the moment is in the hippest part of town, aka Santa Croce. Small and edgy, Blop lures an international crowd with its music theme nights – loads of 60s, hip hop, alternative rock, all sounds in fact. No entrance fee, but first-timers need to buy a membership card (€20).

YAB NIGHTCLUB

(Map p62; www.yab.it; Via de' Sassetti 5r; ⌚9pm-4am Oct-May) It's crucial to pick your night according to your age and tastes at Florence's busiest disco club, around since the 1970s behind Palazzo Strozzi. Thursdays is the evening the over 30s hit the dance floor – otherwise, the set is predominantly student.

Space Club NIGHTCLUB
(Map p62; www.spaceclubfirenze.com; Via Palazzuolo 37r; admission €16 incl one drink; ⏲10pm-4am) Sheer size alone at this vast club in Santa Maria Novella impresses – the moment you walk it, you know you are in for a good night of dancing, drinking, video-karaoke perhaps in the bar, and a mixed student-international crowd. Put drinks on an eletronic card 'tab' and pay at the end of the night (risk forking out €50 if you lose the card).

Twice Club NIGHTCLUB
(Map p82; www.twiceclub.com; Via Giuseppe Verdi 57r; ⏲9pm-4am) There's no admisson but you need to look good to get past the bouncers on the door at this Santa Croce club. Once in, Twice is a relaxed club with stylish decor (chandeliers) and a hip cocktail-quaffing crowd. Music is mainstream dance. Happy hour is 9pm to 11pm; don't expect action on the dance floor until well past midnight.

Full Up NIGHTCLUB
(Map p82; Via della Vigna Vecchia 21r; ⏲11pm-4am Mon-Sat Sep-Jun) A variety of sounds energises the crowd at this popular Florentine nightclub where 20-somethings dance until dawn.

Tenax NIGHTCLUB
(www.tenax.org; Via Pratese 46; admission varies; ⏲10pm-4am Thu-Sun Oct-Apr) The only club in Florence on the European club circuit, with great international guest DJs and wildly popular 'Nobody's Perfect' house parties on Saturday night; find the warehouse-style building out of town near Florence airport. Take bus 29 or 30 from Stazione di Santa Maria Novella.

☆ Entertainment

Hanging out on warm summer nights on cafe and bar terraces aside, Florence enjoys a vibrant entertainment scene thanks in part to its substantial foreign-student population. The city has highly regarded theatres, a bounty of festivals and – from around midnight once *aperitivi* and dinner is done – a fairly low-key but varied dance scene.

Live Music

Most venues are outside town and closed in July and/or August.

La Cité LIVE MUSIC
(Map p62; www.lacitelibreria.info; Borgo San Frediano 20r; ⏲3pm-1am Mon-Thu, 5pm-2am Fri & Sat; 📶) By day this cafe-bookshop is a hip cappuccino stop with an eclectic choice of vintage seating to flop down on and surf. From 10pm the intimate bookshelf-lined space morphs into a vibrant live music space: think swing, fusion, jam-session jazz... The

GO TO JAIL!

Florence's old city jail (1883–1985) and 15th-century nunnery behind the Mercato di Sant'Ambrogio is one of Florence's most exciting and interesting cultural spaces. Arranged around an interior courtyard, the historic red-brick complex is, in itself, compelling: there's absolutely no mistaking the thick sturdy doors leading to the old prison cells, many of which now open onto a bookshop, wine bar, art gallery and so on. **Le Carceri** (Map p82; www.ristorantelecarceri.it; Piazza della Madonna della Neve 3; meals €30; ⏲lunch & dinner) is a restaurant with a lovely terrace overlooking the ensemble, and other spaces within the arts centre host wine tastings, exhibitions, performances, screenings and a gaggle of other hot dates in Florence's increasingly happening arts diary.

But the *pièce de résistance* is **Le Murate Caffè Letterario** (Map p82; ☎055 234 68 72; www.lemurate.it; Piazza delle Murate Firenze; ⏲9-1am), an artsy cafe-cum-bar-cum hangout in the heart of the complex where Florence's literati meet to talk, create and perform over coffee, drinks and light meals. Intended as a melting pot for writers, the literary cafe hosts everything from readings and interviews with authors – Florentine, Italian and international – to film screenings, debates, live music and art exhibitions. Its funky interior embraces a series of retro rooms with vintage chairs and table tops built from recycled window frames. In summer everything spills outside in the wonderful brick courtyard. Check upcoming events online.

staircase next to the bar hooks up with mezzanine seating up top.

Jazz Club JAZZ
(Map p82; www.jazzclubfirenze.com; Via Nuovo de' Caccini 3; ⏲10pm-2am Tue-Sat, closed Jul & Aug) Catch salsa, blues, Dixieland and world music as well as jazz at Florence's top jazz venue.

Be Bop Music Club LIVE MUSIC
(Map p78; Via dei Servi 76r; ⏲8pm-2am) FREE Inspired by the swinging sixties, this beloved retro venue features everything from Led Zeppelin and Beatles cover bands to swing jazz and 1970s funk.

Theatre, Classical Music & Ballet

Teatro del Maggio Musicale Fiorentino OPERA, BALLET
(☎055 28 72 22; www.maggiofiorentino.com; Corso Italia 16) The curtain rises on opera, classical concerts and ballet at this lovely theatre, host to the springtime Maggio Musicale Fiorentina.

Teatro della Pergola THEATRE
(Map p82; ☎055 2 26 41; www.teatrodellapergola.com; Via della Pergola 18) Beautiful city theatre with stunning entrance; host to classical concerts October to April.

Shopping

Tacky mass-produced souvenirs (boxer shorts emblazoned with *David's* packet) are everywhere, not least at the city's two main markets, Mercato Centrale (p79) and **Mercato Nuovo** (Map p62; Loggia Mercato Nuovo; ⏲8.30am-7pm Mon-Sat), awash with cheap imported handbags and other leather goods.

But for serious shoppers keen to delve into a city synonymous with craftsmanship since medieval times, there are plenty of ateliers and studios to visit. In medieval Florence goldsmiths, silversmiths and shoemakers were as *alta moda* as sculptors and artists, and modern Florentines are just as enamoured of design and artisanship – keen to *fare la bella figura* (cut a fine figure), appearances are all-important in this city and high-end shops are patronised by people across the income scale. Some may purchase full wardrobes, others the occasional accessory, but all will be very conscious of the labels they and other people are wearing.

Those keen to take a distinctively Florentine treat home should consider leather goods, jewellery, hand-embroidered linens, designer fashion, perfume, marbled paper, wine, puppets or gourmet foods.

In addition to the following options, try Scuola del Cuoio (p92) behind Basilica di Santa Croce for leather.

If there is one Italian city that screams fashion it's Florence, birthplace of Gucci, Emilio Pucci and Robert Cavalli and a bevy of lesser-known designers who beaver away to ensure Florence's reputation as a city synonymous with beauty, creativity and skilled craftsmanship. Legendary **Via de' Tornabuoni**, a glittering catwalk of designer boutiques, is the place to start. Nearby, **Via della Vigna Nuova**, the street where icon of Florence fashion **Gucci** (Map p62; www.gucci.com; Via de' Tornabuoni 73) started out as a tiny saddlery shop in 1921, is another fashion-hot street. Local designers to look for include Michele Negri, Enrico Coveri, **Patrizia Pepe** (Map p62; www.patriziapepe.com; Via delgi Strozzi

DESIGNER OUTLET STORES

Keen to replenish your wardrobe with a few designer pieces but don't want to break the bank? Then head for Florence's out-of-town outlet malls where you can pick up previous-season designer clothing for 30% to 50% less.

Barberino Designer Outlet (www.mcarthurglen.it; Via Meucci, Barberino di Mugello; ⏲10am-8pm Mon-Fri, to 9pm Sat & Sun) Polo Ralph Lauren, D&G, Prada, Class Roberto Cavalli, Missoni, Furla, Benetton and Bruno Magli are just a few of the 100 labels with stores here. Outlet shuttle buses (adult/reduced return €15/8, 35 minutes) depart from Piazza della Stazione in Florence at 10am and 2.30pm daily, departing for the return journey from the outlet, 40km north in Barberino di Mugello, at 1.30pm and 6pm.

The Mall (www.themall.it; Via Europa 8, Leccio; ⏲10am-7pm) Gucci, Ferragamo, Burberry, Ermenegildo Zegna, Yves Saint Laurent, Tod's, Fendi, Giorgio Armani, Marni, Valentino et al are represented in this mall, 30km from Florence. Hourly buses (€5, up to four daily) depart daily from the SITA bus station. By car, take the Incisa exit off the northbound A1 and follow signs for Leccio.

3; ⏲10am-7pm Mon-Sat, 10am-2pm Sat) and Ermanno Daelli.

★Mrs Macis FASHION

(Map p82; www.mrsmacis.it; Borgo Pinti 38r; ⏲4-7.30pm Mon, 10.30am-1pm & 4-7.30pm Tue-Sat) Workshop and showroom of the talented Carla Macis, this eye-catching boutique – dollhouse-like in design – specialises in very feminine 1950s, '60s and '70s clothes and jewellery made from new and recycled fabrics. Every piece is unique and fabulous.

★Casini Firenze FASHION

(Map p86; www.casinifirenze.it; Piazza Pitti 30-31r; ⏲10am-7pm Mon-Sat, 11am-6pm Sun) One of Florence's oldest and most reputable fashion houses, this lovely boutique across from Palazzo Pitti keeps its edge thanks to American-Florentine designer and stylist Jennifer Tattanelli (she does personal wardrobe consultations).

★Boutique Nadine VINTAGE

(Map p82; www.boutiquenadine.com; Via de' Benci 32r; ⏲2.30-7.30pm Mon, 10.30am-8pm Tue-Sat, noon-7pm Sun) There is no more elegant and quaint address to shop for vintage clothing, jewellery, homewares and other pretty little trinkets. From the wooden floor and antique display cabinets to the period changing cabin, Nadine's attention to detail is impeccable.

★Mio Concept HOMEWARES

(Map p62; www.mio-concept.com; Via della Spada 34; ⏲3-7pm Mon, 10am-1.30pm & 2.30-7pm Tue-Sat) A stunning and fascinating range of design objects for the home – some recycled or upcycled – as well as jewellery, T-shirts and so on, cram this stylish boutique created by German-born globetrotter Antje. A real highlight are the street sign art works by Florence-based street artist CLET.

★Dolce Forte CHOCOLATE

(Map p62; www.dolceforte.it; Via della Scala 21; ⏲10am-1pm & 3.30-7.45pm Wed-Sat & Mon) Elena is the passion and knowledge behind this astonishing chocolate shop that sells only the best. Think black-truffle flavoured chocolate, an entire cherry, stone et al, soaked in grappa and wrapped in white chocolate or – for the ultimate taste sensation – *formaggio di fossa* (a cheese from central Italy) soaked in sweet wine and enrobed in dark chocolate.

★Letizia Fiorini PUPPETS

(Map p62; Via del Parione 60r; ⏲10am-7pm Tue-Sat) This charming shop is a one-woman affair – Letizia Fiorini sits at the counter and makes her distinctive puppets by hand in between assisting customers. You'll find Pulchinella (Punch), Arlecchino the clown, beautiful servant girl Colombina, Doctor Peste (complete with plague mask), cheeky Brighella, swashbuckling Il Capitano and many other characters from traditional Italian puppetry.

★Giulio Giannini e Figlio STATIONERY

(Map p86; www.giuliogiannini.it; Piazza Pitti 37r; ⏲10am-7pm Mon-Sat, 11am-6.30pm Sun) Easy to miss, this quaint old shopfront has watched Palazzo Pitti turn pink with the evening sun since 1856. One of Florence's oldest artisan families, the Gianninis – bookbinders by trade – make and sell marbled paper, beautifully bound books, stationery and so on. Don't miss the workshop upstairs.

Aprosio & Co ACCESSORIES, JEWELLERY

(Map p62; www.aprosio.it; Via della Spada 38; ⏲10.30am-1.30pm & 2.30-5.30pm Mon-Sat) Ornella Aprosio fashions teeny tiny glass and crystal beads into dazzling pieces of jewellery, hair accessories, animal-shaped brooches, handbags, even glass-flecked cashmere. It is all quite magical.

Grevi HATS

(Map p62; www.grevi.com; Via della Spada 11-13r; ⏲10am-2pm & 3-8pm Mon-Sat) It was a hat made by Siena milliner Grevi that actress Cher wore in the film *Tea with Mussolini;* ditto Maggie Smith in *My House in Umbria* (2003). So if you want to shop like a star for a hat by Grevi, this hopelessly romantic boutique is the address. Hats range in price from €30 to unaffordable for many.

Vintage di Antonini Alessandra FASHION

(Map p82; Piazza Piero Calamandrei; ⏲3.30-7.30pm Mon, 10.30am-1.15pm & 3.30-7.30pm Tue-Sat) For Real McCoy haute-couture pieces – Chanel handbags, strappy 1970s Dior sandals – look no further than this stylish boutique off via delle Seggiole.

Alessandro Gherardeschi FASHION

(Map p62; www.alessandrogherardeschi.com; Via della Vigna Nuova 97r; ⏲10am-7pm Mon-Sat) Distinctive men's and women's shirts and blouses, short- and long-sleeved, in dozens of designs – floral, cupcakes, vintage cars, all

1

Florence for Shoppers

Florence is naturally stylish – the city did spawn the Renaissance and Gucci after all – which translates as inspirational shopping. Be it the hottest big-name label to strut down the catwalk or something handmade and unique by a smaller designer, fashion is what many people come to Florence for. Local designers to look for include Michele Negri, Enrico Coveri, Patrizia Pepe, Ermanno Daelli and, for wonderful leather designs, Jennifer Tattanelli at Casini Firenze (p113).

Shopping Streets

The world's luxury brands sit smart on **Via de' Tornabuoni**, Florence's main shopping strip with a dazzling line-up of designers – everyone from Prada to Cartier and home-grown players Gucci, Roberto Cavalli and Ferragamo (with glittering shoe museum to boot). From here, it is a stiletto hop to **Via della Vigna Nuova** and **Via della Spada**, a twin-set of impossibly charming, old-world back streets where some of the city's smartest and most creative designers can be found: milliner Grevi (p113) from Siena and bead designer Ornella Aprosio (p113) are two of many stylish boutiques to have legged it here in the last couple of years. Move east into **Santa Croce** to mingle with Florentine designers specialising in vintage and recycled fashion – Borgo degli Albizi, Borgo Pinti and Via di Mezzo are key streets.

Across the river, **Oltrarno** is the traditional 'working' part of the city, the quarter where the Florentine artisan was born and had his tiny workshop. Borgo San Jacopo and Via Santo Spirito remain great streets for avant-garde fashion,

1. Mercato Nuovo
2. Leather craftsman, Santa Croce
3. High-end fashion, Via de' Tornabuoni

shoes, hand-crafted wood and dazzling jewellery; while steps from the river on Via dell'Olmo, Florence's most playful (and wildly popular) street artist CLET (p113) quietly works in his studio on yet another street sign guaranteed to make you grin.

Handmade

Watching artisans cut bags from tanned calf skin, bookbinders marble paper with peacock patterns, puppeteers stitch, and jewellers pore over gold is what Florence shopping is about: Scuola del Cuoio (p92), Letizia Fiorini (p113) and Giulio Giannini e Figlio (p113) are key addresses to do just that.

Markets

Meandering the sea of open-air stalls at the city's two main markets, **Mercato de San Lorenzo** (Map p62; Piazza San Lorenzo; ⏲9am-7pm Mon-Sat) and Mercato Nuovo (p112), is fun but shoppers on the prowl for a handbag, belt or jacket, be aware: Florence's street markets only hawk cheap, imported leather. For quality Florentine leather head to an old family-run boutique.

BEST BIJOU BOUTIQUES

- ➡ Grevi (p113)
- ➡ Boutique Nadine (p113)
- ➡ Mrs Macis (p113)
- ➡ Desii Lab (p116)
- ➡ Mio Concept (p113)

sorts! – is what this colourful little designer boutique near the river sells.

Desii Lab FASHION

(Map p62; Via della Spada 40r; ⏲10am-7pm Mon-Sat) Be it a pair of glittering lilac and turquoise sequinned Uggs, patent yellow Doc Martens or the latest Converse, this shoe and accessory shop – new and vintage – is the place to go. The street fashion specialist sells scarves and other accessories too; also has a couple of other fashion boutiques in town.

Loretta Caponi FASHION

(Map p62; www.lorettacaponi.com; Piazza degli Antinori 4r; ⏲10am-7pm Mon-Fri & Sat morning Mar-Oct, closed Mon afternoon Nov-Feb) An old family name dressing the aristocracy for eons, this utterly gorgeous shop sells hand-embroidered sleepwear, bed and table linen, as well as slippers, bathrobes and exquisitely smocked children's clothes.

A Piedi Nudi nel Parco FASHION

(Map p62; www.pnp-firenze.com; Via del Proconsolo 1; ⏲10.30am-7.30pm) Specialising in high-end avant-garde designers, this is so chic it even has a tiny bar serving *aperitivi* (from 6pm) while you shop.

Francesco da Firenze SHOES

(Map p62; www.francescodafirenze.it; Via di Santo Spirito 62r; ⏲10am-7pm Mon-Sat, closed 2 weeks Aug) Hand-stitched leather is the cornerstone of this tiny family business specialising in ready-to-wear – and indeed made-to-measure – men's and women's shoes.

Alessandro Dari JEWELLERY

(Map p86; www.alessandrodari.com; Via San Niccolò 115r) Flamboyant jeweller and classical guitarist Alessandro Dari creates unique and extremely beautiful pieces in his atmospheric 15th-century workshop-showroom in San Niccolò. He describes his pieces as 'sculpture that you can wear' and presents them in thematic collections.

Lorenzo Villoresi PERFUME

(Map p86; ☎055 234 11 87; www.lorenzovilloresi.it; Via de' Bardi 14; ⏲10am-7pm Mon-Sat) Villoresi's perfumes and potpourris meld distinctively Tuscan elements such as laurel, olive, cypress and iris with essential oils and essences from around the world. His bespoke fragrances are highly sought after. Visiting his showroom, which occupies his family's 15th-century *palazzo,* is quite an experience. Drop-ins welcome but better to call in advance to arrange your visit.

Le Gare 24 FASHION

(Map p62; Borgo d'Ognissanti 24r; ⏲10am-8pm Mon-Sat) Waltz into this retro boutique near the river, note the bright turquoise sofa with hairy fuschia-pink cushions and know you're in one of the best addresses in town for cutting-edge fashion.

Angela Caputi FASHION

(Map p62; www.angelacaputi.com; Borgo SS Apostoli 42-46; ⏲10am-1pm & 3.30-7.30pm Mon-Sat) The bold and colourful resin jewellery of Angela Caputi, at work in Florence since the 1970s, is much-loved by Florentines. Eye-catching costume gems and jewels are her forté, shown off to perfection against one-of-a-kind women's fashion labels uncovered during her worldwide travels.

Madova GLOVES

(Map p86; www.madova.com; Via Guicciardini 1r; ⏲10am-7pm Mon-Sat) Cashmere lined, silk lined, lambs wool lined, unlined – gloves in whatever size, shape, colour and type of leather you fancy by Florentine glovemakers in the biz since 1919.

La Bottega Moderna ARTS, CRAFTS

(www.labottegamoderna.com; Via Romana 118r; ⏲10am-1pm & 3.30-7.30pm Wed-Sat) This thoroughly modern take on a traditional artist's workshop is a wonderful space to browse. The creation of Simafra Prosperi, a young Florentine painter, decorator and art restorer, the shop is a mix of design objects, art works and decorative pieces for the home; many are made from recycled or upcycled objects.

La Bottega dell'Olio OLIVE OIL

(Map p62; Piazza del Limbo 2r; ⏲10am-1pm & 2-6.30pm Tue-Sat) This bijou boutique takes great care with its displays of olive oils, olive oil soaps, platters made from olive wood and skincare products made with olive oil (the Lepo range is particularly good).

Obsequium WINE

(Map p62; www.obsequium.it; Borgo San Jacopo 17-39r; ⏲11am-7.30pm) Occupying the ground floor of one of the city's best-preserved medieval towers, this shop offers a wide range of fine Tuscan wines, wine accessories and gourmet foods, including truffles.

Officina Profumo-Farmaceutica di Santa Maria Novella PERFUMERY

(Map p62; www.santamarianovella.com.br; Via della Scala 16; ⏲9.30am-7.30pm) In business since

1612, this perfumery-pharmacy began life when the Dominican friars of Santa Maria Novella began to concoct cures and sweet-smelling unguents using medicinal herbs cultivated in the monastery garden. The shop today sells a wide range of fragrances, remedies, teas and skin-care products. A real treasure, it has touchscreen catalogues and a state-of-the-art payment system, yet still manages to ooze vintage charm.

After a day battling crowds at the Uffizi or Accademia, you may want to come here for some Aqua di Santa Maria Novella, said to cure hysterics.

Antico Setifico Fiorentino FABRIC
(Via Bartoini 4; ⌚9am-1pm & 2-5pm Mon-Fri) Precious silks, velvets and other luxurious fabrics are woven on 18th- and 19th-century looms at this world-famous fabric house where opulent damasks and brocades in Renaissance styles have been made since 1786.

Alberto Cozzi STATIONERY
(Map p62; Via del Parione 35r; ⌚10am-7pm) Florence is famous for its exquisite marbled paper and this well-known, fourth-generation bookbinder and restorer has been making sheets of the stuff by hand since 1908. Come here to buy paper, leather-bound journals and colourful cards.

Pineider STATIONERY
(Map p62; www.pineider.com; Piazza della Signoria 13-14r; ⌚10am-7pm) This exclusive stationer opened in 1774 and once designed calling cards for Napoleon. Order your own, or choose from a tempting range of paper products and elegant leather office accessories.

Fabriano Boutique STATIONERY
(Map p62; www.fabrianoboutique.com; Via del Corso 59r; ⌚10am-7.30pm Mon-Sat, 11am-7pm Sun) Luxurious writing paper, origami and pop-up greeting cards, and other lovely paper products entice customers into this thoroughly modern stationery boutique – a refreshing change from the traditional norm. It also organises card-making, calligraphy and origami workshops.

Information

EMERGENCY

Police station (Questura; ☎055 4 97 71; http://questure.poliziadistato.it; Via Zara 2; ⌚24hr)

Tourist police (Polizia Assistenza Turistica; ☎055 20 39 11; Via Pietrapiana 50r; ⌚8.30am-6.30pm Mon-Fri, to 1pm Sat) English-speaking service for filing reports of thefts etc.

MEDICAL SERVICES

24-Hour Pharmacy (Stazione di Santa Maria Novella)

Dr Stephen Kerr: Medical Service (☎335 8361682, 055 28 80 55; www.dr-kerr.com; Piazza Mercato Nuovo 1, 4th fl; ⌚3-5pm Mon-Fri, or by appt) Resident British doctor.

Hospital (Ospedale di Santa Maria Nuova; ☎055 2 75 81; Piazza di Santa Maria Nuova 1)

TOURIST INFORMATION

Tourist office (☎055 31 58 74; Via del Termine, Airport; ⌚9am-7pm Mon-Sat, to 4pm Sun)

MUSEUM PASSES

The **Firenze Card** (www.firenzecard.it; €72) is valid for 72 hours and covers admission to 72 museums (it covers all the biggies), villas and gardens in Florence, as well as unlimited use of public transport. Buy it online (and collect upon arrival in Florence) or in Florence at tourist offices or ticketing desks of the Uffizi (Entrance 2), Palazzo Pitti, Palazzo Vecchio, Museo del Bargello, Cappella Brancacci, Museo di Santa Maria Novella and Giardini Bardini. If you're an EU citizen, your card also covers under 18 year olds travelling with you.

The downside of the Firenze Card is it only allows one admission per museum. So, if you want to split your Uffizi forays into a couple of visits and/or you're not from the EU and are travelling with kids, the annual **Friends of the Uffizi Card** (www.amicidegliuffizi.it; adult/reduced/family of 4 €60/40/100) is a better deal. Valid for a calendar year (expires 31 December), it covers admission to 22 Florence museums (including Galleria dell'Accademia, Museo del Bargello and Palazzo Pitti) and allows as many return visits as you fancy (have your passport on you as proof of ID to show at each museum with your card). Buy online or from the **Amici degli Uffizi Welcome Desk** (☎055 28 56 10; ⌚10am-5pm Tue-Sat) next to Entrance 2 at the Uffizi.

Tourist office (Map p62; ☎055 21 22 45; Piazza della Stazione 4; ⏲9am-7pm Mon-Sat, to 4pm Sun)

Tourist office (Map p78; ☎055 29 08 33, 055 29 08 32; www.firenzeturismo.it; Via Cavour 1r; ⏲8.30am-6.30pm Mon-Sat)

Tourist office (Map p62; ☎055 28 84 96; Piazza San Giovanni 1; ⏲9am-7pm Mon-Sat, to 4pm Sun)

Getting There & Away

AIR

Tuscany's main international airport (p133) is located a 10-minute drive south of Pisa and offers flights to most major European cities.

Florence Airport (www.aeroporto.firenze.it) Also known as Amerigo Vespucci or Peretola airport, 5km northwest of the city centre; domestic and a handful of European flights.

BUS

Services from the **SITA bus station** (Map p62; www.sitabus.it; Via Santa Caterina da Siena 17r; ⏲information office 8.30am-12.30pm & 3-6pm Mon-Fri, to 12.30pm Sat), just west of Piazza della Stazione, are vey limited; generally the train is better.

San Gimignano (Poggibonsi; €7.10, 1¼ hours, 14 daily)

Siena (€7.50, 1¼ hours, at least hourly)

Greve in Chianti (€4.10, one hour, hourly)

CAR & MOTORCYCLE

Florence is connected by the A1 northwards to Bologna and Milan, and southwards to Rome and Naples. The Autostrada del Mare (A11) links Florence with Pistoia, Lucca, Pisa and the coast, but most locals use the FI-PI-LI – a *superstrada* (dual carriageway, hence no tolls); look for blue signs saying FI-PI-LI (as in Firenze-Pisa-Livorno). Another dual carriageway, the S2, links Florence with Siena. The much more picturesque SS67 connects the city with Pisa to the west, and Forli and Ravenna to the east.

TRAIN

Florence's central train station is **Stazione di Santa Maria Novella** (Piazza della Stazione). The **left-luggage counter** (Deposito Bagagliamano; Stazione di Santa Maria Novella; first 5hr €5, then per hr €0.70; ⏲6am-11pm) is located on platform 16; Assistenza Disabili (Disabled Assistance) office is on platform 5. Tickets for all trains are sold in the main ticketing hall, but you can skip the ever-long queue and buy your tickets from the touch-screen automatic ticket-vending machines; machines have an English option and accept cash and credit cards.

Florence is on the Rome-Milan line. Services include the following:

DESTINATION	COST	DURATION
Bologna	€24	one hour to 1¾ hours
Lucca	€7	1½ hours to 1¾ hours
Milan	€50 to €60	2¼ hours to 3½ hours
Pisa	€7.80	45 minutes to one hour
Pistoia	€4.10	45 minutes to one hour
Rome	€20.55 to €43	1¾ hours to 4¼ hours
Venice	€45	2¾ hours to 4½ hours

Getting Around

TO/FROM THE AIRPORT

ATAF operates a Volainbus shuttle (single/return €6/8, 25 minutes) between Florence airport and Florence's Stazione di Santa Maria Novella every 30 minutes between 6am and 11.30pm (5.30am to 11pm from city centre). **Terravision** (www.terravision.eu) runs daily services (one way €4.99, 1¼ hours, hourly) between the bus stop outside Florence's Stazione di Santa Maria Novella on Via Alamanni (under the digital station clock) and Pisa International Airport – buy tickets online, on board or from the Terravision desk inside the Deanna Bar; at Pisa International Airport, the Terravision ticket desk dominates the arrival hall.

A taxi between Florence airport and town costs a flat rate of €20 (€22 on Sundays and holidays, €23.30 between 10pm and 6am), plus €1 per bag. Exit the terminal building, bear right and you'll come to the taxi rank.

Regular trains link Florence's Stazione di Santa Maria Novella with Pisa International Airport (€7.80, 1½ hours, at least hourly from 4.30am to 10.25pm).

CAR & MOTORCYCLE

Nonresident traffic is banned from the centre of Florence for most of the week and our advice, if you can, is to avoid the whole irksome bother of having a car in the city.

BICYCLE & SCOOTER

Milleunabici (www.bicifirenze.it; Piazza della Stazione; per hr/day €2/5; ⏲10am-7pm Mar-Oct) Violet coloured bikes to rent in front of Stazione di Santa Maria Novella; leave ID as a deposit.

Florence by Bike (www.florencebybike.com; Via San Zanobi 120r; ⏲9am-1pm & 3.30-7.30pm Mon-Sat) Top-notch bike shop, itiner-

PARKING IN FLORENCE

There is a strict Limited Traffic Zone in Florence's historic centre between 7.30am and 7.30pm Monday to Friday and 7.30am to 6pm Saturday for all nonresidents, monitored by cyclopean cameras positioned at all entry points. The exclusion also applies on Wednesday, Friday and Saturday from 11pm to 4am mid-May to mid-September. Motorists staying in hotels within the zone are allowed to drive to their hotel to drop off luggage, but must tell reception their car registration number and the time they were in no-cars-land (there's a two-hour window) so that the hotel can inform the authority and organise a permit. If you transgress, a fine of around €150 will be sent to you (or the car-hire company you used). For more information see www.comune.fi.it.

There is free street parking around Piazzale Michelangelo. Pricey (around €20 per day) underground parking can be found around Fortezza da Basso and in the Oltrarno beneath Piazzale di Porta Romana. Otherwise, search for a car park on www.firenzeparcheggi.it or ask if your hotel can arrange parking.

ary suggestions, bike tours and rental outlet (city bike/scooter per day €14.50/68).

PUBLIC TRANSPORT

Buses and electric minibuses run by public transport company **ATAF** (☎199 104245, 800 424500; www.ataf.net) serve the city. Most buses – including bus 13 to Piazzale Michelangelo – start/terminate at the ATAF bus stops opposite the southeastern exit of Stazione di Santa Maria Novella. Tickets valid for 90 minutes (no return journeys) cost €1.20 (€2 on board – drivers don't give change!) and are sold at kiosks, tobacconists and the **ATAF ticket & information office** (Map p78; Piazza della Stazione; 7.30am-7.30pm) adjoining the train station. A travel pass valid for 1/3/7 days is €5/12/18. Upon boarding, time-stamp your ticket (punch on board) or risk a fine. The first **tramline** (www.gestramvia.it) is now up and running, and all tramlines should be ready by 2016.

TAXI

For a taxi, call ☎055 42 42 or ☎055 43 90.

Northwestern Tuscany

Includes ➡

Best Places to Eat

- ➡ Villa Bongi (p141)
- ➡ Osteria Vecchia Mulino (p149)
- ➡ Pepenero (p148)
- ➡ Filippo (p157)

Best Places to Stay

- ➡ Piccolo Hotel Puccini (p138)
- ➡ Locanda Gavarini (p160)
- ➡ Barbialla Nuova (p147)
- ➡ Il Benefizio (p151)

Why Go?

There is far more to this green corner of Tuscany than Italy's iconic Leaning Tower. Usually hurtled through at breakneck speed en route to Florence and Siena's grand-slam queue-for-hours sights, this is the place to take your foot off the brake and go slow – on foot, by bicycle or car. Allow for long lazy lunches of rustic regional specialities to set the pace for the day, before meandering around a medieval hilltop village or along an ancient pilgrimage route.

Even the region's larger towns – university hub Pisa and 'love at first sight' Lucca with its 16th-century walls ensnaring a labyrinth of butter-coloured buildings, Romanesque palaces and gracious piazzas – have an air of tranquillity and tradition that begs the traveller to linger. This is snail-paced Italy, and you're sure to love it.

Road Distances

	Pistoia	Pisa	Lucca	San Miniato
Pisa	55			
Lucca	40	23		
San Miniato	64	47	70	
Pietrasanta	68	31	30	77

Getting Around

Major towns and cities are well connected by the A11 and A12, but it's more fun to veer off the motorways and onto scenic secondary roads and narrow rural routes, particularly in the Lunigiana and Garfagnana. Pisa and Lucca have strictly enforced Limited Traffic Zones (ZTL) in their *centri storici* (historic centres) – be careful where you park! Regular trains link Florence, Pisa, Lucca and Viareggio, but less obvious places such as Lajatico require a car.

THREE PERFECT DAYS

Day 1: Biking Lucca

Hire a bike, provision yourself with Forno Giusti's fresh-from-the-oven focaccias, pizzas and other picnic fare, and free-wheel along the city's medieval streets. Lunch atop the monumental city walls, or pedal east to picnic in a Renaissance villa's grounds. At day's end, listen to a Puccini recital in a medieval church.

Day 2: Backstreet Pisa

Fall in love with backstreet Pisa, squirreling away the tower and Pisa's picture-perfect Piazza dei Miracoli for the latter part of the day – the best shots of the tower are from the pretty cloister garden of the Museo dell'Opera del Duomo. Iconic sight done with, head out of town for a late-afternoon mooch in the crowd-free, Slow Food town of San Miniato. Savour an *aperitivo* (pre-dinner drink accompanied by cocktail snacks) with valley view in one of its lovely quaint cafes and dine after dusk at Pepenero (book in advance) or out-of-town Podere del Grillo. Overnight at Tuscan truffle farm, Barbialla Nuova.

Day 3: Mountain to Sea

Shop for a picnic of local forest produce in Castelnuovo di Garfagnana, then motor up and over the Apuane Alps – allow plenty of time for pulling over to soak up vistas of monumental marble blocks being cut out of the mountainside. Picnic on the Passo del Vestito and visit its botanical garden, then drop down to the sea. In Massa, head north to Carrara (to see a marble quarry) or south to refined Pietrasanta (for contemporary art and creative dining).

Where to Stay

- Pisa is the obvious place to stay, but it is traffic busy and quality accommodation is limited.
- Opt instead for lovely Lucca (tricky parking), a farm around San Miniato, or stylish art gem Pietrasanta: all three are an easy drive to northwestern Tuscany's key sights.

DON'T MISS

The chance to savour *lardo di colannata* (pig fat aged for 12 or 24 months in marble vats of herby olive oil) over lunch in Colannata after visiting Carrara.

Best Food & Wine Experiences

- Barbialla Nuova (p147)
- Mercato della Terra di San Miniato (p147)
- La Barchina (p158)
- L'Enoteca Marcucci (p157)

Best with Kids

- La Citadella di Carnevale (p157)
- Cava di Fantiscritti (p154)
- Grotta del Vento (p152)
- Museo Piaggio (p133)
- Ponte del Diarolo (p153)

Resources

- **Pisa Tourism** (www.pisaturismo.it) Pisa tourist office.
- **Parco Regionale delle Alpi Apuane** (p148) The region's nature park.
- **Toscana Mare** (www.tuscancoast.org) The Tuscan Coast.

North-western Tuscany Highlights

❶ Pedal and picnic atop the lovely Renaissance city walls of **Lucca** (p140).

❷ Meander medieval Pisa and scale its iconic **Leaning Tower** (p125) at sunset.

❸ Hunt white truffles in autumnal woods at **Barbialla Nuova** (p147), near San Miniato.

❹ Shop at the farmer's market, wine taste and dine courtesy of a Tuscan celebrity TV chef in **San Miniato** (p146).

❺ Revel in exciting contemporary art, cuisine and boutique shopping in small-town **Pietrasanta** (p156).

❻ Lose yourself in the best of rural Tuscany in the **Garfagnana** (p148).

❼ See where Michelangelo sourced his marble and visit the quarries in **Carrara** (p153).

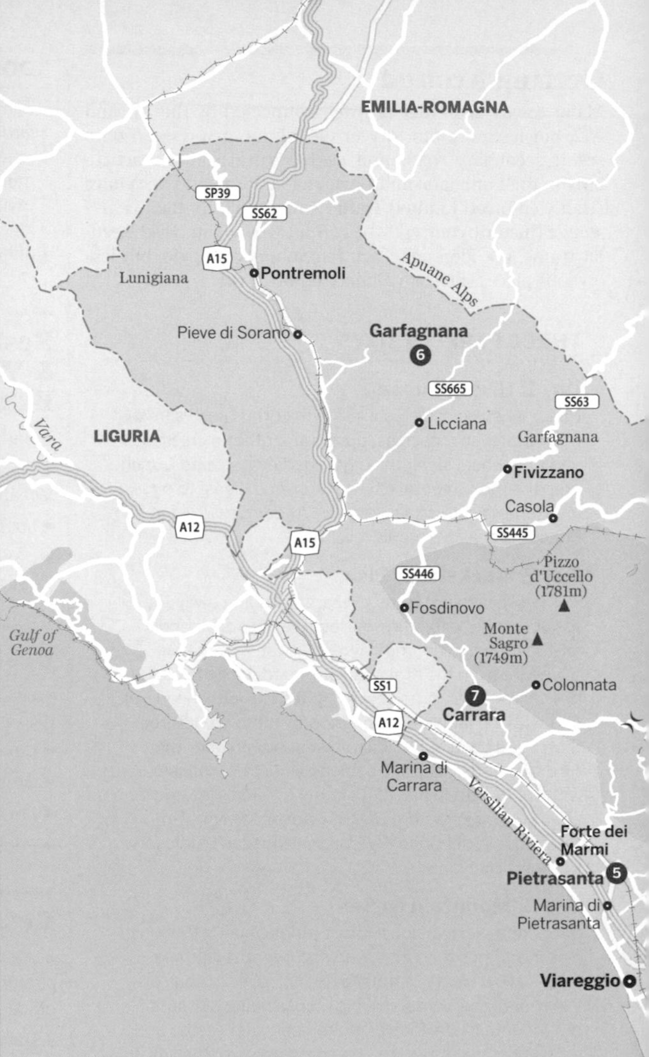

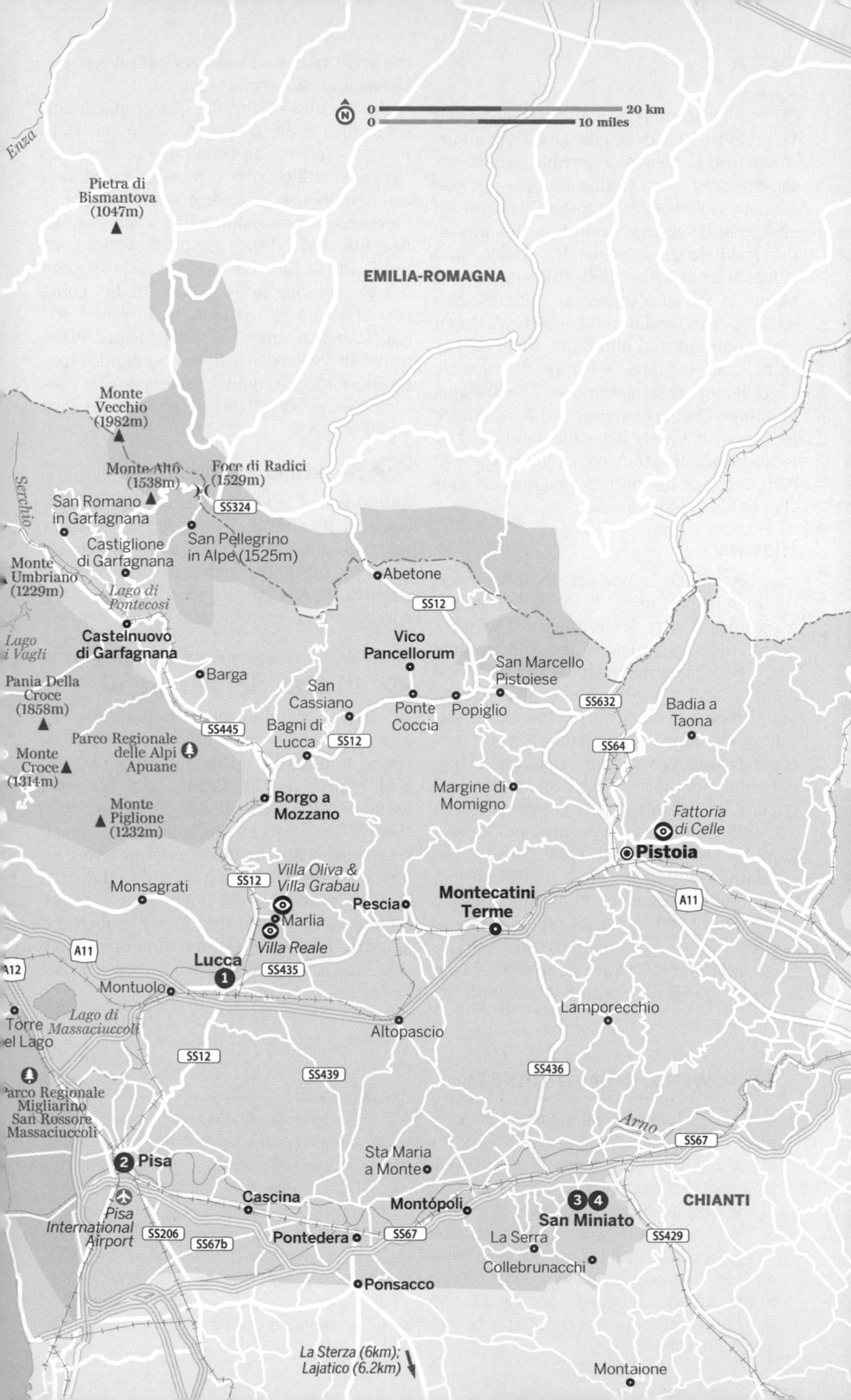

0 20 km
0 10 miles
Enza
Pietra di Bismantova (1047m)
EMILIA-ROMAGNA
Monte Vecchio (1982m)
Monte Alto (1538m)
Foce di Radici (1529m)
SS324
Serchio
San Romano in Garfagnana
Castiglione di Garfagnana
San Pellegrino in Alpe (1525m)
Monte Umbriano (1229m)
Lago di Pontecosi
Abetone
SS12
Lago i Vagli
Castelnuovo di Garfagnana
Vico Pancellorum
San Marcello Pistoiese
Barga
Pania Della Croce (1858m)
San Cassiano
Ponte Coccia
Popiglio
SS632
Badia a Taona
SS445
Bagni di Lucca
SS12
SS64
Parco Regionale delle Alpi Apuane
Monte Croce (1314m)
Borgo a Mozzano
Margine di Momigno
Monte Piglione (1232m)
Fattoria di Celle
Pistoia
SS12
Villa Oliva & Villa Grabau
Monsagrati
Montecatini Terme
Pescia
A11
Marlia
Villa Reale
A11
Lucca
1
A12
SS435
Montuolo
Lago di Massaciuccoli
Torre el Lago
Altopascio
Lamporecchio
SS12
SS439
SS436
Parco Regionale Migliarino San Rossore Massaciuccoli
Arno
SS67
2 Pisa
Sta Maria a Monte
Cascina
Montópoli
3 4
San Miniato
CHIANTI
Pisa International Airport
SS206
SS67b
Pontedera
SS67
La Serra
SS429
Collebrunacchi
Ponsacco
La Sterza (6km); Lajatico (6.2km)
Montaione

PISA

POP 85,500

Once a maritime power to rival Genoa and Venice, Pisa now draws its fame from an architectural project gone terribly wrong. But the world-famous Leaning Tower is just one of many noteworthy sights in this compact and compelling city. Education has fuelled the local economy since the 1400s, and students from across Italy still compete for places in its elite university and research schools. This endows the centre of town with a vibrant and affordable cafe and bar scene, and balances what is an enviable portfolio of well-maintained Romanesque buildings, Gothic churches and Renaissance piazzas with a lively street life dominated by locals rather than tourists – a charm you will definitely not discover if you restrict your visit to Piazza dei Miracoli.

History

Pisa became an important naval base and commercial port under Rome and remained a significant port for centuries. The city's golden days began late in the 10th century, when it became an independent maritime republic and a formidable rival of Genoa and Venice. A century on, the Pisan fleet was sailing far beyond the Mediterranean, successfully trading with the Orient and bringing home new ideas in art, architecture and science. At the peak of its power (the 12th and 13th centuries), Pisa controlled Corsica, Sardinia and the Tuscan coast. Most of the city's finest buildings date from this period, when the distinctive Pisan-Romanesque architectural style with its use of coloured marbles and subtle references to Andalucian architectural styles flourished. Many of these buildings sported decoration by the great father-and-son sculptural team of Nicola and Giovanni Pisano.

Pisa's support for the imperial Ghibellines during the tussles between the Holy Roman Emperor and the pope brought the city into conflict with its mostly Guelph Tuscan neighbours, including Siena, Lucca and Florence. The real blow came when Genoa's fleet inflicted a devastating defeat on Pisa at the Battle of Meloria in 1284. After the city fell to Florence in 1406, the Medici court encouraged great artistic, literary and scientific endeavours and re-established Pisa's university, where the city's most famous son, Galileo Galilei, taught in the late 16th century. During WWII about 40% of old Pisa was destroyed.

Sights & Activities

Many visitors to Pisa arrive by train at Stazione San Rossore and don't get any further than neighbouring Piazza dei Miracoli; those in the know arrive or depart using Pisa's Stazione Centrale allowing casual discovery of the *centro storico* (historic centre).

Piazza dei Miracoli

No Tuscan sight is more immortalised in kitsch souvenirs than the iconic tower teetering on the edge of this gargantuan piazza, also known as the **Campo dei Miracoli** (Field of Miracles) or Piazza del Duomo (Cathedral Sq). With two million visitors every year, crowds are the norm, many arriving by tour bus from Florence for a whirlwind visit.

Each year from 16 June until the last Sunday in August or first in September, the Leaning Tower and Camposanta open their doors to visitors until 11pm – a magical experience not to be missed.

TOWER & COMBO TICKETS

Buy tickets for the Leaning Tower from one of two well-signposted ticket offices: the main **ticket office** behind the tower or the smaller **office** (www.opapisa.it; Piazza dei Miracoli; 8am-8pm summer, 10am-5pm winter) inside Museo delle Sinópie. To guarantee your visit to the tower and to save the long queue in high season, buy tickets in advance online, but note that tickets can only be bought between 20 and 12 days before visiting.

Ticket offices in Pisa also sell combination tickets covering admission to the Baptistry, Camposanto, Museo dell'Opera del Duomo and Museo delle Sinópie: buy a ticket covering one/two/three/four sights costing €5/7/8/9 (reduced €3/4/5/6). Admission to the cathedral is free, but you need to show a ticket – either for one of the other sights or a cathedral coupon distributed at ticket offices. Combination tickets covering four sights are valid two days.

★ Leaning Tower LANDMARK

(Torre Pendente; www.opapisa.it; Piazza dei Miracoli; incl admission to cathedral €18; ⏲8am-8pm summer, 10am-5pm winter) Yes, it's true: the Leaning Tower leans. Construction started in 1173 but stopped a decade later when the structure's first three tiers started tilting. In 1272 work started again, with artisans and masons attempting to bolster the foundations but failing miserably. Despite this, they kept going, compensating for the lean by gradually building straight up from the lower storeys.

Over the centuries, the tower has tilted an extra 1mm each year. By 1993 it was 4.47m out of plumb, more than five degrees from the vertical. The most recent solution saw steel braces slung around the third storey that were then joined to steel cables attached to neighbouring buildings. This held the tower in place as engineers began gingerly removing soil from below the northern foundations. After some 70 tonnes of earth had been extracted from the northern side, the tower sank to its 18th-century level and, in the process, rectified the lean by 43.8cm. Experts believe that this will guarantee the tower's future for the next three centuries.

Access to the Leaning Tower is limited to 40 people at one time – children under eight are not allowed in/up and those aged eight to 12 years must hold an adult's hand. To avoid disappointment, book in advance online or go straight to a ticket office when you arrive in Pisa to book a slot for later in the day. Visits last 30 minutes and involve a steep climb up 300-odd occasionally slippery steps. All bags, handbags included, must be deposited at the free left-luggage desk next to the central ticket office – cameras are about the only thing you can take up.

★ Duomo CATHEDRAL

(Piazza dei Miracoli; admission free with coupon from ticket office; ⏲10am-8pm summer, 10am-1pm & 2-5pm winter) Pisa's cathedral was paid for with spoils brought home after Pisans attacked an Arab fleet entering Palermo in 1063. Begun a year later, the cathedral, with its striking cladding of alternating bands of green and cream marble, became the blueprint floor for Romanesque churches throughout Tuscany. The elliptical dome, the first of its kind in Europe at the time, was added in 1380.

The cathedral was the largest in Europe when it was constructed; its breathtaking proportions were designed to demonstrate Pisa's domination of the Mediterranean. Its main facade – not completed until the 13th century – has four exquisite tiers of columns diminishing skywards, while the vast interior, 96m long and 28m high, is propped up by 68 hefty granite columns in classical style. The wooden ceiling decorated with 24-carat gold is a legacy from the period of Medici rule.

Before stepping foot in the cathedral, study the three pairs of 16th-century bronze doors at the main entrance. Designed by the school of Giambologna to replace the wooden originals destroyed (along with most of the cathedral interior) by fire in 1596, the doors are quite spellbinding – hours can be spent deciphering the biblical scenes illustrating the immaculate conception of the Virgin and birth of Christ (central doors), the road to Calvary and crucifixion of Christ etc, and the Ministry of Christ. Kids can play spot the rhino.

Inside, don't miss the extraordinary early-14th-century octagonal pulpit in the north aisle. Sculpted from Carrara marble by Giovanni Pisano and featuring nude and heroic figures, its depth of detail and heightening of feeling brought a new pictorial expressionism and life to Gothic sculpture. Pisano's work forms a striking contrast to the controversial 2001 pulpit and altar by Italian sculptor Giuliano Vangi.

★ Baptistry RELIGIOUS

(Piazza dei Miracoli; adult/reduced €5/3; ⏲8am-8pm summer, 10am-5pm winter) The unusual round baptistry has one dome piled on top of

LOCAL KNOWLEDGE

PISAN PLAY

Art in Pisa comes in all shapes and sizes. Enter Keith Haring's *Tuttomondo* (1989), the last wall mural the American pop artist painted – on the facade of a convent in Pisa – months before his death in 1990. Play the Pisan: sip a cocktail on the wooden-decking terrace of the hip **Keith** (www.keithcafe.com; Via Zandonai 4; ⏲7am-11pm; wi-fi) cafe–art shop across from the wall and lament the fading, weather-beaten colours of Haring's 30 signature prancing dancing men. Free wi-fi, art exhibitions, knitting evenings, puzzle nights, superb coffee and one of the funkiest outdoor spaces in town ensures the place buzzes.

Why Pisa Leans

In 1160 Pisa boasted 10,000-odd towers, but no *campanile* (bell tower) for its cathedral. Loyal Pisan, Berta di Bernardo, righted this in 1172 when she died and left a legacy of 60 pieces of silver in her will to the city to get cracking on a *campanile*.

Ironically, when Bonnano Pisano set to work on the world's most famous *campanile* in 1173, he did not realise what shaky ground he was on: beneath Piazza dei Miracoli's lawns lay a treacherous mix of sand and clay, 40m deep. And when work stopped five years on, with just three storeys completed, Italy's stump of an icon already tilted. Building resumed in 1272, workers compensating for the lean by building straight up from the lower storeys to create a subtle banana curve. By the 19th century, many were convinced the tower was a mere whimsical folly of its inventors, built deliberately to lean.

In 1838 a clean-up job to remove muck oozing from the base of the tower exposed, once and for all, the true nature of its precarious foundations. In the 1950s the seven bells inside the tower, each sounding a different musical note and rung from the ground by 14 men since 1370, were silenced for fear of a catastrophic collapse. In 1990 the tower was closed to the public. Engineers placed 1000 tonnes of lead ingots on the north side to counteract the subsidence on the south side. Steel bands were wrapped around the 2nd storey to keep it together.

Then in 1995 the tower slipped a whole 2.5mm. Steel braces were slung around the 3rd storey of the tower and attached to heavy hydraulic A-frame

STEVE ALLEN / GETTY IMAGES ©

CHARLES E. ROTKIN / CORBIS ©

1. Pisa's *duomo* (cathedral) and Leaning Tower **2.** Aerial view of Piazza dei Miracoli **3.** Leaning Tower

FIREHORSE / GETTY IMAGES ©

anchors some way from the northern side. The frames were replaced by steel cables, attached to neighbouring buildings. The tower held in place, engineers gingerly removed 70 tonnes of earth from below the northern foundations, forcing the tower to sink to its 18th-century level – and correct the lean by 43.8cm. Success...

A scrub and polish followed and work was completed in 2011. For the first time in 20 years Pisa's Leaning Tower could be viewed as intended – dazzling white, firm, and very firmly leaning.

LEANING CITY

➡ **Duomo & Baptistry** (p125 & p125) The tower's neighbours lean 25cm and 51cm respectively.

➡ **Chiesa di San Nicola** (Map p128; Via Santa Maria) Nicola Pisano's octagonal *campanile* (bell tower) is another sacred edifice not dead straight.

➡ **Chiesa di San Michele degli Scalzi** (Via San Michele degli Scalzi) Note the wonky red-brick square tower.

Pisa

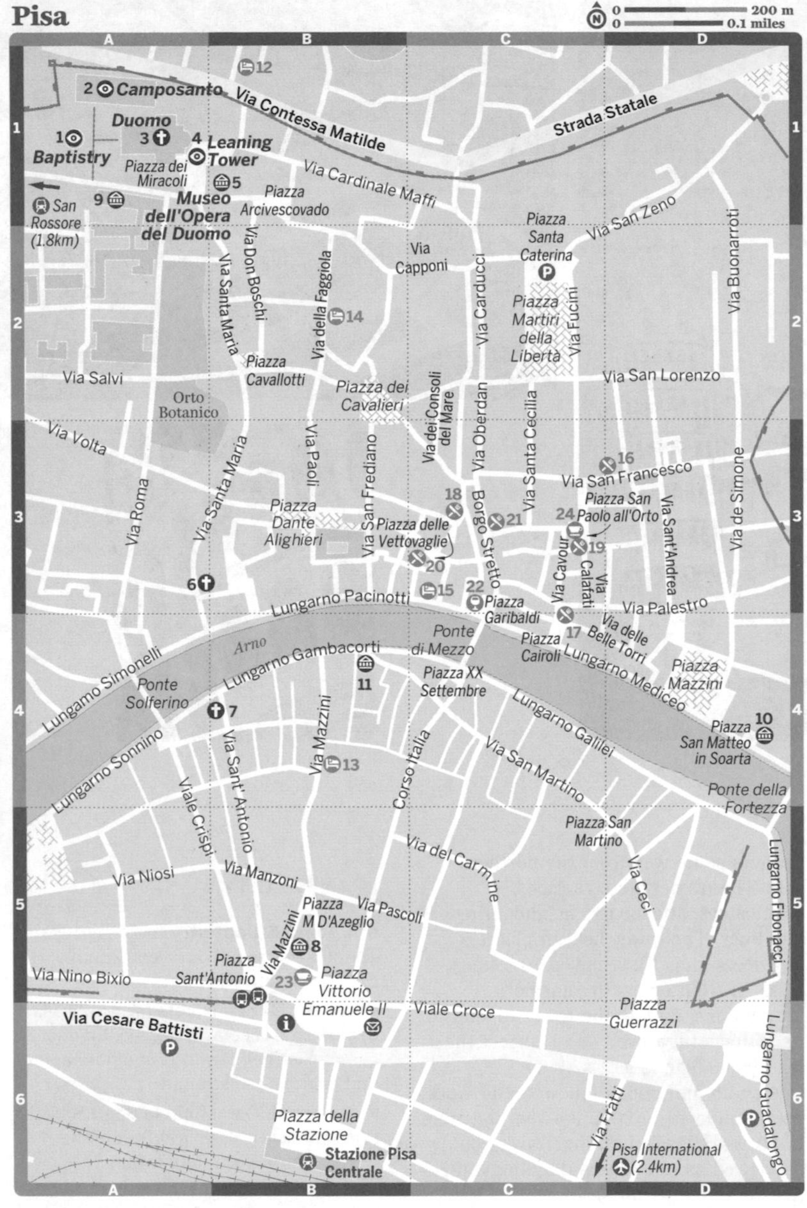

another, each roofed half in lead, half in tiles, and topped by a gilt bronze John the Baptist (1395). Construction began in 1152, but it was remodelled and continued by Nicola and Giovanni Pisano more than a century later and finally completed in the 14th century.

The lower level of arcades is Pisan-Romanesque; the pinnacled upper section and dome are Gothic.

Inside, the hexagonal marble **pulpit** (1260) by Nicola Pisano is the highlight. Pisan scientist Galileo Galilei (who, so the story

Pisa

Top Sights

1 Baptistry ... A1
2 Camposanto ... A1
3 Duomo ... A1
4 Leaning Tower ... A1
5 Museo dell'Opera del Duomo ... B1

Sights

6 Chiesa di San Nicola ... A3
7 Chiesa di Santa Maria della Spina ... B4
8 Domus Mazziniana ... B5
9 Museo delle Sinópie ... A1
10 Museo Nazionale di San Matteo ... D4
11 Palazzo Blu ... B4

Sleeping

12 Hostel Pisa Tower ... B1
13 Hotel Bologna ... B4
14 Hotel Relais dell'Orologio ... B2
15 Royal Victoria Hotel ... C3

Eating

16 biOsteria 050 ... D3
17 Il Crudo ... C4
18 Il Montino ... C3
19 Osteria Bernardo ... C3
20 Osteria del Porton Rosso ... C3
21 Salza ... C3

Drinking & Nightlife

22 Bazeel ... C3
23 Keith ... B5
24 Sottobosco ... C3

goes, came up with the laws of the pendulum by watching a lamp in Pisa's cathedral swing), was baptised in the octagonal font (1246). Don't leave without climbing to the **Upper Gallery** to listen to the custodian demonstrate the double dome's remarkable acoustics and echo effects, every half-hour on the half-hour.

★Camposanto CEMETERY
(Piazza dei Miracoli; adult/reduced €5/3; 8am-8pm summer, 10am-5pm winter) Soil shipped from Calvary during the Crusades is said to lie within the white walls of this hauntingly beautiful, final resting place for many prominent Pisans, arranged around a garden in a cloistered quadrangle. During WWII, Allied artillery destroyed many of the cloisters' frescos, but a couple were salvaged and are now displayed in the **Sala Affreschi** (Frescoes Room).

Most notable is the *Triumph of Death* (133–41), a remarkable illustration of Hell attributed to 14th-century painter Buonamico Buffalmacco. Fortunately, the mirrors apparently once stuck next to the graphic, no-holds-barred images of the damned being roasted alive on spits have since been removed – meaning a marginally less uncomfortable visit for visitors who would have once seen their own faces peering out of the cruel wall painting. Buffalmacco's Last *Judgement & Hell* (1336–41), in the same room, is equally brutal.

★Museo dell'Opera del Duomo MUSEUM
(Piazza dei Miracoli; adult/reduced €5/3; 8am-8pm summer, 10am-5pm winter) A repository for works of art once displayed in the cathedral and baptistry, highlights include Giovanni Pisano's ivory carving of the *Madonna and Child* (1299), made for the cathedral's high altar, and his mid-13th-century *Madonna del colloquio,* originally from a gate of the *duomo*. Don't miss the tranquil cloister garden with great views of the Leaning Tower.

Museo delle Sinópie MUSEUM
(Piazza dei Miracoli; adult/reduced €5/3; 8am-8pm summer, 10am-5pm winter) Home to some fascinating frescoes, this museum safeguards several *sinópie* (preliminary sketches), drawn by the artists in red earth pigment on the walls of the Camposanto in the 14th and 15th centuries before the frescoes were overpainted. The museum is a compelling study in fresco painting, with short films and scale models filling in the gaps.

Along the Arno

Away from the crowded heavyweights of Piazza dei Miracoli, along the Arno river banks, Pisa comes into its own. Splendid *palazzi* (palaces), painted a multitude of hues, line the southern *lungarno* (riverside embankment), from where shopping boulevard **Corso Italia** legs it to the central train station, Stazione Centrale. Don't miss the waterside, triple-spired **Chiesa di Santa Maria della Spina** (Lungarno Gambacorti), an exquisite little Pisan-Gothic church encrusted with tabernacles and statues. It was built between 1230 and 1223 to house a reliquary of a *spina* (thorn) from Christ's crown, but is unfortunately closed today.

Pisa's medieval heart lies north of the water: from **Piazza Cairoli**, with its evening bevy of bars and gelato shops, meander along **Via Cavour** and get lost in the surrounding lanes and alleys. A daily fresh-produce

HOW TO FALL IN LOVE WITH PISA

Sure, the iconic Leaning Tower is the reason everyone wants to go to Pisa. But once you've put yourself through the Piazza dei Miracoli madness (overzealous souvenir sellers, boisterous school groups, photo-posing pandemonium...) most people simply want to get out of town.

To avoid leaving Pisa feeling oddly deflated by one of Europe's great landmarks, save the Leaning Tower & Co for the latter part of the day – or, better still, an enchanting visit after dark (mid-June to August) when the night casts a certain magic on the glistening white monuments and the tour buses have long gone.

Upon arrival, indulge instead in peaceful meanderings along the Arno river, over its bridges and through Pisa's medieval heart. Discover the last monumental wall painting Keith Haring did before he died, enjoy low-key architectural and art genius at the Chiesa di Santa Maria della Spina and Palazzo Blu, and lunch with locals at Sottobosco.

And only once you've fallen in love with the other Pisa, should you head for the tower.

market fills **Piazza delle Vettovaglie**, ringed with 15th-century porticoes and cafe terraces.

Palazzo Blu ART GALLERY
(www.palazzoblu.it; Lungarno Gambacorti 9; ⏲10am-7pm Tue-Fri, to 8pm Sat & Sun) FREE Facing the river is this magnificently restored, 14th-century building that has a striking dusty-blue facade. Inside, its over-the-top 19th-century interior decoration is the perfect backdrop for the Foundation CariPisa's art collection – predominantly Pisan works from the 14th to the 20th centuries, plus various temporary exhibitions.

Museo Nazionale di San Matteo ART GALLERY
(Piazza San Matteo in Soarta; adult/reduced €5/2.50; ⏲8.30am-7pm Tue-Sat, to 1.30pm Sun) This inspiring repository of medieval masterpieces sits in a 13th-century Benedictine convent on the Arno's northern waterfront boulevard. The gallery's collection of paintings from the Tuscan school (c 12th to 14th centuries) is notable, with works by Lippo Memmi, Taddeo Gaddi, Gentile da Fabriano and Ghirlandaio. Don't miss Masaccio's *St Paul,* Fra Angelico's *Madonna of Humility* and Simone Martini's *Polyptych of Saint Catherine*.

Equally engaging is the collection of 14th- and 15th-century Pisan sculptures, including pieces by Nicola and Giovanni Pisano, Andrea and Nino Pisano, Francesco di Valdambrino, Donatello, Michelozzo and Andrea della Robbia.

Domus Mazziniana MUSEUM
(www.domusmazziniana.it; Via Mazzini 71; ⏲9am-12.30pm Mon-Fri) FREE One glimpse of the beautiful renovated facade of Palazzo Nathan-Rosselli, the Pisan mansion where Italian revolutionary and champion of Italian unification Giuseppe Mazzini died in 1872, and a peep (at least) inside is inevitable. Documents, manuscripts, letters handwritten by Mazzini, flags and photographs document Mazzinian and democratic ideology during the Risorgimento (reunification period).

Festivals & Events

Luminaria LIGHT SHOW
The night before Pisa's patron saint's day is magical: thousands upon thousands of candles and blazing torches light up the river and riverbanks while fireworks bedazzle the night sky; 16 June.

Regata Storica di San Ranieri SPORT
The Arno comes to life with a rowing regatta to commemorate the city's patron saint; 17 June.

Gioco del Ponte CULTURE
During Gioco del Ponte (Game of the Bridge), two teams in medieval costume battle it out over the Ponte di Mezzo; last Sunday in June.

Palio delle Quattro Antiche Repubbliche Marinare REGATTA
(Regatta of the Four Ancient Maritime Republics) In the Regatta of the Four Ancient Maritime Republics, the four historical maritime rivals – Pisa, Venice, Amalfi and Genoa – meet yearly in June for a procession of boats and a dramatic race; the next will be held in Pisa in 2017.

Sleeping

Hostel Pisa Tower HOSTEL €
(☎329 7017387, 05 0520 2454; www.hostelpisatower.it; Via Piave 4; dm with shared bathroom

€18-22, apt €49-69; @ wi-fi) This extremely friendly place near PIazza dei Miracoli occupies a suburban villa with garden. Rooms are cheerful, clean and comfortable but lack bathroom facilities (only two showers and two toilets for 22 beds) and communal kitchen. The apartment sleeps two or three, and comes with small kitchen and private car park; free wi-fi but internet access €4 per hour.

Royal Victoria Hotel HOTEL €€
(☎05 094 01 11; www.royalvictoria.it; Lungarno Pacinotti 12; d €110-170, tr €130-170, q €170, s/d with shared bathroom €70/80; ❄ wi-fi) This doyen of Pisan hotels, run with pride by the Piegaja family since 1837, offers old-world luxury accompanied by warm, attentive service. The word on the street says rooms vary, but those we saw were the perfect shabby-chic mix of Grand Tour antique – love the parquet floors and flashes of exposed stone – and modern-day comfort.

The unquestionable highlight is an aperitif flopped on a sofa on the flowery 4th-floor terrace, packed with potted plants. Garage parking/bike hire €20/15 per day, wi-fi €2.50 per hour, breakfast €5.

Hotel Bologna HOTEL €€
(☎05 050 21 20; www.hotelbologna.pisa.it; Via Mazzini 57; d €134-198, tr €188-278, q €194-298; ❄ @ wi-fi) Nicely placed away from the Piazza dei Miracoli mayhem (a 1km walk or bike ride), this four-star choice on the south side of the Arno is a 68-room oasis of peace and tranquillity. Its rooms have wooden floors and high ceilings, and some are nicely frescoed. Those for four make it a practical, if pricey, family choice.

Kudos to the small terrace garden out the back – a dream for breakfast in summer. Courtyard parking/bike hire costs €10/12 per day. Room rates vary enormously depending on the day and the season.

Hotel Relais dell'Orologio HOTEL €€€
(☎05 083 03 61; www.hotelrelaisorologio.com; Via della Faggiola 12-14; s/d from €120/195; ❄ wi-fi) Something of a honeymoon venue, Pisa's dreamy five-star hotel occupies a tastefully restored 14th-century fortified tower house

PIAZZA DEI MIRACOLI WALKING TOUR

No other square has such expansive lawns or such a concentration of Romanesque buildings. From the ticket office (p124) behind the Leaning Tower, walk towards the *duomo* (cathedral; p125) – the first structure built on this almighty piazza. Before strolling its length to reach the main entrance, stop by the **Portale di San Ranieri**, the cathedral doorway facing the Leaning Tower. What you see are copies of 12th-century bronze doors illustrating the life of Christ. The doors are named after Pisa's patron saint, Ranieri.

Continue to the *duomo* main entrance, pausing to savour the gleaming marbled facade. Inside, recover from the shock of the vast gold ceiling, then walk past the pulpit to the **Cappella di San Cappella Ranieri**. Here lies the preserved skeleton of Ranieri, inside a glass-sided marble 'urn'. Arab sculpted decorative elements in the chapel demonstrate just how influential the Islamic world was on Pisa at this time; the 11th-century bronze griffin that stood atop the cathedral until 1828 was booty, probably Egyptian in origin.

Exit the *duomo* and follow the short marble pathway linking it to the baptistry (p125), built almost a century later. Walk upstairs to the crowd-free **Upper Gallery**, the perfect place to listen to the singing custodian demonstrate the extraordinary acoustics. Break afterwards with the **tourist souvenir stalls** along the piazza's south side, pose for the ritual 'prop up the tower' photo shoot, then flee the mayhem for the serenity of Camposanto (p129). Lose yourself in the wonderful medieval frescoes, and learn how they were executed in the Museo delle Sinópie (p129) opposite. This vast building was a shelter for the poor and sick, pilgrims and abandoned children in the 13th century, and was a hospital until 1979.

No museum provides a better round-up of Piazza dei Miracoli's architectural masterpieces than the Museo dell'Opera del Duomo (p129). Close the circle with the original bronze doors of the Portale di San Ranieri and that magnificent griffin that Pisans pilfered to atop their *duomo* with.

This walk takes three to four hours.

in a quiet street. Some rooms have original frescoes and the flowery patio restaurant makes a welcome retreat from the crowds. Garage parking attracts an additional fee. Book through its website to bag the cheapest deal – there are lots of seasonal offers.

Eating

Being a university town, Pisa has a good range of eating places, especially around Borgo Stretto, the university on cafe-ringed Piazza Dante Alighieri – always packed with students – and south of the river in the trendy San Martino quarter.

Local specialities include fresh *pecorino* (sheep's milk cheese) from San Rossore, *zuppe di cavolo* (cabbage soup), *pan ficato* (fig cake) and *castagnaccio* (chestnut-flour cake enriched by nuts).

Il Montino PIZZERIA €
(Vicolo del Monte 1; pizzas €3-6.50; ⌚10.30am-3pm & 5-10pm Mon-Sat) There is nothing flash or fancy about this down-to-earth pizzeria, an icon among Pisans, student or sophisticate alike. Take away or order at the bar then grab a table, inside or out, and munch on house specialities such as *cecina* (chickpea pizza), *castagnaccio* and *spuma* (sweet, nonalcoholic drink). Or go for a *focaccine* (small flat roll) filled with salami, pancetta or *porchetta* (suckling pig).

Hidden in a back alley, the quickest way to find Il Montino is to head west along Via Ulisse Dini from the northern end of Borgo Stretto (opposite the Lo Sfizio cafe at Borgo Stretto 54) to Piazza San Felice where it is easy to spot, on your left, a telling blue neon 'Pizzeria' sign.

Il Crudo SANDWICHES €
(www.ilcrudopisa.it; Piazza Cairoli 7; panini €4.50-6; ⌚11am-3.30pm & 5pm-1am Mon-Thu, to 2am Fri, 11am-2am Sat, 11am-1am Sun) Grab a well-filled *panini* to munch on the move or enjoy one alfresco with a glass of wine at this pocket-sized *panineria* (sandwich shop) and *vineria* (wine bar) strung with ham legs. Find it by the river on one of Pisa's prettiest squares.

Osteria Bernardo MODERN TUSCAN €€
(☎05 057 52 16; www.osteriabernardo.it; Piazza San Paolo all'Orto 1 ; meals €30; ⌚lunch & dinner Tue-Sun) This small *osteria* (tavern) on one of Pisa's loveliest squares, well away from the madding Leaning Tower crowd, is the perfect fusion of easy dining and gourmet excellence. Its menu is small – just four or five dishes to choose from for each course – and cuisine is creative.

Begin perhaps with beef carpaccio marinated in cocoa (yes!), followed by a *primo* (first course) of *pappardelle* (a type of pasta) in a chocolate-scented wild boar sauce, or *paccheri* (short pasta) with baby octopus and zucchini flowers. Divine.

Osteria del Porton Rosso OSTERIA €€
(☎05 058 05 66; www.portonrosso.com; Vicolo del Porton Rosso 11; meals €25; ⌚lunch & dinner Mon-Sat) Don't be put off by the rather dank alley leading to this busy, tip-top *osteria*, a block north of the river. Inside it is all style, charm and excellent regional cuisine from the land and the nearby sea. Pisan specialities such as fresh ravioli with salted cod and chickpeas happily coexist with Tuscan classics such as grilled fillet steak, and the €10 lunchtime deal is unbeatable value.

From riverside Lungarno Pacinotti look for the incongruous neon-sign-lit doorway, a faux entrance a couple of doors down from the Real McCoy.

biOsteria 050 ORGANIC €€
(☎05 054 31 06; Via San Francesco 36; meals €20-30; ⌚lunch Mon-Sun, dinner Tue-Sun; ✎) 
Everything that Marco and Raffaele at Zero Cinquanta cook up is strictly seasonal, local and organic, with products from farms within a 50km radius of Pisa. Try black cabbage, nut and gorgonzola risotto, rabbit with sweet mustard perhaps, or one of the excellent-value daily lunch specials. Ample choice for vegetarians and coeliacs too.

Drinking & Nightlife

Most of the student drinking action takes place on and around Piazza delle Vettovaglie and the university on cafe-ringed Piazza Dante Alighieri, always packed with students.

The local Denominazione d'Origine Controllata e Garantita (DOCG) is Chianti delle Colline Pisane, and though there's no Pisan Denominazione d'Origine Controllata (DOC), Bianco Pisano di San Torpè, a Trebbiano-dominated wine with a delicate, dry flavour, is a popular substitute.

Sottobosco CAFE
(www.sottoboscocafe.it; Piazza San Paolo all'Orto; ⌚10am-midnight Tue-Fri, noon-1am Sat, 7pm-midnight Sun) This creative cafe with a few books for sale and funky furnishings induces love at first sight. Tuck into a doughnut

OFF THE BEATEN TRACK

VESPA TOUR

There's a certain romance to touring Tuscany on the back of a Vespa, Italy's iconic scooter that revolutionised travel when Piaggio launched it from its factory in **Pontedera**, 25km southeast of Pisa, in 1946. The 'wasp', as the two-wheeled utility vehicle was affectionately known, has been restyled 120 times since, culminating most recently in Piaggio's vintage-inspired GTV and LXV models. Yet the essential design remains timeless.

The complete Vespa story, from the Genovese company's arrival in Tuscany in 1921 to its manufacturing of four-engine aircraft and hydroplanes, WWII destruction and rebirth as Europe's exclusive Vespa producer, is grippingly told in Pontedera's **Museo Piaggio** (www.museopiaggio.it; Viale Piagio 7; ⌚10am-6pm Tue-Sat) FREE, in a former factory building.

Should Vespa's free-wheeling, carefree spirit take hold, hook up with Florence-based **Tuscany by Vespa** (www.tuscanybyvespa.com; Via de' Lamberti 1) or **Entroterra Viaggi & Turismo** (www.entroterraturismo.com; Via Rosa Agazzi 28) in San Miniato for your very own Hepburn-style Vespa tour.

and cappuccino at a glass-topped table filled with artists' crayons perhaps, or a collection of buttons. Lunch dishes (salads, pies and pasta) are simple and homemade, and come dusk, jazz bands play or DJs spin tunes.

Bazeel BAR
(www.bazeel.it; Lungarno Pacinotti 1; ⌚5pm-2am) Generous *aperitivo* (predinner drinks accompanied by cocktail snacks) spread, live music or DJs, and a great little terrace out front ensures Bazeel is always busy. Check its Twitter feed for what's on.

Salza CAFE
(Borgo Stretto 44; ⌚8am-8.30pm summer, shorter hr Tue-Sun winter) This old-fashioned cake shop has been tempting Pisans into sugar-induced wickedness since 1898. It's an equally lovely spot for a cocktail – anytime.

Information

Tourist office (☎05 04 22 91; www.pisaunicaterra.it; Piazza Vittorio Emanuele II 16; ⌚9am-7pm Mon-Sat, to 4pm Sun)

Getting There & Away

AIR

Pisa International Airport (☎05 084 93 00; www.pisa-airport.com; Piazzale D'Ascanio) Tuscany's main international airport, a 10-minute drive south of town; flights to most major European cities.

BUS

From its hub on Piazza Sant'Antonio, Pisan bus company **CPT** (www.cpt.pisa.it; Piazza Sant'Antonio) runs buses to/from Volterra (€6.10, two hours, up to 10 daily) and Livorno (€2.75, 55 minutes, half-hourly to hourly).

CAR

Pisa is close to the A11 and A12. The SCG FI-PI-LI (SS67) is a toll-free alternative for Florence and Livorno, while the north–south SS1, the Via Aurelia, connects the city with La Spezia and Rome.

TRAIN

There is a handy **left luggage office** (Deposito Bagagli; 1st 12hr €4, subsequent 12hr €2; ⌚6am-9pm) at **Pisa Centrale** (Piazza della Stazione) train station – not to be confused with north-of-town Pisa San Rossore station. Regional train services to/from Pisa Centrale:

Florence (€7, 1¼ hours, frequent)
Livorno (€2.50, 15 minutes, frequent)
Lucca (€3.30, 30 minutes, every 30 minutes)
Viareggio (€3.30, 15 minutes, every 20 minutes)

Getting Around

TO/FROM THE AIRPORT

Train services run to/from Pisa Centrale (€2.50, five minutes, at least 30 per day); purchase and validate your ticket before boarding the train.

The LAM Rossa (red) bus line (€1.10, 10 minutes, every 10 to 20 minutes) run by CPT (p133) passes through the city centre and the train station en route to/from the airport. Buy tickets from the blue ticket machine, next to the bus stops to the right of the train station exit.

A taxi between the airport and city centre should cost no more than €10. To book, call Radio Taxi Pisa.

BICYCLE

Many hotels rent bikes. Otherwise, stands at the northern end of Via Santa Maria and other streets off Piazza dei Miracoli rent four-wheel rickshaws for up to three/six people (€10/15 per hour) and regular bicycles (€3 per hour).

CAR & MOTORCYCLE

Parking costs up to €2 per hour, but you must be careful that the car park you choose is not in the city's Limited Traffic Zone (ZTL). There's a free car park outside the zone on Lungarno Guadalongo near the Fortezza di San Gallo on the south side of the Arno.

HORSE & CARRIAGE

Easter to October, horse-drawn carriages sit in front of the Museo dell'Opera del Duomo on Piazza dei Miracoli waiting to take tourists for a ride. Count €40 for a 20-minute tour of town.

LUCCA

POP 86,900

Lovely Lucca is a precious pearl of a city that endears itself to everyone who visits. Hidden behind imposing Renaissance walls, its cobbled streets, handsome piazzas and shady promenades make it a perfect destination to explore by foot – as a day trip from Florence or in its own right. At the day's end, historic cafes and restaurants tempt visitors to relax over a glass or two of Lucchesi wine and a slow progression of rustic dishes prepared with fresh produce from the nearby Garfagnana.

If you have a car, the hills to the east of Lucca demand exploration. Home to historic villas and belle Epoque Montecatini Terme where Puccini lazed in warm spa waters, they are easy and attractive day-trip destinations from Lucca.

History

Founded by the Etruscans, Lucca became a Roman colony in 180 BC and a free *comune* (self-governing city) during the 12th century, when it enjoyed a period of prosperity based on the silk trade. In 1314 it briefly fell to Pisa but regained its independence under the leadership of local adventurer Castruccio Castracani degli Anterminelli, and began to amass territories in western Tuscany, including marble-rich Carrara. Castruccio died in 1328 but Lucca remained an independent republic for almost 500 years.

Napoleon ended all this in 1805 when he created the principality of Lucca and placed one of the seemingly countless members of his family in need of an Italian fiefdom (this time his sister Elisa) in control of all of Tuscany. Ten years later the city became a Bourbon duchy before being incorporated into the Kingdom of Italy. It miraculously escaped being bombed during WWII, so the fabric of the *centro storico* has remained unchanged for centuries.

Sights & Activities

Cobbled **Via Fillungo** threads its way through the medieval heart of the old city – cast your eyes above the street-level bustle to appreciate ancient awnings and architectural details. East is one of Tuscany's loveliest piazzas, oval cafe-ringed **Piazza Anfiteatro**, so-called after the amphitheatre that was here in Roman times. Look closely to spot remnants of the amphitheatre's brick arches and masonry on the exterior walls of the medieval houses ringing the piazza.

If you plan to visit the Museo della Cattedrale, Chiesa de SS Giovanni e Reparata and the sacristy inside Cattedrale di San Martino, buy a cheaper combined ticket (adult/reduced €7/5) at any of the sights.

Torre Civica delle Ore CLOCK TOWER

(Via Fillungo; adult/reduced €6/5; ⌚9.30am-6.30pm summer) Break from the boutiques of Via Fillungo with a hike up the 207 wooden steps of Lucca's 13th-century clock tower – at 50m tall, the highest of the city's 130 medieval towers. Views from the top are fabulous.

Legend has it the tower is inhabited by the ghost of Lucida Mansi, a Lucchese lass who sold her soul to the devil in exchange for remaining young and beautiful for three decades. On 14 August 1623 the devil came after her to pay her debt, only for Licida to climb up the clock tower to try and stop time. The devil caught her and took her soul.

★**Palazzo Pfanner** PALACE

(www.palazzopfanner.it; Via degli Asili 33; palace or garden adult/reduced €4.50/4, both €6/5; ⌚10am-6pm summer) Fire the romantic in you with a stroll around this beautiful 17th-century palace where parts of *Portrait of a Lady* (1996) starring Nicole Kidman and John Malkovich were shot. Its baroque-styled garden – the only one of substance within the city walls – is irresistible with its ornamental pond, belle Epoque lemon house and 18th-century statues of Greek gods posing between potted lemon trees.

Climb the grand outdoor staircase to the frescoed and furnished *piano nobile* (main reception room), home to Felix Pfanner, an Austrian émigré who first brought beer to Italy – and brewed it in the mansion's cellars from 1846 until 1929. From the copperpots strung above the hearth in the kitchen to the dining-room table laid for lunch, the rooms vividly evoke daily life in an early-18th-century Lucchese *palazzo* (mansion). In summer watch out for the lovely chamber-music concerts that Palazzo Pfanner hosts.

City Wall CITY WALLS

Lucca's monumental *mura* (wall) was built around the old city in the 16th and 17th centuries and remains in almost perfect condition due to the long periods of peace the city has enjoyed. Twelve metres high and 4km long, the ramparts are crowned with a tree-lined footpath that looks down on the *centro storico* and out towards the Apuane Alps.

This path is the favourite Lucchesi location for a *passeggiata* (traditional evening stroll), be it on foot, bicycle or inline skate. Children's playgrounds, swings and picnic tables beneath shady plane trees add a buzz of activity to Baluardo San Regolo, Baluardo San Salvatore and Baluardo Santa Croce – three of the 11 bastions studding the way – and older kids kick balls around on the vast green lawns of Baluardo San Donato.

★Cattedrale di San Martino CATHEDRAL

(Piazza San Martino; sacristy adult/reduced €3/2, with cathedral museum & Chiesa dei SS Giovanni e Reparata €7/5; ⏲7am-6pm summer, to 5pm winter; sacristy 9.30am-4.45pm Mon-Fri, 9.30am-6.45pm Sat, 11.30am-5pm Sun) Lucca's predominantly Romanesque cathedral dates to the start of the 11th century. Its stunning facade was constructed in the prevailing Lucca-Pisan style and designed to accommodate the pre-existing *campanile* (bell tower). The reliefs over the left doorway of the portico are believed to be by Nicola Pisano.

The cathedral interior was rebuilt in the 14th and 15th centuries with a Gothic flourish. The **Volto Santo** (literally, Holy Countenance) is not to be missed. Legend has it this simply fashioned image of a dark-skinned, life-sized Christ on a wooden crucifix was carved by Nicodemus, who witnessed the crucifixion. In fact, it has recently been dated to the 13th century. A major object of pilgrimage, the sculpture is carried through the streets every 13 September at dusk during the **Luminaria di Santa Croce**, a solemn torchlit procession marking its miraculous arrival in Lucca.

WORTH A TRIP

A VILLA TOUR

Between the 15th and 19th centuries, successful Lucchesi merchants flouted their success to the world by building opulent summer residences in the hills around the city, and though a few have crumbled away or been abandoned, many are still inhabited.

Elisa Bonaparte, Napoleon's sister and short-lived ruler of Tuscany, once lived in handsome **Villa Reale** (www.parcovillareale.it; Via Fraga Alta, Marlia; garden tours €7; ⏲10am-1pm & 2-6pm Tue-Sun summer), 7km north of Lucca in Marlia. The house isn't open to the public, but the statuary-filled gardens can be visited by hourly guided tour.

Neoclassical **Villa Grabau** (www.villagrabau.it; Via di Matraia 269, San Pancrazio; ⏲10am-1pm & 3-7pm Tue-Sun Jul-Aug, shorter hr rest of year, Sun only winter), just north of Lucca in San Pancrazio, sits amid a vast parkland with sweeping traditional English- and Italian-styled gardens, splashing fountains, more than 100 terracotta pots with lemon trees and a postcard-pretty lemon house – host to fashion shows, concerts and the like – dating from the 17th century. It even has a clutch of self-catering properties to rent in its grounds should you happen to fall in love with the estate.

In the same village, the gardens of **Villa Oliva** (www.villaoliva.it; San Pancrazio; ⏲9.30am-12.30pm & 2-6pm summer), a 15th-century country residence designed by Lucchesi architect Matteo Civitali, demand a springtime stroll. Retaining its original design, the fountain-rich park staggers across three levels and includes a romantic cypress alley and stables reckoned to be even more beautiful that those at Versailles. Watch out for concerts held here.

To reach these villas, take the SS12 northeast from Lucca (direction Abetone) and exit onto the SP29 to Marlia. From Marlia, San Pancrazio is a mere 1.2km north.

Lucca

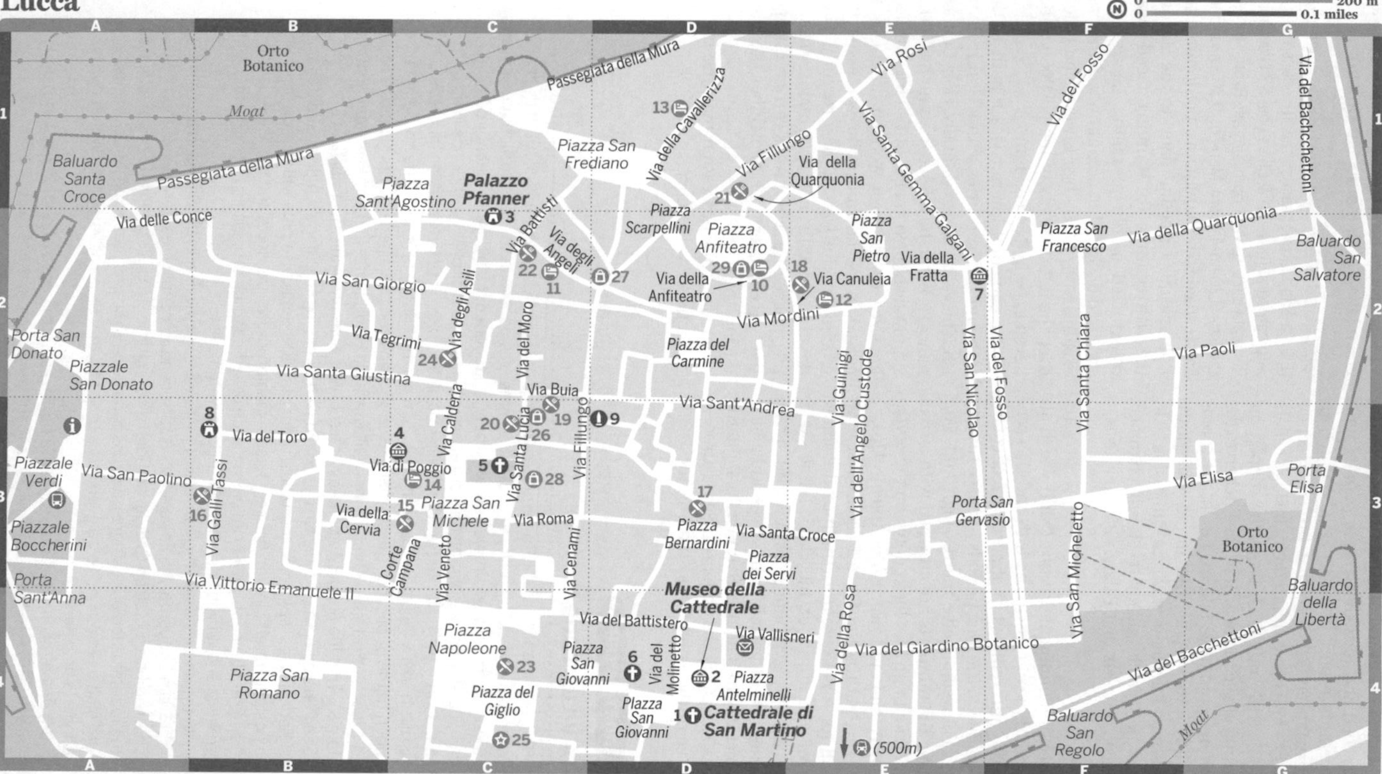
200 m
0.1 miles
Orto Botanico
Moat
Passeggiata della Mura
Baluardo Santa Croce
Via delle Conce
Piazza Sant'Agostino
Palazzo Pfanner
Piazza San Frediano
Via della Cavallerizza
Via Rosi
Via Fillungo
Via della Quarquonia
Via Santa Gemma Galgani
Via del Fosso
Via del Bachcchettoni
Via Battisti
Via degli Angeli
Piazza Scarpellini
Piazza Anfiteatro
Piazza San Pietro
Via della Fratta
Piazza San Francesco
Via della Quarquonia
Baluardo San Salvatore
Via San Giorgio
Via della Anfiteatro
Via Canuleia
Via Mordini
Porta San Donato
Via Tegrimi
Via degli Asili
Via del Moro
Piazza del Carmine
Via San Nicolao
Via del Fosso
Via Santa Chiara
Via Paoli
Piazzale San Donato
Via Santa Giustina
Via Buia
Via Sant'Andrea
Via Guinigi
Via dell'Angelo Custode
Via del Toro
Via Calderia
Via Santa Lucia
Via Fillungo
Piazzale Verdi
Via San Paolino
Via di Poggio
Via Elisa
Porta Elisa
Via Galli Tassi
Via della Cervia
Piazza San Michele
Via Roma
Piazza Bernardini
Porta San Gervasio
Orto Botanico
Piazzale Boccherini
Corte Campana
Via Veneto
Via Cenami
Via Santa Croce
Piazza dei Servi
Via San Micheletto
Porta Sant'Anna
Via Vittorio Emanuele II
Museo della Cattedrale
Baluardo della Libertà
Via del Battistero
Via Vallisneri
Via della Rosa
Via del Giardino Botanico
Piazza Napoleone
Piazza San Giovanni
Via del Molinetto
Piazza Antelminelli
Via del Bacchettoni
Piazza San Romano
Piazza del Giglio
Piazza San Giovanni
Cattedrale di San Martino
(500m)
Baluardo San Regolo
Moat

Lucca

Top Sights
1 Cattedrale di San Martino D4
2 Museo della Cattedrale D4
3 Palazzo Pfanner C2

Sights
4 Casa Natale di Puccini C3
5 Chiesa di San Michele in Foro C3
6 Chiesa e Battistero dei SS Giovanni e Reparata D4
7 Lucca Center of Contemporary Art E2
8 Palazzo Mansi B3
9 Torre Civica delle Ore D3

Sleeping
10 2italia D2
11 Alla Corte degli Angeli C2
12 La Magnolia E2
13 Ostello San Frediano D1
14 Piccolo Hotel Puccini C3

Eating
15 Buca di Sant'Antonio C3
16 Caniparoli B3
17 Cantine Bernardini D3
18 Canuleia E2
19 Da Felice C3
20 Forno Amedeo Giusti C3
21 Osteria Baralla D1
22 Osteria del Manzo C2
23 Ristorante Giglio C4
24 Trattoria da Leo C2

Entertainment
25 Teatro del Giglio C4

Shopping
26 Antica Bodega di Prospero C3
27 Premium D2
28 Taddeucci C3
29 Vi-Ta Playtime D2

The cathedral's many other works of art include a magnificent *Last Supper* by Tintoretto above the third altar of the south aisle and Domenico Ghirlandaio's 1479 *Madonna Enthroned with Saints*. This impressive work by Michelangelo's master is currently located in the **sacristy**. Opposite lies the exquisite, gleaming marble memorial to Ilaria del Carretto carved by Jacopo della Quercia in 1407. The young second wife of the 15th-century lord of Lucca, Paolo Guinigi, Ilaria died in childbirth aged only 24. At her feet lies her faithful dog.

★Museo della Cattedrale — MUSEUM

(www.museocattedralelucca.it; Piazza San Martino; adult/reduced €4/3, with cathedral sacristy & Chiesa dei SS Giovanni & Reparata €7/5; ⏲10am-6pm) Next door to the cathedral, this museum safeguards elaborate gold and silver decorations made for the cathedral's Volto Santo, including a 17th-century crown and a 19th-century sceptre.

Chiesa e Battistero dei SS Giovanni e Reparata — CHURCH

(Piazza San Giovanni; adult/reduced €4/3, with cathedral museum & sacristy €7/5; ⏲10am-6pm summer, to 5pm Sat & Sun winter) The 12th-century interior of this deconsecrated church is a hauntingly atmospheric setting for summertime **opera recitals**; buy tickets in advance inside the church. In the north transept, the Gothic **baptistry** crowns an archaeological area comprising five building levels going back to the Roman period. Don't miss the hike up the red-brick **bell tower** – what a view!

Chiesa di San Michele in Foro — CHURCH

(Piazza San Michele; ⏲7.40am-noon & 3-6pm summer, 9am-noon & 3-5pm winter) One of Lucca's many architecturally significant churches, this lovely Romanesque edifice marks the spot where the city's Roman forum once was. The present building with exquisite wedding-cake facade was constructed on the site of its 8th-century precursor over a period of nearly 300 years, beginning in the 11th century.

Crowning the structure is a figure of the archangel Michael slaying a dragon. Inside, don't miss Filippino Lippi's 1479 painting of Sts Helen, Jerome, Sebastian and Roch (complete with plague sore) in the south transept.

Palazzo Mansi — PALACE

(Via Galli Tassi 43; adult/reduced €4/2; ⏲8.30am-7.30pm Tue-Sat) This 16th-century mansion built for a wealthy Luccan merchant is a wonderful piece of rococo excess. The private apartments are draped head to toe in tapestries, paintings and chintz. The elaborate, gilded bridal suite must have inspired such high jinks in its time.

Lucca Center of Contemporary Art — ART GALLERY

(LuCCA; www.luccamuseum.com; Via della Fratta 36; ⏲10am-7pm Tue-Sun) FREE Lucca's contemporary art museum hosts some riveting temporary exhibitions; check its website for details.

Festivals & Events

Lucca Summer Festival MUSIC

(www.summer-festival.com) This month-long festival in July lures international pop stars to Lucca; James Blunt and Elton John took to the stage on Piazza Napoleone in 2011.

Sleeping

★ **Piccolo Hotel Puccini** HOTEL €

(05 835 54 21; www.hotelpuccini.com; Via di Poggio 9; s/d €73/98;) Snug around the corner from the great man himself (or at least a bronze copy of him) and the house where he was born is this efficiently run, intimate address. Decor is an unobtrusive mix of period furnishings and collectables, and its 14 rooms have great high ceilings and vintage ceiling fans.

Bathrooms are white and modern, and a quintessentially sweet Italian breakfast of bread, jam and tarts, is served at candle-lit tables. Rates are around 30% lower in the depths of winter.

THE PUCCINI TRAIL

Lucca has a particular lure for opera buffs: it was here, in 1858, that the great Giacomo Puccini was born, and baptised the following day in the Chiesa dei SS Giovanni e Reparata (p137). The maestro, who came from a long line of Lucchesi musicians, grew up in an apartment at Corte San Lorenzo 9, which was turned into the house-museum **Casa Natale di Puccini** (www.puccinimuseum.org; Corte San Lorenzo 9; adult/reduced €7/5; 10am-6pm Wed-Mon summer, 11am-5pm Wed-Mon winter) – look for the imposing statue of the maestro at the front. During his teenage years, Puccini played the organ in the Cattedrale di San Martino (p135) and performed as a piano accompanist at the **Teatro del Giglio** (www.teatrodelgiglio.it; Piazza del Giglio 13-15), the 17th-century theatre where the curtain would later rise on some of his best-known operas: *La Bohème* (1896), *Tosca* (1900) and *Madame Butterfly* (1907).

In 1880 Puccini left Lucca to study at Milan's music conservatory, returning after his studies to Tuscany to rent a lakeside house in **Torre del Lago**, 15km west of Lucca on the shore of Lago Massaciuccoli. Nine years later, after the successes of *Manon Lescaut* (1893) and *La Bohème*, he had a villa built on the same lakeshore, undertaking the Liberty-style interior decoration himself. It was here that Puccini with his wife, Elvira, spent his time working, hunting on the lake and carousing with a diverse group of hunters, fishermen and bohemian artists. *Madame Butterfly*, *La Fanciulla del West* (1910), *La Rondine* (1917) and *Il Trittico* (1918) were composed on the Forster piano in his front study, and he wrote his scores on the specially made walnut table in the same room.

The Villa di Torre del Lago, now the **Museo Villa Puccini** (www.giacomopuccini.it; Torre del Lago; adult/reduced €7/3; 3-6.20pm Mon, 10am-12.40pm & 3-6.20pm Tue-Sun summer, to 5.10pm winter), has been preserved almost exactly as it was during Puccini's residence and is hence fascinating to visit (by guided tour every 40 minutes). In summer the villa grounds and lakeshore buzz with the world-famous **Puccini Festival** (www.puccinifestival.it; Torre del Lago), which sees three or four of the great man's operas in a huge purpose-built outdoor theatre. Tickets are like gold dust and need to be bought months in advance.

While living in Torre del Lago, Puccini was a frequent visitor to **Montecatini Terme**, a charming spa resort 56km east, known for its mineral-rich waters – Verdi equally loved the place. May to October, spa lovers still flock to the place today to wallow in warm waters and indulge in various beauty treatments at its *terme* (thermal baths) in grand old buildings overlooking a beautifully maintained park; Leopoldine (1773) is the most impressive. The **tourist office** (05 7377 2244; www.montecatiniturismo.it; Viale Verdi 66-68, Montecatini Terme; 9am-12.30pm & 3-6pm Mon-Sat year-round, 9am-noon Sun summer) on the main street has all the details.

In 1921 Puccini and Elvira moved to a villa in the nearby coastal town of **Viareggio**, where the composer became a regular fixture at **Gran Caffè Margherita** (Viale Regina Margherita 30). He worked on his last opera, the unfinished *Turandot*, during this period. After Puccini's death in 1924, Elvira and son Antonio added a chapel to the Torre del Lago villa; Puccini's remains were interred there in 1926.

La Magnolia B&B €
(☎05 8346 7111; www.lamagnolia.com; Via Mordini 63; s/d €60/90) This atmospheric B&B resides in a beautiful creamy-stone *palazzo* built within the city walls in the 15th century. With a peaceful tree-laden garden to hang out in, it is an accommodation option verging on irresistible.

Ostello San Frediano HOSTEL €
(☎05 8346 9957; www.ostellolucca.it; Via della Cavallerizza 12; dm/s/d/tr/q €22/45/65/80/105; ⊙mid-Feb–Dec;) Slap-bang in the centre of walled Lucca, inside a staggeringly historic building, hostellers won't get closer to the action than this. Top notch in comfort and service, this Hostelling International–affiliated hostel with 141 beds in voluminous rooms is serviced with a bar and grandiose dining room (breakfast €3, lunch or dinner €11). Non-HI members can join on the spot for €2 per year.

★**Locanda Vigna Ilaria** B&B €€
(☎05 833 32 09; www.locandavignailaria.it; Via della Pieve Santo Stefano 967c, St Alessio; d/q €110/120; P) Those on a Tuscan road trip or who love easy parking will be instantly smitten with this lovely stone house in one of Lucca's wealthiest hoods (dump the car, then meander along green lanes, past vast villas bathed in olive groves). The *locanda* (inn) has five rooms, varying in size and each furnished with a mix of old, new and upcycled – lots of wine boxes!

Its downstairs restaurant moreover, open evenings, is a gastronomic fish-driven treat (meals €45, menus €30 to €79). In summer dining is alfresco in the pretty walled garden with wooden decking. Find Locanda Vigna Ilaria 4km north of Lucca's walled city in St Alessio.

2italia APARTMENT €€
(☎392 9960271; www.2italia.com; Via della Anfiteatro 74; apt for 2 adults & up to 4 children €190;) Not a hotel but five family-friendly self-catering apartments overlooking Piazza Anfiteatro, with a communal kids' playroom in the attic. Available on a nightly basis (minimum two nights), the project is the brainchild of well-travelled parents-of-three, Kristin (English) and Kaare (Norwegian). Spacious apartments sleep up to six, have fully equipped kitchen and washing machine, and come with sheets and towels.

Kristin and Kaare have several other apartments and villas to rent in and around Lucca. They can also organise cycling tours, cooking courses, wine tastings and olive pickings for their guests.

Alla Corte degli Angeli BOUTIQUE HOTEL €€
(☎05 8346 9204; www.allacortedegliangeli.com; Via degli Angeli 23; s/d €120/190;) Occupying three floors of a 15th-century townhouse, this four-star boutique hotel with just 10 rooms and a lovely beamed lounge oozes charm. Beautifully frescoed rooms are named after flowers: lovers in the hugely romantic Rosa room can lie beneath a pergola and swallow-filled sky, while guests in Orchidea have their own private shower-sauna. Breakfast €10.

Eating

Lucca is known for its traditional cuisine and prized olive oil. Garfagnana is not far away and local chestnuts, *porcini* mushrooms, honey, *farro* (spelt), sheep's-milk cheese and *formenton* (ground corn) are abundant – and a perfect match with a delicate white Colline Lucchesi or a red Montecarlo di Lucca wine.

Da Felice PIZZERIA €
(www.pizzeriadafelice.com; Via Buia 12; focaccias €1-3, pizza slices €1.30; ⊙10am-8.30pm Mon-Sat) This buzzing local behind Piazza San Michele since 1960 is easy to spot – come noon look for the crowd packed around two tiny tables inside, spilling out the door or squatting on one of two streetside benches. *Cecina,* a salted chickpea pizza served piping-hot from the oven and *castagnacci* (chestnut cakes) are Felice's raison d'être.

Eat in or take away, it comes wrapped in crisp white paper and my, is it good married with a chilled bottle of Maretti beer. To savour the full flavour of this tiny pizzeria, don't miss the snaps of owners Marino Grazzini (aka 'Felice') and wife Pasquina – in 1960 and today – pegged on string and strung in the window.

Trattoria da Leo TRATTORIA €
(☎05 8349 2236; Via Tegrimi 1; meals €25; ⊙lunch & dinner Mon-Sat) A veteran everyone loves, Leo is famed around town for its friendly ambience and cheap food – ranging from plain-Jane acceptable to grandma delicious. Get here early in summer to snag one of 10 checked-tableclothed tables crammed beneath parasols on the narrow street outside. Otherwise, it's noisy dining inside among typically nondescript 1970s decor. The

A WALLTOP PICNIC

When in Lucca, picnicking atop its city walls – on grass or at a wooden picnic table – is as lovely (and typical) a Lucchesi lunch as any.

Buy fresh-from-the-oven pizza and focaccia with a choice of fillings and toppings from fabulous bakery **Forno Amedeo Giusti** (Via Santa Lucia 20; pizzas & filled focaccias per kg €9-16; ⏲7am-1pm & 4-7.30pm Mon-Sat, 4-7.30pm Sun), then nip across the street for a bottle of Lucchesi wine and Garfagnese *biscotti al farro* (spelt biscuits) at **Antica Bodega di Prospero** (Via Santa Lucia 13; ⏲9am-1pm & 4-7.30pm); look for the old-fashioned shop window stuffed with sacks of beans, lentils and other local pulses.

Complete the perfect picnic with accompaniment to a slice of *buccellato*, a traditional sweetbread loaf with sultanas and aniseed seeds, baked in Lucca since 1881. Devour the rest at home, with butter, dipped in egg and pan-fried, or dunked in sweet Vin Santo. Buy it at pastry shop **Taddeucci** (www.taddeucci.com; Piazza San Michele 34; per 300/600/900g loaf of buccellato €4.50/9/13.50; ⏲8.30am-7.45pm, closed Thu winter) for €4.50/9/13.50 per 300/600/900g loaf. Or seduce tastebuds with truffles, white chocolate spread and other heavenly chocolate creations from **Caniparoli** (www.caniparolicioccolateria.it; Via San Paolino 96; ⏲9.30am-1pm & 3.30-9.30pm), the best *cioccolateria* (chocolate maker) in town.

vitello tonnato (cold veal with a tuna and caper sauce) is excellent. No credit cards.

Osteria del Manzo TUSCAN €€
(☎05 8349 0649; Via Battisti 28; meals €25; ⏲lunch & dinner Mon-Sat) A real local favourite with no outside seating, this busy eatery is charmed simplicity in the making. Tuck into typical local dishes beneath a beamed ceiling, observed by – yes – a collection of garden gnomes. Someone clearly collects miniature bottles too.

Cantine Bernardini TUSCAN €€
(☎05 8349 4336; www.cantinebernardini.com; Via del Suffragio 7; meals €40; ⏲lunch & dinner Tue-Sun) This maze of a hybrid *osteria-enoteca*, hidden in the red-brick vaulted cellars of 16th-century Palazzo Bernardini, has got the balance just right. Seasonal Tuscan dishes such as chestnut-flour ravioli in a wild-boar sauce or a springtime flan of violet artichokes tempt on the menu, while the wine list is Tuscan and exceptional. Extra kudos for the kids' menu and Friday-evening DJs and live music.

Canuleia TUSCAN €€
(☎05 8346 7470; Via Canuleia 14; meals €35; ⏲lunch & dinner Tue-Sun) What makes this dining address stand out from the crowd is its secret walled garden out the back – the perfect spot to escape the tourist hordes and listen to birds tweet over partridge risotto, artichoke and prawn spaghetti or a traditional *peposa* (beef and pepper stew).

Osteria Baralla OSTERIA €€
(☎05 8344 0240; www.osteriabaralla.it; Via Anfiteatro 5; meals €30; ⏲lunch & dinner Mon-Sat) This traditional *osteria* dating to 1860 is in every guidebook and for good reason. Feast on local specialities beneath huge red-brick vaults; the soup with new-season olive oil, salt cod and chickpeas is a real highlight. On Thursday it's *bolito misto* (mixed boiled meat) day, Saturday is roast pork day.

★**Ristorante Giglio** TUSCAN €€€
(☎05 8349 4058; www.ristorantegiglio.com; Piazza del Giglio 2; meals €40, 2-person tasting menu €70; ⏲lunch & dinner Thu-Mon, dinner Wed) Don't let the tacky plastic-covered pavement terrace on Lucca's largest pedestrian city square deter. Inside, Giglio is stunning. Dine at white tableclothed tables, sip a complimentary glass of *prosecco*, watch the fire crackle in the ornate marble fireplace and know you're dining in the finest restaurant in town, splendidly at home in the frescoed 18th-century Palazzo Arnolfini no less.

Cuisine is traditional Tuscan with a modern twist, such as fresh artichoke salad served in an edible parmesan-cheese wafer 'bowl', or risotto simmered in Chianti. End with Lucchese *buccellato* (sweetbread) filled with ice cream and berries.

Buca di Sant'Antonio TUSCAN €€€
(☎05 835 58 81; www.bucadisantantonio.com; Via della Cervia 3; meals €50; ⏲lunch & dinner Tue-Sat, lunch Sun) Gosh, what a fabulous collection of copper pots strung from the wood-beamed

ceiling! This atmosphere-laden restaurant has wooed romantic diners since 1782 and is still going strong. The Tuscan cuisine does not quite live up to the exceptional wine list, but it remains a favourite nonetheless. Service is formal – think gents of a certain age in black suits and dicky-bows – and opens with a glass of *prosecco* (sparkling wine) on the house as aperitif.

Shopping

Via Fillungo is the main shopping strip, and what a joy too with its tiny boutiques and car-free mantra. Don't miss the tiny **microbrewery** at No 90 where you can taste and buy Italian craft beers.

Premium FASHION
(www.premiumfashionboutique.it; Via Fillungo 90; ⏲3.30-7.30pm Mon, 10am-1pm & 3.30-7.30pm Tue-Fri , 9.30am-8pm Sat) No fashion boutique has quite so much charm. A 1950s-styled interior complements the mix of hip contemporary and vintage labels that embrace everything from cashmere scarves and handmade hats to the latest in shoe design. Casual chic is the mood.

Vi-Ta Playtime ARTISANAL
(www.vitaplaytime.com; Piazza Anfiteatro 35; ⏲11am-7pm summer, shorter hr winter) Exquisite, creative and wholly unique toys made from cardboard, wood and fabric – all made by hand – is what Lola Murzina, architect-turned-talented-artisan, does best.

Information

Tourist office (☎05 8358 3150; www.comune.lucca.it; Piazzale Verdi; ⏲9am-7pm summer, to 5.30pm winter) Free hotel reservations; bicycle hire and left-luggage service.

Getting There & Away

BUS

From the bus stops around Piazzale Verdi, **Vaibus** (www.vaibus.it) runs services throughout the region, including to the following destinations:

Bagni di Lucca (€3.40, one hour, eight daily)

Castelnuovo di Garfagnana (€4.20, 1½ hours, eight daily)

Pisa airport (€3.20, 45 minutes to one hour, 30 daily)

CAR & MOTORCYCLE

The A11 runs westwards to Pisa and Viareggio and eastwards to Florence. To access the Garfagnana, take the SS12 and continue on the SS445.

The easiest option is to park at Parcheggio Carducci, just outside Porta Sant'Anna. Within the walls, most car parks are for residents only, indicated by yellow lines. Blue lines indicate where anyone, including tourists, can park (€1.50 to €2 per hour). If you are staying within the city walls, contact your hotel ahead of your arrival and enquire about the possibility of getting a temporary resident permit during your stay.

TRAIN

The train station is south of the city walls: take the path across the moat and through the (dank grungy) tunnel under Baluardo San Colombano. Regional train services:

Florence (€7, 1¼ to 1¾ hours, hourly)

Pietrasanta (€4.10, one hour via Viareggio, hourly)

Pisa (€3.30, 30 minutes, every 30 minutes)

Viareggio (€3.30, 25 minutes, hourly)

Getting Around

BICYCLE

Rent regular wheels (per hour/day €3/15; ID required) at the tourist office or one of the following:

LOCAL KNOWLEDGE

VILLA BONGI

Ask anyone from Lucca where to lunch on Sunday or flee the city to escape the stifling summer heat and the reply is invariably **Villa Bongi** (☎05 8351 0479; www.villabongi.it; Via di Cocombola 640, Montuolo; meals €20-25; ⏲dinner Tue-Sat, lunch & dinner Sun; 👪), a dreamy salmon-pink mansion with stone-balustrade verandah, 7km west of town. Born as a convent, the grand old villa overlooks olive groves and has a wonderful tree-shaded terrace on which diners feast alfresco on Tuscan cuisine and green views of soft rolling Lucchesi hills. Pasta is strictly homemade and traditional dishes enjoy a creative seasonal twist – red-cabbage risotto with gorgonzola fondue, saffron-scented *tagliatelle* (ribbon pasta) with prosciutto and prawns. Come winter, dining is all about snuggling up, glass of wine in hand, in front of a roaring fire. Advance reservations essential, especially on Sunday when Lucchese families flock here for Villa Bongi's outstanding-value lunch – three courses, wine, water and coffee for €20 (kids under 10 years €5).

1

LILLISPHOTOGRAPHY / GETTY IMAGES ©

2

4

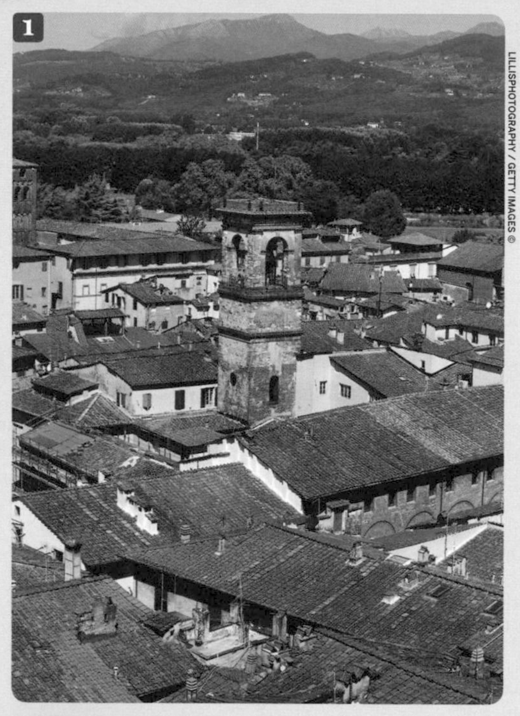

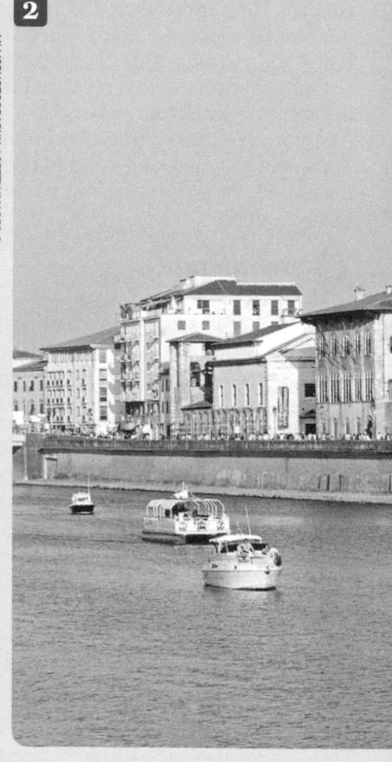

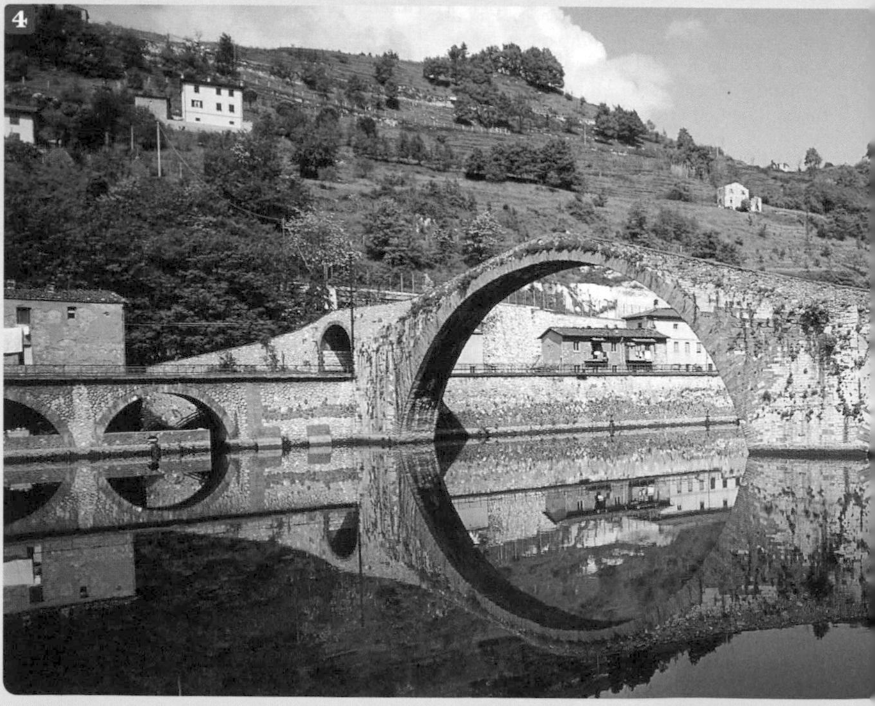

SEPP PUCHINGER / GETTY IMAGES ©

JOHN HESELTINE / GETTY IMAGES ©

PHILIP GAME / GETTY IMAGES ©

1. Lucca (p134)
Lovely Lucca is a precious pearl of a city that endears itself to everyone who visits.

2. Arno river (p129), Pisa
Pisa comes into its own along the peaceful banks of the Arno.

3. Castelnuovo di Garfagnana (p148)
Fresh *porcini*, chestnuts and sacks of *farro* (spelt) fill Castelnuovo di Garfagnana's autumnal markets.

4. Serchio river (p148)
Three stunning valleys have been formed by Serchio and its tributaries.

Biciclette Poli (☎05 8349 3787; www.biciclettepoli.com; Piazza Santa Maria 42; per day €15; ⏲9am-7pm summer)

Cicli Bizzarri (☎05 8349 6682; www.ciclibizzarri.net; Piazza Santa Maria 32; per day €15; ⏲9am-7pm summer)

PISTOIA

POP 89,100

Pretty Pistoia sits snugly at the foot of the Apennines. An easy day trip from Pisa, Lucca or Florence, it deserves more attention than it gets. A town that has grown well beyond its medieval ramparts, its *centro storico* is tranquil, well preserved and guardian to some striking contemporary art.

On Wednesday and Saturday a morning market transforms Pistoia's vast main square, Piazza del Duomo, as well as its surrounding streets into a lively sea of blue awnings and jostling shoppers. Otherwise, on Monday to Saturday you'll find open-air stalls heaped with seasonal fruit and vegetables on tiny Piazza della Sala, west of the cathedral.

Sights

Pistoia's key sights are clustered around its beautiful cathedral square, **Piazza del Duomo**, hemmed by a maze of narrow, shaded pedestrian streets made for hapless meandering.

★Museo Marino Marini ART GALLERY

(www.fondazionemarinomarini.it; Corso Fedi 30; adult/reduced €3.50/2; ⏲10am-6pm Mon-Sat summer, to 5pm winter) This museum-gallery inside the former Palazzo del Tau is devoted to Pistoia's most famous modern son, eponymous sculptor and painter Marino Marini (1901–80). Dozens of his drawings and paintings – mainly of female nudes and horses – hang here.

But the museum's real highlight is **Cappella del Tau**, the tiny 14th-century chapel, frescoed from head to toe and guardian of several Marini sculptures. *The Miracle* (1952) – bronze, monumental and one of dozens of equestrian works by the artist – takes centre stage.

Piazzetta degli Ortaggi PIAZZA

Don't miss pretty this beautiful bijou square with its laid-back cafe life and striking, life-size sculpture of three blindfolded men, **Giro di Sole** (Around the Sun; 1996) by contemporary Pistoia artist Roberto Barni (b 1939). In the 18th century the market square, adjoining Piazza della Sala and once home to a brothel, was the entrance to Pistoia's Jewish ghetto.

★Cattedrale di San Zeno CATHEDRAL

(Piazza del Duomo; silver altar €2/1.50; ⏲8.30am-12.20pm & 3.30-6.45pm, silver altar 9-10am, 11.30am-12.30pm & 3.30-6pm) This cathedral with a beautiful Pisan-Romanesque facade safeguards a lunette of the Madonna and Child between two angels by Andrea della Robbia. Its other highlight, tucked in gloomy **Cappella di San Jacopo** off the north aisle, is the silver **Dossale di San Giacomo** (Altarpiece of St James) begun in 1287 and finished two centuries later by Brunelleschi; buy tickets inside the Battistero di San Giovanni (p144) across the square (on Mondays when the baptistry is shut, cross your fingers and hope a church attendant is around).

★Battistero di San Giovanni RELIGIOUS

(Piazza del Duomo; baptistery admission free, bell tower €6/4.50; ⏲10am-1pm & 3-6pm Tue-Sun) Across from the cathedral is the 14th-century octagonal baptistry, elegantly banded in green-and-white marble to a design by Andrea Pisano. An ornate square marble font and soaring dome enliven the otherwise bare, red-brick interior. Scale its bell tower for bird's-eye city views.

Museo Civico ART GALLERY

(Piazza del Duomo 1; adult/reduced €3.50/2; ⏲10am-6pm Thu-Sun) Pistoia's Gothic **Palazzo Communale** is strung with works by Tuscan artists from the 13th to 20th centuries. Don't miss Bernardino di Antonio Detti's *Madonna della Pergola* (1498) with its modern treatment of St James, the Madonna and Baby Jesus; spot the mosquito on Jesus' arm.

Ospedale del Ceppo & Pistoia Sotterranea MONUMENT

(www.irsapt.it; Piazza Giovanni XXIII 13; guided visits adult/reduced €9/8; ⏲9am-6pm summer, to 5pm winter) The facade of **Ospedale del Ceppo**, with its 16th-century polychrome terracotta frieze by Giovanni della Robbia, stops even the most monument-weary in their tracks. It depicts the *Sette Opere di Misericordia* (Seven Works of Mercy), while the five medallions represent the *Virtù Teologali* (Theological Virtues).

Pistoia

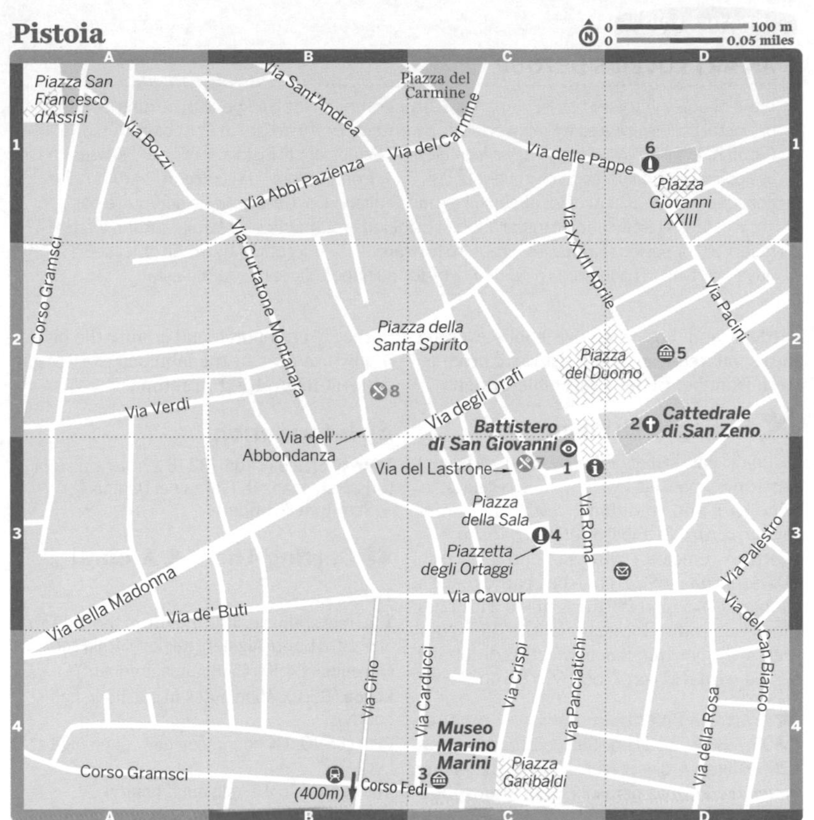

Even more astonishing is the underground labyrinth that weaves its way beneath the ancient hospital.

Known as **Pistoia Sotteranea**, one-hour guided visits take visitors underground into the belly of the 13th-century hospital, an important school of surgery in the 16th century. Ogle at subterranean rivers, old surgical tools, scalpels and all sorts.

Festivals & Events

Giostra dell'Orso CULTURE

Translated as Joust of the Bear, medieval jousting and other equestrian pranks fill Piazza del Duomo during Pistoia's celebration of its patron saint San Giacomo; 25 July.

Sleeping

Tenuta di Pieve a Celle HOTEL €€

(☎05 7391 3087; www.tenutadipieveacelle.it; Via di Pieve a Celle 158; d €160; P ❄ ≋) From the driveway lined with cypress trees to the olive grove and pool, this 1850s country estate 3km outside Pistoia, in the hills, is quintessential Tuscany at its best. Its five pretty rooms with canopy beds overlook expansive

Pistoia

Top Sights

1 Battistero di San Giovanni C3
2 Cattedrale di San Zeno D2
3 Museo Marino Marini C4

Sights

4 Giro di Sole C3
5 Museo Civico D2
6 Ospedale del Ceppo & Pistoia Sotterranea D1

Eating

7 Osteria La BotteGaia C3
8 Trattoria dell'Abbondanza B2

Drinking & Nightlife

Caffètteria Marini .... (see 3)

WORTH A TRIP

AN ART LOVER'S DETOUR

A tea house, aviary and other romantic 19th-century follies mingle with cutting-edge art installations created by the world's top contemporary artists at **Fattoria di Celle** (05 7347 9907; www.goricoll.it; Via Montalese 7 , Santomato di Pistoia; tours free; visits by appointment only Mon-Sat summer) FREE, 5km from Pistoia. The extraordinary private collection and passion of local businessman Giuliano Gori, this unique sculpture park showcases 70 site-specific installations sprinkled around his vast family estate. Visits – reserved for serious art lovers – require forward planning (apply by email at least 30 days in advance) and entail a guided two- to four-hour hike around the estate.

gardens and host Fiorenza cooks evening meals on request using seasonal produce fresh from her organic vegetable garden.

Eating & Drinking

Pistoia's eat street is pedestrian Via del Lastrone, packed with cafes, gelatarie, wine bars and traditional restaurants serving *carcerato* (a type of offal), *frittata con rigatino* (omelette with salt-cured bacon), *farinata con cavalo* (chickpea pancake with cabbage), *migliacci* (fritters made with pig's blood) and other local specialities. End your meal with *berlingozzo,* a sweet traditionally served with a glass of local Vin Santo.

★ Trattoria dell'Abbondanza TUSCAN €€
(05 7336 8037; Via dell'Abbondanza 10; meals €30; lunch & dinner Fri-Tue, dinner Thu) Dine beneath coloured parasols in an atmospheric alley outside or plump for a table inside where homey collections of door bells, pasta jars and so on catch the eye. The cuisine, once you've deciphered the handwriting on the menu, is simple Tuscan.

Osteria La BotteGaia OSTERIA €€
(05 7336 5602; www.labottegaia.it; Via del Lastrone 17; meals €30; lunch & dinner Tue-Sat, dinner Sun) Dishes range from staunchly traditional to experimental at this Slow Food–hailed *osteria,* known for its finely butchered cured meats and interesting wine list. Reserve in advance or, if you fail to snag a table, opt for a salad, *crostini* (bread-based starters) or bruschetta at La BotteGaia's *vineria* (wine bar) at No 4 on the same street.

Caffètteria Marini CAFE
(www.fondazionemarinomarini.it; Corso Fedi 32) This warm, vibrant musem-cafe next to the Museo Marino Marini buzzes with local life. Sip an espresso at the bar, chat with friends over cappuccino at one of four tables in the cosy interior, or flop on a country-style sofa in the covered porch and admire the blooming hydrangeas in the fabulous cloister garden – at its prettiest in summer.

Information

Tourist office (05 732 16 22; www.pistoia.turismo.toscana.it; Piazza del Duomo 4; 9am-1pm & 3-6pm)

Getting There & Around

TRAIN

The train station is 400m south of the Old Town on Piazza Dante Alghieri. Regional train services:

Florence (€4.10, 45 minutes, frequent)

Lucca (€5.10, 45 minutes to one hour, half-hourly)

Pisa (€5.10, 1¾ hours, one daily or change at Lucca)

Viareggio (€6.40, one hour, hourly)

SAN MINIATO & AROUND

POP 27,600

There is one delicious reason to visit this enchantingly sleepy, medieval hilltop town almost equidistant (50km) between Pisa and Florence: to eat, hunt and dream about the *tuber magnatum pico* (white truffle).

San Miniato town's ancient cobbled streets, burnt soft copper and ginger in the hot summer sun, are a delight to meander. Savour a harmonious melody of magnificent palace facades, 14th- to 18th-century churches and an impressive Romanesque cathedral, ending with the stiff hike up San Miniato's reconstructed medieval fortress tower, **Torre di Frederico II** (Tower of Frederick II; admission €3.50; 11am-5pm Tue-Sun), to enjoy a great panorama. Before setting off buy a combined ticket to all the key sites (€5) at the tourist office.

Then knuckle down to the serious business of lunch. Many local restaurants buy their meat from **Sergio Falaschi** (www.sergiofalaschi.it; Via Augusto Conti 18-20), the local *macelleria* (butcher) specialising in products made from *cinta senese* (indigenous Tuscan pig from the area around Siena), including the Slow Food favourite, *mallegato* (blood sausage). Other local products worth looking for on menus are *carciofo San Miniatese* (locally grown artichokes) in April and May; chestnuts and wild mushrooms in autumn (fall); *formaggio di capra delle colline di San Miniato* (the local goat's cheese); and locally raised Chianina beef.

Don't leave town without nipping into **Slow Food** (Via Augusto Conti 39) to ask about tastings, tours, cellar visits, wine itineraries and other great tastebud-tempting activities. It also organises the fabulous **Mercato della Terra di San Miniato** (www.mercatidellaterra.it; Piazzale Dante Alighieri; 9am-2pm), a vibrant farmers' market humming with fresh fruit, veg, meat, raw milk and other local produce from small-scale farmers and artisan producers. It's held on the third Sunday of the month.

Sleeping & Eating

★ Barbialla Nuova FARMSTAY €

(05 7167 7004; www.barbiallanuova.it; Via Casastada 49, Montaione; 2/4/6/8 person apt from €100/160/200/320, minimum 3/7 nights winter/summer; P) Creamy Chianina cows graze on the hillside and wild boars ferret for truffles between tree roots on this heavily wooded, 500-hectare biodynamic farm with just the right mix of adventure (unpaved roads) and panache (stylish decor). Apartments in old farmhouses dotted around the property offer self-catering accommodation and, most memorably, guests get 50% off on the farm's famous truffle hunts.

Staying here is all about feeding the pigs, admiring the livestock, walking (guests get a map of trails around the estate), stocking up on fresh organic produce and truffles at the farm shop – and cooking them up! Barbialla is 20km south of San Miniato on the SP76; look for the white sign on your right 3km after the village of Carrazano.

Podere del Grillo MODERN TUSCAN €

(05 7140 9379; www.poderedelgrillo.eu; Via Serra 3, La Serra; meals €20, tasting platters €10-15; 6-11pm Mon-Sat, 12.30-3.30pm & 6-11pm Sun) The quality of ingredients here is so extraordinary most dishes hardly need cooking or culinary intervention. Everything is sourced from local organic farms and it shows. Top off tasty salads, cold meats and cheeses with an artsy crowd, stylish location in a red-brick farmhouse and a positively urban bar vibe. Occasional live music, art shows, cultural events. Dinner from 8pm.

DON'T MISS

HUNTING WHITE TRUFFLES

An integral part of local culture since the Middle Ages, some 400 *tartufaio* (truffle hunters) in the trio of small valleys around San Miniato snout out the precious fungus, pale ochre in colour, from mid-October to mid-December. The paths and trails they follow are a family secret, passed between generations. The truffles their dogs sniff out are worth a small fortune after all, selling for €1500 per kilogram in Tuscany and four times as much in London and other European capitals.

There is no better time to savour the mystique of this cloak-and-dagger truffle trade than during San Miniato's **Mostra Mercato Nazionale del Tartufo Bianco** (National White Truffle Market), the last three weekends in November, when restaurateurs and truffle tragics come from every corner of the globe to purchase supplies, sample truffle-based delicacies in the town's shops and restaurants, and breathe in one of the world's most distinctive aromas. San Miniato tourist office has a list of truffle dealers and can help you join a truffle hunt.

The best are the early-morning truffle hunts at Barbialla Nuova (p147), a 500-hectare farm, 20km south of San Miniato near Montaione, run by new-generation farmer Guido Manfredi. Two-hour hunts on the estate end with a glass of Chianti and local organic cheese and salami – or go with Guido to a local restaurant and savour your truffle shaved over pasta and after, a *bistecca alla fiorentina* (chargrilled T-bone steak). Famed far and wide for its enviable success rate when it comes to uncovering these nuggets of 'white' gold, Barbialla's *tartufaio* and his dog unearth some 20kg or so of edible booty in a season.

From San Miniato, head south towards Montaione and after a couple of kilometres, play 'Spot pretend cows' (in the parking opposite the red-brick farm).

★Pepenero MODERN TUSCAN **€€€**
(☎05 7141 9523; www.pepenerocucina.it; Via IV Novembre 13; meals €50; ⏲dinner Sat, lunch & dinner Sun & Wed-Fri) Chef and TV star Gilberto Rossi is one of the new breed of innovative Tuscan chefs using traditional products to create modern, seasonally driven dishes at this much-lauded restaurant. To share some of his secrets, sign up for one of his half-day **cooking classes** followed by an informal lunch on the restaurant's terrace. Advance reservations essential.

ℹ Information

Tourist office (☎05 714 27 45; www.sanminiatopromozione.it; Piazza del Popolo 1; ⏲9am-1pm Mon, 9am-1pm & 2-5pm Tue-Sun)

ℹ Getting There & Away

CAR

From Pisa or Florence, take the FI-PI-LI (SS67); car parking on Piazza del Popolo.

TRAIN

Train it to San Miniato then hop on a shuttle bus (€1, every 20 minutes) to the Old Town.

Regional train services:

Florence (€4.10, 45 minutes, hourly)

Pisa (€3.70, 30 minutes, hourly)

THE APUANE ALPS & GARFAGNANA

Rearing up inland from the Versilian Riviera are the Apuane Alps, a rugged mountain range protected by the **Parco Regionale delle Alpi Apuane** (www.parcapuane.it) and beckoning hikers with a trail of isolated farmhouses, medieval hermitages and hilltop villages.

Continue inland, across the Alps' eastern ridge and three stunning valleys formed by the Serchio and its tributaries – the low-lying Lima and Serchio Valleys and the higher Garfagnana Valley, collectively known as the **Garfagnana** – take centre stage. Thickly forested with chestnut woods and unknown to most, this is an unexplored land where fruits of the forest (chestnuts, *porcini* mushrooms and honey) create a very rustic and fabulous cuisine.

The main gateway to this staunchly rural part of Tuscany is Castelnuovo di Garfagnana, home to the regional park visitors centre. If faintly more 'cosmopolitan' rocks your boat as a base, consider Pietrasanta on the Apuane Alps' southern fringe.

FOR THE ULTIMATE ROMANCE

Book the only table – a table for two – at **Peperino** (☎348 7804785; www.peperino.net; Via IV Novembre 1, San Miniato; meal incl wine €210; ⏲lunch & dinner), the world's smallest restaurant plump in the heart of Tuscany's most gourmet village, next to big brother, Pepenero. Decor is in-your-face romantic (think pink silk), furnishings are period and the waiter only comes when diners ring the bell. Reserve months in advance.

Castelnuovo di Garfagnana

POP 6110

The medieval eyrie of Castelnuovo crowns the confluence of the Serchio and its smaller tributary, the Turrite. Its heart is pierced by the burnt-red **Rocca Ariostesca** (Ariosto's Castle), built in the 12th century and named after Italian poet Ariosto who lived here between 1522 and 1525 as governor of the Garfagnana for the House of Este. The castle is now the town hall, with a tiny **archaeological museum** (Piazza Ariosto; ⏲10am-12.30pm & 4-7pm Thu, Sat & Sun) FREE on the ground floor.

Opposite, historic cake shop and chocolate-maker **Fronte delle Rocca** (Piazza Ariosto 1; ⏲9am-1pm & 3-7.30pm Tue-Sun) has been the hub of local life since 1885. Should the hour be right, indulge in a glass of *prosecco* (sparkling wine) in the shade of the Rocca, then follow Via Fulvio Testi to the nearby **duomo** (Piazza del Duomo), with its lovely *Madonna and Two Saints* by Michele di Ridolfo del Ghirlandaio.

Footsteps away, across from the old city gate on Via Dini, sacks of beans, chickpeas, walnuts and *porcini* sit pretty as a picture outside local grocer's shop **Alimentari Poli Roberto** (Via Dini 1; ⏲8.30am-1pm & 3.30-8.30pm) – his chestnut beer, beer made from locally grown *farro*, *farro*-encrusted *pecorino* and honey is a prerequisite for any respectable Garfagnana picnic, as is

OFF THE BEATEN TRACK

AN OPERA BUFF'S DETOUR

Some 35km west of both Barbialla Nuova and San Gimignano, ringed by a natural amphitheatre of soul-stirring hills, is **Lajatico** (pop 1390). This tiny village is the birthplace and family home of opera singer Andrea Bocelli (b 1958) who, each year in July, returns to his village to sing – for just one evening.

His stage is the astonishing **Teatro del Silenzio** (Theatre of Silence; www.teatrodelsilenzio.it), a specially constructed, open-air theatre built in a green meadow on the fringe of the village where the natural silence is broken just once a year – by the Tuscan tenor and his friends (Placido Domingo, José Carreras, Sarah Brightman and Chinese pianist Lang Lang have all performed here). Each year different sculptures by contemporary artists are added to the ensemble, to striking effect. Gently rolling, fresh green hills as far as the eye can see is the astonishing 360-degree backdrop and listening to the tenor sing to an audience of 10,000 is an overwhelming experience. Tickets, usually released each year in March, cost €58 to €230 and are sold by **TicketOne** (www.ticketone.it).

True opera buffs can continue 5km to **La Sterza** to buy wine and olive oil produced on Bocelli's family estate at **Cantina Bocelli** (⌚10am-12.30pm & 4-7pm Mon-Fri), a red-brick vaulted cellar at the southern end of the village on the SR439.

castagnaccio (chestnut cake) and *biroldo* (a type of pork salami spiced with wild fennel).

Thursday morning is market day.

Sleeping & Eating

Pradaccio di Sopra AGRITURISMO €
(☎05 8366 6966; www.agriturismopradaccio.it; Pieve Fosciana; d €60-78, dinner €23; P ≋) Hugged by chestnut woods and *farro* fields, this family farm (wheat, *farro* and corn) is an excellent-value *agriturismo* (farmstay accommodation) option. Rooms are old-world with clean modern bathrooms, and dining translates as copious amounts of homemade *farro* pasta, chestnuts, salads fresh from the veggie patch and meats cooked to perfection in a wood-fuelled oven outside.

Michele, who took over Pradaccio di Sopra with his mother Rosalba in summer 2013, hopes to cook up lunch and dinner too in the future – watch this space. Find the farm 3.5km from Castelnuovo in Pieve Fosciana. No credit cards.

★**Osteria Vecchia Mulino** OSTERIA €
(☎05 836 21 92; www.vecchiomulino.info; Via Vittorio Emanuele 12; tasting menu incl wine €25; ⌚lunch Tue-Sun, evening with advance reservation) Run with passion and humour by the gregarious Andrea Bertucci, this 160-year-old *osteria* has no menu – rather a symphony of cold dishes crafted from local products and brought to shared tables one at a time. Advance reservations essential. Oh, and if you're renting a villa nearby, you can always arrange for Andrea to come to you to host a tasting evening.

Fuori dal Centro GELATO €
(www.fuoridalcentro.com; Piazza Dini 1f; 1/2/3/4/5 ice-cream scoops €1/1.70/2.20/2.70/3.20; ⌚1-8pm Mon-Sat, 11am-8pm Sun) Dare we say it: having tried and tested dozens of Tuscan *gelaterie,* this bright modern ice-cream shop comes out tops. Fuori dal Centro's regional-inspired flavours are magnificent – try chestnut, fig and honey, pine kernel, apple pie, meringue or – most unusually – *crema di farro* (which really does has grains of *farro* in!).

Il Pozzo PIZZERIA €
(☎05 8366 6380; Via Europa 2a, Pieve Fosciana; pizza €5-15; ⌚lunch & dinner Thu-Tue) A great 'cheap meal' address with loads of outside seating, particularly handy on Sunday evening when everything else seems to be shut. Find it 3.5km north of Castelnuovo in Pieve Fosciano.

Information

Centro Visite Parco Alpi Apuane (☎05 836 5169; www.turismo.garfagnana.eu; Piazza delle Erbe 1; ⌚9am-1pm & 3-7pm summer, to 5.30pm winter; 📶) Regional park visitors centre with bags of info on walking, mountain biking, horse riding and other activities in the Apuane Alps; sells maps and has lists of local guides and mountain accommodation. Free wi-fi hotspot complete with sofas for connecting in comfort.

Apuane Alps & Garfagnana

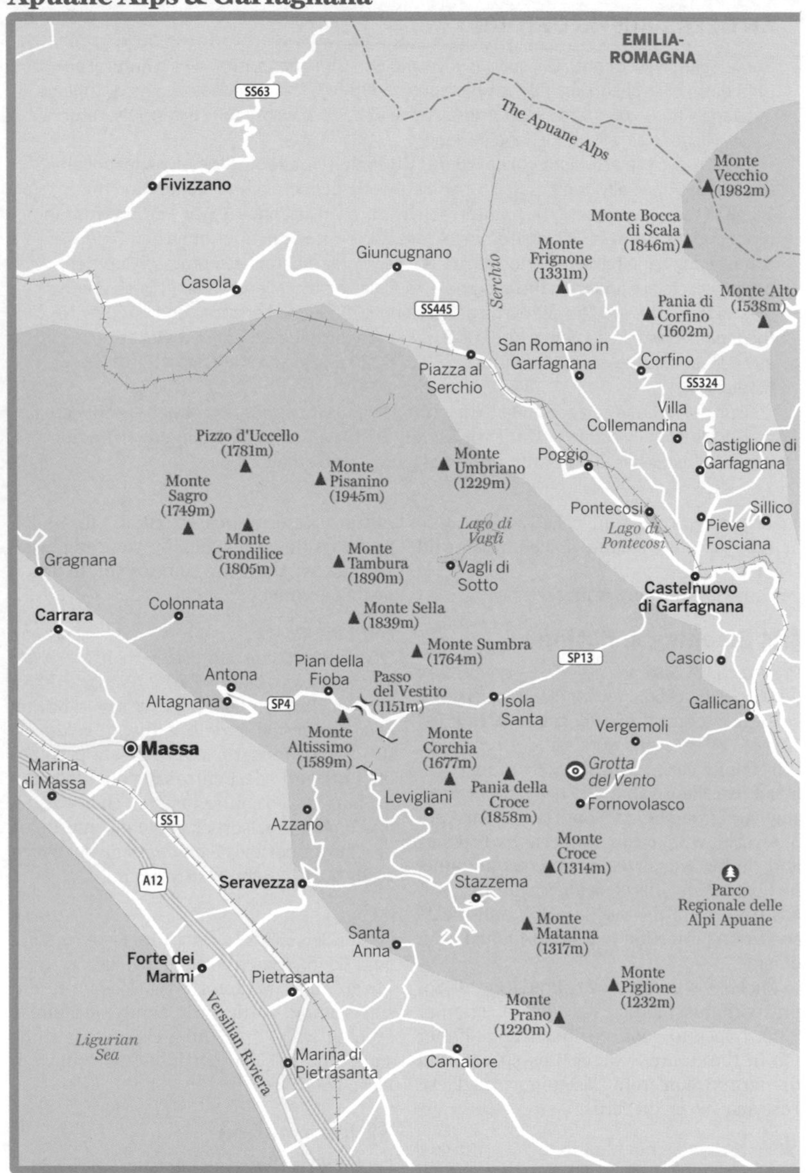

Tourist office (☎05 8364 1007; www.castelnuovagarfagnana.org; Piazza delle Erbe; ⌚9.30am-1pm & 3.30-6.30pm Mon-Sat) Opposite the park visitors centre.

ℹ Getting There & Away

CAR

Take the SS12 from Lucca (direction Abetone) and turn off onto the SS445. There's a car park at Piazza del Genio, off Via Roma on the opposite side of the river to the walled *centro storico*.

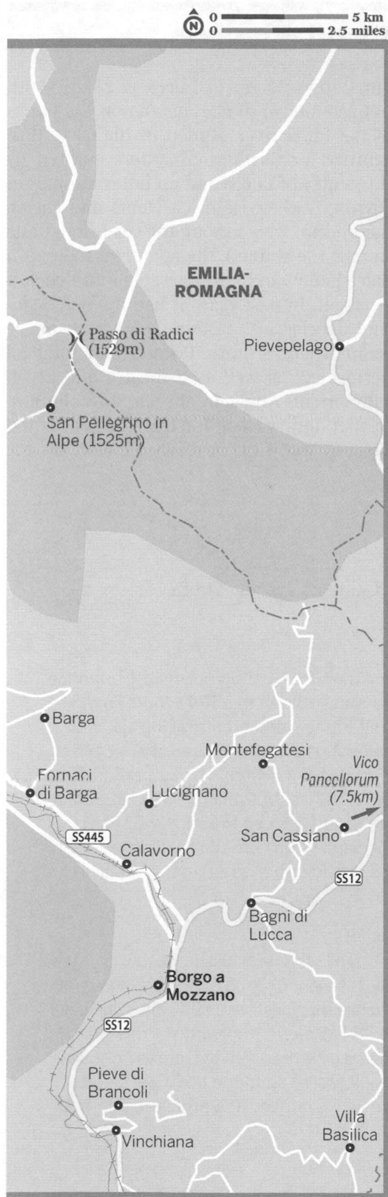

TRAIN

Regional train services:

Lucca (€4.10, one hour, nine daily)

Pisa (€5.10, 1½ hours, four daily)

Barga

POP 10,300

This chic village, 12km south of Castelnuovo di Garfagnana, is one of those irresistibly slow Tuscan hilltop towns with a disproportionately large and dynamic English-speaking community. Churches, artisan workshops, attractive stone houses and palaces built by rich merchants between the 15th and 17th centuries lace the steep streets leading up to the Romanesque **Duomo di San Cristoforo** (Piazza Beato Michele 1). Across the grass from the church, inside Barga's old prison, the **Museo Civico del Territorio di Barga** (Piazza dell'Arringo del Duomo; adult/reduced €3/2; ⏲10am-12.30pm & 3-6pm Thu-Sun Jul & Aug, Sat & Sun only Sep) evokes local history and tradition from prehistory to the 17th century.

Sleeping & Eating

★Il Benefizio AGRITURISMO €

(☎05 8372 2201; www.albenefizio.it; apt from €70; P @ 🛜 🏊) Squeeze your car along the narrow road to this olive farm, framed by acacia and chestnut woods 2km from Barga. It has two well-equipped apartments in the old stables, both with spectacular views. Guests can swim, mountain bike and have use of a BBQ. But the real reason to visit is to get acquainted with owner Francesca, a walking guide and beekeeper.

With her you can visit the apiary, see how honey is extracted, and sign up for an olive oil workshop. Husband Francesco, equally fascinating, is a sound engineer (hence the welcome presence of a state-of-the-art home theatre). No credit cards.

Casa Cordati HOMESTAY €

(☎05 8372 3450; www.casacordati.it; Via di Mezzo 17; s/d/tr €30/44/60; ⏲Mar-Oct; @ 🛜) This atmospheric townhouse is an ode to art, fittingly so given it languishes in the former home and studio of painter Bruno Cordati (1890–1979). The ground-floor gallery (free admission) shows off some of his works, while rooms above tout wooden floors, period decor and an artsy feel. Some bathrooms are shared.

L'Osteria TUSCAN €

(☎335 5387113; www.losteriabarga.com; Piazza Angelio 13-14; meals €20; ⏲lunch & dinner summer, shorter hr winter) This casual *osteria* sits on Barga's prettiest piazza. Cuisine is traditional: *baccalà e ceci* (saltcod and chickpeas), grilled sausage with rosemary- and sage-scented beans, or a simple rack of lamb ribs.

Information

Tourist office (☎05 8372 4745; www.comune.barga.lu.it; Via di Mezzo 47; ⏰9am-1pm Mon-Fri, 9am-1pm & 3-5.30pm Sat summer, shorter hr winter)

Getting There & Away

CAR

Take the SS12 from Lucca (direction: Abetone), veer left onto the SS445 and then turn right onto the SP7 at Fornacci di Barga. Barga is 5km further on.

Bagni di Lucca

POP 6560

Small-town Bagni di Lucca is 28km south of Castelnuovo di Garfagnana on the banks of the Lima river. Famed in the early 19th century for its thermal waters enjoyed by the gentry of Lucca and an international set (Byron, Shelley, Heinrich Heine and Giacomo Puccini were among the celebrity guests to take the waters), the spa town today is a pale shadow of its former splendid neoclassical self. In past years it had its own beautiful neoclassical **casino** (1837) with music room where Strauss, Puccini and Liszt all performed, as well as a theatre and atypically ornate Anglican church, now the municipal library (look for the stucco lion and unicorn motif above each window on the

OFF THE BEATEN TRACK

3 PERFECT ROAD TRIPS

Nerves and stomach depending, dozens of narrow roads spaghetti from Castelnuovo into the Garfagnana's rural depths.

Alpine Flora & Marble Mountain

Head west towards the Med. The first 17km along the SP13 is straightforward, but once you fork right 2km south of Arni (follow signs for Massa along the SP4), motoring becomes a relentless succession of hairpins, unlit tunnels and breathtaking vistas of Carrara's marble quarries as you cross the Apuane Alps over the **Passo del Vestito** (1151m). Stop in **Pian della Fioba** to discover alpine flora in the **Orto Botanico Pietro Pellegrini** (Botanical Garden; www.parcapuane.toscana.it/ob; Pian della Fioba; ⏰9am-noon & 3-7pm May-Sep) and break for coffee at **Rifugio Città di Massa** (☎05 8581 9043; www.rifugiodimassa.it; dm incl breakfast €25; ⏰May-Sep). From here the road drops down, through **Antona** and **Altagnana** clinging to the hilllside, to **Massa** on the Versilian coast. The entire drive is 42km.

Subterranean Rivers & Lakes

The SS445 is a twisting route that leads you through lush green hills pocked with caves. The most accessible and spectacular is **Grotta del Vento** (☎05 8372 2024; www.grottadelvento.com; Grotta del Vento 1, Vergemoli; adult/child 1hr guided visit €9/7, 2hr €14/11, 3hr €20/16; ⏰10am-noon & 2-6pm), 9km west of the SS445 along a horribly narrow road. Inside is a world of underground abysses, lakes and caverns. April to October, choose between a one-, two- or three-hour guided tour – if you're up to the 800/1200 steps involved in the two-/three-hour tour (!) it's worth it. November to March, the one-hour tour (300 steps) is the only choice.

Across a Mountain Pass

Spiralling north from Castelnuovo, a concertina of hairpin bends (the SS324) lifts you to **Castiglione di Garfagnana** and over the scenic **Passo di Radici** mountain pass, across the Apennines, into Emilia-Romagna. A minor parallel road to the south of the pass takes you to **San Pellegrino in Alpe** (www.sanpellegrinoinalpe.it), a hilltop village (at 1525m) with a monastery and, in the old hospital, a **Museo Etnografico** (Ethnographic Museum; Via del Voltone 14; adult/reduced €2.50/1.50; ⏰10am-1pm & 2-6.30pm daily Jul & Aug, closed Mon & shorter hr rest of year) that brings traditional mountain life, scarcely changed for centuries, to life.

vivid burnt-red facade). In the small British cemetery baroque tombs speak volumes.

There are two distinct areas: the smaller casino-clad **Ponte a Serraglio**, clustered around a bridge that crosses the Lima river; and the main town, 2km north, where most shops, restaurants and hotels are.

Sights & Activities

Ponte del Diarolo BRIDGE

(Borgo a Mozzano) Head 2.5km southwest out of town to the tiny riverside hamlet of Borgo a Mozzano, famed for this medieval stone bridge which climbs steeply up and over the Serchio river. The bridge was first mentioned in the 14th century and in 1670 *ceppi* (millstones) were prohibited from using it in a bid to preserve its ancient stone paving. Staggering up to its highest point, dropping stones into the water far below, and skipping down again is great old-fashioned fun.

Bagni di Lucca Terme SPA

(☎05 838 72 21; www.termebagnidilucca.it; Piazza San Martino 11; ⏲8am-12.30pm Mon-Fri & Sun, 8am-12.30pm & 2-4pm Sat) The thermal springs in this area have been popular spots for relaxation and revitalisation since Roman times. Its only spa today has two natural steam grottoes and a wellness centre offering various steam and thermal mud baths (€1 to €24); massages with salt, stone or olive oil (€17 per 30 minutes) and so on. A day ticket for the thermal pool costs €12/15 on weekdays/weekends.

Sorgente La Cova SPRING

(Viale Casino Municipale 84) It might appear to be a simple drinking fountain spouting out of an old stone roadside wall, but this natural *sorgente* (spring) a few doors down from the riverside casino in Ponte a Serraglio, is believed to be the cure of all ills. Its water, fabulously, is hot. Park up like a local and wash your hands in it, bathe tired feet in it, drink it, bottle it.

Eating

Circolo dei Forestieri TUSCAN €

(☎05 838 60 38; Piazza Jean Varraud 10; meals €20; ⏲lunch & dinner Tue-Sun) Quell hunger pangs at the former home of the Foreigners' Club, an elegant belle Epoque building on the river side of Viale Umberto I, southeast of the casino. Its grand dining room, chandeliers et al, provides a splendid setting in which to enjoy good-value Tuscan cuisine.

GET ORGANISED: HIKING, BIKING & EATING

Tuscany Walking (www.tuscanywalking.com) Family-run, English-speaking set-up in Barga offering guided and self-guided hikes.

Eco Guide (www.eco-guide.it) Guided nature tours (on foot and by bicycle) by this creative Lucca-based set-up, including magical night walks in the Garfagnana, kids' walks and a 'Spectacular Apuane Alps' day hike.

Garfagnana Bikers (www.garfagnanabikers.it) The Garfagnana is made for biking and these motorcyclists are the people to help you craft your route.

Sapori e Saperi Gastronomic Adventures (www.sapori-e-saperi.com) Embark on a culinary tour of the Garfagnana with passionate foodie Heather Jarman: learn how bread is traditionally baked, sausages made, *pecorino* cheese produced as it's been done for generations; visit olive farms, harvest chestnuts, meet local cheesemakers and savour age-old recipes in locally endorsed restaurants.

Information

Tourist office (☎05 8380 5745; www.comunebagnidilucca.it; Viale Umberto I 93; ⏲10am-1pm Mon & Wed-Sat)

Getting There & Away

TRAIN

Regional train services:

Lucca (€3.10, 30 minutes, seven daily)

Pisa (€4.10, 1¼ hours, five daily)

Carrara

POP 65,600

Many first-time visitors assume the white mountain peaks forming Carrara's backdrop are capped with snow. In fact, the vista provides a breathtaking illusion – the white is 2000 hectares of marble gouged out of the foothills of the Apuane Alps in vast quarries that have been worked since Roman times.

The texture and purity of Carrara's white marble (derived from the Greek *marmaros*, meaning shining stone) is unrivalled and it was here that Michelangelo selected marble

WORTH A TRIP

VICO PANCELLORUM

Precariously perched above chestnut and walnut forests on a hillock, angled so steeply it threatens to tumble down any second, is the tiny hamlet of **Vico Pancellorum**. Gazing in awe at its dramatic location aside, the main reason to come here is to experience **Buca di Baldabò** (05 838 90 62; bucabaldabo@liberi.it; Via Prati 11, Vico Pancellorum; primi/secondi €8/9; lunch & dinner daily Jun-Aug, dinner Wed-Sun, lunch with reservation mid-Sep–May). This is one of those iconic addresses every local foodie knows about.

Humbly placed at the back of the village bar where locals while away the day playing cards and *boccia* (boules) or watching TV, the much raved-about restaurant has no printed menu. Just listen to what's cooking that day and take your pick from a generous choice of homemade pastas and sauces cooked up daily by Giovanni (Enrico cooks the mains and Luisa the desserts). Game is generally big in the *secondi* (second course) choice (hence the boar's head trophy above the fireplace) and *contorni* (side dishes) are particularly creative (fennel with bitter greens, sweet cabbage with sausage and so on).

To get to Vico Pancellorum from Bagni di Lucca, head 9km north along the scenic SS12 to Abetone and at the northern end of Ponte Coccia take the sharp turning on the left signposted 'Vico Pancellorum'; the restaurant is another 3km from here, at the foot of the hamlet, along a steep, narrow, curvaceous road. Advance reservations (and a double-check of opening hours that do vary depending if there's workmen in the village, a friend's birthday and so on) are essential.

for masterpieces including *David* (actually sculpted from a dud veined block). Today it's a multi-billion-euro industry.

The quarries, 5km out of town, have long been the area's biggest employers. It's hard, dangerous work and on Carrara's central Piazza XXVII Aprile a monument remembers workers who lost their lives up on the hills. These tough men formed the backbone of a strong leftist and anarchist tradition in Carrara, something that won them no friends among the Fascists or, later, the occupying German forces.

Bar the thrill of seeing its mosaic marble pavements, marble street benches, decorative marble putti and marble everything else, the old centre of Carrara doesn't offer much for the visitor. The exception is July to October in even years, when Carrara stages a wonderful contemporary **sculpture biennale** (www.biennialfoundation.org).

Sights & Activities

Museo del Marmo MUSEUM
(Viale XX Settembre; adult/reduced €4/2; 9am-12.30pm & 2.30-5pm Mon-Sat) Opposite the tourist office, Carrara's Marble Museum tells the full story of the marble quarries outside town, from the old chisel-and-hammer days to the 21st-century's high-powered industrial quarrying. It also has a fascinating audiovisual oral history presentation documenting the lives of quarry workers in the 20th century.

Cava di Fantiscritti MARBLE QUARRY
Make your way up the mountain to this dusty, noisy, truck-busy *cava de marmo* (marble quarry), through a dramatic series of tunnels bored through rock and used by trains to transport marble until the 1960s (when trucks took over the weighty task). One of a handful of quarries, this is the easiest to visit.

Pick from a 40-minute **guided tour** (339 7657470; www.marmotour.it; adult/child €9/4; 11am-6pm summer, 9am-4pm winter) by minibus/on foot of the marble quarry inside the mountain, or a 50-minute Bond-style **4WD tour** (05 8577 9673; www.carraramarbletour.it; adult/child €10/5; 11am-6pm summer) of the open-cast quarry above. (Yes, the Bond movie *Quantum of Solace* was shot here). Both tours are dramatic.

Paolo Costa & Co ARTS CENTRE
(05 857 17 40; www.costapaolo.it; Via Carriona 92; 1-4.30pm Mon-Sat) To watch professional sculptors work with Carrara marble, visit these workshops in town. Visiting hours vary considerably, so call ahead.

Eating

The *only* place to lunch is in the hamlet of **Colonnata**, 2km from Fantiscritti, where one of Tuscany's greatest gastronomic treats, *lardo di colonnata* (thinner-than-wafer-thin slices of local pig fat) sits ageing in marble vats of herby olive oil. Once you're hooked, purchase a vacuum-packed slab (from €13.50 per kilogram) to take home from one of the many *larderie* (shops selling *lardo*) in the village.

Ristorante Venanzio TUSCAN €€
(☎05 8575 8062; Piazza Palestro 3, Colonnata; meals €30; ⏲lunch & dinner Mon-Wed, Fri & Sat, lunch Sun) Even those who initially find the idea of noshing on a hunk of fat off-putting are bound to be won over when sampling it melted over piping-hot *focaccette* (small, flat buns made of wheat flour and cornmeal) at this family-run restaurant with classical decor on Colonnata's central, marble-paved square. Its €40 *menu degustazione* (tasting menu; minimum two people) is a real treat.

Locanda Apuana TUSCAN €€
(☎05 8576 8017; www.locandaapuana.com; Via Communale 1, Colonnata; meals €30; ⏲lunch & dinner Tue-Sat, lunch Sun) The other key address in Colonnata, just off central Piazza Palestro, to feast on *crostini caldi con lardo* (warm toasts topped with lardo) et al.

Information

Tourist office (☎05 8584 4136; Viale XX Settembre; ⏲9am-4pm) Opposite the stadium; stop here to pick up a map of Carrara, its marble workshops and out-of-town quarries.

Getting There & Away

TRAIN

The nearest station is Carrara-Avenza, between Carrara and Marina di Carrara. Regional train services:

Pietrasanta (€2.50, 15 minutes, at least twice hourly)

Viareggio (€3.30, 25 minutes, twice hourly)

THE VERSILIAN COAST

The beaches from Viareggio northwards to Liguria are popular with local holiday-makers and some tourists, but have been blighted by beachfront strip development and get unpleasantly packed with Italy's beach-loving hoi polloi during summer. We suggest steering clear of this coastal strip and instead heading inland to explore the hinterland town of Pietrasanta, known for its vibrant arts culture and *centro storico*.

Versilia is a major gateway to both the Apuane Alps, Garfagnana and Lunigiana with roads from the coastal towns snaking their way deep into the heart of the mountains and connecting with small villages and walking tracks.

WORTH A TRIP

MARBLE MOUNTAIN

Zipping down a dank wet unlit tunnel in a dusty white minibus, grubby headlights blazing, driver incongruously dolled up in a shiny shocking-pink bomber jacket, it is all somewhat surreal. Five minutes into the pitch-black marble mountain, everyone is told to get out.

It is 16°C, foggy, damn dirty and slippery on foot and far from being a polished pearly white, it's grey – cold wet miserable grey. Rough-cut blocks, several metres long and almost as wide, are strewn about the place like toy bricks and marble columns prop up the 15m-high ceiling, above which a second gallery, another 17m tall, stands. The place is bigger than several football pitches, yet amazingly there is still plenty of marble left for the five workers employed at Cava di Fantiscritti (p154), 5km north of Carrara, to extract – with the aid of water and mechanical diamond-cutting chains that slice through the rock like butter – 10,000 tonnes of white marble a month. The current market price is €200 to €1000 per tonne, with Carrara's very best commanding double that.

To learn how the Romans did it (with chisels and axes – oh my!), visit the surprisingly informative, open-air **Cava Museo di Walter Danesi** (www.cavamuseo.com; Cava di Fantiscritti; ⏲11am-6pm) FREE, adjoining the souvenir shop across from the quarry entrance. Don't miss the B&W shots of marble blocks being precariously slid down the *lizza* (mountain pathway) to the bottom of the mountain where 18 pairs of oxen would pull the marble to Carrara port. In the 1850s tunnels were built for trains to do the job (hence the tunnel tour groups use to drive into the mountain) – which they did until the 1960s.

Pietrasanta

POP 24,900

Often overlooked by Tuscan travellers, this refined art town is a real unexpected surprise. Its bijou historic heart, originally walled, is car-free and loaded with tiny art galleries, workshops and fashion boutiques – perfect for a day's amble broken only by lunch.

Founded by Guiscardo da Pietrasanta, *podestà* (governing magistrate) of Lucca in 1255, Pietrasanta was seen as a prize by Genoa, Lucca, Pisa and Florence, all of whom jostled for possession of its marble quarries and bronze foundries. As was so often the case, Florence won out and Leo X (Giovanni de' Medici) took control in 1513. Leo put the town's famous quarries at the disposal of Michelangelo, who came here in 1518 to source marble for the facade of San Lorenzo in Florence. The artistic inclination of Pietrasanta dates from this time, and today it is the home of many artists, including internationally lauded Colombian-born sculptor Fernando Botero whose work can be seen here.

Pietrasanta is a great base for exploring the Apuane Alps and a lovely day trip from Pisa or Viareggio.

Sights & Activities

From Pietrasanta train station on Piazza della Stazione head straight across Piazza Carducci, through the Old City gate and onto **Piazza del Duomo**, the main square that poses as an outdoor gallery for sculptures and other large works of art. It is impossible to miss the attractive **Duomo di San Martino** (1256) with its distinctive 36m-tall, red-brick bell tower – actually unfinished (the red brick was meant to have a marble cladding).

Next door, the deconsecrated 13th-century **Chiesa di Sant'Agostino** (Piazza del Duomo; hr vary) is a wonderfully evocative venue for art exhibitions. Inside the convent adjoining the church dozens of moulds of famous sculptures cast or carved in Pietrasanta are showcased by the **Museo dei Bozzetti** (05 8479 5500; www.museodeibozzetti.it; Via Sant'Agostino 1; 2-7pm Tue-Sat, 4-7pm Sun) FREE.

Around the corner from the cathedral is the old-world atmospheric **baptistry** (Baptistery; Via Garibaldi 12; variable). The pair of baptismal fonts – one originally in the cathedral in the 16th century and the other, a hexagonal tub (1389) used two centuries before for full immersion baptisms – form a dramatic ensemble in the tiny candle-lit space. Afterwards stroll the length of pedestrian **Via Garibaldi**, a chic strip peppered with stylish fashion boutiques and art galleries. Highlights guaranteed to tempt include multibrand fashion queen and trendsetter **Zoe** (www.zoecompany.eu; Via Garibaldi 29, & 44-46; 10am-1pm & 5pm-midnight, to 8pm winter) with boutiques for women and men (where Paul Smith's wife bought her husband a scarf); vintage furniture design boutique **Lei** (Via Garibaldi 22); concept store **Dada** (www.dadaconcept.it; Via Garibaldi 39); and fashion designer **Paolo Milani** (Via Garibaldi 11) whose studio is a riot of bold vibrant prints and a wild mix of textures covering the whole sombre-to-sequin-sparkly spectrum.

Holiday money well and truly blown, meander back to the cathedral square and continue the shopping parade on **Via Giuseppe Mazzini**, the town's main shopping strip bookended by contemporary street sculptures. End on an artistic high with the superb **Chiesa della Misericordia** (Via Mazzini 103; variable), frescoed with the *Gate of Paradise* and *Gate of Hell* by Botero (the artist portrays himself in hell). Look for it tucked between shops.

Sleeping

★ **Le Camere di Filippo** B&B €

(05 847 00 10; Via Stagio Stagi 22; d €100; P ❄ @) A fabulous address with two kitchens and four fantastic rooms, each with a different colour scheme and crisp design.

★ **Albergo Pietrasanta** BOUTIQUE HOTEL €€€

(05 8479 3726; www.albergopietrasanta.com; Via Garibaldi 35; s €132-231, d €213-277; P ❄ @) Should you find yourself totally smitten with Pietrasanta and unable to leave, this chic 17th-century *palazzo* – a perfect fusion of old and new – is among Tuscany's loveliest boutique town hotels. After a day spent sightseeing, its gorgeous courtyard, conservatory and beautifully appointed, classically elegant rooms are made for relaxing and pampering.

Eating & Drinking

The historic heart spoils for choice with its many artsy addresses spilling onto flower-pot-adorned summer terraces. Pedestrian Via Stagio Stagi, parallel to main street Via

Mazzini, has several appealing restaurants, while Piazza del Duomo with its many cafes is the alfresco favourite for a coffee or sundowner.

★ Filippo MODERN TUSCAN €€
(☎05 847 00 10; http://ristorantefilippo.com; Via Stagio Stagi 22; meals €30; ⏲lunch & dinner, closed Mon winter) This exceptional foodie address never disappoints. From the home-made bread (all six or so varieties) and focaccia brought warm to your table throughout the course of your meal, to the contemporary fabric on the walls, giant wicker lampshades and modern open kitchen, this bistro is chic. Cuisine is seasonal and as creative as the interior design.

Its salads in particular are superb, as are its unusual pasta *primi* (first course). Arrive before 1pm to ensure a table; reserve in advance to dine after dusk.

San Martino TUSCAN €€
(☎05 8479 3197; Via Garibaldi 19; meals €30; ⏲lunch & dinner) No one feature says more about the place than its name – that of the town's patron saint, casually chalked on a heart-shaped board strung in an otherwise naked window. Vintage chic and stylish, San Martino is a tasty find. Inside, coloured walls mirror a hearty Tuscan cuisine.

Great summertime pavement terrace too!

Pinocchio SEAFOOD €€€
(☎05 847 05 10; Vicolo San Biagio 5; meals €50; ⏲lunch & dinner Tue-Sun) This contemporary restaurant is a hip-crowd favourite. Fish and seafood in various creative guises are its raison d'être, served in a casually refined interior or beneath parasols on its Via Stagio Stagi pavement terrace; the entrance is in the alley around the corner.

★ L'Enoteca Marcucci WINE BAR
(☎05 8479 1962; www.enotecamarcucci.it; Via Garibaldi 40; ⏲10am-1pm & 5pm-1am Tue-Sun) Taste fine Tuscan wine on bar stools at high wooden tables or beneath big parasols on the street outside. Whichever you pick, the distinctly funky, artsy spirit of Pietrasanta's best-loved *enoteca* (wine bar) enthrals. Its house sparkling wine is justly raved about.

ℹ Information

Tourist office (☎05 8428 3375; www.comune.pietrasanta.lu.it; Piazza Statuto; ⏲9am-1pm & 4.30-7pm Mon-Wed, Fri & Sat, 4.30-7pm Thu, 9am-1pm & 4-7.30pm Sun)

ℹ Getting There & Away

TRAIN

Regional train services:

Pisa (€3.30, 25 minutes, frequent)

Viareggio (€2.50, 10 minutes, every 10 minutes)

Lucca (with change of train in Pisa or Viareggio; €4.10, 35 to 50 minutes, every 30 minutes)

Viareggio

POP 64,200

This hugely popular sun and sand resort is known as much for its flamboyant Mardi Gras Carnevale, second only to Venice for party spirit, as for its dishevelled line-up of old art-nouveau facades, once grand, on its seafront that recall the town's 1920s and '30s heyday.

👁 Sights & Activities

Viareggio's vast golden sandy **beachfront** is laden with cafes, climbing frames and other kids' amusements and, bar the short public stretch opposite fountain-pierced **Piazza Mazzini**, is divided into *stabilimenti* (individual lots where you can hire cabins, umbrellas, loungers etc). Only a handful of waterfront buildings retain the ornate stylishness of the 1920s and '30s, notably Puccini's favourite cafe, Gran Caffè Margherita (p138) dating to 1929 and neighbouring wooden **Chalet Martini** (a clothes shop since 1860 with a fabulous interior).

Literature lovers might like to pass by Piazza Shelley, the only tangible reference to the romantic poet who drowned in Viareggio; his body was washed up on the beach and his comrade-in-arts, Lord Byron, had him cremated on the spot.

La Citadella di Carnevale MONUMENT
(Via Santa Maria Goretti; ⏲10am-noon Mon-Fri summer, 10am-noon Mon, Wed & Fri winter) FREE A couple of kilometres from the seafront is 'Carnival City' aka 16 gargantuan hangars which serve as workshops and garage space for the fantastic floats, crafted with a passion by each highly skilled and prized *carrista* (float-builder), for Viareggio's annual carnival.

The largest floats featuring a papier-mâché merry-go-round of clowns, opera divas, skeletons, kings etc are a staggering 20m wide and 14m tall, take five months to build and carry 200 people each during processions. Stroll around the complex and a *carrista* will inevitably invite you into his workshop. Otherwise,

LOCAL KNOWLEDGE

FISH & CHIPS

Forget Viareggio's eateries – too many of which smack of seaside tack – on the seafront. Rather, join locals standing in line at **La Barchina** (☎347 7212848; ⊙noon-3pm Tue-Fri, to 11pm Sat & Sun), a small white boat moored at the harbour which cooks up the morning's catch for lunch. The hot item to order is *fritto misto* (€7), a mix of squid, prawns and octopus battered, deep-fried and served with a huge friendly smile from Sandro Zani or son Andrea in plastic punnets. Friday cooks up *baccalà* (cod) and veggie lovers are catered for on weekdays with small/large punnets of *funghi fritti* (€5/8, fried mushrooms). The queue runs up to 30 minutes in high season, but no one seems to mind. To find the *barchina* (boat), walk to the harbour end of seafront promenade Viale Regina Margherita and duck under the white iron footbridge crossing the canal; the boat is almost opposite Tito del Molo on waterfront Lungomolo Corraldo del Greco.

discover Carnevale history and the art of making *teste in capo* (the giant heads worn in processions) and *mascheroni a piedi* (big walking masks) in the small on-site **Museo del Carnevale** (Carnival Museum).

Consorzio Marittimo Turistico BOAT TRIP
(☎01 8773 2987; www.navigazionegolfodeipoeti.it; adult/child 6-11 €30/15; ⊙mid-Jun–mid-Sep) In summer sail for the day to Porto Venere and Liguria's iconic cluster of medieval seaside villages known collectively as Cinque Terre. There is one boat daily; check the season's timetable online.

Festivals & Events

Carnevale di Viareggio CULTURE
(www.viareggio.ilcarnevale.com) Viareggio's annual moment of glory lasts four weeks in February to early March when the city goes wild during Carnevale – a festival of floats, many featuring giant satirical effigies of political and other topical figures, which also includes fireworks and rampant dusk-to-dawn spirit. Tickets for the 3pm Sunday processions (adult/reduced €15/10) can be bought on the same day from ticket kiosks on the procession circuit or in advance from **Fondazione Carnevale** (☎05 845 80 71; http://viareggio.ilcarnevale.com; Piazza Mazzini 22).

Information

Tourist office (☎05 8496 2233; www.aptversilia.it; Viale Regina Margherita 20; ⊙9am-2pm & 3-7pm Mon-Sat) Across from the clock on the waterfront.

Getting There & Away

TRAIN

To hit the sea from the **train station** (Piazza Dante Alighieri), exit and walk straight ahead along Via XX Settembre for 10 minutes. Regional train services:

Florence (€9, 1½ hours, at least hourly)
Livorno (€5.10, 35 minutes, 16 daily)
Lucca (€3.30, 20 minutes, every 20 minutes)
Pietrasanta (€2.50, 10 minutes, every 10 minutes)
Pisa (€3.30, 15 minutes, every 20 minutes)

THE LUNIGIANA

This landlocked enclave of territory is bordered to the north and east by the Apennines, to the west by Liguria and to the south by the Apuane Alps and the Garfagnana. The few tourists who make their way here tend to be lunching in Pontremoli, a real off-the-beaten-track gastronomic gem, or following in the footsteps of medieval pilgrims along the Via Francigena.

Autumnal visits reward with fresh, intensely scented *porcini* mushrooms that sprout under chestnut trees in fecund woods and hills. Wild herbs cover fields, and 5000 scattered hives produce the region's famous chestnut and acacia honey. These fruits of the forest and other regional delicacies, including Zeri lamb, freshly baked *focaccette,* crisp and sweet *rotella* apples, boiled pork shoulder, *caciotta* (a delicate cow's-milk cheese), *bigliolo* beans, local olive oil and Colli di Luni wines, are reason alone to visit.

Pontremoli

POP 7820

It may be small, but this out-of-the-way town presided over by the impressive bulk of Castello del Piagnaro has a decidedly grand air – a legacy of its strategic location

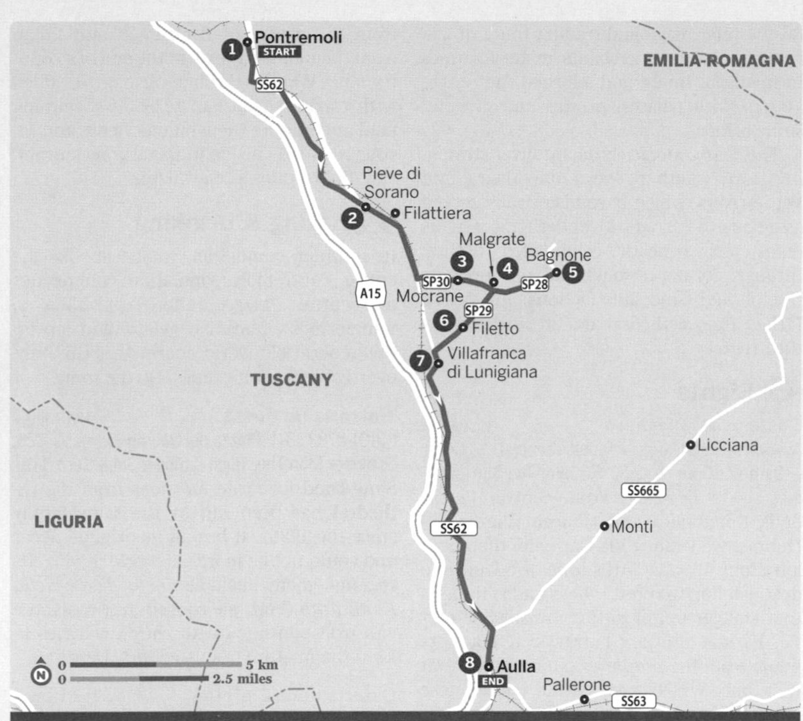

Driving Tour
The Via Francigena

START PONTREMOLI
END AULLA
LENGTH 32KM; TWO TO THREE HOURS

This medieval pilgrimage route connected Canterbury with Rome. It was so popular with pilgrims that in the 8th century the Lombard kings built churches, hospices and monasteries offering shelter for pilgrims along its length. This tour explores some of them.

From **1 Pontremoli** pick up the SS62 (direction La Spezia and Villafranca) and follow it 8km towards Filattiera. In a grassy field on the left, admire the Romanesque **2 Pieve di Sorano** (1148), with traditional *piagnaro* (stone slab) roof and watchtower. Beyond the church, up high, is the old hilltop village. Continue for 2.5km along the SS62 then turn left onto the SP30 (direction Bagnone) and drive 2.3km. In **3 Mocrone** enjoy great views of fortified **4 Malgrate** teetering on the hillside on your left; break for lunch at old-world village inn Locanda Gavarini (p160).

About 4km after Mocrone, **5 Bagnone** is distinctive for its castle, church and eateries. Stretch your legs with a walk above the fiercely gushing river and its dramatic gorges; pick up the 30-minute trail from Piazza Roma and end on main street Via della Republicca. The final leg across the medieval, stone-paved Ponte Vecchio is the stuff of poetry.

From Bagnone, backtrack to Mocrone and onwards towards Villafranca, veering slightly left onto the SP29 to reach the walled medieval hamlet of **6 Filetto**. Park outside the monumental gate and wander through its tiny piazzas and narrow lanes.

Arriving in **7 Villafranca di Lunigiana** 1.5km south, you're on another key stop on the pilgrim route. Set on the Magra river, it is an unassuming place with a small ethnographical museum in an old 15th-century flour mill.

End the tour 12km south in **8 Aulla**, known for its abbey founded in AD 884 and housing the remains of St Caprasio, the hermit monk who inspired the spread of monastic life in Provence from the 5th century.

on the pilgrimage and trading route of Via Francigena. Its merchants made fortunes in medieval times, and adorned the *centro storico* with palaces, piazzas and graceful stone bridges.

The *centro storico* is a long sliver stretching north–south between the Magra and Verde rivers, which have historically served as defensive barriers. Meandering its streets takes you beneath colonnaded arches, through former strongholds of opposing Guelph and Ghibelline factions, and past a 17th-century cathedral and an 18th-century theatre.

Sights

Castello del Piagnaro CASTLE

(www.statuestele.org; adult/reduced €4/2; 9am-12.30pm & 2.30-5.30pm Tue-Sun summer, shorter hr winter) From central Piazza della Repubblica and adjacent Piazza del Duomo, walk along Via Garibaldi then bear left along Vietata l'Affissione or Sdrucciolo del Castello, two pretty alleys and staircases that stagger uphill to this ramshackle castle. Former military barracks, it takes its name from the *piagnaro* (stone slabs) that were once widely used to roof Lunigianese buildings.

Views across town from the castle are impressive and inside is a small museum showcasing primitive stelae statues found nearby. No one knows exactly what these stelae, which have been found throughout the Lunigiana, were for – most depict male and female idols and date from around 3000 BC.

Sleeping

★ **Locanda Gavarini** HOTEL, RESTAURANT €

(01 8749 3115; www.locandagavarini.it; Via Benedicenti 50, Mocrone; s/d €50/70 incl breakfast; P) This country restaurant and inn, in the village of Mocrone at the end of the narrowest street you're ever likely to drive along, is a rural idyll where the only noise is twittering birds and the sunrise cry of the village cockerel. The restaurant (meals €20) is a culinary homage to Lunigianese tradition and is the best local dine for miles around.

Costa d'Orsola HOTEL €€

(01 8783 3332; www.costadorsola.it; Orsola; d/tr/q €120/150/200; P@) For a true taste of this beautiful, untamed region, spend a few nights in the restored stone buildings of this 16th-century village hamlet in Orsola, 3.3km from the centre of Pontremoli and 1.6km from the motorway exit, at the end of a country lane. Wander through olive groves filled with grazing sheep, lounge by the swimming pool and admire the fabulous views, and savour regional cuisine in its tasty restaurant. Half-board rates also available.

Eating & Drinking

In summer, come 5pm, what feels like the entire Pontremoli population congregates on central Piazza della Repubblica to mingle in its cafes, eat gelato, and lap up the general old-world charm that this tiny, overtly rural town exudes. Do the same.

Trattoria Da Bussè TRATTORIA €

(01 8783 1371; Piazza del Duomo 31; meals €25; dinner Mon-Thu, lunch & dinner Sat & Sun) This Slow Food favourite footsteps from the cathedral has been run by the same family since the 1930s. It has all its original decor and could not be more old-world in vibe. Its regional menu includes *torta d'erbe della Lunigiana* (herb pie cooked over coals in a cast-iron pan lined with chestnut leaves to keep the mixture from sticking). Delicious.

Osteria della Bietola OSTERIA €

(01 8783 1949; Via Bietola 49; meals €25; lunch & dinner Fri-Wed) Seating 25, this wonderfully authentic *osteria* hidden down a narrow alley off Via Garibaldi is the place to come for *porcini* mushrooms in season and a very tasty rabbit cooked with herbs. In case you're wondering, *bietola* is a type of chard.

Caffè degli Svizzeri PASTRIES, CAKES €

(01 8783 0160; Piazza della Repubblica 22; 7am-8pm Tue-Sun summer, shorter hr winter) This historic cafe overlooking Pontremoli's central square opened in 1842 and was given an art-nouveau makeover in 1910 that has been lovingly restored. Come here to eat cake – its *spongata degli svizzeri* (almond cake) and *biscotti della salute* (aniseed biscuits) are exceptionally fine, but pale into insignificance when contrasted with the utter delight of the *amor* (wafer filled with zabaglione-style cream, €1 a piece).

Trattoria Pelliccia TRATTORIA €€

(01 8783 0577; Via Garibaldi 137; meals €30; lunch & dinner) Tucked at the end of the *centro storico* is this trattoria, perfect for eating local. Start with *testaroli della lunigiana al pesto* (type of savoury crêpe cut into diamonds, cooked like pasta and served with

pesto), followed by oven-baked *agnello di Zeri* (€13; lamb). End with an unjustly good sorbet (lemon and sage, pistachio and pepper, strawberry and port…).

Information

Terre di Lunigiana (www.terredilunigiana.com) Excellent comprehensive website covering accommodation, nature, activities, dining etc in the Lunigiana.

Tourist office (☎01 8783 2000; Piazza della Repubblica 33; ⊙10am-noon & 3-6pm Sat & Sun)

Getting There & Away

TRAIN

Regional train services:

La Spezia (€5.40, 40 to 55 minutes, frequent)

Pisa (€7.10, 90 minutes, one daily)

Central Coast & Elba

Includes ➡

Best Places to Eat

- Surfer Joe's Diner (p168)
- Le Nuvole (p173)
- Ristorante Capo Nord (p184)
- Il Castagnacciao (p182)
- Enoteca Tognoni (p171)

Best Places to Stay

- Belvedere di Suvereto (p173)
- Podere dell'Orso (p171)
- La Cerreta (p172)
- Tenuta La Chiusa (p181)
- Agriturismo Due Palme (p181)

Why Go?

Despite an enviable setting, this part of Tuscany is not burdened with well-known destinations. Anonymous working cities prevail, including primary-school girl-bully Livorno who dares you to like her – if she doesn't punch your lights out first. But saunter inland, along a trail of vineyards and olive groves, and pride is restored in the form of eye-catching medieval villages and astonishing Etruscan ruins woven together by tiny roads and blind switchbacks. Yes, car, bicycle or foot are the only ways to explore.

Meandering south, several sandy strands are worth a sun-drenched flop and seaside lunch, especially around the bijou Golfo di Baratti. But the best alfresco frolics are a ferry ride away on Elba, a classic Mediterranean island with orange trees, palms and not a single high-rise fronting its many hidden beach-laced coves. Tramp its rugged interior, mountain bike, and don't you dare leave without paddling a sea kayak.

Road Distances

	Suvereto	Livorno	Piombino	Bogheri
Livorno	79			
Piombino	24	86		
Bolgheri	39	50	38	
Portoferrario	24+1hr	86+1hr	1hr	38+1hr

Getting Around

Livorno is a major port with ferries aplenty to Sardinia, Corsica and – closer to home – the tiny island of Capraia in the national-park-protected Tuscan Archipelago; to sail to Elba drive 90km south along the A12 and subsequent SS1 and SP23 to Piombino. Livorno is on the Rome–La Spezia train line and is also connected to Florence and Pisa by train. Bus services are limited; to really explore you need a car, scooter or bicycle.

THREE PERFECT DAYS

Day 1: Stunning Seafood

Livorno does seafood like nowhere else in Tuscany. Examine raw specimens bright and early at the Mercato Centrale, then walk across black-and-white checks on the Terrazza Mascagni followed by a seafood lunch at a Livorno eatery.

Day 2: Along the Strada del Vino e dell'Olio

Start inland from Livorno and wend your way scenically south through a rolling hinterland strung with medieval villages and laced with vineyards. Particularly fine tasting-stops – for wine and food – include San Guido and Bolgheri (linked by a beautiful, 5km-long Cypress Alley), from where it is a very wiggly 20km further south to Sassetta (a great place to overnight is at La Cerreta). Next day focus on Val di Cornia DOC wines in Suvereto, then head 25km southwest to the Golfo di Baratti for a picnic among Etruscan ruins.

Day 3: The Elba Experience

The final leg of the Strada del Vino is across the water on this paradise island. Catch the ferry from Piombino to Portoferraio and spend the day exploring its waterfront, haggling with fishermen for the day's catch, lunching in the Old Town and visiting its forts. Elba's oldest wine estate, Tenuta La Chiusa is the place to stay – and taste/buy Elba's sweet red Aleatico dessert wine. Next day, explore western Elba, not missing a trip up Monte Capanne, an evening *passeggiata* (evening stroll) in Marciana Marina and dinner at Ristorante Capo Nord. If you're with kids, include Rio Marina in your itinerary.

Where to Stay

- Livorno is the obvious place, but it is a busy port town.
- If you're craving peace and tranquillity head to the pine-shaded beaches and vine-framed *agriturismi* (farm stay accommodation) along the unpretentious Etruscan Coast.
- For paradise island accommodation, Elba is the place.

DON'T MISS

The motoring, hiking and biking on Elba is magnificent. But to uncover the island's best beaches, set sail in a sea kayak, fish for your dinner and camp wild beneath the stars.

Best Wine Tasting

- Cantina Nardi (p168)
- Enoteca Tognoni (p171)
- Enoteca dei Difficili (p173)
- Tenuta La Chiusa (p181)
- Fandango (p186)

Best Family Adventures

- Acquario di Livorno (p166)
- Parco Archeominerario di San Silvestro (p172)
- Parco Archeologico di Baratti e Populonia (p173)
- Museo dei Minerali e dell'Arte Mineraria (p186)
- Cabinovia Monte Capanne (p184)

Resources

- **Costa degli Etruschi** (www.costadeglietruschi.it) The Tuscan coast.
- **Tuscan Archipelago Tourist Board** (www.aptelba.it)
- **Info Elba** (www.infoelba.com) Practical Elba guide.

Central Coast & Elba Highlights

1 Revel in the extraordinary hustle, bustle and seafaring cuisine of port town **Livorno** (p166). Enjoy a cinematic moment on Livorno's 1920s **Terrazza Mascagni** (p166), followed by a dip in the sea at old-fashioned baths.

2 Taste Super Tuscans and other wines along the Etruscan Coast's **Strada del Vino e dell'Olio** (p171).

3 Marvel at Tuscany's longest **Cypress Alley** (p171) linking esteemed wine villages San Guido and Bolgheri.

4 Picnic between Etruscan tombs and enjoy majestic sea views in the **Parco Archeologico di Baratti e Populonia** (p173).

5 Set sail to Napoleon's **Elba** (p176); haggle with fishermen and lunch on in Portoferraio's Old Town, or escape to a historic wine estate or olive farm scented with orange blossom.

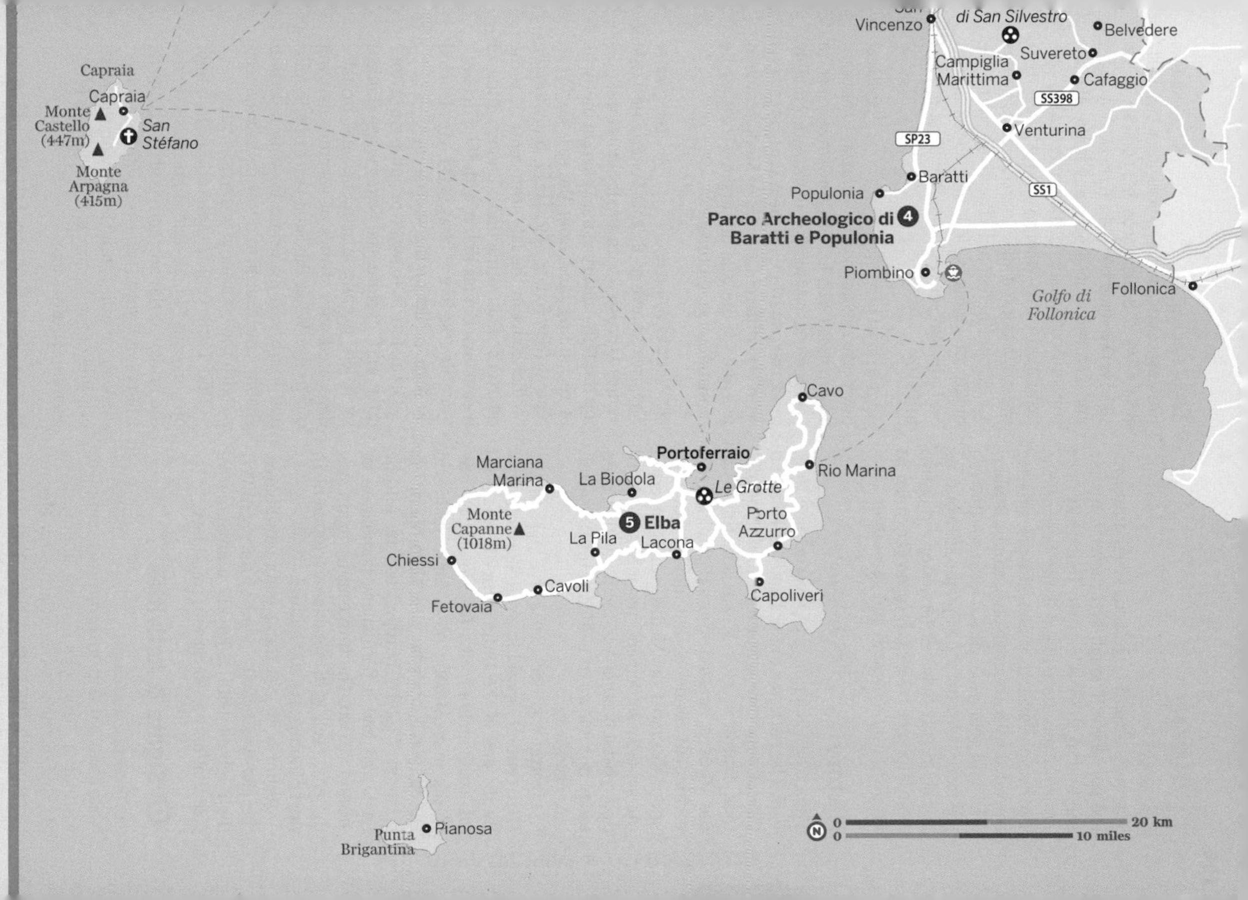

LIVORNO

POP 156,800

Tuscany's second-largest city is a quintessential port town. Though first impressions are rarely kind, this is a 'real' city that really does grow on you. Its seafood is the best on the Tyrrhenian coast, its shabby historic quarter threaded with Venetian-style canals is uber-cool, and pebbly beaches stretch south from the town's elegant belle Epoque seafront. Be it a short stay between ferries or a day trip from Florence or Pisa, Livorno (Leghorn in English) is understated and agreeable.

History

The earliest references to Livorno date from 1017. The port was in the hands of Pisa and then Genoa for centuries, until Florence took control in 1421. It was still tiny – by the 1550s it boasted a grand total of 480 permanent residents. But all that changed under Cosimo I de' Medici, who converted the scrawny settlement into a heavily fortified coastal bastion – to the point that even today it is known as a 'Medici town' by Italians elsewhere.

Livorno was declared a free port in the 17th century, sparking swift development. By the end of the 18th century it was a vital, cosmopolitan city, functioning as one of the main staging posts for British and Dutch merchants who were then operating between Western Europe and the Middle East, and had a permanent population of around 80,000. The 19th century again saw the city swell with notable development in the economy, arts and culture.

As one of Fascist Italy's main naval bases, the city was heavily bombed during WWII then rebuilt with a largely unimaginative face that only a sea captain could love.

Sights & Activities

★Terrazza Mascagni PROMENADE

(Viale Italia) No trip to Livorno is complete without a stroll along (and photo shoot of) this dazzling 'work of art' – an elegant terrace with stone balustrades that sweeps gracefully along the seafront in a dramatic chessboard flurry of black-and-white checks.

When it was built in the 1920s it was called Terrazza Ciano after the leader of the Livorno fascist movement, but 40 years later the city changed its name to that of Livorno-born opera composer Pietro Mascagni (1863–1945).

Bagni Pancaldi SWIMMING

(www.pancaldiacquaviva.it; Viale Italia 56; adult/child €5/4; ⏲8.30am-noon & 3-6pm Sat & Sun summer) Wedged between Terrazza Mascagni and Livorno's naval academy is the elegant soft apricot facade of Bagni Pancaldi, old-fashioned baths where you can swim, rent canoes, hang out in coloured canvas cabins and frolic in the sun. The baths were the height of sophistication, host to tea dances and musical soirées, when they first opened in 1846.

Acquario di Livorno AQUARIUM

(www.acquariodilivorno.it; Terrazza Mascagni; adult/reduced €12/10; ⏲10am-9pm summer, to 6pm weekends only winter) Livorno's thoroughly modern acquarium on the waterfront swims with 300 different species of Mediterranean fish and sea life. Star of the show is Cuba, the monsterous green turtle.

★Piccola Venezia HISTORIC QUARTER

The area known as Piccola Venezia or 'Little Venice' is crossed with small canals built during the 17th century using Venetian methods of reclaiming land from the sea. **Fortezza Nuova** (New Fort; ⏲24hr) FREE, built for the Medici court in the late 16th century, is the quarter's main attraction although little of it remains. Canals link it with the **Fortezza Vecchia** (Old Fort; ⏲24hr) FREE, constructed 60 years earlier on the waterfront.

Great fun is to walk or jump on a tour boat and explore the waterways flanked by faded, peeling apartments and brightly decorated with strings of washing hanging out to dry. What this area lacks in gondolas and tourists, it makes up for with a certain shabby-chic charm, and tow paths intersected with the occasional waterside cafe.

End 'Little Venice' explorations on a high on gorgeous **Piazza dei Domenicani**, across the bridge at the northern end of Via Borra. **Chiesa di Santa Catarina**, with its ancient, thick stone walls, stands sentry on the western side of the square as it did for the Medicis four centuries ago.

Museo Civico Giovanni Fattori ART GALLERY

(Via San Jacopo in Acquaviva 65; adult/reduced €4/2; ⏲10am-1pm & 4-7pm Tue-Sun) This gallery in a pretty park features works by the 19th-century Italian Impressionist Macchiaioli school led by Livorno-born Giovanni Fattori. The group, inspired by the Parisian Barbizon school, flouted stringent academic art conventions and worked directly from nature, emphasising immediacy and freshness through patches, or 'stains' *(macchia)*, of colour.

Museo di Storia Naturale del Mediterraneo MUSEUM
(Via Roma 234; adult/reduced €6/3; 9am-1pm Wed & Fri, to 7pm Tue, Thu & Sat, 3-7pm Sun;)

Livorno's hands-on Natural History Museum is an exhaustive, first-rate museum experience for the natural sciences. Temporary exhibits rotate continually, while the highlight of the permanent collection is a 20m-long common whale skeleton called Annie.

Livorno

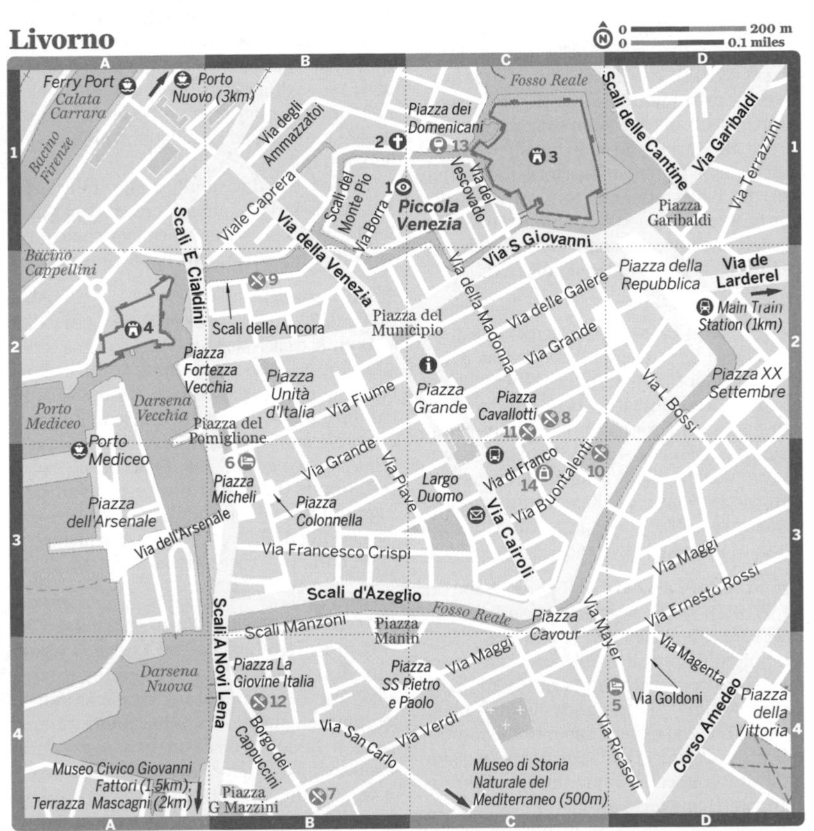

Livorno

Top Sights
1 Piccola Venezia B1

Sights
2 Chiesa di Santa Catarina B1
3 Fortezza Nuova C1
4 Fortezza Vecchia A2

Sleeping
5 Hotel al Teatro D4
6 Hotel Gran Duca B3

Eating
7 Cantina Senese B4
8 La Barrocciaia C2
9 L'Ancora B2
10 Mercato Centrale C3
11 Mercato di Piazza Cavallotti C2
12 Osteria del Mare B4

Drinking & Nightlife
13 La Bodeguita C1

Shopping
14 VAD Formaggi C3

Tours

Giro in Battello BOAT TOUR
(adult/reduced €10/5; 11am, noon & 4pm summer) The tourist office sells tickets for twice- or thrice-daily guided tours by boat (45 minutes) of Livorno's waterways.

Sleeping

★ **Hotel al Teatro** BOUTIQUE HOTEL €
(05 8689 8705; www.hotelalteatro.it; Via Mayer 42; s/d €85/110;) One of Tuscany's loveliest urban hotels, this bijou eight-room address with marble staircase, antique furniture, tapestries and individually designed rooms named after composers is irresistible. But the real stunner is the gravel garden out back where guests can lounge on green wicker furniture beneath a breathtakingly beautiful, 350-year-old magnolia tree.

Camping Miramare CAMPGROUND €
(05 8658 0402; www.campingmiramare.it; Via del Littorale 220; camping 2 people, car & tent €40-80;) Be it tent pitch beneath trees or deluxe version with wooden terrace and sun-loungers on the sandy beach, this campground – open year-round thanks to its village of mobile homes, maxi caravans and bungalows – has it all. Rates out of summer are at least 50% lower. Find the site 8km south of town in Antignano.

Grand Hotel Palazzo LUXURY HOTEL €€
(05 8626 0836; www.grandhotelpalazzo.com; Viale Italia 195; d €140-180;) This shimmering ship of a 19th-century palace on the seafront, with 123 perfectly thought-out rooms and glistening sea views, is belle-Epoque Livorno relived. Dip into the rooftop infinity pool and, afterwards, gorge poolside on a sunset *aperitivo* (predinner drinks accompanied by cocktail snacks) and panoramic sea view. Dining in its rooftop garden restaurant, face to face with the sea and the islet of Gorgona, is equally glam.

Hotel Gran Duca HOTEL €€
(05 8689 1024; www.granduca.it; Piazza Micheli 16; s/d €160/180;) Embedded in the little that survives of Livorno's 16th-century city walls, this hotel with dusty pink facade across from the fishing docks is unique. Its 60 rooms are classic with regal-coloured fabrics; some rooms also have fortress views. For history buffs, those on the 2nd floor with private terrace in the red-brick ramparts of the Medici wall could be straight out of a film set.

Eating & Drinking

Sampling traditional *cacciucco*, a mixed seafood stew, is reason enough to visit Livorno.

★ **Surfer Joe's Diner** AMERICAN €
(05 8680 9211; www.surferjoe.it/diner; Terrazza Mascagni; meals €15-30; noon-1am Tue-Sun) What a burst of dynamism this zesty surf bar on the seafront adds to Livorno drinking and dining scene. American burgers, onion rings, pancakes and smoothies is its culinary bias; 1950s diner is its 'look'; and surf music is its idol. A huge terrace licked by the sea breeze and shaded with bamboo huts is the icing on the cake.

During the day families pile into Surfer Joe. After dark, a younger crowd flocks here for DJ and jam sessions, concerts and various other hip surf-music happenings.

Cantina Nardi TUSCAN €
(05 8680 8006; Via Cambini 6-8; meals €20; lunch & dinner Mon-Sat) In business since 1965, the Nardis know a thing or three about cooking up hearty, wholly affordable Tuscan fare in the company of friendly knowledgeable staff and fabulous wine. As much *enoteca* (wine bar) as Slow Food–hailed restaurant, the bistro organises wine tastings and predinner *aperitivi*. Dine between bottled-filled shelves inside, or outside on bijou patio or street terrace.

La Barrocciaia OSTERIA €
(05 8688 2637; Piazza Cavallotti 13; meals €20; 11am-3pm & 6-11pm Tue-Sat) Livorno's worst-kept dining secret, yes, but locating it takes a careful eye given its tiny facade swamped by market stalls. With luck and timing, score a table to discover why every local speaks of La Barrocciaia with such reverence. The menu fluctuates, as does the wall art, with the exception of grandpa's picture, quietly supervising the third generation of management.

Cantina Senese OSTERIA €
(05 8689 0239; Borgo dei Cappuccini 95; meals €20; lunch & dinner Mon-Sat) Food- and value-conscious harbour workers are the first to fill the long wooden tables at this wonderfully unpretentious and friendly eatery, with neighbourhood families arriving later. Ordering is frequently done via faith in one's server, rather than by menu. The mussels are exceptional, as is the *cacciucco*, both served with piquant garlic bread.

TO MARKET, TO MARKET

For foodie nirvana, get lost in Livorno's late-19th-century **Mercato Centrale** (Via Buontalenti; ⏲6am-2pm Mon-Sat), a magnificent, 95m-long neoclassical gem that miraculously survived Allied WWII bombing intact. Arresting both gastronomically and architecturally, the market is a gargantuan maze of tasty food stalls bursting with local produce, including the most astonishing fish and seafood.

Every Saturday morning, the **Mercato di Piazza Cavallotti** (Piazza Cavallotti; ⏲6am-2pm Mon-Sat) transforms the otherwise quiet square into a sea of open-air stalls bursting with baby violet artichokes, golden courgette flowers, hot red peppers and other seasonal fruit and veg.

Complete the foodie experience with a visit to **VAD Formaggi** (www.vadformaggi.com; Via di Franco 36-38; ⏲7.45am-12.45pm Mon & Wed, 7.45am-12.45pm & 4.40-7.30pm Thu-Sat), the most extraordinary cheese shop, in business since 1955. Its walls are lined floor-to-ceiling with giant rounds of parmesan, and market days see the queue spill out the door.

Osteria del Mare SEAFOOD €€
(☎05 8688 1027; Borgo dei Cappuccini 5; meals €25; ⏲lunch & dinner Fri-Wed) Traditional fish dishes, cooked just like grandma did, lures the punters to this smart old-world *osteria* (tavern) near the water. Go local with *riso nero* (black rice) and the catch of the day, or a simple plate of *fritto misto* (battered and deep-fried mix of thumb-sized fish).

★ **L'Ancora** SEAFOOD €€
(☎05 8688 1401; www.ristoranteancoralivorno.com; Scali delle Ancora 10; meals €35; ⏲lunch & dinner summer, Wed-Mon winter) Gorgeous! Its canalside terrace is the white-hot ticket in good weather, though settling for a table in the elegantly simple 17th-century, barrel-ceilinged, brick boat house is hardly a hardship. You can get *cacciucco* here, but the *carbonara di mare* (seafood and pasta in white sauce) is the family's pride and joy.

La Bodeguita BAR
(Scala Rosciano 9; ⏲9pm-1am Mon-Sat) A red-brick cellar bar with sun-drenched wooden-decking terrace afloat the canal off Piazza dei Domenicani in Piccolo Venezia. Enjoy a cocktail and generously topped bruschetta while members of the local rowing club ply the water with oars in front of you, or dance to live music after dark.

ℹ Information

Tourist office (☎05 8689 4236; www.costadeglietruschi.it; Via Pieroni 18; ⏲8am-5.30pm summer, shorter hr winter)

ℹ Getting There & Away

BOAT

Livorno is a major port. Regular ferries for Sardinia and Corsica depart from Calata Carrara, beside the Stazione Marittima; and ferries to Capraia (via Gorgona) use the smaller Porto Mediceo near Piazza dell'Arsenale. Boats to Spain and Sicily, plus some Sardinia services, use Porto Nuovo, 3km north of the city along Via Salvatore Orlando.

Ferry companies:

Corsica Ferries (www.corsica-ferries.it) Two to seven services per week to Bastia, Corsica (from €36, four hours) and Golfo Aranci, Sardinia (from €45, six to hours).

Grimaldi Lines (www.grimaldi-ferries.com) Weekly sailings to/from Barcelona (€35 to €85, 21 hours) and Tangiers, Morocco (€80 to €240, 58 hours).

Moby (www.moby.it) Boats to/from Bastia, Corsica (from €28, four hours) and Olbia, Sardinia (€46 to €97, six to 10½ hours).

Toremar (www.toremar.it) Services year-round to Capraia (€20, 2¾ hours).

CAR

The A12 runs past the city and the SS1 connects Livorno with Rome. There are several car parks near the waterfront.

TRAIN

From the **main train station** (Piazza Dante) walk westwards (straight ahead) along Viale Carducci, Via de Larderel, then Via Grande into central Piazza Grande, Livorno's main square.

Trains are less frequent to **Stazione Marittima**, the station for the ports.

Florence (€9, 1½ hours, 16 daily)

Pisa (€2.50, 15 minutes, frequent)

Rome (€21.65 to €33, three to four hours, 12 daily)

ℹ Getting Around

ATL (www.atl.livorno.it; Largo Duomo 2) has a service (bus 1) from the main train station to Porto Mediceo (€1.20, on board €1.70), via

OFF THE BEATEN TRACK

MAKING SPAGHETTI

In the medieval hilltop village of Lari (pop 8755), across from the thick red-brick walls of its huge 11th-century fortress, is an address no gastronome should miss: **Martelli** (www.martelli.info; Via San Martino 3; ⏲10am-noon & 3-4pm Mon, Tue, Thu & Fri). Behind the canary-yellow facade of this *pastificio trazionale* (artisanal pasta maker), 35km southeast of Pisa, seven members of the Martelli family beaver away to make 1 tonne of pasta a year – an output any industrial factory would achieve in a matter of hours. Slowly kneaded dough is fed through traditional bronze moulds to create spaghetti and spaghettini, penne, macaroni and fusilli. This is then air-dried for 50 hours (compared to three hours industrially), cut and packaged by hand in Martelli's trademark canary-yellow paper packets, designed to evoke the pre-1960s yellow paper that pasta in Tuscany was traditionally wrapped in at the market before industrial packaging changed it all.

Around since 1926, Martelli pasta – chewier and coarser in texture than many, meaning it marries particularly well with meat sauces and game – is shipped all over the world and sold in many a gourmet store, Harrods of London included. In Lari, buy it for €4 per kilogram around the corner from the workshop at village cafe and tobacconist, **La Bottega delle Specialità** (Via Diaz 12-14); and taste it for lunch at restaurants in the village.

Workshop tours are completely informal. Stick your head around the shopfront, ask to visit (Luca, whose grandfather opened Martelli in 1926, speaks English), then nip down the neighbouring alley to reach the small room where the spaghetti action takes place.

Piazza Grande. To reach Stazione Marittima, take bus 1 to Piazza Grande then bus 5 from Via Cogorano, just off Piazza Grande.

THE ETRUSCAN COAST

The coastline south from Livorno to just beyond Piombino and the ferry to the island of Elba lives up to its historically charged name, Costa degli Etruschi (Etruscan Coast), thanks to a smattering of Etruscan tombs unearthed on its shores. Its basic bucket-and-spade beaches are unstartling, but saunter inland into the hinterland to discover some of Tuscany's lesser-known, but often very good, wines against a backdrop of pretty hilltop villages and winemaking towns.

Those keen to explore by pedal-power can find a wonderfully conceived, detailed list of routes at www.costadeglietruschi.it.

Castiglioncello

Agreeably unpretentious, this small seaside resort 30km south of Livorno is where Italian critic and patron of the arts, Digo Martelli, held court in the late 19th century. He would play host to the Florentine Impressionist artists of the period, giving birth to the artistic movement known as La Scuola di Castiglioncello (Castiglioncello School). The work of contemporary artists who continue to find inspiration in the town can be viewed in the **Centro per l'Arte Diego Martelli** (☎05 8675 9012; Piazza della Vittoria; ⏲3.30-7pm Fri, 10.30am-1.15pm & 3.30-7pm Sat & Sun) FREE, a gallery snug against the gated entrance to **Castello Pasquini** (Piazza della Vittoria). Built in the late 19th century with lovely tree-shaded grounds (a great play park for kids), the crenellated castle is stage to the town's theatre today.

Castiglioncello's best sandy beaches are on the town's northern fringe. Get a map from the **tourist office** (☎05 8675 4890; Via Aurelia 632; ⏲9.30am-12.30pm & 4-6pm), within the train station. The town is linked by a regular train with Livorno (€3.10, 25 minutes).

Sleeping & Eating

★**Pensione Bartoli** HOTEL €

(☎05 8675 2051; www.albergobartoli.com; Via Martelli 9; s/d/tr/q €60/79/96/115, half-board per person €60-70, full board €68-74; ⏲summer; P) Aspiring to the very best of a 1950s boarding house, this impeccably kept villa with shaded garden has bags of character and is wonderful value for money. It's an old-fashioned 'let's stay with grandma' place with 17 well-dusted rooms – five with sea view – and venerable family furniture, photos and knick-knacks. In June to August, it's half- or full-board only.

But dining in is hardly a hardship. With the kitchen (and hotel) firmly in the capable hands of Rosabianca and her mother Aurora (who opened the hotel in 1952), guests eat very well indeed.

★ Podere dell'Orso FARMSTAY €
(☎050 66 26 98; www.poderedellorso.it; Serre di Sotto 1 , Colle Alberti, Lorenzana; d/tr €90/115) The quest for the perfect Tuscan room with a view ends here, at this beautiful 15th-century farmhouse surrounded by fruit orchards, olive groves and a peace and tranquillity you'll never want to leave.

Stylish rooms have big green views and guests can feast on Tuscan classics fuelled with Podere dell'Orso olive oil in the farm *osteria* (open for dinner on Friday and Saturday, and lunch on Sunday, by reservation only).

From Lorenzano, follow signs to Casciana Terme and after 3km turn left towards the hamlet of Colle Alberti.

Grand Hotel Villa Parisi LUXURY HOTEL €€€
(☎05 8675 1698; www.villaparisi.com; Via Romolo Monti 1; s/d €104/198, half-board per person €109-239; Apr-Sep; P ❄ 📶 ≋) With its chic cream facade and wooden shutters, painted racing green, this beautiful seaside villa facing the big blue would not look amiss in a glossy design mag. The top-notch option in town, Villa Parisi oozes panache. Late May to mid-September, half-board is obligatory but given the gorgeous, five-star restaurant who cares?

Caffè Ginori CAFE
(Piazza della Vittoria) With its shaded terrace and interior dating to 1946, Caffè Ginori is where locals drop by to jaw at the bar or gorge on exquisite miniature cakes almost too good to eat. This was the favourite hangout of Italian heart-throb Marcello Mastroianni when he had a summer villa in town.

Bolgheri & Around

This tiny walled village is dominated by its toylike, red-brick castle taking in the city gate and Romanesque Chiesa di SS Giacomo e Cristoro, restructured towards the end of the 19th century. But the main reason people flock here, bar browsing its pricey tourist shops, is to taste wine – notably its locally produced, internationally famous 'Super Tuscan' Sassicaia.

From Bolgheri head 5.7km west along the SP16 to **San Guido** to pick up tasting notes and lists of wine estates where you can taste and buy at the **Strada del Vino e dell'Olio visitor centre** (☎05 6574 9705; Castegneto Carducci 45; 10am-1pm & 2-5pm Mon-Sat), within a pretty walled rose garden; the centre also arranges visits to wineries, olive farms and honey producers.

The short drive is stunning – along a dead-straight, impossibly romantic, century-old **Cypress Alley** built from 2540 trees and made famous by Tuscan poet Giosuè Carducci in his 1874 poem *Davanti a San Guido*. Each year in July the 5km-long tree-lined avenue creates a green backdrop for the arts festival, **Bolgheri Melody** (www.bolgherimelody.com).

Sleeping & Eating

Strada Giulia 16 B&B €€
(☎331 2661699; www.stradagiuliabolgheri.it; Strada Giulia 16; d €150-190; P) Strada Giulia 16 is both the name and address of this hybrid B&B-boutique hotel in a centuries-old house. Location alone, within the historic walls of Bolgheri, renders it instantly charming and its four rooms are glamorously named after famous ladies. Pick from Marilyn, Brigitte, Jacqueline or Lady D.

★ Enoteca Tognoni WINE BAR €€
(☎05 6576 2001; www.enotecatognoni.it; Via Lauretta 5; meals €35; lunch & dinner Thu-Tue) This serious wine bar on Bolgheri's pretty central piazza is a temple to taste, gastronomic and

OFF THE BEATEN TRACK

THE WINE & OIL ROAD

If tasting wine on the seashore or pedalling between olive groves rocks your boat, then trip it – by car, bike or on foot in places – along the **Strada del Vino e dell'Olio** (www.lastradadelvino.com), a 150km tourist itinerary stretching south from Livorno to Piombino and across to Elba. It maps out cellars, wine estates and farms where you can taste and buy local wine and olive oil, and also recommends places to stay and eat. Its visitor centre (p171) is just outside Bolgheri.

oenological. Sassicaia (€22 per 100mL) is among the dozens of different wines to taste and a traditionally Tuscan menu features the best of local products.

Order a mixed plate of antipasti (€12) – a generous feast of salami, cheese, tomato-topped bruschetta, *crostini* (thick slices of Tuscan bread toasted and topped with pâté, oil, tomato and so on) – to accompany your pick of wine and enter foodie heaven.

Castagneto Carducci

POP 8470

South from Bolgheri a densely wooded minor road rolls between vineyards and olive groves before climbing into the hills to this old fortified town. Behind its town walls lies a web of steep, narrow lanes crowded in by brooding houses and dominated by the castle of the Gherardesca clan that once controlled the surrounding area. (The stronghold was turned into a mansion in the 18th century.) The 19th-century poet Giosuè Carducci spent much of his childhood here.

From Castagneto, a winding forested hilly road leads to the tiny hamlet of **Sassetta** (population 580), where houses hang on to their perches for dear life. A map at the entrance marks local walking trails.

Sleeping & Eating

★ **La Cerreta** AGRITURISMO €€

(☎05 6579 4352; www.lacerreta.it; Via Campagna Sud 143, Pian delle Vigne; s/d half-board €80/120; P ≋) Akin to the Tuscan dream, La Cerreta is a biodynamic estate with four stone cottages wedged between woods, vines, fig trees with sweeping views of rolling Tuscan hills. There are horses to ride and the charismatic Daniele takes guests around his 70-hectare farm, explaining how he tends his *cinta senese* (indigenous Tuscan pigs), Maremma cows and rare Livornese chickens.

Everything served for dinner comes from the estate (with the exception of dinner on Friday – fish fresh from wife Vilma's fisherman friend in Piombino). The spirit of the place is 100% in harmony with nature, down to the state-of-the-art thermal spa (admission €20) – a series of pebble rock pools cascading down the hillside. Grapes and olives are harvested in September, chestnuts in October.

San Vincenzo

POP 7020

Italian visitors flock to this moderately attractive seaside town in summer to flop on sandy beaches backed by herb-scented *macchia* (wild scrubland) and pine forest.

In town, yachties moor their vessels in the smart, modern **Marina di San Vincenzo**, well-endowed with a waterside line-up of chic, glass-box boutiques and bars. Those in the know remain staunchly loyal to shabby-chic **Zanzibar** (☎05 6570 2927; Piazza del Porto; meals €40; ⏰lunch & dinner Thu-Tue) with vintage decor, designer nourishment and DJ sets after dark. It's in a former fishermen hut at the northern end of the marina.

A few kilometres inland, the **Parco Archeominerario di San Silvestro** (www.parchivaldicornia.it; adult/reduced €15/11; ⏰9.30am-7.30pm summer, shorter hr rest of year, closed Nov & Dec) explores the valley's 3000-year mining history. Around 50m before the turn-off to the park entrance, a sunken lane on the right signposted *'forni fusori'* leads to the remains of some Etruscan smelting ovens, once used for copper production. The park itself comprises the ruins of the 14th-century mining town **Rocca di San Silvestro**, reached via an underground train that passes through the Temperino **copper and lead mines** (with a small **mineral museum**) en route. Guided tours depart roughly hourly.

Suvereto

POP 3140

Suvereto, seat of a bishopric, was only incorporated into the Tuscan grand duchy in 1815. It is one of Tuscany's most beautiful medieval villages, hence the summer crowd that flocks here after a day on the beach to meander its narrow cobbled streets and steep cream-stone stairways brightened with flower balconies and windowsills. A steep climb up to its crowning glory, the 15th- to 16th-century **rocca** (castle), abandoned in the 1600s and slowly being restored, rewards with a magnificent panorama of surrounding fields and olive groves. On dusky pink summer evenings it is particularly soul-soaring.

Another lovely stroll from main street Via Matteoti, uphill along Via del Crocifisso, brings you to all that remains of the 13th-century Convento di San Francesco: its beautiful red-brick **Chiostro di San Francesco**, used today as a stunning stage for summer concerts, theatre performances and cultural events. Each year in mid-July during Suvereto's annual **Serate Medioevali** (Medieval Evenings), the Romanesque cloister is transformed into a medieval marketplace complete with locals dressed in traditional medieval costume, a medieval banquet, and euro coins being traded for medieval coinage to spend at the many art, craft and food stalls. Should you have the desire to marry your loved one Tuscan medieval-style, this – really! – is the occasion.

Given the accolades of 'Slow Food town', 'wine town' and 'oil town' that it bears, Suvereto is a predictably wonderful place to discover local **Val di Cornia DOC wines** and dine well. The **tourist office** (Via Matteotti 42) has information on where to taste and buy.

Sleeping & Eating

★Belvedere di Suvereto B&B €
(☎328 7158104, 05 6582 7061; www.belvederedisuvereto.it; Piazza San Tommaso 33, Belvedere; s/d/tr/q €58/90/120/140) In nearby Belvedere, this stylish B&B and bistro has fresh white rooms, minimalist country-crafted furnishings and, somewhat predictably, a blockbuster *belvedere* (viewpoint) of sweet Suvereto far far below.

I'Ciocio MODERN TUSCAN €€
(☎05 6582 9947; www.osteriadisuvereto.it; Piazza dei Giudici; meals €35; ⏲lunch & dinner Tue-Sun) Head uphill from Suvereto's main street along Via Piave to this creative *osteria* with an appealing mix of old and new furnishings, a beautiful terrace facing the exquisite red-brick Palazzo Comunale (town hall), and a menu squared firmly at foodies – the 12 different sugar types served after dinner with coffee says it all.

★Le Nuvole MODERN TUSCAN €€€
(☎05 6582 9092; www.lenuvoleristobistro.it; Via Palestro 2; meals €45; ⏲lunch & dinner Tue-Sun) Fabulous Le Nuvole is one of Tuscany's fast-rising culinary stars. Talented chef Timothy Magee, a particular ace at gelato and anything to do with chocolate, cooks up a modern Tuscan cuisine – lots of fish – in the kitchen of this lovely boutique restaurant, while sommelier Cristina works the outstanding wine list.

LOCAL KNOWLEDGE

BELVEDERE

'Belvedere' in Italian means 'viewpoint' or 'panorama', and that is precisely what the hilltop hamlet of **Belvedere** proffers to anyone who drives this far. Hidden on the top of a hill 3km from Suvereto, the hamlet, 280m above sea level, was created in the mid-16th century as an airy escape for rich folk from the malaria-infested plain. Its central square, unpaved, is the most enchanting – and intimate – you're ever likely to encounter in Tuscany (it's rather like brazenly peeking without scruple into the back gardens of every surrounding ginger-stone house). Belvedere's insider address is Belvedere di Suvereto (p173).

Drinking

Enoteca dei Difficili WINE BAR
(Via San Leonardo 2; ⏲6pm-2am Mon, Tue & Thu, to 3am Fri-Sun) This is a spirited spot with brick-and-beam ceiling, stylish vintage chairs and a blockbuster selection of wines. The wine bar has live music (check its Facebook page to see what bands are playing) and serves *crostini, panini,* bruschetta and various €10 *taglieri* (tasting platters of wild boar, salami, cheese etc).

Golfo di Baratti

The drive from San Vincenzo to pretty waterside **Baratti** in the Baratti Gulf is a dead-straight 12km motor south along an avenue lined by sky-high parasol pines backing onto beautiful sandy beaches. Baratti itself is a gorgeous little fishing port with a couple of lovely restaurants.

Sights & Activities

★Parco Archeologico di Baratti e Populonia ARCHAEOLOGICAL SITE
(☎05 6522 6445; www.parchivaldicornia.it; Necropoli or Acropoli adult/child €10/7, entire park adult/child/family €15/11/39; ⏲9.30am-7.30pm Jul & Aug, 10am-6pm Tue-Sun Mar-Jun, Sep & Oct, closed Nov-Feb; 👪) Absolutely fascinating and a real highlight is this vast green archaeological park where five marked walking trails lead to various unearthed remains of several Etruscan tombs. Particularly impressive are the gigantic circular tumulus tombs in the

1

3

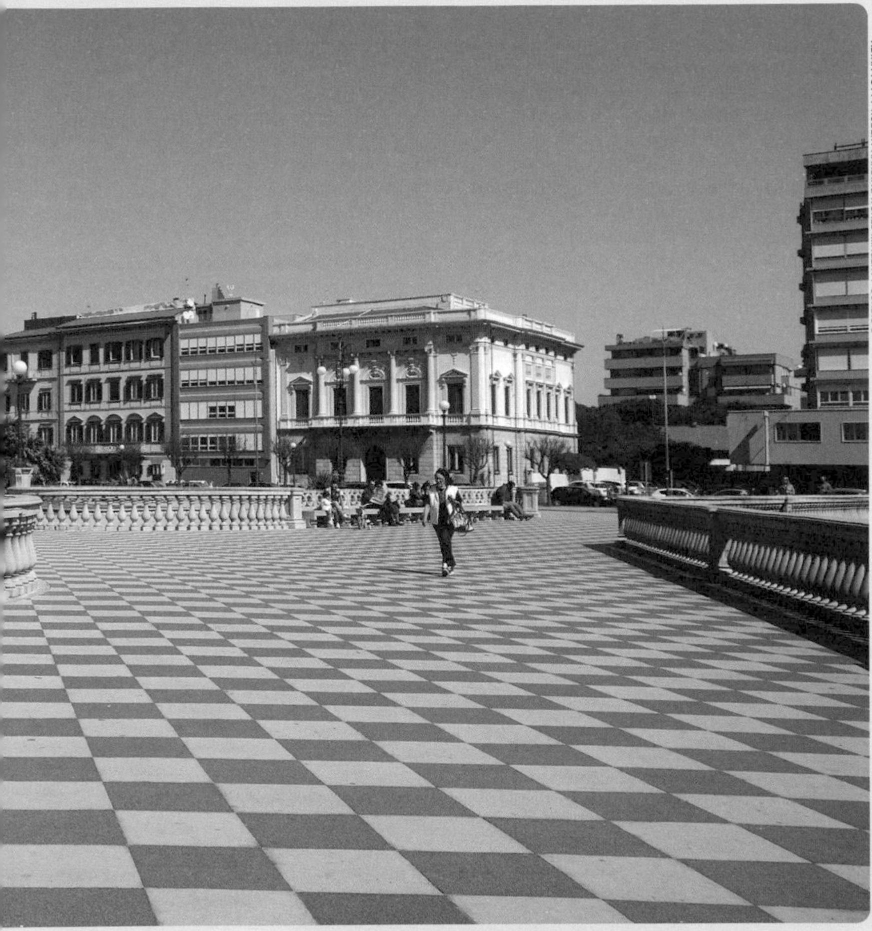

ADINA TOVY / ROBERT HARDING WORLD IMAGERY / CORBIS ©

1. Terrazza Mascagni (p166), Livorno
This elegant promenade sweeps gracefully along Livorno's seafront.

2. Golfo di Baratti (p173)
Golfo di Baratti's sundrenched shoreline is the perfect place for a seaside lunch.

3. Portoferraio (p179), Elba
Portoferraio's Old Town is a spiderweb of narrow streets and alleys that stagger uphill from the old harbour.

UNIVERSAL IMAGES GROUP / DEAGOSTINI / ALAMY ©

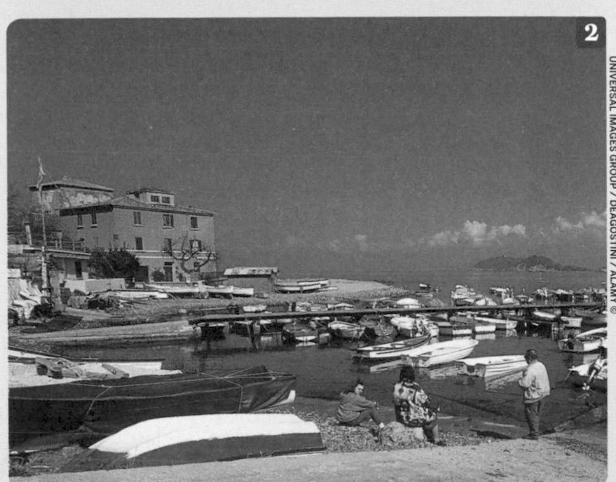

Necropoli di San Cerbone immediately in front of the visitors centre – the **Tomba dei Carri** is an astonishing 28m in diameter.

Great for families (bring your own picnic to make a day of it), the easy **Via delle Cave trail** (two hours) leads through shady woodland to the quarries from which the soft ochre sandstone was extracted and into which tombs were later cut.

More demanding is the **Via della Romanella** (Metal Working Trail; 2½ hours) which leads to the Etruscan acropoli (acropolis) of Populonia. Digs here have revealed the foundations of an Etruscan temple dating to the 2nd century BC, along with its adjacent buildings. If you don't want to walk, you can drive here – follow signs for **Populonia**, a pretty three-street hamlet still owned by a single family and protected by a 15th-century castle with a tower that can be scaled for a fabulous panorama of park and coast.

Bring a sun hat, cream and sturdy shoes.

Sleeping & Eating

Canessa SEAFOOD €€
(☎05 652 9530; www.canessacamere.it; Baratti; d €70-100, meals €30; ⊙lunch & dinner, closed Mon Sep-Jun) What makes this contemporary seafood restaurant so unique is the 15th-century watchtower that the modern building is wrapped around. Cuisine is fishy and fresh, and huge windows look onto the lapping waves. Should you fall in love with quaint Baratti (likely), Canessa has four rooms up top with sea views and romantic terraces on which to savour the outstanding location.

ELBA & THE TUSCAN ARCHIPELAGO

POP 31,000

A local legend says that when Venus rose from the waves, seven precious stones fell from her tiara, creating seven islands off the Tuscan coast. These little-known gems range from the tiny uninhabited island of Gorgona, just 2.23 sq km in size, to the biggest and busiest island, 224-sq-km Elba (Isola d'Elba), best known as the place where Napoleon (poor thing) was exiled to.

National Parks

The **Parco Nazionale dell'Arcipelago Toscano** (Tuscan Archipelago National Park; www.islepark.it) safeguards the delicate ecosystems of the seven islands as well as the 600 sq km of sea that washes around them, making it Europe's largest protected marine area.

Here, typical Mediterranean fish abound and rare species, such as the wonderfully named Neptune's shaving brush seaweed, unique to the archipelago, cling to life. Monk seals, driven from the other islands by human presence, still gambol in the deep underwater ravines off Montecristo. The islands serve as an essential rest stop for birds migrating between Europe and Africa. The shy red partridge survives on Elba and Pianosa and the archipelago supports over a third of the world's population of the equally uncommon Corsican seagull, adopted as the national park's symbol.

On Elba, the national park runs visitors centres in Enfola, Marciana and Rio dell'Elba.

Elba

Napoleon would think twice about fleeing Elba today. Dramatically more congested than when the emperor was charitably dumped here in 1814 (he did manage to engineer an escape in less than a year), the island is an ever-glorious paradise setting of rocky beach-laced coves, vineyards, blue waters, thoroughly fabulous hairpin-bend motoring and mind-bending views crowned by the highest peak on the island, **Monte Capanne** (1018m). All this is supplemented by a very fine seafaring cuisine, some lovely island wines and a rugged terrain just made for hiking, biking and sea-kayaking.

With the exception of high season – actually only the month of August – when the island's beaches are sardine-packed and the few roads clogged to a standstill with too much traffic, Elba is something of a *Robinson Crusoe* paradise. In springtime, early summer and autumn, when grapes and olives are harvested, there are plenty of tranquil nooks on this stunningly picturesque, 28km-long, 19km-wide island.

History

Elba has been inhabited since the Iron Age and the extraction of iron ore and metallurgy were the island's principal sources of economic wellbeing until well into the second half of the 20th century. In 1917 some 840,000 tonnes of iron were produced, but in WWII the Allies bombed the industry to bits. By the beginning of the 1980s, produc-

Elba

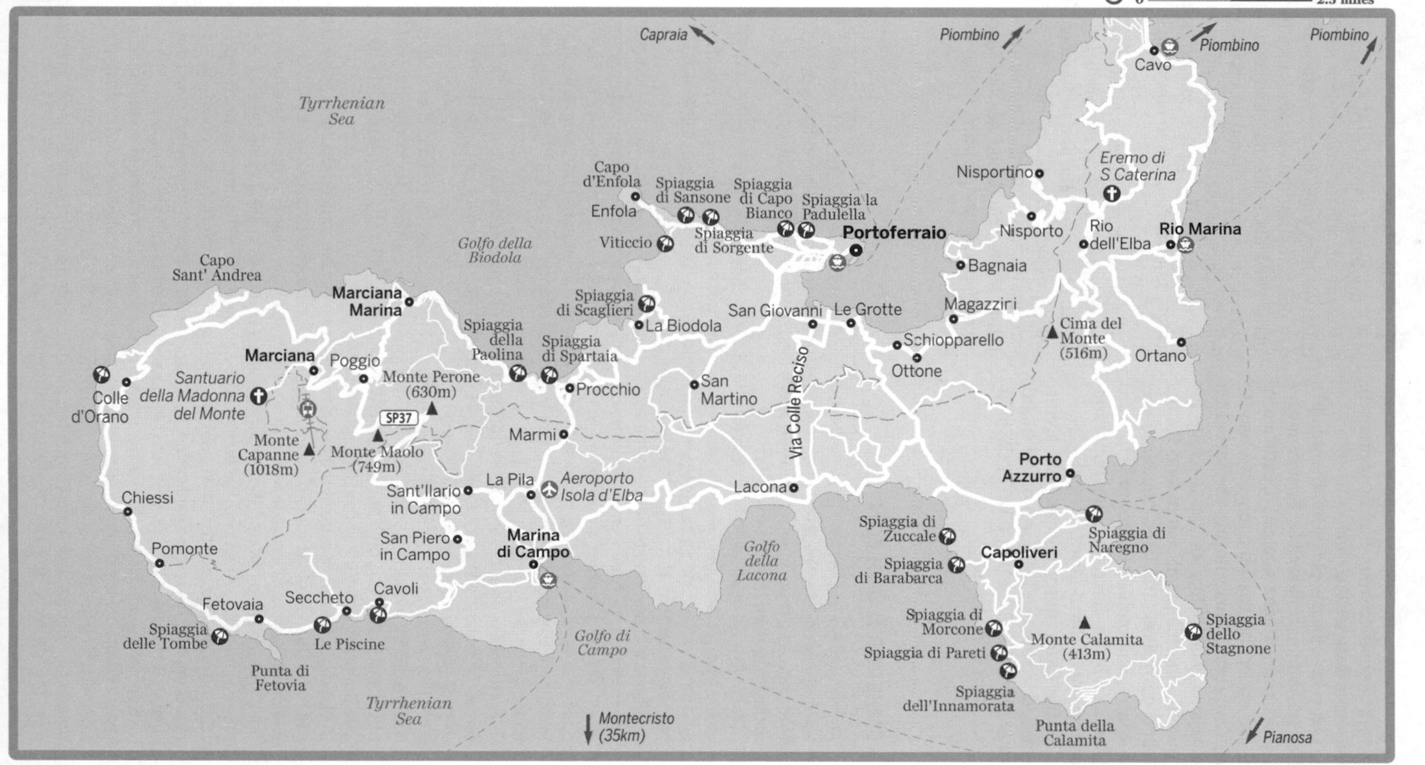
0 5 km
0 2.5 miles
Capraia
Piombino
Piombino
Piombino
Cavo
Tyrrhenian Sea
Nisportino
Eremo di S Caterina
Capo d'Enfola
Enfola
Spiaggia di Sansone
Spiaggia di Capo Bianco
Spiaggia la Padulella
Spiaggia di Sorgente
Viticcio
Golfo della Biodola
Portoferraio
Nisporto
Rio dell'Elba
Rio Marina
Bagnaia
Capo Sant' Andrea
Marciana Marina
Spiaggia di Scaglieri
La Biodola
San Giovanni
Le Grotte
Magazzini
Cima del Monte (516m)
Schiopparello
Ottone
Ortano
Spiaggia della Paolina
Spiaggia di Spartaia
Marciana
Poggio
Monte Perone (630m)
Procchio
San Martino
Colle d'Orano
Santuario della Madonna del Monte
SP37
Via Colle Reciso
Monte Capanne (1018m)
Monte Maolo (749m)
Marmi
Porto Azzurro
La Pila
Aeroporto Isola d'Elba
Sant'Ilario in Campo
Lacona
Chiessi
Spiaggia di Zuccale
Spiaggia di Naregno
San Piero in Campo
Marina di Campo
Golfo della Lacona
Spiaggia di Barabarca
Capoliveri
Pomonte
Fetovaia
Seccheto
Cavoli
Spiaggia di Morcone
Monte Calamita (413m)
Spiaggia dello Stagnone
Spiaggia delle Tombe
Le Piscine
Golfo di Campo
Spiaggia di Pareti
Punta di Fetovia
Spiaggia dell'Innamorata
Tyrrhenian Sea
Montecristo (35km)
Punta della Calamita
Pianosa

tion was down to 100,000 tonnes. You can fossick around to your heart's content in museums dedicated to rocks.

Ligurian tribespeople were the island's first inhabitants, followed by Etruscans and Greeks from Magna Graecia. Centuries of peace under the Pax Romana gave way to more uncertain times during the barbarian invasions, when Elba became a refuge for those fleeing mainland marauders. By the 11th century, Pisa (and later Piombino) was in control and built fortresses to help ward off attacks by Muslim raiders and pirates operating out of North Africa.

In the 16th century, Cosimo I de' Medici grabbed territory in the north of the island, where he founded the port town of Cosmopolis, today's Portoferraio.

Activities

Make the tourist office in Portoferraio your first port of call for information on Elba's many **walking** trails, **biking** paths and other outdoor activities; the visitors centre in Enfola is particularly efficient and maps out a lovely circular walk around the cape starting from in front of the waterside office. From May to October it organises guided botanical and bio-watching (as in observing biodiversity) walks.

Given its gorgeous crystal-clear waters, **diving** and **snorkelling** are predictably big on Elba between June and September. Otherwise, explore the island and its watery surrounds (not to mention a treasure trove of tiny hidden coves and beaches inaccessible on foot) by **sailing boat**, **motor boat** or **kayak**.

EMPEROR NAPOLEON

At precisely 6pm on 3 May 1814, the English frigate *Undaunted* dropped anchor in the harbour of Portoferraio on Elba. It bore an unusual cargo. Under the Treaty of Fontainebleau, the emperor Napoleon was exiled to this seemingly safe open prison, some 15km from the Tuscan coast.

It could have been so much worse for the emperor, but the irony for someone who hailed from Corsica, just over the water, must have been bitter. Napoleon, the conqueror who had stridden across all of Europe and taken Egypt, was awarded this little island as his private fiefdom, to hold until the end of his days.

Elba would never quite be the same again. Napoleon, ever hyperactive, threw himself into frenetic activity in his new, humbler domain. He prescribed a mass of public works, which included improving the operations of the island's iron-ore mines – whose revenue, it is pertinent to note, now went his way. He also went about boosting agriculture, initiating a road-building program, draining marshes and overhauling the legal and education systems.

Some weeks after his arrival, his mother Letizia and sister Paolina rolled up. But he remained separated from his wife, Maria Luisa, and was visited for just two (no doubt hectic) days by his lover, Maria Walewska.

At the Congress of Vienna, the new regime in France called for Napoleon's removal to a more distant location. Austria, too, was nervous. Some participants favoured a shift to Malta, but Britain objected and suggested the remote South Atlantic islet of St Helena. The Congress broke up with no agreed decision.

Napoleon was well aware of the debate. Under no circumstances would he allow himself to be shipped off to some rocky speck in the furthest reaches of the Atlantic Ocean. A lifelong risk taker, he decided to have another roll of the dice. For months he had sent out on 'routine' trips around the Mediterranean a couple of vessels flying the flag of his little empire, Elba. When one, the *Incostante,* set sail early in the morning of 26 February 1815, no one suspected that the conqueror of Europe was stowed away on board. Sir Neil Campbell, his English jail warden, had returned to Livorno the previous day, confident that Napoleon was, as ever, fully immersed in the business of the island.

Napoleon made his way to France, reassumed power and embarked on the Hundred Days, the last of his expansionist campaigns that would culminate in defeat at Waterloo, after which he got his Atlantic exile after all, dying on St Helena in 1821, from arsenic poisoning – contracted, according to the most accepted contemporary theory, probably from the hair tonic he applied to keep that famous quiff glistening.

OFF THE BEATEN TRACK

BIKING & HIKING ON ELBA

A dizzying network of walking and mountain-biking trails blankets Elba. Many start in Portoferraio, but some of the best, far-flung trailheads kick off elsewhere on the island.

Colle Reciso to San Martino and return A 15km (round-trip), medium-difficulty mountain-bike trail that peaks at about 280m. The trail continues past San Martino, and descends into Marmi, but save some breath for the return trip, as circling back to Portoferraio from Marmi on the main road is neither pleasant nor particularly safe in high season.

Marciana to Chiessi A 12km hike starting high up in Marciana, dribbling downhill past ancient churches, sea vistas and granite boulders for about six hours to the seaside in Chiessi.

The Great Elba Crossing A three- to four-day, 60km east–west island crossing, including Monte Capanne, Elba's highest point (1018m), overnighting down on the coast as camping is not allowed on the paths. The highlight is the final 19km leg from Poggio to Pomonte, passing the Santuario della Madonna del Monte and the Masso dell'Aquila rock formation.

Sea Kayak Italy KAYAKING
(☎348 2290711; www.seakayakitaly.com) Sea-kayaking courses, excursions and – the real experience not to be missed – a two-day kayaking trek departing from Marciana Marina with a spot of fishing, an overnight camp on the beach and a campfire dinner of just-caught fish (€140, minimum two people). True enthusiasts can encircle the entire island in seven magical days (€450).

Il Viottolo TREKKING, BIKING
(☎329 7367100; www.ilviottolo.com; Via Fucini 279, Marino di Campo) Vertical trekking, moonlight trekking, archaeological and mineralogy treks, mountain biking, snorkelling and sea kayaking are among the guided expeditions (ranging from two hours to all day) offered by this Marino di Campo–based adventure specialist.

Enfola Diving Center DIVING
(☎339 6791367; www.enfoladivingcenter.it; Enfola; ⏲Jun-Sep) Get set up with gear, tuition and guides at this diving and snorkelling school on Enfola beach, 6km west of Portoferraio.

Diving in Elba DIVING
(www.divinginelba.com) Ogle at coloured walls buzzing with eagle rays, sun fish, barracudas and a couple of wrecks of Roman cargo boats, with this school, the island's largest. It operates 25-odd diving sites along Elba's north coast and has offices in Portoferraio, La Biodola and Procchio.

ℹ Getting There & Away

Elba is a one-hour ferry crossing from Piombino on the mainland to Portoferraio (at least hourly, foot passenger/car & driver €10/50); in high season a handful of boats sail from Piombino to the smaller Elban ports of Cavo and Rio Marina.

Elba's airstrip, **Aeroporto Isola d'Elba** (www.elbaisland-airport.it), is 2km north of Marina di Campo in La Pila.

ℹ Getting Around

Car is the easiest way to get around the island, except in traffic-clogged August when you really won't get very far at all. The island's southwest coast proffers the most dramatic and scenic motoring – with no traffic count one hour to motor the 35km from Procchio to Cavoli.

In Portoferraio, rent a mountain bike, scooter or bike from **Twin Rent** (www.twn-rent.it; Viale Elba 32); or take an ATL bus from the bus station, almost opposite the Toremar jetty.

Portoferraio & Around

POP 11,600

Known to the Romans as Fabricia and later Ferraia (since it was a port for iron exports), this small harbour was acquired by Cosimo I de' Medici in the mid-16th century, when its distinctive fortifications took shape.

Portoferraio can be a hectic place, especially in August when holidaymakers and day-trippers pour off the ferries from Piombino on the mainland every 20 minutes or so. But wandering the streets and steps of the historic centre, indulging in the exceptional eating options and haggling for sardines with fishermen at the old harbour more than makes up for the squeeze.

Sights & Activities

Old Town HISTORIC QUARTER

From the ferry terminal, it's less than a kilometre along the foreshore to the Old Town, a spiderweb of narrow streets and alleys that stagger uphill from the old harbour and waterfront to Portoferraio's defining twinset of forts, **Forte Falcone** and the salmon-pink **Forte Stella** (Via della Stella; adult/reduced €2/1.50; 9am-7pm Easter-Sep) with deserted 16th-century ramparts to wander and seagulls freewheeling overhead.

From central square Piazza Cavour head uphill along Via Garibaldi to the foot of the monumental **Scalinata Medici**, a fabulous mirage of 140 wonky stone steps cascading up through every sun-lit shade of amber to the dark, dimly lit church of 17th-century **Chiesa della Misericordia** (Via della Misericordia). Inside is Napoleon's death mask. Continue to the top of the staircase to reach the forts and Napoleonic villa.

Museo Archeologica della Linguelle ARCHAEOLOGICAL SITE, MUSEUM

(Calata Buccari; adult/reduced €3/2; 10am-1pm & 3.30-7.10pm Fri-Wed summer) Napoleon was 'imprisoned' at the start of his fleeting exile on Elba in 1814 in 16th-century **Torre del Martello**, also called Torre della Linguella. The russet-red, octagonal tower remained a prison until 1877. The archaeological ruins in front of it at its feet were part of a luxurious Roman villa between the 1st and 5th centuries AD, and form part of this modest museum today.

BEST BEACH SPOTS

It pays to know your *spiagge* (beaches), given that Elba's beaches on its 147km-long coast embrace everything in the way of shade and size of sand, pebble and rock. You'll find sandy strands on the south coast and in the Golfo della Biodola on the opposite side of Capo d'Enfola to Portoferraio; **La Biodola** has the nearest sandy beach to Portoferraio. The quietest, prettiest beaches are tucked in bijou rocky coves and often involve a steep clamber down. Parking is invariably roadside and scant.

Enfola

Just 6km west of Portoferraio, it's not so much the grey pebbles as the outdoor action that lures the crowds to this tiny fishing port. There are pedalos to rent, a beachside diving school, and a family-friendly 2.5km-long circular **hiking trail** around the green cape. The **Parco Nazionale dell'Arcipelago Toscano visitors centre** (Tuscan Archipelago National Park; 05 6591 9411; www.islepark.it; Enfola) is also here.

Sansone & Sorgente

This twinset of cliff-ensnared, white-shingle and pebble beaches stands out for its turquoise, crystal-clear waters just made for **snorkelling**. By car from Portoferraio, follow the SP27 towards Enfola. Parking is challenging.

Morcone, Pareti & Innamorata

Find this trio of charming sandy-pebble coves framed by sweet-smelling pine and eucalyptus trees some 3km south of Capoliveri on the southeast part of the island. Rent a kayak and paddle out to sea on Innamorata, the wildest of the three; or fine dine and overnight on Pareti beach at **Hotel Stella Maris** (05 6596 8425; www.albergostellamaris.com; Pareti; half-board per person d €70-110; P ❄), one of the island's few three-star hotels to be found on the sand.

Colle d'Orano & Fetovaia

The standout highlight of these two gorgeous swathes of golden sand on Elba's western coast is the dramatic drive – a real island highlight – between the two. The journey follows the island's splendid southwest coastal road (SP25). Legend has it Napoleon frequented Colle d'Orano to sit and swoon over his native Corsica, which is visible across the water. A heavenly scented, maquis- (herbal scrubland) covered promontory protects sandy Fetovaia, where nudists flop on nearby granite rocks known as **Le Piscine**.

OFF THE BEATEN TRACK

GOURMET ESCAPES

On an island where fine wine and olive oil are abundant, estates producing these products are the natural accommodation idyll for gourmets keen to immerse themselves in local culinary culture.

★ **Tenuta La Chiusa** (☎05 6593 3046; www.tenutalachiusa.it; Magazzini 93; d €65-120, up to 5 people €110-185, d per wk €450-850, up to 5 people per wk €750-1300; P), 8km east of Portoferraio along the SP26 and SP28, is Elba's oldest wine-making estate, and is where Napoleon stayed the night upon landing on Elba in 1814 before heading into Portoferraio. Right on the seashore, this walled estate is stunning. It has a 17th-century farmhouse, an 18th-century villa, almost 8 hectares of vineyards tumbling towards the sea, olive groves, palm trees and 10 apartments to rent – some on the beach in former peasant-worker cottages. Self-catering accommodation (minimum two nights September to July, five nights August) has a simple charm; guests can buy olive oil and wine at reception; and, should you not fancy cooking, harbourside Hotel e Ristorante Mare is a wonderful two-minute stroll away along the pebbly seashore in the tiny harbour of Magazzini. The estate also organises wine-tasting in its cellar.

★ **Agriturismo Due Palme** (☎388 7433736, 05 6593 3017; www.agriturismoelba.it; Via Schiopparello 28, Schiopparello; cottage for 4 people €55-130), on the road to Schiopparello, is another wonderful self-catering option on an olive plantation – the only one on Elba to produce quality-stamped IGP olive oil from its 1200 olive trees covering 6 hectares. Again, guests can taste and buy the silky fresh-green oil (€16 per litre), and traditional accommodation is in five workers' cottages hidden between trees in an astonishingly flowery garden. The springtime scent of orange trees in blossom will linger forever. Tree-shaded deck chairs, a BBQ and grassy promenade between century-old olive trees only heighten the charm of the family estate, created by Fabrizio's grandfather and tended with passion by the elegant Fabrizio today. Due Plame also has a couple of seaside villas with blockbuster sea view to rent as well.

Museo Nazionale della Residenza Napoleoniche HOUSE MUSEUM
(Piazzale Napoleone; ⏲9am-7pm Mon & Wed-Sat, to 1pm Sun) Up on the bastions, between the two forts, is Villa dei Mulini (also known as Palazzo dei Mulini), home to Napoleon during his stint as emperor of this small isle. With its Empire-style furnishings, splendid library, fig-tree-studded Italianate gardens and unbeatable sea view, the emperor certainly didn't want for creature comforts during his brief Elban exile – contrast his Elba lifestyle with the simplicity of his camp bed and travelling trunk when he was on the campaign trail. The museum was closed for renovation at the time of writing.

Museo Villa Napoleonica di San Martino HOUSE MUSEUM
(San Martino; adult/reduced €3/1.50; ⏲9am-7pm Tue-Sat, to 1pm Sun) In San Martino 5km southwest of town, this villa – a remodelled farmhouse topped by a roof terrace with Napoleonic stone eagles – was where Napoleon dropped in to escape the city heat. In the 1850s a Russian nobleman had the rather overbearing gallery built at its base, now host to temporary Napoleon-related exhibitions. Views from the rooftop terrace are lovely.

Sleeping

Half-board is usually the only option in August and many hotels only open April to October. The best places to stay are a short drive from the town centre.

Villa Ombrosa HOTEL €
(☎05 6591 4363; www.villaombrosa.it; Via Alcide de Gasperi 3; d from €95; P 📶) One of the few Portoferraio hotels in town and open year-round, three-star Ombrosa looks out to sea and the pinprick islet of Lo Scoglietto. Decor is a jumble of styles, but summer rates include a lounger and umbrella on a strip of Spiaggia delle Ghiaie (Ghiaie Beach) across the street, and rooms with sea view have pocket-sized balconies. Disabled friendly.

Rosselba Le Palme CAMPGROUND €
(☎05 6593 3101; www.rosselbalepalme.it; Ottone; adult/tent/car €12/14.50/5.40; ⏲mid-Apr–

Sep; P 📶 🏊) Set around a botanical garden backed by Mediterranean forest, few campsites are as leafy or large. The beach is a 400m walk between trees, and accommodation ranges from simple pitches to cute wooden chalets, 'glamping' tents with running water and bathtubs on legs, and apartments in a typical Tuscan villa. Find the ground 9km east of Portoferraio near Ottone.

Hotel e Ristorante Mare HOTEL €€
(☎05 6593 3069; www.hotelmare.org; Magazzini; d €122-178, half-board per person €53-107; ⏱summer; @ 🏊) A modern choice, Hotel Mare has a nautical feel to its architecture and decor – apt given it sits on the waterfront of a picturesque little harbour just across the water from Portoferraio (9km by car from the town centre). And, yes, views of the town and peninsula from its rooftop terrace, pool and waterfront restaurant are magnificent. Minimum three-night stay.

Villa Ottone LUXURY HOTEL €€€
(☎05 6593 3042; www.villaottone.com; Ottone 4; s/d €109/309, d in villa from €309, dinner €30; ⏱summer; P ❄ @ 📶 🏊) Elba doesn't get classier than this. The height of elegance and lap of luxury, this aristocratic 19th-century villa looking out to sea 1km east of Magazzini was home to Tuscan counts until the 1920s. With its own private beach, spa, pool bar, lush gardens, restaurants and so forth, guests want for nothing. Cheaper rooms are in a modern block behind the villa; half-board only.

Eating

★Il Castagnacciao PIZZERIA €
(Via del Mercato Vecchio 5; pizza €4.50-7; ⏱9am-2.30pm & 4.30-11pm Thu-Tue) Hidden in an alley near Piazza Cavour, this iconic address with bench seating at wooden tables is no-frills pizza bliss. Watch your thin-crust, rectangular-shaped pizza go in and out of the wood-fired oven, and save space for dessert – *castagnaccio* (chestnut 'cake') baked in the same oven. To go completely local, start with a lip-smacking plate of *torta di ceci* (chickpea 'pizza').

Caffescondido TRATTORIA €€
(Via del Carmine 65; meals €25; ⏱lunch & dinner Mon-Sat) This Slow Food–endorsed trattoria, footsteps from pretty Piazza Gramsci, makes for the perfect getaway from the waterfront crowds. Options are kept simple – just a handful of *primi* (first courses) and *secondi* (second courses) are chalked on the blackboard which usually stars a local classic such as *baccacà alla marinese* (saltcod with potatoes) or *polpo brisco* (octopus). No credit cards.

Osteria Libertaria TUSCAN €€
(☎05 6591 4978; Calata Giacomo Matteotti 12; meals €30; ⏱lunch & dinner summer) Across from the fishing boats, this waterfront *osteria* cooks up a tasty fish-driven cuisine. Simple dishes such as fried calamari or *tonno in crosta di pistacchi* (pistachio-encrusted tuna fillet) are fresher than fresh and cooked to perfection every time. Dine at one of two tile-topped tables on the traffic-noisy street

DON'T MISS

HAGGLING FOR FISH

Hanging out with locals, waiting for the fishing boats to come in, is a quintessential Portoferraio pastime. The crowd starts to form on the quay around 9.30am and by the time the first boats dock at 10am there is quite a line-up of punters waiting to exchange hand-crumpled bank notes for the catch of the day.

The larger industrial fishing boats with crews of 10 or so dock midway between the ferry terminal and the old-town harbour on **Banchina d'Alto Fondale** (the quayside across the busy road from Piazza del Popolo). Occasionally they'll catch a huge tuna – which draws a real crowd, not to mention the fishing port authorities and all sorts – but in the main its wooden crates of sardines, mackerel and anchovies the crew sell from the side of their boat (€5 for a plastic-bag full).

Smaller boats with just one or two fishermen at most moor alongside **Calata Giacomo Matteotti** at the old harbour each morning any time from 8am onwards. And these are the guys who get the real catch – octopus, lobster, eel and swordfish on good days.

If haggling for fish is simply not your cup of tea, there's always harbourside fishmonger **Pescheria del Porto** (Calata Matteotti 10; ⏱8am-12.30pm Mon-Sat).

outside or on the back-alley terrace. No coffee.

Stella Marina SEAFOOD €€€
(☎05 6591 5983; www.ristorantestellamarina.com; Viale Vittorio Emanuele II, Banchina Alto Fondale; meals €45; ⌚lunch & dinner Tue-Sun) Completely incongruously, Portoferraio's finest dine lies low in an unglamorous building in a car park. Ferry boats moor in front, guaranteeing great entertainment from the terrace. But step inside and it is white tablecloths, smart service and sublime fish and seafood cooked with a fabulous dose of creativity. The black rice risotto with *seppia all' elbana* (mushrooms) is divine. Reservations essential.

Information

Tourist office (☎05 6591 4671; www.isoleditoscana.it; Viale Elba 4; ⌚9am-7pm Mon-Sat, 10am-1pm & 3-6pm Sun summer, 9am-5pm Mon-Thu, to 1pm Fri winter) Helpful staff here have a particularly abundant supply of information on walking and biking paths on the island. Find the office near the ferry port, around the corner from waterfront Calata Italia 33.

Getting There & Away

Year-round regular car and foot passenger ferries sail at least hourly from the Stazione Marittima (ferry port) in Piombino to Portoferraio. Unless it is a summer weekend or August, there is no need to buy a ticket in advance online. Simply buy a ticket from one of the ticket booths at the port. Fares (one-way around €10/50 per person/car and driver) vary according to the season. Sailing time is one hour. Companies include **Blunavy** (www.blunavytraghetti.com), **Moby** (www.mobylines.com) and **Toremar** (www.toremar.it).

Procchio

This small bustling beach town, 10km west of Portoferraio, has one of Elba's longest stretches of golden sand and the island's best gelato and Sicilian *granita* at cafe-gelateria **Scalo 70** (Via del Mare 10; cones €2.20-4.50). Try the rice gelato or nut, fig and caramel. It's also a great spot to rent a bicycle and go for an island spin: **Rent Procchio** (☎335 7567764; www.rentprocchio.it; mountain bikes per day €10), with a stand on the main street, has the wheels and all the info on itineraries. West from Procchio, the road hugs cliffs above **Spiaggia di Spartaia** and **Spiaggia della Paolina**, beautiful little beaches requiring a steep clamber down.

Relais Baia Bianca SELF-CONTAINED €€
(☎0565 209 69 916; www.baiabiancarelais.com; La Biodola 16; d €110-240; ⌚Apr-Sep) A picture-perfect manicured garden with pea-green lawn and wooden decking walkways is the only thing separating this trio of dazzling white, designer chic apartments from the sand. The much raved-about address of the moment, each self-catering apartment has its own (dazzling white) sun-verandah by the water. Find it on the golden sandy beach of La Biodola, northeast of Procchio.

There's a minimum stay of seven nights in June, July and September, and a 14-day minimum in August.

Hotel Hermitage LUXURY HOTEL €€€
(☎0565 9740; www.hotelhermitage.it; La Biodola; half-board per person €130-235; ⌚summer; P ❄ @ ☜ ≋) If James Bond were to parachute onto Elba in a tuxedo, he'd land on the tennis courts here. One of the island's truly luxurious hotels, this is a gorgeous retreat with infinity pool overlooking the sea, golf course just over the fence, beauty centre and many other spoil-yourself treats. Find it in the seaside hamlet of La Biodola, northeast of Procchio.

Marciana

POP 2190

From Portoferraio, cruise 18km west along the coast to **Marciana Marina**, an attractive resort which, unlike typical cookie-cutter marinas, has character and history to complement its pleasant pebble beaches. From here it's a twisting 9km inland to Marciana, the island's oldest and highest (375m) village crowned by a much-knocked-about fort (closed).

It's a joy to meander Marciana's stone streets, past arches, flower boxes and petite balconies to drop-offs revealing views of the coastline below. But the highlight is the short half-day walk from the village to the most important site of pilgrimage on the island.

Sights & Activities

Santuario della Madonna del Monte CHAPEL
Park at the entrance to Marciana and head out of the village on foot along Via delle Fonti and its continuations, Via delle Coste and Via dei Monti, to this much-altered 11th-century church. Inside is a stone upon which a divine hand is said to have painted an image

MARCIANA MARINA: A TRADITIONAL PASSEGGIATA

The loveliest moment of the day in laid-back Marciana Marina is late afternoon and early evening when what feels like the entire town slowly strolls the waterfront for that all-essential, oh-so-Tuscan *passeggiata* (early evening stroll).

Start on **Piazza della Vittoria**, at the eastern end of the seafront promenade, with its gigantic palm tree and restaurant terraces; the hip crowd gathers for *aperitivi* (predinner drinks accompanied by cocktail snacks) on the shabby-chic terrace of **Enoteca Coltelli** (Piazza della Vittoria 11). Around the corner, **Lasvolta** (Via Cairoli 6) is much-loved for its creative *granita* (ices made with coffee or fresh fruit) and gelato – red apple and cinamon, orange and black pepper, coffee and vanilla, and so on.

Walk a couple of minutes west along waterside Viale Margherita and make a quick detour a block inland to Marciana Marina's old central square, **Piazza Vittorio Emanuele**. With its pretty peach-painted church and pristine carpet of perfect cobblestones, this is easily Elba's most beautiful piazza.

Backtrack to the water and continue meandering west past stylish boutiques selling all manner of wares – some great fashion. And, as the sun sinks, find yourself at the far end of the waterfront on **Spiaggia di Capo Nord**, a handsome beach of large smooth pebbles overlooked by a 12th-century Saracen tower.

★**Ristorante Capo Nord** (☎05 6599 6983; meals €50; ⏲lunch & dinner Tue-Sun), an impossibly romantic seafood restaurant with splendid terrace on Spiaggia di Capo Nord is the perfect place to end your *passeggiata*. Enjoy octopus risotto or swordfish while gazing out to sea.

of the Virgin, believed to have miraculous powers. Outside the church a plaque commemorates Napoleon's visits here by horseback in 1814.

It is an invigorating 40-minute uphill walk through scented parasol pine and chestnut woods along an old mule track (lots of wild sage and thyme) and the coastal panorama that unfolds as you get higher is remarkable. Pace yourself with the aid of 14 Stations of the Cross and as you near the hilltop chapel (627m) play 'I Spy Corsica'. Once in situ, drink like Napoleon did from the old stone fountain (1695) across from the church entrance, then continue five minutes along the footpath to ogle at Corsica.

★**Cabinovia Monte Capanne** FUNICULAR
(Cableway; ☎05 6590 1020; single/return €12/18; ⏲10am-1pm & 2.20-5pm summer) If you only have time for one road trip from Portoferraio, make it this. Some 750m south of Marciana on the road to Poggio, the Cabinovia Monte Capanne whisks walkers up in open, barred cabins – imagine riding in a canary-yellow parrot cage – up the mountain to the summit of Elba's highest point, **Monte Capanne** (1019m).

The trip takes 20 minutes and at the top you can scramble around the rocky peak to savour an astonishing 360-degree panorama of the entire island, surrounding Tuscan Archipelago, Etruscan Coast and Corsica 50km away. The scent of *la macchia* (Mediterranean scrub) is heavenly. Keen hikers can buy a one-way ticket and walk back down – a 1½-hour hike along a rocky but well-marked path.

Sleeping & Eating

★**Osteria del Noce** FISH €€
(☎05 6590 1285; Via della Madonna 27; meals €25; ⏲lunch & dinner) This family-run bistro in hilltop Marciana is the type of place where the bread is homemade and flavoured with fennel, chestnut flour and other seasonal treats. The *miso mare del Noce* (mixed fish *antipasti*) makes a fabulous start to any meal – in the company of sweeping coastal views from its cosy terrace, part open, part covered.

Not to be missed: spaghetti laced with Granseolo Elbano (a large crab typical to Elba).

Information

Casa del Parco di Marciana (☎348 7039374, 05 6590 1030; ⏲10am-1pm Mon, 9am-1pm Tue, 9am-1pm & 5.30-7.30pm Wed & Thu, 10am-1pm & 3-7pm Sat, shorter hr mid-season, closed Nov-Mar) National park visitors centre with lots of walking and outdoor-activity info. It's below Fortezza Pisana.

Poggio

A twisting 4km ascent into the mountains from Marciana Marina brings you to the attractive inland village of Poggio on the SP25, famous for its spring water. It's an enchanting little place with steep, cobblestone alleys and stunning coastal views.

Sights & Activities

Monte Perone MOUNTAIN

If you follow the SP37 out of Poggio, park at the picnic site at the foot of Monte Perone (630m) – you can't miss it. To the left (east) you can wander up the mountain, with spectacular views across much of the island. To the right (west) you can scramble fairly quickly to a height that affords broad vistas down to Poggio, Marciana and Marciana Marina.

Monte Maolo MOUNTAIN

From Monte Perone, press on to Monte Maolo (749m), from where the road descends into the southern flank of the island passing en route the granite shell of the Romanesque **Chiesa di San Giovanni** and, shortly after, a ruined tower, the **Torre di San Giovanni**. Two small hamlets, Sant'Ilario in Campo and San Piero in Campo, make simple if uneventful stops to stretch your legs.

Eating

Publius SEAFOOD €€

(05 659 9208; meals €35; lunch & dinner Tue-Sun summer) Another islander favourite, this formal restaurant with white tablecloths sits at the lower end of Poggio village. Cuisine is refined Tuscan with a strong fish bias, and the views from its large sea-facing windows are of the 'big blue' panoramic variety.

Marina di Campo

This small fishing harbour on the south side of the island is Elba's second-largest town. Curling around a picturesque bay, the boats bobbing in the bay add personality to what is otherwise very much a holiday-oriented town. Its beach of bright, white sand pulls in vacationers by the thousands; coves further west, though less spectacular, are more tranquil.

Northeast of town, signposted off the SP30 to Lacona, more than 150 Mediterranean species swim, crawl and wave about in the **Acquario dell'Elba** (www.acquarioelba.com; Marino di Campo; adult/child €7/3; 9am-11pm summer, closed Nov–mid-Mar), a modest aquarium that entertains families on grey or wet days.

Just 6km west of Marina di Campo is the shingle-sand beach of **Cavoli**, suited to families with its beach cafe, sun loungers, pedalos and kids' playground.

Sleeping & Eating

To mingle with local fishermen, linger over a cappuccino or something stronger at **Da Mario**, an institution around since 1952 opposite the fishing boats at the harbour end of the waterfront.

Hotel Montecristo HOTEL €€

(05 6597 6861; www.hotelmontecristo.it; Viale Nomelini; d per person €40-90; P) Low-end rooms are a little spare; otherwise this is a pleasantly posh beachside hotel with flower-framed balconies and a bar and pool overlooking the sea. The large sunny rooms have Scandinavian-style light furnishings and king-size beds. There's a fitness centre, sauna and free bicycles.

Il Cantuccio PIZZERIA €

(05 6597 6775; www.ristoranteilcantuccio.eu; Largo Garibaldi 6; pizza €6-9, meals €25; lunch & dinner) Ignore the menu-touting waiters on the waterfront hoping to entice you in and head to this backstreet trattoria instead – look for the fresh mint facade. In business since 1930, the place is unassuming and excellent value – hence the local crowd who comes here for Tuscan classics, homemade pasta, wood-oven fired pizza and so on.

Capoliveri & Porto Azzurro

From Marina di Campo it's a comparatively long drive along the south coast before climbing up a precipitous ridgeback in the southeast pocket of the island to the hilltop village of **Capoliveri** (population 3840). Its steep, narrow alleys and sandwiched houses are pretty and the panorama of rooftop and sea beyond that fan out from the old stone terrace on its central square, **Piazza Matteotti**, is lovely indeed.

Backtrack down the ridge and head east to **Porto Azzurro** (population 3530), a seaside village overlooked by a fort (now a prison) built by Philip III of Spain in 1603. Its bijou maze of flower-bedecked pedestrian streets is laden with restaurant and cafe terraces, and there is a sweep of good beaches within bicycle shot. It is also a great place for easy wine tasting.

Eating & Drinking

Il Chiasso SEAFOOD €€€
(☎05 6596 8709; Via Cavour 32, Capoliveri; meals €45; ⊙dinner Easter-Oct) Tucked down an alley *(chiasso)* enlivened only by the odd line of washing hung out to dry, Il Chiasso has fishy classics and and excellent wine. For a true taste of Capoliveri go for the fish soup *di Luciano* (€25), cooked up by chef Luciano since time began and swimming with local catch. Advance reservations recommended.

La Taverna dei Poeti TUSCAN €€
(☎05 6596 8306; www.latavernadeipoeti.com; Via Roma 14, Capoliveri; meals €35; ⊙dinner, closed Wed winter) Much-loved by locals, this traditional address sees chef Maximus cook up the very best of Tuscan produce with a generous peppering of simplicity. The menu splits dishes into *'mare'* (sea) and *'terre'* (literally 'earth', meaning meat), and a €50 tasting menu pairs each of the four courses with a different wine.

La Botte Gaia OSTERIA €€
(☎05 659 5607; www.labottegaia.com; Viale Europa 5-7, Porto Azzurro; meals €35; ⊙dinner, closed Mon winter) Slow Food–featured and deservedly so, this is *the* revered dining address in Porto Azzurro – lots of homemade pasta, just-caught fish and island wines.

★ **Fandango** WINE BAR
(Via Cardenti 1, Capoliveri; ⊙Tue-Sun) Steps lead down from the panoramic terrace at the far end of Piazza Matteotti to this *enoteca*. Sitting beneath its vine-clad pergola in the early evening is particularly atmospheric. Cocktails, live music and *piccolo cucina* (light snacks) add real after-dark flair.

Rio dell'Elba & Rio Marina

Time and energy permitting, a final bit of gorgeous driving can be done in the northeast corner of the island to **Rio dell'Elba** (population 1170), the heart of Elba's iron-mining operation, and its coastal sibling 3.5km east, **Rio Marina** (population 2220), where the island's industrial heritage comes to life in the **Museo dei Minerali e dell'Arte Mineraria** (☎05 6596 2088; www.parcominelba.it; Via Magenta 26; adult/reduced €2.50/1.50; ⊙9.30am-12.30pm & 3.30-6.30pm summer). Part of the **Parco Minerario dell'Isola d'Elba**, the museum tells the story of Rio's open-cast iron mines from Etruscan times until 1982 when the mines closed, and exhibits lots of sparkling chunks of golden pyrite and ink-black hematite. The museum is also the place to bag a spot on a seasonal, kid-friendly guided tour (adult/child €12/7.50) of the mining area by electric train; tours last 1½ hours and include a decent stop for passengers to clamber out and dig for minerals (hammers and plastic bags provided!). Before hitting Rio, call ahead to check the day's activities and reserve.

Gorgona, Capraia, Pianosa & Giglio

Pinprick **Gorgona** is the greenest, northernmost of the Tuscan islands and can only be visited with a guide. Two towers built by the Pisans and Medicis of Florence keep watch over its plunging coastline and beautiful interior, part of which has been off-limits as a low-security prison since 1869. Ask for details at the tourist office in Portoferraio.

By contrast the elliptical volcanic island of **Capraia** (population 390), 31km from the French island of Corsica, is 8km long, 4km wide, peaks with Monte Castello (447m) and has a few hotels and restaurants. The island has some great walks (don't miss the trail to Lake Stagnone) and its **tourist office** (☎05 8690 5138; www.prolococapraiaisola.it; Via Assunzione 42; ⊙9am-12.30pm & 4.30-7pm Fri-Wed summer) has maps of hiking and biking routes around the island. A chequered history has seen Genoa, Sardinia, the Saracens from North Africa and Napoleon all have a bash at running it. **Toremar** (www.toremar.it) operates car and passenger ferries from Livorno to Capraia (2½ hours; one or two daily year-round); most days boat schedules allow a return trip in a day but triple-check before setting out.

South of Elba, **Giglio** (population 1500), the second-largest Tuscan island, is 21 km sq and was in the spotlight most as the place where cruise ship *Costa Concordia* met its tragic end in 2012. The wreckage was still being dismantled and removed in summer 2013. Then there is pinprick **Pianosa**, a haven of peace 14km southwest of Elba. It served as a penal colony until 1997.

To get to both these islands, sign up for a day trip with **Aquavision** (☎328 7095470, 0565 97 60 22; www.aquavision.it; Piazza dei Granatieri 203, Marino di Campo), based in Marina di Campo on Elba. Boats depart from Porto Azzuro, Marina di Campo and Portoferraio, on Elba.

Siena & Central Tuscany

Includes ➡

Best Places to Eat

- ➡ Enoteca I Terzi (p200)
- ➡ Il Leccio (p224)
- ➡ I Sette Consoli (p230)
- ➡ La Grotta (p231)

Best Places to Stay

- ➡ La Bandita (p223)
- ➡ La Casa di Adelina (p227)
- ➡ Pensione Palazzo Ravizza (p199)
- ➡ Podere San Lorenzo (p218)

Why Go?

When people imagine classic Tuscan countryside, they usually conjure up images of central Tuscany. However, there's more to this popular region than gently rolling hills, sunkissed vineyards and artistically planted avenues of cypress trees. The real gems here are the historic towns and cities, most of which are medieval and Renaissance time capsules magically transported to the modern day.

This privileged pocket of the country has maintained a high tourist profile ever since the Middle Ages, when Christian pilgrims followed the Via Francigena from Canterbury to Rome. Towns on the route catered to the needs of these pilgrims and local economies prospered as a result. Today, not a lot has changed: tourism is the major industry and travellers are still thick on the ground.

Come here for art, for architecture and for gastronomy. But most of all, come here for enchantment.

Road Distances

	Montepulciano	Siena	San Gimignano	Volterra
Siena	70			
San Gimignano	112	46		
Volterra	120	50	30	
Greve in Chianti	102	48	33	53

DON'T MISS

You'll need to adopt the same breakneck pace as a Palio entrant to do justice to Siena in one day – its Gothic art and architecture deserve leisurely investigation.

Best Wine Tastings

- Antinori nel Chianti Classico (p208) Admire cutting-edge architecture at this flagship wine estate.
- Castello di Ama (p211) Taste award-winning wine and wander through a sculpture garden.
- Poggio Antico (p224) Tour high-tech cellars and taste award-winning Brunellos.

Advance Planning

- Reserve terrace tickets for Siena's Palio a year in advance.
- Book to visit the wine estates of Castello di Ama (p211), Antinori nel Chianti Classico (p208) and Castello di Volpaia (p210).
- Check the website to time your visit to the Abbazia di Sant'Antimo (p225) to coincide with Gregorian chanting.

Resources

- **Terre di Siena** (www.terresiena.it)
- **Toscana & Chianti News** (www.toscanaechiantinews.com)

Getting Around

Siena is the region's major transport hub, with buses zooming up and down the S2 *superstrada* (expressway) between it and Florence and also travelling to other major cities in the country. Buses travel between Siena and smaller towns throughout the area, although services can be infrequent and connections convoluted. There are few primary train routes: the only truly useful service is between Siena and Grosseto. Most towns and cities have strictly enforced *Zone a Traffico Limitato* (Limited Traffic Zones; ZTLs) in their historic centres.

THREE PERFECT DAYS

Day 1: Touring Chianti

Spend a day visiting grand wine estates and sampling modern Tuscan cuisine. Prime your palate at the recently opened Antinori nel Chianti Classico (p208) near Florence and then wend your way south to Siena through scenic secondary roads in the Chianti Fiorentino and Chianti Senese, stopping for tastings and lunch along the way.

Day 2: Val d'Elsa

Two of the region's most compelling attractions are perched atop hills in the Val d'Elsa. Spend the morning exploring the cobbled streets of Volterra, admiring artefacts in the Museo Etrusco Guarnacci (p216) and visiting alabaster ateliers where artisans have worked for millennia. Then head to the perfectly preserved medieval town of San Gimignano (p211) to follow an artistic itinerary that balances the gravitas of the old (Collegiata) with the exhilaration of the new (Galleria Continua).

Day 3: Around Montalcino

Another wine-related day (you are in Tuscany, after all!). Start at the majestic medieval abbey of Sant'Antimo (p225), where you might be lucky enough to hear the resident monks chanting during mass. Then drive through vineyards laden with sangiovese grapes to enjoy lunch with local winemakers at Il Leccio (p224). In the afternoon, head to the fortified town of Montalcino (p222), home to one of the world's great wines, Brunello.

Off the Beaten Track

- To avoid Siena's madding crowds, make your way to the Orto de' Pecci (p197), an urban farm, vineyard and medieval garden spread over one of the city's green valleys.
- Tramp along parts of the medieval pilgrimmage route known as the Via Francigena (p216).
- Meditate in the tranquil environs of the Abbazia di San Galgano (p222), a ruined 13th-century abbey south of Siena.

SIENA

POP 52,800

The rivalry between historic adversaries Siena and Florence continues to this day, and participation isn't limited to the locals – most travellers tend to develop a strong preference for one over the other. These allegiances often boil down to aesthetic preference: while Florence saw its greatest flourishing during the Renaissance, Siena's enduring artistic glories are largely Gothic.

Sadly, the city has been seriously affected by the financial mismanagement of the Banca Monte dei Paschi di Siena – the world's oldest bank and until now a source of immense local pride, employment and arts patronage. For more on this, see p272.

History

Legend tells us that Siena was founded by the son of Remus, and the symbol of the wolf feeding the twins Romulus and Remus is as ubiquitous in Siena as it is in Rome. In reality the city was probably of Etruscan origin, although it didn't begin to grow into a proper town until the 1st century BC, when the Romans established a military colony here called Sena Julia.

In the 12th century, Siena's wealth, size and power grew along with its involvement in commerce and trade. Its rivalry with neighbouring Florence grew proportionately, leading to numerous wars during the first half of the 13th century between Guelph Florence and Ghibelline Siena. In 1230 Florence besieged Siena and catapulted dung and donkeys over its walls. Siena's revenge came at the Battle of Montaperti in 1260, when it decisively defeated its rival, but victory was short-lived. Only 10 years later, the Tuscan Ghibellines were defeated by Charles of Anjou and Siena was forced to ally with Florence, the chief town of the Tuscan Guelph League.

In the ensuing century, Siena was ruled by the *Consiglio dei Nove* (Council of Nine), a bourgeois group constantly bickering with the feudal nobles. It enjoyed its greatest prosperity during this time, and the Council commissioned many of the fine buildings in the Sienese-Gothic style that give the city its striking appearance, including lasting monuments such as the *duomo* (cathedral), Palazzo Comunale and Piazza del Campo.

The Sienese school of painting also had its origins at this time and reached its peak in the early 14th century, when artists such as Duccio di Buoninsegna and Ambrogio Lorenzetti were at work.

A plague outbreak in 1348 killed two-thirds of Siena's 100,000 inhabitants and led to a period of decline that culminated in the city being handed over to Florence's Cosimo I de' Medici, who barred the inhabitants from operating banks and thus severely curtailed its power.

This centuries-long economic downturn in the wake of the Medici takeover was a blessing in disguise, as lack of funds meant that its city centre was subject to very little redevelopment or new construction. In WWII, the French took Siena virtually unopposed, sparing it discernible damage. All of this has led to the historic centre's listing on Unesco's World Heritage list as the living embodiment of a medieval city.

Sights

★Piazza del Campo — PIAZZA

This sloping piazza, popularly known as Il Campo, has been Siena's civic and social centre since being staked out by the *Consiglio dei Nove* in the mid-12th century. It was built on the site of a former Roman marketplace, and its pie-piece paving design is divided into nine sectors to represent the number of members of the council.

In 1346 water first bubbled forth from the **Fonte Gaia** (Happy Fountain; Piazza del Campo) in the upper part of the square. These days the fountain's panels are reproductions; the severely weathered originals, sculpted by Jacopo della Quercia in the early 15th century, are on display in the Complesso Museale Santa Maria della Scala.

At the lowest point of the square stands the spare, elegant **Palazzo Comunale** (Palazzo Pubblico), purpose-built in the late 13th century as the piazza's centrepiece and now home to the **Museo Civico**. One of the most graceful Gothic buildings in Italy, it has an ingeniously designed concave facade that mirrors the opposing convex curve formed by the piazza.

Entry to the *palazzo's* ground-floor central courtyard is free. From it soars the graceful **Torre del Mangia** (admission €8; ⏲10am-6.15pm Mar–mid-Oct, to 3.15pm mid-Oct–Feb), 102m high and with 500-odd steps. The views from the top are magnificent, but if you want to see them you should expect to wait in high season, as only 30 people are allowed up at any time.

Siena & Central Tuscany Highlights

1. Eat, drink and sleep in style while exploring the world-famous wine region of **Chianti** (p202).
2. Gorge on Gothic architecture and *panforte* (a rich cake of almonds, honey and candied fruit) in sublimely beautiful **Siena** (p189).
3. Meditate while listening to Gregorian chants at the Romanesque **Abbazia di Sant'Antimo** (p225).
4. Wander the magically preserved medieval streets of gorgeous **San Gimignano** (p211).
5. Savour Vino Nobile and locally raised Chianina beef in **Montepulciano** (p227).
6. Admire Etruscan artefacts and alabaster artworks in the artistic enclave of **Volterra** (p216).
7. Taste-test Tuscany's most famous wine in and around medieval **Montalcino** (p222).
8. Detour onto scenic back roads in the World Heritage-listed **Val d'Orcia** (p222).

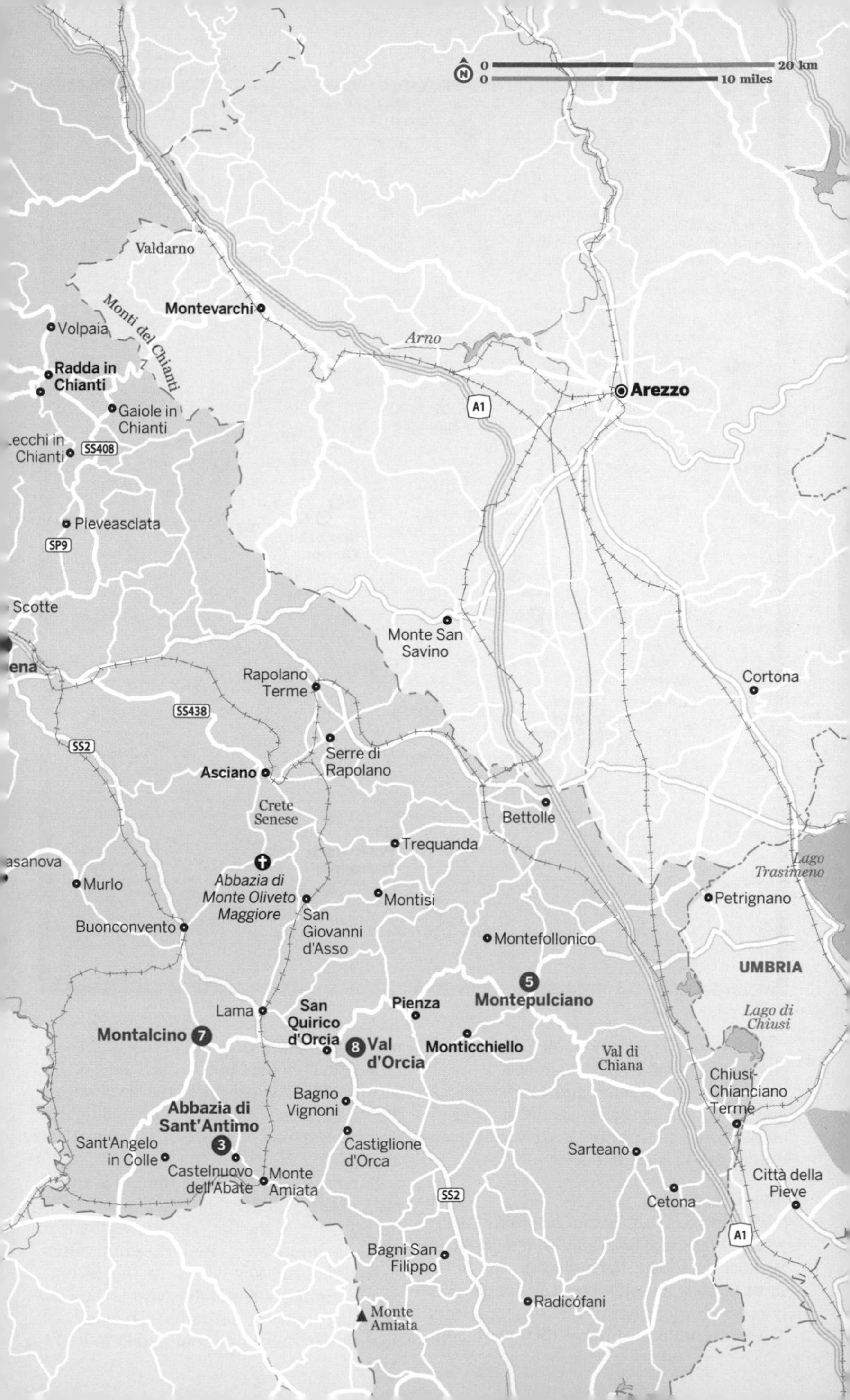
0 20 km
0 10 miles
Valdarno
Monti del Chianti
Montevarchi
Volpaia
Radda in Chianti
Gaiole in Chianti
Lecchi in Chianti
SS408
Pieveasclata
SP9
Arno
Arezzo
A1
Scotte
Monte San Savino
Rapolano Terme
SS438
SS2
Serre di Rapolano
Asciano
Crete Senese
Bettolle
Cortona
Trequanda
Abbazia di Monte Oliveto Maggiore
Murlo
Montisi
San Giovanni d'Asso
Buonconvento
Lago Trasimeno
Petrignano
Montefollonico
UMBRIA
5
Montepulciano
Lama
San Quirico d'Orcia
Pienza
Montalcino
7
8
Val d'Orcia
Monticchiello
Lago di Chiusi
Val di Chiana
Chiusi-Chianciano Terme
Bagno Vignoni
Abbazia di Sant'Antimo
3
Castiglione d'Orca
Sant'Angelo in Colle
Castelnuovo dell'Abate
Monte Amiata
Sarteano
Città della Pieve
Cetona
SS2
A1
Bagni San Filippo
Radicófani
Monte Amiata

Siena

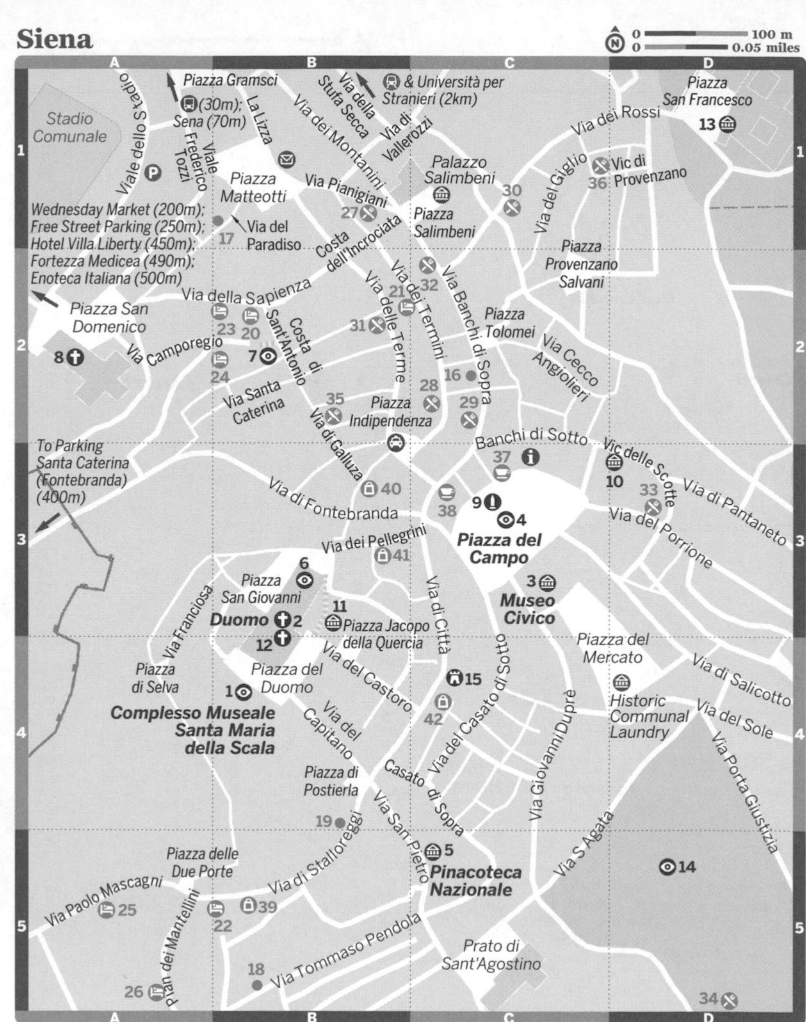

The Campo is the undoubted heart of the city. Its magnificent pavement acts as a carpet on which students and tourists picnic and relax, and the cafes around the perimeter are the most popular *aperitivo* (predinner drink) spots in town.

★ Museo Civico MUSEUM

(www.comune.siena.it; Palazzo Comunale, Il Campo; adult/EU reduced €8/4.50; ⏲10am-6.15pm mid-Mar–Oct, to 5.15pm Nov–mid-Mar) The city's most famous museum occupies rooms richly frescoed by artists of the Sienese school. These are unusual in that they were commissioned by the governing body of the city, rather than by the Church, and many depict secular subjects instead of the favoured religious themes of the time. The highlight is Simone Martini's huge *Maestà* (Virgin Mary in Majesty).

Purchase your ticket at the office to the right of the entrance then head upstairs past the gift shop to the **Sala del Risorgimento**, with its impressive late-19th-century frescoes serialising key events in the Risorgimento (unification of Italy). Next is the **Sala di Balia** (Rooms of Authority). The 15 scenes depicted in frescoes around the walls re-

Siena

Top Sights
1 Complesso Museale Santa Maria della Scala B4
2 Duomo B3
3 Museo Civico C3
4 Piazza del Campo C3
5 Pinacoteca Nazionale C5

Sights
6 Battistero di San Giovanni B3
7 Casa Santuario di Santa Caterina B2
8 Chiesa di San Domenico A2
Cripta .... (see 6)
9 Fonte Gaia C3
10 Museo delle Tavolette di Biccherna D3
11 Museo dell'Opera del Duomo B3
12 Opera della Metropolitana di Siena B4
13 Oratorio di San Bernardino D1
14 Orto de' Pecci D5
15 Palazzo Chigi-Saracini C4
Palazzo Comunale .... (see 3)
Panorama del Facciatone .... (see 11)
Torre del Mangia .... (see 3)

Activities, Courses & Tours
Accademia Musicale Chigiana ..... (see 15)
16 Centro Guide Turistiche Siena e Provincia C2
17 Scuola Leonardo da Vinci B1
18 Società Dante Alighieri B5
19 Tuscan Wine School B4

Sleeping
20 Albergo Bernini B2
21 Antica Residenza Cicogna B2
22 Bed and Breakfast Alle Due Porte B5
23 Campo Regio Relais B2
24 Hotel Alma Domus B2
25 Hotel Athena A5
26 Pensione Palazzo Ravizza A5

Eating
27 Consorzio Agrario di Siena B1
28 Enoteca I Terzi C2
29 Grom C2
30 Kopa Kabana C1
31 La Compagnia dei Vinattieri B2
32 Morbidi C2
33 Osteria Le Logge D3
34 Ristorante All'Orto de' Pecci D5
35 Ristorante Grotta Santa Caterina da Bagoga B2
36 Tre Cristi C1

Drinking & Nightlife
37 Bar Il Palio C3
38 Caffè Fiorella C3

Shopping
39 Bottega d'Arte B5
40 Il Pellicano B3
41 Panificio Il Magnifico B3
42 Pizzicheria de Miccoli C4

count episodes in the life of Pope Alexander III (the Sienese Rolando Bandinelli), including his clashes with the Holy Roman Emperor Frederick Barbarossa. Straight ahead is the **Sala del Concistoro** (Hall of the Council of Clergymen), dominated by the allegorical ceiling frescoes of the Mannerist Domenico Beccafumi; and through a vestibule to the left are the Anticappella (Chapel entrance hall) and Cappella (Chapel). The **Anticappella** features frescoes painted in 1415 by Taddeo di Bartolo. These include figures representing the virtues needed for the proper exercise of power (Justice, Magnanimity, Strength, Prudence, Religion), as well as depictions of some of the leading Republican lights of ancient Rome. The **Cappella** contains a fine *Holy Family and St Leonard* by Il Sodoma. Next to the Anticappella is the **Vestibolo** (Vestibule), whose star attraction is a bronze wolf, the symbol of the city.

The best is saved for last, though. From the vestibule, you emerge into the **Sala del Mappamondo** (Hall of the World Map), where you can admire Simone Martini's powerful and striking *Maestà* (Virgin Mary in Majesty; 1315). It features the Madonna beneath a canopy surrounded by saints and angels and is Martini's first known work. On the other side of the room is another work attributed to Martini, his oft-reproduced fresco (1328–30) of Guidoriccio da Fogliano, a captain of the Sienese army.

The next room, the **Sala dei Nove** (or Hall of the Nine), is where the Council of Nine was based. It is decorated with Ambrogio Lorenzetti's fresco cycle known as the *Allegories of Good and Bad Government* (c 1338–40). The central allegory portrays scenes with personifications of Justice, Wisdom, Virtue and Peace, all unusually (at the time) depicted as women, rendered along with scenes of criminal punishment and rewards for righteousness. Set perpendicular from it are the frescoes *Allegory of Good Government* and *Allegory of Bad Government*, which feature intensely contrasting scenes set in the recognisable environs of Siena. The good depicts a sunlit, idyllic, serene city, with joyous citizens and a countryside filled with crops; the bad city is filled with vices, crime and disease. These frescoes are often described as the most important secular paintings of the Renaissance, and shouldn't be missed.

Opera della Metropolitana di Siena CATHEDRAL

(www.operaduomo.siena.it; Piazza del Duomo; OPA SI pass Mar-Oct €12, Nov-Feb €8) Siena's *duomo* is one of Italy's greatest Gothic churches, and is the focal point of this important group of ecclesiastical buildings, consisting of the *duomo*, Museo dell'Opera del Duomo, baptistry and crypt. The OPA SI Pass offers discounted admission to all of the attractions here.

➡ Duomo

(www.operaduomo.siena.it; Piazza del Duomo; Mar-Oct €4, Nov-Feb free; ⌚10.30am-6.30pm Mon-Sat, 1.30-5.30pm Sun Mar-Oct, to 5pm Nov-Feb) Construction of the *duomo* started in 1215 and work continued well into the 14th century. The magnificent facade of white, green and red polychrome marble was designed by Giovanni Pisano (the statues of philosophers and prophets are copies; you'll find the originals in the Museo dell'Opera).

In 1339 the city's leaders planned to enlarge the cathedral and create one of Italy's biggest churches. Known as the Duomo Nuovo (New Cathedral), the remains of this project are on Piazza Jacopo della Quercia, on the eastern side of the cathedral. The daring plan, to build an immense new nave with the present church becoming the transept, was scotched by the plague of 1348.

The interior of the duomo is truly stunning. Walls and pillars continue the black-and-white-stripe theme of the exterior, while the vaults are painted blue with gold stars. The inlaid-marble floor, decorated with 56 panels by about 40 artists and executed over the course of 200 years (14th to 16th centuries), depicts historical and biblical subjects. The older rectangular panels, including Wheel of Fortune (1372) and The She-Wolf of Siena with the Emblems of the Confederate Cities (1373), are graffiti designs by unknown artists, both restored in 1864. Domenico di Niccoló dei Cori was the first known artist to work on the cathedral, contributing several panels between 1413 and 1423, followed by renowned painter Domenico di Bartolo, who contributed Emperor Sigismund Enthroned in 1434. In the 15th century, director Alberto Aringhieri and celebrated Sienese artist Domenico Beccafumi created the dramatic expansion of the floor scheme. These later panels were done in more advanced multicoloured marble, inlaid with hexagon and rhombus frames. Unfortunately, about half are obscured by unsightly, protective covering, and are revealed only from 21 August through to 27 October each year (admission is €6 during this period), and dates vary slightly each year.

Other drawcards include the exquisitely crafted marble and porphyry pulpit carved by Nicola Pisano, assisted by Arnolfo di Cambio, who later designed the duomo in Florence. Intricately carved with vigorous, realistic crowd scenes, it's one of the masterpieces of Gothic sculpture.

Through a door from the north aisle is the enchanting **Libreria Piccolomini** (Piccolomini Library; included in duomo ticket Mar-Oct, Nov-Feb €2), built to house the books of Enea Silvio Piccolomini, better known as Pius II. The walls of the small hall are decorated with vividly coloured narrative frescoes painted between 1502–07 by Bernardino Pinturicchio depicting events in the life of Piccolomini.

➡ Museo dell'Opera del Duomo

(Piazza del Duomo; admission €7; ⌚10.30am-6.30pm Mon-Sat, 1.30-5.30pm Sun Mar-Oct, to 5pm Nov-Feb) The collection here showcases artworks that formerly adorned the cathedral, including the 12 statues of prophets and philosophers by Giovanni Pisano that decorated the facade. Their creator designed them to be viewed from ground level, which is why they look so distorted as they crane uncomfortably forward.

The museum's highlight is Duccio di Buoninsegna's striking *Maestà* (1311), which was painted on both sides as a screen for the *duomo*'s high altar. The main painting portrays the Virgin surrounded by angels, saints and prominent Sienese citizens of the period; the rear panels (sadly incomplete) portray scenes from the Passion of Christ. Duccio also designed and painted the vibrant stained-glass window downstairs; it was originally in the *duomo*.

➡ **Battistero di San Giovanni**

(Piazza San Giovanni; admission €4; ⏲10.30am-6.30pm Mon-Sat, 1.30-5.30pm Sun Mar-Oct, to 5pm Nov-Feb) Behind the *duomo,* down a steep flight of steps is the Baptistry, richly decorated with frescoes. At its centre is a hexagonal marble font by Jacopo della Quercia, decorated with bronze panels depicting the life of St John the Baptist by artists including Lorenzo Ghiberti *(Baptism of Christ* and *St John in Prison)* and Donatello *(The Head of John the Baptist Being Presented to Herod).*

➡ **Cripta**

(Piazza San Giovanni; admission incl audioguide €6; ⏲10.30am-6.30pm Mon-Sat, 1.30-5.30pm Sun Mar-Oct, to 5pm Nov-Feb) This Crypt below the cathedral's pulpit was rediscovered and restored in 1999 after having been filled to the roof with debris in the 1300s. The walls are completely covered with *pintura a secco* ('dry painting', better known as 'mural painting', as opposed to frescoes, which are painted on wet plaster, making them more durable) dating back to the 1200s. There's some 180 sq metres' worth, depicting several biblical stories, including the Passion of Jesus and the Crucifixion.

➡ **Panorama del Facciatone**

(⏲10.30am-6.30pm Mon-Sat, 1.30-5.30pm Sun Mar-Oct, to 5pm Nov-Feb) For a great panoramic view, haul yourself up the 131-step, narrow corkscrew stairway to the Panorama del Facciatone at the top of the facade of the putative Nuovo Duomo. Entrance is included in the Museo dell'Opera ticket.

★ **Complesso Museale Santa Maria della Scala** CULTURAL BUILDING

(www.santamariadellascala.com; Piazza del Duomo 1; adult/reduced/child under 11 €6/3.50/free; ⏲10.30am-4pm, to 6.30pm in high season) This former hospital, parts of which date to the 13th century, was built as a hospice for pilgrims travelling the Via Francigena. Located opposite the *duomo,* its highlight is the upstairs *Pellegrinaio* (Pilgrim's Hall), with vivid 15th-century frescoes by Lorenzo Vecchietta, Priamo della Quercia and Domenico di Bartolo lauding the good works of the hospital and its patrons.

The building now functions as a cultural centre and houses three museums – the Archaeological Museum, Art Museum for Children and Center of Contemporary Art (SMS Contemporanea) as well as a variety of historic halls, chapels and temporary exhibition spaces. Don't miss the atmospheric Archaeological Museum housed in the basement tunnels and the medieval *fienile* (hayloft) on level three, which houses Jacopo della Quercia's original Fonte Gaia sculptures.

★ **Pinacoteca Nazionale** ART GALLERY

(Via San Pietro 29; adult/reduced €4/2; ⏲10am-5.45pm Tue-Sat, 9am-12.45pm Sun & Mon) Occupying the once grand but now sadly dishevelled 14th-century Palazzo Buonsignori, this labyrinthine gallery displays an extraordinary collection of Gothic masterpieces from the Sienese school. The highlights are all on the 2nd floor, including magnificent and uplifting works by Duccio di Buoninsegna, Simone Martini, Niccolò di Segna, Lippo Memmi, Ambrogio and Pietro Lorenzetti, Bartolo di Fredi and Taddeo di Bartolo.

The collection demonstrates the gulf cleaved between artistic life in Siena and Florence in the 15th century. While the Renaissance flourished 70km to the north, Siena's masters and their patrons remained firmly rooted in the Byzantine and Gothic precepts that had stood them in such good stead from the early 13th century. Religious images and episodes predominate, typically pasted lavishly with gold and generally lacking any of the advances in painting (eg perspective, emotion or movement) that artists in Florence were exploring. That's not to say that the works here are second-rate – many are among the most beautiful and important creations of their time.

There are too many knock-'em-dead canvasses to list here, but you should be sure not to miss Duccio's *Madonna and Child* (Room 2), *Madonna with Child and Four Saints* (Room 4) and *Santa Maria Maddalena* (Room 5); Simone Martini's *Madonna della Misericordia* and *Madonna with Child* (both in Room 4), *Madonna and Child* (Room 6) and *Blessed Agostino* altarpiece (Room 6); Lippo Memmi's *Adoration of the Magi* (Room 6); Ambrogio Lorenzetti's luminous *Annunciation* and *Madonna with Child* (both in Room 8); Pietro Lorenzetti's *Madonna Enthroned with Saint Nicholas and the Prophet Elia* and *Crucifixion* (both in Room 8); and Taddeo di Bartolo's *The Annunciation of the Virgin Mary* (Room 11).

Note that the gallery occasionally rearranges its exhibits; we have cited the room numbers that applied when we last visited.

COMBINED PASSES

If you are planning to visit the major monuments, be sure to purchase one or more of the money-saving combined passes on offer:

- OPA SI Pass (*duomo*, Libreria Piccolomini, Museo dell'Opera, Battistero di San Giovanni, Cripta and Oratorio di San Bernardino; €12 Mar-Oct, €8 Nov-Feb, valid for three days)
- SIA Summer (Museo Civico, Complesso Museale Santa Maria della Scala, Museo dell'Opera, Battistero di San Giovanni, Oratorio di San Bernardino and Chiesa di San Agostino; €17, valid for seven days during period 15 March to 31 October)
- SIA Winter (Museo Civico, Complesso Museale Santa Maria della Scala, Museo dell'Opera and Battistero di San Giovanni; €14, valid for seven days during period 1 November to 14 March)
- Museo Civico and Torre del Mangia (€13)
- Musei Comunali (Museo Civico and Complesso Museale Santa Maria della Scala; €11, valid for two days)

The OPA SI Pass can be booked in advance at www.operaduomo.siena.it; all other passes are purchased directly at the museums.

Chiesa di San Domenico CHURCH
(Piazza San Domenico; 9am-12.30pm & 3-7pm) St Catherine was welcomed into the Dominican fold within this imposing church, and its **Cappella di Santa Caterina** is adorned with frescoes by Il Sodoma depicting events in her life. Catherine died in Rome, where most of her body is preserved, but her head was returned to Siena (it's in a 15th-century tabernacle above the altar in the chapel).

Also here are her desiccated thumb (in a small window box to the right of the chapel) and a nasty-looking chain that the saint is said to have flagellated herself with.

Casa Santuario di Santa Caterina RELIGIOUS
(Costa di Sant'Antonio 6; 9am-6.30pm Mar-Nov, 10am-6pm Dec-Feb) FREE If you want more of Santa Caterina – figuratively speaking – visit this pilgrimage sight where the saint, her parents and 24 siblings lived (locals like to joke that her mother must have been a saint, too). The rooms in the house were converted into small chapels in the 15th century.

The lower-level bedroom, frescoed in 1893 by Alessandro Franchi, includes her untouched, nearly bare cell. The largest of the chapels is minded by nuns, and is closed during their lunchtime (12.30pm to 3pm).

Oratorio di San Bernardino ART GALLERY
(www.operaduomo.siena.it; Piazza San Francesco 9; adult/reduced €3/2.50; 10.30am-7pm Mar-Oct) Nestled in the shadow of the huge Gothic church of San Francesco is this 15th-century oratory, which is dedicated to St Bernardino and decorated with Mannerist frescoes by Il Sodoma, Beccafumi and Pacchia. Upstairs, the small **Museo Diocesano di Arte Sacra** has some lovely paintings, including a *Madonna del Latte* (Nursing Madonna, c 1340) by Ambrogio Lorenzetti.

Note that admission to the oratory is included in the OPA SI Pass.

Museo delle Tavolette di Biccherna MUSEUM
(http://archiviostato.si.it, in Italian; Banchi di Sotto 52; guided tours 9.30am, 10.30am & 11.30am Mon-Sat) FREE Siena's state archives are housed in magnificent **Palazzo Piccolomini**, a Renaissance-era building close to the Campo. Enter from the courtyard and take the elevator to the fourth floor to visit this charming museum, which takes its name from the pride of its collection, a series of small late 13th-century paintings known as the 'Tavolette di Biccherna'.

Originally created as covers for the municipal accounts books, the *tavolette* were painted by Sienese artists including Ambogio Lorenzetti. They and other historically significant documents from the archive (many medieval) can be seen on the compulsory guided tour (in Italian only).

Courses

Accademia Musicale Chigiana MUSIC
(0577 2 20 91; www.chigiana.it; Via di Città 89) Competitive-entry classical-music masterclasses and workshops every summer.

Fondazione Siena Jazz MUSIC
(☎0577 27 14 01; www.sienajazz.it; Fortezza Medicea 1) One of Europe's foremost institutions of its type, offering courses and workshops for experienced jazz musicians.

Scuola Leonardo da Vinci LANGUAGE
(☎0577 24 90 97; www.scuolaleonardo.com; Via del Paradiso 16) Italian-language school with supplementary cultural programs.

Società Dante Alighieri LANGUAGE
(☎0577 4 95 33; www.dantealighieri.com; Via Tommaso Pendola 37) Language and cultural courses southwest of the city centre.

Tuscan Wine School WINE TASTING
(☎333 7229716; www.tuscanwineschool.com; Via Stalloreggi 26) Daily two-hour wine-tasting classes introducing Italian and Tuscan wines (€40).

Università per Stranieri LANGUAGE
(University for Foreigners; ☎0577 24 01 00; www.unistrasi.it; Piazza Carlo Rosselli 27-28) Offers various courses in Italian language and culture. You'll find it near the train station.

Tours

Centro Guide Turistiche Siena e Provincia TOUR
(☎0577 4 32 73; info@guidesiena.it; Galleria Odeon, Via Banchi di Sopra 31; ⏲10am-1pm & 3-5pm Mon-Fri) This association of accredited professional tour guides operates four recommended tours between Easter and October: a one-hour tour of the *duomo* (11am, noon & 4pm daily; €5 plus entrance fee); a 90-minute Classical Siena Walking Tour (11am Monday to Saturday; €20 including *duomo* entrance fee); and a 90-minute Secret Siena Walk (11am Sun; €20 including Complesso Museale Santa Maria della Scala entrance fee). The *duomo* tour departs from the OPA SI ticket office next door, and the walking tours depart from outside the tourist office in the Campo; all are in English and Italian. Bookings are advisable. Children under 11 are free.

The centre also operates private guided tours in Siena and throughout the region (3/6 hours €150/280).

Festivals & Events

The Accademia Musicale Chigiana presents three highly regarded series of concerts featuring classical musicians from around the world: **Micat in Vertice** from November to April, **Settimana Musicale Senese** in July and **Estate Musicale Chigiana** in July and August. Venues include the Teatro dei Rinnovati in the Campo, Teatro dei Rozzi in Piazza Indipendenza, Chiesa di Sant'Agostino and **Palazzo Chigi-Saracini** (Via di Città, near Piazza del Duomo).

For more information about events, go to www.terresiena.it.

Sleeping

★**Hotel Alma Domus** HOTEL €
(☎0577 4 41 77; www.hotelalmadomus.it; Via Camporegio 37; s €40-48, d without view €60-75, d with view €65-85, q €95-125; ❄@🛜) Owned by the Catholic diocese and still home to six Dominican nuns, this convent now operates as a budget hotel. And though its prices are low, the standard of its recently renovated 4th floor rooms are anything but. Most of these have new bathrooms and beds, air-con and views over the narrow green Fontebranda valley across to the *duomo*.

Families are welcome, and will be charmed by the particularly lovely room 12, which sleeps four and has a balcony. Note that there's a 1am curfew.

Antica Residenza Cicogna B&B €
(☎0577 28 56 13; www.anticaresidenzacicogna.it; Via dei Terme 67; s €65-90, d €85-110, ste €120-150;

OFF THE BEATEN TRACK

ORTO DE' PECCI

Head behind the Palazzo Comunale and down the hill past Piazza del Mercato and the city's historic, now decommissioned communal laundry to discover **Orto de' Pecci** (www.ortodepecci.it; ⏲24hr) FREE, an urban oasis. Kids love visiting the geese, goats, ducks and donkeys that live here, and locals can often be found hiding from the tourist masses in its green spaces (perfect for picnics or an afternoon snooze). There's a cooperative organic farm that grows fruit and vegetables and supplies the on-site **restaurant** (⏲12.30-2.30pm & 7.30-10pm Tue-Sat, 12.30-2.30pm Sun Mar-Oct, 12.30-2.30pm & 7.30-10pm Fri & Sat, 12.30-2.30pm Sun Nov-Feb) with produce, a medieval garden and an experimental vineyard which Siena University's agriculture department has planted with clones of medieval vines. On summer evenings, concerts are sometimes held here, too.

) Charming host Elisa supervised the restoration of this 13th-century building and will happily recount its history (it's been owned by her family for generations). The seven rooms are clean and well maintained, with comfortable beds, painted ceilings and tiled floors. There's also a tiny lounge where you can relax over complimentary Vin Santo and *cantucci* (hard, sweet almond biscuits).

Note that reception has limited core hours (8am to 1pm), so you should arrange the time of your arrival in advance.

Bed and Breakfast Alle Due Porte B&B €
(0577 28 76 70; www.sienatur.it; Via Stalloreggi 51; s €65, d €75-85;) Taking its name from the nearby city gate, this well-located B&B has loads of character and a real 'home away from home' feel. Run by an elderly couple, it offers three rooms (two with air-con) and a small breakfast room on the first floor of a rebuilt 12th-century tower house.

Hotel Athena HOTEL €
(0577 28 63 13; www.hotelathena.com; Via Paolo Mascagni 55; s €55-140, superior d €65-180, deluxe d €90-280; closed Feb; P) Hotel man-

ST CATHERINE OF SIENA

One of the two patron saints of Italy (with St Francis) and one of only three female Doctors of the Church (with St Teresa of Avilà and St Thérèse of Liseux), St Catherine was born in Siena in 1347, the 23rd child out of 25. Like a true prodigy, she had a religious fixation at a very early age. She is said to have entertained plans to impersonate a man so she could be a Dominican friar and occasionally raced out to the road to kiss the place where Dominicans had walked.

At the age of seven, Catherine consecrated her virginity to Christ, much to her family's despair. At 18 she assumed the life of a Dominican Tertiary (lay affiliate) and lived as a recluse in the family's basement, focusing her attention on devotion and spiritual ecstasy. She was noted for her ability to fast for extended periods, living only on the Blessed Sacrament, which, as nutritionists might attest, probably contributed to a delirium or two. Catherine described one such episode as a 'mystical marriage' with Jesus. Feeling a surge of humanity, she emerged from her cloistered path and began caring for the sick and poor at the Ospedale Santa Maria della Scala.

Another series of visions – this time set in Hell, Purgatory and Heaven – compelled Catherine to take her work to the next level and she began an ambitious and fearless letter-writing campaign to all variety of influential people, including lengthy correspondence with Pope Gregory XI. She beseeched royalty and religious leaders for everything from peace between Italy's republics to reform within the clergy. This go-getting, early form of activism was considered highly unusual for a woman at the time and her no-holds-barred style, sometimes scolding cardinals and queens like naughty children, was gutsy by any standard. And yet, rather than being persecuted for her insolence, she was admired, her powers of persuasion often winning the day where so many others had failed. She is said to have experienced the stigmata, but this event was suppressed as it was considered bad form at the time to associate the stigmata with anyone but St Francis.

Acting as an ambassador to Florence, Catherine went to Avignon and was able to convince Gregory XI to bring the papacy back to Rome after a 73-year reign in France. A few years later she was invited to Rome by newly elected Pope Urban VI to campaign on his behalf during the pope/anti-pope struggle (the Great Western Schism), where she did her best to undo the effects that his temper and shortcomings were having on Rome. This heroic, utterly exhausting effort likely contributed to her untimely death in 1380 at the age of 33.

Catherine's abundant post-mortem accolades started relatively soon after her death, when Pope Pius II canonised her in 1461. More recently, Pope Paul VI bestowed Catherine with the title of Doctor of the Church in 1970 and Pope John Paul II made her one of Europe's patron saints in 1999. She is also one of the three patron saints of Siena (the others being Saints Ansanas and Ambrose).

For information about guided and self-guided walking tours of St Catherine's Siena, go to www.viaesiena.it.

THE PALIO

Dating from the Middle Ages, this spectacular annual event includes a series of colourful pageants and a wild horse race on 2 July and 16 August. Ten of Siena's 17 *contrade* (town districts) compete for the coveted *palio* (silk banner). Each *contrada* has its own traditions, symbol and colours plus its own church and *palio* museum.

The race is staged in the Campo. From about 5pm, representatives from each *contrada* parade in historical costume, all bearing their individual banners. For scarcely one exhilarating minute, the 10 horses and their bareback riders tear three times around a temporarily constructed dirt racetrack with a speed and violence that makes spectators' hair stand on end.

The race is held at 7.45pm in July and 7pm in August. Join the crowds in the centre of the Campo at least four hours before the start if you want a place on the rails, but be aware that once there you won't be able to leave for toilet or drink breaks until the race has finished. Alternatively, the cafes in the Campo sell places on their terraces; these cost between €350 and €400 per ticket, and can be booked through the tourist office up to one year in advance.

Note that during the Palio, hotels raise their rates between 10% and 50% and enforce a minimum-stay requirement.

agement schools looking for an exemplar of a well-run business could easily cite the Athena. Operated by the Bianciardi family for the past four decades, it's clean, comfortable, meticulously maintained and friendly. The deluxe countryside rooms are knockouts (well worth the price) and the summertime terrace bar and restaurant is the stuff of which lasting holiday memories are made.

Standard rooms on the lower floors are not nearly as attractive as the superior and deluxe versions upstairs, but they are considerably cheaper – check the website for deals. On-site parking is free and easy to access.

Albergo Bernini PENSION €
(☎0577 28 90 47; www.albergobernini.com; Via della Sapienza 15; d with/without bathroom €85/65; 📶) Pros: this is a welcoming, family-run hotel with 10 neat rooms and a gorgeous terrace sporting views across to the *duomo* and Chiesa di San Domenico. Cons: uncomfortable beds and the fact that only two rooms – the single and triple – have air-con. Breakfast costs €3 to €7.50, rates are negotiable in winter and payment is cash only.

★Pensione Palazzo Ravizza BOUTIQUE HOTEL €€
(☎0577 28 04 62; www.palazzoravizza.it; Pian dei Mantellini 34; loft r €80-150, d €100-220, ste €180-320; P ❄ @ 📶) Occupying a Renaissance-era *palazzo* located in a quiet but convenient corner of the city, this extremely friendly hotel offers rooms with frescoed ceilings, huge beds and small but well-equipped bathrooms. Suites are even more impressive, with views over the delightful rear garden. The free on-site parking is a major draw and low-season rates are a huge bargain.

Note that the three cheapest rooms are in the loft and, though charming, have small windows and even smaller bathrooms.

Hotel Villa Liberty HOTEL €€
(☎0577 4 49 66; www.villaliberty.it; Viale Vittorio Veneto 11; s €62-167, d €102-294, ste €122-368; ❄ 📶) Located in a tree-lined boulevard opposite the Fortezza Medicea, this Liberty-style villa has been converted into a 17-room hotel and is one of the city's best midrange choices. Though the Campo is only a 15-minute walk away, the area is less touristy than the historic centre and there is free (but highly contested) parking right outside the hotel.

Rooms are light and modern, with comfortable beds and small but perfectly adequate bathrooms; the superior versions have free tea- and coffee-making facilities.

★Campo Regio Relais BOUTIQUE HOTEL €€€
(☎0577 22 20 73; www.camporegio.com; Via della Sapienza 25; s €150-300, d €190-300, ste €250-600; ❄ @ 📶) Siena's most charming hotel has only six rooms, all individually decorated and luxuriously equipped. Breakfast is served in the sumptuously decorated lounge or on the terrace, with a sensational view of the *duomo* and Torre del Mangia.

Villa Scacciapensieri BOUTIQUE HOTEL €€€
(☎0577 4 14 41; www.villascacciapensieri.it; Via Scacciapensieri 10; s €65-140, d €100-315, ste €210-345; P ❄ 📶 ≋) Around 2.5km north of Siena, this 19th-century villa with two annexes is set in formal gardens and has plenty of amenities, including a swimming pool, restaurant (dinner Thursday to Tuesday €40) and tennis court. Guests driving through the region can leave their cars here and catch the bus into Florence for day trips (the bus stop is directly outside the property).

Eating

Among many traditional Sienese dishes are *panzanella* (summer salad of soaked bread, basil, onion and tomatoes), *ribollita* (a rich vegetable, bean and bread soup), *pappardelle con la lepre* (ribbon pasta with hare) and *panforte* (a rich cake of almonds, honey and candied fruit). Keep an eye out for dishes featuring the region's signature *cinta senese* (indigenous Tuscan pig).

Morbidi DELI €
(www.morbidi.com; Via Banchi di Sopra 75; meal €12; ⏲9am-8pm Mon-Sat, lunch buffet 12.30-2.30pm) Local gastronomes shop here as the range of cheese, cured meats and imported delicacies is the best in Siena. Also notable is the downstairs lunch buffet, which offers fantastic value. For a mere €12, you can graze on platters of antipasti, salads, pastas and a dessert of the day. Bottled water is supplied, wine and coffee cost extra.

Consorzio Agrario di Siena DELI €
(Via Pianigiani 13; ⏲8am-7.30pm Mon-Sat) Operating since 1901, this farmer's co-op is a rich emporium of food and wine, much of it locally produced. There's a small bar area where you can purchase and eat a slab of freshly cooked pizza (€12 to €14.30 per kg).

Grom GELATO €
(www.grom.it; Via Banchi di Sopra 11-13; gelato €2.50-5.50; ⏲11am-midnight Sun-Thu, to 12.30am Fri & Sat Apr-Sep, 11am-11pm Sun-Thu, to midnight Fri & Sat Oct-Mar) Delectable gelato with flavours that change with the season; many of the ingredients are organic or Slow Food-accredited. Also serves milkshakes.

Kopa Kabana GELATO €
(www.gelateriakopakabana.it; Via dei Rossi 52-55; gelati €1.80-4.30; ⏲noon-8pm mid-Feb–mid-Nov, later hr in warm weather) Come here for fresh gelato made by self-proclaimed ice-cream master Fabio (we're pleased to concur).

★**Enoteca I Terzi** MODERN TUSCAN €€
(☎0577 4 43 29; www.enotecaiterzi.it; Via dei Termini 7; meals €35, antipasto plate €9; ⏲11am-1am Mon-Sat) Close to the Campo but off the well-beaten tourist trail, this classy modern *enoteca* (wine bar) is a favourite with sophisticated locals, who linger over working lunches, *aperitivi* sessions and casual dinners featuring top-notch *salumi* (cured meats), delicate handmade pasta, flavoursome risotto and succulent grilled meats. The wine list is fantastic, and includes an excellent choice by the glass. Go.

Ristorante Grotta Santa Caterina da Bagoga TUSCAN €€
(☎0577 28 22 08; www.bagoga.it; Via della Galluzza 26; meals €28; ⏲12.30-2.30pm & 7.30-10.30pm Tue-Sat, 12.30-2.30pm Sun) Pierino Fagnani ('Bagogoga'), one of Siena's most famous Palio jockeys, swapped his saddle for an apron in 1973 and has been operating this much-loved restaurant near the Casa Santuario di Santa Caterina ever since. Traditional Tuscan palate pleasers feature on the menu, and are perhaps best appreciated in the four-course 'tipico' (€35) or 'degustazione' (€50 with wine) menus.

La Compagnia dei Vinattieri WINE BAR €€
(☎0577 23 65 68; www.vinattieri.net; Via delle Terme 79; antipasto platter €7-9, meals €35; ⏲noon-10pm, closed late Feb–late Mar) Duck down the stairs to enjoy a quick glass of wine and a meat or cheese platter in this cellar, or settle in for a leisurely meal accompanied by your choice from an impressive wine list. It's popular with locals and tourists alike – you'll need to try your luck for a drink, and book in advance for a meal.

Tre Cristi SEAFOOD €€€
(☎0577 28 06 08; www.trecristi.com; Vicolo di Provenzano 1; 3-course tasting menus €35-45, 5-course menus €65; ⏲12.30-3pm & 7.30-10.30pm Mon-Sat) Seafood restaurants are thin on the ground in this meat-obsessed region, so the long existence of Tre Cristi (it's been around since 1830) should be heartily celebrated. The menu here is as elegant as the decor, and added touches such as a complimentary glass of *prosecco* (dry sparkling wine) at the start of the meal add to the experience.

Osteria Le Logge MODERN TUSCAN €€€
(☎0577 4 80 13; www.osterialelogge.it; Via del Porrione 33; meals €55; ⏲noon-2.45 & 7-10.30pm Mon-Sat) This place changes its menu of creative Tuscan cuisine almost daily. The best tables

are in the downstairs dining room – once a pharmacy and still retaining its handsome display cabinets – or on the streetside terrace. We've found that the antipasti and *primi* (first courses) are consistently delicious, but the mains can be disappointing.

Drinking

Caffè Fiorella CAFE
(www.torrefazionefiorella.it; Via di Città 13; 7am-8pm Mon-Sat) Squeeze into this tiny space behind the Campo to enjoy Siena's best coffee. In summer, the coffee granita with a dollop of cream is a wonderful indulgence.

Enoteca Italiana WINE BAR
(www.enoteca-italiana.it; Fortezza Medicea; noon-1am Mon-Sat Apr-Sep, to midnight Oct-Mar) The former munitions cellar and dungeon of this Medici fortress has been artfully transformed into a classy *enoteca* that carries over 1500 Italian labels. You can take a bottle with you, ship a case home or enjoy a glass or two in the attractive courtyard or atmospheric vaulted interior of the wine bar. There's usually food available, too.

Bar Il Palio CAFE
(Piazza del Campo 47; 8am-midnight) The best coffee on the Campo; drink it standing at the bar or suffer the financial consequences.

Shopping

Panificio Il Magnifico FOOD
(www.ilmagnifico.siena.it; Via dei Pellegrini 27; 7.30am-7.30pm Mon-Sat) Lorenzo Rossi is Siena's best baker, and his *panforte*, *ricciarelli* (sugar-dusted chewy almond biscuits) and *cavallucci* (almond biscuits made with Tuscan millefiori honey) are a weekly purchase for most local households. Try them at his bakery and shop behind the *duomo*, and you'll understand why.

Bottega d'Arte ART
(www.arteinsiena.it; Via Stalloreggi 47) Inspired by the works of Sienese masters of the 14th and 15th centuries, artists Chiara Perinetti Casoni and Michelangelo Attardo Perinetti Casoni create exquisite icons in tempera and 24-carat gold leaf. Expensive? Yes. Worth it? You bet.

Il Pellicano CERAMICS
(0577 24 79 14; www.siena-ilpellicano.it; Via Diacceto 17a; 10.30am-7pm Easter-Oct, to 7pm Mon-Sat Nov-Easter) Elisabetta Ricci has been making traditional hand-painted Sienese ceramics for over 30 years. She shapes, fires and paints her ceramic creations – often using Renaissance-era styles or typical *contrade* designs – at her atelier near Parking Santa Caterina and sells them at this shop near the *duomo*. Elisabetta also conducts lessons in traditional ceramic techniques – contact her for details.

Wednesday Market MARKET
(7.30am-1pm) Spreading around Fortezza Medicea and towards the Stadio Comunale, this is one of Tuscany's largest markets and is great for foodstuffs and cheap clothing. An antiques market is also held here on the third Sunday of each month.

Pizzicheria de Miccoli FOOD
(Via di Città 93-95; 8am-8pm) Richly scented, de Miccoli has a stuffed boar's head over its entrance and windows festooned with sausages, stacks of cheese and sacks of *porcini* mushrooms. It also sells filled *panini* to go.

Information

Hospital (0577 58 51 11; Viale Bracci) Just north of Siena at Le Scotte.

Police station (0577 20 11 11; Via del Castoro 6)

Tourist office (0577 28 05 51; www.terresiena.it; Piazza del Campo 56; 9.30am-6.30pm Easter-Sep, to 5.30pm Mon-Fri, to 12.30pm Sun Oct-Easter) Reserves accommodation, sells a map of Siena (€1), organises car and scooter hire, and sells train tickets (commission applies). Also takes bookings for a range of day tours operated by the My Tour company. These include a package for the Palio, cooking classes, hot-air balloon rides, horse-riding, and trips to Chianti, Montalcino, San Gimignano and Montepulciano.

Getting There & Away

BUS

Siena Mobilità (800 570530; www.sienamobilita.it), part of the **Tiemme** (0577 20 42 46; www.tiemmespa.it) network, runs services between Siena and other parts of Tuscany. It has a **ticket office** (6.30am-7.30pm Mon-Fri, 7am-7.30pm Sat & Sun) underneath the main bus station in Piazza Gramsci; there's also a left-luggage office here (per 24 hours €5.50).

A Siena Mobilità bus travels between Pisa airport and Siena (one-way/return €14/26, two hours), leaving Siena at 7.10am and Pisa at 1pm. Tickets should be purchased at least one day in advance from the bus station or online.

Frequent 'Corse Rapide' (Express) buses race up to Florence (€7.80, 1¼ hours); they are a better option than the 'Corse Ordinarie' services, which stop in Poggibonsi and Colle di Val d'Elsa en route. Other regional destinations include San Gimignano (€6, one to 1½ hours, 10 daily either direct or changing in Poggibonsi), Poggibonsi (€4.35, 50 minutes, every 40 minutes), Arezzo (€6.60, 1½ hours, eight daily) and Colle di Val d'Elsa (€3.40, 30 minutes, hourly), with connections for Volterra (€2.75). Note that all services run to dramatically reduced timetables on Sunday and holidays. Services to Montalcino (€4.90, 1½ hours, six daily), Montepulciano (€6.60, one hour, two daily) and Pienza (€5.50, 70 minutes, two daily) depart from outside the train station.

Sena (☎861 199 19 00; www.sena.it) buses run to/from Rome TIbertina (€23, 3½ hours, six daily), Fiumicino Airport (€23, 3¾ hours, two daily), Turin (€36, 8¼ hours, one daily), Milan (€36, 4¼ hours, two daily), Venice (€29, 5½ hours, one daily) and Perugia (€12, 1½ hours, one daily). Its **ticket office** (⌚8.30am-7.45pm Mon-Sat) is also underneath the bus station in Piazza Gramsci.

CAR & MOTORCYCLE

For Florence, take the Siena–Florence *S2 superstrada* (expressway) or the more scenic SR222.

TRAIN

Siena isn't on a major train line so buses are generally a better alternative; the exception is the direct service to Grosseto (€9, 1½ hours, eight daily). You'll need to change at Chiusi for Rome and at Empoli for Florence and Pisa.

ℹ Getting Around

BUS

Siena Mobilità operates city bus services (€1.10 per 90 minutes). Buses 8 and 9 run between the train station and Piazza Gramsci.

CAR & MOTORCYCLE

There's a ZTL in the historical centre, although visitors can drop off luggage at their hotel, then get out (don't forget to have reception report your licence number or risk receiving a hefty fine).

Large, conveniently located car parks are at the Stadio Comunale and around the Fortezza Medicea, both just north of Piazza San Domenico. Some free street parking (look for white lines) is available in Viale Vittorio Veneto, on the southern edge of the Fortezza Medicea, but it is hotly contested. The paid car parks at San Francesco and Santa Caterina (aka Fontebranda) each have a *scala mobile* (escalator) to take you up into the centre.

All paid car parks charge €1.70 per hour. For more information on parking, go to www.siena parcheggi.com (in Italian).

CHIANTI

The ancient vineyards in this photogenic part of Tuscany produce the grapes used in the ruby-red Chianti and Chianti Classico DOCGs, blends of red grapes with a minimum 75% (Chianti) or 80% (Chianti Classico) Sangiovese component. Both are sold under the Gallo Nero (Black Cockerel/ Rooster) trademark. They're not the only wines produced in this region, though: the Colli dell'Etruria Centrale, Pomino, Vin Santo del Chianti and Vin Santo del Chianti Classico DOCs are local drops, too. The biggest wine-producing estates have *cantine* (cellars) where you can taste and buy wine, but few vineyards – big or small – can be visited without an advance reservation.

Split between the provinces of Florence (Chianti Fiorentino) and Siena (Chianti Senese), Chianti is usually accessed via the SR222 (Via Chiantigiana) and is criss-crossed by a picturesque network of *strade provinciale* (provincial roads) and *strade secondaria* (secondary roads), some of which are unsealed. You'll pass immaculately maintained vineyards and olive groves, honey-coloured stone farmhouses, dense forests, graceful Romanesque *pieve* (rural churches), handsome Renaissance villas and imposing stone castles built by Florentine and Sienese warlords during the Middle Ages.

Chianti Festival (www.chiantifestival.com), a program of arts events, is staged in June and July.

For information about the Consorzio Vino Chianti Classico (the high-profile consortium of local producers), go to www.chianti classico.com. In May and June the *consorzio* organises a popular 10-day festival featuring wine and food events called Chianti Classico E (www.classico-e.it).

The northern half of this region (Chianti Fiorentino) is a popular day trip from Florence, with visitors arriving by bus, car and bicycle.

Though it's now part of the province of Siena, the southern section of Chianti (Chianti Senese) was once the stronghold of the Lega del Chianti, a military and administrative alliance within the city-state of Florence that comprised Castellina, Gaiole and Radda.

🛏 Sleeping

Ostello del Chianti HOSTEL **€**
(☎055 805 02 65; www.ostellodelchianti.it; Via Roma 137, Tavarnelle Val di Pesa; dm €14-16, q with private/shared bathroom €70/76; ⌚reception

8.30-11am & 4pm-midnight, hostel closed Nov–mid-Mar; P @) This is one of Italy's oldest hostels and though it occupies an ugly building in the less-than-scenic town of Tavarnelle Val di Pesa, the friendly staff and bargain prices compensate. Dorms max out at six beds and bike hire can be arranged for €8 per day. Breakfast costs €2. Florence is easily accessed by SITA bus (€3.30, one hour).

Fattoria di Rignana AGRITURISMO **€€**
(055 85 20 65; www.rignana.it; Rignana; d with/without bathroom in fattoria €90/100, d villa €110-130; P @) This old farmstead and noble villa 3.8km from Badia a Passignano has everything you'll need for the perfect Chianti experience – an historic setting, glorious views, a large swimming pool and walking access to a decent local eatery. Two accommodation options are on offer: elegant rooms in the 17th-century villa and more rustic rooms in the adjoining *fattoria* (farmhouse).

Villa I Barronci HOTEL **€€**
(055 82 05 98; www.villaibarronci.com; Via Sorripa 10, San Casciano Val di Pesa; s €85-150, d €115-230; P @) Located on the northwestern edge of Chianti between Florence and Pisa, this extremely comfortable and modern country hotel offers exemplary service and amenities. You can relax in the bar and restaurant, rejuvenate in the spa, laze by the pool or head off for easy day trips to Volterra, San Gimignano and Siena.

Villa Il Poggiale BOUTIQUE HOTEL **€€**
(055 82 83 11; www.villailpoggiale.it; Via Empolese 69, San Casciano Val di Pesa; d €80-250, ste €120-350; closed mid-Jan–mid-Feb; P @) Accommodation in Chianti is often prohibitively expensive, but this Renaissance-era villa in an elevated location looking toward the Val d'Elsa (Il Poggiale means 'Top of the Hill') bucks the trend. It offers a labyrinthine arrangement of 24 spacious and individually decorated rooms and suites; some have four-poster beds and frescoed ceilings, and all have tea- and coffee-making facilities.

The villa's downstairs spa has a sauna and jacuzzi, and the swimming pool commands an amazing view. Guests enjoy the complimentary afternoon tea that is served in the gracious reception salon, and appreciate the buffet dinner after a big day of sightseeing in the region.

Locanda La Capannuccia RURAL INN **€€**
(0577 74 11 83; www.lacapannuccia.it; Borgo di Pietrafitta; s €80-90, d €96-130, two-night minimum; closed Nov-Feb; P) Tucked down a valley at the end of a 1.5km dirt road, this is a true Tuscan getaway. A pretty country inn, it offers five simple but comfortable rooms and can provide dinner for guests if they book in advance (€25 to €30). To get here, head north along the SR222 from Castellina in Chianti and turn right to Pietrafitta.

DRIVING IN CHIANTI

Chianti's roads can be frighteningly narrow and frustratingly difficult to navigate – to cut down on driving stress, be sure to purchase a copy of *Le strade del Gallo Nero* (€2.50), a useful map of the wine-producing zone that shows both major and secondary roads and also includes a comprehensive list of wine estates. It's available at newsstands in the region.

★ **Villa Sassolini** BOUTIQUE HOTEL **€€€**
(055 970 22 46; www.villasassolini.it; Largo Moncioni, Località Moncioni; d €198-355, ste €324-443, dinner €50; closed Nov–mid-Mar;) It would be almost impossible to top the romantic credentials of this gorgeous hotel perched high in dense forest on the border of Chianti and the Valdarno. Luxe rooms, an intimate restaurant and a spectacular pool terrace are three of many elements contributing to an utterly irrestistible package – proximity to the Valdarno's designer clothing outlet stores being another.

Villa Le Barone BOUTIQUE HOTEL **€€€**
(055 85 26 21; www.villalebarone.com; Via San Leolino 19, Panzano in Chianti; r €195-365, dinner €32; P) Surrounded by a rose garden and commanding panoramic views, this tastefully converted manor house was once occupied by members of the famous Della Robbia family of Renaissance sculptors, so has a historical pedigree as impressive as its facilities (swimming pool, tennis court, fitness trail, restaurant). The 28 rooms are scattered between the villa, cottages and a converted barn.

Castello delle Serre BOUTIQUE HOTEL **€€€**
(338 5040811; www.castellodelleserre.com; Piazza XX Settembre 1, Serre di Rapolano; r €250, ste €300-375; P @) Though not officially in the Chianti Senese (it's in the Crete Senesi), the prospect of spending the night in this fabulous medieval castle makes the 41km trip from Gaiole in Chianti well worth

the effort. Meticulously restored by Italian-American host Salvatore Gangale, it features huge rooms and a swish pool area.

For a once-in-a-lifetime experience, book into the deluxe suite in the turret, which has a private terrace commanding suitably regal views.

La Locanda BOUTIQUE HOTEL €€€
(☎0577 73 88 32; www.lalocanda.it; Montanino di Volpaia; r €220-290, ste €290-310; ⏲closed Nov–mid-Apr; P ❄ 📶 🏊) Overlooking the medieval village of Volpaia near Radda in Chianti, this country hotel offers seven charming rooms in the converted 16th-century farmhouse, as well as a lounge, library and dining room (dinner Monday, Wednesday and Friday, €35) in the former stables.

Eating & Drinking

Il Giglio GELATO €
(www.gelateriailgiglio.it; Via del Giglio 13, San Donato in Poggio; gelato €1.50-4; ⏲3-11pm Easter-Oct) The fortified medieval village of San Donato is on the Siena–Florence *superstrada*, close to Tavarnelle Val di Pesa and a short drive from Badia a Passignano. It has three claims to fame: a charming main street with a Renaissance *palazzo*; a beautiful 12th-century *pieve;* and this *gelateria artiginale* (artisan ice-cream shop), which has a pretty rear courtyard.

Bar Ucci WINE BAR €
(www.bar-ucci.it; crostoni €4.50-6, antipasti plates €8, salads €4-8; ⏲8am-9pm Tue-Sun) Paola Barucci's small bar/cafe in the medieval hamlet of Volpaia is a deservedly popular stop with those touring the Chianti Senese. There's a good choice of Chianti by the bottle and a choice of Volpaia's own Chianti Classico or Riserva by the glass. Snacks include salads and *crostoni* (toasted bread) with a multitude of toppings.

La Locanda di Pietracupa GASTRONOMIC €€
(☎055 807 24 00; www.locandapietracupa.com; Via Madonna di Pietracupa 31, San Donato in Poggio; meals €40; ⏲closed Tue; P 📶) The prices at this restaurant near the late-Renaissance sanctuary of the Madonna di Pietracupa are remarkably reasonable considering the quality of the modern Tuscan cuisine on offer. You can enjoy a long lunch on the outdoor terrace, or book one of the four B&B rooms (single/double €70/80) and settle in for an indulgent dinner in the elegant dining room. As befits a top restaurant in this region, the wine list is as impressive as the food menu.

Rinuccio 1180 MODERN TUSCAN €€
(☎055 235 97 20; www.antinorichianticlassico.it; Via Cassia per Siena 133, Bargino; meals €32, tasting platters €9-12; ⏲noon-4pm) Imagine lunching inside a glass box on a terrace with an intoxicating 180-degree Dolby-esque surround of pea-green vines, hills and birdsong. This is what the latest starlet of the Chianti dining scene – the restaurant at the new Antinori cellar in Bargino – is about. Cuisine is Tuscan, modern, seasonal and sassy.

We love the fact that the water glasses are made from recycled wine bottles, the menu is cork-plated and the wine list is – naturally – fabulous. Advance reservations are essential.

La Cantinetta di Rignana TUSCAN €€
(☎055 85 26 01; www.lacantinettadirignana.it; meals €40; ⏲noon-3pm & 7-10pm Wed-Mon) Idyllically nestled in the old oil mill on the Rignana estate, this eatery offers quintessential Tuscan views from its large terrace. The food is rustic and will please most palates. It's a 15-minute drive from Badia a Passignano, between Panzano in Chianti and Mercatale Val di Pesa, and is approached via a long unsealed road.

L'Antica Scuderia TUSCAN €€
(☎055 807 16 23; www.ristorolanticascuderia.com; Via di Passignano 17, Badia a Passignano; meals €44, pizzas €7-15; ⏲12.30-2.30pm & 7.30-10.30pm Wed-Mon) If you fancy the idea of lunching on a garden terrace overlooking one of the Antinori vineyards, this casual eatery may well fit the bill. Lunch features antipasti, pastas and traditional grilled meats, while dinner sees plenty of pizza-oven action. Kids love the playground set, and adults love the fact that it's at the opposite end of the garden.

Osteria Le Panzanelle TUSCAN €€
(☎0577 73 35 11; www.lepanzanelle.it; Lucarelli; meals €35; ⏲noon-2.30pm & 7.30-9.30pm Tue-Sun, closed part of Jan & Feb) A great lunch stop en route from Greve in Chianti to Siena, this roadside inn serves traditional Tuscan dishes in its pretty garden and downstairs bar/dining room. The menu changes monthly, reflecting what is in season. Find it 5km south of Panzano in Chianti on the SP2 to Radda in Chianti. Bookings are advisable.

Osteria di Passignano GASTRONOMIC €€€
(☎055 807 12 78; www.osteriadipassignano.com; Via di Passignano 33; meals €70; ⏲12.15-2.15pm & 7.30-10pm Mon-Sat) This elegant dining room on the Antinori Estate at Badia a Passignano has long been one of Tuscany's most glamor-

ous dining destinations. Dishes utilise local produce and are decidedly Tuscan in inspiration, but could be overly fussy for some diners. It's no surprise that the wine list is mighty impressive, with Antinori offerings aplenty (by glass €7 to €35).

Greve in Chianti

POP 13,888

Located 26km south of Florence, Greve in Chianti is the main town in the Chianti Fiorentino. As well as being the hub of the local wine industry, it is home to the enthusiastic and entrepreneurial Falorni family, who operate the town's three main tourist attractions.

Greve's annual **wine fair** is held in the first or second week of September – book accommodation well in advance if you plan to visit at this time.

Sights & Activities

Museo del Vino MUSEUM

(Museum of Wine; www.museovino.it; Piazza Nino Tirinnanzi 10; hr vary) Opened in 2010, the privately established and operated Museo del Vino is a labour of love for brothers Lorenzo and Stefano Falorni, who have spent over 40 years documenting the history of the local wine industry and adding to their father's collection of artefacts and materials associated with it.

The collection is as extensive as it is eclectic – including historic postcards featuring Chianti scenes, wine manuals and catalogues, wine-making machinery and implements, barriques (a type of wine barrel) and more. An audioguide provides a fascinating narrative, as does an interview-based audiovisual presentation. At the time of research, the museum was welcoming visitors by appointment only. Email for an update.

Le Cantine di Greve in Chianti WINE TASTING

(www.lecantine.it; Galleria delle Cantine 2; 10am-7pm) Another Falorni family enterprise, Le Cantine di Greve in Chianti is a vast commercial *enoteca* stocking more than 1200 varieties of wine. To indulge in some of the 140 different wines available for tasting here (including Toscana IGTs – sometimes dubbed 'Super Tuscans' – top DOCs and DOCGs, Vin Santo and grappa), buy a prepaid wine card costing €10 to €25 from the central bar, stick it into one of the many taps and out trickles your tipple of choice.

Any unused credit will be refunded when you return the card. They are fabulous fun, though somewhat distressing for designated drivers. Fortunately, it's also possible to purchase bottles to drink back at the hotel or ship home. To find the cantine, look for the supermarket on the main road – it's down a staircase opposite the supermarket entrance.

LOCAL KNOWLEDGE

OUTLET SHOPPING

Follow local bargain-hunters to the Valdarno area in northeast Chianti to unleash your inner fashionista (and your credit cards). Bargains from the previous season's collections can be sourced at a number of outlets, the most popular of which are the **Mall** (www.themall.it; Via Europa 8; 10am-7pm or 8pm) in Leccio Regello; **Dolce & Gabbana** (055 833 13 00; Via Pian dell'Isola 49, Località Santa Maria Maddalena; 10am-7pm Mon-Sat, 3-7pm Sun), off the SR69 near Incisa Val d'Arno; and **Prada** (055 28 34 39; www.prada.com; Space Factory Outlets, Via Levanella Becorpi, Località Levanella; 10.30am-7.30pm Mon-Fri & Sun, 9.30am-7.30pm Sat), off the SR69 on the southern edge of Montevarchi.

Eating

Osteria Mangiando Mangiando TUSCAN €€

(055 854 63 72; www.mangiandomangiando.it; Piazza Matteotti 80, Greve in Chianti; meals €36; noon-2.30pm & 7-10pm Feb-Dec) It may be the much-lauded recipient of a coveted Slow Food snail of excellence, but this unpretentious place on Greve's main piazza has a friendly and casual vibe, a cheerful but simple decor, and a menu balancing Tuscan standards and some light and flavoursome options (especially soups) that differ from the usual local menu.

Shopping

Antica Macellerìa Falorni FOOD

(www.falorni.it; Piazza Matteotti 71; 8am-1pm & 3.30-7.30pm Mon-Sat, 10am-1pm & 3.30-7pm Sun) This atmospheric *macellerìa* (butcher shop) in the main square was established by the Falornis way back in 1729. Known for its *finocchiona briciolona* (pork salami made with fennel seeds and Chianti), it's the perfect pit stop if you're after picnic provisions.

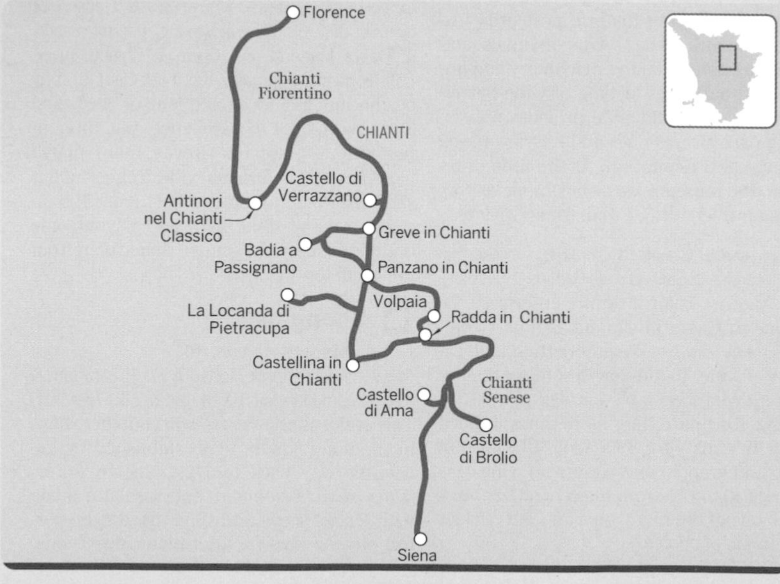
Florence
Chianti Fiorentino
CHIANTI
Castello di Verrazzano
Antinori nel Chianti Classico
Greve in Chianti
Badia a Passignano
Panzano in Chianti
Volpaia
La Locanda di Pietracupa
Radda in Chianti
Castellina in Chianti
Chianti Senese
Castello di Ama
Castello di Brolio
Siena

JOHN ELK / GETTY IMAGES ©

ROCCO FASANO / GETTY IMAGES ©

Top: Vineyards in Chianti
Bottom: Generations of winemakers at work

Wine Tour of Chianti

Tuscany has more than its fair share of highlights, but few can match the glorious indulgence of a leisurely drive through Chianti. On offer is an intoxicating blend of scenery, acclaimed restaurants and ruby-red wine.

From **Florence**, take the *superstrada* (expressway) towards Siena, exit at Bargino and follow the signs to **Antinori nel Chianti Classico** (p208), a recently opened wine estate featuring an architecturally innovative ageing cellar. Take a tour, prime your palate with a wine tasting and enjoy lunch in the estate's Rinuccio 1180 restaurant.

Head southeast along the SS2, SP3 and SS222 (Via Chiantigiana) towards Greve in Chianti. Stop at historic **Castello di Verrazzano** (p209) for a tasting en route.

On the next day, make your way to **Greve in Chianti** to visit its Museo del Vino (p205) and then test your new-found knowledge over a self-directed tasting in the nearby Cantine di Greve in Chianti (p205). For lunch, eat a Tuscan-style burger at Dario DOC (p209) in **Panzano in Chianti** or linger over lunch at **La Locanda di Pietracupa** (p204). Your destination in the afternoon should be **Badia a Passignano** (p208), an 11th-century, still-functioning Vallombrosian abbey surrounded by an Antinori wine estate. Enjoy a tasting in the *enoteca* (wine bar) and consider staying for an early pizza dinner at L'Antica Scuderia (p204) opposite the abbey, where you'll be able to watch the sun set over the vineyards.

On day three, pop into the pretty hilltop hamlet of **Volpaia** near **Radda in Chianti** and take a tour of the Castello di Volpaia (p210) cellars before relaxing over lunch at Bar Ucci (p204) or heading to the Michelin-starred Ristorante Albergaccio (p209) in **Castellina in Chianti**.

On the final day, head towards **Siena**. Along the way, take a guided tour of the **Castello di Brolio** (p210), ancestral home of the aristocratic Ricasoli family. Their wine estate is the oldest in Italy, so be sure to sample some Baron Ricasoli Chianti Classico at the estate's *cantina* (cellar) or over lunch in its *osteria* (casual tavern). Afterwards, investigate award-winning wines and contemporary art at **Castello di Ama** (p211).

CYCLING CHIANTI

Exploring Chianti by bicycle is a highlight for many travellers. The tourist office in Greve in Chianti publishes a brochure listing walking and cycling routes in the Greve area, and you can rent bicycles from **Ramuzzi** (☎055 85 30 37; www.ramuzzi.com; Via Italo Stecchi 23; touring bike/125cc scooter per day €20/55; ⏱9am-1pm & 3-7pm Mon-Fri, 9am-1pm Sat) in the town. A number of companies offer guided cycling tours leaving from Florence:

Florence by Bike (Map p82; ☎055 48 89 92; www.florencebybike.it; Via San Zanobi 120r) Day tour of northern Chianti, with lunch and wine tasting (€76; March to October).

I Bike Italy (☎342 9352395; www.ibikeitaly.com) Offers a day tour including lunch at a winery (€83; mid-March to October). A shuttle takes you from Florence to the starting point in Chianti. Students receive a 10% discount.

I Bike Tuscany (☎335 8120769; www.ibiketuscany.com) Year-round one-day tours (€120 to €150) for riders of all levels. The company transports you from your Florence hotel to Chianti by minibus, where you join the tour. Both hybrid and electric bikes are available, as is a support vehicle. Also offers one-day Florence to Siena tours (€145).

Information

The **tourist office** (☎055 854 62 99; Piazza Matteotti 11; ⏱10am-7pm) is located in Greve's main square.

Getting There & Around

SITA buses travel between Greve in Chianti and Florence (€3.30, one hour, hourly).

Greve is located on the Via Chiantigiana. There is free parking in the two-level, open-air car park on Piazza della Resistenza, on the opposite side of the main road to Piazza Matteotti. On Fridays, don't park overnight in the paid spaces in Piazza Matteotti – your car will be towed away to make room for Saturday market stalls.

Around Greve in Chianti

A narrow road leads from Greve in Chianti up to the medieval village of **Montefioralle**, the ancestral home of Amerigo Vespucci (1415–1512). An explorer, navigator and cartographer who made two early voyages to America following the route charted by Columbus, Vespucci wrote excitedly about the New World on his return to Europe, inspiring cartographer Martin Waldseemüller (creator of the 1507 *Universalis Cosmographia*) to name the new continent in his honour. It's an extremely steep walk or bike ride, but the panoramic view makes it worth the effort.

Sights & Activities

★Antinori nel Chianti Classico WINERY
(www.antinorichianticlassico.it; Via Cassia per Siena 133, Località Bargino; tour & tasting €20, bookings essential; ⏱11am-6pm Mon-Sat, to 2pm Sun) Visiting this cellar complex is a James Bond-esque experience. Show a print-out of your reservation at the gated, guarded entrance and then approach the sculptural main building, which is built into the hillside. Inside, your one-hour guided tour (English and Italian) finishes with a tasting of three Antinori wines in an all-glass tasting room suspended above barrels in the cellar (wow!).

There is a shop (naturally) to buy wine, glasses and other wine-related paraphernalia and within this there's a state-of-the-art bar where you can taste 16 different wines (€4 to €9 per tasting); have a 'guided tasting' of three different wines with the sommelier (€9 or €12); or simply drink a glass of wine (ranging from €7 for a glass of Marchese Antinori 2009 to €35 for a glass of Solaia 2009). Afterwards, be sure to enjoy lunch in the Rinuccio 1180 (p204) restaurant.

Bargino is a scenic 20km drive northwest of Greve via the SS222, SP3 and SS2.

Badia a Passignano WINERY
(www.osteriadipassignano.com) This 11th-century abbey located 6km west of Montefioralle is owned by the Vallumbrosans, a Benedictine religious order. It is surrounded by a picturesque wine estate owned by the Antinoris, one of Tuscany's best known winemaking families. The main building is closed for a restoration that doesn't look as if it will be completed for many years, but the vineyards and historic cellars can be visited on a guided tour.

The most popular of these is the four-hour 'Antinori at Badia a Passignano' tour (€150;

11.15am and 6.15pm Monday to Saturday), which includes a visit to the vineyard and cellars followed by lunch or dinner in the estate's Osteria di Passignano restaurant accompanied by four of Antinori's signature wines.

Other options include visits to the Tignanello vineyard (where the grapes for the Tignanello and Solaia Super Tuscans are grown). Alternatively, you can enjoy a tour of the cellars and a paid tasting of four wines (€80; 4pm Monday to Saturday; minimum booking of six people).

Bookings for all of these tours are essential. It's also possible to taste and purchase Antinori wines and olive oil at La Bottega, the estate's wine shop. You don't need to make a reservation for this.

Castello di Verrazzano WINERY
(055 85 42 43; www.verrazzano.com; Via Citille, Greti) This castle 3km north of Greve was once home to Giovanni da Verrazzano (1485–1528), who explored the North American coast and is commemorated in New York by the Verrazano Narrows bridge (the good captain lost a 'z' from his name somewhere in the mid-Atlantic). Today it presides over a 220-hectare historic wine estate.

There are a number of guided tours on offer, each of which incorporate a short visit to the historic wine cellar and gardens and tastings of the estate's wines (including its flagship Chianti Classico) and other products (perhaps honey, olive oil or balsamic vinegar). The 'Classic Wine Tour' (1½ hours, €16, 3pm Monday to Friday) includes a tasting of wines; the 'Chianti Tradition Tour' (2½ hours, €32, 11am Monday to Friday) includes a tasting of wine and gastronomic specialities; the 'Wine and Food Experience' (three hours, €54, noon Monday to Friday) includes a four-course lunch with estate wines; and the 'Executive Wine Tour' (€115, Tuesday to Thursday) includes a private guide, lunch with estate wines and transport to/from Florence; the price is based on a minimum of four persons. Bookings for all tours are advisable.

Castellina in Chianti

POP 2873

Established by the Etruscans and fortified by the Florentines in the 15th century as a defensive outpost against the Sienese, Castellina in Chianti is now a major centre of the wine industry, as the huge cylindrical silos brimming with Chianti Classico attest. To taste some of the local product, head to **Antica Fattoria la Castellina** (Via Ferruccio 26), the town's best-known wine shop.

From the southern car park, follow Via Ferruccio or the panoramic path next to the town's eastern defensive walls to access the atmospheric **Via delle Volte**, an arched medieval passageway that was originally used for ancient sacred rites and later enclosed with a roof and incorporated into the Florentine defensive structure.

Etruscan archaeological finds from the local area are on display at the **Museo Archeologico del Chianti Senese** (www.museoarcheologicochianti.it; Piazza del Comune 18; adult/reduced €5/3; 10am-6pm Apr-May & Sep-Oct, 11am-7pm Jun-Aug, 10am-5pm Sat & Sun Nov-Mar), located in the town's medieval *rocca* (castle). Room 4 showcases artefacts found in the 7th-century-BC Etruscan tombs of **Montecalvario** (Ipogeo Etrusco di Monte Calvario; 24hr) FREE, which is located on the northern edge of town off the SR222.

Eating

Ristorante Albergaccio GASTRONOMIC €€€
(0577 74 10 42; www.albergacciocast.com; Via Fiorentina 63, Castellina in Chianti; 4-course menu

L'ANTICA MACELLERÌA CECCHINI

The small town of Panzano in Chianti southwest of Greve in Chianti is known throughout Italy for the *macellerìa* (butcher shop) owned and run by extrovert butcher, **Dario Cecchini** (www.dariocecchini.com; Via XX Luglio 11; 9am-4pm). This Tuscan celebrity has carved out a niche for himself as a poetry-spouting guardian of the *bistecca* (steak) and other Tuscan meaty treats, and he operates three eateries here as well as the *macellerìa*: **Officina della Bistecca** (055 85 21 76; set menu €50; from 8pm Tue, Fri & Sat, from 1pm Sun), with a simple set menu built around the famous *bistecca;* **Solociccia** (055 85 27 27; set menu €30; from 7pm & 9pm Thu, Fri & Sat, from 1pm Sun), where guests share a communal table to sample meat dishes other than *bistecca;* and **Dario DOC** (burger €10-15, light menu €20; noon-3pm Mon-Sat), his casual lunchtime-only eatery. Book ahead for the Officina and Solociccia.

€58, 5-course menu €68, 3-course kids menu €27; lunch & dinner Mon-Sat, closed parts of Dec-Mar) One kilometre outside Castellina in Chianti on the road to San Donato in Poggio, this upmarket restaurant in a restored farmhouse showcases what it describes as 'the territory on the table', making full use of local, seasonal and organic produce. The menu is innovative, making it a favourite with local and international foodies. There's a thoughtful and well-priced wine list.

Information

The **tourist office** (0577 74 13 92; ufficio turistico@comune.castelina.si.it; Via Ferruccio 40; 10am-noon & 3-6pm Tue, Thu, Sat & Sun mid-Mar–May, 10am-1pm & 3-7pm Jun-Oct, 3-6pm Sat & Sun Nov, 10am-noon Fri & 10am-noon & 3-6pm Sat & Sun Dec–mid-Jan) can book visits to wineries and cellars. It also provides maps, accommodation suggestions and other information.

Getting There & Around

Siena Mobilità buses travel between Castellina in Chianti and Siena (€3.40, 35 minutes, 10 daily). The most convenient car park is at the southern edge of town off Via IV Novembre (€1/5 per hour/day).

Radda in Chianti

POP 1688

Shields and escutcheons add a dash of drama to the facade of 16th-century **Palazzo del Podestà** on the main square of this important wine centre 11km east of Castellina in Chianti. The **tourist office** (0577 73 84 94; proradda@chiantinet.it; Piazza Castello 2; 10am-1pm & 3-7pm Easter-Sep, 10.30am-12.30pm & 3.30-6.30pm Oct-Easter) can book accommodation and tours for this pocket of Chianti, and also supplies information about walks in the area.

Around Radda in Chianti

Castello di Brolio CASTLE

(0577 73 02 80; www.ricasoli.it; self-guided tour of garden, chapel & crypt €5, guided tour of museum, chapel & crypt €8; 10am-5.30pm mid-Mar–Nov, guided tours every 30 minutes 10am-1pm & 2.30-5.30pm Tue-Sun) The ancestral estate of the aristocratic Ricasoli family dates from the 11th century and is the oldest winery in Italy. Currently home to the 32nd baron, it opens its formal garden, panoramic terrace and museum to day-trippers, who often adjourn to the on-site *osteria* for lunch after taking a guided tour of the castle's small but fascinating museum.

Occupying three rooms in the castle's tower, the museum is dedicated to documenting the fascinating life of Baron Bettino Ricasoli (1809–1880), the second prime minster of the Republic of Italy and a true polymath (scientist, farmer, winemaker, statesman, businessman). A leading figure in the Risorgimento, his greatest claim to fame (in our view, at least) is that he invented the formula for Chianti Classico that is enshrined in current DOC regulations.

The chapel dates from the early 14th century; below it is a crypt where generations of Ricasolis are interred.

The estate produces wine and olive oil, and the huge terrace commands a spectacular view of the vineyards and olive groves. Surrounding the castle is a *bosco Inglese* (English garden) where, near the estate carpark, you'll find the estate's **Osteria del Castello** (0577 73 02 90; four-course tasting menu with wines €50; noon-2.30pm & 7.30-9.30pm Fri-Wed late Mar–Oct). Just outside the estate's entrance gates, on the SP484, is a modern **cantina** (9am-7pm Mon-Fri, 11am-7pm Sat & Sun Mar-Dec, 9am-6pm Mon-Fri Jan & Feb) where you can taste the estate's well-regarded Chianti Classico.

Castello di Volpaia WINERY

(0577 73 80 66; www.volpaia.it; Località Volpaia) Wines, olive oils, vinegars and honey have been produced for centuries at this wine estate based in the medieval hill-top hamlet of Volpaia (the name is misleading, as there's no actual castle here). Book ahead to enjoy a tour of the estate's cellars, or pop into its *enoteca,* which is inside the main tower of the castle.

While here, consider enjoying a snack at Bar Ucci or a more formal meal at **Ristorante La Bottega** (0577 73 80 01; www.labottegadivolpaia.it; meals €25; noon-2.30pm & 7.30-10pm Wed-Mon Easter-Jan), a pretty restaurant serving *cucina contadina* (food from the farmers' kitchen). Both are operated by members of the local Barucci family, and are located on the main square of the hamlet. The restaurant's outdoor terrace (which has lovely views) is next to the Baruccis' productive kitchen garden.

VAL D'ELSA

A convenient base for visiting the rest of Tuscany, this valley stretching from Chianti to the Maremma can be relied upon to tick many of the boxes on your Tuscan 'must-do' list, with plenty of opportunities to enjoy food, wine, museums and scenery. The valley's major towns are Colle di Val d'Elsa and Poggibonsi, but the major tourist drawcard is San Gimignano. Note that we have included nearby Volterra in this section despite the fact that it is officially located in the Val di Cecina, a province of Pisa.

San Gimignano

POP 7638

As you crest the hill coming from the east, the 15 towers of this walled hill town look like a medieval Manhattan. Originally an Etruscan village, the town was named after the bishop of Modena, San Gimignano, who is said to have saved the city from Attila the Hun. It became a *comune* (local government) in 1199 and was very prosperous due in part to its location on the Via Francigena – building a tower taller than that of one's neighbour (there were originally 72) became a popular way for the town's prominent families to flaunt their power and wealth. In 1348 plague wiped out much of the population and weakened the local economy, leading to the town's submission to Florence in 1353. Today, not even the plague would deter the swarms of summer day-trippers, who are lured by the town's palpable sense of history, intact medieval streetscapes and enchanting rural setting.

Sights

Triangular Piazza della Cisterna is named after the 13th-century cistern at its centre. In Piazza del Duomo, the cathedral looks across to the late-13th-century **Palazzo del Podestà** (Piazza del Duomo) and its tower, the **Torre della Rognosa**.

★Collegiata CHURCH

(Duomo Collegiata o Basilica di Santa Maria Assunta; Piazza del Duomo; adult/child €3.50/1.50; ⏲10am-7.10pm Mon-Fri, to 5.10pm Sat, 12.30-7.10pm Sun Apr-Oct, shorter hr rest of year, closed 2nd half Nov & Jan) San Gimignano's Romanesque cathedral is commonly known as the Collegiata, a reference to the college of priests who originally managed it. Parts of the building date back to the second half of the 11th century, but its remarkably vivid frescoes, which resemble a vast medieval comic strip, date from the 14th century.

Entry is via the side stairs and through a loggia that was originally covered and functioned as the baptistry. After entering the main space, face the altar and look to your left (north). On the wall are scenes from Genesis and the Old Testament by Bartolo di Fredi, dating from around 1367. The top row runs from the creation of the world through to the forbidden fruit scene. This in

SCULPTURE PARKS

To indulge in some art appreciation between wine tastings, take a scenic drive to these sculpture parks located in the Chianti Senese.

Castello di Ama (☎0577 74 60 31; http://arte.castellodiama.com; guided tours €15, with wine & oil tasting €35; ⏲year round, by appt) The highly regarded Castello di Ama estate produces a range of wines including the internationally renowned 'L'Apparita' Merlot, the 'Haiku' Sangiovese/Cabernet Franc/Merlot blend and a delicious 'Vigneto Bellavista' Chianti Classico. In recent years it has also developed a sculpture park showcasing 13 site-specific artworks by artists including Louise Bourgeois, Chen Zhen, Anish Kapoor, Kendell Geers and Daniel Buren. Guided tours of the cellar, villa and sculpture park are in English, French, Italian or German. The estate is 11km southwest of Gaiole, near Lecchi in Chianti.

Parco Sculture del Chianti (Chianti Sculpture Park; ☎0577 35 71 51; www.chiantisculpturepark.it; adult/child €10/5; ⏲10am-sunset Apr-Oct, by appointment Nov-Mar; 👪) This 13-acre green wooded area studded with 26 site-specific contemporary artworks can be explored on a 1km walking trail. You'll find it 12km southwest of Gaiole and only 7km north of Siena off the SS408. While here, be sure to explore the nearby village of **Pievasciata**, whose streets are home to an ever-growing number of site-specific contemporary international artworks (don't miss Yu Zhaoyang's hilarious *Town Ostriches* next to the cypress trees).

GALLERIA CONTINUA

It may seem strange that we're highlighting a showcase of contemporary art in this medieval time capsule of a town, but we do so for good reason. **Galleria Continua** (tel, info 0577 94 31 34; www.galleriacontinua.com; Via del Castello 11; 2-7pm Tue-Sat) FREE is one of the best commercial art galleries in Europe, showing the work of its stable of 40 big-name artists, including Ai Weiwei, Daniel Buren, Carlos Garaicoa, Moataz Nasr, Kendell Geers, Liu Jianhua and Sophie Whettnall. Spread over three venues (an old cinema, a medieval tower and a medieval vaulted cellar), the gallery is one of San Gimignano's most compelling attractions.

turn leads to the next level and fresco, the expulsion of Adam and Eve from the Garden of Eden, which has sustained some war damage. Further scenes include Cain killing Abel, and the stories of Noah's ark and Joseph's coat. The last level continues with the tale of Moses leading the Jews out of Egypt, and the story of Job.

On the right (south) wall are scenes from the New Testament by the workshop of Simone Martini (probably led by Lippo Memmi, Martini's brother-in-law), which were completed in 1336. Again, the frescoes are spread over three levels, starting in the six lunettes at the top. Commencing with the Annunciation, the panels proceed through episodes such as the Epiphany, the presentation of Christ in the temple and the massacre of the innocents on Herod's orders. The subsequent panels on the lower levels summarise the life and death of Christ, the Resurrection and so on. Again, some have sustained damage, but most are in good condition.

On the inside wall of the front facade, extending onto adjoining walls, is Taddeo di Bartolo's striking depiction of the Last Judgment – on the upper-left side is a fresco depicting *Paradiso* (Heaven) and on the upper-right *Inferno* (Hell). The fresco of San Sebastian under them is by Benozzo Gozzoli.

Off the south aisle, near the main altar, is the **Cappella di Santa Fina**, a Renaissance chapel adorned with naive and touching frescoes by Domenico Ghirlandaio depicting events in the life of one of the town's patron saints. These featured in Franco Zeffirelli's 1999 film *Tea with Mussolini*.

★Museo Civico — MUSEUM

(Piazza del Duomo 2; adult/reduced €5/4; 9.30am-7pm Apr-Sep, 11am-5.30pm Oct-Mar) The 12th-century **Palazzo Civico** has always been the centre of local government; its **Sala di Dante** is where the great poet addressed the town's council in 1299, urging it to support the Guelph cause, and its **pinacoteca** has a charming collection of paintings from the Sienese and Florentine schools of the 12th to 15th centuries.

The Sala di Dante (also known as the Sala del Consiglio) is home to Lippo Memmi's early-14th-century *Maestà*, which portrays the enthroned Virgin and Child surrounded by angels, saints and local dignitaries – the kneeling noble in red-and-black stripes was the *podestà* (chief magistrate) of the time. Other frescoes in the room portray jousts, hunting scenes, castles and other medieval goings-on.

On the floor above the Sala di Dante is the small but charming pinacoteca. Highlights of its collection are two large *Annunciation* panels (1482) by Filippino Lippi, *Madonna of Humility Worshipped by Two Saints* (1466) and *Madonna and Child with Saints* (1466) by Benozzo Gozzoli and an altarpiece by Taddeo di Bartolo (1401) illustrating the life of St Gimignano.

In the **Camera del Podestà**, at the top of the stairs, is a meticulously restored cycle of frescos by Memmo di Filippuccio illustrating a moral history – the rewards of marriage are shown in the scenes of the husband and wife naked in the bath and in bed.

While here, be sure to climb the 154 steps of the *palazzo*'s **Torre Grossa** for a spectacular view over the town and surrounding countryside.

Chiesa di Sant'Agostino — CHURCH

(Piazza Sant'Agostino; 9am-noon & 3-7pm mid-Mar–Oct, to 6pm Nov-Dec, 4-6pm Mon, 10am-noon & 3-6pm Tue-Sun Jan–mid-Mar) This late-13th-century church at the northern end of town is best known for Benozzo Gozzoli's charming fresco cycle illustrating the life of St Augustine. You'll find it behind the altar and will need €0.50 to illuminate it.

Gozzoli also painted the highly unusual fresco of San Sebastian on the north wall, which shows the fully clothed saint protecting the citizens of San Gimignano, helped by

San Gimignano

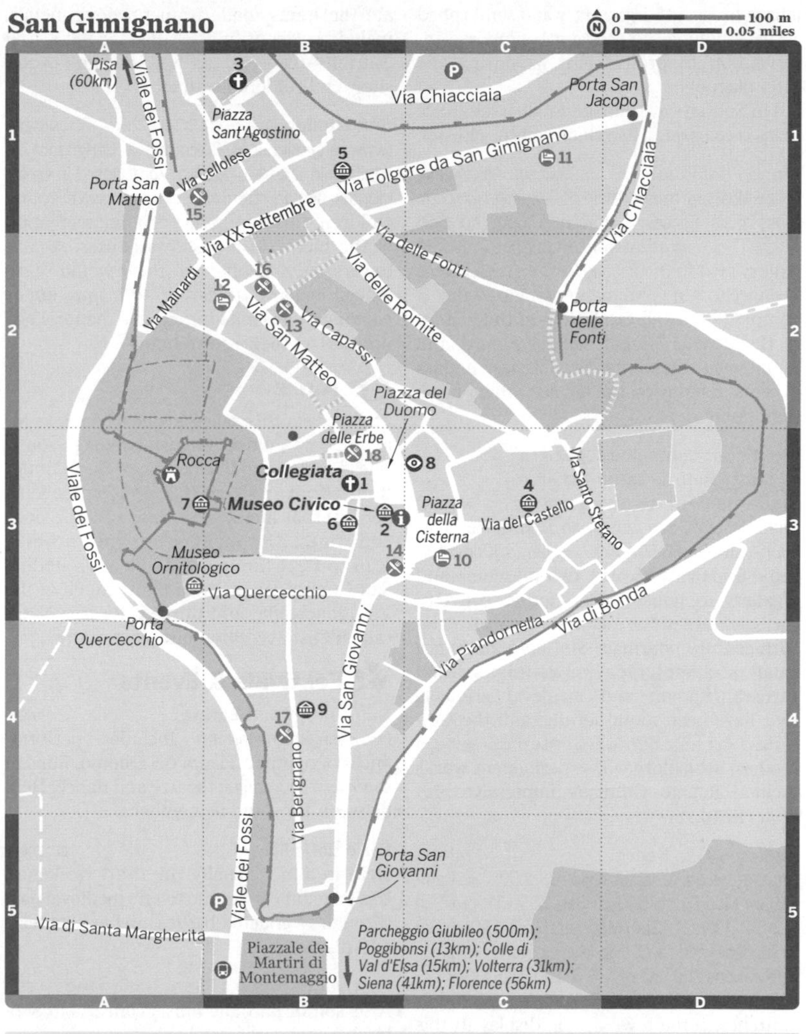

San Gimignano

Top Sights

1 Collegiata B3
2 Museo Civico B3

Sights

3 Chiesa di Sant'Agostino B1
4 Galleria Continua C3
5 Museo Archeologico, Speziera di Santa Fina & Galleria d'Arte Moderna e Contemporanea B1
6 Museo d'Arte Sacra B3
7 Museo del Vino A3
8 Palazzo del Podestà C3
9 San Gimignano del 1300 .... B4

Sleeping

10 Al Pozzo dei Desideri C3
11 Foresteria Monastero di San Girolamo C1
12 Hotel L'Antico Pozzo B2

Eating

13 Dal Bertelli B2
14 Gelateria Dondoli B3
15 Il Pino A1
16 Perucà B2
17 Ristorante La Mandragola B4
18 Thursday Morning Market B3

a bare-breasted Virgin Mary and semi-robed Jesus (it alluded to the saint's supposed intervention to protect citizens during the 1464 plague).

On Sundays at 11am, an English-language mass is celebrated in a chapel off the cloister.

Museo del Vino MUSEUM, WINE TASTING
(Wine Museum; museodelvino@sangimignano.com; Parco della Rocca; ⊙11.30am-6.30pm Apr-Oct) FREE This operation housed in an unmarked gallery next to the *rocca* (fortress) celebrates Vernaccia, San Gimignano's famous wine. It comprises a small exhibition on the history of the varietal (Italian language only) and an *enoteca* where you can purchase a glass of wine to enjoy on the terrace, which has a panoramic view.

Museo Archeologico, Speziera di Santa Fina & Galleria d'Arte Moderna e Contemporanea MUSEUM
(Via Folgore da San Gimignano 11; both museums adult/reduced €3.50/2.50; ⊙11am-5.30pm Apr-Sep, 2-6pm Oct-Sep & Mar) Two museums and a gallery are housed in this former convent: the **Speziera di Santa Fina**, a reconstructed 16th-century pharmacy and herb garden; a small **archaeological museum** featuring Etruscan/Roman and medieval artefacts that have been found locally; and the **Galleria d'Arte Moderna E Contemporanea**, a modern art gallery whose permanent works include Renato Guttuso's impressive *Marina* (1970).

Museo d'Arte Sacra MUSEUM
(Piazza Pecori 1; adult/child €3/1.50; ⊙10am-7.10pm Mon-Fri, to 5.10pm Sat, 12.30-7.10pm Sun Apr-Oct, 10am-4.40pm Mon-Sat, 12.30-4.40pm Sat & Sun Nov–mid-Jan & Feb-Mar, closed for religious celebrations 2nd half of Nov & Jan) Works of religious art from the Collegiata and other churches in the town are on display in this modest museum. Those who are interested in medieval religious objects will appreciate the items made from precious metals, including beautifully crafted chalices and thuribles (censers), as well as some exquisitely embroidered textiles.

San Gimignano del 1300 MUSEUM
(www.sangimignano1300.com; Via Berignano 23; adult/child €3/free; ⊙10am-7pm, closed in winter months;) Particularly popular with young children, this handmade ceramic recreation of the medieval city shows houses, streets, towers and people as they would have looked in 1300. It's certain to inspire junior visitors to attempt bigger and better Lego projects on their return home.

> **COMBINED TICKETS**
>
> Two combined tickets can save you money. The first (adult/child €7.50/5.50) gives admission to the Museo Civico, the Museo Archeologico complex and the town's small ornithological museum (Museo Ornitologico). The second (adult/child €5.50/2.50) gets you into the Collegiata and Museo d'Arte Sacra.

Tours

The tourist office takes advance bookings for a range of guided English-language tours. These include a **Vernaccia di San Gimignano Vineyard Visit** (€20; ⊙5-7pm Tue & Thu Apr-Oct) that includes tastings of local foods and wines. Also on offer are **nature walks** (€15 to €22) through the hills surrounding San Gimignano; along a 6km stretch of the Via Francigena; and through Riserva Naturale di Castelvecchio, southwest of town.

Festivals & Events

San Gimignano Estate ARTS
(www.sangimignano.com) Includes performances of opera in Piazza del Duomo, films in the *rocca*, concerts, theatre and dance. Held between June and September.

Ferie delle Messi CULTURAL
Held in June (usually the third weekend), this pageant evokes the town's medieval past through re-enacted battles, archery contests and plays.

Festival Barocco di San Gimignano MUSIC
A season of Baroque music concerts in September and early October.

Sleeping

★**Al Pozzo dei Desideri** B&B €
(☎370 3102538, 0577 90 71 99; www.alpozzodeidesideri.it; Piazza della Cisterna 32; d €75-110, tr €95-120, q €115-160;) Three rooms-with-a-view (two over the Tuscan countryside and one over the town's main piazza) are on offer in this recently opened B&B. All have a charming decor, stylish modern bathrooms, a fridge and tea- and coffee-making facilities. No breakfast, but there's a good cafe close by.

Foresteria Monastero di San Girolamo HOSTEL €
(☎0577 94 05 73; www.monasterosangirolamo.it; Via Folgore da San Gimignano 26-32; s/tw/tr €37.50/75/112.50) This is an excellent budget choice. Run by friendly Benedictine Vallumbrosan nuns, it has basic but comfortable rooms sleeping two to five people; all have attached bathrooms. Parking and kitchen use are available for a small fee. Book in advance at www.monasterystays.com, as it's usually full.

If you don't have a reservation, arrive between 9am and 12.30pm or between 3.30pm and 5.45pm and ring the monastery bell (not the Foresteria one, which is never answered).

Hotel L'Antico Pozzo BOUTIQUE HOTEL €€
(☎0577 94 20 14; www.anticopozzo.com; Via San Matteo 87; s €80-95, d €90-135, superior d €169-180; closed 1st 2 wks Nov & Jan;) Named after the old, softly illuminated *pozzo* (well) just off its lobby, this hotel occupies a 15th-century *palazzo* on busy Via San Matteo. Most rooms feature high ceilings, simple but elegant decor and good-sized if dated bathrooms; the superior rooms are particularly attractive. We suggest avoiding the cheaper top-floor rooms. There's a handsome breakfast room and a pretty rear courtyard.

Eating & Drinking

San Gimignano is known for its *zafferano* (saffron). You can purchase meat, vegetables, fish and takeaway food at the **Thursday morning market** (Piazza delle Erbe) in and around Piazzas Cisterna, Duomo and Erbe.

Dal Bertelli SANDWICHES €
(Via Capassi 30; panini €3-5, glass of wine €1.50; 1-7pm Mar–early Jan) The Bertelli family has lived in San Gimignano since 1779, and its current patriarch is fiercely proud of both his heritage and his sandwiches. Brunello Bertelli sources his salami, cheese, bread and wine from local artisan producers and sells his generously sized offerings from an atmospheric space as far away as possible from what he calls the town's 'tourist grand bazaar'. Fabulous.

Gelateria Dondoli GELATO €
(www.gelateriadipiazza.com; Piazza della Cisterna 4; gelati €2-3; 8.30am-11pm Mar–mid-Nov;) Master gelato-maker Sergio Dondoli uses only the choicest ingredients to create his creamy and icy delights. Get into the local swing of things with a *Crema di Santa Fina* (saffron cream) gelato or a Vernaccia sorbet.

★ **Ristorante La Mandragola** TUSCAN €€
(☎0577 94 03 77; www.locandalamandragola.it; Via Berignano 58; meals €37, set menus €14-25, kids menu €10; noon-2.30pm & 7.30-9.30pm, closed Thu Nov–early Mar) Locals wouldn't dream of eating at the tourist restaurants on Via San Giovanni, but they love La Mandragola. Built into the city walls, it's big enough to seat regulars, day-tripping Italians and foreign tour groups and still have space for the rest of us. Great food (especially pastas), an excellent house Vernaccia and friendly staff contribute to the winning formula.

Perucà TUSCAN €€
(☎0577 94 31 36; www.peruca.eu; Via Capassi 16; meals €30; 12.30-2pm & 7.30-10pm Tue-Sun mid-Feb–early Dec, open Mon Apr-Sep) The lady owner here is as knowledgeable about regional food and wine as she is enthusiastic, and the food is excellent. Try the house speciality of *fagottini del contadino* (ravioli with *pecorino*, pears and saffron cream) with a glass of Fattoria San Donato's Vernaccia – it's a match made in heaven.

Il Pino MODERN TUSCAN €€
(☎0577 94 04 15; www.ristoranteilpino.it; Via Cellolese 8-10; meals €44; noon-2.30pm & 7-9.30pm Fri-Sat & Mon-Wed, noon-2.30pm Sun) An elegant vaulted space where a seasonal menu including excellent homemade pasta and bread is served. It's the only restaurant in town recommended by the highly regarded *Gambero Rosso* restaurant guide, so you're bound to be dining alongside foodies.

Information

The extremely helpful **tourist office** (☎0577 94 00 08; www.sangimignano.com; Piazza del Duomo 1; 10am-1pm & 3-7pm Mar-Oct, 10am-1pm & 2-6pm Nov-Feb) organises tours, supplies maps and can book accommodation. It also has information on the *Strada del Vino Vernaccia di San Gimignano* (Wine Road of the Vernaccia di San Gimignano).

Free wi-fi is available in and around Piazza del Duomo.

Getting There & Away

The **bus station** is next to the Carabinieri (Police Station) at Porta San Giovanni. Buy bus tickets at the tourist office. Buses run to/from Florence

OFF THE BEATEN TRACK

THE VIA FRANCIGENA

Devise a holiday with a difference by walking or driving parts of the **Via Francigena**, a medieval pilgrimage route connecting Canterbury with Rome. In Central Tuscany, the route goes past or through towns including San Gimignano, Monteriggioni, San Quirico d'Orcia and Radicófani. Globalmap publishes *Via Francigena in Toscana*, an excellent hiking map (1:50,000) with detailed routes and information about accommodation for pilgrims. You'll find it for sale in tourist offices and bookshops throughout the region. You can also check www.francigenalibrari.beniculturali.it for route maps and GPS coordinates.

(€6.80, 1¼-2 hours, 14 daily) but often require a change at Poggibonsi. Buses also run to/from Siena (€6, one to 1½ hours, 10 daily Monday to Saturday). For Volterra you need to go to Colle di Val d'Elsa (€3.40, 35 minutes, four daily Monday to Saturday) and then buy a ticket for Volterra (€2.75, 50 minutes, four daily).

From Florence and Siena, take the Siena–Florence *superstrada*, then the SR2 and finally the SP1 from Poggibonsi. From Volterra, take the SR68 east and follow the turn-off signs north to San Gimignano on the SP47.

Parking is expensive here. The cheapest option (per hour/24 hours €1.50/6) is at Parcheggio Giubileo on the southern edge of town; the most convenient is at Parcheggio Montemaggio next to Porta San Giovanni (per hour/24 hours €2/20).

The closest train station is located at Poggibonsi (by bus €2.50, about 30 minutes, frequent).

Volterra

POP 10,675

Volterra's well-preserved medieval ramparts give the windswept town a proud, forbidding air that author Stephanie Meyer deemed ideal for the discriminating tastes of the planet's principal vampire coven in her wildly popular *Twilight* book series. Fortunately, the reality is considerably more welcoming, as a wander through the winding cobbled streets (refreshingly populated by locals rather than tourists) attests.

The Etruscan settlement of Velathri was an important trading centre and senior partner of the Dodecapolis. It is believed that as many as 25,000 people lived here in its Etruscan heyday. Partly because of the surrounding inhospitable terrain, the city was among the last to succumb to Rome – it was absorbed into the Roman confederation around 260 BC and renamed Volaterrae. The bulk of the old city was built in the 12th and 13th centuries under a fiercely independent free *comune*. The city first entered Florence's orbit in 1361, but the people of Volterra fought hard against Medici rule – their rebellion was brought to a brutal end when Lorenzo Il Magnifico's soldiers sacked the city in 1472. There was another rebellion in 1530 – again brutally crushed by the Florentines – but Volterra would never again achieve self-government, moving from Florentine rule to that of the Grand Duchy of Tuscany before unification in 1860.

Sights & Activities

★**Museo Etrusco Guarnacci** MUSEUM
(Via Don Minzoni 15; adult/student €8/6; 9am-7pm mid-Mar–Oct, 10am-4.30pm Nov–mid-Mar) One of Italy's most impressive collections of Etruscan artefacts is exhibited here. These were unearthed locally and include a vast collection of some 600 funerary urns carved mainly from alabaster and tufa and displayed according to subject and period. The best examples (those dating from later periods) are on the 2nd and 3rd floors.

Highlights include the Urn of the Sposi, a strikingly realistic terracotta rendering of an elderly couple; a crested helmet excavated from the Tomba del Guernero at nearby Poggio alle Croci; and the *L'Ombra della Sera* (Shadow of the Evening), an elongated bronze nude figurine that bears a striking resemblance to the work of the Italian sculptor Alberto Giacometti.

★**Cattedrale di Santa Maria Assunta** CATHEDRAL
(Duomo di Volterra; Piazza San Giovanni; 8am-12.30pm & 3-6pm Sat-Thu, 4-6pm Fri) Built in the 12th and 13th centuries, the interior of the *duomo* was remodelled in the 16th century and features a handsome coffered ceiling. The **Chapel of Our Lady of Sorrows**, on the left as you enter from Piazza San Giovanni, has two sculptures by Andrea della Robbia and a small fresco of the *Procession of the Magi* by Benozzo Gozzoli.

In front of the *duomo*, a 13th-century **baptistry** (Piazza San Giovanni) features a small marble font (1502) by Andrea Sansovino.

Palazzo dei Priori HISTORIC BUILDING
(Piazza dei Priori; adult/child/family €4/2.50/8 incl tower; ⊙10.30am-5.30pm daily mid-Mar–Oct, 10am-4pm Sat & Sun Nov–mid-Mar) Volterra's 13th-century town hall is the oldest seat of local government in Tuscany. Highlights inside are a fresco on the staircase of the Crucifixion by Piero Francesco Fiorentino and a magnificent cross-vaulted council hall. The **bell tower** was significantly rebuilt in the 19th century and can be accessed by lift or stairs.

Palazzo Pretorio (Piazza del Priori), opposite, dates back to the same era. From it thrusts the **Torre del Porcellino** (Piglet's Tower), so named because of the wild boar protruding from its upper section.

Pinacoteca Comunale ART GALLERY
(Via dei Sarti 1; adult/student €8/6; ⊙9am-7pm mid-Mar–early Nov, 10am-4.30pm early Nov–mid-Mar) Occupying the Palazzo Minucci Solaini, this modest collection of local, Sienese and Florentine art includes Taddeo di Bartolo's lovely *Madonna Enthroned with Child* (1411) and Rosso Fiorentino's strikingly modern representation of the *Deposition from the Cross* (1521).

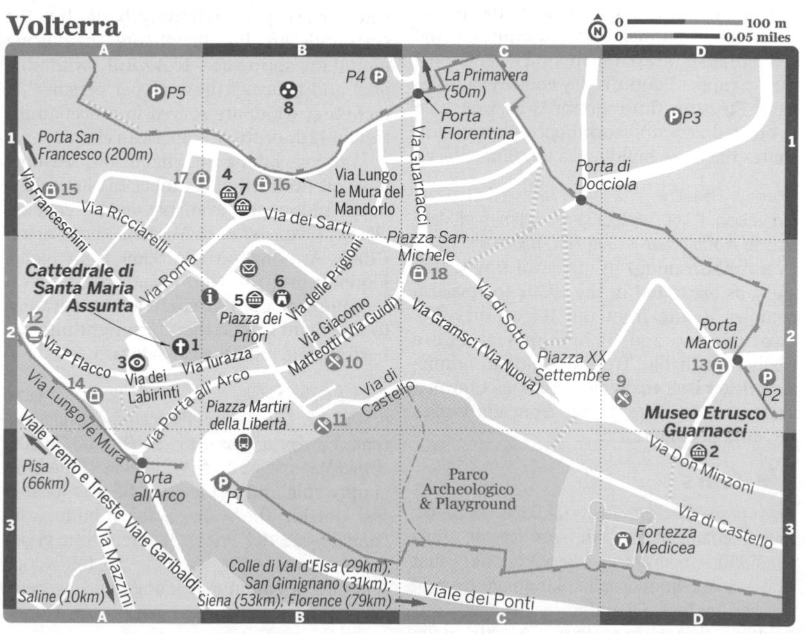

Volterra

Top Sights
1 Cattedrale di Santa Maria Assunta ... A2
2 Museo Etrusco Guarnacci ... D3

Sights
3 Baptistry ... A2
4 Ecomuseo dell'Alabastro ... B1
5 Palazzo dei Priori ... B2
6 Palazzo Pretorio ... B2
7 Pinacoteca Comunale ... B1
8 Roman Theatre ... B1
Torre del Porcellino ... (see 6)

Eating
9 La Carabaccia ... D2
10 L'Incontro ... B2
11 Ristorante-Enoteca Del Duca ... B2

Drinking & Nightlife
12 Caffè dei Fornelli ... A2

Shopping
13 Alab'Arte ... D2
14 Alessandro Marzetti ... A2
15 Emporio del Gusto ... A1
16 Fabula Etrusca ... B1
17 Opus Artis ... A1
18 Paolo Sabatini ... C2

COMBINED TICKETS

A *biglietto cumulativo* (adult/student & child/family €10/6/20) gives admission to the Museo Etrusco Guarnacci, the Pinacoteca Comunale and the Ecomuseo dell'Alabastro.

Ecomuseo dell'Alabastro MUSEUM
(Via dei Sarti 1; admission incl in Pinacoteca entrance ticket; 9.30am-7pm mid-Mar–Oct, 10.30am-4.30pm Nov–mid-Mar) As befits a town that has hewn the precious rock from nearby quarries since Etruscan times, Volterra is the proud possessor of an alabaster museum. On the ground floor are contemporary creations; the two upper floors display choice examples from Etruscan times onwards as well as a re-created artisan's workshop. The museum shares the same building as the Pinacoteca.

Roman Theatre ARCHAEOLOGICAL SITE
(admission €3.50; 10.30am-5.30pm mid-Mar–Oct, to 4.30pm Sat & Sun Nov–mid-Mar) Used as a rubbish dump in medieval times, this site was excavated in the 1950s to reveal a complex dating from the 1st century BC. Two stairways and 19 rows of seating are easily identifiable. Truth be told, an admission ticket isn't really necessary, as there's a great view over the theatre from Via Lungo Le Mura del Mandorlo.

Tours

Volterra Walking Tour (0588 08 62 01; www.volterrawalkingtour.com; per person [min three] €10; 6pm Apr-Jul & Sep-Oct) offers just that – a one-hour English-language tour of the city by foot. Operated by licensed tour guides, it leaves from Piazza Martiri della Libertà; bookings aren't necessary and payment is cash only.

Between mid-June and mid-September, Volterra's tourist office runs a 90-minute **Volterra by Night** (www.volterratur.it/en/volterra-by-night; adult/child €10/free; 9.30pm Sat mid-Jun–mid-Sep) walking tour in English and Italian. Advance bookings are essential.

Festivals & Events

Volterra AD 1398 CULTURAL
(www.volterra1398.it; day pass €9) On the third and fourth Sundays of August, the citizens of Volterra roll back the calendar some 600 years, take to the streets in period costume and celebrate all the fun of a medieval fair.

Volterragusto FOOD
(www.volterragusto.com) Events in mid-March, late October and early November showcase local produce, including cheese, white truffles, olive oil and chocolate.

Sleeping

★ **Podere San Lorenzo** AGRITURISMO €
(0588 3 90 80; www.agriturismo-volterra.it; Via Allori 80; B&B d €100, 2-/3-/4-bed apt without breakfast €100-130;) This model of slow tourism is located on an olive farm 3.4km outside Volterra. The two rooms and five self-catering apartments (two with private terraces) are relatively basic, but the surrounds are bucolic, there's an alluring mountain spring–fed biological swimming pool and gourmet dinners (per person €30 including wine) are served in a decommissioned 12th-century Franciscan chapel.

Walking, biking and hands-on, seasonal olive-oil production (October to November) opportunities are available, as are cooking classes given by chef Mariana (per person €100). Arriving on the SS68 from Siena, Florence and San Gimignano, you'll pass a sculpture of the red circle at the entrance to town and should then turn right into the narrow lane after the car saleyard.

★ **La Primavera** B&B €
(0588 8 72 95; www.affittacamere-laprimavera.com; Via Porta Diana 15; s/d/tr €50/75/100; mid-Mar–mid-Nov; P) Silvia Pineschi's simply splendid home-style B&B is located just outside the walls, a five-minute walk from Piazza dei Priori. It offers four good-sized rooms with soothing pastel colour schemes, a communal lounge and a pretty garden. The free on-site parking is a huge asset. No credit cards.

Molina d'Era HOTEL €
(0588 3 32 20; www.molinodera.com; SR439; s €54-79, d €64-89; closed Jan, Feb and Sun-Thu Mar; P) Here's a life lesson: don't be fooled by appearances. When we arrived at this modern building 6.4km north of Volterra we were underwhelmed. Frankly, the place is ugly. But then we stayed the night. Rooms are simple but comfortable, staff are helpful, the restaurant serves hearty home-style Tuscan cooking and the breakfast is great (including excellent coffee). Love it.

Chiosco delle Monache HOSTEL €
(0588 8 66 13; www.ostellovolterra.it; Via del Teatro 4, Località San Girolamo; dm €16-20, B&B

s €48-53, B&B d €62-69; ⊙ mid-Mar–Oct; P ☎) Opened in 2009 after a major renovation, this excellent private hostel occupies a 13th-century monastery complete with a frescoed refectory where breakfast is served. Airy rooms overlook the cloisters and have good beds and bathrooms; dorms sleep up to six. Breakfast (for those in dorms) costs €6.

The hostel is located outside town, near the hospital, but the historic centre is only a 30-minute (albeit steep) walk away and local buses from Piazza Martiri della Libertà stop right outside the entrance (€1). Reception is open 8am to noon and 5pm to 11pm, but often stays open for the full day in high summer.

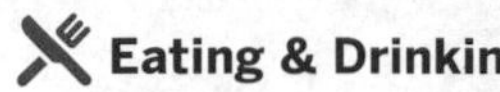

Eating & Drinking

La Carabaccia TUSCAN €
(☎0588 8 62 39; www.lacarabacciavolterra.it; Piazza XX Settembre 4-5; meals €20; ⊙ noon-2.30pm & 7.30-9.30pm, closed Mon Oct-Easter; ✎) Sisters Sara, Lalla and Patrizia have put their heart and soul into this fantastic trattoria, which is the city's best lunch option. Named after a humble Tuscan vegetable soup, it has a small menu that changes daily according to what local producers are offering and always has vegetarian options. Sit in the rustic interior or on the front terrace.

L'Incontro CAFE €
(Via G Matteotti 18; sandwiches €2.50-3.50; ⊙ 6.30am-1am Thu-Tue) L'Incontro's rear *salone* (room) is a great spot to grab a quick antipasto plate or *panino* for lunch, and its front bar area is always crowded with locals enjoying a coffee or *aperitivo*. The house-baked biscuits are noteworthy – try the chewy and nutty *brutti mai buoni* ('ugly but good') or its alabaster-coloured version, *ossi di morto* (bones of the dead).

Ristorante-Enoteca Del Duca TUSCAN €€
(☎0588 8 15 10; www.enoteca-delduca-ristorante.it; Via di Castello 2; 5-course tasting menus €45; ⊙ 12.30-2.30pm & 7.30-10pm) Volterra's only fine-dining establishment serves traditional Tuscan dishes in its vaulted dining areas and lovely rear courtyard. It has an excellent wine list – not surprising considering the owner has his own vineyard.

Caffè dei Fornelli CAFE, BAR
(www.caffedeifornelli.it; Piazza dei Fornelli 3-4; ⊙ 9am-late, closed Thu in winter) The city's bohemian set congregates here, drawn by genial host Carlo Bigazzi, cheap house wine (€1.50 per glass), live jazz, poetry readings and exhibitions. Though the cafe's interior is pleasant, the most sought-after tables are on the streetside terrace.

Shopping

For information about artisans in Volterra, see www.arteinbottegavolterra.it.

Emporio del Gusto FOOD
(Via San Lino 2; ⊙ 9.30am-1pm & 4.30-8pm Mon-Fri) This food co-op is sponsored by the *comune* and sells produce from around the region. It stocks olive-oil products (including toiletries), fresh milk and yoghurt, cheese, vegetables, locally grown saffron, truffles, pasta, bread and wine.

Fabula Etrusca JEWELLERY
(www.fabulaetrusca.it; Via Lungo Le Mura del Mandorlo 10; ⊙ 10am-7pm Easter-Christmas) Distinctive pieces in 18-carat gold – many based on

OFF THE BEATEN TRACK

ABBAZIA DI MONTE OLIVETO MAGGIORE

Still a retreat for Benedictine monks, the congregation of this **medieval abbey** (☎0577 70 76 11; www.monteolivetomaggiore.it; admission free but library donation requested; ⊙ 9.15am-noon & 3.15-5pm Mon-Sat, to 6pm in summer, 9am-12.30pm Sun), 39km southeast of Siena, was founded in 1313 by John Tolomei, although construction didn't begin on the monastery until 1393. Visitors come here for the wonderful fresco series in the Great Cloister, painted by Luca Signorelli and Il Sodoma, which illustrates events in the life of St Benedict, founder of the order.

You can also visit the church, which features magnificent choir stalls of inlaid wood; the refectory, frescoed by Paolo Novelli; the magnificent library, built in 1518; the pharmacy; and the chapter house.

Downhill from the main building is the abbey's 14th-century **Cantina Storica** (Historic Wine Cellar; www.agricolamonteoliveto.com; ⊙ 10am-1pm & 2.30-6.30pm, to 6pm winter), where it is possible to take a guided tour and enjoy a wine tasting.

LEEMAGE / GETTY IMAGES ©

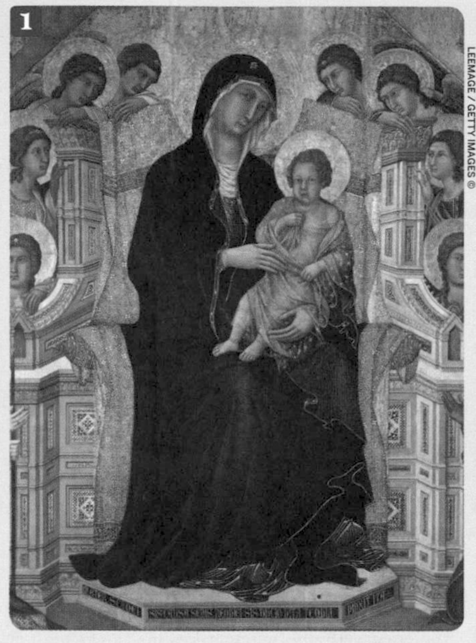

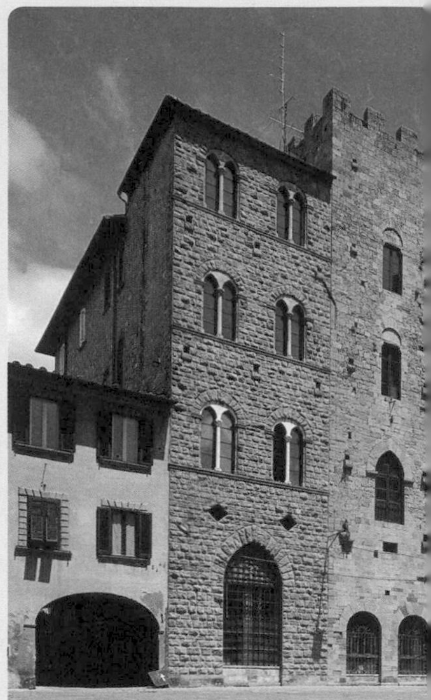

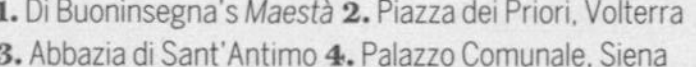

1. Di Buoninsegna's *Maestà* **2.** Piazza dei Priori, Volterra
3. Abbazia di Sant'Antimo **4.** Palazzo Comunale, Siena

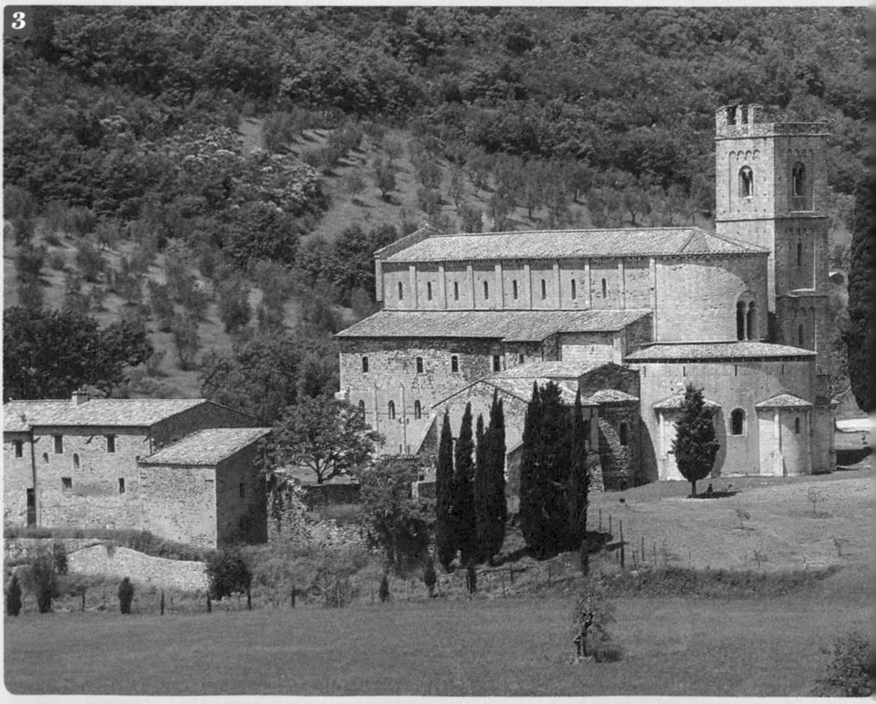

Medieval Masterpieces

We reckon the Middle Ages get a bad rap in the history books. This period may have been blighted by famines, plagues and wars, but it also saw an extraordinary flowering of art and architecture. Cities such as Siena, San Gimignano and Volterra are full of masterpieces dating from this time.

Palazzo Comunale, Siena

Built on the cusp of the Middle Ages and the Renaissance, Siena's city hall (p189) is a triumph of Gothic secular architecture. Inside, the Museo Civico showcases a collection that is modest in size but monumental in quality.

Abbazia di Sant'Antimo

Benedictine monks have been performing Gregorian chants in this Romanesque abbey (p225) near Montalcino ever since the Middle Ages. Dating back to the time of Charlemagne, its austere beauty and idyllic setting make it an essential stop on every itinerary.

Piazza dei Priori, Volterra

Ringed by medieval palaces, Volterra's central square (p217) is presided over by the handsome Palazzo dei Priori and Palazzo Pretorio, the latter crowned by the Torre del Porcellino (Piglet's Tower), named for the wild boar protruding from its upper section.

Duccio di Buoninsegna's Maestà, Siena

Originally displayed in Siena's *duomo* (cathedral) and now the prize exhibit in the Museo dell'Opera, Duccio's altarpiece (p194) portrays the Virgin surrounded by angels, saints and prominent Sienese citizens of the period.

Collegiata, San Gimignano

Don't be fooled by its modest facade. Inside, the walls of this Romanesque cathedral (p211) are adorned with brightly coloured frescoes resembling a vast medieval comic strip.

Etruscan designs – are handmade in this workshop on the city's northern walls.

Alabaster Workshops ARTISANAL
Volterra is known as the city of alabaster, and has a number of shops specialising in hand-carved alabaster items; many of these double as ateliers where the artisans work. Among the best are **Opus Artis** (www.opusartis.com; Piazza Minucci 1); **Paolo Sabatini** (www.paolosabatini.com; Via G Matteotti 56); and the atelier of sculptor **Alessandro Marzetti** (www.alessandromarzetti.it; Via dei Labirinti). To watch alabaster being carved, head to **alab'Arte** (Via Orti San Agostino 28; 9.30am-12.30pm & 3-7pm Mon-Sat).

Information

The extremely efficient **tourist office** (0588 8 72 57; www.volterratur.it; Piazza dei Priori 19-20; 9.30am-1pm & 2-6pm) provides free maps, offers a free hotel-booking service and rents out an audioguide tour (€5) of the town.

Getting There & Around

The bus station is in Piazza Martiri della Libertà. **CPT** (800 570530; www.cpt.pisa.it) buses connect the town with Pisa (€6.10, two hours, up to 10 daily).

You'll need to go to Colle di Val d'Elsa (€2.75, 50 minutes, four daily) to catch connecting bus services to San Gimignano (€3.40, 35 minutes, four daily) and Siena (€3.40, two hours, four daily). For Florence, you'll need only one ticket (€8.35, two hours, three to four daily), but you'll usually need to change buses at Colle di Val d'Elsa. Note that all bus services are greatly reduced on Sundays. Bus tickets can be purchased at the **Associazione Pro Loco Volterra** (0588 8 61 50; www.provolterra.it; Piazza dei Priori 10; 9.30am-12.30pm & 3-6pm) office.

Volterra is accessed via the SR68, which runs between Cecina on the coast and Colle di Val d'Elsa, just off the Siena–Florence *superstrada*.

A ZTL applies in the historic centre. The most convenient car park is beneath Piazza Martiri della Libertà (per hour/day €1.50/11), but there are other car parks around the circumference – P5, P6 and P8 are free. Don't park in P5 overnight on Friday, as the city's weekly produce market is held there on Saturday morning.

VAL D'ORCIA

This picturesque agricultural valley is a Unesco World Heritage site, as is the town of Pienza on its northeastern edge. Its distinctive landscape features flat chalk plains out of which rise almost conical hills topped with fortified settlements and with magnificent abbeys that were once important staging points on the Via Francigena.

Montalcino

POP 5155

Managing to hold out against Florence even after Siena had fallen (hence its former title of 'the Republic of Siena in Montalcino'), this medieval-era hill town eventually gave up on politics and channelled its energies into winemaking. Today, it is known as the home of one of the world's great wines, Brunello di Montalcino.

Sights & Activities

The main activity in town is visiting *enoteche*. For nonalcoholic diversion, purchase a combined ticket (€6) for entry to the *fortez-*

OFF THE BEATEN TRACK

ABBAZIA DI SAN GALGANO

About 52km southwest of Siena via the SS73 are the evocative ruins of this 13th-century Cistercian **Abbazia di San Galgano** (www.sangalgano.org; adult/reduced/family €2/1.50/6; 9am-7pm Apr-Jun & Sep-Oct, 9am-8pm Jul & Aug, 9.30am-5.30pm Nov-Mar), in its day one of the country's finest Gothic buildings. It's well worth a visit, particularly during the **San Galgano Opera Festival** (www.festivalopera.it) held in summer.

On a hill overlooking the abbey is the tiny, round Romanesque **Cappella di Monte Siepi**, home to badly preserved frescoes by Ambrogio Lorenzetti depicting the life of local soldier and saint, San Galgano, who lived his last years here as a hermit.

Near the approach to the abbey is a **fattoria** (farmhouse) with a **cafe** (panino €3.50 to €4) and **restaurant** (meals €22).

If you are heading towards Siena, Montalcino, Pienza or Montepulciano after your visit here, be sure to take the SS73 south and then veer east onto the SP delle Pinete (dir: San Lorenzo a Merse), a scenic drive through protected forest.

LA BANDITA

Sophisticated urban style melds with stupendous scenery at **La Bandita** (☎333 4046704; www.la-bandita.com; d €195-500; ⊙Mar-Dec; P ❄ @ ☎ ≋), a rural retreat set amid working sheep farms in one of the most stunning sections of the Val d'Orcia. Owned and operated by former NYC music executive John Voigtmann and his travel-writer wife (non-Lonely Planet, we hasten to add), it offers comfortable rooms, amenities galore (we love the Ortigia toiletries), wonderful meals and impressive levels of personalised service. Put simply, it's the type of retreat we all fantasise about owning, though few of us could afford to do so. Base yourself here to visit nearby Pienza, Montepulciano and Montalcino.

za's ramparts and to the Museo Civico e Diocesano d'Arte Sacra. These are available from the tourist office.

Fortezza HISTORICAL BUILDING
(Piazzale Fortezza; courtyard free, ramparts adult/child €4/2; ⊙9am-8pm Apr-Oct, 10am-6pm Nov-Mar) This imposing 14th-century structure was expanded under the Medici dukes and now dominates the town's skyline. You can sample and buy local wines in its *enoteca* (tasting of 2/3/5 Brunellos €9/13/19) and also climb up to the fort's ramparts. Buy a ticket for the ramparts at the bar.

Museo Civico e Diocesano d'Arte Sacra MUSEUM
(☎0577 84 60 14; Via Ricasoli 31; adult/child €4.50/3; ⊙10am-1pm & 2-5.50pm Tue-Sun) Occupying the former convent of the neighbouring **Chiesa di Sant'Agostino**, this collection of religious art from the town and surrounding region includes a triptych by Duccio and a *Madonna and Child* by Simone Martini. Other artists represented include the Lorenzetti brothers, Giovanni di Paolo and Sano di Pietro.

Festivals & Events

Benvenuto Brunello WINE
The new vintage is celebrated at this weekend of tastings and award presentations in February. It's organised by the **Consorzio del Vino Brunello di Montalcino** (www.consorziobrunellodimontalcino.it).

International Chamber Music Festival MUSIC
(www.musica-reale.com) Staged in July.

Sagra del Tordo CULTURAL
(www.comunedimontalcino.it) A procession and traditional archery competition held on the last weekend in October.

Sleeping

Hotel Vecchia Oliviera BOUTIQUE HOTEL €€
(☎0577 84 60 28; www.vecchiaoliviera.com; Via Landi 1; s €70-85, d €120-190, ste €200-240; ⊙closed Dec–mid-Feb; P ❄ ☎ ≋) Just beside the Porta Cerbaia, this former olive mill has been tastefully restored and converted into a stylish small hotel. Each of the 11 rooms is individually decorated; the superior ones come with view and Jacuzzi. The garden terrace has stunning views, and the pool is in an attractive garden setting.

Hotel Il Giglio HOTEL €€
(☎0577 84 81 67; www.gigliohotel.com; Via Soccorso Saloni 5; s €95, d €135-145, annex s/d €60/95, apt €100-150; P ☎) The comfortable wrought-iron beds here are each gilded with a painted *giglio* (lily), and all doubles in the main building have a panoramic view. Room 1 has a private terrace, and the small single is very attractive.

Eating & Drinking

★**Osticcio** WINE BAR €€
(www.osticcio.it; Via Matteotti 23; antipasto plates €13-24, meals €37; ⊙noon-4pm & 7-11pm Fri-Wed, noon-7pm Thu mid-Feb–mid Jan) A huge selection of Brunello and its more modest – but still very palatable – sibling Rosso di Montalcino joins dozens of bottles of wine from around the world at this excellent *enoteca*. After browsing the selection of wines downstairs, claim a table in the upstairs dining room for a glass of wine with an antipasto plate or pasta.

Fiaschetteria Italiana 1888 CAFE
(Piazza del Popolo 6; ⊙7.30am-midnight, closed Thu Oct-Easter) We doff our hats to this atmosphere-laden *enoteca*/cafe on the main piazza, which has been serving coffee and glasses of Brunello to locals since 1888 and

BRUNELLOPOLI

In 2008, Montalcino drew the attention of the international wine world when a number of local producers were accused of secretly adulterating their vintages of Brunello di Montalcino with 'foreign' grapes such as merlot and cabernet sauvignon. The Disciplinare di Produzione dei Vini a Denominazione di Origine Controllata (Law Controlling Wine Appellations in Italy) decrees that Brunello must be 100% Sangiovese, so this breach was taken extremely seriously by the government, wine industry and international wine media.

As a result of the accusations, the USA blocked some imports of Brunello, hitting Montalcino's economy hard (approximately 25% of each vintage ends up in the States). Seventeen producers faced commercial fraud charges and possible jail sentences, and the local industry's reputation (not to mention that of its product) suffered as a consequence.

The scandal – known as Brunellopoli or Brunellogate – raised the question of whether winemakers should be able to vary the DOCG decree and add other grapes to broaden Brunello's marketing appeal, particularly for palates attuned to New World wines. Heated debates have occurred within the Consorzio del Vino Brunello, the peak consortium of local producers, about whether upholding tradition equates to halting progress.

At present, the vast majority of the consortium's 700-odd members believe that the 100% local Sangiovese rule should stand, arguing that it is the purest expression of terroir and the wine's strongest claim to quality and marketability. They also argue that allowing blending would simply be another step towards global wine homogenisation. Proponents of change argue that blending with other varieties makes economic sense and leads to the creation of better wines.

Only one thing is sure: the debate is unlikely to be resolved any time soon.

has managed to retain both its decor and charm for the duration.

Information

The **tourist office** (☎0577 84 93 31; www.prolocomontalcino.com; Costa del Municipio 1; ⏲10am-1pm & 2-5.50pm) is just off the main square. It can book cellar door visits and accommodation.

Getting There & Away

Siena Mobilità buses (€4.90, 1½ hours, six daily Mon-Sat) run to/from Siena.

From Siena, take the SR2 (Via Cassia) and exit onto the SP14 at Lama. There's plenty of parking around the *fortezza* (€1.50 per hr 8am-8pm).

Around Montalcino

Poggio Antico WINERY

(☎0577 84 80 44; www.poggioantico.com; ⏲cantina 10am-6pm, restaurant 12.30-2.30pm & 7.30-9.30pm Tue-Sun Apr-Oct, 12.30-2.30pm Tue-Sun Nov-Dec & Feb) Located 4.5km outside Montalcino on the road to Grosseto, Poggio Antico makes award-winning wines (try its Brunello Altero or Riserva), conducts free cellar tours in Italian, English and German, offers paid tastings (approx €25 depending on wines) and has an on-site restaurant (tasting menus without wine €40 to €50). Tours must be booked in advance.

★Il Leccio TUSCAN €€

(☎0577 84 41 75; www.illeccio.net; Costa Castellare 1/3, Sant'Angelo in Colle; meals €40; ⏲12.30-2.30pm & 7.30-9.30pm Thu-Tue) Sometimes simple dishes are the hardest to perfect, and perfection is the only term to use when discussing this trattoria in Brunello's heartland. Watching the chef make his way between his stove and kitchen garden to gather produce for each order puts a whole new spin on the word 'fresh', and both the results and the house Brunello are spectacular.

Sant'Angelo in Colle is 10km southwest of Montalcino along Via del Sole, and 10km west of the Abbazia di Sant'Antimo along an unsealed but signed road through vineyards.

Pienza

POP 2134

If the primary road to Montepulciano didn't pass right through town, Pienza might still be the sleepy hamlet it was before Enea Silvio Piccolomini (later Pius II) decided to rebuild it in magnificent Renaissance style. And, frankly, that could be a very good thing. Summer weekends here are horrendous, with tourists outnumbering locals by a ratio of around 50:1. Come midweek if at all possible.

Unesco added Pienza's historic centre to its World Heritage list in 1996, citing the revolutionary vision of urban space realised in Piazza Pio II and the buildings around it.

Sights

Piazza Pio II PIAZZA

Stand in this magnificent square and spin 360 degrees. You have just taken in Pienza's major monuments. Gems of the Renaissance constructed in a mere three years between 1459 and 1462, they are arranged according to the urban design of Bernardo Rossellino, who applied the principles of Renaissance town planning devised by his mentor, Leon Battista Alberti.

The space available to Rossellino was limited, so to increase the sense of perspective and dignity of the great edifices that he had been commissioned to design, he set them off at angles to the cathedral around a magnificently paved piazza. It was a true masterstroke.

➡ Palazzo Piccolomini

(www.palazzopiccolominipienza.it; 30min guided tours adult/reduced €7/5; 10am-6pm Tue-Sun mid-Mar–mid-Oct, to 4pm mid-Oct–mid-Mar) This magnificent palace was the pope's residence and is considered Rossellino's masterpiece. Located to your right as you face the *duomo,* it was built on the site of former Piccolomini family houses and features a fine courtyard, handsome staircase and the former papal apartments, which are filled with an assortment of period furnishings, minor art and the like. To the rear, a three-level loggia offers a spectacular panorama over the Val d'Orcia below. There are guided tours of the 1st floor every 30 minutes, but you can peek into the courtyard for free.

➡ Duomo

(Piazza Pio II; 8.30am-1pm & 2.15-6.30pm) The piazza's focal point, this cathedral was built on the site of the Romanesque Chiesa di Santa Maria, of which little remains. The Renaissance facade, in travertine stone, is of clear Albertian inspiration. The interior of the building, a strange mix of Gothic and Renaissance, contains a collection of five altarpieces painted by Sienese artists of the period, as well as a superb marble tabernacle by Rossellino containing a relic of St Andrew the Apostle, Pienza's patron saint. The papal bull of 1462 forbade any changes to the church, so revel in the thought that its appearance is virtually the same now as it was in the Middle Ages.

ABBAZIA DI SANT'ANTIMO

This beautiful Romanesque **Abbazia di Sant'Antimo** (www.antimo.it; Castelnuovo dell'Abate; 10.30am-12.30pm & 3-6.30pm Mon-Sat, 9.15-10.45am & 3-6pm Sun) FREE lies in an isolated valley just below the village of Castelnuovo dell'Abate, 10.5km from Montalcino. It's best visited in the morning, when the sun, streaming through the east windows, creates an almost surreal atmosphere. At night, too, it's impressive, lit up like a beacon.

Tradition tells us that Charlemagne founded the original monastery here in 781. The exterior, built in pale travertine stone, is simple except for the stone carvings, which include various fantastical animals. Inside, study the capitals of the columns lining the nave, especially the one representing Daniel in the lion's den (second on the right as you enter). Below it is a particularly intense polychrome 13th-century Madonna and Child and there's a haunting 12th-century Crucifixion above the main altar.

Monks perform Gregorian chants in the abbey during daily services – check times on the website.

Three to four buses per day (€1.50, 15 minutes, Monday to Saturday) connect Montalcino with the village of Castelnuovo dell'Abate.

It's a two-to-three-hour walk from Montalcino to the abbey. The route starts next to the police station near the main roundabout in town; many visitors choose to walk there and return by bus – check the timetable with the tourist office.

The abbey has a **guesthouse** (foresterie@antimo.it) offering simple accommodation for pilgrims.

➡ **Palazzo Vescovile**
(Piazza Pio II) To the left as you face the *duomo* is this *palazzo*, modified and enlarged in 1492 by Roderigo Borgia, the future Pope Alexander VI. It and the adjoining **Palazzo Borgia e Jouffrey** are now home to the **Museo Diocesano** (☎0578 74 99 05; Corso Rossellino 30; adult/reduced €4.50/3; ⊙10am-1pm & 2-5pm Wed-Mon mid-Mar–Oct, 10am-4pm Sat & Sun Nov–mid-Mar), as well as the tourist office (enter via the courtyard onto Corso Rossellino). Tucked in behind Palazzo Vescovile, next to the *duomo*, is the **Casa dei Canonici** (House of the Church Canons).

Pieve di Corsignano CHURCH
(⊙9am-6pm Jun-Nov, from 10am Dec-May) This Romanesque church at the entrance to town dates from the 10th century, when Pienza was called Corsignano, and boasts a strange circular bell tower with eight arched windows. Look closely to discern the carving of a two-headed siren over the main doorway and scenes of the Three Kings and Nativity on the side doorway to the right.

Inside the church is the baptismal font where Pius II was christened.

Sleeping

★**La Bandita Townhouse** BOUTIQUE HOTEL €€€
(☎0578 74 90 05; www.labanditatownhouse.com; Corso Rossellino 111; r €195-495, ste €275-695; P❄@🛜) Conceived to give travellers a glimpse into Tuscan village life, this recently opened offshoot of the fabulous La Bandita rural retreat is Pienza's best sleeping option. Occupying a remodelled Renaissance-era convent, it offers 12 luxurious rooms and suites with a minimalist decor, a communal library/lounge and a laid-back cafe and wine bar.

> LOCAL KNOWLEDGE
>
> **BAGNI SAN FILIPPO**
>
> Medieval pilgrims walking the Via Francigena from Canterbury to Rome loved pausing in this part of central Tuscany to enjoy a long therapeutic soak in one of its thermal springs. If you're keen to do the same, we suggest avoiding the famous thermal institute and hotels in Bagno Vignoni and instead heading to the open-air cascades in this tiny village 16km southwest of Pienza. You'll find them just uphill from Hotel le Terme – follow a sign marked 'Fosso Bianco' down a lane for about 150m to limestone outcrops and you'll come to a set of warm tumbling cascades that get more spectacular the further downhill you walk. It's a pleasant if slightly whiffy spot for a picnic, and you can take a dip for free.

Eating

Osteria Sette di Vino TUSCAN €
(☎0578 74 90 92; Piazza di Spagna 1; meals €16; ⊙12.30-2.30pm & 7.30-10pm Thu-Tue) Known for its *zuppa di pane e fagioli* (bread and white-bean soup), *bruschette* and range of local *pecorino* cheese, this simple place is run by the exuberant Luciano, who is immortalised as Bacchus in a copy of Caravaggio's famous painting hanging above the main counter. There are indoor and outdoor tables. Cash only; no coffee; book ahead.

Pummarò PIZZERIA €
(Via del Giglio 4; slice €2.20, pizza €5.50-9; ⊙to 11pm Tue-Sun; 🛜) Look for bicycles painted red, white and green parked in a laneway off Via Rossellino and you'll find this teensy pizzeria, which is a great place to source a cheap and quick snack. Try the *pizza pummarò* (with cherry tomatoes, *mozzarella di bufala* and basil).

Townhouse Caffè MODERN TUSCAN €€
(☎0578 74 90 05; www.labanditatownhouse.com; Via Rossellino 111, enter from Via San Andrea; breakfast €10, light lunch €15, dinner €30; ⊙7-11pm Mon & Tue, 8am-11pm Wed-Sun,) After visiting Piazza Pio II, consider spending an hour or two lingering over a light lunch, coffee or glass of wine in this cafe's medieval walled garden. The menu relies heavily on local organic produce for its inspiration (fancy a burger made with Chianina beef and topped with melted fresh *pecorino* and mint mayonnaise?) and there's a well-considered wine list.

Il Rossellino TUSCAN €€
(☎0578 74 90 64; www.rossellino.it; Piazza di Spagna 4; meals €40; ⊙12.30-2.30pm & 7.30-9.30pm Fri-Wed) Run by a husband and wife team (she's in the kitchen, he's front of house), this old-fashioned place has a small number of tables and a big reputation for its hand-made pasta and perfectly cooked meat dishes. There's a great wine list.

Information

Tourist office (☎0578 74 99 05; info.turismo@comune.pienza.si.it; Corso Rossellino 30; ⏰10am-1pm & 2-5pm Wed-Mon mid-Mar–Oct, 10am-4pm Sat & Sun Nov–mid-Mar) Located on the ground floor of Palazzo Vescovile.

Getting There & Away

Two Siena Mobilità buses run Monday to Saturday between Siena and Pienza (€5.50, 70 minutes) and nine travel to/from Montepulciano (€2.50). The bus stops are just off Piazza Dante Alighieri. Buy tickets at one of the nearby bars.

Finding a car park is extremely difficult on weekends as the public car park near the centre fills quickly. It costs €1.50 per hour. Be warned that local traffic officers are quick to fine cars that overstay their ticket.

Monticchiello

A 15-minute drive southeast from Pienza will bring you to Monticchiello, a semi-comatose, pretty-as-a-picture medieval hilltop village.

★La Casa di Adelina B&B €

(☎0578 75 51 67; www.lacasadiadelina.eu; Piazza San Martino 3; s €55, d €85-115, 4-bed apt €90-110; ⏰closed 2 weeks in Nov; @📶) Laden with art and atmosphere, this place has friendly hosts, a communal lounge with wood stove (great in winter) and four comfortable B&B rooms. There's also a well-appointed two-bedroom apartment nearby that is perfect for those wanting to base themselves in the area for a week or two (discounts available for extended stays).

Osteria La Porta TUSCAN €€

(☎0578 75 51 63; Via del Piano 3; meals €40; ⏰cafe 9am-12.30pm & 3-7pm, restaurant 12.30-3pm & 7.30-10.30pm) Positioned just inside the town's main gate, this highly regarded place has a small terrace with panoramic views of Val d'Orcia and a reputation for food and service that behoves a reservation, even in low season. The €18 fixed lunch menu offers great value, and *spuntini* (snacks) such as bruschettas, olives and cheese plates are served outside usual meal hours.

VAL DI CHIANA

Straddling the provinces of Siena and Arezzo, this scenic valley is known for its food and wine. Dining in its major town, Montepulciano, is a highlight – particularly if you opt for the local Chianina beef washed down with a glass or two of the famous Vino Nobile.

FATTORIA LE CAPEZZINE

This **wine estate** (☎0578 72 43 04; www.avignonesi.it; Via Colonica 1, Valiano di Montepulciano; ⏰9am-6pm May-Oct, 9am-5pm Mon-Fri Nov-Apr), 15km northeast of Montepulciano, is part of the highly regarded Avignonesi company, which produces Vino Nobile di Montepulciano, Rosso di Montepulciano, Vin Santo, grappa and olive oil. Spread over 19 hectares, the estate is known for its 'Round Vineyard', which was designed to establish to what extent the quality of wine is influenced by density of planting and type of rootstock. Book in advance to enjoy a two-hour **tour** (standard/premium tasting €15/38; ⏰tours 10am & 3pm May-Oct, 9am-5pm Mon-Fri Nov-Apr) of the vineyards, ageing cellars and vinsantaia (where Vin Santo is aged), followed by a tasting of Avignonesi wines; details are on the website.

Montepulciano

POP 14,188

Exploring this reclaimed narrow ridge of volcanic rock will push your quadriceps to their failure point. When this happens, self-medicate with a generous pour of the highly reputed Vino Nobile while drinking in the spectacular views over the Val di Chiana and Val d'Orcia.

A late-Etruscan fort was the first in a series of settlements here. During the Middle Ages, the town was a constant bone of contention between Florence and Siena. Florence eventually won the day in 1404 and the Marzocco, or lion of Florence, came to replace the she-wolf of Siena as the city's symbol. The new administration invited architects including Michelozzo and Sangallo il Vecchio to design new buildings and endow this Gothic stronghold with some Renaissance grace and style. That intriguing mix alone makes the steep climbs worthwhile.

Sights

Il Corso STREET

Montepulciano's main street – called in stages Via di Gracciano, Via di Voltaia, Via

Montepulciano

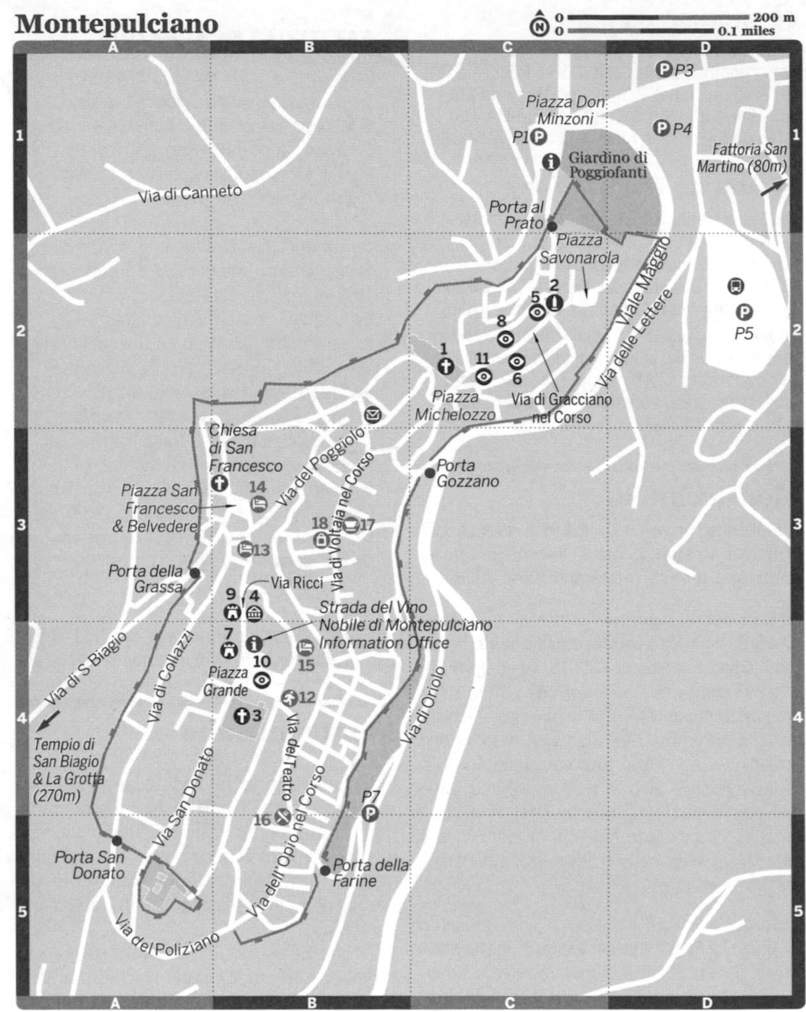

dell'Opio and Via d'Poliziano – climbs up the eastern ridge of the town from Porta al Prato and loops to meet Via di Collazzi on the western ridge. To reach the centre of town (Piazza Grande) take a dog-leg turn into Via del Teatro.

In Piazza Savonarola, up from the Porta al Prato, is the **Colonna del Marzocca**, erected in 1511 to confirm Montepulciano's allegiance to Florence. The splendid stone lion, squat as a pussycat atop this column is, in fact, a copy; the original is in the town's Museo Civico. The late-Renaissance **Palazzo Avignonesi** is at No 91 and other notable buildings include the **Palazzo di Bucelli** at No 73 (look for the recycled Etruscan and Latin inscriptions and reliefs on the lower facade), and **Palazzo Cocconi** at No 70.

Continuing uphill, you'll find Michelozzo's **Chiesa di Sant'Agostino**, with its lunette above the entrance holding a terracotta Madonna and Child, John the Baptist and St Augustine. Opposite, the **Torre di Pulcinella**, a medieval tower house, is topped by the town clock and the hunched figure of Pulcinella (Punch of Punch and Judy fame), which strikes the hours. After passing historic Caffè Poliziano (p231), the

Montepulciano

Sights
1 Chiesa di Sant'Agostino C2
2 Colonna del Marzocca C2
3 Duomo B4
4 Museo Civico B3
5 Palazzo Avignonesi C2
6 Palazzo Cocconi C2
7 Palazzo Comunale B4
8 Palazzo di Bucelli C2
9 Palazzo Ricci B3
10 Piazza Grande B4
11 Torre di Pulcinella C2

Activities, Courses & Tours
Cantina del Redi .... (see 9)
12 Cantine Contucci B4

Sleeping
13 Camere Bellavista B3
14 Locanda San Francesco B3
15 Meublé Il Riccio B4

Eating
16 Osteria Acquacheta B5

Drinking & Nightlife
17 Caffè Poliziano B3
E Lucevan Le Stelle .... (see 14)

Shopping
18 Maledetti Toscani B3

Corso continues straight ahead and Via del Teatro veers off to the right.

Piazza Grande PIAZZA
This is the town's highest point and the shooting location for the main crowd scene in *New Moon,* the second film in the *Twilight* series. The 14th-century **Palazzo Comunale** (panoramic terrace €2) and the late-16th-century **Duomo** (Piazza Grande), with its unfinished facade, are the piazza's major landmarks. Behind the high altar in the *duomo* is Taddeo di Bartolo's lovely *Assumption* triptych (1401).

Via Ricci STREET
From Piazza Grande, Via Ricci runs downhill past **Palazzo Ricci** (www.palazzoricci.com; Via Ricci 9-11), now home to a German music academy. From the *palazzo*'s courtyard, stairs lead down to the historic **Cantina del Redi** (Via Ricci; fee for tastings; 10.30am-7pm mid-Mar–early Jan, Sat & Sun only early Jan–mid Mar) wine cellar. The street terminates in **Piazza San Francesco**, where you can admire a panoramic view of the Val di Chiana.

Museo Civico MUSEUM, ART GALLERY
(www.museocivicomontepulciano.it; Via Ricci 10; adult/reduced €5/3; 10am-1pm & 3-6pm Tue-Sun Mar-July & Sep-Oct, 10am-7pm Tue-Sun Aug, 10am-1pm & 3-6pm Sat & Sun Nov-Feb) The town's museum/Pinacoteca occupies Palazzo Neri Orselli. The pride of its collection is a portrait recently attributed to Caravaggio.

Cantine Contucci WINE TASTING
(www.contucci.it; Via del Teatro 1; fee for tastings; 9.30am-12.30pm & 2.30-6pm Mon-Fri, from 9.30am Sat & Sun) Occupying three levels in the bowels of the handsome 13th-century *palazzo* of the same name are the historic cellars of the Contucci estate, in business since the Renaissance and one of the first producers of Vino Nobile.

Courses & Tours

The office of the **Strada del Vino Nobile di Montepulciano** (www.stradavinonobile.it) organises a range of tours and courses, including cooking courses (€60 to €180), vineyard tours (€18 to €48), Slow Food tours (€100 to €155), wine-tasting lessons (€37) and walking tours in the vineyards culminating in a wine tasting (€45 to €60). You can make bookings at its information office in Piazza Grande.

Festivals & Events

Musica di Stelle ARTS
(Music of the Stars; www.fondazionecantiere.it) Performances of opera, theatre and classical and contemporary music are staged in venues throughout the town.

Bravio delle Botti CULTURAL
(www.braviodellebotti.com) Members of the city's eight *contrade* race to push 80kg wine barrels uphill in this race held on the last Sunday in August.

Festival of Chamber Music MUSIC
(www.palazzoricci.com) Held at Palazzo Ricci in late-August and September.

Sleeping

Camere Bellavista HOTEL €
(347 8232314; www.camerebellavista.it; Via Ricci 25; s €65-70, d €75; P) Nearly all of the 10

high-ceilinged double rooms at this excellent budget hotel have fantastic views; room 6 also has a private terrace (€100). No-one lives here so phone ahead in order to be met and given a key (if you've omitted this stage, there's a phone in the lobby from where you can call). No breakfast.

★ Locanda San Francesco B&B €€
(☎349 6721302; www.locandasanfrancesco.it; Piazza San Francesco 5; r €150-240; ⊙closed mid-Jan; P❄@📶) Four handsome rooms with magnificent views and lovely bathrooms await at this luxury B&B. Host Cinzia Caporali runs both it and the attached E Lucevan Le Stelle wine bar with friendly efficiency.

★ Fattoria San Martino AGRITURISMO €€
(☎0578 71 74 63; www.fattoriasanmartino.it; Via di Martiena 3; r €140-180; ⊙closed Dec-Easter; P📶🏊) Dutch-born Karin and Italian Antonio met when working in Milan's high-velocity fashion industry, but eventually decided that organic farming was more to their liking than haute couture. The homespun-chic rooms in this rebuilt 12th-century farmhouse and purpose-built annexe are sure to please, as will the all-vegetarian meals (dinner €35 plus wine), pretty garden, biological filtered pool and emphasis on sustainability.

Meublé Il Riccio B&B €€
(☎0578 75 77 13; www.ilriccio.net; Via Talosa 21; standard r €100-110, superior r €120-160; P❄@📶) Not many buildings have been owned by the same family for 800 years, but this one has. Now a hugely atmospheric B&B, it showcases art, antiques and chandeliers acquired over the centuries and offers guests a choice of standard and superior rooms – opt for a superior if possible (some of these have balconies and all have views).

There's an impressive breakfast salon and a terrace with a spectacular view. Breakfast costs €8.

Eating & Drinking

Osteria Acquacheta OSTERIA €
(☎0578 71 70 86; www.acquacheta.eu; Via del Teatro 22; meals €20; ⊙12.15-4pm & 7.30-10.30pm Wed-Mon) Hugely popular with locals and tourists alike, this bustling place specialises in *bistecca alla fiorentina* (chargrilled T-bone steak), which comes to the table in huge, lightly seared and exceptionally flavoursome slabs (don't even *think* of asking

WORTH A TRIP

ORVIETO

This Umbrian city looms over the A1 *superstrada* (expressway) in truly spectacular fashion. Perched precariously on a craggy volcanic landform, its skyline is dominated by a huge **cathedral** (www.opsm.it; Piazza Duomo; admission €3, incl Cappella di San Brizio €5; ⊙9.30am-7pm Apr-Sep, 9.30am-6pm Mar & Oct, 9.30am-1pm & 2.30-5pm Nov-Feb), one of the great masterpieces of medieval architecture. Construction of the cathedral commenced in 1290 and took three centuries to complete. Its facade is perhaps the most beautiful to grace any Italian church and inside the stark but ethereally beautiful interior is Luca Signorelli's *The Last Judgment* fresco cycle. Signorelli began work on these extraordinary frescoes in 1499, and Michelangelo is said to have taken inspiration from them.

Orvieto is a mere one-hour drive from both Montepulciano and Arezzo, so can easily be visited in a day if you're staying in the Val di Chiana. The **tourist office** (☎0763 34 17 72; info@iat.orvieto.tr.it; Piazza Duomo 24; ⊙8.15am-1.50pm & 4-7pm Mon-Fri, 10am-1pm & 3-6pm Sat & Sun) is opposite the cathedral, and one of Umbria's best restaurants, **I Sette Consoli** (☎0763 34 39 11; www.isetteconsoli.it; Piazza Sant'Angelo 1a; meals €40, 6-course degustazion menu €42; ⊙12.30-3pm & 7.30-10pm Thu-Tue), is nearby. When we last visited, this was offering a fabulous-value €20 set weekday lunch (three courses plus one glass of wine, water and service).

Trains run to/from Florence (*regionale veloce*, €15, 2¼ hours, eight daily) and Rome (*regionale veloce* €7.50, 80 minutes, eight daily). From the train station you'll need to take the *funicolore* (cable car; €1 each way, €0.80 with train ticket; every 10 minutes 7.05am-8.25pm Mon-Fri, every 15 minutes 8.15am-8pm Sat & Sun) up to the town centre. Tickets are available from the *tabacchi* (tobacconist) at the station.

The carpark next to the *funicolore* station in the upper town charges €1.20 per hour between 8am and 8pm.

for it to be served otherwise). Lunch sittings are at 12.15pm and 2.15pm; dinner at 7.30pm and 9.15pm – book ahead.

★ **La Grotta** TRADITIONAL ITALIAN €€€

(☎0578 75 74 79; www.lagrottamontepulciano.it; Via San Biagio 15; meals €44, 6-course tasting menu €48; ⊙12.30-2.30pm & 7.30-10pm Thu-Tue, closed mid-Jan–mid-Mar) Facing the High Renaissance Tempio di San Biagio on the road to Chiusi, La Grotta has elegant dining rooms and a gorgeous courtyard garden that's perfect for summer dining. The food is traditional with a modern twist or two, and service is exemplary. A hint: don't skip dessert.

E Lucevan Le Stelle WINE BAR

(www.locandasanfrancesco.it; Piazza San Francesco 5; ⊙11.30am-11pm Easter-Oct;) Comfy couches, cool jazz (both on the sound system and live) and modern art on the walls are the hallmarks at this laid-back wine bar and bistro. Dishes (antipasto plates €4.50 to €8, *piadinas* (Italian flatbread) €6, pastas €6.50 to €9) are simple but tasty and there's an outdoor terrace that's a perfect spot for an *aperitivo*.

Caffè Poliziano CAFE

(Via di Voltaia nel Corso 27;) Established as a cafe in 1868, Poliziano was lovingly restored to its original form 20 years ago and is the town's favourite cafe. A sit-down coffee is expensive, but will be worth the outlay if you manage to score one of the tiny, precipitous balcony tables.

Shopping

Maledetti Toscani LEATHER GOODS

(www.maledettitoscani.com; Via di Voltaia nel Corso 44-46) In the leather goods business since 1848, local success-story Maledetti manufactures good-quality shoes, bags, coats and belts. This is the women's store; the men's store is at number 40.

Information

Strada del Vino Nobile di Montepulciano Information Office (☎0578 71 74 84; www.stradavinonobile.it; Piazza Grande 7; ⊙10am-1pm & 3-6pm Mon-Fri) Books accommodation and arranges courses and tours.

Tourist office (☎0578 75 73 41; www.prolocomontepulciano.it; Piazza Don Minzoni 1; ⊙9.30am-12.30pm & 3-7pm Mon-Sat, 9am-1pm Sun Easter-Sep, 9.30am-12.30pm & 3-6pm Mon-Sat, 9.30am-12.30pm Sun Oct-Easter) Reserves accommodation, offers internet access (€3.50 per hour), supplies maps of the town, rents mountain bikes (per hour/day €2.50/15) and scooters and sells bus and train tickets (commission applies for train tickets).

Getting There & Around

The bus station is next to Car Park No 5. Siena Mobilità runs four buses daily between Siena and Montepulciano (€6.60, one hour) stopping at Pienza (€2.50) en route. There are three services per day to/from Florence (€11.20, 90 minutes).

Regular buses connect with Chiusi-Chianciano Terme (€3.40, 40 minutes), from where you can catch a train to Florence (€12.50, two hours, frequent) via Arezzo (€6.40, 50 minutes).

Coming from Florence, take the Valdichiana exit off the A1 (direction Bettolle-Sinalunga) and then follow the signs; from Siena, take the Siena–Bettolle–Perugia autostrada.

A 24-hour ZTL applies in the historic centre between May and September; in October and April it applies from 8am to 8pm, and from November to March it applies from 8am to 5pm. Your hotel can usually supply a permit. The most convenient car park is at Piazza Don Minzoni (€1.30 per hour April to October, free November to March), from where minibuses (€1) weave their way up the hill to Piazza Grande.

Southern Tuscany

Includes ➡

Best Places to Eat

- ➡ Grantosco (p247)
- ➡ Il Pellicano (p250)
- ➡ Il Tufo Allegro (p244)
- ➡ La Tana del Brillo Parlante (p240)

Best Places to Stay

- ➡ La Fattoria di Tatti (p237)
- ➡ Le Camere del Ceccottino (p243)
- ➡ Montebelli Agriturismo & Country Hotel (p241)
- ➡ Pieve di Caminino (p241)

Why Go?

Diversity reigns supreme in southern Tuscany. Here, it's possible to travel from sandy beaches to snow-capped mountains in the space of a few hours, passing marshy coastal plains teeming with wildlife, vine-covered slopes and dramatically sited hill towns along the way. Matched to these landscapes are activities of every description – visitors can swim, walk, horse ride, mountain-bike ride and bird-watch to their hearts' content, spending days in the fresh air and nights relaxing in atmospheric *agriturismi* (accommodation on working farms or wine estates).

But there's more to the region than the great outdoors. Locals are fiercely proud of the ancient customs of the Maremma, as the region is commonly called, and history resonates in every town. There's a wealth of Etruscan archaeological sites and medieval and Renaissance settlements with historic streets, churches and museums that are sure to keep you busy.

Road Distances

	Vetulonia	Massa Marittima	Grosseto	Pitigliano
Massa Marittima	38			
Grosseto	52	48		
Pitigliano	129	120	75	
Parco Regionale della Maremma	28	67	20	56

Getting Around

You'll need a car to explore this pocket of Tuscany thoroughly – veer off the S1 autostrada and explore secondary roads whenever possible. Train travel won't get you far – the *Frecciabianca* stops in Grosseto on its Rome–Genoa trip and *regionale* (slow regional) trains servicing that route also stop in Orbatello-Monte Argentario, but the only other rail link is between Siena and Grosseto. Bus travel is worse, with limited routes and infrequent services.

THREE PERFECT DAYS

Day 1: Città del Tufa

Though the Etruscans have left their mark on towns, cities and landscapes throughout this region, the southeast corner is a particularly rich repository of their heritage. Make your way to picturesque Pitigliano, where you should have lunch, and then explore the neighbouring settlements of Sorano and Sovana to see Etruscan necropolises, visit archaeological museums and explore a network of mysterious *vie cave* (sunken roads). If there's any time left in your day, consider a brief stop at the Società Agricola Terenzi to sample its award-winning Morellino di Scansano.

Day 2: Parco Regionale della Maremma

Head to this regional park to walk, bicycle, canoe or horse-ride through the wild natural scenery. While here, enjoy a farm experience at Agienza Regionale Agricola di Alberese, where the famous *butteri* (Maremmese cowboys) ride the range. At the end of the day, consider visiting the quirky Giardino dei Tarocchi, a sculpture garden near Capalbio.

Day 3: Massa Marittima

Not many tourists make it to this medieval hill town crowning the Colline Metallifere (metal-producing hills) at the top end of the region, but that's their loss. Spend the morning wandering the narrow streets and handsome piazzas of the historic centre (be sure to visit the *duomo*) before moving on to explore the geologically fascinating sites around Monterotondo Marittimo, or the Etruscan-era settlement at Vetulonia.

Advance Planning

- For summer travel, reserve accommodation near the coast well in advance.
- Book ahead for boat or bike tours of the Riserva Naturale Provinciale Diaccia Botrona, farm experiences at the Agienza Regionale Agricola di Alberese or tours in the Parco Regionale della Maremma.

DON'T MISS

Don't miss this region's famed Etruscan sights, the most impressive of which are the Museo Civico Archeologico 'Isidoro Falchi' and Scavi di Città, both in Vetulonia, the Parco Archeologico 'Città del Tufa' near Sovana and the Archaeological Site at Roselle, near Grosseto.

Best Walks

- **Pitigliano to Sovana** (p242) Incorporating sections of *vie cave*.
- **Le Biancane, Monterotondo Marittimo** (p240) Through a strange geothermal landscape.
- **Parco Regionale della Maremma** (p248) Explore beaches, wetlands, forests and a ruined 12th-century tower.

Best Festivals

- Torciata di San Giuseppe (p242), Pitigliano
- Balestro del Girifalco (p236), Massa Marittima

Resources

- **Maremma Tourism** (www.turismoinmaremma.it)
- **Parco degli Etruschi** (www.parcodeglietruschi.it)

Southern Tuscany Highlights

❶ Become a Maremmese cowboy for the day in the **Parco Regionale della Maremma** (p248).

❷ Admire a saucy fresco and one of Tuscany's most magnificent piazzas in **Massa Marittima** (p236).

❸ Embark on a hike with a difference amid the strange geothermal landscape of **Monterotondo Marittimo** (p240).

❹ Observe exciting Etruscan excavation works at the archaeological site of **Vetulonia** (p241).

❺ Visit a historic synagogue, where the largest Jewish community in Italy once worshipped in the hilltop stronghold of **Pitigliano** (p242).

❻ Walk in the footsteps of Etruscans while exploring the enigmatic landscape around **Sovana** (p244).

❼ Follow tens of thousands of migrating birds to the unspoiled natural landscape of the **Riserva Naturale Provinciale Diaccia Botrona** (p248).

0 10 km
0 5 miles
Buonconvento
SS223
Bagni di Petriolo
Castelnuovo dell'Abate
Monte Amiata
SS2
Monte Amiata (1736m)
Abbadia San Salvatore
Cinigiano
Arcidosso
Santa Fiora
Roselle
Arcille
Roccalbegna
Castel Azzara
SS322
Semproniano
Monte Elmo (829m)
Scansano
Sorano
San Quirico
Società Agricola Terenzi
Terme di Saturnia
Sovana
6
Parco Archeologico 'Città del Tufa'
5
Pitigliano
SS322
SS323
Magliano in Toscana
Manciano
Talamone
SS1
SS74
Monte Bellino (516m)
L'Oasi WWF di Orbetello
Albinia
Monte Maggiore (379m)
LAZIO
Laguna di Ponente
Orbetello Scalo
Orbetello
Capalbio
Giardino dei Tarocchi
Laguna di Levante
Capalbio Scalo
Monte Argentario
Porto Ercole
Lago di Burano
Riserva Naturale WWF Lago di Burano

THE ALTA MAREMMA

The Alta (Upper) Maremma starts south of Livorno and continues down to Grosseto, incorporating Massa Marittima and the surrounding Colline Metallifere (metal-producing hills) that are now part of Unesco's European Geopark Network. It also covers inland territory including the hill towns south of the Crete Senesi and the mountainous terrain surrounding Monte Amiata.

Massa Marittima

POP 8620

Drawcards at this tranquil hill town include an eccentric yet endearing jumble of museums, an extremely handsome central piazza and largely intact medieval streets that are blessedly bereft of tour groups.

Briefly under Pisan domination, Massa Marittima became an independent *comune* (city-state) in 1225 but was swallowed up by Siena a century later. A plague in 1348 was followed by the decline of the region's lucrative mining industry after 50 years, reducing the town to the brink of extinction, a situation made even worse by the prevalence of malaria in surrounding marshlands. Fortunately, the draining of marshes in the 18th century and the re-establishment of mining shortly afterwards brought Massa Marittima back to life.

The town is divided into three districts: the Città Vecchia (Old Town), Città Nuova (New Town) and Borgo (Borough). Access from the Città Vecchia to the Città Nuova is via the massive **Arco Senese** (Sienese Arch; Piazza Matteotti), which links defensive bastions in the old city walls to the **Torre del Candeliere**, a tower commanding stupendous views over the town.

Sights & Activities

★Cattedrale di San Cerbone CATHEDRAL

(Piazza Garibaldi; 8am-noon & 3-5pm) Presiding over photogenic Piazza Garibaldi (aka Piazza Duomo), Massa Marittima's asymmetrically positioned 13th-century *duomo* is dedicated to St Cerbonius, the town's patron saint, who is always depicted surrounded by a flock of geese. Inside, don't miss the freestanding *Maestà* (Madonna and Child enthroned in majesty; 1316) attributed by some experts to Duccio di Buoninsegna.

The *duomo*'s other treasures include a carved marble urn known as the *Arca di San Cerbone* (St Cerbone's Ark; 1324) behind the high altar and an early-14th-century polychrome wooden crucifix carved by Giovanni Pisano on the altar itself.

On the facade, above the main doorway, are carved panels depicting scenes from St Cerbone's life.

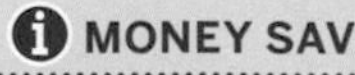

A **cumulative ticket** (adult/child €15/10) gives access to all of Massa Marittima's museums and monuments.

★Museo di Arte Sacra MUSEUM

(Museum of Sacred Art; www.museiartesacra.net; Corso Diaz 36; adult/child €5/3; 10am-1pm & 3-6pm Tue-Sun summer, 11am-1pm & 3-5pm Tue-Sun winter) Housed in the former monastery of San Pietro all'Orto, this museum houses a splendid *Maestà* (c 1335–37) by Ambrogio Lorenzetti, as well as sculptures by Giovanni Pisano that originally adorned the *duomo*'s facade. The collection of primitive grey alabaster bas-reliefs also came from the *duomo,* but date from an earlier era.

Museo Archeologico MUSEUM

(Piazza Garibaldi 1; adult/child €3/2; 10am-12.30pm & 3.30-7pm Tue-Sun summer, 10am-12.30pm & 3-5pm Tue-Sun winter) The 13th-century **Palazzo del Podestà** houses a musty archaeological museum whose only truly noteworthy exhibit is *La Stele del Vado all'Arancio,* a simple but compelling stone stela (funeral or commemorative marker) dating from the 3rd millennium BC.

Albero della Fecondità MONUMENT

Downhill from Piazza Garibaldi, opposite the main car park, is a 13th-century building that was once used to store wheat. Under its loggia is the *Fonte dell'Abbondanza* (Fountain of Abundance), a now decommissioned public drinking fountain topped by an extraordinary fresco known as the *Albero della Fecondità* (Fertility Tree). Look closely to see what type of fruit the tree bears!

Festivals & Events

Balestro del Girifalco CULTURE

(Contest of the Falcon's Heart; www.societaterzieri massetani.it) This crossbow competition is held twice yearly on the first Sunday after 20 May, and on a Sunday in either July or August (usually the second Sunday in August). Twenty-four crossbowmen from the

Massa Marittima

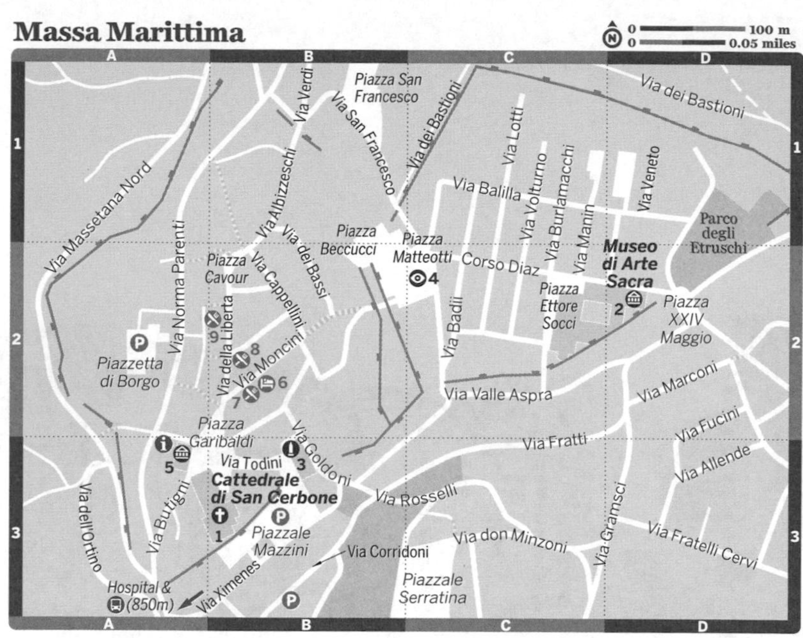

Massa Marittima

Top Sights

1 Cattedrale di San Cerbone B3
2 Museo di Arte Sacra D2

Sights

3 Albero della Fecondità B3
4 Arco Senese C2
5 Museo Archeologico A3
Palazzo del Podestà .... (see 5)
Torre del Candeliere .... (see 4)

Sleeping

6 Residenza d'Epoca Palazzo Malfatti B2

Eating

7 Il Bacchino B2
8 La Tana del Brillo Parlante B2
9 L'Osteria da Tronca B2

town's three *terzieri* (town districts) dress in medieval costume and compete for a golden arrow and a large silk painting.

Sleeping

The town's clutch of hotels leave a lot to be desired, but there is one apartment hotel worthy of recommendation as well as some impressive B&Bs and *agriturismi* dotted through the surrounding area.

★La Fattoria di Tatti B&B €
(☎05 6691 2001; www.tattifattoria.it; Via Matteotti 10, Tatti; s €50-80, d €90-115; ⊙closed Nov–mid-Mar; P@) Built in the 18th century, this restored *fattoria* (farm building) in Tatti, a hilltop village 25km southeast of Massa Marittima, offers eight simple but stylish rooms. Manager Maria prepares a delicious breakfast each morning, and guests are welcome to use the kitchen at other times. A nearby playground and pizzeria/trattoria make it a great choice for families.

Residenza d'Epoca Palazzo Malfatti APARTMENT €
(☎05 6690 4181; www.palazzomalfattiresidenzadepoca.com; Via Moncini 10; d €60-115, t €90-165, q €120-230, 5-bed €150-290;) These seven apartments in a 13th-century *palazzo* overlooking Piazza Garibaldi are an attractive option for self-catering guests who want to stay for a while (rates drop for stays of more than two nights). The building's conversion hasn't been handled as cleverly as it could have been, but the strangely arranged spaces are comfortable and reasonably well equipped, with good bathrooms.

3

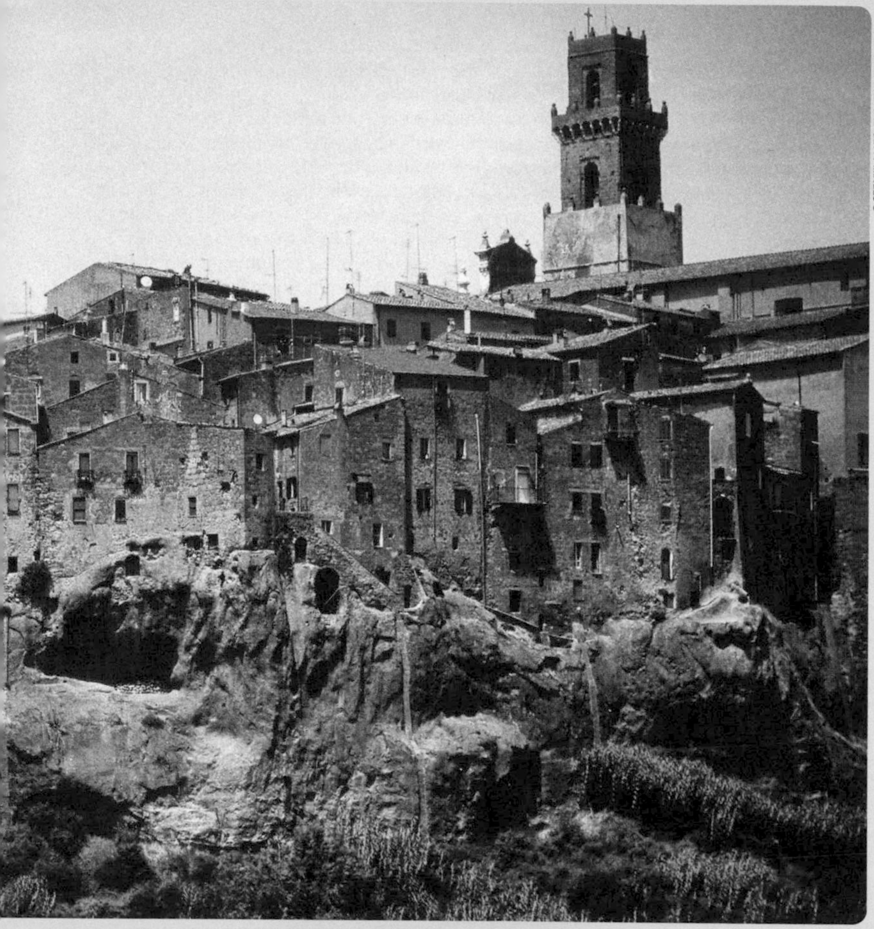

WAYNE WALTON / GETTY IMAGES ©

1. Pitigliano (p242)
This spectacular hilltop village sprouts from a volcanic rocky outcrop that towers over the surrounding country.

2. Massa Marittima (p236)
This tranquil hill town boasts an eccentric yet endearing jumble of museums, an extremely handsome central piazza and largely intact medieval streets.

3. Near Porto Ercole, Monte Argentario (p249)
Porto Ercole, on the less-crowded, southern side of Monte Argentario, has a small and attractive harbour nestled between Spanish forts.

CHARLES BOWMAN / GETTY IMAGES ©

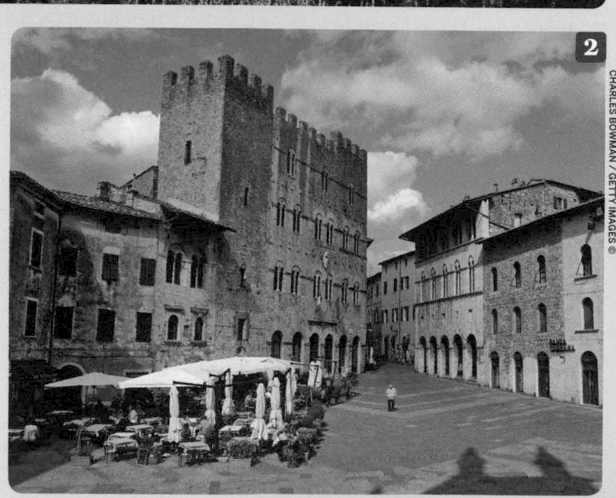

THE COLLINE METALLIFERE

Massa Marittima's handsome buildings and artistic treasures are the legacy of the town's location in the centre of Tuscany's Colline Metallifere (metal-producing hills). Mining occurred in these hills over three millenniums, and has shaped the region's physical and cultural landscapes – a fact acknowledged by the recent addition of the **Parco Nazionale Technologico Archeologico delle Colline Metallifere Grossetane** (National Technological & Archaeological Park of the Colline Metallifere; www.parcocollinemetallifere.it) to the Unesco-auspiced European Geopark Network. The national park aims to preserve and promote the history of metallurgy and mining activities in the region.

The national park incorporates many sites, including **Le Biancane** (information office 10.30am-12.30pm & 3-5.30pm Tue-Sun summer, 10.30am-12.30pm Tue & Thu, 10.30am-12.30pm & 3-5pm Sat & Sun winter) FREE in **Monterotondo Marittimo**, a geothermal park 21km north of Massa Marittima where steam has been converted into power by vapour turbines since 1916, supplying power to one million Tuscan households (and meeting 25% of Tuscany's overall energy demands). Visitors can take a two-hour walk through wooded terrain belching steam from under the earth's crust and sheltering amazing clumps of sulphur crystals.

Another site well worth a visit is the **Parco Minerario Naturalistico Gavorrano** (www.parcominerario.it; Località Ex Bagnetti, Gavorrano; adult/reduced €10/8; 10am-1pm & 4-7pm Tue-Sun mid-Jun–mid-Sep; Sat & Sun only May–mid-Jun & mid-Sep–Dec, closed Jan-Apr), a museum and education centre in a huge former pyrite mine that operated from 1898 to 1984 and was once the largest mine in Europe. A section of the mine's 180km of underground galleries can be visited in a fascinating guided tour incorporating social history commentary and interactive displays.

Podere Riparbella AGRITURISMO €€
(05 6691 5557; www.riparbella.com; Località Sopra Pian di Mucini; s €82-94, d €164-184; closed early Jan–mid-Apr; P) The Swiss owners of this 46-hectare estate 5km outside town have spent the last 20-odd years building an ecologically sustainable farm operation. The 11 guest rooms are in a charming old building with communal lounge and terrace. A delicious four-course dinner uses home-grown and local products and is included in the room price. No credit cards.

Eating & Drinking

Il Bacchino DELI €
(Via Moncini 8; 9am-10pm Mar-Jan, closed Sun & Mon Feb) Owner Magdy Lamei may not be a local (in fact, he's from Cairo), but it would be hard to find anyone else as knowledgeable and passionate about local artisanal produce. Come here for a tasting of local wines, or to stock up on picnic provisions including wine, jams, cheese and cured meats.

★**La Tana del Brillo Parlante** TUSCAN €€
(05 6690 1274; Vicolo del Ciambellano 4; meals €32; noon-2.30pm & 7.30-10pm Thu-Tue Dec-Oct) Satisfying the Slow Food checklist to the letter, this self-described 'smallest *osteria* in Italy' seats a mere 10 people (in summer up to another six can squeeze into tiny alley tables) and serves deliciously authentic Maremmese dishes. If you intend to dine here in summer or on the weekend, reserve well in advance. No credit cards.

L'Osteria da Tronca TUSCAN €€
(05 6690 1991; Vicolo Porte 5; meals €28; 7.30-10.30pm Thu-Tue Mar-Jul & Sep–mid-Dec, 7.30-10pm Aug) Squeezed into a side street (it's behind Hotel Il Sole), this stone-walled restaurant specialises in the rustic dishes of the Maremma. Specialities include *acquacotta* (a hearty vegetable soup with bread and egg), *tortelli alla maremma* (pasta parcels filled with ricotta and a type of spinach) and *coniglio in porchetta* (roasted stuffed rabbit).

Information

Tourist office (05 6690 2756; www.altamaremmaturismo.it; Via Todini 3-5; 9.30am-1pm & 2-6.30pm Tue-Sun) Down a side street beneath the Museo Archeologico.

Getting There & Away

BUS

The bus station is near the hospital on Piazza del Risorgimento, 1km down the hill from Piazza Garibaldi. There is one bus daily to Grosseto

(€3.70, one hour), and two to Siena (€5.30, two hours) at 7.05am and 4.40pm. To get to to Volterra you'll need to change at Monterotondo Marittimo. **Massa Veternensis** (Piazza Garibaldi 18) sells both bus and train tickets.

CAR

There's a convenient car park (€1 per hour during the day, free at night) close to Piazza Garibaldi; head up the hill and you'll find it on your left. There's also a free car park at Piazzetta di Borgo further down the hill.

TRAIN

The nearest train station is in Follonica, 22km southwest of Massa, and it is served by a regular shuttle bus (€2.60, 25 minutes, 10 daily).

Vetulonia & Around

Originally an important Etruscan settlement, this windswept hilltop village 23km northwest of Grosseto was colonised by the Romans in 224 BC. It retains important traces of both eras.

Sights

★Museo Civico Archeologico 'Isidoro Falchi' MUSEUM
(museovetulonia@libero.it; Piazza Vatluna; adult/child €4.50/2.50; ⏲10am-1pm & 4-9pm Tue-Sun Jun-Sep, 10am-1pm & 2-5pm Tue-Sun Mar-May) Vetulonia's main piazza boasts spectacular views over the surrounding countryside, and is home to this small but extremely impressive museum bringing Etruscan history to life through its rich display of artefacts excavated from local Etruscan tombs and settlements. Highlights include the furnishings of the tomb of the *Fibula d'Oro* (Golden Brooch), including the precious brooch itself.

Sleeping

★Montebelli Agriturismo & Country Hotel AGRITURISMO €€
(☎05 6688 7100; www.montebelli.com; Località Molinetto Caldana; economy agriturismo r €68-145, standard agriturismo r €84-185, deluxe country hotel r €110-225; ⏲closed Jan-end Mar; P❄📶🏊) A country-club feel prevails on this sprawling biodynamic wine and olive-oil estate 10km north of Vetulonia. The facilities are sensational – tennis court, two swimming pools (one indoor, one outdoor), horse-riding lessons, restaurant (five-course dinner adult/child €30/15) and sleek health centre. Choose between cheaper (but more atmospheric) rooms in the *agriturismo* or deluxe air-con rooms in the modern 'country hotel'.

★Pieve di Caminino AGRITURISMO €€
(☎05 6456 9736; www.caminino.com; Via Provinciale di Peruzzo, Roccatederighi; s & d €110-130, d & tr €140-190, 4-person apt €150-250; P❄📶🏊) Few sleeping options can boast an historic atmosphere to equal this now-decommissioned 11th-century monastery 25km northeast of Vetulonia. Set on a 500-hectare estate planted with olive trees and vines, it offers six charmingly decorated suites and two apartments with panoramic terraces. Each has a sitting area and basic kitchen, four have wi-fi and three have air-conditioning. Breakfast (optional) costs €5 to €10.

Eating

★La Vecchia Hosteria TUSCAN €€
(☎05 6684 4980; www.lavecchiahosteria.it; Viale Marconi 249, Bagno di Gavorrano; meals €28; ⏲noon-2.30pm & 7-10pm Fri-Wed Feb-Dec) The unassuming exterior of this neighbourhood eatery on Bagno di Gavorrano's main street gives no clue as to the excellence of its kitchen. The handmade pasta is sensational (we highly recommend the *tortelli di ricotta*) and the rustic mains pack a flavoursome punch. You'll find the town 14km north of

ETRUSCAN EXCAVATIONS

Since 2009 a small team of archaeologists has been excavating the foundations of a 2300-year-old Etruscan *domus* (house) at the **Scavi di Città** (⏲10.10am-6.50pm Mon, Wed & Fri-Sun summer, 8.30am-4.50pm Mon, Wed & Fri-Sat winter) FREE located on the main road just below Vetulonia. Led by Dr Simona Rafanelli, the team has uncovered dry-stone walls, a brick floor, a small terracotta altar, plenty of amphorae and a small fragment of wall fresco. Dr Rafanelli claims that this is the most intact villa from the Etruscan-Roman era in existence and believes that there are other houses, shops and temples still to be discovered here.

Earlier excavations in the area include two (sadly empty) Etruscan tombs, situated a couple of kilometres further downhill and along a turn-off to the right.

Vetulonia, near the Parco Minerario Naturalistico Gavorrano.

Getting There & Away

Driving to Vetulonia, exit the SS1 at Montepescali/Braccagni (heading towards Braccagni) and follow the SP152 and SP72 uphill to the village.

CITTÀ DEL TUFA

The picturesque towns of Pitigliano, Sovana and Sorano form a triangle, enclosing a dramatic landscape where local buildings have been constructed from the volcanic porous rock called 'tufa' since Etruscan times. This area is called the Città del Tufa (City of the Tufa) or, less commonly, the Paese del Tufa (Land of the Tufa).

Pitigliano

POP 3840

Check your car mirrors before screeching to a halt and indulging in an orgy of photography on the approach to this spectacularly sited hilltop stronghold. Organically sprouting from a volcanic rocky outcrop towering over the surrounding country, Pitigliano is surrounded by gorges on three sides, constituting a natural bastion which is completed to the east by a man-made fort. Within the town, twisting stairways disappear around corners, cobbled alleys bend tantalisingly out of sight beneath graceful arches, and quaint stone houses are crammed next to each other in higgledy-piggledy fashion.

Originally built by the Etruscans, Pitigliano came under Roman rule before becoming a fiefdom of the wealthy Aldobrandeschi and Orsini families; the Orsinis, who were from Rome, enlarged the fortress, reinforced the defensive walls and built the imposing aqueduct. Their rule came to an end in 1608 when the town was absorbed into the grand duchy of Tuscany under Cosimo I de' Medici.

In 1944, 88 local residents were killed and many buildings were damaged during Allied bombings. A plaque near Piazza della Repubblica commemorates the victims.

Sights & Activities

La Piccola Gerusalemme MUSEUM

(Little Jerusalem; ☎05 6461 4230; www.lapiccolagerusalemme.it; Vicolo Manin 30; adult/reduced €4/3; ⏲10am-1.30pm & 2.30-6.30pm Sun-Fri summer, 10am-12.30pm & 3-5.30pm Sun-Fri winter)

VIE CAVE

There are at least 15 *vie cave* (sunken roads) hewn out of tufa in the valleys below Pitigliano. These enormous – up to 20m deep and 3m wide – passages are popularly believed to be sacred routes linking the necropolises and other sites associated with the Etruscan religious cult. A more mundane explanation is that these strange megalithic corridors were used to move livestock or as some kind of defence, allowing people to move from village to village unseen. Whatever the reason, every spring on the night of the equinox (19 March) there is a torch-lit procession down the Via Cava di San Giuseppe, which culminates in a huge bonfire in Pitigliano's Piazza Garibaldi. Known as the **Torciata di San Giuseppe**, the procession serves as a symbol of purification and renewal that marks the end of winter.

Two particularly good examples of *vie cave* – the Via Cava di Fratenuti and the Via Cava di San Giuseppe – are found 500m west of Pitigliano on the road to Sovana. Fratenuti has high vertical walls and Etruscan markings, and San Giuseppe passes the Fontana dell'Olmo, a fountain carved out of solid rock. From it stares the sculpted head of Bacchus, the Roman god of fruitfulness.

There's a fine walk from Pitigliano to Sovana (8km) that incorporates parts of the *vie cave*. For a description and map, go to www.trekking.it and download the pdf in the Maremma section. There's also an enjoyable 2km walk from the small stone bridge in the gorge below Sorano along the Via Cava San Rocco (2km) to the **Necropoli di San Rocco**, another Etruscan burial site.

The open-air **Museo Archeologico all'Aperto 'Alberto Manzi'** (Alberto Manzi Open-Air Archaeology Museum; Via Cava del Gradone, off SS74; adult/reduced €4/2; ⏲10am-5pm Wed-Mon Jun-Aug, 10am-5pm Sat & Sun Easter-Jun & Sep-Oct), south of Pitigliano on the road to Saturnia, contains sections of *vie cave* and several necropolises.

Head down Via Zuccarelli and turn left at a sign indicating 'La Piccola Gerusalemme' to visit this fascinating time capsule of Pitigliano's rich but sadly near-exinct Jewish culture. It incorporates a tiny, richly adorned synagogue (established in 1598 and one of only five in Tuscany), ritual bath, kosher butcher, bakery, wine cellar and dyeing workshops.

Interpretative panels recount the history: in the course of the 16th century, a Jewish community settled in Pitigliano, growing considerably when Pope Pius IV banned Jews from Rome in 1569. Under Medici rule, its members were moved into this tiny ghetto, where they remained until 1772. From then until well into the following century, the local community of about 400 flourished, forming the largest Jewish community in Italy and leading to the town being dubbed 'Little Jerusalem'. By the time the Fascists introduced the race laws in 1938, most Jews had moved away; only 80 or so were left and very few survived the war. Those that did survive were hidden from the Fascists by locals.

Palazzo Orsini MUSEUM

(www.palazzo-orsini-pitigliano.it; Piazza della Fortezza; adult/reduced €4/3; ⏰10am-1pm & 3-7pm Tue-Sun summer, 10am-1pm & 3-5pm Tue-Sun winter) Interlinked Piazza Petruccioli and Piazza Garibaldi provide a majestic walkway towards this 13th-century castle, which was enlarged by the Orsinis in the 16th century, became the residence of the local bishop and is now a museum. Its rooms are filled with an eclectic collection of artworks and ecclesiastic oddments from churches in the diocese.

Museo Civico Archeologico di Pitigliano MUSEUM

(Piazza della Fortezza; adult/child €3/2; ⏰10am-5pm Mon, Thu & Fri, to 6pm Sat & Sun Jun-Aug, 10am-5pm Sat & Sun Easter-May) Accessed via a stone staircase opposite the entrance to Palazzo Orsini, this small but well-run museum has a rich display of finds from local Etruscan sites. Highlights include some huge intact *bucchero* (black earthenware pottery) urns dating from the 6th century BC and a collection of charming pinkish-cream clay oil containers in the form of small deer.

Festivals & Events

Wines, including the town's signature Bianco di Pitigliano, a dry and lively white varietal, are celebrated each year over the first weekend in September at **Settembre diVino – Festa delle Cantine** (Festival of the Wine Cellars). At this time, *cantine* (cellars) in the town and surrounding areas are open for tastings. Check www.comune.pitigliano.gr.it for details.

> **COMBINED TICKET**
>
> If you're keen to investigate the area's Etruscan heritage, buy the **combined ticket** (adult/child €6/3) giving entry to both the Museo Civico Archeologico di Pitigliano and the Museo Archeologico all'Aperto 'Alberto Manzi' (p242) outside town.

Sleeping

Il Tufo Rosa PENSION €

(☎05 6461 7019; www.iltuforosa.com; Piazza Petruccioli 97-101; s €42-48, d €55-75; ❄📶) The owner of this old-fashioned *pensione* is very proud of her spick-and-span rooms, each of which is individually decorated and named after an Aldobrandeschi, Orsini or Medici countess. The rooms are located in an old bastion of the fortress on Piazza Petruccioli, conveniently near the town's main bus stop. No breakfast is offered, and air-con is only available in a few rooms.

★**Le Camere del Ceccottino** PENSION €€

(☎05 6461 4273; www.ceccottino.com; Via Roma 159; r €80-150; ❄📶) Owned and operated by the extremely helpful Chiara and Alessandro, who live on-site and also run a nearby *osteria* and *enoteca* (wine bar) of the same name, this *pensione* boasts an excellent location near the *duomo* and four immaculately maintained and well-equipped rooms. Opt for the superior or prestige room if possible, as the standard versions are slightly cramped. No breakfast.

Eating & Drinking

Enoteca La Corte del Ceccottino WINE BAR €

(Via Vignoli; plates from €8; ⏰variable hours Fri-Wed mid-Mar–mid-Jan) This sunken courtyard is an atmospheric spot to sample a glass or two of the local vino, accompanied by a simple antipasto plate or a bowl of pasta.

La Rocca WINE BAR €

(Piazza della Repubblica 92; panino €3.50, meals €24; ⏰10am-11pm Tue-Sun) Generous pourings of local wine and *prodotti tipici* (typical local products), including rustic pastas, antipasti platters and *panini* stuffed with pecorino cheese and cured meats, are on offer at this cavernous wine bar, cafe and restaurant.

★**Il Tufo Allegro** TRADITIONAL ITALIAN €€
(☎05 6461 6192; www.iltufoallegro.com; Vicolo della Costituzione 5; meals €35; ⊙noon-1.30pm Thu-Mon & 7.30-9.30pm Wed-Mon Mar-Dec) The aromas emanating from the kitchen door off Via Zuccarelli should be enough to draw you down the stairs and into the cosy dining rooms, which are carved out of tufa. Chef Domenico Pichini offers two menus – one traditional and one modern – and all of his creations rely heavily on local produce for inspiration. It's near Piccola Gerusalemme.

Hostaria del Ceccottino TRADITIONAL ITALIAN €€
(☎05 6461 4273; www.ceccottino.com; Piazza San Gregorio VII 64; meals €40; ⊙noon-2.30pm & 7.30-10pm mid-Mar–mid-Jan, closed Thu Oct-May) Nestled in the shadow of the town's Baroque *duomo*, Ceccottino subscribes to both the Slow Food philosophy and the Km0 movement. It specialises in beef from certified local Chianina and Maremmana cows, but there are also excellent vegetarian options (especially pasta) on offer. Tables on the piazza are hotly contested during summer.

OFF THE BEATEN TRACK

SOCIETÀ AGRICOLA TERENZI

Awarded the prestigious 'Emerging Winery of the Year' accolade in Gambero Rosso's 2013 *Vini d'Italia* (Wines of Italy) guide, this **wine estate** (☎05 6459 9601; www.terenzi.eu; Località Montedonico, Scansano) is located on a scenic road just outside the town of Scansano, a 50-minute drive from Pitigliano on a secondary route to Grosseto. It's best known for its Morellino di Scansano DOCG, a ruby-red Sangiovese with berry and violet overtones that can be tasted over a meal at the winery's **restaurant** (⊙noon-3pm Easter-Dec) or purchased at its **cantina** (⊙8.30am-1pm & 2-5.30pm Mon-Fri, 9am-2pm & 6-8pm Sat, 9am-noon Sun). There's even a **locanda** (d €110-155, ste €140-175; P ❄ 📶 🏊) for travellers wanting to soak up the wonderful views and wine on offer here over the course of a few days.

Information

The **tourist office** (☎05 6461 7111; www.comune.pitigliano.gr.it; Piazza Garibaldi 12; ⊙10am-12.20pm & 3.30-6pm Tue-Sat summer, 10am-12.30pm & 2.30-5pm Fri & Sat, 10am-12.30pm Sun winter) is in the piazza just inside the Old City's main gate.

Getting There & Away

BUS

Rama Mobilità (☎199 848787; www.ramamobilita.it) buses travel between Via Santa Chiara, just off Piazza Petruccioli, and Grosseto four times daily (€5.80, two hours). There's also one daily service to Siena (€8.50, three hours), four services to Sorano (€1.35, 10–20 minutes) and one service to Sovana (€1.35, 10–20 minutes). Buses don't usually operate on Sundays. Buy tickets at **Bar Guastini** in Piazza Petruccioli.

CAR

There are plenty of free car parks around town; look for white lines. Alternatively, the car park near Piazza Petruccioli charges €0.50 per hour from 8am to 1pm and from 3pm to 8pm.

Sovana

The main attractions at this postcard-pretty town are a cobbled main street that dates from Roman times, two austerely beautiful Romanesque churches and a museum showcasing a collection of ancient gold coins.

Sights

Duomo CATHEDRAL
(Concattedrale dei Santi Pietro e Paolo; ⊙10am-1pm & 2.30-6pm) Built over a 200-year period starting in the 1100s, this Romanesque cathedral was commissioned by local boy-made-big Pope Gregory VII (Hildebrand of Sovana; c 1015–85). Its strangely positioned doorway is decorated with carvings of people, animals and plants, and its huge interior has a beauty that owes nothing to artworks and everything to the genius of its architect.

Museo di San Mamiliano MUSEUM
(Piazza del Pretorio; adult/child €4/2; ⊙10am-1pm & 3-7pm Thu-Tue summer, daily in Aug, to 6pm Oct, 10am-1pm & 2-5pm Sat & Sun Nov & Dec) In 2004, archaeologists excavating beneath the ruined 9th-century Church of St Mamiliano made the discovery of a lifetime – a cache of 498 gold coins that had been buried in a small vase 2.44m under the church floor in the 5th century AD. Most are now displayed

in this small museum of Roman times, which occupies the restored church.

Santa Maria Maggiore CHURCH
(Piazza Pretorio) Designed in a Romanesque-Gothic transitional style, this church is notable for the 16th-century frescoes in the apse and an unusual and quite lovely stone ciborium (vaulted canopy over the altar) dating from the 9th century.

Eating

La Tavernetta TRATTORIA €
(Via del Pretorio 3; meals €20, pizzas €4-7; ⊙daily summer, Wed-Mon winter) Serving traditional Maremmese dishes all day and pizzas from its wood-fired oven at night, this casual eatery near the tourist office is a safe choice for a simple meal.

Information

The extremely helpful **tourist office** (☎05 6461 4074; ⊙10am-1pm & 3-7pm Fri-Wed summer only) is in the Palazzo Pretorio on the main piazza.

Getting There & Away

Rama Mobilità (p244) buses travel to/from Pitigliano (€1.35, 10–20 minutes, once daily) and Sorano (€1.35, 15 minutes, once or twice daily).

The car park at the entrance to town charges €0.50 per hour.

Around Sovana

Tuscany's most significant Etruscan tombs are found within the **Parco Archeologico 'Città del Tufa'** (Necropoli di Sovana; www.leviecave.it; €5; ⊙10am-7pm summer, 10am-5pm Sat & Sun Nov & Mar), 1.5km east of town. Interpretative panels in Italian and English impart interesting information about the site.

There are four tombs in total. The **Tomba dei Demoni Alati** (Tomb of the Winged Demons) was discovered in 2004 and features a headless recumbent figure in terracotta. The carving of a sea demon with huge wings that was the original centrepiece of the tomb is now protected in a roofed enclosure nearby. The **Tomba Ildebranda**, named after Gregory VII, still bears traces of its carved columns and stairs and is the park's headline exhibit. The **Tomba del Tifone** (Tomb of the Typhoon) is about 300m down a trail running alongside a rank of tomb facades cut from the rock face. Two arresting lengths of *via cave* (one known as 'Cavone' and the other 'Poggio Prisca') are nearby.

> **COMBINED TICKET**
>
> If you're planning to visit the Museo di San Mamiliano, the Parco Archeologico 'Città del Tufa' outside town and the Fortezza Orsini in Sorano, a **combined ticket** (adult/child €10/5) will save you money.

On the opposite side of the site is the **Tomba della Sirena** and another *via cava* ('San Sebastiano'), which was closed due to safety concerns at the time of research.

At the **Area Archeologica di Vitozza** (⊙24hr) FREE, due east of the village and signposted from the main square, you will find more than 200 rock caves peppering a high rock ridge. One of the largest troglodyte dwellings in Italy, the complex was first inhabited in prehistoric times. To explore the site, you'll need two hours and sturdy walking shoes.

Sorano

POP 3590

Sorano's setting isn't quite as dramatic as Pitigliano's, but it comes pretty close. Astride a rocky outcrop, its weather-worn stone houses are built along a ridge overlooking the Lente gorge and river. Below the ridgeline are *cantine* (cellars) dug out of tufa, as well as a series of terraced gardens, many hidden from public view.

Sights & Activities

Fortezza Orsini FORT
(☎05 6463 3767; admission €4; ⊙10am-1pm & 3-7pm Tue-Sun summer (open daily Aug), to 6pm Oct, 10am-1pm & 2-5pm Sat & Sun Nov) Standing sentinel over the town, this massive fortress was built in the 11th century and added to over the centuries. It has two bastions connected by sturdy walls and surrounded by a dry moat. The highlight of any visit is undoubtedly a guided tour of the subterranean passages (11am and 2pm).

Sleeping

★**Sant'Egle** AGRITURISMO €€
(☎34 8888 4810; www.santegle.it; Case Sparse Sant'Egle 18; d €110, ste €160; P ☎) Atmosphere-laden rooms, a pretty garden setting and a strong commitment to sustainability make Sant'Egle a great choice. Occupying a

TERME DI SATURNIA

The sulphurous thermal baths at **Terme di Saturnia** (☎05 6460 0111; www.termedisaturnia.it; day admission €44, after 3pm €39; ⊙9.30am-7.30pm summer, to 5.30pm winter) are 2.5km downhill from the village of the same name, which is 35km from Sorano and 26km from Pitigliano. You can happily do as the Romans did and spend a whole day dunking yourself in the hot pools and indulging in spa treatments at this luxury resort, or you can take the econo-bather option and avail yourself of the waters running parallel to the road for several hundred metres, starting just south of the Terme di Saturnia turn-off. Look for the telltale sign of other bathers' cars parked on the road, then forage down the dirt path until you find a suitable spot of gratis cascading water, with temperatures at a constant 37.5°C. Another alternative is to overnight in the **Hotel Saturno Fontepura** (☎05 6460 1313; www.hotelsaturnofontepura.com; r €130-180; P ❄ 📶 ≋), a spa resort with its own thermal pool. It's on the highway overlooking the *terme* (thermal baths).

meticulously restored 17th-century customs house on an organic farm between Sorano and Pitigliano, it offers attractive rooms and a restaurant serving dinners (€30) featuring home-grown fruit and vegetables, handmade pasta and bread and free-range meats. Mountain bikes are available for guests' use.

Hotel della Fortezza HOTEL €€
(☎05 6463 3549; www.fortezzahotel.it; Piazza Cairoli 5; d €75-140, ste €115-160; P) Fancy the idea of sleeping in a medieval castle? If so, this comfortable hotel inside one of the fortress' bastions is just what you're looking for. Many of its 16 rooms have spectacular views, but the best is undoubtedly the massive 'La Torre' (Tower) suite.

Drinking

Cantina L'Ottava Rima WINE BAR
(www.cantinaottavarima.com; Via del Borgo 25; ⊙noon-3pm & 6pm-midnight summer, 6pm-midnight Thu & noon-3pm & 6pm-midnight Fri-Sun winter) Carved out of the tufa, this casual *cantina* (wine bar) on a terraced walkway is a great place to sample local wines, micobrewed beers and simple dishes (antipasto plates €12) that highlight quality Maremmese produce. It's the best of a lacklustre range of cafes/eateries in the town.

Information

The best **tourist office** (☎05 6463 3099; ⊙10am-1pm & 3-7pm Tue-Sun) is at the *fortezza;* a second branch in the centre of town isn't at all helpful.

Getting There & Away

Rama Mobilità (p244) buses travel to/from Pitigliano (€1.35, 10–20 minutes, four daily) and Sovana (€1.35, 15 minutes, one daily).

The car park outside the Town Hall charges €0.50 per hour from 8am to 1pm and from 3pm to 8pm daily. Parking at the *fortezza* is free.

THE BASSA MAREMMA

The Bassa (Lower) Maremma starts at Grosseto and travels along the coast, incorporating the peninsula of Monte Argentario and the Parco Regionale della Maremma.

Grosseto

POP 78,500

Poor Grosseto. Its uninviting name, unattractive surrounds and lack of headline sites lead to it being ignored by most tourists, relegated to a mere navigational marker for travellers taking the coastal highway south to Rome. However, like all Tuscan cities it has a distinct character and is worth a short stop.

One of the last Sienese-dominated towns to fall into Medici hands (in 1559), Grosseto's bastions, fortress, and hexagonal-shaped, 2.5km-long walls were raised by the Florentines in order to protect what was then an important grain and salt depot for the grand duchy. These days the city is the provincial capital of the Maremma and its *centro storico* (historic centre) is one of the rare places in Tuscany where the oft-proclaimed 'no car zone' means almost that, making it a perfect place to wander during the day and to experience the *passeggiata* (evening stroll) along Corso Carducci.

The city is renowned for its heavy rainfalls in November, which have caused catastrophic floods in the past.

Sights & Activities

Cattedrale di San Lorenzo CATHEDRAL

(Piazza del Duomo; 7.30am-noon & 3.30-7pm) Grosseto's late-13th-century *duomo* has a distinctive Sienese character and a particularly beautiful rose window. The building has been altered over time, with much of the facade renewed along neo-Romanesque lines during the 19th century. Inside, look for the the *Madonna delle Grazie* in the left transept, part of a larger painting by Sienese artist Matteo di Giovanni.

Also notable are the baptismal font, which dates from 1470, and the two 15th-century stained-glass windows depicting saints.

Museo Archeologico e d'Arte della Maremma MUSEUM

(Piazza Baccarini 3; adult/reduced €5/2.50; 10am-5.30pm Tue-Sat, later in summer) Grosseto's major tourist drawcard, this complex houses an archaeological museum on the ground floor and a museum of ecclesiastical art upstairs. On show are Etruscan and Roman artefacts unearthed from Roselle, Vetulonia and other Etruscan sites, as well as a collection of paintings from the 13th to the 17th centuries.

Festivals & Events

Grosseto's patron saint, St Lawrence, is celebrated at the **Festa di San Lorenzo** held on August 9th and 10th each year.

Sleeping

There are very few decent accommodation options in Grosseto, so most visitors choose to stay in nearby *agriturismi*. The only decent budget option is a B&B close to Caffè Ricasoli and is thus too noisy to recommend.

Grand Hotel Bastiani HOTEL €€

(05 642 00 47; www.hotelbastiani.com; Piazza Gioberti 64; s from €80, d from €118, ste from €178;) This old-fashioned hotel is located just inside the main gate into the *centro storico,* conveniently close to a public car park. Housed within a grand old building complete with a *Gone with the Wind*–style dance-down-me staircase, it offers comfortable if slightly faded rooms, efficient and friendly service, and a lavish breakfast buffet.

Eating & Drinking

★**Grantosco** TUSCAN €€

(05 642 60 27; www.grantosco.it; Via Solferino 4; meals €35; 7-10pm Mon, noon-2.30pm & 7-10pm Tue-Sat, noon-2.30pm Sun) Succulent meat dishes including Maremmese beef, *cinta senese* (Tuscan pork), and *cinghiale* (wild boar) marinated in Morellino di Scansano wine are the show-stoppers on the menu at this restaurant and wine bar, but the pastas and desserts are pretty damn fine, too. Walls adorned with bottles of wine, high ceilings and warm lighting provide an atmospheric setting.

The bar and streetside tables are popular for early-evening *aperitivi* (predinner drinks accompanied by cocktail snacks); at dinner, it's advisable to book a table.

Rosso e Vino WINE BAR €€

(Piazza Pacciardi 2; meals €38, glass of wine €5-10; noon-2.30pm & 8-10pm Thu-Tue, wine bar 5pm-late, closed Jul) Owned by Fattoria Le Pupille, a highly regarded local winery, this sleek *enoteca* is Grosseto's style hub and a great place to enjoy a meal or *aperitivo*. The restaurant seating spills out onto Piazza Pacciardi, and the *enoteca* entrance is around the corner on Via Garibaldi. An excellent wine list is complemented by modern Tuscan cuisine.

Caffè Ricasoli BAR, CAFE

(www.caffericasoli.it; Strada Ricasoli 20; 8am-midnight Mon-Sat;) The city's nightlife revolves around this pumping bar-cafe just off Piazza Dante Alighieri. It offers free wi-fi, has a DJ spinning Italian pop towards the end of the week and hosts occasional poetry readings and live music – check the website for details.

Shopping

Dolci Tradizioni dalla Maremma Toscana FOOD

(Via Garibaldi 60; daily) Specialising in local delicacies including *lo sfratto,* a traditional Jewish pastry made with honey and walnuts, this wonderful *pasticceria* (pastry shop) opposite the Medici fortress makes all of its products by hand and sells them in beautifully wrapped packages.

Information

There is a **tourism information point** (05 6448 8208; www.turismoinmaremma.it; Corso Carducci 1; 9am-1pm & 4-7pm Mon-Thu, 9am-1pm & 5-8pm Fri & Sat) close to the *duomo*.

Getting There & Away

BUS

Buses usually leave from the train station. There is only one direct bus daily to Massa Marittima

(€3.70, one hour). Other destinations include Porto Santo Stefano (€3.70, one hour, three daily), Siena (€7.80, 80 minutes, 13 daily) and Pitigliano (€5.80, two hours, four daily). Buy tickets at the **Tiemme office** near the train station.

CAR

A Limited Traffic Zone (ZTL) applies in the *centro storico*. There's plenty of paid car parking surrounding the city walls; the most convenient is at Porta Corsica, next to the city gate on Viale Zimenes near Piazza Lamaremma (per hour €1).

TRAIN

The main coastal train line runs between Rome and Pisa via Grosseto (Intercity €21.50, two hours) and Livorno. A ticket from Grosseto to Livorno (75 minutes) or Pisa (90 minutes) costs €16.50. The high-speed *Frecciabianca* runs between Rome and Genoa, stopping at Grosseto (€27.50, 90 minutes). A ticket from Grosseto to Livorno (one hour) or Pisa (75 minutes) costs €21.50. There are also eight direct *regionale* (slow local train) services to Siena daily (€9, 90 minutes).

Around Grosseto

Riserva Naturale Provinciale Diaccia Botrona PARK

(☎05 642 02 98; www.maremma-online.it) The marshes surrounding the coastal town of Castiglione della Pescaia are an important shelter for migrating birds, and this 1272ha nature reserve off the SS322 is a wonderful stop for those keen on spending an afternoon exploring the flat yet fascinating local landscape. Daily **boat tours** (adult/child €12/6; ⊙5pm & 6.30pm Tue-Sun mid-Jun–mid-Sep) enable visitors to spot waterfowl, herons, flamingos and other species; advance bookings recommended.

The boat tours depart from the **visitor centre** (multimedia display adult/reduced €3.50/2.50; ⊙3.30-8.30pm Tue-Sun mid-Jun–mid-Sep, 3.30pm-sunset Thu-Sun mid-Sep–mid-Jun), which occupies the **Casa Rossa Ximenes**, a handsome sluice-house commissioned by Grand Duke Pietro Leopoldo I of Lorraine in the mid-18th century as part of his huge project to reclaim the marshes for agriculture and at the same time reduce the horrifyingly high levels of malaria that existed in the region. Inside the building there is a multimedia display (in Italian only) about the reserve and its wildlife, the building and the history of the reclamation project.

Guided mountain-**bike tours** (adult/child €8/5) of the reserve depart from the nearby town of Castiglione della Pescaia from late May to early October; again, advance booking is essential.

Roselle ARCHAEOLOGICAL SITE

(SS 223; adult/reduced €4/2; ⊙8.30am-7pm May-Aug, to 6.30pm Mar, Apr, Sep & Oct, to 5.30pm Nov-Feb) Less than 7km northeast of Grosseto's *centro storico*, Roselle (Rusellae) was a middle-ranking Etruscan town populated as early as the 7th century BC. It came under Roman control in the 3rd century BC. Although there are no great monuments left standing, the site retains its Roman defensive walls, an oddly elliptical amphitheatre, traces of houses, the forum and streets.

Parco Regionale della Maremma

This spectacular **regional park** (www.parco-maremma.it; adult/reduced €10/5, mountain bike hire per day €15) incorporates the Uccellina mountain range, a 600-hectare pine forest, marshy plains and a 20km stretch of unspoiled coastline. The main **visitor centre** (☎05 6440 7098; Via del Bersagliere 7-9; ⊙8.30am-6pm mid-Jun–mid-Sep, 8.30am-5pm mid-Sep–mid-Nov, 8.30am-2pm mid-Nov–mid-Jun) is in Alberese, on the park's northern edge. A smaller **visitor centre** (☎05 6488 7173; Via Nizza 12; ⊙9am-noon & 3-5pm Jul & Aug) adjoins the **Talamone Aquarium** at the park's southern extremity (the aquarium showcases the local lagoon environment and works to protect local turtles).

Park access is limited to 13 signed walking trails, varying in length from 2.5km to 13km; the most popular is A2 ('Le Torri'), a 5.8km walk to the beach. The entry fee is paid at the visitor centres and there's a park-operated bus that can transport you from the Alberese visitor centre to your chosen route. From 15 June to 15 September the park can only be visited on a guided tour due to possible bushfire threat. At the time of research these tours were being conducted regularly in Italian, as well as in German (on Wednesdays from mid-June to mid-September at 4pm), but it is wise to call ahead to check tour language and time.

As well as the walking trails, there are four guided mountain-bike tours (€10 to €15 plus bike hire, two to six hours) and a guided 2½-hour canoe tour (adult/child €16/10); book these at the Alberese visitor centre. A number of private operators offer horse and pony treks through the park – contact **Il Gelsomino** (☎347 774 64 76; www.ilgelsomino.com; Via Strada del Barbicato 4, Alberese) or **Circolo Ippico Uccellina** (☎334 979 71 81; www.circoloippicouccellina.it; Località Collecchio 38, Magliano in Toscana); both offer accommodation and horse-riding treks and lessons.

There are free tastings of local food and wine (mid-June to mid-September) in the upstairs *degustazion* (tasting) room at the Alberese visitor centre, conduced by the Consorzio Naturalmente Toscana, an association of local farms. Opposite the centre are a bar-cafe and **I Briganti al Parco**, a small and friendly *enoteca* with variable opening hours where you can grab a sandwich, *antipasto* plate or pasta accompanied by a glass of locally produced wine.

Parts of the regional park are farmed as they have been for centuries, mainly to graze the famous Maremmana breed of cattle. The huge **Agienza Regionale Agricola di Alberese** (☎05 6440 7180; www.alberese.com; Via della Spergolaia) farm operation produces beef, wine, olive oil and its own organic pasta and is a regional headquarters for the Slow Food organisation. It offers a **farm experience** (☎05 6440 7100; €25; ⊙10am-1pm Thu Jul & Aug, other times by reservation), including an introduction to the work of the Maremma's famed *butteri* (traditional cowboys) and tastings of farm produce. Experienced horse riders can also sign up for work experience with a *buttero* (€50; daily from 7am to noon). The farm's **fattoria** (farmhouse; Via dell'Artigliere 4; ⊙8.30am-12.30pm & 4.30-7.30pm Tue & Thu-Sun), located near the Alberese visitor centre, sells its own products and those of other Slow Food–accredited producers. It's a great place to stock up on supplies if you're self-catering (its Morellino di Scansano – a robust red wine – costs a mere €2 or so per litre, so bring a couple of bottles to fill!).

The farm offers accommodation at the **Villa Fattoria Granducale** (☎05 6440 7100; www.alberese.com/fattoria-granducale; B&B d & tr €90-100, self-contained apt €75-125 (both 2-night min)), a 15th-century villa. It also rents out simple apartments in surrounding farm buildings; check the website for details.

Orbetello

POP 14,700

Set on a balance-beam isthmus running through a lagoon south of the Parco Regionale della Maremma, Orbetello is a relatively laid-back seaside destination. Its modest main attraction is the **cathedral** (Piazza della Repubblica; ⊙9am-noon & 3-6pm), which has retained its 14th-century Gothic facade despite being remodelled in the Spanish style during the 16th century. Other reminders of the Spanish garrison that was stationed in the city for nearly 150 years include the **viceroy's residence** on Piazza Eroe dei Due Mondi, the **fort** and the **city walls**, parts of which are the original Etruscan fortification.

The best place for observing bird life on Orbetello Lagoon (where as many as 140 species have been identified) is at the **L'Oasi WWF di Orbetello** (www.wwf.it; SS Aurelia, Località Ceriolo; adult/reduced €5/3; ⊙guided visits 9.30am & 1.30pm Sat & Sun Sep-Apr) north of town, which is owned and operated by the Italian branch of the WWF.

OFF THE BEATEN TRACK

MAGLIANO IN TOSCANA

A 23km drive inland from Orbetello will get you to this hilltop town, fortified by monumental walls built between the 14th and 16th centuries. There's not much to see other than the Romanesque churches of San Martino and San Giovanni Battista (the latter with a remodelled Renaissance facade), but the trip is well rewarded by lunch in the pretty sheltered garden at **Antica Trattoria Aurora** (☎05 6459 2030; Via Chiasso Lavagnini 12/14; meals €45; ⊙noon-2.30pm & 7.30-10pm Thu-Tue Mar-Dec), a restaurant serving excellent modern Tuscan cuisine. Those after a more casual, less expensive lunch can eat in the restaurant's attached *cantina* (dishes €5 to €12). To get to the town, take the Albinia exit off the SS1 and then turn left onto the SS323.

Monte Argentario

POP 12,500

Once an island, this rugged promontory came to be linked to the mainland by an accumulation of sand that is now the isthmus of Orbetello. Further sandy bulwarks form the Tombolo della Giannella and Tombolo di Feniglia to the north and south. They enclose a lagoon that is now a protected **nature reserve**. Sadly, overdevelopment has spoiled the northern side of the promontory, particularly around the crowded harbour of

OFF THE BEATEN TRACK

GIARDINO DEI TAROCCHI

Twenty-two oversized Gaudí-influenced sculptures tumble down a hillside at this fantastic **sculpture garden** (www.nikidesaintphalle.com; Località Garavicchio-Capalbio; adult/reduced €12/7; ⌚2.30-7.30pm summer) created by Franco-American artist Niki de Saint Phalle (1930–2002). On a theme-park scale, the whimsical, mosaic-covered sculptures skilfully merge with the surrounding nature, creating what the artist described as a 'garden of joy'. This colossal effort depicts the main players from the tarot card pack – the Moon, the Fool, Justice, the Falling Tower etc – and include one used by De Saint Phalle as a home during the garden's construction. Sculptor Jean Tinguely contributed sculptural elements to many of the figures and the visitor centre was designed by Swiss architect Mario Botta. Your interest in divination notwithstanding, these pleasing exhibits transcend aesthetic leanings and are particularly popular with young children. To get here, take the Pescia Fiorentina exit from the SS1.

Porto Santo Stefano, a favourite weekend getaway for Romans in the summer. Ambitious hotel and restaurant prices make it poor value in the high season, and parking is cutthroat; we suggest visiting on a day trip and then hightailing it inland for accommodation options.

If you're driving, follow signs for the narrow and sometimes dangerously overcrowded **Via Panoramica**, a circular route offering great coastal views over the water to the hazy whaleback of the Isola de Giglio.

There are several good **beaches**, mainly of the pebbly variety, just to the east and west of Porto Santo Stefano.

On the less-crowded southern side of the promontory is **Porto Ercole**, a smaller and more attractive harbour nestled between three Spanish forts. Here you can wander the hillside *centro storico* past the sandwiched Chiesa di Sant'Erasmo and up towards the largest of the **fortresses**. Down by the water, the beach is relatively clean but is cluttered with deck chairs and umbrellas.

Eating & Drinking

★**Il Pellicano** GASTRONOMIC €€€
(☎05 6485 8275; www.pellicanohotel.com; Località Lo Sbarcatello, Porto Ercole; set menu €150; ⌚dinner daily summer) Proud possessor of two Michelin stars (one of only four such recipients in Tuscany), this classy restaurant at the five-star hotel of the same name specialises in seafood and has two outdoor terraces with spectacular views. There's also a more casual and slightly less expensive poolside grill and bar here that is open for both lunch and dinner.

Giulia CAFE
(Via del Molo 16/17, Porto Santo Stefano; ⌚6.30am-4am Tue-Sun, daily summer) Almost at the end of the *lungomare* (port promenade) and with outdoor seating, Porto Santo Sefano's best cafe is a great spot for a morning coffee, *panino* (sandwich) lunch or late-afternoon *aperitivo*.

Information

Orbetello tourist office (☎05 6486 0447; proorbet@ouverture.it; Piazza Giovanni Paolo II 2; ⌚9am-1pm & 4-8pm) Opposite the cathedral.

Porto Santo Stefano tourist office (☎05 6481 4208; info@infopointargentario.it; Piazzale Sant'Andrea; ⌚9am-1pm & 4-8pm) Appallingly located at the eastern end of the port.

Getting There & Away

Frequent **Rama Mobilità** (p244) buses connect most towns on Monte Argentario with central Orbetello (€2.60, 20 minutes) and continue to the train station. They also run to Grosseto (€3.70, one hour, up to four daily).

If driving, follow signs for Monte Argentario from the SS1, which connects Grosseto with Rome.

Eastern Tuscany

Includes ➡

Best Places to Eat

- ➡ Il Tirabusciò (p266)
- ➡ LAB Pasticceria (p258)
- ➡ Ristorante Da Ventura (p262)
- ➡ Ristorante La Nena (p259)
- ➡ Trattoria del Leone (p258)

Best Places to Stay

- ➡ Borgo Corsignano (p265)
- ➡ Casa Chilenne (p269)
- ➡ Relais Palazzo Magi (p262)
- ➡ Villa Fontelunga (p258)
- ➡ Villa Marsili (p269)

Why Go?

The eastern edge of Tuscany is beloved by local and international film directors, who have immortalised its landscape, medieval hilltop towns and laid-back locals in a range of critically acclaimed and visually splendid films. Despite this, the region is strangely bereft of foreign tourists (Cortona is a notable exception) and so offers uncrowded trails to those visitors who decide to devote a week or so to exploration here. The attractions are many and varied: spectacular mountain scenery and walks in the Casentino; magnificent art and architecture in the medieval cities of Arezzo, Sansepolcro and Cortona; one of Italy's most significant Catholic pilgrimage sites; and Tuscany's best *bistecca alla fiorentina* (chargrilled T-bone steak) in the Val di Chiana. Your travels may be solitary but they'll always be rewarding – a particularly unusual and felicitous combination.

Road Distances

	Assisi	Arezzo	Cortona	Sansepolcro
Arezzo	94			
Cortona	65	29		
Sansepolcro	76	38	52	
Poppi	132	36	62	71

DON'T MISS

Close to the Umbrian border and well off the well-trodden tourist trail, the city of Sansepolcro is known for its handmade lace, its preponderance of neighbourhood churches and its wonderful Museo Civico.

Best Museums

- Museo Civico, Sansepolcro (p259) Home to three magnificent paintings by Piero della Francesca.
- Museo Diocesano, Cortona (p268) Has a small but sensational collection of religious art.
- Casa Museo di Ivan Bruschi, Arezzo (p257) Showcases an antique dealer's eclectic personal collection.

Medieval Pageants

- Giostra del Saracino (p257), Arezzo
- Palio della Ballestra (p262), Sansepolcro
- Giostra dell'Archidado (p269), Cortona

Resources

- **Arezzo & surrounds** (www.benvenutiadarezzo.it)
- **The Casentino** (www.casentino.net)
- **Parco Nazionale delle Foreste Casentinesi, Monte Falterona e Campigna** (www.parcoforestecasentinesi.it)

Getting Around

Arezzo is on the Florence–Rome train line, as is Camucia, a 15-minute shuttle-bus ride from Cortona's historic centre. Regional rail lines link Arezzo with the Casentino, and Sansepolcro with Perugia. Buses in this part of Tuscany are few and far between – you can travel from Arezzo to Sansepolcro via Anghiari, or from Arezzo to Cortona via Castiglion Fiorentino, but that's about it. To explore the Casentino and Val di Chiana, you'll need a car.

THREE PERFECT DAYS

Day 1: Arezzo

Two major films are set in Eastern Tuscany's major city, Arezzo. Spend the day exploring the historic streets and piazzas where Roberto Benigni filmed scenes of *La vita è bella* (Life is Beautiful). On your wanders, pop into both the *duomo* and the Pieve di Santa Maria and be sure to pay homage to Piero della Francesca's genius by viewing his frescoes in the Basilica di San Francesco's Capella Bacci, where Anthony Minghella shot the most memorable scene of *The English Patient*.

Day 2: Della Robbia Trail

This famous family of sculptors took ceramics way beyond teacups in the 15th century, creating magnificent devotional sculptures for churches throughout Tuscany. Visit the medieval monasteries at Camaldoli and La Verna in the Parco Nazionale delle Foreste Casentinesi, Monte Falterona e Campigna to admire masterpieces in glazed terracotta by the most famous member of the family, Andrea (1435–1525).

Day 3: Val di Chiana

Home to apple orchards, olive groves and lush pastures where porcelain-white Chianina cattle graze, the huge Val di Chiana is worth exploring when travelling between Arezzo and Cortona, or from either town to central Tuscany. Make your way off the beaten track to visit hilltop towns such as Castiglion Fiorentino, Foiano della Chiana and Lucignano.

Off the Beaten Track

- History buffs will love the unspoiled medieval hilltop town of **Anghiari**, near Sansepolcro, where the famous battle of the same name occurred in 1440.
- To visit a typical Casentinesi hill town, head to unassuming **Bibbiena**, between Poppi and Arezzo.
- The town of **Stia**, in the Casentino, has a pretty setting on the Arno and is known for its fascinating wool-making heritage.

AREZZO

POP 98,000

Arezzo may not be a Tuscan centrefold, but those parts of its historic centre that survived merciless WWII bombings are as compelling as any destination in the region.

Once an important Etruscan trading post, Arezzo was later absorbed into the Roman Empire. A free republic as early as the 10th century, it supported the Ghibelline cause in the violent battles between pope and emperor and was eventually subjugated by Florence in 1384.

Today, the city is known for its churches, museums and cultural life. It's also known for its shopping – Arentini (residents of Arezzo) flock to the huge antiques fair held in Piazza Grande on the first weekend of every month, and love nothing more than combining the *passeggiata* with a spot of upmarket retail therapy on Corso Italia.

Sights & Activities

★Cappella Bacci CHURCH

(☎0575 35 27 27; www.pierodellafrancesca.it; Piazza San Francesco; adult/reduced €8/5; ⌚9am-6.30pm Mon-Fri, to 5.30pm Sat & 1-5.30pm Sun May-Aug; 9am-5.30pm Mon-Fri, to 5pm Sat & 1-5pm Sun Sep-Apr) Gracing the apse of the 14th-century **Basilica di San Francesco** is the Capella Bacci, a chapel housing one of the greatest works of Italian art, Piero della Francesca's fresco cycle of the *Legend of the True Cross*. Painted between 1452 and 1466, it relates in 10 episodes the story of the cross on which Christ was crucified.

This medieval legend is as entertaining as it is inconceivable. The illustrations follows the story of the tree that Seth plants on the grave of his father, Adam, and from which the True Cross is made. Another scene shows the long-lost cross being rediscovered by Helena, mother of the emperor Constantine; behind her, the city of Jerusalem is represented by a medieval view of Arezzo. Other scenes show the victory of Heraclius over the Persian king Khosrau, who had been accused of stealing the cross; Constantine sleeping in a tent on the eve of his battle with Maxentius; and Constantine carrying the cross into battle.

Two of the best-loved scenes depict the meeting of the Queen of Sheba and King Solomon. In the first half she is kneeling on a bridge over the Siloam River and meeting with the king; she and her attendants are depicted wearing rich Renaissance-style gowns. In the second half, King Solomon's palace seems to be modelled on the designs of notable architect Leon Battista Alberti.

Only 25 people are allowed into the chapel every half-hour (maximum 30-minute visit), so advance booking is recommended. The ticket office is down the stairs located at the basilica's entrance.

★Pieve di Santa Maria CHURCH

(Corso Italia 7; ⌚8.30am-12.30pm & 3-7pm May-Sep, to noon & 3-6pm Oct-Apr) This 12th-century church (Arezzo's oldest) has a magnificent Romanesque arcaded facade adorned with dozens of carved columns, each uniquely decorated. Above the central doorway are 13th-century carved reliefs known as the *Cyclo dei Mesi*, which represent the months of the year. January's figure has two faces: one looks back on the previous year and the other looks forward.

Inside, the undoubted highlight is Pietro Lorenzetti's polyptych, *Madonna and Saints* (1320–24), beneath the semidome of the apse. Below the altar is a 14th-century silver bust reliquary of the city's patron saint, San Donato. Other treasures include a 13th-century crucifix by Margarito di Arezzo, which hangs near the door to the sacristy, and a fresco by Andrea di Nerio (1331–69) on a column behind the alter (left-hand side) of Saints Francesco and Domenico.

Piazza Grande PIAZZA

This lopsided and steeply sloping piazza is located behind the *pieve* (rural church) and is overlooked at its upper end by the porticos of the **Palazzo delle Logge Vasariane**, completed in 1573. The church-like **Palazzo della Fraternità dei Laici** in the northwest corner was started in 1375 in the Gothic style and finished after the onset of the Renaissance.

In addition to being the venue for the famous Giostra del Saracino (p257), the piazza is the venue for Arezzo's famous antiques fair, one of the largest in Italy.

★Duomo di Arezzo CATHEDRAL

(Cattedrale di SS Donato e Pietro; Piazza del Duomo; ⌚7am-12.30pm & 3-6.30pm) Though construction started in the 13th century, Arezzo's *duomo* (cathedral) wasn't completed until the 15th century. In the northeast corner, to the left of the intricately carved main altar, is an exquisite fresco of *Mary Magdalene* (c 1459) by Piero della Francesca. Also notable are five splendid, glazed terracottas by Andrea della Robbia and his studio.

Eastern Tuscany Highlights

❶ Marvel at the frescoes in the Capella Bacci before joining the locals for a *passeggiata* (evening stroll) along fashionable Corso Italia in **Arezzo** (p253).

❷ Admire the work of Renaissance painter Piero della Francesca in his birthplace of **Sansepolcro** (p259).

❸ Explore a well-preserved medieval castle in the fortified hamlet of **Poppi** (p263).

❹ Commune with nature and a higher power when making a pilgrimage to two medieval monasteries located in the secluded setting of the **Parco Nazionale delle Foreste Casentinesi, Monte Falterona e Campigna** (p265).

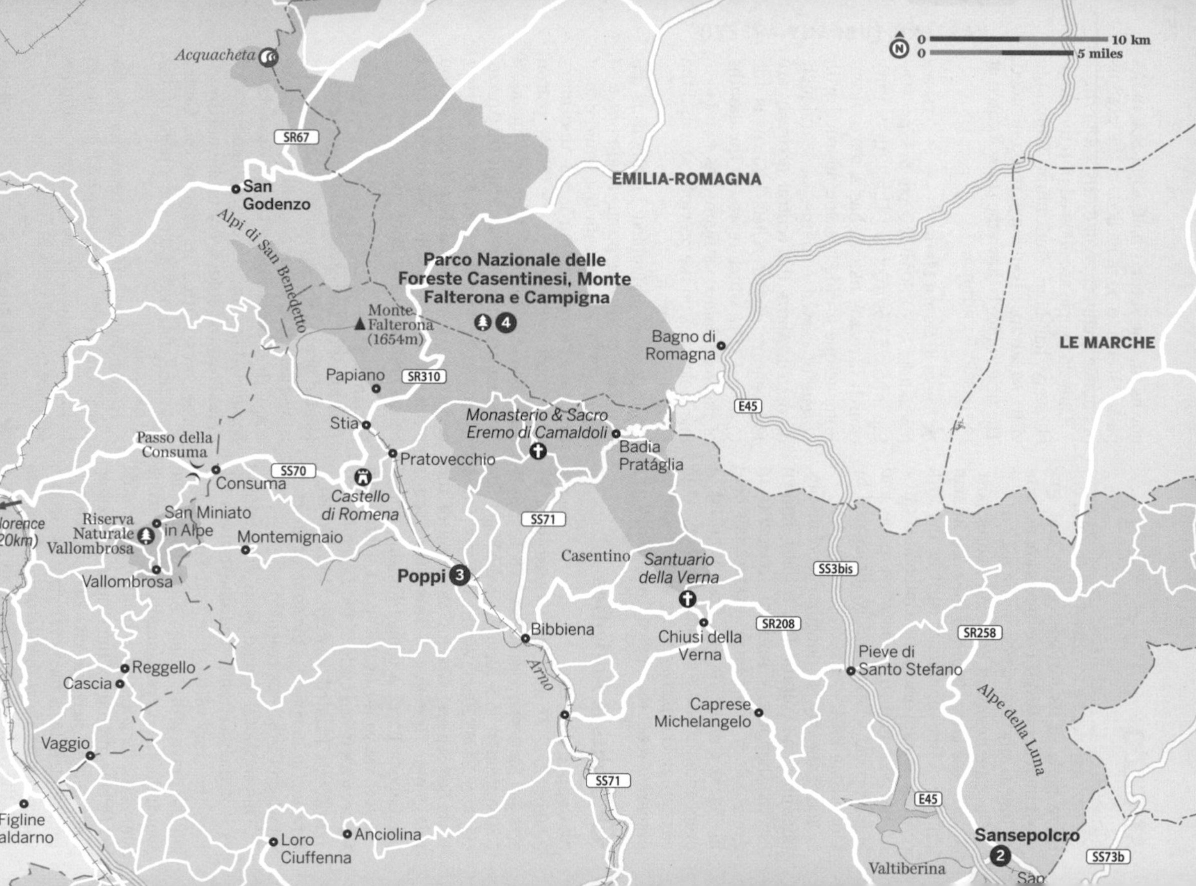

5 Laze away a couple of days visiting churches and museums in the spectacularly sited hilltop town of **Cortona** (p267).

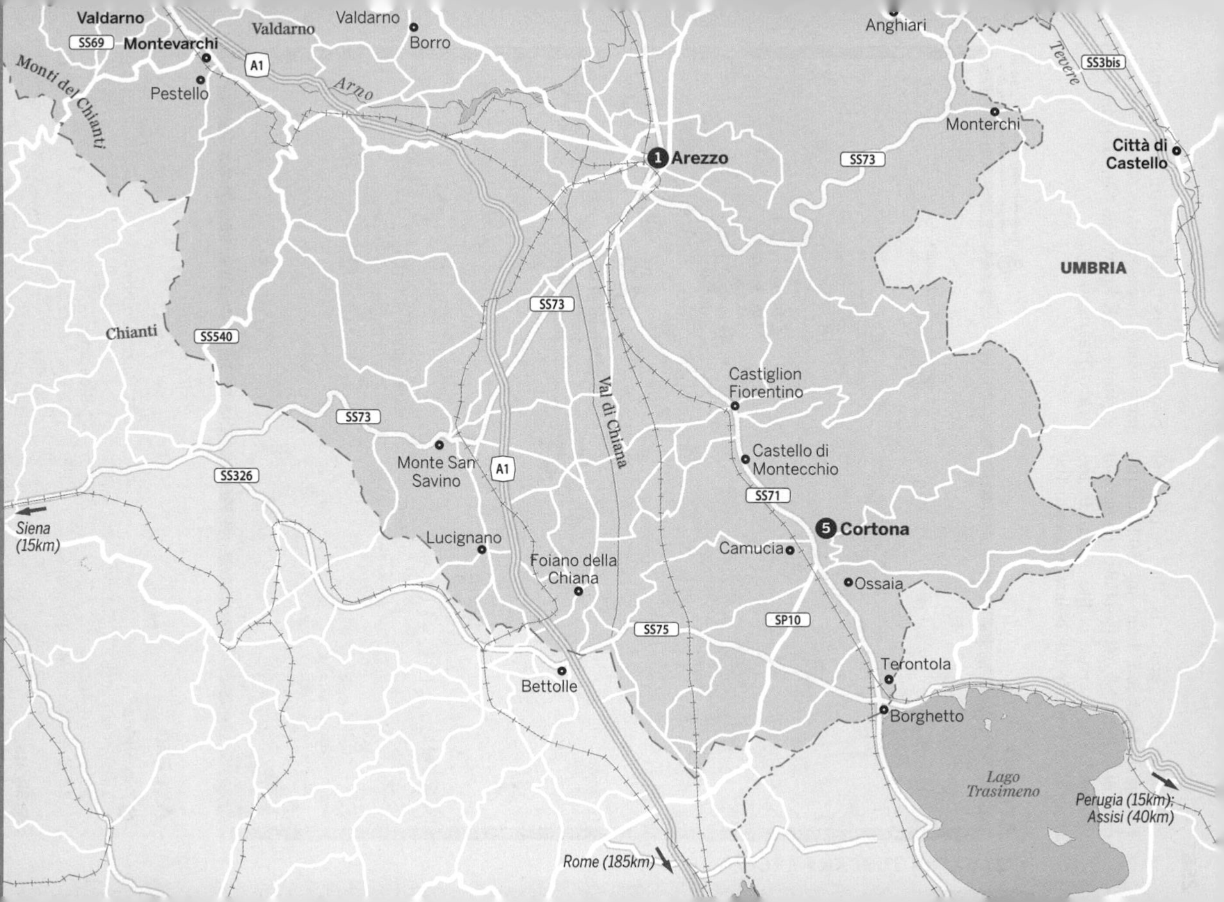

Behind the *duomo* is the pentagonal **Fortezza Medicea**, built in 1502 on the crest of one of Arezzo's two hills (the *duomo* was built on the crest of the other). In the early 14th century the hollow between the two hills was filled to form a large public park where horse-races were held; it's now a public park known as the **Giardino del Prato** (Prato Garden).

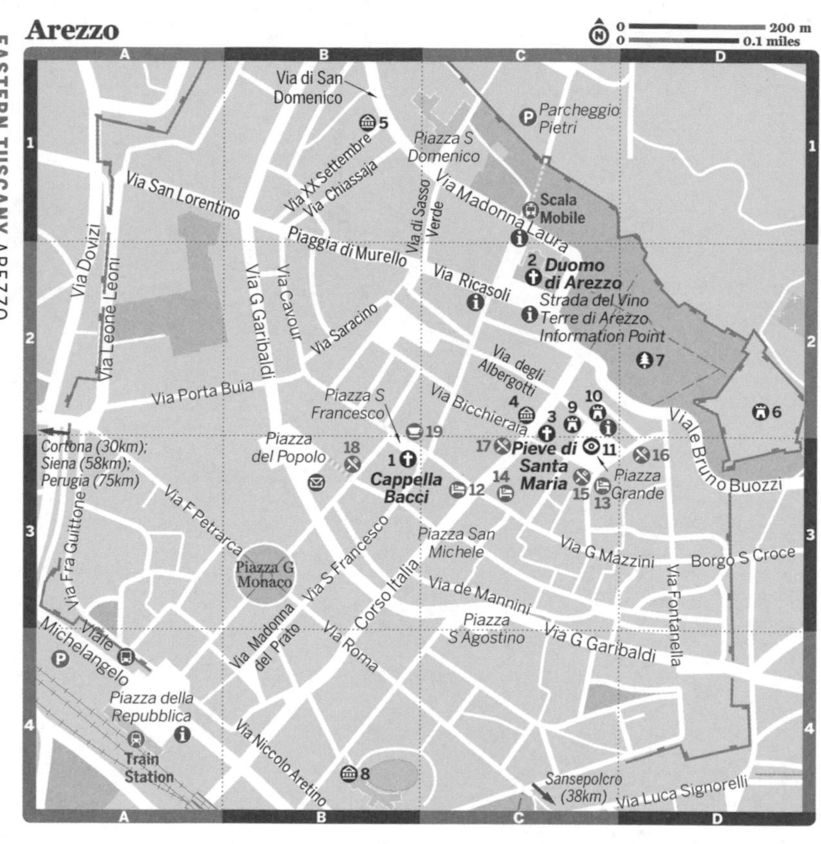

Arezzo

Top Sights

1 Cappella Bacci B3
2 Duomo di Arezzo C2
3 Pieve di Santa Maria C2

Sights

Basilica di San Francesco .... (see 1)
4 Casa Museo di Ivan Bruschi C2
5 Casa Vasari B1
6 Fortezza Medicea D2
7 Giardino del Prato D2
8 Museo Archeologico Nazionale 'Gaio Cilnio Mecenate' B4
9 Palazzo della Fraternità dei Laici C2
10 Palazzo delle Logge Vasariane C2
11 Piazza Grande C3

Sleeping

12 Graziella Patio Hotel C3
13 La Corte Del Re C3
14 Palazzo dei Bostoli C3

Eating

15 La Bottega di Gnicche C3
16 La Torre di Gnicche D3
17 LAB Pasticceria C3
18 Trattoria del Leone B3

Drinking & Nightlife

19 Caffè dei Costanti B2

Museo Archeologico Nazionale 'Gaio Cilnio Mecenate' MUSEUM

(Via Margaritone 10; adult/reduced/child €6/3/free; ⌚8.30am-7.30pm early Mar–mid-Jan, to 2pm mid-Jan–early Mar) Overlooking the remains of a Roman amphitheatre that once seated up to 10,000 spectators, this museum in a 14th-century convent building has a sizeable collection of Etruscan and Roman artefacts. The highlight is the *Cratere di Euphronios,* a large 6th-century-BC Etruscan vase decorated with vivid scenes showing Hercules in battle. It's in Room 6, upstairs.

Also of note is an exquisite tiny portrait of a bearded man; it's executed in chrysography, where a very fine sheet of gold is engraved and then encased between two pieces of glass. This dates from the second half of the 3rd century AD. It's in Room 2, upstairs.

Casa Museo di Ivan Bruschi MUSEUM

(www.fondazionebruschi.it; Corso Italia 14; adult/reduced €5/3; ⌚10am-6pm Tue-Sun late Mar–Oct, 10am-1pm & 2-6pm Tue-Sun Nov–late Mar) The 13th-century Palazzo del Capitano del Popolo opposite the *pieve* was restored in the 1960s by Ivan Bruschi, a wealthy antiques dealer. Since his death, the Palazzo has opened its doors as a private house museum showcasing Bruschi's eclectic personal collection of furniture, art, coins, jewellery, costumes and ceramics dating from the prehistoric, Etruscan, Greek, Roman, medieval and Renaissance periods. Admission is discounted to €1 if you have a ticket for the Cappella Bacci.

Casa Vasari MUSEUM

(Via XX Settembre 55; adult/reduced €4/2; ⌚9am-7pm Mon & Wed-Sat, to 1pm Sun) Built and sumptuously decorated by the Arezzo-born painter, architect and art historian Giorgio Vasari (1511–74), this small museum is where Vasari lived and worked, and where the original manuscript of his *Lives of the Most Excellent Painters, Sculptors and Architects* (1550) – still in print under the title *The Lives of the Artists* – is kept.

The most important room is the **Sala della Virtu** (Room of Virtue), which he decorated in 1548 while writing *Lives*. It features episodes in the lives of the most famous painters of antiquity. Vasari's contemporaries were celebrated in the **Camera della Fama e delle Art** (Room of Fame and Art), where the seven portraits include Michelangelo, Andrea del Sarto and – in a display of hubris – Vasari himself.

Ring the bell to be granted entrance.

MONEY SAVER

A combined ticket (€12) gives entry to the Cappella Bacci, Museo Archeologico Nazionale and Casa Vasari.

Tours

Two-hour guided English-language **walking tours** (☎0575 40 33 19, 334 3340608; www.centroguidearezzo.it; adult/child €10/free) are conducted every Thursday from 11am between May and October. Book ahead.

Festivals & Events

Fiera Antiquaria di Arezzo ANTIQUES

(Arezzo Antique Fair; www.arezzofieraantiquaria.org) Tuscany's most famous antiques fair is held in Piazza Grande on the last Saturday and first Sunday of every month.

Giostra del Saracino CULTURAL

(Joust of the Saracen; www.giostradelsaracino.arezzo.it; Piazza Grande) This medieval jousting competition is held in Piazza Grande on the third Saturday of June and first Sunday of September. It's the highlight of the year for the city's four *quartieri* (quarters), each of which puts forward a team of 'knights'.

Sleeping

Palazzo dei Bostoli B&B €

(☎334 1490558; www.palazzobostoli.it; 2nd fl, Via G Mazzini 1; s/d/tr €50/70/90; ❄📶) This old-fashioned place offers five simple but comfortable rooms in a 13th-century *palazzo* close to Piazza Grande. The breakfast – a coffee and *cornetto* (croissant) – is served at Bar Stefano in nearby Corso Italia.

Graziella Patio Hotel BOUTIQUE HOTEL €€

(☎0575 40 19 62; www.hotelpatio.it; Via Cavour 23; s €115-190, d €145-225, ste €265-280; ❄@📶) Each of the 10 themed rooms in Arezzo's most character-rich hotel is dedicated to one of Bruce Chatwin's travel books and is decorated accordingly. The nicest room is 'Utz', so request this one if you can. The location is hard to beat.

La Corte Del Re B&B €€

(☎0575 40 16 03; www.lacortedelre.com; Via Borgunto 5; s €80-100, d €90-120; ❄📶) Owner Franca has a bubbly personality and is remarkably helpful (she even picks guests up from the railway station). Located centimetres from Piazza Grande, her B&B has nine

OFF THE BEATEN TRACK

VILLA FONTELUNGA

Gorgeous is the only word to use when describing **Villa Fontelunga** (☎0575 66 04 10; www.fontelunga.com; Via Cunicchio 5, Foiano della Chiana; d/tw €160-350, ste €210-395; ⏱closed Nov–early Mar; P ❄ @ ᯤ ≋), a 19th-century villa in Foiano della Chiana, 30 minutes southwest of Arezzo. Restored, decorated and run by three charming friends (one an architect, one a landscape designer and one a former international banker), it perfectly balances traditional Tuscan elegance with jet-set pizazz. There's a two-night minimum stay.

simple rooms; some have kitchenettes and views of the square, and most suffer from a lack of noise insulation. Breakfast is brought to your room at a pre-agreed time.

Eating & Drinking

★LAB Pasticceria PATISSERIE €
(www.pasticcerialab.com; Corso Italia 40; coffee & cake €3.50; ⏱10am-1.30pm & 4.30-8.30pm Wed-Sun) There are no mad scientists working in this glass-fronted lab, just a team of pastry chefs who who delight Arentini with their exquisite sweet creations. Enter through the covered courtyard off Corso Italia and you'll discover a super-stylish cafe with indoor and outdoor seating, friendly staff, and glass display cases filled with cakes, pastries, biscuits and *grissini* (breadsticks).

★Trattoria del Leone MODERN TUSCAN €€
(☎0575 35 79 27; Scalinata Camillo Berneri 2; meals €28; ⏱noon-2.30pm Tue-Sun & 7.30-10pm Tue-Sat, closed Aug) A perfect example of the trattoria model that is trending in Tuscany today, del Leone is found in a slightly obscure location on some stairs leading down into Piazza del Popolo, and has a clever, design-driven interior. The food is delicious – small-ish portions of beautifully prepared modern riffs on Tuscan classics, with homemade pasta, *bruschette* and salads featuring.

La Torre di Gnicche WINE BAR €
(www.latorredignicche.it; Piaggia San Martino 8; soup €7, meat & cheese platters €11; ⏱noon-3pm & 6pm-1am Thu-Tue, closed 2 wks in Jan) This cosy bottle-lined room just off Piazza Grande offers a huge choice of Tuscan wine (by the glass or bottle), platters of cheese and meat, and rustic tummy-fillers including *pappa al pomodoro* (a thick bread and tomato soup served in summer) and *ribollita* (a 'reboiled' bean, vegetable, cabbage and bread soup served in winter).

La Bottega di Gnicche SANDWICHES €
(www.bottegadignicche.com; Piazza Grande 4; panini €3-5; ⏱11am-8pm Thu-Tue) There's a delectable array of artisan meats and cheeses to choose from when you order a *panini imbottiti* (roll filled with meat and cheese) at this wonderful *alimentari* (grocery store) on Arezzo's main piazza.

Caffè dei Costanti CAFE
(www.caffedeicostanti.it; Piazza San Francesco 19-20; ⏱8.30am-9.30pm Wed-Sun, to 2am summer) Arezzo's oldest and most atmospheric cafe is located directly opposite the Basilica di San Francesco, so it's a perfect coffee stop before or after a visit to the Cappella Bacci. The coffee is excellent, as are the home-baked pastries. The outdoor tables are popular with the *aperitivo* set.

Information

Centro di Accoglienza Turistica Benvenuti ad Arezzo (☎0575 40 19 45; www.benvenutiadarezzo.it; Palazzo Comunale, Via Ricasoli; ⏱10am-1pm & 2-7pm Mon-Fri, 10am-1pm Sat & Sun Jun-Sep, to 4pm Oct-May) The region's main tourist office is located opposite the *duomo*. There's another branch (Piazza della Repubblica 22-23) with similar hours in Piazza della Repubblica next to the train station.

Una Vetrina per Arezzo e Le Sue Vallate (☎0575 182 27 70; ⏱9am-7pm) A private tourist office located on the *scala mobile* leading

TERRE DI AREZZO

The Arezzo region boasts one DOCG and five DOC wines: Chianti Colli Arentini DOCG, Vinsanto del Chianti Colli Arentini DOC, Vinsanto del Chianti Colli Arentini Occhio di Pernice DOC, Valdichiana DOC, Cortona DOC and Pietraviva DOC. To investigate these fully, you can follow the **Strada del Vino Terre di Arezzo** (www.stradadelvino.arezzo.it) or take full advantage of their regular appearances on the wine menus of restaurants across the region. For information and a map, pop into the **Strada del Vino Terre di Arezzo Information Point** (☎0575 29 40 66; Via Ricasoli 38-40; ⏱9.30am-3pm Mon-Fri) in Arezzo.

OFF THE BEATEN TRACK

ANGHIARI

This unspoilt medieval hill town looms over the plain where the army of the Italian League, spearheaded by the Republic of Florence, famously defeated Milan's numerically superior forces in 1440. Enclosed by massive walls, it is an easy detour for those travelling between Arezzo and Sansepolcro. The walls enclose steep cobbled lanes lined by houses, shops, churches and the **Museo Statale di Palazzo Taglieschi** (Piazza Mameli 16; adult/child €2/1; ⌚10am-7pm Tue-Sun May-Sep, 9am-6pm Tue-Sun Oct-Apr), which has a modest collection of 15th- and 16th-century sculptures and paintings. The town's helpful **tourist information office** (☎0575 74 92 79; www.anghiari.it; Corso Giacomo Matteotti 103; ⌚9.30am-12.30pm & 4-6.30pm) is located next to the post office on the almost vertical Corso Giacomo Matteotti just outside the walls, as is the excellent **Ristorante La Nena** (☎0575 78 94 91; www.ristorantenena.it; Corso Giacomo Matteotti 10-14; meals €35; ⌚noon-2.30pm & 7.30-10pm Tue-Sun), an old-fashioned place that is beloved of Slow Food devotees. There's convenient and cheap parking in Piazza Baldaccio (aka Piazza del Mercato) opposite the tourist information office.

up to Piazza del Duomo. Offers toilet facilities (€0.50) and maps (€0.50). It operates another branch (Piazza Grande; ⌚10.30am-5.30pm Sat & Sun) in Piazza Grande.

Nuovo Ospedale San Donato (☎0575 25 50 01; Via A de Gasperi) Hospital located outside the city walls.

Police (☎0575 31 81; Via Fra Guittone 3)

Getting There & Away

Siena Mobilità (www.sienamobilita.it) buses go to Siena (€6.60, 1½ hours, seven daily) and **Etruria Mobilità** (www.etruriamobilita.it) buses go to Sansepolcro (€4.10, one hour, frequent on weekdays, fewer services on weekends) and Cortona (€3.50, one hour, frequent). Buses depart from Piazza della Repubblica.

To **drive** here from Florence, take the A1; the SS73 heads west to Siena. There is car parking (some spaces free, some €0.70 per hour or €5 per day) at Via Pietri, from where a *scala mobile* takes you up to Piazza del Duomo. Parking at the train station costs €1.50 per hour.

Arezzo is on the Florence–Rome **train** line, and there are frequent services to Florence (*Regionale* €7.80, 1½ hours) and Rome (Intercity €19-25, two hours). There are also hourly *regionale* services to Cortona (€3.30, 20 minutes).

SANSEPOLCRO

POP 16,100

The term 'hidden gem' is bandied about with gay abandon in travel brochures and books, but this is one place that truly deserves the description. Dating from the year 1000, Sansepolcro (called 'Borgo' by locals) reached its current size in the 15th century and was walled in the 16th century. Today, its historic centre remains blessedly untouched by development or tourism – something that can't be said of many other Tuscan towns.

Sights

The historic centre is littered with *palazzi* and churches – look out for the **Chiesa di Sant'Antonio Abate** (cnr Via San Antonio & Via del Campaccio; ⌚8.30am-1pm & 3-6pm), which houses a processional banner painted by Luca Signorelli in 1505; the deconsecrated 16th-century **Chiesa di San Lorenzo** (cnr Via di San Croce & Via Lucca Pacioli), where you'll find the Rosso Fiorentino masterpiece *Deposition of Christ* dating from 1528 (ring the bell at 2 Via di San Croce for entrance); and the16th-century **Chiesa di Santa Maria delle Grazie** (Piazza Beato Ranieri; ⌚8.30am-1pm & 3-6pm), built by members of the Fraternity of Death (men who cared for plague sufferers) and home to the *Madonna delle Grazie* (1555), a painting of a pregnant Madonna that may slightly predate Piero's *Parto* in Monterchi. The artist was Raffaellino del Colle, a member of the fraternity, who included a skull at the Madonna's feet as a reference to the fraternity's sombre work.

★**Museo Civico** MUSEUM

(www.museocivicosansepolcro.it; Via Niccolò Aggiunti 65; adult/reduced/child €8/5/3; ⌚9.30am-1.30pm & 2.30-7pm mid-Jun–mid-Sep, 9.30am-1pm & 2.30-6pm mid-Sep–mid-Jun) The town's flagship museum is home to a small but top-notch collection of artworks, the highlights of which are three Piero della Francesca masterpieces: *Resurrection* (1458–74), the *Madonna della Misericordia* polyptych (1445–56) and *Saint Julian* (1455–58).

1

2

DANITA DELIMONT / ALAMY ©

1. Basilica di San Francesco 2. Abbazia di Monte Oliveto Maggiore 3. Monasterio & Sacro Eremo di Camaldoli

3

Magnificent Monasteries

Consider yourself warned: after visiting these medieval monasteries in Tuscany and nearby Umbria, you may well find yourself entertaining serious thoughts about leaving your fast-paced urban existence to embrace the contemplative life.

Basilica di San Francesco, Assisi

Every year, more than five million pilgrims make their way to St Francis' birthplace (p267) in Umbria to visit the huge basilica and monastery that is dedicated to his legacy, as well as the suitably modest basilica that is dedicated to his friend and follower, St Clare.

Abbazia di Monte Oliveto Maggiore

The Benedictine monks living in this medieval abbey (p219) southeast of Siena tend the vineyard and olive grove, study in one of Italy's most important medieval libraries and walk through a cloister frescoed by Luca Signorelli and Il Sodoma.

Monasterio & Sacro Eremo di Camaldoli

Deep in the forest of the Casentino, amid a landscape that has changed little for centuries, lie this Benedictine monastery and hermitage (p266). Treasures include paintings by Vasari and Bronzino, as well as one of Andrea della Robbia's greatest terracotta sculptures.

Santuario della Verna

St Francis of Assisi is said to have received the stigmata at this spectacularly located monastery (p266) on the southeastern edge of the Casentino. Pilgrims flock here to worship in the Cappella delle Stimmate and to admire the della Robbia artworks in the church.

Eremo Le Celle

A babbling stream, old stone bridge and terraces of olive trees contribute to the fairy-tale feel of this picturesque Franciscan hermitage (p269) just outside Cortona.

Piero's authorship of a fourth work, *Saint Louis of Toulouse* (1460), is disputed by some art historians – see what you think.

The museum also holds paintings by Raffaellino del Colle, Matteo di Giovanni and Santi di Tito. In the main exhibition room, look out for two works by the studio of Andrea della Robbia: a polychrome terracotta called *The Nativity and Adoration of the Shepherds* (1485) and a gorgeous tondo (circular sculpture) known as the *Virgin and Child with Manetti Coat of Arms* (1503).

Cattedrale di San Giovanni Evangelista CATHEDRAL

(Duomo di Sansepolcro; Via Giacomo Matteotti 4; 8.30am-12.30pm & 3-7pm mid-Jun–mid-Sep, to 6pm mid-Sep–mid-Jun) Sansepolcro's 14th-century *duomo* contains an *Ascension* by Perugino, a *Resurrection* by Raffaellino Dal Colle and a polyptych by Niccolò di Segna that is thought to have influenced Piero's *Resurrection*. Left of the main alter is the striking *Volto Santo* (Sacred Face), a wooden crucifix with a wide-eyed Christ that dates back to the 9th or 10th century.

Festivals & Events

On the second Sunday of September, Sansepolcro hosts the **Palio della Ballestra**, a crossbow tournament between local archers and rivals from nearby Gubbio. Contestants and the crowd dress in medieval costumes and a great time is had by all.

Sleeping

★**Relais Palazzo Magi** B&B €

(0575 74 04 77; www.hotelmagisansepolcro.it; Via XX Settembre 160-162; s €65-80, d €90-100, ste €120-200;) Comfort and charm are perfectly aligned at Sansepolcro's best sleeping option. Located in a 15th-century *palazzo* in the heart of the historic centre, it offers sixteen comfortable rooms (some with frescoed walls), a billiard room and a comfortable TV lounge. In the low season, reception is only open during the day and guests are provided with keys for evening access.

Eating & Drinking

The first three places below also offer simple B&B accommodation.

★**Ristorante Da Ventura** TRADITIONAL ITALIAN €€

(0575 74 25 60; www.albergodaventura.it; Via Niccolò Aggiunti 30; meals €32; noon-2.30pm Tue-Sun, 7.30-10pm Tue-Sat) Beware the trollies at this fabulous local eatery! Heavily laden with the huge joints of roasted meat that the place is famous for (roast pork, beef stewed in Chianti Classico and roasted veal shank), these zoom around the old-fashioned dining room pushed by waiters intent on piling diners' plates high.

Vegetarians have no need to fear, though – the *uova con tartufo marzolino fresco* (omelette topped with shaved black truffles) is a triumph, as are the home-made pasta served with truffles or fresh porcini mushrooms, the antipasti spread and the tasty side dishes.

Ristorante Fiorentino TRADITIONAL ITALIAN €€

(0575 74 20 33; www.ristorantefiorentino.it; Via Luca Pacioli 60; meals €40; 12.30-2.30pm & 7.30-10.30pm Thu-Tue) No wonder locals come here to celebrate birthdays and big dates – the dining room is adorned with antique furniture, chandeliers and objets d'art, and genial host Alessio makes everyone feel like special guests. The food is traditional with an occasional modern twist, and there's an excellent wine list.

Enoteca Guidi WINE BAR

(0575 74 19 07; www.locandaguidi.it; Via Luca Pacioli 44-46; 11am-midnight Thu-Sat, Mon & Tue, 6-11pm Sun) Owner Saverio presides over the teensy *enoteca* but also keeps a close eye on the rear dining space, where simple meals (€34) are served. Enjoy a local artisanal beer (Saverio recommends 'La Tipografica') or a glass of vino (everything from local drops to fashionable Super Tuscans).

Torrefazione Alessandrini CAFE

(Via Luca Pacioli 31; 7.45am-1pm & 4.30-8pm Mon-Sat Jun-Sep, 7.45am-1pm & 4-7.30 Mon-Sat Oct-May) The interior of the town's best-loved cafe has hardly changed over the decades, and neither have its opening hours (staff close the doors for three hours to go home for lunch with their families). A bag of the aromatic house blend – roasted on site – is an essential weekly purchase for most locals.

Shopping

Fuselli e Ricamo HANDICRAFTS

(Via Niccolò Aggiunti 42; 4-8pm Mon, 9am-1pm & 4-8pm Tue-Sat) Sansepolcro is known for the quality of its handmade linen lace, and this shop is the best place to purchase it. Aficionados should also visit the **Spazio del**

Merletto (Lace Space; Piazza Garibaldi 2), where generations of local women have gathered to learn and practice the art of lacemaking – if you're lucky, one of the ladies will show you their small museum.

Information

The extremely helpful **tourist office** (☎0575 74 05 36; info@valtiberinaintoscana.it; Via Giacomo Matteotti 8; ⏱9.30am-1pm & 2.30-6.30pm daily Apr-Oct, 10am-1pm daily & 3-5pm Fri-Sun Nov-Mar; 📶) is opposite the *duomo*. Visitors can email in advance of their arrival for updates on events and suggested route itineraries in the region. There's also free public internet and wi-fi access in the office.

Getting There & Away

Etruria Mobilità (p259) buses link Sansepolcro with Anghiari (€1.30, 10 minutes, frequent on weekdays, fewer on weekends) and Arezzo (€4.10, one hour, frequent on weekdays, fewer on weekends). **Sulga** (www.sulga.it) operates one daily service to Rome and Fiumicino Airport (€18.50, 3½-4¼ hours), leaving at 7am every day except Sunday. All buses leave from the bus station off Via G Marconi, near the Porta Fiorentina; purchase tickets at the Bar Autostazione.

Umbria Mobilità (www.umbriamobilita.it) operates a Ferroviaria e Interscambio FS (train) service between Sansepolcro and Perugia (€4.60, two hours, seven daily Monday to Saturday, three on Sunday).

A Zona a Traffico Limitato (ZTL; Limited Traffic Zone) applies within the city walls; you'll find free parking just outside.

THE CASENTINO

The northeastern corner of Tuscany is home to spectacular mountains, historic monasteries and little-visited hamlets where traditional customs and cuisine are proudly maintained.

Poppi

POP 6198

Seeming to float in the clouds above the Arno plain, Poppi Alta (the historic upper section of the town) is crowned by the commanding presence of the Castello dei Conti Guidi. The kiosk in the piazza outside the castle is the social hub during the summer months; at other times locals tend to socialise in Ponte a Poppi (the lower town).

Sights

Castello dei Conti Guidi CASTLE

(www.buonconte.com; Piazza Repubblica 1; adult/child €6/5; ⏱10am-6.30pm summer, to 4.30pm Thu-Sun winter) Castello dei Conti Guidi was built in the late 13th century by Count Simone da Battifolle, head of the Guidi family. Inside, there's a fairy-tale courtyard, a handsome staircase, a library full of medieval manuscripts and a chapel with frescoes by Taddeo Gaddi. The scene of Herod's Feast shows Salome apparently clicking her fingers as she dances, accompanied by a lute player, while John the Baptist's headless corpse lies slumped in the corner.

PIERO DELLA FRANCESCA

Though many details about his life are hazy, it is believed that this great Renaissance painter was born around 1420 in Sansepolcro and died in 1492. Trained as a painter from the age of 15, his distinctive use of perspective, mastery of light and skilful synthesis of form and colour set him apart from his artistic contemporaries, and the serene grace of his figures remains unsurpassed to this day. In his book *The Lives of the Artists,* Piero's fellow townsman Giorgio Vasari called him the 'best geometrician of his time' and lamented the fact that so few of his works were preserved for posterity, leading to him being 'robbed of the honour that [was] due to his labours'.

Piero's most famous works are the *Legend of the True Cross* in Arezzo's Cappella Bacci, his *Resurrection* in Sansepolcro's Museo Civico and his panel featuring *Federico da Montefeltro and Battista Sforza, the Duke and Duchess of Urbino* in the Uffizi, but he is perhaps most fondly remembered for his luminous **Madonna del Parto** (Pregnant Madonna; Via della Reglia 1; adult/reduced/child & pregnant women €5.50/€4/free; ⏱9am-1pm & 2-7pm Apr-Oct, 9am-1pm & 2-5pm Wed-Mon Nov-Mar) on display in Monterchi, a village located in the Tiber Valley between Sansepolcro and Arezzo.

Devotees can follow a trail of Piero's paintings through the region of Arezzo by picking up a copy of the brochure *Piero della Francesca: In and Around Arezzo* from museums and tourist offices throughout the region.

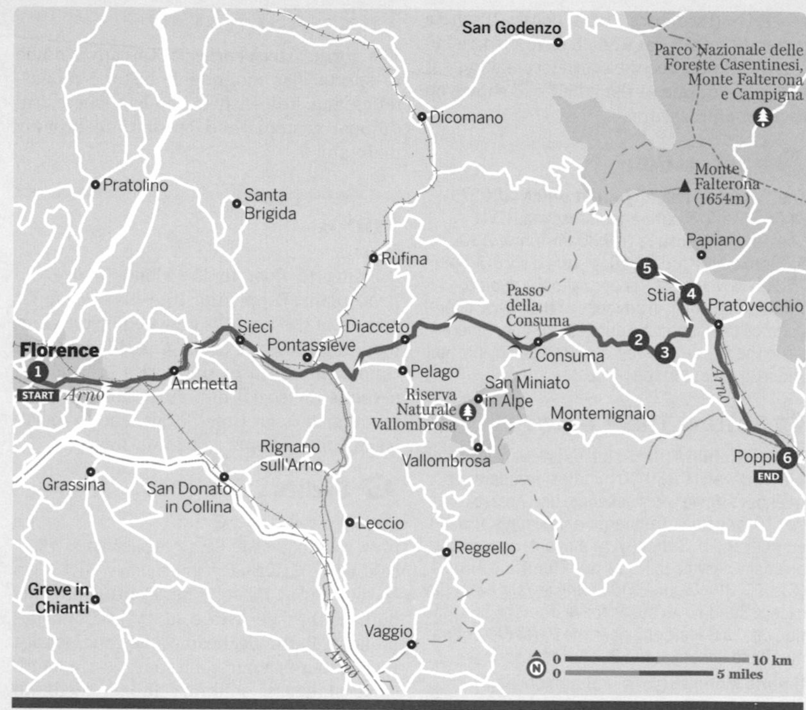

Driving Tour
The Casentino

START FLORENCE
END POPPI
LENGTH 59KM; SIX HOURS

For a foray into this little-visited corner of Tuscany, head southeast (direction Firenze Sud) from 1 **Florence** and drive alongside the Arno river through Pontassieve and over the Passo della Consuma (SS70), a scenic mountain pass through this Tuscan section of the Apennine Mountains (follow the signs for Consuma and Bibbiena). The road will eventually bring you to the turn-off to the 2 **Castello di Romena**, on the left-hand-side of the road. After wandering around this ruined 11th-century castle that Dante once visited, walk or drive down the hill to the exquisite 3 **Pieve di Romena**, a Romanesque church with interior capitals featuring primitive carvings of human and animal figures. To gain entry, try knocking on the door of the adjoining building. Next, follow the road signs to the town of 4 **Stia**. This is where the Arno meets its first tributary, the Staggia, and the town was for many years the centre of the local wool industry. It's now home to the Lanificio di Stia, an impressive wool museum that occupies a handsome, centuries-old mill that was the Casentino's major employer until it closed in 2000. Near the museum's entrance is Tessilnova, a shop selling examples of the brightly coloured and 'nubby' woollen blankets and clothing that the Casentino is famous for, as well as other top-quality, Italian-made woollen clothing.

From Stia, it's a short drive northwest to the 5 **Chiesa Santa Maria delle Grazie**, a gorgeous Renaissance church – see if you can find a local who will let you inside to admire a fresco by Ghirlandaio and two very pretty ceramic lunettes by Benedetto Buglioni. Backtracking to Stia, proceed south through Pratovecchio and continue on to the regional centre of 6 **Poppi**, where you can visit the magnificent Castello dei Conti Guidi and wander the picturesque streets of the upper town before heading to your accommodation for the night.

Sleeping

Albergo San Lorenzo B&B €

(☎0575 52 01 76; www.poppi-sanlorenzo.com; Piazza Bordoni 2-5, Poppi Alta; d €84; ⊙mid-Mar–mid-Nov; @☜✿) There can't be too many B&Bs that incorporate a historic chapel housing a gallery and performance space, but the San Lorenzo does. Next to the wall of Poppi's castle, this arty B&B offers nine smallish rooms with tiled floors and frescoed or beamed ceilings. There's a terraced garden with wonderful views, and a light and airy breakfast room.

The owners, who are German, can organise gastronomic tours of the region.

Poggio a Poppi AGRITURISMO €

(☎0575 52 98 86; www.poggioapoppi.it; Via Magrete 13; d €70-80, apt €80-100; ⊙closed Nov) Surrounded by corn fields and an orchard, this old stone manor house outside Poppi offers six double rooms and two self-catering apartments. It's an attractive proposition in summer, when guests make the most of the large swimming pool, outdoor pizza-oven and expansive views, but it can be bleak in the colder weather.

★**Borgo Corsignano** RESORT €€

(☎0575 50 02 94; www.borgocorsignano.it; Località Corsignano; 1-bedroom apt €100-130, 2-bedroom apt €180-200, 3-bedroom apt €250-300; P@☜✿) Occupying a *borgo* (medieval village) that was once home to Camaldoli monks, this gorgeous country hotel is the best accommodation option in the Casentino. A mere five-minute drive from Poppi, it offers self-contained apartments and a wealth of facilities, including two swimming pools, a little wellness centre with sauna and jacuzzi (€15), tennis court, childrens' playground and sculpture-filled gardens.

Wi-fi is available in the reception area.

Eating

L'Antica Cantina TUSCAN €€

(☎0575 52 98 44; www.anticacantina.com; Via Lapucci 2; meals €39; ⊙noon-2.30pm & 8-11pm Tue-Sun, closed Jan) Come to 'The Old Cantina' for an old-fashioned dining experience under an atmospheric vaulted ceiling. The menu offers no surprises, but should have something to please most palates. It's on a steep side street off Via Cesare Battisti in Poppi Alta.

Information

The **tourist office** (☎0575 52 05 11; consorzio@casentino.toscana.it; Via Roma 203, Ponte a Poppi; ⊙9am-1pm & 3-6pm Mon-Thu, 9am-1pm Fri) is in the ugly modern Unione dei Comuni Montani del Casentino building at the eastern edge of town, near the turn-off to Camaldoli.

> **LOCAL KNOWLEDGE**
>
> **PRATOVECCHIO**
>
> Most visitors zoom through this unremarkable town on their drive between Stia and Poppi, but it's well worth a pitstop around mealtimes. In the evening, tables at **La Tana degli Orsi** (☎0575 58 33 77; Via Roma 1; meals €38; ⊙7.30-10.30pm Thu-Mon) are hotly contested, so book ahead if you're keen to savour the traditional Casentino dishes that its chef creates with love and local produce. At lunch or *aperitivo*, the more modern **Toscana Twist** (☎0575 58 21 20; Via della Libertà 3; pastry & coffee €4, lunch €20; ⊙6am-7.30pm Tue-Thu, to 11pm Fri, to 9pm Sat) is the destination of choice. Toscana Twist doesn't accept credit cards.

Getting There & Away

Etruria Mobilità (p259) buses travel between Florence and Bibbiena, stopping in Poppi en route (€5, two hours, six daily). Unfortunately, local services within the Casentino are few and far between.

From Florence, take the SR67 and SR69 (Via Aretina) and veer onto the SS70 (Passo della Consuma). To Arezzo, take the SR70 and SS71.

Frequent **Trasporto Ferroviario Toscano** (TFT; www.trasportoferroviariotoscano.it) trains link Poppi with Arezzo (€3.40, one hour), Bibbiena (€1.40, 10 minutes) and Stia (€1.40, 15 minutes).

Parco Nazionale delle Foreste Casentinesi, Monte Falterona e Campigna

One of only three national parks in Tuscany, this protected **nature reserve** (www.parcoforestecasentinesi.it) straddles the Tuscany–Emilia-Romagna border, taking in some of the most scenic stretches of the Apennines and protecting the largest and best preserved forest and woodlands in the country.

One of the highest peaks, **Monte Falterona** (1654m), marks the source of the Arno. Apart from the human population, which includes the inhabitants of two his-

OFF THE BEATEN TRACK

BIBBIENA

It may be short on headline attractions, but Bibbiena is one of the oldest settlements in the Casentino and its upper town has a sleepy charm. The **Chiesa di Santi Ippolito e Donato** (aka the Pieve), off the central piazza, is the proud possessor of artworks such as a 13th-century crucifix by the Master of San Polo in Rosso and a 15th-century *Madonna and Child Enthroned with Angels* by Arcangelo di Cola da Camerino. Visit it before or after enjoying a meal at **Il Tirabusciò** (0575 59 54 74; www.tirabuscio.it; Via R Scoti 12; meals €30; 12.30-2.30pm Wed-Sun & 7.30-10pm Wed-Mon), which is known for the excellence of its modern Tuscan cuisine.

toric monasteries, the park is also home to a rich assortment of wildlife plus nearly 100 bird species. Nine self-guided walking trails have been created within the park; the most popular is the 4.5km uphill hike to the Acquacheta waterfall.

The major settlement in the park is **Badia Pratáglia**, a small village in the Alpe di Serra, near the border with Emilia-Romagna.

Sights

Monasterio & Sacro Eremo di Camaldoli MONASTERY

(www.camaldoli.it; monastery 8am-1pm & 3.30-6pm, hermitage 9am-noon & 3-5pm, pharmacy 9am-12.30pm & 2.30-6pm) Hidden in the dense forest of the national park are the Benedictine monastery and hermitage of Camaldoli, founded between 1024 and 1025 by St Romuald and now home to a community of approximately 20 monks.

From Poppi, take Via Camaldoli (SR67) and follow it up through the forest. You will come to a fork in the road – the hermitage is uphill to the right and the monastery is downhill to the left.

You can visit the monastery's church, which houses three paintings by Vasari. Down a set of stairs off the main road are the forbidding 11th-century cloisters and the austere Cappella dello Spirito Santo, a stone space with an exhibition about daily life in the monastery. Pop into the 16th-century *farmacia* (pharmacy), accessed from the side of the main building, which sells soap, perfumes and other items made by members of the monastic community.

The hermitage has a small church with a Bronzino altarpiece of the Crucifixion and Four Saints, but the highlight is the Cappella di San Antonio Abate, to the left as you enter the church building. Inside is an exquisite altarpiece by Andrea della Robbia.

Santuario della Verna MONASTERY

(www.santuariolaverna.org; Via del Santuario 45; 6.30am-sunset) Dramatically positioned on a windswept mountainside, this Franciscan monastic complex is where St Francis of Assisi is said to have received the stigmata and is thus a major pilgrimage destination.

The **Basilica** houses some remarkably fine polychrome glazed ceramics by Andrea della Robbia and his studio – a *Madonna and Child Enthroned between Saints* to your right as you enter the church, a *Nativity* on the right before the altar, an *Adoration* in the small chapel to the right of the altar, saints on either side of the altar, a huge *Ascension* (c 1480) in the chapel to the left of the altar and a beautiful *Annunciation* in the second chapel to the left.

The **Corridoio delle Stimmate**, decorated with modern frescoes recounting St Francis' life, leads to the **Cappella delle Stimmate**, built in 1263 on the spot where the saint supposedly received the stigmata. It's decorated with a magnificent *Crucifixion* by Andrea della Robbia and a smaller *Madonna and Child* tondo attributed to Andrea's studio.

By car, follow signs just outside the hamlet of Chiusi della Verna for the sanctuary or take the mildly taxing but agreeable 30-minute uphill hike from the **information point** (0575 53 20 98; cv.chiusiverna@parcoforestecasentinesi.it; Parco Martiri della Libertà 21; 10am-noon & 3-6pm Jul & Aug, 10am-noon & 2.30-5pm 18 Sep & 4 Oct). The sanctuary is 23km east of Bibbiena and is accessed via the SP208. There is a guesthouse (€55 per person), refectory (set lunch €18) and bar/cafe on site. Parking is €1 per hour.

Information

Badia Pratáglia's **visitor centre** (0575 55 94 77; cv.badiaprataglia@parcoforestecasentinesi.it; Via Nazionale 14; 9am-12.30pm & 3.30-6pm Jul & Aug, 9am-12.30pm Sat & Sun Sep-Jun) carries a wealth of information about the park and also hires out mountain bikes (€6 per half day, €10 per day).

VAL DI CHIANA

This wide green valley stretches south from Arezzo and is punctuated by gently rolling hills crowned with medieval villages. Its prized agricultural land is rich in orchards and olive groves, but is primarily known as the home of Tuscany's famed Chianina cows, one of the oldest breeds of cattle in the world and the essential ingredient in Tuscany's signature dish, *bistecca alla fiorentina*.

Castiglion Fiorentino

POP 13,178

If you're driving from Arezzo to Cortona, be sure to stop en route at this picturesque walled town to visit its impressively restored **Cassero**. Inside this huge medieval fortress are the **Pinacoteca Comunale** (adult/reduced/child €3/2/0.50; ⏲10am-12.30pm & 4-6.30pm Tue-Sat, 4-7pm Sun Apr-Oct, 10am-12.30pm & 3.30-6pm Tue-Sun Nov-Mar), with a small collection including Taddeo Gaddi's delightful *Virgin and Child;* the **Museo Archeologico Sezione Antica e Medievale** (adult/reduced/child €3/2/0.50; ⏲10am-12.30pm & 4-6.30pm Tue-Sat, 4-7pm Sun Apr-Oct, 10am-12.30pm & 3.30-6pm Tue-Sun Nov-Mar), which incorporates the remains of an Etruscan temple dating from the end of the 6th century BC and an Etruscan house from the end of the 4th century BC; and the **Torre del Cassero** (admission €1.50; ⏲10am-1pm & 4-7pm Sun May-Sep), a medieval tower commanding panoramic views over the valley. A combined ticket costs €5 for adults, €1 for children and €3 for a discounted ticket. There are wonderful views over the Val di Chiana from the belvedere in Piazza del Comune, just below the Cassero.

A ZTL applies in the streets immediately surrounding the Cassero, but a public car park is close by at Porta Fiorentina (€1 per hour). Also here is a **tourist information booth** (☎0575 65 82 78; proloco.castiglioni@tin.it; ⏲10am-noon & 4-6pm Tue & Fri, 10am-noon Wed, Thu & Sat).

Cortona

POP 22,487

Rooms with a view are the rule rather than the exception in this spectacularly sited hilltop town. In the late 14th century Fra'

WORTH A TRIP

ASSISI

Thanks to St Francis, who was born here in 1182, this medieval hilltop town in the neighbouring region of Umbria is a major destination for millions of pilgrims. Its major drawcard is the **Basilica di San Francesco** (Piazza di San Francesco; ⏲upper church 8.30am-6.45pm summer, to 6pm winter, lower church 6am-6.45pm summer, to 6pm winter), which comprises two churches filled with magnificent Renaissance art. The **upper church** was built between 1230 and 1253 in the Italian Gothic style and features a superb fresco cycle by Giotto. Downstairs, in the dimly lit **lower church**, there's a series of colourful frescoes by Simone Martini, Cimabue and Pietro Lorenzetti. The crypt where St Francis lies buried is below the church.

To book English-language guided tours of the basilica, contact its **information office** (☎075 819 00 84; www.sanfrancescoassisi.org; ⏲9.15am-noon & 2.15-5.30pm Mon-Sat) or fill out the form on the website. The **tourist office** (☎0758 13 86 80; www.assisi.regioneumbria.eu; ⏲8am-2pm & 3-6pm Mon-Sat, 10am-1pm Sun) on Piazza del Comune can supply general information about the town.

Assisi is a popular overnight destination, so you'll need to book ahead during peak times: Easter, August, September and the Feast of St Francis (4 October). For a comfortable and well located sleeping option, try **Hotel Alexander** (☎075 81 61 90; www.hotelalexanderassisi.it; Piazza Chiesa Nuova 6; s €60-80, d €80-140; ❄📶). To eat, head to **Trattoria Pallotta** (☎075 81 26 49; www.pallottaassisi.it; Vicolo della Volta Pinta; set menus €18-27; ⏲lunch & dinner Wed-Mon; 🖉) or **Trattoria Da Erminio** (☎075 81 25 06; www.trattoriadaerminio.it; Via Montecavallo 19; mains €7-11, set menus €16; ⏲lunch & dinner Fri-Wed, closed Feb & 1st half of Jul) for traditional Umbrian dishes.

Sulga buses connect Assisi with Florence (€12.50, 2½ hours, twice weekly). A Zona a Traffico Limitato (ZTL; Limited Traffic Zone) applies in the historic centre, but there are plenty of paid car parks (€1.15 per hour, €10 per day) just outside the walls.

Angelico lived and worked here, and fellow artists Luca Signorelli and Pietro da Cortona were both born within the walls – all three are represented in the Museo Diocesano's small but sensational collection. More recently, large chunks of *Under the Tuscan Sun,* the soap-in-the-sun film of the book by Frances Mayes, were shot here.

Sights

★Museo Diocesano MUSEUM
(Piazza del Duomo 1; adult/child €5/3, audioguide €3; ⏲10am-7pm Tue-Sun Apr-Oct, to 5pm Tue-Sun Nov-Mar) Little is left of the original Romanesque character of Cortona's **duomo**, which is situated northwest of Piazza Signorelli and has been rebuilt several times in a less-than-felicitous fashion. Fortunately, its wonderful artworks have been saved and are on display in this museum, which occupies the former church of the Gesù on the opposite side of the piazza.

Room 1 features a remarkable Roman sarcophagus decorated with a frenzied battle scene between Dionysus and the Amazons, but the real treasures are in Room 3. These include a moving *Crucifixion* (1320) by Pietro Lorenzetti and two beautiful works by Fra' Angelico: *Annunciation* (1436) and *Madonna with Child and Saints* (1436–7).

★Museo dell'Accademia Etrusca MUSEUM
(MAEC; www.cortonamaec.org; Piazza Signorelli 9; adult/child 6-12yr €10/7; ⏲10am-7pm daily Apr-Oct, to 5pm Tue-Sun Nov-Mar) The rather plain facade of the 13th-century **Palazzo Casali** (Piazza Signorelli) was added to the original building in the 17th century. Inside, this fascinating museum displays substantial local Etruscan and Roman finds, Renaissance globes, 18th-century decorative arts and contemporary paintings. The Etruscan collection is the highlight, particularly those objects excavated from the tombs at Sodo, just outside town.

Basilica di Santa Margherita CHURCH
(Piazza Santa Margherita; ⏲8am-noon & 3-7pm Apr-Oct, 9am-noon & 3-6pm Nov-Mar) For the most effective cardiovascular workout in Tuscany, hike up to this largely 19th-century

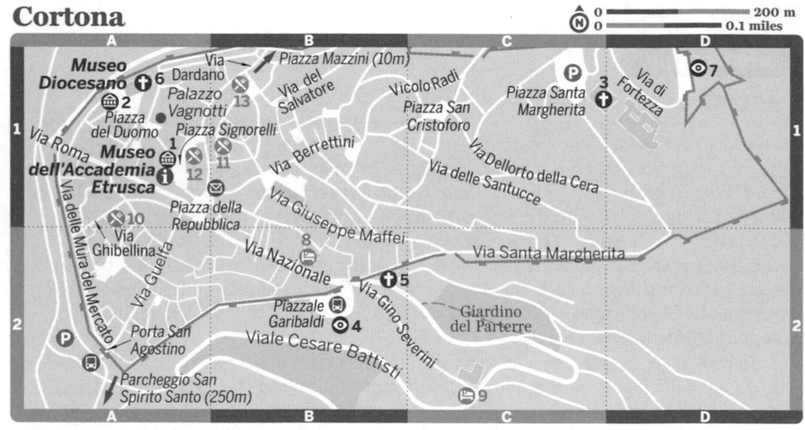

Cortona

Top Sights
1 Museo dell'Accademia Etrusca A1
2 Museo Diocesano A1

Sights
3 Basilica di Santa Margherita C1
4 Belvedere B2
5 Chiesa di San Domenico B2
6 Duomo A1
7 Fortezza Medicea D1
Palazzo Casali .... (see 1)

Sleeping
8 Casa Chilenne B2
9 Villa Marsili C2

Eating
10 La Bucaccia A1
11 Osteria del Teatro B1
12 Taverna Pane e Vino A1
13 Trattoria Dardano B1

church through the warren of steep cobbled lanes in the eastern part of town. Inside, the remains of St Margaret, patron saint of Cortona, are on display in a 14th-century, glass-sided tomb above the main altar.

Chiesa di San Domenico CHURCH
(Largo Beato Angelico; ⌚9am-6pm) Close to the belvedere at the eastern end of Via Nazionale is this 15-century church, which is home to a 1515 painting of the *Madonna and Saints* by local luminary, Luca Signorelli.

Fortezza Medicea LANDMARK
(adult/child €3/1.50; ⌚10am-1pm & 3-6pm Sat & Sun May & Jun, 10am-1pm & 4-7pm Jul-Sep) There's a stupendous view over the Val di Chiana to Lago Trasimeno in Umbria from the remains of this Medici fortress, which stands atop the highest point in town. For the less fit, a **belvedere** at the eastern end of Via Nazionale, down in the centre of town, also has a panoramic view.

Eremo Le Celle MONASTERY
(www.lecelle.it; Strada dei Cappuccini 1; ⌚dawn-dusk) This Franciscan hermitage is set amid dense woodland 3km north of Cortona. Its buildings sit next to a picturesque stream with an 18th-century stone bridge, and the only sounds to disturb the tranquil atmosphere are the bells that call the resident friars to vespers and mass in the cave-like **Chiesa Cella di San Francesco**.

Tours

English-language **walking tours** (☎334 3340608, 0575 40 33 19; www.centroguidearezzo.it; adult/reduced €10/free) are conducted every Monday from 11am to 1pm between May and October. The ticket includes entrance to Museo dell'Accademia Etrusca. Bookings essential.

Festivals & Events

Giostra dell'Archidado CULTURAL
(www.giostraarchidado.com) A full week of medieval merriment in May or June (the date varies to coincide with Ascension Day) culminates in a crossbow competition.

Festival of Sacred Music MUSIC
(www.cortonacristiana.it) Held in late June and early July each year.

Cortona Mix Festival ARTS
(www.mixfestival.it) Arts festival held in late July and early August each year.

MONEY SAVER

A combined ticket (adult €13, child €9) gives entry to the Museo dell'Accademia Etrusca and the Museo Diocesano.

Cortonantiquaria ANTIQUES
(www.cortonantiquaria.it) Cortona's well-known antiques market sets up in the beautiful 18th-century halls of Palazzo Vagnotti in late August and early September each year

Sleeping

★**Casa Chilenne** B&B €
(☎0575 60 33 20; www.casachilenne.com; Via Nazionale 65; s €80-85, d €88-110; ❄@📶) Run by American-born Jeanette and her Cortonese husband Luciano, this wonderfully welcoming B&B has it all – great hosts, a central location, comfortable rooms, a lavish breakfast spread and keen prices. Each of the five rooms has a satellite TV, but there's also a communal lounge with TV, small terrace and cooking corner.

★**Villa Marsili** HOTEL €€
(☎0575 60 52 52; www.villamarsili.net; Viale C Battisti 13; s €90-110, d €99-250, ste €240-340; ❄@📶) Service is the hallmark at this attractive villa nestled against the city walls. Guests rave about the helpful staff, lavish breakfast buffet and early-evening *aperitivo*, which is served in the garden. Consider booking one of the suites, which have jacuzzis and wonderful views across the Val di Chiana to Lago Trasimeno.

Eating & Drinking

Taverna Pane e Vino WINE BAR €
(www.pane-vino.it; Piazza Signorelli 27; bruschetta €4, meat & cheese platters €6-11, pasta €6.50-9; ⌚noon-11pm Tue-Sun Easter-Jan, 5-11pm Tue-Sat & noon-11pm Sun Feb & Mar) Serving over 900 wines, this casual place is a perfect spot for a light lunch, afternoon drink or rustic dinner. Claim a table in the front courtyard or vaulted interior, settle back over a glass of wine or two and relax with the local bon vivants.

Trattoria Dardano TUSCAN €
(☎0575 60 19 44; www.trattoriadardano.com; Via Dardano 24; meals €20; ⌚noon-3pm & 4.45-10.30pm Thu-Tue) You'll be elbow-to-elbow with locals when you claim a table in one of the two dining rooms at this humble trattoria. The food is honest rather than inspired,

but the bustling atmosphere and low prices compensate. No credit cards.

La Bucaccia TUSCAN **€€**

(☎0575 60 60 39; www.labucaccia.it; Via Ghibellina 17; meals €35; ⊙noon-2.30pm & 7.30-10pm Tue-Sun) Set in a medieval stable that was incorporated into a Renaissance *palazzo,* this is an atmospheric and enjoyable dinner venue, but it's a bit dark at lunchtime. The set menu (€29) of four courses, one glass of wine and water offers extremely good value.

Osteria del Teatro TRADITIONAL ITALIAN **€€**

(☎0575 63 05 56; www.osteria-del-teatro.it; Via Giuseppe Maffei 2; meals €36; ⊙12.30-2.30pm & 7.30-9.30pm Thu-Tue) The walls are clad with photos of actors who have dined here after performing in the nearby theatre, and service is suitably theatrical – waiters wield what could well be the biggest pepper grinder in the world, and blocks of locally produced chocolate are attacked with a butcher's knife for a sweet finale. The menu relies heavily on seasonal local produce.

Information

The **tourist office** (☎0575 63 72 23; infocortona@apt.arezzo.it; Palazzo Comunale; ⊙9am-1pm & 3-6pm Mon-Sat, 9am-1pm Sun late Apr–Sep, 9am-1pm & 3-6pm Mon-Fri, 9am-1pm Sat Oct–late Apr) stocks maps and can book hotels.

Getting There & Away

From Piazza del Mercato or Piazzale Garibaldi (at the time of writing authorities were considering changing from the former to the latter), **Etruria Mobilità** buses connect the town with Arezzo (€3.50, one hour, frequent) via Castiglion Fiorentino (€2.30).

The city is on the north–south SS71 that runs to Arezzo. It's also close to the Siena–Bettolle–Perugia autostrada, which connects to the A1. There are paid car parks around the circumference of the city walls and a free car park at Parcheggio San Spirito Santo that is connected to the historical centre by a *scala mobile*. A ZTL applies inside the walls.

The nearest train station is located about 6km away at Camucia, and can be accessed via a local bus (€1.30, 15 minutes, hourly). Destinations include Arezzo (€3.30, 25 minutes, hourly), Florence (€9.80, 1¾ hours, hourly), Rome (€11.15, 2¼ hours, eight daily), Perugia (€4.25, 55 minutes, six daily) and Orvieto (€7, 55 minutes, seven daily).

Note that Camucia station has no ticket office, only machines. If you need assistance purchasing or booking tickets, you'll need to go to the station at Terontola, south of Camucia, instead.

Understand Florence & Tuscany

Florence & Tuscany Today

Tuscany – with its world-class fashion, Super Tuscan wines and farmsteads romantically lost in cinematic rushes of hills, vineyards, cypress alleys and wheat fields – is an enviable part of the world. Agriculture and travel are defining features of the region: 'go slow' is the spindle around which the Tuscan cart turns, just as it did three millennia ago. But it is not all fabled romance. Italy's privileged land of autumnal gold vineyards and silvery olive groves is as susceptible to modern-day trouble and strife as any other.

Best in Print

The Stones of Florence (Mary McCarthy; 1956) Timeless portrait of Florence.

The Birth of Venus (Sarah Dunant, 2003) The daughter of a wealthy merchant falls in love with a fresco painter in 15th-century Florence.

The Decameron (Giovanni Boccaccio, 1353) A bawdy masterpiece.

A Tabernacle for the Sun (Linda Proud, 1997) Book One of the Botticelli Trilogy.

Best in Film

Life is Beautiful (Robert Benigni, 1998) Bittersweet comedy-drama set during the Holocaust.

A Room with a View (James Ivory, 1985) Exquisitely rendered screen version of EM Forster's 1908 novel.

Tea with Mussolini (Franco Zeffirelli, 1999) Semi-autobiographical film, opening in Florence in 1935.

The English Patient (Anthony Minghella, 1996) Arezzo's Cappella Bacci is the Tuscan star of this romantic drama.

Trouble at the Bank

As Europe's floundering economy limped from bad to dire in 2012 in a crisis considered to be the worst since the 1930s Great Depression, Tuscany found itself sucked in. The region had stood up well to initial troubles in 2007, but as Italy entered its third year of recession, resistance was wavering: Italy's economy shrunk by 2.3% in 2012; and national unemployment hit 12% in April 2013, with youth unemployment hovering around 40%.

The Tuscan crunch came with the Monte dei Paschi di Siena bank scandal. In January 2013 the Banca Monte dei Paschi di Siena – Italy's third-largest lender and the world's longest-operating bank, in business in a gorgeous *palazzo* (palace) in Siena since 1472 – revealed losses of €730 million on a trio of derivative deals, made between 2007 and 2009 and hidden from regulators. While former high-ranking officials at the pedigree bank grappled with corruption, fraud and bribery allegations, the government came to the rescue with a €4.1 billion bail-out. Tuscan taxpayers, still reeling from the new home property tax and other tough austerity measures introduced by short-lived prime minister Mario Monti in 2011 and 2012, were far from impressed with such government 'spending'.

Future restructuring at the bank, essential for survival, will see 400 of its 1900 countrywide branches close and 4600 redundancies made by 2015. But the fallout of the scandal reaches far beyond job cuts. For decades 'il Monte' (as Tuscans know the bank) sustained Siena's vibrant cultural life. Through the foundation, Fondazione Monte dei Paschi di Siena, it funded part of the city's university, hospital, football team, Palio horse race and so on – effectively providing around 10% of Siena's local government budget. For Siena (and Tuscany) the social and economic impact of their sugar daddy's dramatic fall from grace is catastrophic.

A Chest of Treasures

As state coffers diminish, museums are increasingly unable to afford a full quota of staff; hence the necessity to open certain floors or rooms to visitors for limited hours only, often by 'guided tour'. Yet milestones have been reached in Tuscany's endless quest to safeguard its chest of treasures, unmatched in Europe. In Florence the €65 million 'New Uffizi' refurbishment project surges forward with the opening of dozens more rooms, while the bronze doors Ghiberti sculpted for Florence's baptistery are again on show after 27 years of restoration.

Tuscany's portfolio of 14 palatial villas and gardens, built in the countryside around Florence between the 15th and 18th centuries for the Medicis, became a Unesco World Heritage site in 2013. Siena (www.2019si.eu) meanwhile is competing with Venice, Palermo, Amalfi and a handful of other Italian cities to become Italy's chosen European Capital of Culture in 2019 (and thereby scoop a desperately-needed EU windfall of €1.5 million to invest in cultural events, infrastructure, on-going or scuppered museum projects such as the Complesso Museale Santa Maria della Scala); the winning candidate will be announced in 2015.

Going Green

In a region borne out of agriculture, ecofriendly travel is naturally of increasing importance. In traffic-clogged Florence, smart young city mayor Matteo Renzi is considering a London-style scheme limiting the number of cars entering downtown Florence. The obvious moment to introduce it would be 2016, when Florence's state-of-the-art tramlines will be completed – the first line is already functional and, if Florentines are lucky, Line 2 could be complete by the end of 2014.

Ecological disaster was narrowly averted after the *Costa Concordia* cruise ship ran aground on rocks off the Tuscan island of Giglio in January 2012. The clean-up operation to salvage all 114,500 tonnes of the shipwreck from the protected waters – part of the Tuscan Archipelago National Park and Europe's largest protected marine park – continues more than a year later.

POPULATION: **3.67 MILLION**

AREA: **22,994 SQ KM**

GDP: **€105.9 BILLION**

ANNUAL INFLATION: **2.2%**

UNEMPLOYMENT RATE: **12%**

if Tuscany were 100 people

91 would be Italian
2 would be Albanian
2 would be Romanian
5 would be Other

belief systems

(% of population)

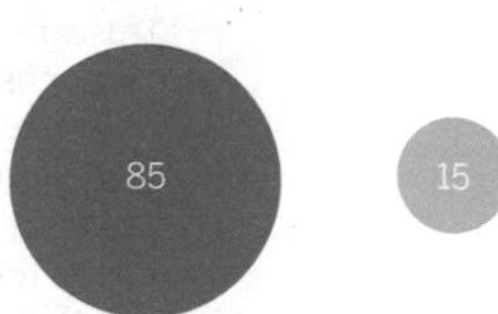

population per sq km

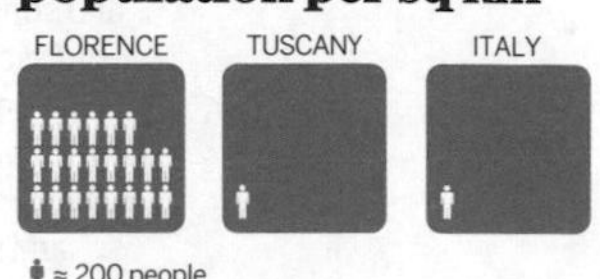

History

Tuscan history is an opera that quietly opens with the wine-loving Etruscans around the 9th century BC, staccatos with feisty clashes between medieval city-states, and crescendos with Florence's powerful Medici dynasty and the birth of the Renaissance. To this day, it is the Renaissance with its extraordinary art and architecture that defines the region's largest city and remains the region's greatest period; Tuscany has not been at the cusp of such momentous change since.

Learn to speak Etruscan at Etruscology: www.etruskisch.de/pgs/vc.htm. Favourite words: *netshvis* (a fortune teller who reads animal entrails) and *thuta* (which can mean either 'chaste' or 'only married once').

The Etruscans

No one knows exactly why the ancient Etruscans headed to Tuscany in the 9th century BC, but Etruscan artefacts give clues as to why they stayed: dinner. The wild boar roaming the Tuscan hills was a favourite on the menu, and boar hunts are a recurring theme on Etruscan ceramics and tomb paintings. In case the odd boar bristle tickled the throat while eating, Etruscans washed down their meals with plenty of wine, thereby introducing viticulture to Italy.

Tomb paintings show Etruscan women keeping pace with men in banquets so decadent they scandalised even the orgy-happy Romans. Many middle-class and aristocratic women had the means to do what they wished, including indulging in music and romance, participating in politics and overseeing a vast underclass of servants. Roman military histories boast of conquests of Etruscan women along with Etruscan territory starting in the 3rd century BC. According to recent genetic tests, Etruscans did not mingle much with their captors – their genetic material is distinct from that of modern Italians, who are the descendants of ancient Romans.

Etruscans didn't take kindly to Roman authority, nor were they keen on being enslaved to establish Roman plantations. They secretly allied themselves with Hannibal to bring about the ignominious defeat of the Romans – one of the deadliest battles in all of Roman history – at Lago Trasimeno in neighbouring Umbria: 16,000 Roman soldiers were lost in approximately three hours.

After that, Rome took a more hands-off approach with the Etruscans, granting them citizenship in 88 BC to manage their own affairs in the

TIMELINE

9th century BC

Etruscans bring highly civilised wine, women and song to the hills of Tuscany – never has life been so good. Unfortunately they fail to invite the Romans and war ensues.

265 BC

Etruria falls to Rome, but it remains unruly and conspires with Hannibal against Rome during the Punic Wars.

59 BC

After emerging victorious from a corrupt election campaign for the position of Roman consul, Julius Caesar establishes a soldier-retiree resort called Florentia.

new province of Tuscia (Tuscany), and in return securing themselves safe passage along the major inland Roman trade route via the Via Flaminia. Little did the Romans realise when they paved the road that they were also paving the way for their own replacements in the 5th to 8th centuries AD: first came German emperor Theodoric, then Byzantine emperor Justinian, then the Lombards and finally Charlemagne in 800.

Medieval Scandal

Political power constantly changed hands in medieval Tuscany. Nevertheless, two notorious women wielded power effectively against a shifting backdrop of kings and popes. The daughter of a Roman senator and a notorious prostitute-turned-senatrix, Marozia already had one illegitimate son by her lover Pope Sergius III and was pregnant again when she married the Lombard duke of Spoleto, Alberic I, in 909 AD. He was hardly scrupulous himself: he'd achieved his position by murdering the previous duke, and he soon had Sergius III deposed. When Alberic was in turn killed, Marozia married Guy of Tuscany and conspired with him to smother Pope John X and install (in lethally rapid succession) Pope Leo VI and Stephen VIII.

After Guy's death, Marozia wooed his half-brother Hugh of Arles, the new king of Italy. No matter that he already had a wife: his previous marriage was soon annulled. But at the wedding ceremony, Marozia's son, Alberic II, who had been named Pope John XI, had the happy couple arrested. Marozia spent the rest of her life in prison, but her legacy lived on: ultimately five popes were her direct descendants.

Countess Matilda of Tuscany (1046–1115) was another powerful woman. Rumour has it that she was more than just an ally to Pope Gregory VII, and there's no doubt she was a formidable strategist. To consolidate her family's Tuscan holdings, she married her own stepbrother, Godfrey the Hunchback. She soon arranged for him to be sent off to Germany, annulling that marriage then marrying a powerful prince 26 years her junior.

When Matilda's ally Pope Gregory VII excommunicated Holy Roman Emperor Henry IV in 1077 (for threatening to replace him with an antipope), the emperor showed up outside her castle barefoot and kneeling in the snow to beg the pope's forgiveness. Gregory, who was Matilda's guest, kept him waiting for three days before rescinding the excommunication. Henry retaliated for what he saw as Matilda's complicity in his humiliation, conspiring with Matilda's neighbours to seize her property, and even turning her trophy husband against her – but Matilda soon dislodged Henry's power base in the north with the support of his own son, Conrad. Disgraced by his own family and humbled on the battlefield by a woman, Henry died in 1106.

Best Etruscan Ruins

- *Vie Cave, Pitigliano*
- *Parco Archeologico di Baratti e Populonia, Golfi di Baratti*
- *Necropoli, Sovana*

570–774

The Lombards rule Italy as far south as Florence, and manage to turn the tiny duchy of Spoleto into a booming trade empire.

773–74

Charlemagne crosses the Alps into Italy, fighting the Lombards and having his ownership of Tuscany, Emilia, Venice and Corsica confirmed by Pope Hadrian I.

1080

Henry IV deposes Pope Gregory VII for the second time, installing Clement III in his place and marching against Gregory's supporter Matilda of Tuscany, confiscating her territory.

1082

Florence picks a fight with Siena over the ownership of the Chianti region, starting a bitter rivalry that will last the next 400 years.

A New Law & Order

By the 13th century Tuscans wanted change. Farmers who had painstakingly reclaimed their fields wanted to get their produce to market alive; merchants needed peaceful piazzas in which to conduct their business; and the populace at large began to entertain hopes of actually living past the age of 40.

Best Roman Relics

Area Archeologica, Fiesole

Roman theatre, Volterra

Vetulonia

In a bid to reorganise their communities in a more civilised fashion, *comuni* (town councils) were established in Florence, Siena and other towns. In this new power-sharing arrangement, representatives were drawn from influential families, guilds and the merchant classes. Building projects were undertaken to give citizens a new sense of shared purpose and civic identity. Hospitals and public charities helped serve the needy, and new public squares, marketplaces and town halls became crucial meeting places for civic society.

Law and order were kept by a *podestà*, an independent judiciary often brought in from outside the city for limited terms of office to prevent corruption. Each *comune* (city-state) developed its own style of government: Siena's was the most imaginative. To curb bloody turf battles among its *contrade* (neighbourhoods), Siena channelled its fighting spirit into organised boxing matches, bullfights and Il Palio, an annual horse race. Anyone who broke the peace was fined and the city's coffers soon swelled

FLAGELLATING MONKS & NUNS

The first known case of religious self-flagellation dates from the mid-13th century in Perugia in neighbouring Umbria, when a strange, spontaneous parade of believers began whipping themselves while singing.

By 1260 roving bands of Flagellants appeared in major Tuscan cities, stripped to the waist, hooded and ecstatically whipping themselves while singing *laudi* (songs about the passion of Christ). They made quite an impression in Florence and Siena where adherents formed *scuole di battuti* (schools of beatings) and built *case di Dio* (houses of God) that served as charity centres, hospices and hosts to mass flagellation sessions.

The Church remained neutral on the issue until the fledgling Flagellants claimed their activities could grant temporary relief from sin. This posed direct competition to the Church's practice of confession, not to mention its steady business in indulgences, pardons and tithes. The Flagellant movement was banned in 1262, only to regain momentum a century later during the plague and recur periodically until the 15th century, when the Inquisition subjected Flagellants to the ultimate mortification of the flesh: death by burning at the stake.

Self-flagellation processions continued to be held in Tuscany under the Church's guidance into the late 19th century.

1136

Scrappy, seafaring Pisa adds Amalfi to its list of conquests, which included Jerusalem, Valencia, Tripoli and Mallorca, plus colonies in Constantinople and Cairo, among others.

1167

Siena's *comune* (town council) establishes a written constitution, declaring that elected terms should be short and money should be pretty; it's soon amended to guarantee Sienese public boxing matches.

1314–21

Dante Alighieri writes his *Divina Commedia*, told in the first person, using Tuscan dialect instead of the usual formal Latin, and peppered with political satire, pathos, adventure and light humour.

DALLAS STRIBLEY / GETTY IMAGES ©

➜ Statue of Dante, Florence

with monies collected in the city's *osterie* (casual taverns or eateries presided over by a host) for cursing.

After Florence won yet another battle against Siena by cutting off the town's water supply, Siena's *comune* was faced with a funding choice: build an underground aqueduct to avoid Florence's attacks or a cathedral to establish Siena as the creative capital of the medieval world. The council voted unanimously for the latter.

Dante's Circle of Hell

'Midway on our life's journey, I found myself in dark woods, the right road lost...' So begins the ominous year 1300 in Dante Alighieri's *Inferno,* where our hero Dante (1265–1321) escapes from one circle of hell only to tumble into the next. In the 14th century, Dante and his fellow Tuscans were to endure a hellish succession of famine, economic collapse, plague, war and tyranny.

When medieval mystics predicted the year 1300 would bring doom, they were off by barely 50 years. Approximately two-thirds of the population were decimated in cities across Tuscany in the bubonic plague outbreak of 1348, and since the carriers of the plague (fleas and rats) weren't identified or eradicated, the Black Death ravaged the area for decades. Entire hospital and monastery populations were wiped out, leaving treatment to opportunists promising miracle cures. Flagellation, liquor, sugar and spices were prescribed, as was abstinence from bathing, fruit and olive oil.

Painful though those days must have been to record, writers such as Boccaccio, Dante and Marchione di Coppo Stefani (c 1336–85) wrote frank assessments of their time, believing their critiques might one day serve the greater good. More than any painterly tricks of perspective or shading, it's this rounded view of humanity that brought truth to Renaissance art.

Medieval Tuscany was just criminal: leaders of powerful families were stabbed by rivals while attending Mass; peasants were ambushed by brigands; bystanders were maimed in neighbourhood disputes that all too easily escalated to murderous brawls. Petty crimes were punished with steep fines, corporal punishment and public flogging or mutilation.

Renaissance Belligerence & Beauty

The Renaissance was a time of great art and great tyrants, between which there was an uneasy relationship. The careful balance of power of the *comuni* became a casualty of the plague in the 14th century; political control was mostly left to those who survived and were either strong enough or unscrupulous enough to claim it. In *comuni* such as Florence and Siena, powerful families assumed control of the *signoria,* the city council ostensibly run by guild representatives and merchants.

Cities, commercial entities and individual families took sides with either the Rome-backed Guelphs or the imperial Ghibellines, loyalists of the Holy Roman Empire. Since each of these factions was eager to put

1348–50

Black Death ravages Tuscany, wiping out approximately two-thirds of the population in dense urban areas. It doesn't stop there: further outbreaks are recorded until 1500.

1375–1406

Colluccio Salutati serves as chancellor of Florence, promoting a secular civic identity to trump old feudal tendencies; it's a bold, new model of citizenship for Europe that occasionally even works.

1378

The Florentine *signoria* (city council) ignores a petition from the city's *ciompi* (wool carders), who want guild representation: cue the Revolt of Ciompi, an ultimately unsuccessful democratic uprising.

1469–92

Lorenzo de' Medici unofficially rules Florence, despite the 1478 Pazzi Conspiracy, an attempted overthrow that left his brother Giuliano torn to shreds in the *duomo*.

itself on the map, this competition might have meant a bonanza for artists and architects – but shifting fortunes in the battlefield meant funds for pet art projects could disappear just as quickly as they appeared.

Relive 14th-century Florence: visit Dante's Florentine home with the chapel where he met his muse and with a traditional tripe shop. For Dante with a pop-culture twist, read Sandow Birk's and Marcus Sanders' *The Divine Comedy*, which sets *Inferno* in Los Angeles' traffic, *Purgatorio* in foggy San Francisco and *Paradiso* in New York.

Tuscany began to resemble a chess game, with feudal castles built only to be overtaken, powerful bishops aligning with nobles before being toppled, and minor players backed by key commercial interests occasionally rising to power. Nowhere was the chess game harder to follow than in the Ghibelline *comune* of Pistoia: first it was conquered by the Florentine Guelphs, then it was divided into White and Black Guelph splinter groups, then it was captured by Lucca (which was at that time Ghibelline backed) before being reclaimed by the Florentines.

The Medicis

The Medici family were not exempt from the usual failings of Renaissance tyrants, but early on in his rise to power Cosimo the Elder (1389–1464) revealed a surprisingly enlightened self-interest and an exceptional eye for art. Although he held no elected office, Cosimo served as ambassador for the Church, and through his behind-the-scenes diplomatic skills managed to finagle a rare 25-year stretch of relative peace for Florence. When a conspiracy led by competing banking interests exiled him from the city in 1433, some of Cosimo's favourite artists split town with him, including Donatello and Fra' Angelico.

But they weren't gone long: Cosimo's banking interests were too important to Florence, and he returned triumphant after just one year to crush his rivals, exert even greater behind-the-scenes control and sponsor masterpieces such as Brunelleschi's legendary dome for Florence's *duomo* (cathedral).

But sponsorship from even the most enlightened and powerful patrons had its downside: their whims could make or break artists and they attracted powerful enemies. Lorenzo de' Medici (Lorenzo Il Magnifico; 1449–92) was a legendary supporter of the arts and humanities, providing crucial early recognition and support for Leonardo da Vinci, Sandro Botticelli and Michelangelo Buonarroti, among others.

The Medici have nothing to hide – at least, not anymore. Dig your own dirt on Florence's dynamic dynasty in the archives at www.medici.org.

But after Lorenzo escaped an assassination attempt by a conspiracy among the rival Florentine Pazzi family, the king of Naples and the pope, the artists he supported had to look elsewhere for sponsorship until Lorenzo could regain his position. Religious reformer Savonarola took an even darker view of Lorenzo and the classically influenced art he promoted, viewing it as a sinful indulgence in a time of great suffering. When Savonarola ousted the Medici in 1494, he decided that their decadent art had to go, too, and works by Botticelli, Michelangelo and others went up in flames in the massive 'Bonfire of the Vanities' on Florence's Piazza della Signoria.

1478–80

A confusing set of overlapping wars break out among the papacy, Siena, Florence, Venice, Milan and Naples, as individual families broker secret pacts and the dwindling Tuscan population pays the price.

1494

The Medici are expelled by Charles VIII of France, and Savonarola declares a theocratic republic with his Consiglia di Cinquecento.

1498

To test Savonarola's beliefs, rival Franciscans invite him to a trial by fire. He sends a representative to be burned instead, but is eventually tortured, hung and burned as heretic.

1527–30

Florentines run the Medici out of town. The Republic of Florence holds out for three years, until the emperor's and pope's combined cannon power reinstalls the Medici.

Galileo

One of the most notable faculty members at the revitalised University of Pisa was a professor of mathematics named Galileo Galilei (1564–1642). To put it in mathematical terms, Galileo was a logical paradox: a Catholic who fathered three illegitimate children; a man of science with a poetic streak, who lectured on the dimensions of hell according to Dante's *Inferno;* and an inventor of telescopes whose head was quite literally in the clouds, yet who kept in close contact with many friends who were the leading intellectuals of their day.

Galileo's meticulous observations of the physical universe attracted the attention of the Church, which by the 16th century had a difficult

HOW MACHIAVELLIAN!

Few names have such resonance as Niccolò Machiavelli (1469–1527), the Florentine scholar and political thinker who said 'the times are more powerful than our brains'. He was born into a poor offshoot of one of Florence's leading families and his essential premise – 'the end justifies the means' – is one that continues to live with disturbing terrorism five centuries on.

Impoverished as Machiavelli's family was, his father had a well-stocked library, which the young Machiavelli devoured. When he was 29 Machiavelli landed a post in the city's second chancery. By 1500 he was in France on his first diplomatic mission in the service of the Republic. Indeed, so impressed was he by the martial success of Cesare Borgia and the centralised state of France that Machiavelli concluded that Florence, too, needed a standing army – which he convinced the Republic to do in 1506. Three years later it was bloodied in battle against the rebellious city of Pisa.

The return to power of the Medici family in 1512 was a blow for Machiavelli. Suspected of plotting against the Medici, he was thrown into Florence's Le Stinche (the earliest known jail in Tuscany, dating from 1297 and among the first in Europe) in 1513 and tortured with six rounds of interrogation on the prison's notorious rack. Yet he maintained his innocence. Once freed, he retired a poor man to a small property outside Florence.

But it was during these years that Machiavelli did his greatest writing. *Il Principe* (The Prince) is his classic treatise on the nature of power and its administration, a work reflecting the confusing and corrupt times in which he lived and his desire for strong and just rule in Florence and beyond. He later wrote an official history of Florence, the *Istorie Fiorentine*.

In 1526 Machiavelli joined the papal army in its futile fight against imperial forces. By the time the latter had sacked Rome in 1527, Florence had again rid itself of Medici rule. Machiavelli hoped he would be restored to a position of dignity, but to no avail. He died frustrated and, as in his youth, impoverished.

1633

Galileo Galilei is condemned for heresy in Rome. True to his observations of a pendulum in motion, the Inquisition's extreme repression yielded an opposite reaction: Enlightenment.

➡ Statue of Galileo, Florence

1656

The plague kills at least 300,000 people across central and southern Italy.

1737

Maria Theresa ends the Medici's dynastic rule by installing her husband as grand duke of Tuscany. She remains the brains of the operation, reforming Tuscany from behind the scenes.

relationship with the stars. Pope Paul III kept several astrologers on hand, and no major papal initiative or construction project could be undertaken without first searching the sky with an astrolabe for auspicious signs. Yet theologian (and sometime astrologer) Tommaso Campanella was found guilty of heresy for dissenting views that emphasised observation. Research into the universe's guiding physical principles was entrusted by Paul III to his consulting theologians, who determined from close examination of the scriptures that the sun must revolve around the earth.

Tuscany's Renaissance legacy was almost lost in the 1966 Great Flood of Florence that left thousands homeless and three million manuscripts and thousands of art works under mud, stone and sewage. Those heroes who helped dig out the treasures are honoured as *gli angeli del fango* (angels of mud).

Equipped with telescopes that he'd adjusted and improved, Galileo came to a different conclusion. His observations supported Nicolaus Copernicus' theory that the planets revolved around the sun, and a cautious body of Vatican Inquisitors initially allowed him to publish his findings as long as he also presented a case for the alternate view. But when Galileo's research turned out to be dangerously convincing, the Vatican reversed its position and tried him for heresy. By then Galileo was quite ill, and his weakened state and widespread support may have spared him the usual heretic's sentence of execution. Under official threat of torture, Galileo stated in writing that he may have overstated the case for the Copernican view of the universe, and was allowed to carry out his prison sentence under house arrest. Pope Urban VIII alternately indulged his further studies and denied him access to doctors, but Galileo kept on pursuing scientific research even after he began losing his sight. Meanwhile, Tommaso Campanella was taken out of prison and brought to Rome, where he became Urban VIII's personal astrologer in 1629.

Gold Gilt: Going for Baroque

See Galileo's preserved middle finger (and other body parts) in Florence's superb and wholly interactive Museo Galileo, just around the corner from the Uffizi. Online, explore Galileo's life, times, religious context and scientific advances in The Galileo Project (http://galileo.rice.edu).

With his astrologers on hand, the pope might have seen Italy's foreign domination coming. Far from cementing the Church's authority, the Inquisition created a power vacuum on the ground while papal authorities were otherwise occupied with lofty theological matters. While local Italian nobles and successful capitalists vied among themselves for influence as usual, the Austrian Holy Roman Empress Maria Theresa took charge of the situation in 1737, and set up her husband Francis as the grand duke of Tuscany.

Napoleon Bonaparte conquered swathes of Tuscany in 1799. So appreciative was Napoleon of the area's cultural heritage, in fact, that he decided to take as much as possible home with him. What he couldn't take he gave as gifts to various relatives – never mind that all those Tuscan villas and church altarpieces were not technically his to give. When Habsburg Ferdinando III took over the title of grand duke of Tuscany in 1814, Napoleon's sister Elisa Bonaparte and various other relations refused to budge from the luxe Lucchesi villas they had usurped, and concessions had to be made to accommodate them all.

1760s

Florence, along with Venice, Milan and Turin, becomes an essential stop for British aristocrats on the Grand Tour, a trend that continues until the 1840s.

1765–90

Enlightenment leader Leopold I continues his mother Maria Theresa's reforms. Moved by Cesare Beccaria's case for criminal justice reform, he makes Tuscany the first sovereign state to outlaw the death penalty.

1796–1801

Italy becomes a battleground between Napoleon, the Habsburgs and their Russian allies, and Tuscans witness much of their cultural patrimony divvied up as spoils of war.

1805–14

Napoleon establishes himself as king of Italy, with the military assistance of Italian soldiers he'd conscripted; when his conscripts desert, Napoleon loses Tuscany to Grand Duke Ferdinando III in 1814.

Still more upmarket expats arrived in Tuscany with the inauguration of Italy's cross-country train lines in 1840. Soon no finishing-school education would be complete without a Grand Tour of Italy, and the landmarks and museums of Tuscany were required reading. Train-loads of debutantes, dour chaperones and career bachelors arrived, setting the stage for EM Forster novels, Tuscan time-share investors and George Clooney wannabes.

Red & Black: A Chequered Past

While an upper-crust expat community was exporting Romantic notions about Italy, the country was facing harsh realities. Commercial agriculture provided tidy sums to absentee royal Austrian landlords while reducing peasants to poverty and creating stiff competition for small family farms. In rural areas, three-quarters of the family income was spent on a meagre diet of mostly grains. The promise of work in the burgeoning industrial sector lured many to cities, where long working hours and dangerous working conditions simply led to another dead end, and 70% of family income was still spent on food. Upward mobility was rare, since university admissions were strictly limited, and the Habsburgs were cautious about allowing locals into their imperial army or bureaucratic positions. Increasingly, the most reliable means for Tuscans to support their families was emigration to the Americas.

Austrian rule provided a common enemy that united Italians across provinces and classes. The Risorgimento (reunification period) was not so much a reorganisation of some previously unified Italian states (which hadn't existed since Roman times) as a revival of the city-state ideals of an independent citizenry. The secret societies that had flourished right

A BLOW TO INTELLECTUAL THOUGHT

Savonarola's theocratic rule over Florence (1494–98) only lasted four years, until his denunciation of decadence got him excommunicated and executed by Pope Alexander VI. The pope didn't appreciate Savonarola criticising his extravagant spending, illegitimate children and pursuit of personal vendettas under papal guise.

But Savonarola's short reign had an impact on Tuscany for centuries to come: it made the Church see a need to exert more direct control over the independent-minded region, and to guard against humanist philosophies that might contradict the its divine authority. The result: the Inquisition, where heretical ideas were made punishable by death, leading to an understandably chilling effect on intellectual inquiry. Celebrated universities in Pisa and Siena were subjected to close scrutiny, and the University of Pisa was effectively closed for about 50 years until Cosimo I de' Medici (1519–74) reinaugurated it in 1543.

1861

Two decades of insurrections culminate in a new Italian government, with a parliament and a king. Florence becomes Italy's capital in 1865, despite widespread poverty and periodic bread riots.

1871

After French troops are withdrawn from Rome, the forces of the Kingdom of Italy defeat the Papal States to take power in Rome; the capital moves there from Florence.

1915

Italy enters WWI fighting a familiar foe: the Austro-Hungarian Empire. War casualties, stranded POWs, heating-oil shortages and food rationing make for a hard-won victory by 1918.

1921

Mussolini forms the Fascist Party, and Tuscan supporters fall in line by 1922. The 1924 elections are 'overseen' by Fascist paramilitary groups, and the Fascists win a parliamentary majority.

under French noses as a local check on colonial control formed a network of support for nationalist sentiment. During 1848 and 1849 revolution broke out, and a radical government was temporarily installed in Florence.

Nervous that the Austrians would invade, conservative Florentine leaders invited Habsburg Leopold II to return as archduke of Tuscany. But when rural unrest in Tuscany complicated Austria's return to power, Austrian retaliation and brutal repression galvanised nationalist sentiment in the region. Although Italy was united under one flag in 1861, this early split between radicals and conservatives would define Tuscany's future political landscape.

Unification didn't end unemployment or unrest; only 2% of Italy's population gained the right to vote in 1861. Strikes were held to protest working conditions, and their brutal suppression gave rise to a new Socialist Party in 1881. The new Italian government's money-making scheme to establish itself as a colonial power in Abyssinia (modern-day Ethiopia and Eritrea) proved a costly failure: 17,000 Italian soldiers were lost near Adowa in 1896. When grain prices were raised in 1898, many impoverished Italians could no longer afford to buy food, and riots broke out. Rural workers unionised, and when a strike was called in 1902, 200,000 rural labourers came out en masse.

Finally Italian politicians began to take the hint and initiated some reforms. Child labour was banned, working hours fixed and the right to vote extended to all men over the age of 30 by 1912 (women would have to wait until 1945). But as soon as the government promised the Socialists to fund an old-age pension scheme, it reneged, and opted to invade Tunisia instead.

GENEROUS TO A FAULT

Austrian Holy Roman Empress Maria Theresa (1717–80; mother of 16 children – including the now-notorious Marie Antoinette) was generous to a fault. A self-taught military strategist, she held local potentates in check and pushed through reforms that curbed witch burning, outlawed torture, established mandatory education and allowed Italian peasants to keep a modest share of their crops. She also brought the Habsburgs' signature flashy style to Tuscany, and kicked off a frenzy of redecoration that included flamboyant frescoes packed with cherubs, ornate architectural details that were surely a nightmare to dust, and gilding whenever and wherever possible.

Perhaps fearing that her family's priceless art collection might factor into Maria Theresa's redecorating plans, Medici heiress Anna Maria Luisa de' Medici willed everything to the city of Florence upon her death in 1743, on the condition that the entire inheritance must remain in the city. Generous to a fault.

1940–43

The Fascist Italian Empire joins Germany in declaring war on Great Britain and France. The Italian government surrenders in 1943; Mussolini refuses to comply and war continues.

1943–45

The Italian Resistance joins the Allies against Mussolini and the Nazis; Tuscany is liberated. When civil warfare ends in 1945, a coalition government is formed.

1946

Umberto II is exiled after a referendum to make Italy a republic is successful; 71.6% of Tuscans vote for a republic.

1959–63

Italy's economy revives via industrialisation, entrepreneurship and US Marshall Plan investments designed to stop it from joining the Soviet Bloc.

Italy got more war than it had budgeted for when WWI broke out in 1914. A prominent young Socialist firebrand named Benito Mussolini (1883–1945) led the call for Italy to intervene in support of the Allies, though most Socialists were opposed to such an action. As a result, Mussolini was expelled from the Socialist Party and went on to join the Italian army. After being injured and discharged, he formed the Italian Combat Squad in 1919, the forerunner of the National Fascist Party.

Inter-War Blues

Though Italy had been on the winning side in WWI, few Italians were in the mood to celebrate. In addition to war casualties, 600,000 Italians served time as prisoners of war, and 100,000 had died (primarily due to the Italian government's failure to send food, clothing and medical supplies to its own soldiers). Wartime decrees that extended working hours and outlawed strikes had made factory conditions so deplorable that women led mass strikes. Bread shortages and bread riots spread nationwide. Mussolini had found support for his call to order in the Tuscan countryside, and by 1922 his black-shirted squads could be seen parading through Florence, echoing his call for the ousting of the national government and the purging of socialists and communists from all local positions of power. In 1922 the Fascists marched on Rome and staged a coup d'etat, installing Mussolini as prime minister.

No amount of left-wing purges prevented the country from plunging into recession in the 1930s after Mussolini demanded a revaluation of the Italian lira. While the free-fall of wages won Mussolini allies among industrialists, it created further desperation among his power base. New military conquests in Libya and Ethiopia initially provided a feeble boost to the failing economy, but when the enormous bill came due in the late 1930s, Mussolini hastily agreed to an economic and military alliance with Germany. Contrary to the bold claims of Mussolini's propaganda machine, Italy was ill-prepared for the war it entered in 1940.

Post-WWII: the Tuscan Left

A new Italian government surrendered to the Allies in 1943, but Mussolini refused to concede defeat, and dragged Italy through two more years of civil war, Allied campaigns and German occupation. Tuscany emerged from these black years redder than ever, and became a staunch Socialist power base.

Immediately after the war, three coalition governments succeeded one another. Italy became a republic in 1946 and the newly formed right-wing Democrazia Cristiana (DC; Christian Democrats) – led by Alcide de Gasperi, who remained prime minister until 1953 – won the first elections under the new constitution in 1948.

Best Historical Reads

Renaissance Florence on Five Florins a Day (2010), Charles FitzRoy

Tuscany: A History (2011), Alistair Moffat

Queen Bee of Tuscany: The Redoubtable Janet Ross (2013), Ben Downing

A powerful Resistance movement emerged in Tuscany during WWII, but not soon enough to prevent hundreds of thousands of Italian casualties, plus a still-unknown number of Italians shipped off to 23 Italian concentration camps (including one near Arezzo) and death camps in Germany.

1966

The Arno bursts its banks, submerging Florence in metres of mud and water. Some 5000 people are left homeless and thousands of art works and manuscripts are destroyed.

1969

Strikes and university-student uprisings demand social change and promote sweeping reforms, not just in working conditions but also in housing, social services, pensions and civil rights.

1970s–'80s

The Anni di Piombo (Years of Lead) terrorise the country with extremist violence and reprisals; police kill anarchist Franco Serantini in Pisa, and Red Brigades kill Florence's mayor in 1986.

1993

A car bomb at the Uffizi kills six and causes US$10 million damage to artworks. The mafia is suspected, but never indicted. The same year 200,000 people protest mafia violence.

America was named after Amerigo Vespucci, a Florentine navigator who, from 1497 to 1504, made several voyages of discovery in what would one day be known as South America.

Until the 1980s the Partito Comunista Italiano (PCI; Italian Communist Party), despite being systematically kept out of government, played a crucial role in Italy's social and political development. The popularity of the party – founded in the port town of Livorno in 1921 – prompted the so-called *anni di piombo* (years of lead) in the 1970s, dominated by terrorism and social unrest. In 1978 the Brigate Rosse (Red Brigades, a group of young left-wing militants responsible for several bomb blasts and assassinations) claimed their most important victim – former DC prime minister Aldo Moro. His kidnap and murder (54 days later) shook the country.

Despite the disquiet, the 1970s enjoyed positive change: divorce and abortion became legal, and legislation was passed allowing women to keep their own names after marriage. Regional governments with limited powers were formed in 15 of the country's 20 regions, including Tuscany.

And, in a predictable Tuscan centre-left fashion, from its creation in 1970 until 1983, Tuscany's regional government was headed up by Italy's dominant leftist party, the Partito Socialista Italiano (PSI; Italian Socialist Party).

With the disbanding of the Socialist party following the Tangentopoli ('kickback city') scandal, which broke in Milan in 1992, the door was

THE BIKER, THE FRIAR & THE ACCOUNTANT

Unbelievable as it may sound, this trio became heroes of the Italian Resistance during WWII. Giorgio Nissim was a Jewish accountant in Pisa who belonged to a secret Tuscan Resistance group that helped Jewish Italians escape from fascist Italy. The network was discovered by the Fascists, and everyone involved was sent to concentration camps, except for Giorgio, who remained undetected.

It seemed nowhere was safe for Jewish refugees – until Franciscan friar Rufino Niccacci helped organise the Assisi Underground, which hid hundreds of Jewish refugees from all over Italy in convents and monasteries across Umbria in 1943 and 1944. In Assisi, nuns who'd never met Jewish people before learned to cook kosher meals for their guests, and locals risked their lives to provide shelter to total strangers.

The next problem was getting forged travel documents to the refugees, and quick. Enter Gino Bartali, world-famous Tuscan cyclist, Tour de France winner and three-time champion of the Giro d'Italia. After his death in 2003, documents revealed that during his 'training rides' during the war years, Bartali had carried Resistance intelligence and falsified documents that were used to transport Jewish refugees to safe locations. Suspected of involvement, Bartali was once interrogated at the dreaded Villa Triste in Florence, where political prisoners were held and tortured – but he revealed nothing. Until his death he refused to discuss his efforts to save Jewish refugees, even with his children, saying, 'One does these things, and then that's that.'

1995

Maurizio Gucci, heir to the Florence-born Gucci fashion empire, is gunned down outside his Milan offices. Three years later, his estranged wife Patrizia Reggiani is jailed for ordering his murder.

2005

Regional elections in Tuscany see centre-left president Claudio Martini win a second term in office, with a landslide victory, reconfirming Tuscany as Italy's true bastion of the left.

2007

Almost a decade after the renovation project was announced, the first crane is spotted above Florence's Uffizi gallery. The multimillion-euro project will double the gallery size. Completion date unknown.

2008

Silvio Berlusconi and his right-wing allies triumph in the national elections. Tuscany's traditional support of leftist candidates and parties is diluted, with support for the Rainbow Left coalition falling dramatically.

left open in Tuscany's political arena for the Partito Democratico della Sinistra (Democratic Party of the Left; PDS) – an equally socialist political party created in 1991 to replace the disbanded PCI – to dominate the decade: on a national level, the PDS was part of Romano Prodi's winning centre-left coalition that defeated Berlusconi in 1996 (only for Berlusconi to sweep back into power with an unassailable majority at the head of a right-wing coalition known as Popolo della Libertà; PdL).

Regional elections in 2005 saw incumbent Tuscan president Claudio Martini of the left-wing Democratici di Sinistra (DS; Democrats of the Left) win a second term in office. Born in Tunis in 1951, he moved to Italy aged 10 and worked tirelessly to revamp the healthcare system during his time in office. He rid Tuscany of a serious health-service deficit and forged closer ties with the rest of Europe and Tuscans abroad.

Tuscany Now

Tuscany has been a stronghold of the Italian left ever since rapid industrialisation post-WWII. And regional elections in 2010 proved no exception. With much-loved incumbent Regione Toscane president Claudio Martini choosing not to stand for a third term, fellow centre-left candidate Enrico Rossi (b 1958) stormed into office with a landslide victory over the centre-right. What made the red Tuscan politician's victory so poignant was the fact that other like-minded, traditionally left regions in Italy fell to Berlusconi's governing centre-right coalition – while famously red Tuscany stood firm.

Tuscans rapidly warmed to their new president, who tweets at @rossipresidente and uses Facebook to converse and communicate key developments in Tuscany – such as the region-wide switch to digital TV in 2011; Pisa being hailed as one of Italy's most wi-fi–connected cities; and the opening of the first leg of the controversial, Rome-bound toll motorway that will run from just south of Livorno to Civitavecchia, 206km further south, once completed in 2016.

Tuscany's regional government is headed by the president, elected every five years. In turn he is aided by 10 ministers and a legislative regional council comprising 65 members, also elected by proportional representation for the same five-year term. Keep tabs on regional government and council at www.regione.toscana.it and www.consiglio.regione.toscana.it respectively.

2009
Italy's Constitutional Court overturns a law giving Berlusconi immunity from persecution while in office, opening the possibility that he could stand trial in several court cases. He refuses to resign.

2010
Regional elections see a new centre-left president, Enrico Rossi, in power for a five-year term; the next elections will be held in 2015.

2011
Skilled economist Mario Monti is drafted in as prime minister to head a government of unelected technocrats, introducing tough austerity measures in a bid to stave off economic disaster.

2011–13
Berlusconi stands trial for sex with an underage prostitute, abusing power, tax fraud and breaching confidentiality. He is found guilty of all four crimes.

The Tuscan Way of Life

Romanticised the world over, Tuscany has impassioned more writers, designers and filmmakers than any other region. Yet what is it that makes the birthplace of Gucci, Cavalli and the Vespa scooter so inspiring, so *dolce* (sweet)? Florence takes the lead with its artistic heritage and tradition of master craftsmanship, its inhabitants whose natural style, grace and appreciation of beauty finds expression in an extraordinary attention to detail, quest for perfection and pride in local dialect and history. Enter the cornerstones of Tuscan lifestyle...

Unesco World Heritage Sites

- *Historic centre of Florence*
- *Piazza dei Miracoli, Pisa*
- *Historic centre of Siena*
- *Val d'Orcia*
- *Historic centre of San Gimignano*
- *Historic centre of Pienza*
- *Medici villas and gardens, Tuscany*

Rural Roots

Deeply attached to their patch of land, people in this predominantly rural neck of the woods are not simply Italian or Tuscan. Harking back to centuries of coexistence as rival political entities with their own style of architecture, school of painting, bell tower and so on, it is the *paese* (home town) or, in the case of Siena and other towns, the *contrada* (neighbourhood) in which one is born that reigns supreme. For most, such *campanilismo* (literally, loyalty to one's bell tower) is all-consuming. 'Better a death in the family than a Pisan at the door' says an old Florentine proverb, referencing the historic rivalry between the Tuscan towns.

Passionate, proud, reserved, hard-working, family-oriented, fond of food and wine, thrifty, extremely self-conscious and proud of their appearance are characteristics attributed to Tuscans across the board.

Brash, no, but in Florence Florentines like to make it known where they stand in society. From oversized doorknobs to sculpted stonework, overt statements of wealth and power are everywhere in this class-driven city, whose dialect – penned for the world to read by literary greats Dante, Boccaccio and Petrarch in the 14th century – is deemed the purest form of Italian.

La Dolce Vita

Life is *dolce* (sweet) for this privileged pocket of Italy, one of the country's wealthiest enclaves where the family reigns supreme, and tradition and quality reign over quantity. From the great names in viticulture to the flower-producing industry of Pescia and the small-scale farms of rural Tuscany, it is family-run businesses handed between generations that form the backbone of this proud, strong region.

In Florence – the only city with a faint hint of the cosmopolitan – daily life is the fastest paced. Florentines rise early, drop their kids at school by 8am then flit from espresso to the office by 9am. Lunch is a lengthy affair for these food- and wine-mad people, as is the early-evening *aperitivo* (pre-dinner drinks), enjoyed in a bar with friends to whet the appetite for dinner. For younger Florentines, who bear the biggest brunt of Florence's ever-rising rent and salaries that scarcely rise, it is quite common to treat the lavish *aperitivo* spread like dinner – enter *apericena*. Smokers, fast dwindling, puff on pavements outside.

There is no better time of day or week than late Sunday afternoon to witness the *passeggiata* (early evening stroll), a wonderful tradition that sees Tuscans in towns don a suitable outfit and walk – to get a gelato, chat, meet friends, mooch, contemplate the sunset and, quite simply, relish the close of the day at an exceedingly relaxed pace.

Theatre, concerts, art exhibitions (the free opening on Thursday evenings at Florence's Palazzo Strozzi is always packed) and *il calcio* (football) entertain after hours. Tuscany's top professional football club, ACF Fiorentina, has a fanatical fan base (check the memorabilia in Florence's Trattoria Mario).

Weekends see many flee their city apartments for less urban climes, where the din of *motorini* (scooters) whizzing through the night lessens and there's more space and light: green countryside is a mere 15-minute getaway from lucky old Florence, unlike many urban centres where industrial sprawl really sprawls.

Best Passeggiata Strips

- *Via de' Tornabuoni & Ponte Vecchio, Florence*
- *Via Fillungo, Lucca*
- *Via Banchi di Sopra, Siena*
- *'The Corso' (aka Corso Italia), Arezzo*
- *Corso Carducci, Grosetto*

Casa Dolce Casa

By their very nature, family-orientated Tuscans travel little (many spend a lifetime living in the town of their birth) and place great importance on *casa dolce casa* (home sweet home) – the rate of home ownership in Tuscany is among Europe's highest.

Rural lifestyle is slavishly driven by close-knit, ancient communities in small towns and villages, where local matters and gossip are more important than national or world affairs. Everyone knows everyone to the point of being clannish, making assimilation for outsiders hard – if not impossible. Farming is the self-sufficient way of life, albeit one that is becoming increasingly difficult – hence the mushrooming of *agriturismi* (farm-stay accommodation), as farmers stoically utilise every resource they have to make ends meet.

At one time the domain of Tuscany's substantial well-off British population (there's good reason why playwright John Mortimer dubbed Chianti 'Chiantishire' in his 1988 novel and 1989 TV adaptation *Summer's Lease*), the region's bounty of stylish stone villas and farmhouses with terracotta floors, wood-burning fireplaces and terraces with views are now increasingly passing back into the hands of Tuscans eagerly rediscovering their countryside.

Urban or rural, children typically remain at home until they reach their 30s, often only fleeing the nest to wed. In line with national trends, Tuscan families are small – one or two kids, with around 20% of families

No title better delves into the essence of Tuscan lifestyle than *The Wisdom of Tuscany: Simplicity, Security and the Good Life – Making the Tuscan Lifestyle Your Own* by Ferenc Màté.

COFFEE CULTURE

Coffee is not just a drink but a way of life for Tuscans, whose typical day is regimentally punctuated with caffeine, the type of coffee depending wholly on time of day and occasion.

The number one cardinal rule: cappuccino (espresso topped with hot, frothy milk), caffè latte (milkier version with less froth) and latte macchiato (warmed milk 'stained' with a spot of coffee) are only ever drunk at breakfast or in the early morning. If you're truly Tuscan, though, the chances are you'll probably grab a speed espresso (short, sharp shot of strong, black coffee) or *caffè doppio* (double espresso) standing up at the bar with everyone else at your favourite cafe on the way to work.

Lunch and dinner only end one way, with *un caffè* (literally 'a coffee', meaning an espresso and nothing else), although come dusk it is quite acceptable to perhaps finish with *un caffè corretto* (espresso with a dash of grappa or other spirit).

Sitting down at a table in a cafe to have a coffee is four times more expensive than drinking it standing at the bar.

childless and 26% of households being single. Despite increasing numbers of women working, chauvinistic attitudes remain well entrenched in more rural areas.

La Festa

Delve into the mindset of a Tuscan and a holy trinity of popular folklore, agricultural tradition and religious rite of passage dances before your eyes – which pretty much translates as *la festa* (party!). No cultural agenda is more jam-packed with ancient festivity than theirs: patron saints alone provide weeks of celebration given that every village, town, profession, trade and social group has a saint they call their own and venerate religiously.

Known in Florence as 'the book that broke all the rules', *Italians Dance and I'm a Wallflower* by Florence-based author Linda Malcone provides a cracking insight into local behaviour and cultural expression. The title is one of several to be published by local publishing house, The Florentine Press (www.theflorentinepress.com).

La festa climaxes, not once but twice, with Siena's soul-stirring Il Palio, a hot-blooded horse race conceived in the 12th century to honour the Virgin Mary and revamped six centuries on to celebrate the miracles of the Madonna of Provenzano (2 July) and Assumption (16 August). Deeply embroiled in its religious roots is a fierce *contrada* rivalry, not to mention a fervent penchant for dressing up and a widespread respect of tradition that sees horses blessed before the race, jockeys riding bareback and the silk banner for the winner of August's race ritually designed by local Sienese artists and July's by nonSienese. Legend says that a Sienese bride marrying in far-off lands took with her earth from her *contrada* to put beneath the legs of her marital bed to ensure her offspring would be conceived on home soil.

Although it's by no means the social force it once was, Catholicism (the religion of 85% of the region) and its rituals nevertheless play a key role in daily lives: first Communions, church weddings and religious feast days are an integral part of Tuscan society.

Bella Figura

A sense of style is vital to Tuscans, who take great pride in their dress and appearance to ensure their *bella figura* (good public face). Dressing impeccably comes naturally to most Tuscans and for most Florentines, chic is a byword. Indeed, it was in their naturally beautiful city that the Italian fashion industry was born and bred.

Guccio Gucci and Salvatore Ferragamo got the haute-couture ball rolling in the 1920s with boutiques in Florence. And in 1951 a well-heeled Florentine nobleman called Giovanni Battista Giorgini held a fashion soirée in his Florence home to spawn Italy's first prét-à-porter fashion shows. The catwalk quickly shifted to Florence's Palazzo Pitti, where Eu-

VIRTUAL TUSCAN LIFESTYLE

- **Florence Night & Day** (http://lovingflorence.blogspot.com) Compelling diary of a 30-something Florentine gal.
- **One Hundred Years Later in Florence** (http://bellabiker.blogspot.com) A New York executive follows her Italian ancestors to Florence and becomes a bike-tour leader.
- **Girl in Florence** (http://girlinflorence.com) Insider musings, reflections, practical tips and (excellent) recommendations from an American called Georgette very much at home in Florence.
- **Maple Leaf Mamma** (www.mapleleafmamma.com) Sharp, pithy prose on navigating motherhood in a traditional macho country from a feminist perspective; penned by a Canadian in Florence.
- **A Dusty Olive Green** (www.adustyolivegreen.com) A blog from Florence by a Danish photographer.

rope's most prestigious fashion shows dazzled until 1971 (when the women's shows moved to Milan). The menswear shows stayed put, though, and top designers still leg it to Florence twice a year to unveil their menswear collections at the Pitti Immagine Uomo fashion shows and their creations for *bambini* (kids) at Pitti Bimbo.

Tuscany continues to inspire fashion and the fashionable. Take American actor and dandy John Malkovich, who chose the Tuscan town of Prato to create his designer fashion label **Technobohemian** (www.technobohemian.it).

Tuscan Icons

The Vespa scooter

Gucci

Chianti wine

Michelangelo's David

Renaissance art

The Tuscan Table

Be it by sinking your teeth into a beefy blue *bistecca alla fiorentina* (chargrilled T-bone steak), wine tasting in Chianti, savouring Livorno fish stew or devouring white truffles unearthed around San Miniato near Pisa, travelling Tuscany is a memorable banquet of gastronomic and viticultural experiences.

Best Traditional Tuscan Cuisine

Trattoria Mario, Florence

Trattoria Cibrèo, Florence

La Grotta, Montepulciano

I Sette Consoli, Orvieto

Il Leccio, Sant'Angelo in Colle

For tips on when to go and what to eat, see p36. For guidance on what to expect to spend eating out, see p322.

A Country Kitchen

It was above an open wood fire in *la cucina contadina* (the farmer's kitchen) that Tuscan cuisine was cooked up. Its basic premise: don't waste a crumb.

During the 13th and 14th centuries, when Florence prospered and the wealthy started using silver cutlery instead of fingers, simplicity remained the hallmark of dishes served at lavish banquets thrown by feuding families as a show of wealth. And while the Medici passion for flaunting the finer things in life during the Renaissance gave Tuscan cuisine a fanciful kick, with spectacular sugar sculptures starring alongside spit-roasted suckling pig, ordinary Tuscans continued to rely on the age-old *cucina povera* (poor dishes) to keep hunger at bay.

Contemporary Tuscan cuisine remains faithful to these humble roots, using fresh local produce and eschewing fussy execution.

A Bloody Affair: Meat & Game

The icon of Tuscan cuisine is Florence's *bistecca alla fiorentina,* a chargrilled T-bone steak rubbed with olive oil, seared on the chargrill, seasoned, and served *al sangue* (blue and bloody). A born-and-bred rebel, this feisty cut of meat is weighed before it's cooked and priced on menus by *l'etto* or 100g.

Tuscan markets conjure up animal parts many wouldn't dream of eating. In the past, prime beef cuts were the domain of the wealthy and offal was the staple peasant fare: tripe was simmered for hours with onions, carrots and herbs to make *lampredetto* or with tomatoes and herbs to make *trippa alla fiorentina* – two classics that are still going strong.

Pasto, a gruesome mix of *picchiante* (cow's lungs) and chopped potatoes, is not even a gastronomic curiosity these days – unlike *cibrèo* (chicken's kidney, liver, heart and cockscomb stew) and *colle ripieno* (stuffed chicken's neck), two dishes that can still be found. Another golden oldie featured on many a medieval fresco is *pollo al mattone* – boned chicken splattered beneath a brick, rubbed with herbs and baked beneath the brick. The end result is handsomely crispy.

Cinghiale (wild boar), hunted in autumn, is turned into *salsicce di cinghiale* (wild-boar sausages) or simmered with tomatoes, pepper and herbs to create a rich stew.

In Tuscany the family pig invariably ends up on the plate as a salty slice of *soprassata* (head, skin and tongue boiled, chopped and spiced with garlic, rosemary and other herbs and spices), *finocchiona* (fennel-spiced sausage), prosciutto, nearly black *mallegato* (spiked with nutmeg, cinnamon, raisins and pine kernels from San Miniato) or *mortadella* (a smooth-textured pork sausage speckled with cubes of white fat). *Lardo di colonnata* (thin slices of local pork fat aged in a mix of herbs and oils for at least six months) is a treat hard to find outside Tuscany.

Best on Friday: Fish

Livorno leads the region in seafood: *cacciucco* (one 'c' for each type of fish thrown into it) is the signature dish. Deriving its name from the Turkish *kukut*, meaning 'small fry', *cacciucco* is a stew of five fish simmered with tomatoes and red peppers, served atop stale bread. *Triglie alla livornese* is red or white mullet cooked in tomatoes, and *baccalà alla livornese*, also with tomatoes, features cod traditionally salted aboard the ships en route to the old Medici port. *Baccalà* (salted cod), not to be confused with *stoccofisso* (unsalted air-dried stockfish) is a trattoria mainstay, served on Fridays as tradition and old-style Catholicism demands.

Poor Man's Meat: Pulses, Grains & Vegetables

Poor man's meat was precisely what pulses were to Tuscans centuries ago. Jam-packed with protein, cheap and available year-round (eaten fresh in summer, dried in winter), pulses go into traditional dishes like *minestra di fagioli* (bean soup), *minestra di pane* (bread and bean soup) and *ribollita* (a 'reboiled' bean, vegetable and bread soup with black cabbage, left to sit for a day before being served).

Of the dozens of bean varieties, *cannellini* and dappled *borlotti* are the most common; both are delicious drizzled with olive oil to accompany meat. The round yellow *zolfino* from Pratomagno and silky smooth *sorano* bean from Pescia are prized. Of huge local pride to farmers in Garfagnana is *farro della garfagnana* (spelt), an ancient grain grown in Europe as early as 2500 BC.

Tuscany's lush vegetable patch sees medieval vegetables grow alongside tomatoes. Wild fennel, black celery (braised as a side dish), sweet red onions (delicious oven-baked), artichokes and zucchini flowers (stuffed and oven-baked), black cabbage, broad beans, chicory, chard, thistle-like cardoons and green tomatoes are among the more unusual ones to look out for.

Prized as one of the most expensive spices, saffron is all the rage around San Gimignano where it was enthusiastically traded in medieval

ETIQUETTE

Bread Is plentiful, unsalted and butter-less; don't expect a side plate (put it on the table).

Spaghetti Twirling it around your fork as if you were born twirling is the only way – no spoons please.

Fussy kids It is OK to ask for a plate of pasta with butter and Parmesan.

Coffee Never order a cappuccino after 11am, and certainly not after a meal, when an espresso is the only respectable way to end a dining experience (with, perhaps, a digestive of grappa or other fiery liqueur).

Il conto (the bill) Whoever invites pays.

Splitting the bill Common enough.

Tipping If there is no *servizio* (service charge), leave 10% to 15% tip.

Dress Decent is best, particularly in Florence where working Florentines go home to freshen up between *aperitivo* and dinner.

times. Fiery red and as fine as dust by the time it reaches the kitchen, saffron in its rawest state is the dried flower stigma of the saffron crocus.

Where's the Salt: Bread

One bite and the difference is striking: Tuscan *pane* (bread) is unsalted, creating a disconcertingly bland taste many a bread lover might never learn to love.

Yet it is this centuries-old staple, deliberately unsalted to ensure it lasted for a good week and to complement the region's salty cured meats, that forms the backbone of Tuscany's most famous dishes: *pappa al pomodoro* (bread and tomato soup), *panzanella* (tomato and basil salad mixed with a mush of bread soaked in cold water) and *ribollita*. None of the sound or look particularly appetising, but their depth of flavour is extraordinary.

Thick-crusted *pane toscana* is the basis of two antipasti delights: *crostini* (lightly toasted slices of bread topped with liver pâté) and *fettunta* or Tuscan bruschetta (also called *crogiantina*; toast fingers doused in garlic, salt and olive oil).

A Dowry Skill: Cheese

So important was cheesemaking in the past that it was a dowry skill. Still respected, the sheep's-milk *pecorino* crafted in Pienza ranks among Italy's greatest *pecorini:* taste it young and mild with fava beans, fresh pear or chestnuts and honey; or try it mature and tangy, spiked with *toscanello* (black peppercorns) or as *pecorino di tartufo* (infused with black-truffle shavings). *Pecorino* massaged with olive oil during the ageing process turns red and is called *rossellino*.

Festive Frolics: Sweets, Chocolate & Ice

Be it the honey, almond and sugar-cane sweets served at the start of 14th-century banquets in Florence, or the sugar sculptures made to impress

GO SLOW TUSCANY

Born out of a desire to protect the world from McDonaldisation, **Slow Food** (www.fondazioneslowfood.com) preserves local food traditions and encourages interest in the food we eat, its origins and how it tastes. Created by Italian wine writer, Carlo Petrini, the foundation works in over 130 countries and has also spawned **Slow City** (www.cittaslow.blogspot.com). Slow City towns – Anghiari, Barga, Castelnuovo Berardenga, Civitella in Val di Chiana, Greve in Chianti, Massa Marittima, Pratovecchio, San Miniato, San Vincenzo and Suvereto in Tuscany – have a visible and distinct culture; rely on local resources rather than mass-produced food and culture; work to reduce pollution; and increasingly rely on sustainable development, such as organic farming and public transport.

Industrialisation, globalisation and environmental dangers threaten traditional, indigenous edibles. Enter Slow Food's **Ark of Taste**, a project born and headquartered in Florence that aims to protect and promote endangered food products including, in Tuscany: Chianina beef, *lardo di colonnata*, Certaldo onions, Casola chestnut bread, Cetica red potatoes, Garfagnana potato bread and *farro* (spelt), Carmignano dried figs, *cinta senese* (the indigenous Tuscan pig), Londa Regina peaches, Pistoian Mountain *pecorino* cheese, Orbetello *bottarga* (salted mullet roe) and Zeri lamb. Among the many cured meats that make the list: San Miniato *mallegato,* Prato mortadella (smooth-textured pork sausage made dull-pink with drops of alkermes liqueur and speckled white with cubes of fat), Sienese *buristo* (a type of pork salami made in the province of Siena), Valdarno *tarese* (a 50cm-to-80cm-long pancetta spiced with red garlic, orange peel and covered in pepper), Florentine *bardiccio* (fresh fennel-flavoured sausage encased in a natural skin of pig intestine and eaten immediately) and *biroldo* (spiced blood sausage made in Garfagnana from pig's head and blood).

Sampling any of these Tuscan items guarantees an authentic tasting experience.

OLIVE OIL

Olive oil heads Tuscany's culinary trinity (bread and wine are the other two) and epitomises the earthy simplicity of Tuscan cuisine: dipping chunks of bread into pools of this liquid gold or biting into a slice of oil-doused *fettunta* (bruschetta) are sweet pleasures here.

The Etruscans were the first to cultivate olive trees and press the fruit to make oil, a process refined by the Romans. As with wine, strict rules govern when and how olives are harvested (October to December), the varieties used, and so on.

The best Tuscan oils wear a Chianti Classico DOP or Terre di Siena DOP label and an IGP certificate of quality issued by the region's Consortium of Tuscan Olive Oil. In Florence look out for prize-winning oils from local olive oil producer, Marchesi de' Frescobaldi.

at the flamboyant 16th- and 17th-century feasts of the power-greedy Medici, *dolci* (sweets) have always been reserved for festive occasions. In more humble circles street vendors sold *bomboloni* (doughnuts) and *pandiramerino* (rosemary-bread buns), while carnival in Florence was marked by *stiacchiata* (Florentine flat bread made from eggs, flour, sugar and lard, then dusted with icing sugar).

As early as the 13th century, servants at the Abbazia di Montecelso near Siena paid tax to the nuns in the form of *panpepato* (a pepper and honey flat bread), although legend tells a different tale: following a siege in Siena, Sister Berta baked a revitalising flat cake of honey, dried fruit, almonds and pepper to pep up the city's weakened inhabitants. Subsequently sweetened with spices, sprinkled with sugar and feasted on once a year at Christmas, Siena's *panforte* (literally 'strong bread') – a flat, hard cake with nuts and candied fruit – is now eaten year-round. An old wives' tale says it stops couples quarrelling.

Unsurprisingly, it was at the Florentine court of Catherine de' Medici that Italy's most famous product, *gelato* (ice cream), first appeared. It's all thanks to court maestro Bernardo Buontalenti (1536–1608), who engineered a way of freezing sweetened milk and egg yolks. For centuries, ice cream and sherbets – a mix of shaved ice and fruit juice served between courses at Renaissance banquets to aid digestion – only appeared on tables of the wealthy.

Tuscan *biscotti* (biscuits) – once served with candied fruits and sugared almonds at the start of and between courses at Renaissance banquets – are dry, crisp and often double baked. *Cantucci* are hard, sweet biscuits studded with almonds. *Brighidini di lamporecchio* are small, round aniseed-flavoured wafers; *ricciarelli* are almond biscuits, sometimes with candied orange; and *lardpinocchiati* are studded with pine kernels. In Lucca, locals are proud of their *buccellato* (a sweet bread loaf with sultanas and aniseed seeds), a treat given by godparents to their godchild on their first Holy Communion and eaten with alacrity at all other times.

ORGANIC PRODUCE

Cibo biologico (organic food) is increasingly popular in farm-rich Tuscany, where several stand-out dining choices – such as Podere del Grillo near San Miniato, La Cerreta near Sassetta, Pisa's biOsteria 050 – serve meals created solely from organic farm produce. Florentine enoteca Vivanda notably marries organic cuisine with organic wine.

Buone Feste

Be it harvest, wedding, birth or religious holiday, traditional celebrations are intrinsically woven into Tuscan culinary culture. They are not as raucous as festivals of the past, when an animal was sacrificed, but most remain meaty affairs.

Tuscans have baked breads and cakes such as ring-shaped *berlingozzo* (Tuscan sweet bread) and *schiacciata alla fiorentina* (a flattish, spongey bread-cum-cake best made with old-fashioned lard) for centuries during Carnevale, the period of merrymaking leading up to Ash Wednesday. Fritters are another sweet Carnevale treat: *cenci* are plain twists (literally 'rags') of fried, sweet dough sprinkled with icing sugar; *castagnole* look like puffed-up cushions; and *fritelle di mele* are slices of apple battered, deep fried and eaten warm with sugar.

On Easter Sunday, families take baskets of hard-boiled white eggs covered in a white-cloth napkin to church to be blessed, and return home to a luncheon feast of roast lamb gently spiced with garlic and rosemary, pre-empted by the blessed eggs.

September's grape harvest sees grapes stuck on top of *schiacciata* to make *schiacciata con l'uva* (grape cake), and autumn's chestnut harvest brings a flurry of chestnut festivals and *castagnaccio* (chestnut cake baked with chestnut flower, studded with raisins, topped with a rosemary sprig and served with a slice of ricotta) to the Tuscan table.

Come Christmas, *bollito misto* (boiled meat) with all the trimmings is traditional for many families: various animal parts, trotters et al, are thrown into the cooking pot and simmered for hours with a vegetable and herb stock. The meat is later served with mustard, green salsa and other sauces. A whole pig – notably the recently revived ancient white-and-black *cinta senese* indigenous breed – roasted on a spit, is the other option.

PASTA

Pasta is as much Tuscan as it is Italian, and no Tuscan banquet would be quite right without a *primo* (first course) of homemade *maccheroni* (wide, flat ribbon pasta), *pappardelle* (wider flat ribbon pasta) or Sienese *pici* (a thick, hand-rolled version of spaghetti) served with a duck, hare, rabbit or boar sauce.

On the Wine Trail

There's far more to this vine-rich region than cheap, raffia-wrapped bottled Chianti – *that* was the 1970s, darling! Something of a viticulture powerhouse, Tuscany excites oenophiles with its myriad full-bodied, highly respected reds. Wine tasting is an endless pleasure and the region is peppered with *enoteche* (wine bars) and *cantine* (wine cellars) designed especially for tasting and buying.

Many are planted on Tuscany's *strade del vino* (wine roads), signposted itineraries that lead motorists and cyclists along wonderfully scenic back roads into the heart of Tuscan wine country.

Tuscan white amounts to one label loved by Renaissance popes and artists alike: the aromatic Vernaccia di San Gimignano, best drunk as an aperitif on a terrace in or around San Gimignano.

Brunello di Montalcino

Brunello is up there at the top with Italy's most prized: count on up to €15 for a glass, €30 to €100 for an average bottle and €5000 for a 1940s collectible. The product of Sangiovese grapes grown south of Siena, it must spend at least two years ageing in oak. It is intense and complex with an ethereal fragrance, and is best paired with game, wild boar and roasts. Brunello grape rejects go into Rossi di Montalcino, Brunello's substantially cheaper but wholly drinkable kid sister.

Vino Nobile di Montepulciano

Prugnolo Gentile grapes (a clone of Sangiovese) form the backbone of the distinguished Vino Nobile di Montepulciano (2006 was an exceptional

TOP WINE & OIL ROADS

Meander past olive groves, vines and farms plump with local produce with these delightful *strade del Vino e dell'Olio.*

Strada del Vino e dei Sapori Colli di Maremma (www.stradavinimaremma.it) This route southeast of Grosseto highlights several DOC and DOCG wines, extra-virgin olive oil Toscano IGP, and the Maremma breed of cattle.

Strada del Vino e dell'Olio Lucca Montecarlo e Versilia (www.stradavinoeoliolucca.it) From Seravezza in the Apuane Alps to Lucca, then east to Montecarlo and Pescia: features Lucca's famous DOP olive oil and the Colline Lucchesi and Montecarlo di Lucca DOCs.

LABELS OF QUALITY

Quality and origin of Tuscan wine is flagged with these official classifications:

DOC (Denominazione d'Origine Controllata; Protected Designation of Origin) Must be produced within a specified region using defined methods to meet a certain quality; the rules spell out production area, grape varietals and viticultural/bottling techniques.

DOCG (Denominazione d'Origine Controllata e Garantita; Protected Designation of Origin and Quality) The most prestigious stamp of quality, DOCG wines are particularly good ones, produced in subterritories of DOC areas. Of Italy's 44 DOCGs, eight are Tuscan – Brunello di Montalcino, Carmignano, Chianti, Chianti Classico, Morellino di Scansano, Vernaccia di San Gimignano, Vino Nobile di Montepulciano and Elba Aleatico Passito.

IGT (Indicazione Geografica Tipica; Protected Geographical Indication) High-quality wines that don't meet DOC or DOCG definitions, such as Super Tuscans.

year). Its intense but delicate nose and dry, vaguely tannic taste make it the perfect companion to red meat and mature cheese.

Chianti

This cheery, full and dry fellow is known the world over as being easy to drink, suited to any dish and wholly affordable. More famous than good in the 1970s, contemporary Chianti gets the thumbs up from wine critics today. Produced in seven subzones from Sangiovese and a mix of other grape varieties, Chianti Classico – the traditional heart of this long-standing wine-growing area – is the best known, with a DOCG (Denominazione d'Origine Controllata e Garantita; Protected Designation of Origin and Quality) guarantee of quality and a Gallo Nero (Black Cockerel) emblem that once symbolised the medieval Chianti League. Young, fun Chianti Colli Senesi from the Siena hills is the largest subzone; Chianti delle Colline Pisane is light and soft in style; and Chianti Rùfina comes from the hills east of Florence.

Best Creative Tuscan Cuisine

- *Il Santo Bevitore, Florence*
- *Filippo, Pietrasanta*
- *Ristorante Albergaccio, Castellina in Chianti*
- *Grantosco, Grosseto*
- *La Locanda di Pietracupa, San Donato in Poggio*

Super Tuscans

One result of Chianti's 'cheap wine for the masses' reputation in the 1970s was the realisation by some Tuscans – including the Antinoris, Tuscany's most famous wine-producing family – that wines with a rich, complex, internationally acceptable taste following the New World tradition of blending mixes could be sold for a lot more than local wines. Thus, innovative, exciting wines were developed and cleverly marketed to appeal to buyers both in New York and in Florence. And when an English-speaking scribe dubbed the end product 'Super Tuscans', the name stuck. (Although Italian winemakers prefer the term IGT – Indicazione Geografica Tipica.) Sassacaia, Solaia, Bolgheri, Tignanello and Luce are all superhot Super Tuscans.

More and more international wine producers are turning to Tuscan soil to blend Super Tuscans and other modern wines. American-owned Castello Banfi, in the Tuscan biz for over three decades, scooped the prestigious Vinitaly wine prize in 2011, quietly underscoring the demise of winemaking as the exclusive domain of old, blue-blooded Tuscan wine-making families. These days, in this ancient land first cultivated by the Etruscans, Tuscany's oldest craft is open to anyone with wine-wizardry nous.

Celebrity Wine

With the birth of Super Tuscans a gaggle of celebrity-backed wine was born: Sting owns an estate near Figline Valdarno in Chianti, where he produces a Chianti Colli Aretini known as Il Serrestori (after the silk-weaving family who once owned his pad). It is sold under his own private label, limited and signed.

Best Wine Bars

Le Volpi e l'Uva, Florence

Il Santino, Florence

Enoteca Marcucci, Pietrasanta

Osticcio, Montalcino

Rosso e Vino, Grosseto

Sinatra Family Estates (yes, Frank) owns a three-hectare vineyard in the Fiesole hills near Florence where grapes are grown to make La Voce (literally 'the Voice'), a limited-edition Super Tuscan blend of Colorino and Sangiovese grapes.

Other celebrity wines to look out for are the Super Tuscan reds produced by the son of Florentine designer Roberto Cavalli, at Tenuta degli Dei outside Panzano in Chianti (top-of-the-range bottles are packaged in a typical Cavalli, flashy leopard-print box); and those produced southeast of Pisa on the family estate of opera singer Andrea Bocelli, sold at Cantina Bocelli in La Sterza.

If celebrity design is more your cup of tea, taste wine at the subterranean, design-driven **Rocca di Frassinello** (www.roccadifrassinello.it) winery near Grosseto by Renzo Piano; or the equally breathtaking **Petra** (www.petrawine.it) winery by Swiss architect Mario Botta in the Etruscan hills near Suvereto.

Then, of course, there is the spectacular new Antinori cellar in Bargino, ground-breaking in design – quite literally: An entire hillside in the heart of Chianti Classico was dug up, a designer cellar was popped inside and earthed over, and new vines were planted leaving just two giant slashes (the panoramic terraces of the 26,000 sq metre building) visible from the opposite rolling Chianti hill.

Tuscany on Page & Screen

It's no wonder that so many books, films and television productions are set in Tuscany. Few places have such a rich history and landscape to draw on for inspiration, and even fewer offer authors, actors and crews such a sybaritic location in which to research, write and shoot their works. The birthplace of Italian literature (courtesy of the great Dante Alighieri) and the setting for the greatest Italian film of recent decades *(Life is Beautiful)*, Tuscany offers the visitor plenty of options when it comes to pre-departure reading and viewing.

Tuscany in Print

In the late Middle Ages, a cheeky chap named Dante Alighieri decided that he would shake up the literary establishment by writing in Italian rather than Latin. In so doing, he laid the foundations for the development of a rich literary culture that continues to nurture both local and foreign writers to this day.

In 2010, the US video-game developer Electronic Arts released its version of Dante's *Inferno* for Xbox 360 and PlayStation 3 consoles.

Local Voices

Prior to the 13th century, Italian literature was written in Latin. But all that changed with Florentine-born Dante Alighieri (c 1265–1321). One of the founders of the Dolce Stil Novo (Sweet New Style) literary movement – whose members wrote lyric poetry in the Tuscan vernacular –

THE REAL ADVENTURES OF PINOCCHIO

In the early 1880s, Carlo Collodi (1826–90), a Florentine journalist, wrote a series for *Il Giornale dei Bambini*, the first Italian newspaper for children. Entitled *Storia di un burattino (Story of a Puppet)* and subsequently renamed, *Pinocchio* would have made Collodi (real name Lorenzini) a multimillionaire had he lived to exploit the film and translation rights.

The character of Pinocchio is a frustrating mix of the likeable and the odious. At his worst he's a wilful, obnoxious, deceitful little monster who deserves just about everything he gets. Humble and blubbering when things go wrong, he has the oh-so-human tendency to resume his wayward behaviour when he thinks he's in the clear.

The story, weaving between fantasy and reality, is a mine of references, some more veiled than others, to the society of late-19th-century Italy – a troubled country with enormous socio-economic problems compounded by the general apathy of those in power. Pinocchio waits the length of the story to become a real boy. But, while his persona may provoke laughter, his encounters with poverty, petty crime, skewed justice and just plain bad luck constitute a painful education in the machinations of the 'real' world.

Disney made a much-loved animated film of the story in 1940. It won two Academy Awards – one for Best Original Score and one for Best Original Song ('When You Wish Upon a Star'). A number of Italian adaptations have also been made, including one directed by Roberto Benigni in 2002.

Dante went on to use the local language when writing the epic poem that was to become the first, and greatest, literary work published in the Italian language: *La grande commedia (The Great Comedy),* published around 1317 and later renamed *La divina commedia (The Divine Comedy)* by his fellow poet Boccaccio. Divided into three parts – *Inferno, Purgatorio* and *Paradiso* – *The Divine Comedy* delivered an allegorical vision of the afterlife that made an immediate and profound impression on readers and, through its wide-reaching popularity, established the Tuscan dialect as the new standardised form of written Italian.

Another early adopter of the new language of literature was Giovanni Boccaccio (1303–75), who hailed from Certaldo. His masterpiece, *Decameron,* was written in the years following the plague of 1348. A collection of 100 allegorical tales recounted by 10 characters, it delivered a vast panorama of personalities, events and symbolism to contemporary readers and was nearly as popular and influential as *The Divine Comedy*.

The remaining member of the influential triumvirate that allowed for the development of a rich literature in Italian was Petrarch (Francesco Petrarca; 1304–74), born in Arezzo to Florentine parents. Although most of his writings were in Latin, he wrote his most popular works, his poems, in Italian. *Il canzoniere* (*Songbook;* c 1327–68) is the distilled result of his finest poetry. Although the core subject is his unrequited love for a woman named Laura, the breadth of human grief and joy is treated with a lyrical quality hitherto unmatched. His influence spread far and across time: the Petrarchan sonnet form, rhyme scheme and even subject matter was adopted by English metaphysical poets of 17th-century England such as John Donne.

Another outstanding writer of this period was Niccolò Machiavelli (1469–1527), known above all for his work on power and politics, *Il Principe* (*The Prince;* 1532).

Britons Abroad

Pictures from Italy (Charles Dickens; 1846)

Along the Road (Aldous Huxley; 1925)

Etruscan Places (DH Lawrence; 1932)

Americans Abroad

Italian Hours (Henry James; 1909)

The Stones of Florence (Mary McCarthy; 1956)

The City of Florence (RWB Lewis; 1995)

The 19th Century Onwards

After its stellar start during the Renaissance, Tuscany took a literary break in the 17th and 18th centuries. It wasn't until the 19th century that the scene started to regain some momentum.

Giosue Carducci (1835–1907) was one of the key figures of 19th-century Tuscan literature. Born in the Maremma, he spent the second

TUSCAN MEMOIRS

After visiting Tuscany, many people dream of purchasing their own piece of paradise. The following writers did just that, some establishing wildly successful literary franchises in the process.

- **Dario Castagno** (*Too Much Tuscan Sun; A Day in Tuscany; Too Much Tuscan Wine;* 2004–2009)
- **Mark Gordon Smith** (*Tuscan Echoes; Tuscan Light: Memories of Italy;* 2003–2007)
- **Sam Hilt** (*Turning Tuscan: A Step-By-Step Guide to Going Native*; 2012)
- **David Leavitt & Mark Mitchell** (*In Maremma: Life and a House in Southern Tuscany*; 2002, updated 2011)
- **Ferenc Máté** (*The Hills of Tuscany; A Vineyard in Tuscany: A Wine-Lover's Dream; The Wisdom of Tuscany;* 1999–2009)
- **Frances Mayes** (*Under the Tuscan Sun: At Home in Italy; Bella Tuscany; In Tuscany; Every Day in Tuscany;* 1996–2010)
- **Don McPherson** (*Ah! Tuscany: The Enlightenment of an Expatriate;* 2006)
- **Eric Newby** (*A Small Place in Italy;* 1994)

MURDER MOST TUSCAN

Tuscany features as the setting for some great crime fiction written by local and international authors.

- **Michael Dibdin** His popular Aurelio Zen novels include *And Then You Die* (2002), set on the Tuscan coast.
- **Michele Giuttari** A former high-ranking Florentine policeman, Giuttari has set four of his Michele Ferrara novels here: *A Florentine Death* (2008), *A Death in Tuscany* (2009), *Death of a Mafia Don* (2010) and *The Black Rose of Florence* (2012).
- **Lucretia Grindle** The Inspector Pallioti novels – *The Faces of Angels* (2006), *The Villa Triste* (2010) and *The Lost Daughter* (2011) – are set in Florence.
- **John Spencer Hill** The late Canadian writer set two historical crime titles here: *The Last Castrato* (1995) in Florence and *Ghirlandaio's Daughter* (1996) in Lucca.
- **Christobel Kent** Her Florentine-based private detective Sandro Cellini features in *A Florentine Revenge* (2006), *A Time of Mourning* (aka *The Drowning River;* 2009), *A Fine and Private Place* (aka *Murder in Tuscany;* 2010), *The Dead Season* (2012) and *A Darkness Descending* (2013).
- **Magdalen Nabb** The prolific British crime writer wrote 14 novels featuring Florentine policeman Marshal Guarnaccia.
- **Iain Pears** The Jonathan Argyll/Flavia di Stefano series includes *The Raphael Affair* (1991), set in Siena; *Giotto's Hand* (1994), set in Florence; and *The Immaculate Deception* (2000), set in various Tuscan locations.
- **Marco Vichi** Italian crime fiction writer who writes the Inspector Bordelli series. His latest title is *Death in Florence* (2013).
- **Elizabeth George** In *Just One Evil Act* (2013), the first of the Lynley books to be set outside Britain, the Inspector travels to Lucca in search of a missing British child.

half of his life in Bologna. The best of his poetry, written in the 1870s, ranged in tone from pensive evocations of death (such as in 'Pianto antico') or memories of youthful passion ('Idillio Maremmano') to a historic nostalgia harking back to the glories of ancient Rome.

Florence's Aldo Palazzeschi (1885–1974) was in the vanguard of the Futurist movement during the pre-WWI years. In 1911 he published arguably his best work, *Il codice di Perelà (Perelà's Code),* an at times bitter allegory that in part becomes a farcical imitation of the life of Christ.

Another Florentine, Vasco Pratolini (1913–91), set four highly regarded Neorealist novels in his birthplace: *Le ragazze di San Frediano* (1949), *Cronaca familiare* (1947), *Cronache di poveri amanti* (1947) and *Metello* (1955).

Tuscan-born Dacia Maraini (b 1936), for many years the partner of author Alberto Moravia, is one of Italy's most lauded contemporary writers, with novels, plays and poetry to her credit. Her best-known works include *Buio* (1999), which won the Premio Strega, Italy's most prestigious literary award, and *La lunga vita di Marianna Ucrìa* (published in English as *The Silent Duchess;* 1990).

Food forms the subject of many Tuscan memoirs. Two good examples are *A Culinary Traveller in Tuscany: Exploring & Eating Off The Beaten Track* (Beth Elon; 2006) and *The Tuscan Year: Life and Food in an Italian Valley* (Elizabeth Romer; 1985).

Through Foreign Eyes

The trend of setting English-language novels in Tuscany kicked off during the era of the Grand Tour, when wealthy young men from Britain and Northern Europe travelled around Europe to view the cultural legacies of classical antiquity and the Renaissance, completing their liberal educations and being introduced to polite society in the process. The Grand Tour's heyday was from the mid-17th century to the mid-19th century.

With the advent of rail travel in the 1840s, the prospect of a cultural odyssey opened to the middle classes. Wealthy travellers from Britain, America and Australasia flocked to Italy, some of whom wrote about their experiences. Notable among them were Henry James, who set parts of *The Portrait of a Lady* (1881) and *Roderick Hudson* (1875) here; George Eliot, whose *Romola* (1862) was set in 15th-century Florence; and EM Forster, who set *A Room with a View* (1908) in Florence and *Where Angels Fear to Tread* (1905) in San Gimignano (fictionalised as Monteriano).

ON LOCATION IN TUSCANY

Tuscany has been a popular location for international film and TV shoots, including the following:

➡ *The English Patient* (Anthony Minghella; 1996) Includes scenes shot in a monastery outside Pienza but is predominantly remembered for its lyrically beautiful sequence when Kip (Naveen Andrews) takes Hana (Juliette Binoche) into Arezzo's Cappella Bacci and hoists her aloft on ropes so that she can see Piero della Francesa's frescoes by the light of a flare.

➡ *Gladiator* (Ridley Scott; 2000) Those glorious shots of fields of wheat rippling in the breeze were shot near Pienza.

➡ *Hannibal* (Ridley Scott; 2001) Parts of the sequel to *The Silence of the Lambs* were shot in Florence.

➡ *Miracle at St Anna* (Spike Lee; 2008) Based on James McBride's novel about four black American soldiers who get trapped in a Tuscan village near Lucca during WWII.

➡ *Much Ado about Nothing* (Kenneth Branagh; 1993) Branagh, Emma Thompson and Keanu Reeves star in this adaptation of Shakespeare's comedy; shot in Chianti.

➡ *New Moon* (Chris Weitz; 2009) Parts of the second film in the Twilight trilogy were shot in Montepulciano's main piazza, despite the fact that in the book the action occurs in Volterra.

➡ *Obsession* (Brian De Palma; 1976) Clearly influenced by Hitchcock's *Vertigo*, this lacklustre effort is only redeemed by some lovely shots of Florence.

➡ *The Portrait of a Lady* (Jane Campion; 1996) Features a couple of scenes shot in Florence.

➡ *Quantum of Solace* (Marc Forster; 2008) The 22nd Bond film featured great action sequences shot in Carrara and Siena.

➡ *A Room with a View* (James Ivory; 1985) Hugely popular period drama set in Florence; there was also a 2007 UK ITV adaptation by Andrew Davies.

➡ *September Affair* (William Dieterle; 1950) Joseph Cotten and Joan Fontaine fall in love in Florence; features Kurt Weill's famous 'September Song'.

➡ *Stealing Beauty* (Bernardo Bertolucci; 1996) In her first film role, Liv Tyler grapples with grief and burgeoning sexuality in the lush Tuscan countryside.

➡ *Summer's Lease* (Martyn Friend; 1989) Award-winning BBC television adaptation of John Mortimer's 1998 novel. Stars John Gielgud.

➡ *Under the Tuscan Sun* (Audrey Wells; 2003) A lightweight film version of the wildly popular memoir set in Cortona.

➡ *Up at the Villa* (Philip Haas; 2000) Sean Penn and Kristin Scott Thomas star in an adaptation of Somerset Maugham's novel.

➡ *Where Angels Fear to Tread* (Charles Sturridge; 1991) A fine cast including Helen Mirren, Judy Davis and Helena Bonham Carter stars in this period film shot in San Gimignano.

Things slowed down in the early 20th century, with only a few major novelists choosing to set their work here. These included Somerset Maugham (*Up at the Villa;* 1941) and Aldous Huxley (*Time Must Have a Stop;* 1944).

In recent decades, a number of highly regarded novels have been set in Tuscany. Perhaps the best known of these are by English writer Linda Proud, whose Botticelli trilogy – *A Tabernacle for the Sun, Pallas and the Centaur* and *The Rebirth of Venus* – is set in Renaissance Florence during the Pazzi Conspiracy, the Medici exile and the rise of Savonarola. The historical detail in all three is exemplary, and each is a cracking good read. Her novel about Botticelli's master Fra' Filippo Lippi, *A Gift for the Magus,* was published in 2012.

Other writers who have used Renaissance Florence as a setting include Sarah Dunant (*The Birth of Venus;* 2003), Salman Rushdie (*The Enchantress of Florence;* 2008), Michaela-Marie Roessner-Hermann (*The Stars Dispose;* 1997, and *The Stars Dispel;* 1999) and Jack Dann (*The Memory Cathedral;* 1995). Of these, Dann wins the prize for constructing the most bizarre plot, setting his novel in a version of the Renaissance in which Leonardo da Vinci actually constructs a number of his inventions (eg the flying machine) and uses them during a battle in the Middle East while in the service of a Syrian general.

Also set in Florence are *Innocence* (1986) by Booker Prize–winning novelist Penelope Fitzgerald, which is set during the 1950s; *The Sixteen Pleasures* (1994) by Robert Hellenga, set after the devastating flood of 1966; *The English Patient* (1992) by Michael Ondaatje; and *Inferno* (2013) by Dan Brown of *The De Vinci Code* fame (or should that be infamy?).

Tuscany on Film

Cinema heavyweight Franco Zeffirelli was born in Florence in 1923 and has set many of his films in the region. His career has taken him from radio and theatre to opera (both stage productions and film versions) and his films include *Romeo and Juliet* (1968), *Brother Sun, Sister Moon* (1972), *Hamlet* (1990) and the semiautobiographical *Tea with Mussolini* (1999).

Actor, comedian and director Roberto Benigni was born near Castiglion Fiorentino in 1952. He picked up four Oscars and created a genre all of his own – Holocaust comedy – with the extraordinarily powerful *La vita é bella* (*Life is Beautiful;* 1998), a film that he directed, co-wrote and starred in. Often compared with Charlie Chaplin and Buster Keaton, he has directed nine films (two set in Tuscany) and acted in many more, including three directed by American independent film-maker Jim Jarmusch.

Four films based on Neorealist novels by Vasco Pratolini were shot in Florence: *Le ragazze di San Frediano* (*The Girls of San Frediano;* Valerio Zurlini; 1954), *Cronache di poveri amanti* (*Chronicle of Poor Lovers*; Carlo Lizzani; 1954), *Cronaca familiare* (*Family Diary;* Valerio Zurlini; 1962) and *Metello* (Mauro Bolognini; 1970).

Award-winning film-makers Paolo and Vittorio Taviani were born in San Miniato and have set parts of three of their films in Tuscany: *La notte di San Lorenzo* (aka *The Night of the Shooting Stars;* 1982), *Le affinità elettive* (*Elective Affinities;* 1996) and *Good Morning Babylon* (1987).

Don't Miss

- *Life is Beautiful*
- *A Room with a View*
- *The Night of the Shooting Stars*

Don't Bother

- *Under the Tuscan Sun*
- *New Moon*
- *Obsession*

Decameron on Screen

- *Decameron Nights (Hugo Fregonese; 1953)*
- *Decameron (Pier Paolo Pasolini; 1971)*
- *Virgin Territory (David Leland; 2007)*

Art & Architecture

In many respects, the history of Tuscan art is also the history of Western art. Browse through any text on the subject and you'll quickly develop an understanding of how influential the Italian Renaissance – which kicked off and reached its greatest flowering in Florence – has been over the past 500 years. Indeed, it's no exaggeration to say that architecture, painting and sculpture rely on its technical innovations and take inspiration from its major works to this very day.

Top Etruscan Museums

Museo Etrusco Guarnacci, Volterra

Museo dell'Accademia Etrusca, Cortona

Museo Civico Archeologico 'Isidoro Falchi', Vetulonia

Museo Archeologico Nazionale 'Gaio Cilnio Mecenate', Arezzo

The Etruscans

Roughly 2800 years before we all started dreaming of a hilltop getaway in Tuscany, the Etruscans had a similar idea: hill towns that they founded are dotted throughout the countryside.

From the 8th to the 3rd centuries BC, Etruscans held their own against friends, Romans and countrymen, worshipped their own gods and goddesses, and farmed lowlands using sophisticated drainage systems of their own invention. How well they lived between sieges and war is unclear, but they sure knew how to throw a funeral. Etruscan *necropoli* (tombs) are found throughout southern, central and eastern Tuscany. Excavation of these tombs often yields a wealth of jewellery, cinerary urns (used for body ashes) made from terracotta and alabaster, earthenware pottery (particularly the glossy black ceramic known as *bucchero*) and bronze votive offerings.

Of course, the Romans knew a good thing when they plundered it. After conquering swaths of Etruscan territory in Tuscany in the 3rd century BC, they incorporated the Etruscans' highly refined, geometric style into their own art and architecture.

Enter Christianity

Roman centurions weren't in the area for long before Christianity began to take hold. After abandoning his studies and a promising career in Rome to adopt the contemplative life around AD 500, a young man from the region named Benedict went on to achieve a number of miracles, establish 12 monasteries and inspire the founding of many more. His story is visually narrated in great detail in the stunning fresco series (1497–1505) by Il Sodoma and Luca Signorelli in the Great Cloister at the Abbazia di Monte Oliveto Maggiore, near Siena.

One early Benedictine monastery, San Pietro in Valle, was built in neighbouring Umbria by order of the Longobard duke of Spoleto, Faroaldo II. It kick-started a craze for the blend of Lombard and Roman styles known as Romanesque, and many local ecclesiastical structures were built in this style. The basic template was simple: a stark nave stripped of extra columns ending in a domed apse, surrounded by chapels usually donated by wealthy patrons.

In the 11th century the Romanesque style acquired a distinctly Tuscan twist in Pisa, when the coloured marble banding and veneering of the city's *duomo* (cathedral) set a new gold standard for architectural decoration. This new style (sometimes described as Pisan) was then applied to a swath of churches throughout the region, including the Chiesa di San Miniato al Monte, in Florence, and the Chiesa di San Michele in Foro and Cattedrale di San Martino, both in Lucca.

Siena was not about to be outdone in the architectural stakes by its rivals, Florence and Pisa, and so in 1196 its city council approved a no-expenses-spared program to build a new *duomo*. They certainly got their money's worth, ending up with a spectacular Gothic facade by Giovanni Pisano, a pulpit by Nicola Pisano and a rose window designed by Duccio di Buoninsegna.

While Tuscany's churches were becoming increasingly spectacular, nothing prepared pilgrims for what they would find inside the upper and lower churches of the Basilica di San Francesco in Assisi, Umbria. Not long after St Francis' death in 1226, an all-star team of Tuscan artists was hired to decorate these churches in his honour, kicking off a craze for frescoes that wouldn't abate for centuries. Cimabue, Giotto, Pietro Lorenzetti and Simone Martini captured the life and gentle spirit of St Francis while his memory was still fresh in the minds of the faithful. For medieval pilgrims unaccustomed to multiplexes and special effects, entering a space that had been covered from floor to ceiling with stories told in living colour must have been a dazzling, overwhelming experience.

The Middle Ages: The Rise of the Comune

While communities sprang up around hermits and holy men in the hinterlands, cities took on a life of their own from the 13th and 14th centuries. Roman road networks had been serving as handy trade routes starting in the 11th century, and farming estates and villas began to spring up outside major trading centres as a new middle class of merchants, farmers and skilled craftspeople emerged. Taxes and donations sponsored the building of hospitals such as the Ospedale Santa Maria della Scala in Siena. Streets were paved, town walls erected and sewage systems built to accommodate an increasingly sophisticated urban population not keen on sprawl or squalor.

Once townsfolk came into a bit of money, they weren't necessarily keen to part with it, and didn't always agree how their tax dollars should be spent. *Comuni* (local governments) were formed to represent the various interests of merchants, guilds and competing noble families, and the first order of business on the agenda in major medieval cities, such as Siena, Florence and Volterra, was the construction of an impressive town hall to reflect the importance and authority of the *comune*. The greatest example is Siena's Palazzo Comunale.

In addition to being savvy political lobbyists and fans of grand architectural projects that kept their constituents gainfully employed, medieval *comuni* were masters of propaganda, and fully understood the influence that art and architecture could wield. A perfect case in point is Ambrogio Lorenzetti's *Allegories of Good and Bad Government* fresco series in Siena's Palazzo Comunale, which is better and bigger than any political billboard could ever be. In the *Allegory of Good Government*, Lorenzetti's grey-bearded figure of Legitimate Authority is flanked by an entourage who'd certainly put White House interns to shame: Peace, Fortitude, Prudence, Magnanimity, Temperance and Justice. Above them flit Faith, Hope and Charity, and to the left Concord sits confidently on her throne while the reins of justice are held taut overhead.

Next to this fresco is another depicting the effects of good government: townsfolk make their way through town in an orderly fashion, pausing to do business, greet one another, join hands and dance a merry jig. But things couldn't be more different in the *Allegory of Bad Government*, where horned and fanged Tyrannia rules over a scene of chaos

Best Art Galleries

- *Uffizi Gallery, Florence*
- *Galleria dell'Accademia, Florence*
- *Pinacoteca Nazionale, Siena*
- *Museo Nazionale di San Matteo, Pisa*
- *Galleria Palatina, Palazzo Pitti, Florence*

1

PIETRO LORENZETTI / GETTY IMAGES ©

2

4

RICHARD I'ANSON / GETTY IMAGES ©

1. Fresco in Basilica di San Francesco (p267), Assisi

Assisi's major drawcard is this basilica, which comprises two churches filled with magnificent Renaissance art.

2. Pinturicchio's frescoes in the *duomo* (p194), Siena

Inside Siena's *duomo*, the small Libreria Piccolomini's walls are decorated with vividly coloured narrative frescoes.

3. Masaccio's frescoes in Basilica di Santa Maria del Carmine (p85), Florence

Masaccio's fresco cycle illustrating the life of St Peter is considered among his greatest works, representing a definitive break with Gothic art and a plunge into new worlds of expression.

4. Museo di San Marco (p80), Florence

Fra' Angelico's frescoes portray religious figures in all-too-human moments of uncertainty, reflecting the humanist spirit of the Renaissance.

JULIET COOMBE / GETTY IMAGES ©

surrounded by winged vices, and Justice lies unconscious, her scales shattered. Like the best campaign speeches, this cautionary tale was brilliantly rendered, but not always heeded.

Romanesque Churches

- *Duomo di San Cristoforo, Barga*
- *Collegiata, San Gimignano*
- *Abbazia di Sant'Antimo, near Montalcino*
- *Pieve di Corsignano, Pienza*
- *Duomo, Sovana*
- *Pieve di Santa Maria, Arezzo*

On the World Stage

When they weren't busy politicking, late-medieval farmers, craftspeople and merchants did quite well for themselves. Elegant, locally made ceramics, tiles and marbles were showcased in churches across Tuscany; became all the rage throughout Europe and the Mediterranean when pilgrims returned home to England and France with examples after following the Via Francigena pilgrimage route from Canterbury to Rome. Artisans were kept busy applying their skills to civic works projects and churches, which had to be expanded and updated to keep up with the growing numbers and rising expectations of pilgrims in the area.

With outside interest came outside influence, and local styles adapted to international markets. Florence became famous for lustrous, tin-glazed *maiolica* (majolica ware) tiles and plates painted with vibrant metallic pigments that were inspired by the Islamic ceramics of Majorca (Spain). The prolific della Robbia family started to create richly glazed ceramic reliefs that are now enshrined at the Museo del Bargello in Florence and in churches and museums across the region.

Modest Romanesque cathedrals were given an International Gothic makeover befitting their appeal to pilgrims of all nations, but the Italian take on the French style was more colourful than the grey-stone spires and flying buttresses of Paris. The local version often featured a simple layout and striped stone naves fronted by multilayer birthday-cake facades, which might be frosted with pink paint, glittering mosaics and rows of arches capped with sculptures. The most famous example of this confectionery approach is the *duomo* in Siena.

The evolution from solid Romanesque to airy Gothic to a yin and yang balance of the two can be witnessed in buildings throughout the region, many of which blend a relatively austere Romanesque exterior with high Gothic drama indoors. This set a new ecclesiastical architecture standard that was quickly exported into Tuscany and on to the rest of Europe.

As well as endowing churches, building palaces and funding frescoes, wealthy merchant families of the Renaissance commissioned plenty of portraits. Cosimo I de' Medici's favourite portrait painter was Agnolo di Cosimo (1503–72), called Bronzino because of his dark complexion. Look for his Medici portraits in the Uffizi, Florence.

Dark Times

By the 14th century, the smiling Sienese townsfolk of Ambrogio Lorenzetti's *Allegory of Good Government* must have seemed like the figment of a fertile imagination. After a major famine in 1329 was followed by a bank collapse, Siena's *comune* went into debt to maintain roads, continue work on the *duomo*, help the needy and jump-start the local economy. But just when it seemed set for a comeback, the plague devastated the city in 1348. Three-quarters of Siena's population – including artists Pietro and Ambrogio Lorenzetti – died, and virtually all economic and artistic activity ground to a halt. Another plague hit in 1374, killing 80,000 Sienese, and was swiftly followed by a famine. It was too much – the city never entirely recovered.

Florence was also hit by the plague in 1348, and despite fervent public prayer rituals, 96,000 Florentines died in just seven months. Those who survived experienced a crisis of faith, making Florence fertile territory for humanist ideals – not to mention macabre superstition, attempts to raise the dead, and a fascination with corpses that the likes of Leonardo da Vinci would call 'science' and others 'morbid curiosity'.

At plague's end, a Florentine building boom ensued. Upstart merchants such as Cosimo I de' Medici (Cosimo the Elder) and Palla Strozzi competed to put their stamp on a city that needed to be reimagined after the horrors it had undergone.

GIOTTO DI BONDONE

The 14th-century Tuscan poet Giovanni Boccaccio wrote in *Decameron* that his fellow Tuscan Giotto di Bondone (c 1266–1337) was 'a genius so sublime that there was nothing produced by nature...that he could not depict to the life'.

Boccaccio wasn't the only prominent critic of the time to consider Giotto extraordinary – Giorgio Vasari was also a huge fan, arguing that Giotto initiated the 'rebirth' (*rinascità* or *renaissance*) in art. In his paintings, Giotto abandoned popular conventions such as the three-quarter view of head and body, and presented his figures from behind, from the side or turning around, just as the story demanded. Giotto had no need for lashings of gold paint and elaborate ornamentation to impress the viewer with the significance of the subject. Instead, he enabled the viewer to feel the dramatic tension of a scene through a naturalistic rendition of figures and a radical composition that created the illusion of depth.

Giotto's important works in Tuscany include an altarpiece portraying the Madonna and Child among angels and saints in Florence's Uffizi Gallery, a painted wooden crucifix in the Basilica di Santa Maria Novella and frescoes in the Basilica di Santa Croce. His magnificent *Life of St Francis* fresco cycle graces the walls of the upper church of the Basilica di San Francesco in Assisi, Umbria.

Many Renaissance painters included self-portraits in their major works. Giotto didn't, possibly due to the fact that friends such as Boccaccio described him as the ugliest man in Florence. With friends like those...

The Renaissance

It wasn't only merchants who were jockeying for power at this time. To put an end to the competing claims of the Tuscan Ghibelline faction that was allied with the Holy Roman Empire, the Rome-backed Guelph faction had marked its territory with impressive new landmarks, predominantly in Florence. Giotto – often described as the founding artist of the Renaissance – had been commissioned to design the city's iconic 85m-tall square *campanile* (bell tower) and thus one-up the 57m-tall tower under construction in Ghibelline Pisa that was already looking a bit off kilter. And this was only one of many such projects.

'Mess with Florence, and you take on Rome' was the not-so-subtle hint delivered by Florentine architects, who made frequent reference to the glories of the ancient power and its classical architecture when designing the new churches, *palazzi* and public buildings that sprouted across the city during the *Trecento* (14th century) and proliferated in the *Quattrocentro* (15th century). This new Florentine style became known as Renaissance or 'rebirth', and really hit its swing after architect Filippo Brunelleschi (p308) won a competition to design the dome of Florence's *duomo*. Brunelleschi was heavily influenced by the achievements of the classical masters, but he was able to do something that they hadn't been able to do themselves – discover and record the mathematical rules by which objects appear to diminish as they recede from us. In so doing, he gave local artists and architects a whole new visual perspective and a means to glorious artistic ends.

Gothic Churches

- *Duomo, Siena*
- *Abbazia di San Galgano, south of Siena*
- *Chiesa di Santa Maria della Spina, Pisa*

To decorate the new buildings, artists enjoyed a bonanza of commissions to paint heroic battle scenes, fresco private chapels and carve busts of the latest power players – works that sometimes outlived their patrons' clout. A good example is the Peruzzi family, whose members had risen to prominence in 14th-century Florence as bankers with interests reaching from London to the Middle East. They set the trend for art patronage by commissioning Giotto to fresco the family's memorial chapel in Santa Croce, completed in 1320. When Peruzzi client King Edward III of England defaulted on loans the family went bankrupt – but as patrons of Giotto's explorations in perspective and Renaissance illusionism, their legacy set the tone for the artistic flowering of Florence.

One Florentine family to follow the Peruzzis' lead was the prominent Brancacci, who commissioned Masolino da Panicale and his precocious assistant Masaccio to decorate a chapel in the Basilica di Santa Maria del Carmine in Florence. After Masaccio's premature death aged only 27, the frescoes were completed by Filippino Lippi. In these dramatic frescoes, framed in astonishingly convincing architectural sets, scenes from the life of St Peter allude to pressing Florentine concerns of the day: the new income tax, unfair imprisonment and hoarded wealth. Masaccio's image of the expulsion of Adam and Eve from the Garden of Eden proved especially prophetic: the Brancacci were allied with the Strozzi family, and were similarly exiled by the Medici before they could see the work completed.

But the patrons with the greatest impact on the course of art history were, of course, the Medicis. Patriarch Cosimo the Elder was exiled in 1433 by a consortium of Florentine families who considered him a triple threat: powerful banker, ambassador of the Church, and consummate politician with the savvy to sway emperors and popes. But the flight of capital from Florence after his departure created such a fiscal panic that the banishment was hastily rescinded and within a year the Medicis were well and truly back in town. To announce his return in grand style, Cosimo funded the 1437 rebuilding of the Convento di San Marco (now Museo di San Marco) by Michelozzo, and commissioned Fra' Angelico to fresco the monks' quarters with scenes from the life of Christ. Another artist pleased to see Cosimo return was Donatello, who had completed his lithe bronze statue of *David* (now in the city's Museo del Bargello) with his patronage.

FILIPPO BRUNELLESCHI

Many Renaissance men left their mark on Florence, but few did so with as much grace and glory as Filippo Brunelleschi (1377–1446). An architect, mathematician, engineer and sculptor, Brunelleschi trained as a master goldsmith and showed early promise as a sculptor – he was an entrant in the 1401 competition to design the doors of the baptistry in Florence (won by fellow goldsmith Lorenzo Ghiberti) and shortly after travelled to Rome with Donatello, another goldsmith by training, to study that city's ancient architecture and art. When he returned to Florence in 1419 he took up an architectural commission from the silk merchant's guild to design a hospital for foundlings on Piazza della Santissima Annunziata in San Marco. Known as the Ospedale degli Innocenti (Hospital of the Innocents), his classically proportioned and detailed building featured a distinctive nine-arched loggia and was a radical departure from the High Gothic style that many of his artistic contemporaries were still embracing. Its design was sober, secular and sophisticated, epitomising the new humanist age.

In 1419, after completing his work on the foundling hospital, Brunelleschi moved on to a commission that was to occupy him for the next 42 years – the dome of Florence's *duomo*. His mathematical brain and talent for devising innovative engineering solutions enabled him to do what many Florentines had thought impossible: deliver the largest dome to be built in Italy since antiquity.

Brunelleschi's other works in Florence include the Basilica di San Lorenzo, the Basilica di Santo Spirito and the Cappella de' Pazzi in the Basilica di Santa Croce. Vasari said of him: 'The world having for so long been without artists of lofty soul or inspired talent, heaven ordained that it should receive from the hand of Filippo the greatest, the tallest, and the finest edifice of ancient and modern times, demonstrating that Tuscan genius, although moribund, was not yet dead.' He is buried in the *duomo*, under the dome that was his finest achievement.

Through such commissions, early Renaissance innovations in perspective, closely observed realism and chiaroscuro (the play of light and dark) began to catch on throughout the region. In Sansepolcro, a painter named Piero della Francesca earned a reputation for figures who were glowing with otherworldly light, and who were caught in personal predicaments that people could relate to: Roman soldiers snoozing on the job, crowds left goggle-eyed by miracles, bystanders distressed to witness cruel persecution. His fresco series *Legend of the True Cross,* commissioned by the Bacci family for a chapel in Arezzo's Chiesa di San Francesco, was one of the supreme artistic achievements of the time.

The High Renaissance

The decades leading up to and starting the *Cinquecento* (16th century) are often seen as a kind of university faculty meeting, with genteel, silver-haired sages engaged in a collegial exchange of ideas. A bar brawl might be closer to the metaphorical truth, with artists, scientists, politicians and clergy mixing it up and everyone emerging bruised. The debate was never as simple as Church versus state, science versus art or seeing versus believing; in those days, politicians could be clergy, scientists could be artists, and artists could be clergy.

There were many artistic superstars during this period, and most were locals who ended up honing their skills in Florence and then moving elsewhere in Italy. Their careers were well documented by Giorgio Vasari in his gossipy *Lives of the Artists* (see p316).

Inspired by Masaccio, tutored by Fra' Filippo Lippi and backed by Lorenzo de' Medici, Sandro Botticelli was a rising Florentine art star who was sent to Rome to paint a fresco celebrating papal authority in the Sistine Chapel. The golden boy who'd painted the *Birth of Venus* for Lorenzo de' Medici's private villa in 1485 (now in Florence's Uffizi Gallery) could do no wrong until he was accused of sodomy in 1501. The charges didn't stick but the rumours did, and Botticelli's work was critiqued as too decadently sensual for religious subjects. When religious reformer Savonarola ousted the Medici and began to purge Florence of decadent excess in the face of surely imminent Armageddon, Botticelli paintings went up in flames in the massive 'Bonfire of the Vanities'. Botticelli repudiated mythology and turned his attention to Madonnas, some of whom bear a marked family resemblance to his Venus.

Michelangelo was another of Lorenzo de' Medici's protégées, and his classically inspired work was uniformly admired until the Medicis were ousted by Savonarola in 1494. By some accounts, Savonarola tossed rare early paintings by Michelangelo onto his bonfires (ouch). Without his Medici protectors, Michelangelo seemed unsure of his next move: he briefly hid in the basement of San Lorenzo and then roamed around Italy. In Rome he carved a Bacchus for Cardinal Raffaele Riaro that the patron deemed unsuitable – which only seemed to spur Michelangelo to make a bigger and still more sensuous statue of *David* in 1501. It's now exhibited in Florence's Galleria dell'Accademia.

Leonardo, who hailed from Vinci, southwest of Florence, had so many talents that it is hard to isolate only a few for comment. In his painting, he took what some critics have described as the decisive step in the history of Western art – namely, abandoning the balance that had previously been maintained between colour and line and choosing to modulate his contours using shading. This technique is called sfumato and it is perfectly displayed in his *Mona Lisa* (now in the Louvre in Paris). Few of his works live in her birthplace; the exceptions are his *Adoration of the Magi* and *Annunciation,* both in the Uffizi.

Filippo Lippi (1406–69), one of the greatest Tuscan painters of his era, entered the Carmelite order as a monk aged only 14 but renounced his vows after meeting (and subsequently eloping with) a novice who was sitting for the figure of the Madonna in a fresco he was painting for the *duomo* in Prato.

As madness and profligacy often run through families, so too does artistic genius. Italian artistic dynasties include the della Robbias (Luca, Marco, Andrea, Giovanni and Girolamo), Lorenzettis (Ambrogio and Pietro) and Pisanos (Nicola and Giovanni, Andrea and Nino).

1

2

DE AGOSTINI / GETTY IMAGES ©

. Fra' Angelico's *Annunciation* **2.** Botticelli's *Primavera*
. Di Buoninsegna's *Madonna with Child and Siz Angels*

3

Tuscan Artists

Plenty of big names jostle for precedence in the pantheon of Tuscan artists, so narrowing any list down to a 'Top Five' is a near impossible task. Here's our best attempt.

Michelangelo Buonarroti (1475–1564)

The quintessential Renaissance man. A painter, sculptor and architect with more masterpieces to his credit than any other artist either before or since. In Florence, view his *David* in the Galleria dell'Accademia and his *Tondo Doni* (Holy Family) in the Uffizi.

Sandro Botticelli (c 1444–1510)

His Renaissance beauties charmed commissions out of the Medicis and continue to exert their siren call on the millions who visit the Uffizi Gallery each year. Don't miss his *Primavera* and *Birth of Venus*.

Giotto di Bondone (c 1266–1337)

Giotto kick-started the Renaissance with action-packed frescoes in which each character pinpoints emotions with facial expressions and poses that need no translation. Make the pilgrimage to Assisi to see his *Life of St Francis* fresco cycle.

Fra' Angelico (c 1395–1455)

Few artists are saints – they're far more likely to be sinners. One of the exceptions was Il Beato Angelico, who was canonised in 1982. His best-loved work is the *Annunciation*, versions of which are on display in Florence's Museo di San Marco and Cortona's Museo Diocesano.

Duccio di Buoninsegna (c 1255–1318)

Head honcho of the Sienese school; known for his riveting Madonnas with level gazes and pale-green skin against glowing gold backgrounds. His masterwork is the *Maestà* in the Museo dell'Opera in Siena.

In 1542 the Inquisition arrived in Italy, marking a definitive end to the Renaissance exploration of humanity in all its glorious imperfections. Tuscan art and architecture would never again lead the world by example.

A Stop on the Grand Tour

A 'Grand Tour' of Italy became an obligatory display of culture and class status by the 18th century, and Tuscany was a key stop on the itinerary. German and English artists enraptured with Michelangelo, Perugino and other early High Renaissance painters took the inspiration home, kick-starting a neoclassicist craze. Conversely, trends from northern Europe (impressionism, plein-air painting and romanticism) became trendy among Italian artists, as witnessed in the collection at Florence's Galleria d'Arte Moderna in the Palazzo Pitti, which is dominated by late-19th-century works by artists of the Tuscan Macchiaioli school (the local equivalent of impressionism). These include Telemaco Signorini (1835–1901) and Giovanni Fattori (1825–1908).

In architecture, the most fascinating case of artistic import-export is Italian art nouveau, often referred to as Liberty after the London store

RENAISSANCE FRESCOES

They may look like ordinary bible stories now, but in their heyday, Renaissance frescoes provided running social commentary as well as religious inspiration. In them, human adversity looked divine, and vice versa.

Fantastic examples are found throughout Tuscany, but to see the very best head to the following churches and museums:

➡ **Collegiata, San Gimignano** (p211) There are hardly any undecorated surfaces in this cathedral, with every wall sporting huge, comic-strip-like frescoes by Bartolo di Fredi, Lippo Memmi, Domenico Ghirlandaio and Benozzo Gozzoli. The highlight is Taddeo di Bartolo's gleefully grotesque *Final Judgment* (1396).

➡ **Libreria Piccolomini, Duomo, Siena** (p194) Umbrian artist Bernardino Pinturicchio extols the glory of Siena in 10 vibrant fresco panels (c 1502–1507) celebrating Enea Silvio Piccolomini, aka the humanist Pope Pius II. St Catherine of Siena makes a cameo appearance.

➡ **Museo di San Marco, Florence** (p80) Fra' Angelico's frescoes portray religious figures in all-too-human moments of uncertainty, reflecting the humanist spirit of the Renaissance. The highlight is his *Annunciation* (c 1440).

➡ **Museo Civico, Siena** (p192) Magnificent is the only word to use when describing Ambrogio Lorenzetti's *Allegories of Good and Bad Government* (1338–40) and Simone Martini's *Maestà* (Virgin Mary in Majesty; 1315).

➡ **Cappella Brancacci, Florence** (p85) Masaccio's *The Expulsion of Adam and Eve from Paradise* and *The Tribute Money* (c 1427) showcase architectural perspective and sly political satire.

➡ **Cappella Bacci, Chiesa di San Francesco, Arezzo** (p253) Piero della Francesca's *Legend of the True Cross* (c 1452–66) displays a veritable smorgasbord of Renaissance painting tricks (directional lighting, steep perspective etc).

➡ **Chiesa di Sant'Agostino, San Gimignano** (p212) Benozzo Gozzoli's bizarre fresco of San Sebastian (c 1464) shows the fully clothed saint protecting the citizens of San Gimignano, helped by a bare-breasted Virgin Mary and semi-robed Jesus. Wins the prize for the weirdest religious iconography.

➡ **Cappella dei Magi, Palazzo Medici-Riccardi, Florence** (p78) More Gozzoli, but this time there's nothing strange about his subject matter, which has members of the Medici family making a guest appearance in the *Procession of the Magi to Bethlehem* (c 1459–63).

that put William Morris' Italian-inspired visual ideals into commercial action.

The 20th Century

After centuries under the thumbs of popes and sundry imperial powers, Tuscany had acquired a certain forced cosmopolitanism, and local artists could identify with Rome, Paris or other big cities in addition to their own *contrada* (neighbourhood). The two biggest stars in the early decades of this century were Livorno-born painter and sculptor Amedeo Modigliani (1884–1920), who lived most of his adult life in Paris, and Greek-born painter Giorgio de Chirico (1888–1978), who studied in Florence and painted the first of his 'Metaphysical Town Square' series there.

Other than Modigliani and di Chirico, no Tuscan painters of note were represented within the major Italian artistic movements of the century: Futurismo (Futurism), Pittura Metafisica (Metaphysical Painting), Spazialismo (Spatialism) and Arte Povera (conceptual art using materials of little worth). Architecture didn't have many local stars either, with the only exception being Giovanni Michelucci (1891–1990), whose buildings include Santa Maria Novella Railway Station in Florence (1932–34).

In the 1980s, there was a return to painting and sculpture in a traditional (primarily figurative) sense. Dubbed 'Transavanguardia', this movement broke with the prevailing international focus on conceptual art and was thought by some critics to signal the death of avant-garde. Tuscan artists who were part of this movement include Sandro Chia (b 1946).

Tuscany has a wealth of sculpture gardens showcasing site-specific contemporary works in gorgeous surrounds. These include the Fattoria di Celle, near Pistoia, Giardino dei Tarocchi in southern Tuscany, and Castello di Ama, in Chianti.

SCULPTURE

Contemporary Art

A heritage of rich artistic traditions spanning three millennia means job security for legions of Tuscan art conservation specialists and art historians, but can have a stultifying effect on artists attempting to create something wholly new. Fortunately, there's more going on than the daubs being created by sidewalk artists outside major museums and tourist attractions would seem to indicate.

One of the most notable visual artists working here is Massimo Bartolini (b 1962), who radically alters the local landscape with just a few deceptively simple (and quintessentially Tuscan) adjustments of light and perspective that fundamentally change our experience: a bedroom where all the furniture appears to be sinking into the floor, Venice style, or a gallery where the viewer wears special shoes that subtly change the lighting in the gallery with each step. Bartolini has also changed the local flora of the tiny Tuscan town of Cecina, near Livorno, where he lives and works, attracting colourful flocks of contemporary art collectors and curators.

The bijou town of Pietrasanta in the hinterland of the Versilian coast in northwestern Tuscany has a vibrant arts community and is home to the much-lauded Colombian-born sculptor Fernando Botero (b 1932).

Also notable is San Gimignano's Galleria Continua, a world-class commercial gallery whose stable of artists includes Tuscans Giovanni Ozzola (b 1982) and Luca Pancrazzi (b 1961).

Art & Architecture Glossary

Annunciation	the appearance of the Angel Gabriel to Mary to tell her that she will bear the Son of God
apse	a vaulted semicircular or polygonal recess, especially at the end of a choir in a church
architrave	1. the part of the entablature that holds columns in place; 2. a band of mouldings or other ornamentation atop or around openings or panels

Tuscan Architecture

Italy has more than its share of great buildings, and a large percentage of these are in Tuscany. Brunelleschi and Michelangelo both designed masterpieces here, and every town and city seems to have at least one notable Romanesque, Gothic or Renaissance structure.

Churches

Tuscany's *chiese* (churches) are headline attractions where worship can take many forms. Every village, town and city has at least one church, and many are repositories of great art. Florence has masterpieces galore (don't miss Santa Maria Novella, Santa Croce and San Lorenzo), but Siena, Pisa and San Gimignano are richly endowed, too, with their respective *duomos* (cathedrals) being the best-loved and most distinctive buildings in town. On the border of Tuscany and Umbria, Orvieto's *duomo* is one of the most beautiful in the country.

Baptistries

Important cathedrals often have a detached *battistero* (baptistry) with a dedicated altar and font. Pisa's cupcake-shaped example in the Piazza dei Miracoli, with its exquisite hexagonal marble pulpit carved by Nicola Pisano, is wonderful, as is Florence's Romanesque version with its famous door panels sculpted by Lorenzo Ghiberti.

Hospitals

Funded by the church, the *comune* (municipality) or wealthy philanthropists, *ospedali* (hospitals) have historically been among the largest and grandest of civic buildings. Siena's Santa Maria della

1. Aerial view of Piazza del Campo (p189), Siena **2.** Orvieto's *duomo* (cathedral; p230)

Scala is perhaps the best known, but architecture buffs adore Brunelleschi's Ospedale degli Innocenti in Florence.

Palaces

The Medicis weren't the only dynasty with a penchant for building *palazzi* (palaces). In the medieval and Renaissance periods, wealthy families in every city built houses aimed to impress, as did ambassadors, popes, cardinals and *podestàs* (chief magistrates). Architecturally notable examples include Palazzo Strozzi, Palazzo Pitti and Palazzo Medici-Riccardi in Florence; Palazzo Piccolomini, Palazzo Salimbeni and Palazzo Chigi-Saracini in Siena; and Palazzo Piccolomini in Pienza.

Piazzas

These triumphs of town planning are the lifeblood of every Tuscan community, the places where locals come to connect with their neighbours and where important institutions such as churches and town halls are almost inevitably situated. The two most famous examples, Piazzo Pio II in Pienza and Piazza dei Miracoli in Pisa, feature in Unesco's World Heritage List. Worthy of an honourable mention are Livorno's Piazza dei Domenicani, Arezzo's Piazza Grande and Massa Marittima's Piazza Garibaldi.

Town Halls

Built to showcase wealth and civic pride, the *palazzo comunale* (municipal palace) is often the most impressive secular building in a Tuscan town. Noteworthy examples include those on Siena's Piazza del Campo, Volterra's Piazza dei Priori and Florence's Piazza della Signoria.

GIORGIO VASARI'S 'LIVES OF THE ARTISTS'

Painter, architect and writer Giorgio Vasari (1511–74) was one of those figures rightfully described as a 'Renaissance man'. Born in Arezzo, he trained as a painter in Florence, working with artists such as Andrea del Sarto and Michelangelo (whome he idolised). As a painter, he is best remembered for his floor-to-ceiling frescoes in the Salone dei Cinquecento in Florence's Palazzo Vecchio. As an architect, his most accomplished work was the elegant loggia of the Uffizi Gallery (he also designed the enclosed, elevated corridor that connected the Palazzo Vecchio with the Uffizi and Palazzo Pitti and was dubbed the 'Corridoio Vasariano' in his honour). But posterity remembers him predominantly for his work as an art historian. His *Lives of the Most Excellent Painters, Sculptors and Architects, from Cimabue to Our Time,* an encyclopaedia of artistic biographies published in 1550 and dedicated to Cosimo I de' Medici, is still in print (as *The Lives of the Artists*) and is full of wonderful anecdotes and gossip about his artistic contemporaries in 16th-century Florence.

Memorable passages include his recollection of visiting Donatello's studio one day only to find the great sculptor staring at his extremely life-like statue of the *Prophet Habakkuk* and imploring it to talk (we can only assume that Donatello had been working too hard). Vasari also writes about a young Giotto painting a fly on the surface of a work by Cimabue that the older master then tried to brush away.

atrium	forecourt
badia	abbey
baldacchino	canopy, usually over a high altar in a basilica
basilica	an early or medieval Christian church with a ground plan similar to or derived from the Roman basilica
bas-relief	sculpture in low relief
battistero	a church building in which baptism was/is administered
Byzantine	art and architecture of the Byzantine Empire; predated the Romanesque, Gothic and Renaissance movements
campanile	bell tower
cappella	chapel
cartoon	a full-size preparatory drawing for a painting or fresco
cella	sanctuary of a temple
cenacolo	scene of the Last Supper (often in the refectory of a convent or monastery)
chiaroscuro	literally 'light-dark'; artistic distribution of light and dark areas in a painting
chiostro	cloister; a rectangular open space surrounded by a covered walkway
clerestory	upper part of the nave wall of a church featuring windows
coffer	ornamental sunken panel in a ceiling
colonnade	a series of columns set at regular intervals, and usually supporting an entablature, a roof or a series of arches
cornice	1. a horizontal moulded projection that crowns or finishes a wall or building; 2. the uppermost division of an entablature, resting on the frieze; 3. the moulding(s) between the walls and ceiling of a room
cortile	courtyard
cruciform	cross-shaped
crypt	underground chamber or vault used as a burial place

cupola	a rounded vault or dome
diptych	painting or carving with two panels; usually small and portable and often used as an altarpiece
duomo	cathedral
entablature	sits on top of a row of columns on a classical facade; includes an architrave, the decorative frieze atop that and the triangular pediment to cap it off
exedra	semicircular recess
ex-voto	tablet or small painting expressing gratitude to a saint
font	receptacle, usually made of stone, that holds the water used in baptisms
fresco	painting executed on wet plaster
frieze	the part of an entablature between the architrave and the cornice, commonly ornamented with sculpture
Gothic	style of art and architecture in the late medieval period; popular from the 12th century
grisaille	technique of monochrome painting in shades of grey
loggia	1. covered area on the side of a building; 2. porch; 3. lodge
lunette	semicircular space in a vault or ceiling or above a door or window; often decorated with a fresco or painting
Madonna della Misericordia	literally 'Madonna of Mercy'; in art, an iconic formula showing a group of people seeking protection under the outspread cloak of the Madonna
Maestà	literally 'Majesty'; in art, an iconic formula of the enthroned Madonna with Christ Child, often surrounded by angels and saints
mausoleo	mausoleum; stately and magnificent tomb
narthex	vestibule along the facade of an early Christian church
nave	the main body, or middle part (lengthwise), of a church, flanked by aisles and extending typically from the entrance to the *apse*
necropolis	ancient cemetery or burial site
oculus	round window
pediment	a low triangular gable crowned with a projecting cornice, especially over a portico or porch at the end of a gable-roofed building
piano nobile	main floor of a palace
Pietà	literally 'pity' or 'compassion'; sculpture, drawing or painting of the dead Christ being held by the Madonna
pietra forte	fine sandstone used as a building material
pietra serena	greenish-grey 'serene stone'
pieve	parish church, usually in a rural setting
pinacoteca	art gallery
podium	a low continuous structure serving as a base or terrace wall
polyptych	painting or carving consisting of more than three panels; usually used as an altarpiece
porphyry	dark blue-, purple- or red-coloured rock
portico	a structure consisting of a roof supported by columns or piers forming the entrance to a church or other building
predella	small painting or panel attached below a large altarpiece

The term 'Macchiaioli' (the name given to a 19th-century group of Tuscan plein-air artists) was coined by a journalist in 1862. It mockingly implied that the artists' finished works were no more than sketches, and was drawn from the phrase *darsi alla macchia* (to hide in bushes or scrubland).

MACCHIAIOLI

presbytery	eastern part of a church chancel, beyond the choir
pulpit	a platform or raised structure in a church from which a priest delivers a sermon
quadriporto	four-sided porch
quatrefoil	four-lobed design
relief	an apparent projection of parts in a sculpture or frieze giving the appearance of the third dimension
Renaissance	cultural movement that started in Florence; period c 14th to 17th centuries
Romanesque	architecture of the early Western Christian empire c 6th to 12th centuries
rose window	circular window divided into sections by stone mullions and tracery; usually found in Gothic churches
rustification	stone with a chiselled, rough-hewn look
sacristy	room in a church where the sacred vessels, vestments etc are kept
sanctuaio	sanctuary; the part of a church above the altar
sfumato	hazy blending of colours and blurring of outlines; used in painting
sgraffito	a surface covered with plaster, then scratched away to create a 3D trompe l'œil effect of carved stone or brick
sinopia	working sketch for a fresco
spolia	creative reuse of ancient monuments in new structures
stele	upright stone with carved inscription or image
stemma	coat of arms
stigmata	marks appearing on a saint's body in the same places as the wounds of Christ
stucco	plasterwork
tabernacle	in Christianity, a locked box in which the communion wafers and wine are stored
tempera	powdered pigment bound together with a mixture of egg and water; used in painting
tesoro	treasury
tesserae	small cubes of marble, stone or glass used in mosaic work
tondo	circular painting or relief
transept	the transverse portion(s) of a cruciform church
travertine	limestone used in paving and building
triptych	painting or carving over three panels, hinged so that the outer panels fold over the middle one; often used as an altarpiece
tufa	soft volcanic rock
vault	arched structure forming a ceiling or roof
vestibule	passage, hall or antechamber between the outer door and interior parts of a building

RENAISSANCE PAINTING

Masaccio's *Trinity*, a wall painting in the Basilica di Santa Maria Novella in Florence, is often described as one of the founding works of Renaissance painting and the inspiration for Leonardo da Vinci's *Last Supper* fresco.

Survival Guide

Directory A–Z

Accommodation

See p33 for information on accommodation in Tuscany.

Customs Regulations

Visitors coming into Italy from non-EU countries can import the following items duty free:

- 1L spirits (or 4L wine)
- 200 cigarettes
- up to a total of €430 (€150 for travellers aged under 15) for other goods, including perfume and eau de toilette.

Anything over these limits must be declared on arrival and the appropriate duty paid. On leaving the EU, non-EU citizens can reclaim any Value Added Tax (VAT) on any purchases over €154.94.

For more information, go to www.agenziadogane.it. See also p323.

Discount Cards

Free admission to many galleries and cultural sites is available to youths under 18 and seniors over 65 years old. In addition, visitors aged between 18 and 25 often qualify for a 50% discount. In many cases, these discounts only apply to EU citizens. In our reviews, we have indicated this by using the description 'reduced' when citing admission charges.

When in Florence, consider purchasing a **Firenze Card** (www.firenzecard.it; €72), which is valid for 72 hours and covers admission to 72 museums, villas and gardens in Florence, as well as unlimited use of public transport.

You can also often save money with a *biglietto cumulativo* (combined ticket), which allows admission to a number of associated sights for less than the combined cost of separate admission fees.

Youth, Student & Teacher Cards

If you're aged under 30, the European Youth Card (*Carta Giovani Europea*; www.cartagiovani.it, http://eyca.org; €5-19 depending on where it is purchased) offers thousands of discounts on Italian hotels, museums, restaurants, shops and clubs and is available for purchase online. Student, teacher or youth travel cards (www.isic.org) can save you money on flights to Italy and are available worldwide from student unions, hostelling organisations and youth travel agencies such as **STA Travel** (www.statravel.com). Options include the International Student Identity Card (for full-time students), Interna-

Climate

Florence

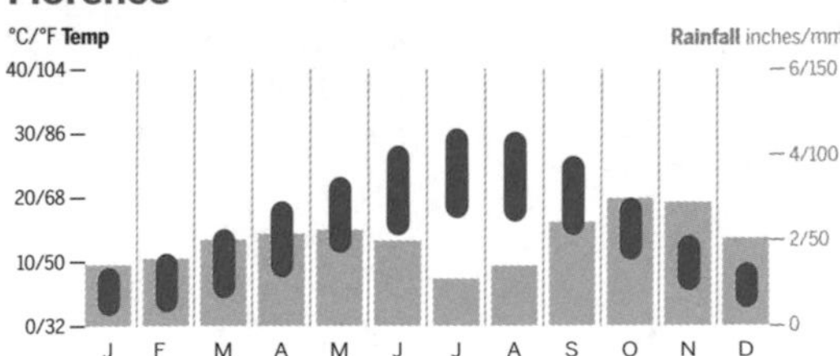

Elba

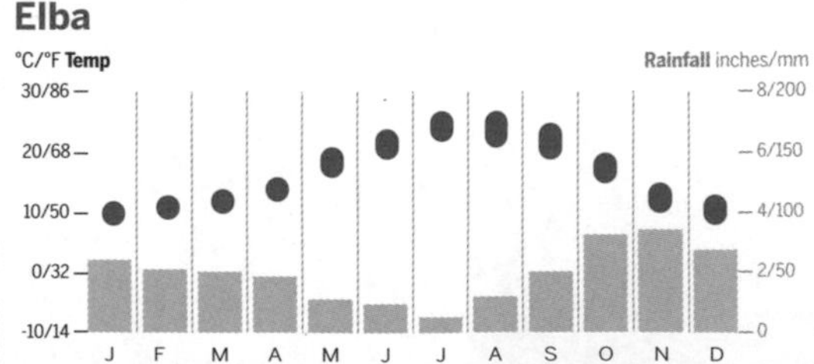

tional Teacher Identity Card (for full-time teachers) and the International Youth Travel Card (for travellers under 26 years).

Note that many places in Italy give discounts according to age rather than student status. An ISIC may not always be accepted without proof of age (eg passport).

Electricity

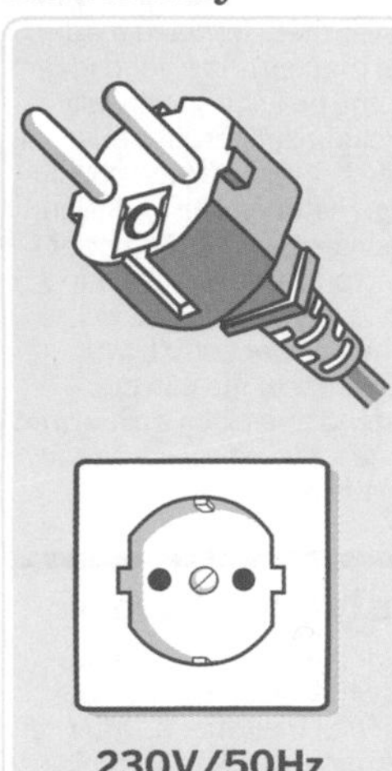

230V/50Hz

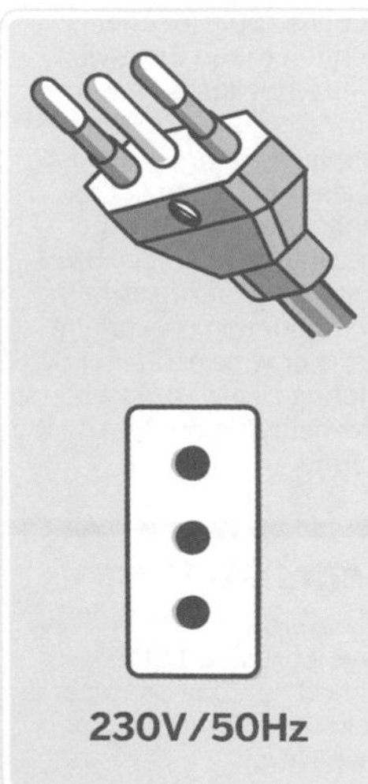

230V/50Hz

BOOK YOUR STAY ONLINE

For more accommodation reviews by Lonely Planet authors, check out http://lonelyplanet.com/hotels/. You'll find independent reviews, as well as recommendations on the best places to stay. Best of all, you can book online.

Embassies & Consulates

For foreign embassies and consulates in Italy that are not listed here, look under 'Ambasciate' or 'Consolati' in the telephone directory. In addition to the following, some countries run honorary consulates in other cities.

Australian (www.italy.embassy.gov.au) Rome (06 85 27 21; Via Antonio Bosio 5); Milan (02 7767 4217; www.austrade.it; 3rd fl, Via Borgogna 2)

Austrian Rome (06 844 01 41; www.aussenministerium.at/rom; Via Pergolesi 3); Milan (02 78 37 43; www.aussenministerium.at/mailandgk; Piazza del Liberty 8/4)

Canadian (www.canadainternational.gc.ca/italy-italie) Rome (06 85444 2911; Via Zara 30); Milan (02 6269 4238; Piazza Cavour 3)

Dutch (www.olanda.it) Rome (06 3228 6001; Via Michele Mercati 8)

French (www.ambafrance-it.org) Rome (06 68 60 11; Piazza Farnese 67); Milan (02 655 91 41; www.ambafrance-it.org/-Milan-; Via della Moscova 12; M Turati)

German Rome (06 49 21 31; www.rom.diplo.de; Via San Martino della Battaglia 4); Milan (02 623 11 01; www.mailand.diplo.de; Via Solferino 40; M Moscova)

Irish (06 585 23 81; www.ambasciata-irlanda.it; Villa Spada, Via Giacomo Medici 1, Rome)

Japanese (www.it.emb-japan.go.jp) Rome (06 48 79 91; Via Quintino Sella 60); Milan (02 624 11 41; Via Cesare Mangili 2/4; M Turati)

New Zealand (www.nzembassy.com/italy) Rome (06 853 75 01; Via Clitunno 44); Milan (02 7217 0001; Via Terraggio 17; M Cadorna)

Slovenian (www.rim.veleposlanistvo.si) Rome (06 8091 4310; Via Leonardo Pisano 10, Rome)

Swiss (www.eda.admin.ch) Rome (06 80 95 71; www.eda.admin.ch/roma; Via Barnaba Oriani 61, Rome); Florence (055 22 24 34; Piazzale Galileo 5, Florence)

UK (http://ukinitaly.fco.gov.uk) Rome (06 4220 0001; Via XX Settembre 80a, Rome); Milan (06 4220 2431; Via San Paolo 7; M San Babila)

US (http://italy.usembassy.gov) Rome (06 4 67 41; Via Vittorio Veneto 121, Rome); Florence (055 26 69 51; Lungarno Vespucci 38, Florence)

Food

In this book reviews are listed by author preference within price categories. We include approximate meal prices in our restaurant reviews. For more on food, see p36 and p290.

Gay & Lesbian Travellers

Homosexuality is legal in Italy and well accepted in the major cities. On the Tuscan coast, Torre del Lago has a lively gay scene, best expressed by **Friendly Versilia** (www.friendlyversilia.it), a summer campaign that encourages gays and lesbians to revel in Torre del Lago's

EATING PRICE RANGES

Food review prices are based on a *primo* (first course), *secondo* (main course/entrée), *contorno* (side dish), *bicchiere di vino della casa* (glass of house wine) and *coperto* (cover charge). The food pricing system is as follows:

€ less than €25

€€ €25 to €45

€€€ more than €45

fun-in-the-sun frolics from late April to September.

Resources include the following:

Arcigay (www.arcigay.it) Bologna-based national organisation for the LGBTI community.

Azione Gay e Lesbica Firenze (☎055 22 02 50; www.azionegayelesbica.it; Via Pisana 32r) Active Florence-based organisation for gays and lesbians.

GayFriendlyItaly.com (www.gayfriendlyitaly.com) English-language site produced by Gay.it, featuring information on everything from hotels to homophobia issues and the law.

Gay.it (www.gay.it) Website featuring LGBT news, feature articles and gossip.

Pride (www.prideonline.it) National monthly magazine of art, music, politics and gay culture.

Health

Recommended Vaccinations

No jabs are required to travel to Italy. However, the World Health Organization (WHO) recommends that all travellers should be covered for diphtheria, tetanus, the measles, mumps, rubella and polio, as well as hepatitis B.

Health Insurance

If you're an EU citizen (or from Switzerland, Norway or Iceland), a European Health Insurance Card (EHIC) covers you for most medical care in public hospitals free of charge, but not for emergency repatriation home or non-emergencies. The card is available from health centres and (in the UK) from post offices. Citizens from other countries should find out if there is a reciprocal arrangement for free medical care between their country and Italy (Australia, for instance, has such an agreement; carry your Medicare card).

If you do need health insurance, make sure you get a policy that covers you for the worst possible scenario, such as an accident requiring an emergency flight home. Find out in advance if your insurance plan will make payments directly to providers or reimburse you later for overseas health expenditures.

Availability of Health Care

Pharmacists can give you valuable advice and sell over-the-counter medication for minor illnesses. They can also advise you when more specialised help is required and point you in the right direction.

Pharmacies generally keep the same hours as other shops, closing at night and on Sundays. However, in big cities a handful remain open on a rotation basis *(farmacie di turno)* for emergency purposes. These are listed online at www.miniportale.it/miniportale/farmacie/Toscana.htm. You can also check the door of any pharmacy that is closed for business – it will display a list of the nearest emergency pharmacies.

If you need an ambulance, call ☎118. For emergency treatment, head straight to the *pronto soccorso* (casualty) section of a public hospital, where you can also get emergency dental treatment.

Insurance

A travel-insurance policy to cover theft, loss and medical problems is a good idea. Some policies specifically exclude dangerous activities, which can include scuba diving, motorcycling and even hiking – read the fine print.

Worldwide travel insurance is available at www.lonelyplanet.com/travel-insurance. You can buy, extend and claim online any time – even if you're already on the road.

Internet Access

Throughout this guide we use the @ icon to indicate venues that offer an internet terminal (an actual computer or tablet) for guests' use, and the wi-fi icon to designate places with a wi-fi network. If charges apply for either, we mention this in the review.

Internet access has improved markedly in the past couple of years, with most locals now having home connections and a large percentage of hotels, B&Bs, hostels and *agriturismi* (accommodation on working farms or wine estates) now offering free wi-fi. As a result, internet cafes are thin on the ground.

Legal Matters

The average tourist will only have a brush with the law if robbed by a bag-snatcher or pickpocket, or if their car is towed away.

See p330 for information on traffic laws.

Maps

You can choose from a number of sheet maps covering the region, including Michelin's *Toscana* (1:200,000), Marco Polo's *Toscana/Tuscany* (1:200,000) and Touring Editore's *Toscana* (1:200,000).

Money

The euro is Italy's currency. Notes come in denominations of €500, €200, €100, €50, €20, €10 and €5. Coins are in denominations of €2 and €1, and 50, 20, 10, five, two and one cents.

For the latest exchange rates, see p19.

ATMs

Bancomats (ATM machines) are widely available throughout Tuscany and are the best way to obtain local currency.

Credit Cards

International credit and debit cards can be used at any *bancomat* displaying the appropriate sign. Cards are also good for payment in most hotels, restaurants, shops, supermarkets and tollbooths.

If your card is lost, stolen or swallowed by an ATM, you can telephone toll free to have an immediate stop put on its use:

Amex (☎800 928391)

Diners Club (☎800 864064)

MasterCard (☎800 870866)

Visa (☎800 819014)

Moneychangers

You can change money in banks, at the post office or in a *cambio* (exchange office). Post offices and banks tend to offer the best rates; exchange offices keep longer hours, but watch for high commissions and inferior rates.

Taxes & Refunds

A Value Added Tax (VAT) of 21%, known as IVA (Imposta di Valore Aggiunto), is slapped on most goods and services in Italy; a discounted rate of 10% applies in restaurants, bars and hotels. If you are a non-EU resident and spend more than €155 (€154.94 to be precise!) on a purchase, you can claim a refund when you leave. The refund only applies to purchases from affiliated retail outlets that display a 'tax free for tourists' (or similar) sign. You have to complete a form at the point of sale, then have it stamped by EU customs as you leave the zone (if you are visiting one or more EU countries after visiting Italy, you'll need to submit the form at your final port of exit). For information, visit **Tax Refund for Tourists** (www.taxrefund.it) or pick up a pamphlet on the scheme from participating stores.

See p35 for information about the recently introduced *tassa di soggiorno* (hotel occupancy tax).

Opening Hours

In this book, we include opening times for most individual businesses. As a general rule:

Banks 8.30am to 1.30pm and 3.30pm to 4.30pm Monday to Friday

Bars & pubs 10am to 1am

Cafes 7.30am to 8pm

Nightclubs 10pm to late

Pharmacies 9am to 12.30pm and 3.30pm to 7pm Monday to Friday, 9am to 12.30pm Saturday and Sunday

Post offices (main) 8am to 7pm Monday to Friday, 8.30am to noon Saturday

Post offices (branch) 8am to 2pm Monday to Friday, 8.30am to noon Saturday

Restaurants 12.30pm to 2.30pm and 7.30pm to 10pm

Shops 9am to 1pm and 3.30pm to 7.30pm (or 4pm to 8pm) Monday to Saturday

Post

Le Poste (www.poste.it), Italy's postal system, is reasonably reliable but if you are sending a package you might want to use DHL or FedEx, which are safer.

ITALY'S POLICE FORCES

There are six national police forces in Italy, as well as a number of local police forces. The three main forces are shown in the table below.

ORGANISATION	JURISDICTION	UNIFORM
polizia di stato (civil national police)	thefts, visa extensions and permits; based at the local *questura* (police station)	powder blue trousers with a fuchsia stripe and a navy blue jacket
arma dei carabinieri (military police)	general crime, public order and drug enforcement (often overlapping with the *polizia di stato*)	black uniforms with a red stripe
polizia municipale (aka *vigili urbani*; municipal police)	parking tickets, towed cars, public order, petty crime	varies according to province

Francobolli (stamps) are available at post offices and authorised *tabacchi* (tobacconists; look for the official sign: a big 'T', often white on black). Since letters often need to be weighed, what you get at the tobacconist for international airmail will occasionally be an approximation of the proper rate. *Tabacchi* keep regular shop hours.

Public Holidays

Most Italians take their annual holiday in August, with the busiest period occurring around 15 August, known locally as Ferragosto. This means that many businesses and shops close for at least a part of that month. Settimana Santa (Easter Week) is another busy holiday period for Italians.

Individual towns have public holidays to celebrate the feasts of their patron saints. National public holidays:

New Year's Day (Capodanno or Anno Nuovo) 1 January

Epiphany (Epifania or Befana) 6 January

Anniversary of the Unification of Italy (Anniversario dell'Unità d'Italia) 17 March

Easter Sunday (Domenica di Pasqua) March/April

Easter Monday (Pasquetta or Lunedì dell'Angelo) March/April

Liberation Day (Giorno della Liberazione) On 25 April – marks the Allied Victory in Italy, and the end of the German presence and Mussolini, in 1945.

Labour Day (Festa del Lavoro) 1 May

Republic Day (Festa della Repubblica) 2 June

Feast of the Assumption (Assunzione or Ferragosto) 15 August

All Saints' Day (Ognissanti) 1 November

Feast of the Immaculate Conception (Immaculata Concezione) 8 December

Christmas Day (Natale) 25 December

Boxing Day (Festa di Santo Stefano) 26 December

Telephone

Domestic Calls

Italian telephone area codes all begin with 0 and consist of up to four digits. The area code is followed by a number of anything from four to nine digits. The area code is an integral part of the telephone number and must always be dialled, even when calling from next door. Mobile-phone numbers begin with a three-digit prefix such as 330. Toll-free (free-phone) numbers are known as *numeri verdi* and usually start with 800. Nongeographical numbers start with 840, 841, 848, 892, 899, 163, 166 or 199. Some six-digit national rate numbers are also in use (such as those for Alitalia, and rail and postal information).

As elsewhere in Europe, Italians choose from a host of providers of phone plans and rates, making it difficult to make generalisations about costs.

International Calls

The cheapest options for calling internationally are free or low-cost computer programs such as Skype, cut-rate call centres or international calling cards, which are sold at newsstands and *tabacchi*. Cut-price call centres can be found in all of the main cities, and rates can be considerably lower than from Telecom Italia payphones for international calls. You simply place your call from a private booth inside the centre and pay for it when you've finished. Direct international calls can also easily be made from public telephones with a phonecard. Dial ☎00 to get out of Italy, then the relevant country and area codes, followed by the telephone number.

To call Italy from abroad, call the international access number (☎011 in the USA, ☎00 from most other countries), Italy's country code (39) and then the area code of the location you want, including the leading 0.

Mobile Phones

Italy uses GSM 900/1800, which is compatible with the rest of Europe and Australia but not with North American GSM 1900 or the totally different Japanese system (though some GSM 1900/900 phones do work here). If you have a GSM phone, check with your service provider about using it in Italy and beware of calls being routed internationally (very expensive for a 'local' call).

Italy has one of the highest levels of mobile-phone penetration in Europe, and

PRACTICALITIES

- Italy uses the metric system for weights and measures.
- Smoking is banned in all closed public spaces.
- The major daily newspapers are **Corriere della Sera** (www.corriere.it/english), which publishes in both Italian and English, and the Florentine edition of **La Repubblica** (www.firenze.repubblica.it), which is only in Italian.
- For news, views and classifieds in English, pick up a copy of the free bimonthly newspaper **The Florentine** (www.theflorentine.net), distributed at select hotels, cafes, bookshops and bars in Florence.

you can get a temporary or prepaid account from several companies if you already own a GSM, dual- or tri-band mobile phone. Always check with your mobile-service provider in your home country to ascertain whether your handset allows use of another SIM card. If yours does, it can cost as little as €20 to activate a local prepaid SIM card (sometimes with €10 worth of calls on the card). You'll need to register with a mobile-phone shop, bring your passport and wait for approximately 24 hours for your account to be activated. After that, buy *ricarica* (prepaid minutes) from your selected mobile company at shops and *tabacchi* everywhere. If you have an internet-enabled phone, be sure to turn off your data roaming function when you're not using it, as this devours credit.

TIM (Telecom Italia Mobile; www.tim.it), **Vodafone** (www.vodafone.it) and **Wind** (www.wind.it) have the densest networks of outlets across the country.

Payphones & Phonecards

You'll find Telecom Italia payphones on the streets, in train stations and in Telecom offices. Most payphones accept only *carte/schede telefoniche* (phonecards), although some also accept credit cards. Telecom offers a wide range of prepaid cards for both domestic and international use; for a full list, see www.telecomitalia.it/telefono/carte-telefoniche. You can buy phonecards (most commonly €3, €5 or €10) at post offices, *tabacchi* and newsstands. You must break off the top left-hand corner of the card before you can use it. All phonecards have an expiry date, printed on the face of the card.

Time

Italy operates on a 24-hour clock. It is one hour ahead of GMT/UTC. Daylight-saving time starts on the last Sunday in March, when clocks are put forward one hour. Clocks are put back an hour on the last Sunday in October. This is especially valuable to know in Italy, as 'summer' and 'winter' hours at museums and other sights (cited in this book) are usually based on daylight-saving time.

Tourist Information

Practically every village and town has a tourist office of sorts. These operate under a variety of names but are often known as 'Pro Loco'.

Italy's recent economic downturn has had a significant impact on the tourism sector in Tuscany, with tourist promotion and information budgets being cut in every region. This has led to the closure of some tourist information offices, and the introduction of reduced opening times at others.

When this book went to print, the situation lacked clarity. We have included addresses and opening hours for the tourist offices that were open during our research, but cannot be sure that this information will remain accurate.

Travellers with Disabilities

Italy is not an easy country for travellers with disabilities and getting around can be a problem for wheelchair users. Even a short journey in a city or town can become a major expedition if cobblestone streets have to be negotiated. Although many buildings have lifts, they are not always wide enough for wheelchairs. Not an awful lot has been done to make life for the hearing impaired and/or blind any easier, either.

Italy's national rail company, **Trenitalia** (www.trenitalia.com) offers a helpline for disabled passengers at ☎199 303060 (7am to 9pm daily).

Two companies that specialise in accessible travel:

Accessible Italy (www.accessibleitaly.com) Based in the Republic of San Marino, this outfit specialises in holiday services for the disabled, ranging from tours to the hiring of adapted transport to the organisation of weddings.

Sage Traveling (www.sagetraveling.com) European accessible travel specialists who can organise customised tours; its website offers tips and advice on accessible travel in Florence.

Visas

Italy is one of 26 member countries of the Schengen Convention, under which EU countries (except Bulgaria, Cyprus, Ireland, Romania and the UK) plus Iceland, Liechtenstein, Norway and Switzerland have abolished permanent checks at common borders.

Legal residents of one Schengen country do not require a visa for another. Residents of 28 non-EU countries, including Australia, Brazil, Canada, Israel, Japan, New Zealand and the USA, do not require visas for tourist visits of up to 90 days.

All non-EU and non-Schengen nationals entering Italy for more than 90 days, or for any reason other than tourism (such as study or work) may need a specific visa. For details, visit www.esteri.it or contact an Italian consulate.

You should also have your passport stamped on entry as, without a stamp, you could encounter problems if trying to obtain a residence permit *(permesso di soggiorno)*. If you enter the EU via another member state, get your passport stamped there.

EU citizens do not require any permits to live or work in Italy but, after three months' residence, are supposed to register themselves at the municipal registry office where they live and offer proof of work or sufficient funds to support themselves. Non-EU foreign citizens with five years' continuous legal residence may apply for permanent residence.

Permesso di Soggiorno

Non-EU citizens planning to stay at the same address for more than one week are supposed to report to the police station to receive a *permesso di soggiorno*. Tourists staying in hotels are not required to do this.

A *permesso di soggiorno* only really becomes a necessity if you plan to study, work (legally) or live in Italy. Obtaining one is never a pleasant experience; it often involves long queues and the frustration of arriving at the counter only to find you don't have the necessary documents.

The exact requirements, such as specific documents and *marche da bollo* (official stamps), can change. In general, you will need a valid passport (if possible containing a stamp with your date of entry into Italy), a special visa issued in your own country if you are planning to study (for non-EU citizens), four passport photos and proof of your ability to support yourself financially. You can apply at the *ufficio stranieri* (foreigners' bureau) of the police station closest to where you're staying.

EU citizens do not require a *permesso di soggiorno*.

Study Visas

Non-EU citizens who want to study at a university or language school in Italy must have a study visa. These can be obtained from your nearest Italian embassy or consulate. You will normally require confirmation of your enrolment, proof of payment of fees and adequate funds to support yourself. The visa covers only the period of the enrolment. This type of visa is renewable within Italy but, again, only with confirmation of ongoing enrolment and proof that you are able to support yourself (bank statements are preferred).

Transport

GETTING THERE & AWAY

Entering the Country

EU and Swiss citizens can travel to Italy with their national identity card alone. All other nationalities must have a valid passport and may be required to fill out a landing card at airports.

By law you are supposed to have your passport or ID card with you at all times. You'll need one of these documents for police registration every time you check into a hotel.

In theory, there are no passport checks at land crossings from neighbouring countries, but random customs controls do occasionally still take place between Italy and Switzerland.

Air

High season for air travel to Italy is mid-April to mid-September. Shoulder season runs from mid-September to the end of October and from Easter to mid-April. Low season is generally November to March, but tickets around Christmas and Easter increase in price or sell out. Flights, tours and rail tickets can be booked at lonelyplanet.com/bookings.

Airlines

Domestic flights in and out of the region:

Air One (www.flyairone.it) Pisa International Airport to/from Olbia and Catania.

Alitalia (www.alitalia.it) Pisa International Airport, Florence Airport and Bologna Airport to/from Rome and Catania.

Meridiana Fly (www.meridiana.it) Bologna Airport to/from Olbia, Cagliari, Lampedusa and Catania.

Ryanair (www.ryanair.com) Pisa International Airport to/from Trapani, Palermo, Bari, Brindisi and Cagliari; Umbria International Airport to/from Cagliari and Trapani; Bologna Airport to Bari, Brindisi, Trapani and Palermo.

Volotea (www.volotea.com) Florence Airport to/from Catania and Palermo.

Land

Border Crossings

Entering Italy is relatively simple. If you are arriving from a neighbouring EU country, you do not require a passport check.

Bus

Buses are the cheapest overland option to Italy, but services are less frequent, less comfortable and significantly slower than the train, so we do not recommend them.

AIRPORTS SERVICING TUSCANY

AIRPORT	ALTERNATIVE NAMES	LOCATION	WEBSITE
Pisa International Airport (PSA)	Aeroporto Galileo Galilei	Pisa	www.pisa-airport.com
Florence Airport (FLR)	Amerigo Vespucci; Peretola	Florence	www.aeroporto.firenze.it
Umbria International Airport (PEG)	S Egidio	Perugia, Umbria	www.airport.umbria.it
Bologna Airport (BLQ)	Aeroporto G Marconi	Bologna, Emilia-Romagna	www.bologna-airport.it

CLIMATE CHANGE & TRAVEL

Every form of transport that relies on carbon-based fuel generates CO_2, the main cause of human-induced climate change. Modern travel is dependent on aeroplanes, which might use less fuel per kilometre per person than most cars but travel much greater distances. The altitude at which aircraft emit gases (including CO_2) and particles also contributes to their climate change impact. Many websites offer 'carbon calculators' that allow people to estimate the carbon emissions generated by their journey and, for those who wish to do so, to offset the impact of the greenhouse gases emitted with contributions to portfolios of climate-friendly initiatives throughout the world. Lonely Planet offsets the carbon footprint of all staff and author travel.

Car & Motorcycle

Every vehicle travelling across the border should display a valid national licence plate and an accompanying registration card.

Train

Milan is the major rail hub in northern Italy, so if you are arriving from a European destination you will usually arrive there and change trains to get to Florence. From France, you can also change at Turin to catch a connecting service to Pisa, or book onto the Thello sleeper train that travels from Paris-Gare de Lyon to Rome, stopping at Firenze Campo di Marte en route.

For timetables, go to www.eurail.com.

Sea

Ferries connect Italy with its islands and other countries all across the Mediterranean. However, the only options for reaching Tuscany directly by sea are the ferry crossings to Livorno from Spain, Sardinia, Corsica and Sicily.

For a comprehensive guide to all ferry services into and out of Italy, check out **Traghettionline** (www.traghettionline.com). The website lists every route and includes links to ferry companies, where you can buy tickets or search for deals.

EXPRESS TRAINS FROM CONTINENTAL EUROPE

FROM	TO	FREQUENCY	DURATION (HR)	COST (€)
Geneva	Milan	4 daily	4	78
Munich	Verona	5 daily	5½	74
Ventimiglia	Milan	6 daily	4	9-19
Paris	Florence	nightly	12¾	80-100
Paris	Milan	3 daily	7-10	55-80
Vienna	Florence	nightly	10½	89
Zurich	Milan	6 daily	3¾	71

GETTING AROUND

To/From the Airport

Buses and trains connect Pisa International Airport with Pisa and Florence, and there is also one bus per day between Pisa airport and Siena. Buses link Florence airport with central Florence. If you fly into Bologna airport, **Appennino Shuttle** (www.appenninoshuttle.it) buses travel to Florence (€19, 90 minutes, 10 daily). From Umbria International Airport you'll need to take a taxi to Perugia (15km) and then a bus or train to Tuscany.

Bicycle

Cycling is a national pastime in Italy. Bikes are prohibited on the autostrada (expressway), but there are few other special road rules.

Bikes can be taken on any train that carries the bicycle logo. The cheapest way to do this is to buy a separate bicycle ticket (€3.50 for *regionale* (slow local train) services and €12 for international services), which are available even at the self-service kiosks. You can use this ticket for 24 hours, making a day trip quite economical. Bicycles that are dismantled and stored in a bag can be taken for free, even on night trains, and all ferries allow free bicycle passage.

Boat

Regular ferries connect Piombino on the mainland with Portoferraio on Elba; in summer, a handful of boats sail from Piombino to the smaller Elban ports of Cavo and Rio Marina. From Livorno, ferries run to the island of Capraia via Gorgona.

Bus

Although trains are the most convenient and economical way to travel between major towns, a bus is often the best link between small towns and villages. For a few intercity routes, such as the one between Florence and Siena, the bus is your best bet.

Dozens of different companies – loosely affiliated under the **Tiemme** (www.lfi.it) network – service the region. Most reduce or even drop services on holidays and weekends, especially Sundays; we cite frequency of services on weekdays. Local tourist offices often carry bus timetables.

You can purchase tickets at most *tabacchi* (tobacconists) and news-stands, or from ticket booths and dispensing machines at bus stations; they must be validated in the machine on board. Tickets are also usually available on board for a slightly higher cost. In larger cities, ticket companies often have offices at the bus terminal and some larger cities offer good-value daily tourist tickets.

Turn up on time; in defiance of deep-seated Italian tradition, buses are almost always punctual.

BUS COMPANIES IN TUSCANY

REGIONAL BUS COMPANY	WEBSITE (MOST IN ITALIAN ONLY)	SERVICES
ATL	www.atl.livorno.it	Livorno
CAT	www.catspa.it	Lunigiana & Massa-Carrara
CPT	www.cpt.pisa.it	Pisa & Volterra
Etruria Mobilità	www.etruriamobilita.it	eastern Tuscany
Rama Mobilità	www.ramamobilita.it	southern Tuscany
Siena Mobilità	www.sienamobilita.it	Siena & around
SITA	www.sitabus.it	Florence & Chianti
Vaibus	www.vaibus.it	Lucca, Garfagnana & Versilia

Car & Motorcycle

Automobile Associations

The **Automobile Club d'Italia** (ACI; from non-Italian phone account ☎800 116800, roadside assistance ☎803 116; www.aci.it) is a driver's best resource in Italy. For 24-hour roadside emergency service, dial ☎803 116. Foreigners do not have to join but instead pay a per-incident fee.

Hire

CAR

To rent a car you must be at least 25 years old and have a credit card. Car-rental agencies expect you to bring the car back with a full tank of petrol and will charge astronomically if you don't. You should also make sure that the office where you are returning your car will be open when you arrive – we receive many complaints from travellers who have been hit with late fines because offices were closed when they tried to return their hire vehicles.

Make sure you understand what is included in the price (unlimited kilometres, tax, insurance, collision damage waiver and so on). Also consider vehicle size carefully: high fuel prices, extremely narrow streets and tight parking conditions mean that smaller is always better.

MOTORCYCLE

Agencies throughout Tuscany rent everything from small Vespas to larger touring bikes.

Most agencies will not rent motorcycles to people aged under 18. Many require a sizeable deposit, and you could be responsible for reimbursing part of the cost of the bike if it is stolen.

You don't need a licence to ride a scooter under 50cc. The speed limit is 40km/h, you must be 14 or over and you can't carry passengers. To ride a motorcycle or scooter between 50cc and 125cc, you must be aged 16 or over and have a licence (a car licence will do). For motorcycles over 125cc you will need a motorcycle licence.

On a motorcycle, you can ride freely in the heart of cities that have Zona a Traffico Limitato (ZTLs; Limited Traffic Zones), including Florence.

Driving Licence

All EU member states' driving licences are fully recognised throughout Europe. Drivers with a non-EU licence are supposed to obtain an International Driving Permit (IDP) to accompany their national licence, though anecdotal testimonies indicate that this rule is rarely enforced.

Fuel & Spare Parts

Italy's petrol (gas) prices are among the highest in Europe and vary from one service station *(benzinaio, stazione di servizio)* to another. During the time of research, lead-free gasoline (*senza piombo;* 95 octane) averaged €1.73 per litre, with diesel *(gasolio)* averaging €1.61 per litre. Many petrol stations are unattended at lunchtime, at night and on weekends; at these times credit cards may be used for payment (note, though, that not all foreign cards are accepted).

Spare parts are available at many garages or via the 24-hour ACI motorist assistance number (☎803 116).

Insurance

Always carry proof of vehicle ownership and evidence of third-party insurance. If driving an EU-registered vehicle, your home country insurance is sufficient. Ask your insurer for a European Accident Statement (EAS) form, which can simplify matters in the event of an accident.

Parking

Parking spaces outlined in blue are designated for paid parking (look for a nearby ticket machine and display the ticket on your dashboard). White outlines indicate free parking; yellow outlines indicate that residential permits are needed. Traffic police generally turn a blind eye to motorcycles or scooters parked on footpaths.

Road Network

Tuscany has an excellent road network, including autostradas, superstradas (dual carriageways) and major highways. Most of these are untolled, with the main exceptions being the A11 and A12 (FI-PI-LI) autostrada connecting Florence, Pisa and Livorno and the A1 autostrada linking Milan and Rome via Florence and Arezzo. For information about driving times and toll charges on these, check www.autostrade.it/en/.

There are several minor road categories, listed below in descending order of importance.

Strade statali (state highways) Represented on maps by 'S' or 'SS'. Vary from toll-free, four-lane highways to two-lane main roads. The latter can be extremely slow, especially in mountainous regions.

Strade regionali (regional highways connecting small villages) Coded SR or R.

Strade provinciali (provincial highways) Coded SP or P.

Strade locali Often not even paved or mapped.

Road Rules

Cars drive on the right and overtake on the left. Unless otherwise indicated, you must always give way to cars entering an intersection from a road on your right.

Seatbelt use (front and rear) is required by law; violators are subject to an on-the-spot fine. Children under 12 must travel in the back seat, and those under four must use child seats.

In the event of a breakdown, a warning triangle is compulsory, as is use of an approved yellow or orange safety vest if you leave your vehicle.

Italy's blood-alcohol limit is 0.05%, and random breath tests take place. If you're involved in an accident while under the influence, the penalties can be severe.

Speeding fines follow EU standards and are proportionate with the number of kilometres that you are caught driving over the speed limit, reaching up to €2000 with possible suspension of your driving licence.

On all two-wheeled transport, helmets are required. The speed limit for scooters is 40km/h. Headlights are compulsory day and night for all vehicles on the autostradas, and advisable for motorcycles even on smaller roads.

Many Tuscan towns and cities have a ZTL in their historic centre. This means that only local vehicles with parking permits can enter – all other vehicles must stay outside the ZTL or be hit with a hefty fine. Being in a hire car will not exempt you from this rule – we receive regular reports from travellers who have unknowingly breached a ZTL and have ended up with a hefty charge (fine plus administrative fee) on their credit card.

SPEED LIMITS

- Urban areas: 50km/h
- Secondary roads: 70-90km/h (look for signs)
- Main roads: cars 110km/h (90km/h in rain)
- Autostradas: cars 130km/h (110km/h in rain)

Local Transport

Taxi

You can usually find taxi ranks at train and bus stations, or you can telephone for taxis. It's best to go to a designated taxi stand, as it's illegal for taxis to stop in the street if hailed. If you phone a taxi, bear in mind that the meter starts running from the moment of your call rather than when the taxi picks you up.

Tram

Florence has a new tram network, but it services residential areas rather than tourist hotspots.

Train

The train network throughout Tuscany is limited. Local *regionale* trains are slow and stop at nearly all stations; *regionale veloce* (fast regional) trains stop at fewer stations. Next fastest are Intercity (IC) services.

High-speed services include the high-speed *frecce* (arrow) trains that link major towns and cities. These include the *Frecciabianca*, *Frecciargento* and – fastest of all – *Frecciarossa* trains.

Train Routes

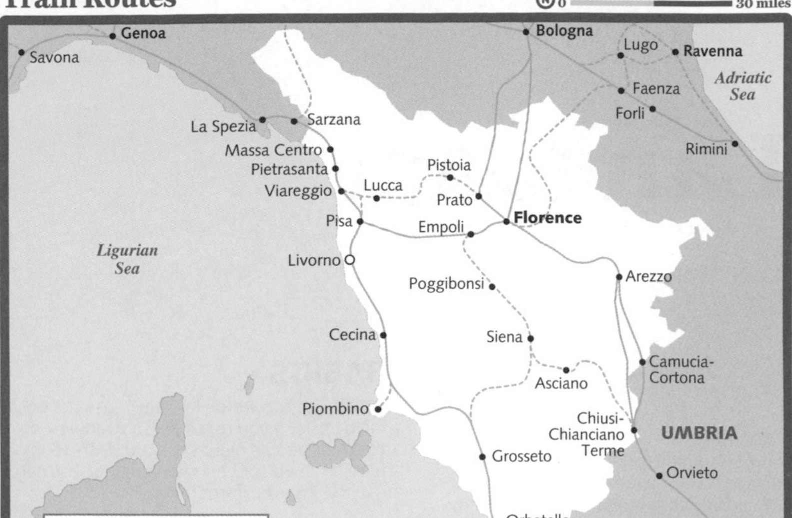

Trenitalia (☎Italian speaking 800 892021; www.trenitalia.com) is the partially privatised state train system, which runs most of the services in Italy.

Advance reservations are not really necessary unless you are travelling on a *freccia*. Tickets can be purchased from the ticket office or automated ticket machines when you get to the station.

Almost all train journeys require you to validate your ticket *before* boarding – just punch it in the yellow *convalida* machines installed at the entrance to all train platforms. On many buses, you'll need to validate your ticket on the bus itself. Getting caught freeloading or with a ticket that hasn't been validated risks a fine of at least €50. It's paid on the spot to an inspector who will be kind enough to escort you to an ATM if you don't have the cash on you. Don't even think about trying the '*Ma sono turista!*' line; it won't wash.

Train timetables at stations generally display *arrivi* (arrivals) on a white background and *partenze* (departures) on a yellow one.

Classes & Costs

There are 1st and 2nd classes on most Italian trains; a 1st-class ticket costs just less than double the price of a 2nd-class one. There's not a huge amount of difference between the two – just a bit more space in first class, along with complimentary tea and coffee.

If you are taking a short trip, check the difference between the *regionale* and IC/*freccia* ticket prices, as *regionale* tickets are always considerably cheaper – you might arrive 10 minutes earlier on an IC or *freccia* service, but you'll also pay €5 or more for the privilege. Check up-to-date prices of routes on www.trenitalia.com.

Left Luggage

Most train stations have either a guarded left-luggage office or self-service lockers. The guarded offices are usually open 24 hours or 6am to midnight and charge around €4 per 12 hours for each piece of luggage. In Florence, it's €5 for the first five hours, and then €0.70 per hour from six to 12 hours and €0.30 per hour after that.

Train Passes

Trenitalia offers various discount passes, including the *Carta Verde* for young people aged 12-26 and *Carta d'Argento* for seniors (60+), but these only pay for themselves with regular use over an extended period. See www.trenitalia.com for details.

Language

Modern standard Italian began to develop in the 13th and 14th centuries, predominantly through the works of Dante, Petrarch and Boccaccio – all Tuscans – who wrote chiefly in the Florentine dialect. The language drew on its Latin heritage and many dialects to develop into the standard Italian of today. Although many dialects are spoken in everyday conversation in Italy, standard Italian is understood throughout the country. Despite the Florentine roots of standard Italian – and the fact that standard Italian is widely used in Florence and Tuscany – anyone who has learned some Italian will notice the peculiarity of the local accent. In Florence, as in other parts of Tuscany, you are bound to hear the hard 'c' pronounced as a heavy 'h'. For example, *Voglio una cannuccia per la Coca Cola* (I want a straw for my Coca Cola) sounds more like *Voglio una hannuccia per la Hoha Hola*.

Italian pronunciation is relatively easy as the sounds used in spoken Italian can all be found in English. If you read our coloured pronunciation guides as if they were English, you'll be understood. The stressed syllables are indicated with italics. Note that ai is pronounced as in 'aisle', ay as in 'say', ow as in 'how', dz as the 'ds' in 'lids', and that r is a strong and rolled sound. Keep in mind that Italian consonants can have a stronger, emphatic pronunciation – if the consonant is written as a double letter, it should be pronounced a little stronger, eg *sonno son*·no (sleep) versus *sono so*·no (I am).

WANT MORE?

For in-depth language information and handy phrases, check out Lonely Planet's *Italian Phrasebook*. You'll find it at **shop.lonelyplanet.com**, or you can buy Lonely Planet's iPhone phrasebooks at the Apple App Store.

BASICS

Italian has two words for 'you' – use the polite form *Lei* lay if you're talking to strangers, officials or people older than you. With people familiar to you or younger than you, you can use the informal form *tu* too.

Hello.	*Buongiorno.*	bwon·*jor*·no
Goodbye.	*Arrivederci.*	a·ree·ve·*der*·chee
Yes./No.	*Sì./No.*	see/no
Excuse me.	*Mi scusi.* (pol) *Scusami.* (inf)	mee *skoo*·zee *skoo*·za·mee
Sorry.	*Mi dispiace.*	mee dees·*pya*·che
Please.	*Per favore.*	per fa·*vo*·re
Thank you.	*Grazie.*	*gra*·tsye
You're welcome.	*Prego.*	*pre*·go

How are you?
Come sta/stai? (pol/inf) — *ko*·me sta/stai

Fine. And you?
Bene. E Lei/tu? (pol/inf) — *be*·ne e lay/too

What's your name?
Come si chiama? — *ko*·me see *kya*·ma

My name is ...
Mi chiamo ... — mee *kya*·mo ...

Do you speak English?
Parla/Parli inglese? (pol/inf) — *par*·la/*par*·lee een·*gle*·ze

I don't understand.
Non capisco. — non ka·*pee*·sko

ACCOMMODATION

Do you have a ... room?	*Avete una camera ...?*	a·*ve*·te *oo*·na *ka*·me·ra ...
double	*doppia con letto matrimoniale*	*do*·pya kon *le*·to ma·tree·mo·*nya*·le
single	*singola*	*seen*·go·la

How much is it per ...?	*Quanto costa per ...?*	*kwan*·to *kos*·ta per ...
night	*una notte*	*oo*·na *no*·te
person	*persona*	per·*so*·na

Is breakfast included?
La colazione è compresa? — la ko·la·*tsyo*·ne e kom·*pre*·sa

air-con	*aria condizionata*	*a*·rya kon·dee·tsyo·*na*·ta
bathroom	*bagno*	*ba*·nyo
campsite	*campeggio*	kam·*pe*·jo
guesthouse	*pensione*	pen·*syo*·ne
hotel	*albergo*	al·*ber*·go
youth hostel	*ostello della gioventù*	os·*te*·lo de·la jo·ven·*too*
window	*finestra*	fee·*nes*·tra

DIRECTIONS

Where's ...?
Dov'è ...? — do·*ve* ...

What's the address?
Qual'è l'indirizzo? — kwa·*le* leen·dee·*ree*·tso

Could you please write it down?
Può scriverlo, per favore? — pwo *skree*·ver·lo per fa·*vo*·re

Can you show me (on the map)?
Può mostrarmi (sulla pianta)? — pwo mos·*trar*·mee (soo·la *pyan*·ta)

at the corner	*all'angolo*	a·*lan*·go·lo
at the traffic lights	*al semaforo*	al se·*ma*·fo·ro
behind	*dietro*	*dye*·tro
far	*lontano*	lon·*ta*·no
in front of	*davanti a*	da·*van*·tee a
left	*a sinistra*	a see·*nee*·stra
near	*vicino*	vee·*chee*·no
next to	*accanto a*	a·*kan*·to a
opposite	*di fronte a*	dee *fron*·te a
right	*a destra*	a *de*·stra
straight ahead	*sempre diritto*	*sem*·pre dee·*ree*·to

EATING & DRINKING

What would you recommend?
Cosa mi consiglia? — *ko*·za mee kon·*see*·lya

What's in that dish?
Quali ingredienti ci sono in questo piatto? — *kwa*·li een·gre·*dyen*·tee chee *so*·no een *kwe*·sto *pya*·to

KEY PATTERNS

To get by in Italian, mix and match these simple patterns with words of your choice:

When's (the next flight)?
A che ora è (il prossimo volo)? — a ke o·ra e (eel *pro*·see·mo *vo*·lo)

Where's (the station)?
Dov'è (la stazione)? — *do*·ve (la sta·*tsyo*·ne)

I'm looking for (a hotel).
Sto cercando (un albergo). — sto cher·*kan*·do (oon al·*ber*·go)

Do you have (a map)?
Ha (una pianta)? — a (*oo*·na *pyan*·ta)

Is there (a toilet)?
C'è (un gabinetto)? — che (oon ga·bee·*ne*·to)

I'd like (a coffee).
Vorrei (un caffè). — vo·*ray* (oon ka·*fe*)

I'd like to (hire a car).
Vorrei (noleggiare una macchina). — vo·*ray* (no·le·*ja*·re oo·na *ma*·kee·na)

Can I (enter)?
Posso (entrare)? — *po*·so (en·*tra*·re)

Could you please (help me)?
Può (aiutarmi), per favore? — pwo (a·yoo·*tar*·mee) per fa·*vo*·re

That was delicious!
Era squisito! — e·ra skwee·*zee*·to

Cheers!
Salute! — sa·*loo*·te

Please bring the bill.
Mi porta il conto, per favore? — mee *por*·ta eel *kon*·to per fa·*vo*·re

I'd like to reserve a table for ...	*Vorrei prenotare un tavolo per ...*	vo·*ray* pre·no·*ta*·re oon *ta*·vo·lo per ...
(two) people	*(due) persone*	(*doo*·e) per·*so*·ne
(eight) o'clock	*le (otto)*	le (*o*·to)

I don't eat ...	*Non mangio ...*	non *man*·jo ...
eggs	*uova*	*wo*·va
fish	*pesce*	*pe*·she
nuts	*noci*	*no*·chee
(red) meat	*carne (rossa)*	*kar*·ne (*ro*·sa)

Key Words

bar	*locale*	lo·*ka*·le
bottle	*bottiglia*	bo·*tee*·lya
breakfast	*prima colazione*	*pree*·ma ko·la·*tsyo*·ne

cafe	*bar*	bar
cold	*freddo*	*fre*·do
dinner	*cena*	*che*·na
drink list	*lista delle bevande*	*lee*·sta *de*·le be·*van*·de
fork	*forchetta*	for·*ke*·ta
glass	*bicchiere*	bee·*kye*·re
grocery store	*alimentari*	a·lee·men·*ta*·ree
hot	*caldo*	*kal*·do
knife	*coltello*	kol·*te*·lo
lunch	*pranzo*	*pran*·dzo
market	*mercato*	mer·*ka*·to
menu	*menù*	me·*noo*
plate	*piatto*	*pya*·to
restaurant	*ristorante*	ree·sto·*ran*·te
spicy	*piccante*	pee·*kan*·te
spoon	*cucchiaio*	koo·*kya*·yo
vegetarian (food)	*vegetariano*	ve·je·ta·*rya*·no
with	*con*	kon
without	*senza*	*sen*·tsa

Meat & Fish

beef	*manzo*	*man*·dzo
chicken	*pollo*	*po*·lo
(dried) cod	*baccalà*	ba·ka·*la*
crab	*granchio*	*gran*·kyo
duck	*anatra*	*a*·na·tra
fish	*pesce*	*pe*·she
(cured) ham	*prosciutto*	pro·*shoo*·to
herring	*aringa*	a·*reen*·ga
lamb	*agnello*	a·*nye*·lo
lobster	*aragosta*	a·ra·*gos*·ta
meat	*carne*	*kar*·ne
mussels	*cozze*	*ko*·tse
octopus	*polpi*	*pol*·pee
oysters	*ostriche*	*o*·stree·ke
pork	*maiale*	ma·*ya*·le
prawn	*gambero*	*gam*·be·ro
rabbit	*coniglio*	ko·*nee*·lyo
salmon	*salmone*	sal·*mo*·ne
sausage	*salsiccia*	sal·*see*·cha
scallops	*capasante*	ka·pa·*san*·te
seafood	*frutti di mare*	*froo*·tee dee *ma*·re
shrimp	*gambero*	*gam*·be·ro
squid	*calamari*	ka·la·*ma*·ree
thinly sliced raw meat	*carpaccio*	kar·*pa*·cho
tripe	*trippa*	*tree*·pa
trout	*trota*	*tro*·ta
tuna	*tonno*	*to*·no
turkey	*tacchino*	ta·*kee*·no
veal	*vitello*	vee·*te*·lo

Signs

Entrata/Ingresso	Entrance
Uscita	Exit
Aperto	Open
Chiuso	Closed
Informazioni	Information
Proibito/Vietato	Prohibited
Gabinetti/Servizi	Toilets
Uomini	Men
Donne	Women

Vegetables

artichokes	*carciofi*	kar·*cho*·fee
asparagus	*asparagi*	as·*pa*·ra·jee
aubergine/ eggplant	*melanzane*	me·lan·*dza*·ne
beans	*fagioli*	fa·*jo*·lee
black cabbage	*cavolo nero*	*ka*·vo·lo *ne*·ro
cabbage	*cavolo*	*ka*·vo·lo
capsicum	*peperone*	pe·pe·*ro*·ne
carrot	*carota*	ka·*ro*·ta
cauliflower	*cavolfiore*	ka·vol·*fyo*·re
cucumber	*cetriolo*	che·tree·*o*·lo
fennel	*finocchio*	fee·*no*·kyo
lentils	*lenticchie*	len·*tee*·kye
lettuce	*lattuga*	la·*too*·ga
mushroom	*funghi*	*foon*·gee
nuts	*noci*	*no*·chee
olive	*oliva*	o·*lee*·va
onions	*cipolle*	chee·*po*·le
peas	*piselli*	pee·*ze*·lee
potatoes	*patate*	pa·*ta*·te
rocket	*rucola*	*roo*·ko·la
salad	*insalata*	een·sa·*la*·ta
spinach	*spinaci*	spee·*na*·chee
tomatoes	*pomodori*	po·mo·*do*·ree
vegetables	*verdura*	ver·*doo*·ra

Fruit & Gelato Flavours

apple	*mela*	*me*·la
cherry	*ciliegia*	chee·lee·*e*·ja
chocolate	*cioccolata*	cho·ko·*la*·ta

chocolate and hazelnuts	*bacio*	*ba*·cho
forest fruits (wild berries)	*frutta di bosco*	*froo*·ta dee *bos*·ko
fruit	*frutta*	*froo*·ta
grapes	*uva*	*oo*·va
hazelnut	*nocciola*	no·*cho*·la
lemon	*limone*	lee·*mo*·ne
melon	*melone*	me·*lo*·ne
orange	*arancia*	a·*ran*·cha
peach	*pesca*	*pe*·ska
pear	*pere*	*pe*·re
pineapple	*ananas*	*a*·na·nas
plum	*prugna*	*proo*·nya
strawberry	*fragola*	*fra*·go·la
trifle	*zuppa inglese*	*tsoo*·pa een·*gle*·ze
vanilla	*vaniglia*	va·*nee*·ya
wild/sour cherry	*amarena*	a·ma·*re*·na

Other

bread	*pane*	*pa*·ne
butter	*burro*	*boo*·ro
cheese	*formaggio*	for·*ma*·jo
cream	*panna*	*pa*·na
cone	*cono*	*ko*·no
cup	*coppa*	*ko*·pa
eggs	*uova*	*wo*·va
honey	*miele*	*mye*·le
ice	*ghiaccio*	*gya*·cho
jam	*marmellata*	mar·me·*la*·ta
noodles	*pasta*	*pas*·ta
oil	*olio*	*o*·lyo
pepper	*pepe*	*pe*·pe
rice	*riso*	*ree*·zo
salt	*sale*	*sa*·le
soup	*minestra*	mee·*nes*·tra
soy sauce	*salsa di soia*	*sal*·sa dee *so*·ya
sugar	*zucchero*	*tsoo*·ke·ro

Question Words

How?	*Come?*	*ko*·me
What?	*Che cosa?*	ke *ko*·za
When?	*Quando?*	*kwan*·do
Where?	*Dove?*	*do*·ve
Who?	*Chi?*	kee
Why?	*Perché?*	per·*ke*

truffle	*tartufo*	tar·*too*·fo
vinegar	*aceto*	a·*che*·to

Drinks

beer	*birra*	*bee*·ra
coffee	*caffè*	ka·*fe*
(orange) juice	*succo (d'arancia)*	*soo*·ko (da·*ran*·cha)
milk	*latte*	*la*·te
red wine	*vino rosso*	*vee*·no *ro*·so
soft drink	*bibita*	*bee*·bee·ta
tea	*tè*	te
(mineral) water	*acqua (minerale)*	*a*·kwa (mee·ne·*ra*·le)
white wine	*vino bianco*	*vee*·no *byan*·ko

For additional food and drink terms, check out the Eat & Drink Like a Local chapter (p36).

EMERGENCIES

Help!
Aiuto! — a·*yoo*·to

Leave me alone!
Lasciami in pace! — *la*·sha·mee een *pa*·che

I'm lost.
Mi sono perso/a. (m/f) — mee *so*·no *per*·so/a

There's been an accident.
C'è stato un incidente. — che *sta*·to oon een·chee·*den*·te

Call the police!
Chiami la polizia! — *kya*·mee la po·lee·*tsee*·a

Call a doctor!
Chiami un medico! — *kya*·mee oon *me*·dee·ko

Where are the toilets?
Dove sono i gabinetti? — *do*·ve *so*·no ee ga·bee·*ne*·tee

I'm sick.
Mi sento male. — mee *sen*·to *ma*·le

It hurts here.
Mi fa male qui. — mee fa *ma*·le kwee

I'm allergic to ...
Sono allergico/a a ... (m/f) — *so*·no a·*ler*·jee·ko/a a ...

SHOPPING & SERVICES

I'd like to buy ...
Vorrei comprare ... — vo·*ray* kom·*pra*·re ...

I'm just looking.
Sto solo guardando. — sto *so*·lo gwar·*dan*·do

Can I look at it?
Posso dare un'occhiata? — *po*·so *da*·re oo·no·*kya*·ta

How much is this?
Quanto costa questo? — *kwan*·to *kos*·ta *kwe*·sto

It's too expensive.
È troppo caro/a. (m/f) e tro·po *ka*·ro/a

Can you lower the price?
Può farmi lo sconto? pwo *far*·mee lo *skon*·to

There's a mistake in the bill.
C'è un errore nel conto. che oo·ne·*ro*·re nel *kon*·to

ATM	*Bancomat*	*ban*·ko·mat
post office	*ufficio postale*	oo·*fee*·cho pos·*ta*·le
tourist office	*ufficio del turismo*	oo·*fee*·cho del too·*reez*·mo

TIME & DATES

What time is it?	*Che ora è?*	ke *o*·ra e
It's one o'clock.	*È l'una.*	e *loo*·na
It's (two) o'clock.	*Sono le (due).*	*so*·no le (*doo*·e)
Half past (one).	*(L'una) e mezza.*	(*loo*·na) e *me*·dza

in the morning	*di mattina*	dee ma·*tee*·na
in the afternoon	*di pomeriggio*	dee po·me·*ree*·jo
in the evening	*di sera*	dee *se*·ra

yesterday	*ieri*	*ye*·ree
today	*oggi*	*o*·jee
tomorrow	*domani*	do·*ma*·nee

Monday	*lunedì*	loo·ne·*dee*
Tuesday	*martedì*	mar·te·*dee*
Wednesday	*mercoledì*	mer·ko·le·*dee*
Thursday	*giovedì*	jo·ve·*dee*
Friday	*venerdì*	ve·ner·*dee*
Saturday	*sabato*	*sa*·ba·to
Sunday	*domenica*	do·*me*·nee·ka

January	*gennaio*	je·*na*·yo
February	*febbraio*	fe·*bra*·yo
March	*marzo*	*mar*·tso
April	*aprile*	a·*pree*·le
May	*maggio*	*ma*·jo
June	*giugno*	*joo*·nyo
July	*luglio*	*loo*·lyo
August	*agosto*	a·*gos*·to
September	*settembre*	se·*tem*·bre
October	*ottobre*	o·*to*·bre
November	*novembre*	no·*vem*·bre
December	*dicembre*	dee·*chem*·bre

Numbers

1	*uno*	*oo*·no
2	*due*	*doo*·e
3	*tre*	tre
4	*quattro*	*kwa*·tro
5	*cinque*	*cheen*·kwe
6	*sei*	say
7	*sette*	*se*·te
8	*otto*	*o*·to
9	*nove*	*no*·ve
10	*dieci*	*dye*·chee
20	*venti*	*ven*·tee
30	*trenta*	*tren*·ta
40	*quaranta*	kwa·*ran*·ta
50	*cinquanta*	cheen·*kwan*·ta
60	*sessanta*	se·*san*·ta
70	*settanta*	se·*tan*·ta
80	*ottanta*	o·*tan*·ta
90	*novanta*	no·*van*·ta
100	*cento*	*chen*·to
1000	*mille*	*mee*·lel

TRANSPORT

Public Transport

At what time does the ... leave/arrive?	*A che ora parte/ arriva ...?*	a ke *o*·ra *par*·te/ a·*ree*·va ...
boat	*la nave*	la *na*·ve
bus	*l'autobus*	*low*·to·boos
ferry	*il traghetto*	eel tra·*ge*·to
metro	*la metropolitana*	la me·tro·po·lee·*ta*·na
plane	*l'aereo*	la·*e*·re·o
train	*il treno*	eel *tre*·no

... ticket	*un biglietto ...*	oon bee·*lye*·to
one-way	*di sola andata*	dee *so*·la an·*da*·ta
return	*di andata e ritorno*	dee an·*da*·ta e ree·*tor*·no

bus stop	*fermata dell'autobus*	fer·*ma*·ta del *ow*·to·boos
platform	*binario*	bee·*na*·ryo
ticket office	*biglietteria*	bee·lye·te·*ree*·a
timetable	*orario*	o·*ra*·ryo
train station	*stazione ferroviaria*	sta·*tsyo*·ne fe·ro·*vyar*·ya

Does it stop at ...?
Si ferma a ...? — see *fer*·ma a ...

Please tell me when we get to ...
Mi dica per favore quando arriviamo a ... — mee *dee*·ka per fa·*vo*·re kwan·do a·ree·*vya*·mo a ...

I want to get off here.
Voglio scendere qui. — *vo*·lyo *shen*·de·re kwee

Driving & Cycling

I'd like to hire a/an ...	*Vorrei noleggiare un/una ...* (m/f)	vo·*ray* no·le·*ja*·re oon/*oo*·na ...
bicycle	*bicicletta* (f)	bee·chee·*kle*·ta
car	*macchina* (f)	*ma*·kee·na
motorbike	*moto* (f)	*mo*·to

bicycle pump	*pompa della bicicletta*	*pom*·pa *de*·la bee·chee·*kle*·ta
child seat	*seggiolino*	se·jo·*lee*·no
helmet	*casco*	*kas*·ko
mechanic	*meccanico*	me·*ka*·nee·ko
petrol/gas	*benzina*	ben·*dzee*·na
puncture	*gomma bucata*	*go*·ma boo·*ka*·ta
service station	*stazione di servizio*	sta·*tsyo*·ne dee ser·*vee*·tsyo

Is this the road to ...?
Questa strada porta a ...? — *kwe*·sta *stra*·da *por*·ta a ...

(How long) Can I park here?
(Per quanto tempo) Posso parcheggiare qui? — (per *kwan*·to *tem*·po) *po*·so par·ke·*ja*·re kwee

The car/motorbike has broken down (at ...).
La macchina/moto si è guastata (a ...). — la *ma*·kee·na/*mo*·to see e gwas·*ta*·ta (a ...)

I have a flat tyre.
Ho una gomma bucata. — o *oo*·na *go*·ma boo·*ka*·ta

I've run out of petrol.
Ho esaurito la benzina. — o e·zow·*ree*·to la ben·*dzee*·na

I've lost my car keys.
Ho perso le chiavi della macchina. — o *per*·so le *kya*·vee *de*·la *ma*·kee·na

GLOSSARY

For art and architecture terms, see p313.

abbazia – abbey
aeroporto – airport
affittacamere – rooms for rent in private houses
agriturismo – farm-stay accommodation
albergo – hotel
alimentari – grocery shop
alto – high
ambulanza – ambulance
anfiteatro – amphitheatre
aperitivo – predinner drinks accompanied by cocktail snacks
autostazione – bus station/terminal
autostrada – motorway, highway

basilica – Christian church with a rectangular hall, aisles and an apse at the end
battistero – baptistry
biblioteca – library
biglietto – ticket
biglietto cumulativo – combined ticket that allows entrance to a number of associated sights
borgo – ancient town or village; farm hamlet

cabinovia – two-seater cable car
calcio – football
camera doppia – room with twin beds
camera matrimoniale – room with a double bed
camera singola – single room
campanile – bell tower
campeggio – camping
campo – field
cantinetta – small cellar where wine is served
cappella – chapel
carabinieri – military police
Carnevale – carnival period between Epiphany and Lent
casa – house, home
castello – castle
cattedrale – cathedral
cava – quarry
centro – city centre
centro storico – literally, 'historical centre'; old town
chiesa – church
colle – hill
colonna – column
comune – equivalent to a municipality; town or city council; historically, a commune (self-governing town or city)
contrada – town district
convalida – ticket-stamping machine
coperto – cover charge
corso – main street, avenue

deposito bagagli – left luggage
dolce – sweet; also dessert course
duomo – cathedral

enoteca – wine bar (see also *fiaschetteria*)

fattoria – farmhouse
ferrovia – train station
festa – festival
fiaschetteria – small tavern serving wine and snacks (see also *enoteca*)
fontana – fountain
forno – bakery
foro – forum

gelateria – ice-cream shop
golfo – gulf
grotta – cave

isola – island

lago – lake
largo – small square

libreria – bookshop
locanda – inn, small hotel
loggia – covered area on the side of a building; porch
lungomare – seafront road, promenade

macchia – scrub, bush
macellerìa – butcher shop
mare – sea
mercato – market
monte – mountain, mount
motorino – scooter
municipio – town hall
museo – museum

nave – ship
necropoli – ancient cemetery, burial site

osteria – casual tavern or eatery presided over by a host

palazzo – palace; a large building of any type, including an apartment block
parcheggio – car park
parco – park
passeggiata – traditional evening stroll
pasticceria – shop selling cakes and pastries
pensione – small hotel
permesso di soggiorno – residence permit
piazza – square
piazzale – large open square
pinacoteca – art gallery
ponte – bridge
porta – door, city gate
portico – walkway, often on the outside of buildings
porto – port

questura – police station

rifugio – mountain hut
rocca – fort

sagra – festival (usually with a culinary theme)
sala – room in a museum or a gallery
santuario – sanctuary
scalinata – flight of stairs
scavi – excavations
spiaggia – beach
stazione – station
stazione di servizio – service/petrol station
stazione marittima – ferry terminal
strada – street, road
superstrada – expressway; highway with divided lanes

tabaccheria/tabaccaio – tobacconist's shop/ tobacconist
teatro – theatre
tempio – temple
terme – thermal bath
torre – tower
trattoria – simple restaurant

ufficio stranieri – foreigners' bureau
uffizi – offices

via – street, road
vicoli – alley, alleyway

ZTL – *(Zona a Traffico Limitato)* Limited Traffic Zone

Behind the Scenes

SEND US YOUR FEEDBACK

We love to hear from travellers – your comments keep us on our toes and help make our books better. Our well-travelled team reads every word on what you loved or loathed about this book. Although we cannot reply individually to postal submissions, we always guarantee that your feedback goes straight to the appropriate authors, in time for the next edition. Each person who sends us information is thanked in the next edition – the most useful submissions are rewarded with a selection of digital PDF chapters.

Visit **lonelyplanet.com/contact** to submit your updates and suggestions or to ask for help. Our award-winning website also features inspirational travel stories, news and discussions.

Note: We may edit, reproduce and incorporate your comments in Lonely Planet products such as guidebooks, websites and digital products, so let us know if you don't want your comments reproduced or your name acknowledged. For a copy of our privacy policy visit lonelyplanet.com/privacy.

OUR READERS

Many thanks to the travellers who used the last edition and wrote to us with helpful hints, useful advice and interesting anecdotes:

Alexandre Abreu, Alma Sesti, Andrew McIntosh, Assen Totin, Carmen Germaine, Chiara Cavedoni, Graham Hardman, Karen Kiang, Kelley Eckmair, M Greenwood, Margaret A Simpson, Peter Williams, Piero Giadrossi

AUTHOR THANKS

Virginia Maxwell

Love and thanks to my partner and travelling companion, Peter Handsaker. Thanks also to Ilaria Crescioli, Alberto Peruzzini, Roberta Vichi, Eva Zettelmayr, Sigrid Fuchs, Chiara Ponzuoli, Luigina Benci, Cecilia Rosa, Fulvia in San Gimignano, Arturo Comastri, Sean Lawson, Silvia Bucci and Italia Luchini. Finally, *grazie mille* to my co-author Nicola Williams and commissioning editor Joe Bindloss.

Nicola Williams

Grazie mille to everyone who helped me delve deep into the Tuscan heart: in Florence, Krista Ricchi (@allafiorentina), Marquis Vanni and Susanna Torrigiani Malaspina (what a beautiful garden), Guido Manfredi (no farm is finer), Alessandro Gargani (New York to Florence), Antje d'Almeida (for directing me to CLET), Roberta Romoli, and Freya Middleton (guide extraordinaire); on Elba, Anna Galletti and third-generation olive farmer Fabrizio Galletti; elsewhere, Maria Genova (Suvereto), husband Matthias and our trilingual tribe of fearless young road-trippers.

ACKNOWLEDGMENTS

Climate map data adapted from Peel MC, Finlayson BL & McMahon TA (2007) 'Updated World Map of the Köppen-Geiger Climate Classification', *Hydrology and Earth System Sciences*, 11, 163344.
Illustrations p66-7 by Javier Zarracina.
Cover photograph: Val d'Elsa, Luca Da Ros/4Corners Images ©.

THIS BOOK

This 8th edition of Lonely Planet's *Florence & Tuscany* guidebook was researched and written by Virginia Maxwell and Nicola Williams. The same authors wrote the 7th edition, and the 6th edition was written by Virginia Maxwell, Alex Leviton and Leif Pettersen. This guidebook was commissioned in Lonely Planet's London office, and produced by the following:

Commissioning Editors Joe Bindloss, Helena Smith
Coordinating Editors Barbara Delissen, Briohny Hooper
Senior Cartographers Anthony Phelan, Valentina Kremenchutskaya
Coordinating Layout Designer Wibowo Rusli
Managing Editors Brigitte Ellemor, Bruce Evans, Annelies Mertens, Angela Tinson
Managing Layout Designer Jane Hart
Assisting Editors Kate Evans, Paul Harding, Jodie Martire, Jeanette Wall
Cover Research Naomi Parker
Internal Image Research Aude Vauconsant
Language Content Branislava Vladisavljevic

Thanks to Anita Banh, Ryan Evans, Larissa Frost, Genesys India, Jouve India, Karyn Noble, Wayne Murphy, Catherine Naghten, Katie O'Connell, Trent Paton, Gerard Walker

Index

Map Pages **000**
Photo Pages **000**

Map Pages **000**
Photo Pages **000**

N

O

P

Map Pages **000**
Photo Pages **000**

NOTES

Map Legend

Sights

- Beach
- Bird Sanctuary
- Buddhist
- Castle/Palace
- Christian
- Confucian
- Hindu
- Islamic
- Jain
- Jewish
- Monument
- Museum/Gallery/Historic Building
- Ruin
- Sento Hot Baths/Onsen
- Shinto
- Sikh
- Taoist
- Winery/Vineyard
- Zoo/Wildlife Sanctuary
- Other Sight

Activities, Courses & Tours

- Bodysurfing
- Diving
- Canoeing/Kayaking
- Course/Tour
- Skiing
- Snorkelling
- Surfing
- Swimming/Pool
- Walking
- Windsurfing
- Other Activity

Sleeping

- Sleeping
- Camping

Eating

- Eating

Drinking & Nightlife

- Drinking & Nightlife
- Cafe

Entertainment

- Entertainment

Shopping

- Shopping

Information

- Bank
- Embassy/Consulate
- Hospital/Medical
- Internet
- Police
- Post Office
- Telephone
- Toilet
- Tourist Information
- Other Information

Geographic

- Beach
- Hut/Shelter
- Lighthouse
- Lookout
- Mountain/Volcano
- Oasis
- Park
- Pass
- Picnic Area
- Waterfall

Population

- Capital (National)
- Capital (State/Province)
- City/Large Town
- Town/Village

Transport

- Airport
- Border crossing
- Bus
- Cable car/Funicular
- Cycling
- Ferry
- Metro station
- Monorail
- Parking
- Petrol station
- S-Bahn/Subway station
- Taxi
- T-bane/Tunnelbana station
- Train station/Railway
- Tram
- Tube station
- U-Bahn/Underground station
- Other Transport

Note: Not all symbols displayed above appear on the maps in this book

Routes

- Tollway
- Freeway
- Primary
- Secondary
- Tertiary
- Lane
- Unsealed road
- Road under construction
- Plaza/Mall
- Steps
- Tunnel
- Pedestrian overpass
- Walking Tour
- Walking Tour detour
- Path/Walking Trail

Boundaries

- International
- State/Province
- Disputed
- Regional/Suburb
- Marine Park
- Cliff
- Wall

Hydrography

- River, Creek
- Intermittent River
- Canal
- Water
- Dry/Salt/Intermittent Lake
- Reef

Areas

- Airport/Runway
- Beach/Desert
- Cemetery (Christian)
- Cemetery (Other)
- Glacier
- Mudflat
- Park/Forest
- Sight (Building)
- Sportsground
- Swamp/Mangrove

OUR STORY

A beat-up old car, a few dollars in the pocket and a sense of adventure. In 1972 that's all Tony and Maureen Wheeler needed for the trip of a lifetime – across Europe and Asia overland to Australia. It took several months, and at the end – broke but inspired – they sat at their kitchen table writing and stapling together their first travel guide, *Across Asia on the Cheap*. Within a week they'd sold 1500 copies. Lonely Planet was born.

Today, Lonely Planet has offices in Melbourne, London and Oakland, with more than 600 staff and writers. We share Tony's belief that 'a great guidebook should do three things: inform, educate and amuse'.

OUR WRITERS

Virginia Maxwell

Coordinating Author; Siena & Central Tuscany; Southern Tuscany; Eastern Tuscany Based in Australia, Virginia spends part of every year in Italy indulging her passions for history, art, architecture, food and wine. She has written two previous editions of this guide and covers both Tuscany and other parts of the country for the *Italy* and *Western Europe* books. Though reticent to nominate a favourite Tuscan destination (arguing that they're all wonderful), she usually nominates Florence if pressed. For this book Virginia also wrote most of the Plan Your Trip section, Tuscany on Page & Screen, Art & Architecture and the Survival Guide section.

Read more about Virginia at:
lonelyplanet.com/members/virginiamaxwell

Nicola Williams

Florence; Northwestern Tuscany; Central Coast & Elba A British writer and editorial consultant, Nicola has lived on the southern shore of Lake Geneva for over a decade. Thankfully for her Italianate soul, it is an easy hop through the Mont Blanc Tunnel to Italy where she has spent years eating her way around and revelling in its extraordinary art and landscape. Nicola has worked on numerous Lonely Planet titles, including *Italy*, *Milan, Turin & Genoa* and *Piedmont*. She blogs at tripalong.wordpress.com and tweets @tripalong. For this book Nicola also wrote Eat & Drink Like a Local, Outdoor Experiences and most of the Understand section.

Read more about Nicola at:
lonelyplanet.com/members/nicolawilliams

Published by Lonely Planet Publications Pty Ltd
ABN 36 005 607 983
8th edition – Jan 2014
ISBN 978 1 74220 718 6

10 9 8 7 6 5 4 3 2 1
Printed in China